The American Heritage®
Dictionary of Business Terms

The American Heritage®
Dictionary of Business Terms

David L. Scott, PhD
Professor Emeritus of Finance
Valdosta State University
Valdosta, Georgia

650.03
S 425q

11/09

Houghton Mifflin Harcourt
Boston   New York

Visit our website: www.hmhbooks.com

Library of Congress Cataloging-in-Publication Data
Scott, David Logan, 1942-
  The American heritage dictionary of business terms / David L. Scott.
    p. cm.
  ISBN-13: 978-0-618-75525-7
  ISBN-10: 0-618-75525-X
  1. Business--Dictionaries. 2. Finance--Dictionaries. I. Title.
  HF1001.S348 2009
  650.03--dc22
                                    2008042657
Manufactured in the United States of America

Book design by Jean Hammond

1 2 3 4 5 6 7 8 9 10-VB-15 14 13 12 11 10 09

▪ Contents

▪ Tips from the Experts: Contributor Panel

Scott Alderman
Broker and President
First Commercial Real Estate
Valdosta, GA

Brooke Barber
Vice President
Middle Market Banking
Atlanta, GA

Peter M. Bergevin, PhD
Professor of Accounting
School of Business
University of Redlands
Redlands, CA

Deaver Brown
Publisher
Simplysoftwarecd.com
Lincoln, MA

Michael W. Butler, PhD
Professor of Economics
Angelo State University
San Angelo, TX

Richard S. Campbell, CIMA®
Senior Vice President, Wealth Management
Portfolio Management Director
Smith Barney
Valdosta, GA

Paul G. Holland, Jr., JD, LLM
Director, Wealth Planning
MiddleCove Capital
Centerbrook, CT

Phyllis G. Holland, PhD
Professor and Head
Department of Management
Langdale College of Business
Valdosta State University
Valdosta, GA

Helen M. Kemp
Division Counsel and Assistant Director
Retirement and Benefit Services
Office of the State Comptroller
State of Connecticut

Joan A. Koffman, Esq.
Real Estate Attorney
Koffman & Dreyer
Newton, MA

Stephen F. Lappert
Partner
Trusts and Estates Department
Carter Ledyard & Milburn LLP
New York, NY

E. Mace Lewis
Vice President, Business Development
QD Healthcare Group
Greenwich, CT

Tom Mesereau
Principal
Mesereau Public Relations
Parker, CO

Noah L. Myers, CFP®
Principal and Chief Investment Officer
MiddleCove Capital
Centerbrook, CT

■ Preface

Years ago a colleague and I were discussing the testing of students in our principles of finance course. We talked about a variety of topics, including the advantages and disadvantages of various types of examinations and how to best test the students' knowledge. As always, we complained about lack of student preparation, poor study habits, and dreadful test performance. I was initially surprised when my colleague mentioned that his exams included questions related to finance terminology. When I asked the reason, he replied, "You can't master a subject without understanding the language." He was correct, of course, and I subsequently modified my own exams to include terminology questions related to the assigned material. I also began devoting class time to discussing various business terms students were likely to encounter at work and in the media. The learning never ends, because the language is constantly changing.

Recent years have witnessed rapid changes in all areas of business. New and innovative investment vehicles (some good, some questionable, and some impossible to understand, as per structured investment vehicles from the subprime debacle) have been developed for sale to individuals and institutions. The Internet continues to evolve and offer new and efficient avenues for advertising, shopping, delivering content, and transferring and evaluating data. Improvements in communications and transportation have facilitated globalization and altered the manner in which businesses operate. Companies in developed countries have increasingly transferred jobs overseas to take advantage of lower wages and less expensive manufacturing and service facilities. Global competition and the quest for increased profitability have caused businesses to require employees to accept greater responsibility for their own retirement and health care. Defined-benefit retirement plans have been phased out as employees were shifted to self-directed 401b plans. Employees have found it necessary to assume greater control of their health care as business-provided health benefits were scaled back with higher premiums, increased deductibles, and added wrinkles such as Health Savings Accounts and Health Reimbursement Arrangements. In many instances business-sponsored health insurance has simply been discontinued. All these changes have been accompanied by an evolution in the language of business. Greater responsibility for making decisions relative to your own financial and business affairs makes it increasingly important to keep up with changes in the language so that you can understand the information that is being presented.

The American Heritage Dictionary of Business Terms is the product of more than two years of scouring business and general media to identify common and specialized business terms that most of us are likely to encounter. Not too specialized, of course. No dictionary of such broad subject matter can be exhaustive. Thus, the task was not only to identify business terms, but also to determine which of the identified terms are appropriate for inclusion in a general business dictionary. My hope is that the selection of terms and their accompanying definitions, examples, and expert tips will help you to better understand the business terms you are likely to come across in your job and in the news. Knowledge may be power, but knowledge can be gained only when you are able to interpret the information that is being conveyed.

I wish to express my appreciation to the staff at Houghton Mifflin Harcourt, especially publisher Marge Berube, who approached me with the idea for a business dictionary. I previously worked with Marge on five finance books including *Wall Street Words* and was gratified by her faith that I would be able to produce a manuscript of such broad scope. I would like to commend the organizational skills of managing editor Chris Leonesio, who was able to successfully schedule important editorial and production dates around my frequent travels. I am indebted to editor Diane Fredrick, who certainly did a thorough job of ferreting out the omissions and mistakes I overlooked. Although I was initially uncertain whether I had the time or the energy to undertake such a major project, an evaluation of positives and negatives caused me to think back to the earlier discussion with my colleague about the importance of understanding the language of finance. This conversation and the resulting awareness of the importance of learning the language of business were key factors in my decision to commit several years of effort to what I considered a worthwhile endeavor. Authoring a business dictionary offered the added benefit of forcing me to examine material outside my main interest of personal finance and investing. The result of this work is now before you. I hope you find it useful.

David L. Scott
Valdosta, Georgia

A

A An upper-medium grade assigned to a debt obligation by a rating agency to indicate a strong capacity to pay interest and repay principal. This capacity is susceptible to impairment in the event of adverse developments.

AA A grade assigned to a debt obligation by a rating agency to indicate a very strong capacity to pay interest and repay principal. Such a rating indicates only slightly lower quality than the top rating of AAA. —Also called *Aa.*

AAA The highest grade assigned to a debt obligation by a rating agency. It indicates an unusually strong capacity to pay interest and repay principal. —Also called *triple A.*

AACSB —See ASSOCIATION TO ADVANCE COLLEGIATE SCHOOLS OF BUSINESS.

AAII —See AMERICAN ASSOCIATION OF INDIVIDUAL INVESTORS.

abandonment 1. The voluntary surrender of an asset without compensation and without identifying a new owner. **2.** In insurance, surrender of an insured asset by the insured to the underwriter. For example, an insured vehicle owner may abandon to the insurance company a wrecked vehicle that has been declared a total loss. **3.** Termination of a patent application, generally because of a failure on the part of the applicant to reply to a request from the U.S. Patent and Trademark Office. **4.** —See EXPIRATION.

abatement The reduction or elimination of an expense or series of expenses. For example, a loan agreement may include a provision for payment abatement under certain circumstances. —See also TAX ABATEMENT.

abbrochment The purchase of all merchandise offered at wholesale in a particular market in order to control sales in that market.

ABC method Classification of inventory into categories based on an established criterion such as unit or dollar volume of sales.

above par Of or relating to a security that sells at more than face value or par value. For example, a $1,000 par bond that trades at a market price of $1,050 is selling above par. A fixed-income security is most likely to sell above par if market rates of interest have declined since the time the security was issued. —Compare BELOW PAR. —See also PREMIUM BOND.

above the line 1. Describing expenses that can be deducted for tax purposes before arriving at adjusted gross income. Alimony and contributions to an IRA are examples of deductions taken prior to calculating adjusted gross income. **2.** Of or relating to paid advertising using mass media, including print, radio, television, and the Internet, that reach large audiences. —Compare BELOW THE LINE.

abrogate To revoke or annul an agreement or law.

absolute advantage In economics, the ability of a firm, region, or country to produce a good or service at a lower cost. For example, Florida has an absolute advantage in growing citrus, and China has an absolute advantage in the production of textiles. —Compare COMPARATIVE ADVANTAGE. —See also ACQUIRED ADVANTAGE.

absolute auction A public sale in which items are sold to the highest bidder without any minimum bid requirement. —Also called *without reserve.*

absolute net —See NET LEASE.

absolute priority rule The principle that senior creditors are paid in full prior to any payment being made to junior creditors, and that all creditors have seniority to equity holders.

absolute sale Transfer of title by a seller to a buyer without any restrictions other than payment of an agreed-upon amount of money.

absorb 1. To allocate costs. **2.** To offset sell orders on a new security offering with buy orders. **3.** To accept certain expenses rather than pass them on to a customer. For example, a manufacturer might absorb freight costs for shipments to customers.

absorption costing In accounting, applying all variable and fixed manufacturing costs in calculating the expense of producing units of output. —See also DIRECT COST.

abstract of title A condensed history of transactions relative to a specific parcel of land. The abstract includes changes of ownership and liens or encumbrances. —See also CHAIN OF TITLE.

abstract of trust A shortened version of a living trust that omits the identity of the beneficiaries and the specifics of what is included in the trust.

abusive tax shelter A tax shelter in which an improper interpretation of the law is used to produce tax benefits that are disproportionate to economic reality.

Accelerated Cost Recovery System (ACRS) An accounting technique for calculating the depreciation of tangible assets on the basis of the estimated-life classifications into which the assets are placed. The Economic Recovery Act of 1981 initiated ACRS with the goal of making investments more profitable by sheltering large amounts of income from taxation during the early years of an asset's life. The initial law established classifications of 3, 5, 10, and 15 years; these classifications were subsequently modified in order to reduce depreciation and increase the government's tax revenues. The classification into which an asset is placed determines the percentage of the cost potentially recoverable in each year. —See also MODIFIED ACCELERATED COST RECOVERY SYSTEM.

accelerated death benefit A rider to a life insurance policy that allows the insured to collect benefits to cover medical expenses during a terminal illness. Accelerated death benefits are offset by a reduction in the death benefit paid to the beneficiary at the time of the insured's death.

accelerated depreciation An Accelerated Cost Recovery System method for writing off the cost of a capital asset by taking the largest deductions in the early years of the asset's life. The purpose of using accelerated depreciation is to delay the payment of taxes so that cash savings from the deferral can be reinvested to earn additional income. —Compare STRAIGHT-LINE DEPRECIATION. —See also DECLINING-BALANCE METHOD; DOUBLE-DECLINING-BALANCE DEPRECIATION; MODIFIED ACCELERATED COST RECOVERY SYSTEM; SUM-OF-THE-YEARS'-DIGITS METHOD.

acceleration clause A provision in a bond indenture that, in the event of default, allows the trustee or the holders of 25% of the principal amount of the outstanding issue to declare all of the principal and interest due immediately. Calling for an acceleration is likely to cause the borrower to cure the default or seek bankruptcy protection.

acceptance 1. An agreement to purchase goods subject to specified conditions. **2.** —See BANKER'S ACCEPTANCE.

acceptance sampling A statistical methodology for judging whether batches of products or data meet an acceptable standard of quality. A random sample of a given size is examined in order to determine if the sample is acceptable.

accepting bank A financial institution that endorses and agrees to pay a time draft upon maturity.

accommodation endorsement Guarantee without compensation by a third party to a promissory note. The endorser is liable in the event of a default.

accommodative monetary policy The Federal Reserve policy of increasing the supply of money to make credit more readily available. An accommodative monetary policy tends to lower interest rates, especially the short-term ones, at the time credit is made plentiful. Such a policy is likely to result eventually in increased inflation and interest rates. —Compare MONETARY POLICY.

account 1. A contractual relationship between two parties. For example, an individual may have an account with a bank or brokerage firm. 2. The record of a firm's or person's transactions and balances. —Also called *account statement.* 3. In accounting, a record of transactions related to segments of an income statement and balance sheet including income, expenses, assets, liabilities, and stockholders' equity.

account aging —See AGING.

accountant A person who maintains and audits financial information and who prepares financial statements and tax returns.

accountant's opinion —See OPINION 1.

account executive 1. In advertising, the person who coordinates and administers the account of one of the firm's clients. 2. —See REGISTERED REPRESENTATIVE.

account hold A warning attached to an account at a financial institution. A hold might limit an account holder's access to funds when the account is being used as collateral for a loan or when funds have not been collected from a recent deposit.

accounting cycle The series of procedures for recording an accounting event from the initial transaction to the effect on the financial statements.

accounting equation The relationship of assets always being equal to liabilities plus equity.

accounting exposure A change in the value of an entry on an accounting statement because of a change in currency exchange rates.

accounting information systems (AIS) The processing, presentation, and use of accounting information for internal reporting to managers and external reporting to shareholders, creditors, and government.

accounting period —See FISCAL PERIOD.

accounting principles Guidelines regarding how transactions and financial statements are to be treated for accounting purposes.

Accounting Principles Board (APB) A group of accountants appointed by the American Institute of Certified Public Accountants to determine accounting principles for financial record keeping. The APB was terminated in 1973 with the founding of the Financial Accounting Standards Board.

accounting procedure The manner in which financial data are utilized in a business.

accounting rate of return Average annual profits divided by the average amount of money invested in assets that produce the profits. This is generally considered an inferior measure of profitability compared to net present value and internal rate of return, which use discounted cash flows rather than accounting profits.

accounting system The formal arrangement by which an organization develops its financial statements.

accounts payable Money a business owes to others. Accounts payable are current liabilities incurred in the normal course of business as a firm purchases goods or services with the understanding that payment is due at a later date. No accounts payable will appear on the balance sheet of a firm that pays cash for all of its purchases.

accounts receivable Money owed to a business by customers who have bought goods or services on credit. Accounts receivable are current assets that are continually converted into cash as customers pay their bills. —Also called *receivables.*

accounts receivable financing Borrowing the funds that are used to pay for short-term loans to customers. The customer loans are generally used as collateral for this type of financing. —See also FACTOR².

accounts receivable turnover The number of times in each accounting period that a firm converts credit sales into cash. A high turnover indicates effective granting of credit and collection from customers by the firm's management. Accounts receivable turnover is calculated by dividing the average amount of receivables into annual credit sales. —Also called *receivables turnover.* —See also ACTIVITY RATIO; COLLECTION PERIOD.

account statement —See ACCOUNT 2.

accredited investor An investor with sufficient income or wealth to qualify for restricted offerings and limited partnerships. Accredited investors include banks, insurance companies, registered investment companies, charitable organizations with assets over $5 million, and individuals with annual income exceeding $200,000 ($300,000 for joint returns) or a net worth exceeding $1 million. Raising funds from accredited investors allows companies an exemption from registering securities with the Securities and Exchange Commission.

accreted value The current value of an original-issue discount bond, taking into account imputed interest that has accumulated since the date the bond was issued.

accretion 1. The accumulation of theoretical gains in value on discount bonds with the expectation that the securities will be redeemed at maturity. Excluding municipals, the amount of annual accretion is taxable on an original-issue discount bond even though only a small amount of interest or no interest at all is paid each year. —See also IMPUTED INTEREST. **2.** The gradual accumulation of land due to natural causes. For example, sediment carried in a stream is deposited along its banks.

accrual accounting A method of accounting that recognizes expenses when incurred and revenue when earned rather than when payment is made or received. Thus, it is the act of sending the goods or receiving an inventory item that is important in determining when transactions are posted on financial statements. For example, under accrual accounting, sales are recorded as revenue when goods are shipped even though payment is not expected for days, weeks, or months. Most firms use the accrual basis of accounting in recording transactions. —Compare CASH BASIS ACCOUNTING.

accrual bond —See ZERO-COUPON BOND.

accrued expense An expense incurred but not yet paid. A firm incurs certain expenses such as wages, interest, and taxes that are paid only periodically. From the time expenses are incurred until the date they are paid, expenses accrue in a firm's balance sheet as liabilities.

accrued interest 1. Interest owed but not yet paid. Like other accrued expenses, accrued interest is listed as a liability on the borrower's balance sheet. **2.** The amount of interest added to the price at which bonds are traded. For example, if a 12% coupon bond's last record date for an interest payment was two months ago, the buyer must pay the seller $20 (two months' interest at 1% per month on $1,000 principal) in accrued interest in addition to the quoted price. This additional expense will be recovered when the new owner receives six months' interest after holding the bond only four months.

accrued market discount The gain in the value of a bond that occurs because the bond has been bought at a discount from face value. For example, a $1,000 par bond maturing in ten years and selling at $800 can be expected to rise gradually in price throughout its remaining life. The accrued market discount is the portion of any price rise caused by the gradual increase (as opposed to an increase caused by a fall in interest rates).

accrued revenue Money that has been earned, but the funds have not yet been received. For example, a firm might sell $1,000 of products to a customer who is not required to pay for 60 days. The sale is recorded on the income statement as revenue and on the balance sheet as a current asset even though no money will be received until later.

accumulate To purchase a relatively large amount of an asset during a given period. For example, an investment group might accumulate shares of stock in a company the investment group feels is undervalued.

accumulated depreciation The total amount of depreciation that has been recorded for an asset since its date of acquisition. For example, a computer with a five-year estimated life that was purchased for $2,000 would have accumulated depreciation of $800 [($2,000/5) × 2] and a book value of $1,200 ($2,000 − $800) after two years of straight-line depreciation. —Also called *allowance for depreciation*; *depreciation reserve*.

accumulated dividend —See DIVIDENDS IN ARREARS.

accumulated earnings tax A federal tax on a company's retained earnings that are considered in excess of what is reasonable. The purpose of an accumulated earnings tax is to make it more difficult for owners of a business to defer taxes.

accumulation The purchase of a particular asset throughout a period of time. For example, the accumulation of a substantial quantity of silver may take place over a period of several weeks or months in order to avoid driving up the price of silver. An individual's accumulation of shares of a mutual fund may occur over a period of many years.

acid-test ratio —See QUICK RATIO.

acquired advantage The theory that a cost advantage in producing goods and services can be achieved through improvements in knowledge and technology in addition to natural resources. —See also ABSOLUTE ADVANTAGE; COMPARATIVE ADVANTAGE.

acquisition The purchase of an asset such as a plant, division, or even an entire company. For example, Sacramento, CA–based McClatchy Company made a major acquisition in 2006 when the firm purchased the Knight Ridder newspaper chain for cash and stock worth nearly $6.5 billion. McClatchy, which wanted to extend its reach in the newspaper industry, later sold some of the Knight Ridder papers.

acquisition cost The price plus all additional charges to acquire an asset. Additional charges might include transportation, attorney fees, and appraisal costs.

acquisition premium The difference in the amount offered by the acquirer and the preacquisition valuation of the firm being acquired. For example, offering $150 million for a firm with a market value of $110 million involves an acquisition premium of $40 million. An acquisition premium helps convince managers and owners of the firm to be acquired that it is in their financial interest to approve the acquisition. A large acquisition premium is likely to deter other potential suitors.

ACRS —See ACCELERATED COST RECOVERY SYSTEM.

acting in concert Two or more investors acting together to achieve a common goal. For example, several wealthy investors may accumulate a major position in a firm's common stock in an attempt to influence the firm's management decisions.

action device In direct marketing, an advertising add-on designed to induce the recipient to take a particular action. For example, a direct mailing may include stamps that can be peeled off and attached to a return-reply card.

active Of or relating to an asset in which there is a large amount of buying and selling. Active assets are easier to buy and sell without affecting price. In securities trading, an active stock or bond usually has a smaller spread between the bid and ask price.

active income Income derived from performing services. Active income includes tips, wages, salaries, commissions, and returns from active participation in a business. Active income is distinguished from portfolio income and passive income.

active investment management The management of an investment portfolio that involves active trading of securities in an attempt to produce above-average returns on a risk-adjusted basis. Active management is predicated on the belief that it is possible to beat the market averages consistently. —Compare PASSIVE INVESTMENT MANAGEMENT.

active market An asset market or the market for a particular asset in which trading is relatively heavy. Frequently used to describe a securities market in which there is heavy trading volume. An active market makes it easier to acquire or dispose of large positions without affecting price.

activity The amount of relative trading volume in an asset.

activity charge A fee resulting from servicing an account. For example, a financial institution may levy an activity charge on an account in which transactions exceed the maximum number permitted. Likewise, some financial institutions charge a fee for ATM withdrawals.

activity ratio An indicator of how rapidly a firm converts various accounts into cash or sales. In general, the sooner management can convert assets into sales or cash, the more effectively the firm is being run. —See also FIXED-ASSET TURNOVER; INVENTORY TURNOVER; TOTAL ASSET TURNOVER.

act of God An unexpected and destructive natural catastrophe such as a hurricane, tornado, or earthquake.

Act of State Doctrine The principle that actions that occur within a sovereign nation are not subject to the courts of another nation.

actual In commodities, the physical asset (that is, the commodity) as opposed to a futures contract on that asset. —Also called *cash commodity*.

actual cash value The amount of cash to be received by the holder of a whole life insurance policy in the event the policy is surrendered. Cash value results from a policyholder paying premiums that more than cover the cost of the death benefit.

actual cost The price paid for an asset, generally including any freight and installation costs.

actuarial table —See MORTALITY TABLE.

actuary An insurance company professional trained in mathematics and statistics who calculates premiums, dividends, pensions, reserves, employee benefits, and risks.

ADA —See AMERICANS WITH DISABILITIES ACT.

addendum An addition or attachment to a book or document. For example, a contract may include an addendum with additional specifications not spelled out in the main text.

additional paid-in capital Stockholder contributions that are in excess of a stock's stated or par value. For example, if a firm issues stock with a par value of $1 per share but sells the stock to investors at $10 per share, the firm's financial statements will show $1 in common stock and $9 in additional paid-in capital for each share issued. —Also called *capital contributed in excess of par value; capital surplus; paid-in surplus.*

additur A court-ordered increase in a jury award. For example, a judge decides a jury award is inadequate.

add-on Funds that are added to a certificate of deposit after its date of purchase and that earn the same rate of interest as funds deposited with the original certificate. The add-ons allowed by some savings institutions provide an important benefit to savers during periods of declining interest rates.

add-on financing —See FOLLOW-ON OFFERING.

add-on interest Interest that is calculated on and added to the original principal of a loan. Add-on interest essentially increases the amount of the loan and results in a stated interest rate that is artificially low. For example, borrowing $1,000 for one year at add-on interest of 8% would result in an original balance of $1,080 and monthly payments of $1,080/12, or $90.

address of record The official location of a person, business, or organization.

ademption Failure of a specific bequest in a will because the designated property is not available for transfer. For example, a father's will designates a daughter as beneficiary of the family home that is later sold by the father prior to death. The home is unavailable for transfer by the will.

adequacy of coverage The degree to which an asset owner is protected with insurance against loss of value. For example, a homeowner's insurance policy may provide coverage for only 60% of a home's replacement cost. —See also OVERINSURED; UNDERINSURED.

adhesion contract A one-sided agreement offered by the stronger party on a take-it-or-leave-it basis. For example, an insurance contract is presented by a large insurance company to an individual who must accept the terms of the contract or go elsewhere.

ad hoc Latin, meaning "for a special purpose." A company may appoint members to an ad hoc committee to study methods that will reduce the firm's energy costs. The ad hoc committee is dissolved when the charge is completed.

ad infinitum Without end. For example, an issue of preferred stock has no maturity date and pays dividends ad infinitum.

adjudication Rendering a final judgment in a legal proceeding.

adjustable life insurance Life insurance that permits the insured to change the amount of the premium, the amount of coverage, the period of protection, and the length of coverage.

adjustable peg Fixed currency exchange rates with intermittent adjustment in the rates.

adjustable-rate mortgage (ARM) A real estate loan on which the interest rate is periodically adjusted, generally semiannually. The rate is set based on some short-term interest rate such as the six-month U.S. Treasury bill rate. Adjustable-rate mortgages generally include a maximum amount the interest rate can increase during a given year and over the life of the loan. For example, an adjustable-rate loan with a starting interest rate of 5% might limit annual changes to 2% and limit the lifetime change to 5%. In this case, the interest rate on the loan could not rise above 10%. Adjustable-rate loans tend to transfer risk from the lender to the borrower. —Compare FIXED-RATE LOAN. —Also called *variable-rate mortgage.* —See also ADJUSTMENT PERIOD; ANNUAL CAP; CONVERSION OPTION; CONVERTIBLE ARM; TWO-STEP MORTGAGE.

adjustable-rate preferred stock —See FLOATING-RATE PREFERRED STOCK.

adjusted basis The acquisition cost of an asset after it has been adjusted to reflect changes in cost basis that result from the occurrence of certain events after the date of acquisition. The cost basis of real estate may be adjusted for depreciation or improvement. Stock dividends, stock splits, and dividends deemed to be returned on capital cause a downward adjustment in the cost basis of a security. Conversely, commissions result in an upward adjustment in the cost basis. Adjusted basis is used in calculating gains and losses for tax purposes.

adjusted gross estate The monetary value of an estate after subtracting court costs, attorney fees, and debts of the deceased, but not estate taxes. —See also TAXABLE ESTATE.

adjusted gross income The amount of taxable income that remains after certain allowed business-related deductions—such as alimony payments, contributions to a Keogh retirement plan, and in some cases, contributions to an IRA—are subtracted from an individual's gross income. Adjusted gross income and gross income will be the same for many taxpayers.

adjuster A property and casualty insurance company employee who settles claims filed by the firm's customers. The adjuster must determine the validity and dollar value of claims.

adjusting entry In accounting, an end-of-period bookkeeping entry that assigns income and/or expenses to an earlier period.

adjustment bond —See INCOME BOND.

adjustment in conversion terms An alteration in the terms under which a convertible security may be exchanged. For example, if an issuer implements a two-for-one split (resulting in a doubling of the number of shares) in the common stock into which its convertible security may be exchanged, the issuer will nearly always be required to reduce the convertible's conversion price by half. Automatic price adjustments also may be scheduled throughout the life of a convertible security.

adjustment period The period between interest rate changes for adjustable-rate loans. A one-year adjustment period means the interest rate can change only once every 12 months.

adjustments to income Any of various amounts a taxpayer is allowed to subtract from his or her gross income when calculating adjusted gross income. These adjustments are permitted even if the taxpayer does not itemize deductions during a tax year. Allowable adjustments of particular interest to investors are interest penalties on early savings withdrawals and payments into IRAs and Keogh plans. —See also ADJUSTED GROSS INCOME.

administered price The price of a good or service that is established by an administrative process such as a government commission decision or business collusion. The federal minimum wage is an example of an administered price.

administrative law The body of law covering agencies created by the U.S. Congress or state legislatures. Much of administrative law addresses benefits administered by the agencies.

administrator or administratrix 1. A person who performs managerial duties. 2. The court-appointed person or institution charged with handling the estate of someone who has died without a will. —See also EXECUTOR.

administrator's deed A legal document used by the executor of an estate to transfer assets.

admitted assets In insurance, assets that are permitted by state insurance regulators in determining whether an insurance or reinsurance company is solvent. Only admitted assets may be listed on an insurance company's balance sheet.

ADR 1. —See AMERICAN DEPOSITARY RECEIPT. 2. —See ASSET DEPRECIATION RANGE.

ADR ratio The number of foreign shares represented by one American Depositary Receipt.

ad valorem tariff A customs duty whose size is based on the value of the goods being brought into the country. For example, a tariff is calculated as 10% of the value of merchandise being imported. —Compare SPECIFIC TARIFF.

ad valorem tax A tax that is computed as a percentage of the value of specific property. For example, local governments typically levy an annual tax on real estate. Some states levy an annual tax on the market value of an investor's securities as of a certain date. —Also called *property tax.* —See also TAX-EXEMPT PROPERTY.

advance 1. Money provided by an employer to an employee before the money is earned. For example, a new employee may seek an advance to pay for moving expenses and necessities. —Also called *cash advance.* 2. Prepayment for a good or service. Authors often get an advance against royalties from publishers. 3. An increase in the price of a security.

advance death benefit Reduced amount paid directly to a life insurance policyholder who has a short life expectancy.

advance refunding —See PREREFUNDING.

adversary An opponent. For example, two firms manufacturing the same type of product are likely to be adversaries in that they have the same pool of potential customers.

adverse action Any act that negatively affects a consumer. For example, an insurance company denies coverage to an applicant or a credit card issuer increases the interest rate charged on outstanding balances of an existing cardholder.

adverse opinion An opinion by a firm's auditors that the firm's financial statements do not accurately present its operating results or financial position. This unusual opinion is a strong warning that something at the firm may be very wrong. —Compare CLEAN OPINION. —See also QUALIFIED OPINION; SUBJECT TO OPINION.

adverse possession Acquiring title to land by continuous and open use of the land for a specified period of time defined by the state government in which the land is located. —Also called *squatter's rights.*

adverse selection 1. The likelihood that goods and services of inferior quality will dominate a market in which buyers have difficulty judging quality. Thus, consumers are likely to make an adverse selection and choose goods and services of poor quality. **2.** The predisposition of people most likely to file an insurance claim to purchase insurance coverage. For example, people in poor health are most likely to buy health insurance. —See also MORAL HAZARD.

adverse use Gaining access and utilizing property without the owner's permission.

advertising Paid communication that attempts to influence opinion regarding products, services, or thoughts.

advertising elasticity The responsiveness of quantity demanded in relation to a change in funds spent on advertising. Advertising elasticity is a measure of the effectiveness of advertising expenditures and should be an important consideration in the allocation of an advertising budget among various products.

advertising substantiation The Federal Trade Commission requirement that advertisers and advertising agencies have a reasonable basis (objective evidence) for advertising claims before the claims are disseminated. For example, a company that advertises that "four out of five individuals who tried the new product preferred it over their regular brand" must be able to provide the results of a reliable survey that support the claim.

> **CASE STUDY** The Federal Trade Commission announced in early 2007 that it would levy a $25 million fine against the marketers of four weight-loss pills including Xenadrine EFX, One A Day Weight Smart, CortiSlim, and TrimSpa. The FTC charged the marketers of these pills with making false advertising claims relating to weight loss and health benefits. The marketers had made a variety of health claims including reductions in the risk of Alzheimer's and cancer. According to the FTC, the firms did not have advertising substantiation for the claims, and in one case actually possessed a study indicating that individuals taking a placebo lost more weight than individuals taking their product. The FTC chairman stated that although the firms would be required to quit making the false claims, the pills would remain available for sale. The chairman also indicated a portion of the fines would be returned to consumers.

advertorial An advertisement that is designed and presented to resemble an editorial or news story.

advised credit A letter of credit for which the beneficiary has been notified of terms and conditions by the advising bank.

Advisers Act —See INVESTMENT ADVISERS ACT OF 1940.

advisers' sentiment A contrarian technical indicator derived from market forecasts regarding the future course of security prices and predicated on the theory that when

---

advertising

I operate a small service company and am trying to determine the most effective way to advertise. With limited funds available for advertising should I concentrate on the local newspaper, or should I purchase time on radio or television?

It's not so much with which medium you choose to advertise as the frequency of your message. Too many companies blow their budget with long, elaborate spots on television or radio or full pages in newspapers. It's better to have a campaign of smaller ads than to spend all of your money making a big splash that is forgotten quickly.

■ Tom Mesereau, Principal, Mesereau Public Relations, Parker, CO

---

most advisers expect a certain market movement, the opposite movement is most likely to occur. For example, strong bullish sentiment from investment advisers is often considered a bearish sign, while strong bearish sentiment is considered a bullish sign. —Compare SENTIMENT INDEX.

advising bank A correspondent bank that handles letters of credit on behalf of a foreign bank. The advising bank notifies the exporting firm of the terms and opening of the letter of credit.

advisory account A brokerage account in which the broker may make limited investment decisions without consulting the customer. Securities traded in the account are confined to those that meet the customer's investment goals. —Compare DISCRETIONARY ACCOUNT.

advisory fee —See MANAGEMENT FEE 1.

affiant The person who makes and signs an affidavit.

affidavit A written legal document with facts and statements sworn under oath to be true.

affiliate An organization that is related to another organization through some type of control or ownership. For example, a U.S.–based company may have a foreign affiliate that handles overseas sales.

affiliated chain A collection of retail stores that buy as a group in order to obtain lower prices from suppliers. For example, an independent grocery store might join an association that offers bulk purchasing and lower prices than the store could obtain on its own.

affiliated person A person who is in a position to influence a firm's management decisions. Affiliated persons usually include directors, officers, owners of more than 10% of the firm's outstanding stock, and family members or close associates of these groups. —Also called *control person*.

affinity card A debit or credit card issued through an agreement between a card issuer and a sponsoring organization. The card is offered to the organization's members and often provides users with special benefits, such as reduced interest rates or no annual fee, and the sponsoring organization with compensation.

affinity diagram A chart of opinions, ideas, or concepts sorted into related groups. Affinity diagrams are used to bring some semblance of order to seemingly unrelated information.

affinity fraud Investment scams that target members of identifiable groups, including elderly, ethnic, professional, and religious groups. Perpetrators of affinity fraud are often either members of the targeted group or individuals who enlist the assistance of leaders in order to exploit the trust of members of the group. —See also PYRAMID[1].

affirmative action Measures taken in recruitment, hiring, and advancement to provide members of identified groups with improved economic and educational opportunities. —See also REVERSE DISCRIMINATION.

affreightment A contract between a shipper and a cargo carrier for transport of cargos, often over a period of time.

AFL-CIO A federation of labor unions formed in 1955 by the merger of the American Federation of Labor and the Congress of Industrial Organizations. —See also CHANGE TO WIN.

after-acquired clause **1.** In mortgage lending, a clause specifying that property acquired by the borrower following the signing of the mortgage will be included as collateral in the lien. The clause improves the quality of the lender's claim. **2.** In asset-based lending, a clause specifying that additional receivables and inventories acquired by the borrower will be included as collateral for the loan agreement. An after-acquired clause is a particularly important component of loans backed by current assets that are continually replaced during the normal course of business.

after-acquired title A deed to real property that was not properly held by the seller at the time of the transaction but must be conveyed to the buyer or his successors when subsequently obtained.

after-hours trading —See EXTENDED-HOURS TRADING.

aftermarket —See SECONDARY MARKET.

aftertax proceeds Funds that remain from the sale of an asset after all expenses and taxes have been paid.

aftertax profit —See NET INCOME.

aftertax yield The rate of return on an investment after taxes have been calculated and subtracted. Aftertax yield, as opposed to pretax yield, is generally a preferred basis for comparing investment alternatives.

age discrimination The use of age as a consideration in employment decisions. For example, a business, concerned about the escalating cost of health benefits, requires employees to retire upon reaching age 55. Most employees are protected from age discrimination by a series of federal laws including the Age Discrimination Employment Act of 1967.

agency **1.** A relationship between an agent and a principal in which the agent acts for and represents the principal on the basis of the principal's instructions. **2.** A security issued by a federal agency or federally sponsored corporation. —See also FEDERAL AGENCY SECURITY; FEDERALLY SPONSORED CORPORATE SECURITY.

agency disclosure Revealing the party for whom an agent is working. For example, most states require real estate agents to provide a written disclosure of whether they are working for the seller, buyer, or both.

agency risk The possibility a firm's managers will not act in the best interest of its stockholders. For example, if managers attempt to ensure their job tenure by making low-risk investment decisions, such decisions may penalize the firm's profitability and the stockholders' return. Likewise, managers may spend the firm's money to benefit themselves rather than stockholders.

agency shop An organization in which a union represents all employees. Employees of an agency shop are not required to be union members but are required to pay union dues.

agency disclosure
I am in the process of buying a house. How can I make certain that a real estate agent is working in my interest?

You must hire the agent and the agent's company to represent you by signing a contract typically referred to as a "buyer brokerage agreement." The real estate company (and its agents) promise to legally represent you and work in your best interests as they show you houses, negotiate price and terms, prepare a contract, and help you close the deal. As the buyer, you promise to use only this company in your home search. Typically there are no fees paid in advance, and the company is paid at closing from a portion of the commission paid by the seller.

Most real estate companies also list properties for sale, in which case they are representing the seller. So if you buy a home listed by the company you hired, does that company represent you or the seller? The answer is both, through a relationship known as "dual agency." Dual agency occurs often and is hardly ever an issue, unless the agent you are working with is also the listing agent of the home you want to buy. In this case, the company's broker/manager has the option of designating another agent within the company to assist you in buying the home. This provides some degree of "arm's length" separation among the parties so the seller and buyer can have more assurance that their interests are being properly represented without any conflict.

In reality, most buyers do not hire a company in advance, because they do not want to be tied down to one agent or company in their home search. If they find a home they want to buy through an agent, the sales contract they sign will designate the agent's company as representing the buyer in this particular transaction only.

▪ Scott Alderman, Broker and President, First Commercial Real Estate, Valdosta, GA

agent An individual or organization that acts on behalf of and is subject to the control of another party. For example, in executing an order to buy or sell a security, a broker is acting as a customer's agent. Likewise, an insurance professional is acting as an agent when selling and servicing insurance policies. —See also SUBAGENT.

aggregate demand In economics, the total amount of spending during a period on goods and services by consumers, businesses, and governments. Aggregate demand drives economic activity.

aggregate supply In economics, the overall production of goods and services that are made available to satisfy demand from consumers, businesses, and government.

aggressive Of or relating to an investment philosophy that seeks to achieve above-average returns by accepting above-average risks. An example of an aggressive investment posture would be confining one's investments to the common stocks of companies in young industries with high growth potential. Likewise, purchasing undeveloped real estate is more aggressive than acquiring rental property.

aggressive growth fund An investment company that attempts to maximize capital gains by investing in the stocks of companies that offer the potential for very rapid growth. Aggressive growth funds tend to produce very high returns in bull markets and relatively large losses in bear markets. Shares of an aggressive growth fund produce very little current income and are subject to wide variations in value. —Also called *performance fund.*

aging A technique for evaluating the composition of a firm's accounts receivable to determine whether irregularities exist. It is carried out by grouping a firm's accounts receivable according to the length of time accounts have been outstanding. For example, a financial analyst may use aging to determine whether a firm carries many overdue debtors that may never pay their bills. —Also called *account aging; receivables aging.*

agrarian Of or describing an economy or society that is heavily dependent on breeding and raising livestock and growing agricultural products. Agrarian economies are generally associated with a relatively low standard of living.

agreement A mutually acceptable verbal or written arrangement between two or more parties.

agreement among underwriters A contract signed by members of an underwriting syndicate that specifies the syndicate manager, additional managers, member liability, and life of the group. —Compare UNDERWRITING AGREEMENT.

agreement corporation —See EDGE ACT CORPORATION.

agribusiness Commercial operations related to the production, marketing, and supply of farm products and services.

AI —See ARTIFICIAL INTELLIGENCE.

AICPA —See AMERICAN INSTITUTE OF CERTIFIED PUBLIC ACCOUNTANTS.

AIS —See ACCOUNTING INFORMATION SYSTEMS.

aleatory contract An agreement between parties in which the performance by one party is dependent on an uncertain event or contingency. A liability insurance policy is an example of an aleatory contract in that payment by the insurance company is dependent on an event that results in a liability of the insured.

algorithm A precise set of rules for solving a problem. An algorithm can be as simple as a recipe for vegetable soup or as complicated as a complex computer program.

alias An alternate or assumed name for something. For example, in computer use an alias may be assigned to a file name.

alienation In real estate, the transfer of title and possession of real property to another person.

alienation clause —See DUE-ON-SALE CLAUSE.

alien corporation —See FOREIGN CORPORATION.

alimony Court-ordered support to a separated or divorced person by a spouse. Alimony payments must meet certain requirements, such as being paid via check or cash, in order to be deductible for tax purposes.

allegation In law, a formal accusation that must be proved or supported with evidence.

all-holders rule An SEC rule that prohibits bidders and target companies from excluding a stockholder or a group of stockholders from a tender offer. —See also EXCLUSIONARY TENDER OFFER.

all-in cost The total expense of a financial transaction, including interest, fees, and discounts. All-in cost is generally stated as an annualized rate. A loan with a stated interest rate of 6% may have an all-in cost of 6.75%.

allocate 1. To spread systematically a single monetary amount over a number of time periods, usually years. For example, depreciation allocates the cost of a capital asset over its useful life. **2.** To distribute cost or revenue throughout a number of operations or products. For example, a business must decide how to allocate the costs of running its headquarters over all its operations to determine the profitability of each of those operations.

allocation of resources —See RESOURCE ALLOCATION.

allodial system An arrangement of land ownership in which real property is owned without any rent or service owed to the government.

all-or-none offering In investing, a securities offering in which the entire issue must be sold or the securities will be withdrawn from distribution. With an all-or-none offering, no sale is considered final until the issuer has determined that the entire issue has been distributed.

all-or-none order A limit order by an investor in which the broker is directed to attempt to fill the entire amount of the order or, failing that, to fill none of it. —See also FILL-OR-KILL ORDER.

allotment Securities apportioned to members of an underwriting syndicate for resale to investors.

allowance 1. Funds set aside for a potential expense. 2. Funds allocated for a regular expenditure such as the expense of operating a personal vehicle for business purposes. 3. A benefit offered to a distributor or retailer in exchange for a specific activity, such as product placement or advertising. —See also TRADE ALLOWANCE.

allowance for bad debts —See ALLOWANCE FOR DOUBTFUL ACCOUNTS.

allowance for depreciation —See ACCUMULATED DEPRECIATION.

allowance for doubtful accounts A balance-sheet account established to offset expected bad debts. If a firm has made a sufficient provision in its allowance for doubtful accounts, reported earnings will not be penalized by bad debts when the bad debts occur. If uncollectible accounts are larger than expected, however, the firm will have to increase the size of the account and reduce reported income. —Also called *allowance for bad debts; reserve for bad debts.*

all-risk insurance Comprehensive insurance coverage for all perils unless a peril is specifically excluded. For example, a homeowner's insurance policy is likely to exclude losses due to damage from earthquakes and flooding.

alpha The mathematical estimate of the return on a security when the market return as a whole is zero. Alpha is derived from a in the formula $R_i = a + bR_m$, which measures the return on a security (R_i) for a given return on the market (R_m) where b is beta. —See also CAPITAL-ASSET PRICING MODEL.

alt-A loan Credit provided to someone with a generally clean credit record but who suffers some deficiency such as incomplete documentation, an unsteady income, or an inability or unwillingness to make a regular down payment. Alt-A loans fall between prime loans and subprime loans, although the actual boundaries are vague.

alternate beneficiary A person or organization to whom property passes through a will or trust when the primary beneficiary is unable or declines to accept the property. For example, an alternate beneficiary of an insurance policy receives proceeds of the policy when the primary beneficiary is deceased.

alternate valuation date In federal estate taxes, the valuation of an estate six months following the date of death, or the date on which the assets are disposed of if this occurs within the six-month period. The alternate valuation date can be chosen to value estate assets if the value at this date is lower than at the time of death.

alternative minimum tax (AMT) A parallel federal tax on taxable income as adjusted for specific deductions and tax-preference items, such as passive losses from tax shelters and interest paid on certain municipal bonds. The intent of the AMT is to ensure that nearly all individuals, especially those with high gross incomes, much of which is sheltered under normal reporting, pay at least some tax. The AMT was designed without automatic inflation adjustments, resulting in the tax impacting increasing numbers of middle-income taxpayers. —Also called *minimum tax.* —See also PRIVATE ACTIVITY BOND.

alternative mortgage instrument (AMI) A loan with real property as collateral that differs in one or more ways from a standard mortgage that has a fixed interest rate, a level premium, and a fixed term at the end of which the loan is fully repaid. Mortgages with a variable interest rate and interest-only loans are classified as alternative mortgage instruments.

amass To accumulate an unusually large amount of an asset. For example, a wealthy investor may amass a large stock of gold, or a profitable business with few investment alternatives may amass cash.

Ambac Assurance Corporation A subsidiary of publicly traded Ambac Financial Group that provides financial guarantees for municipal borrowers and for asset-backed and structured issues. Ambac was founded in 1971 as a subsidiary of MGIC Investment Corporation and later owned by Baldwin-United and Citibank. —Formerly called *American Municipal Bond Assurance Corporation.*

A. M. Best Company A firm that is widely recognized for its ratings of insurers. The highest Best rating for insurers is A++, and some financial advisers suggest that individuals limit selections to companies rated A++ and A+.

ambush marketing A promotion tactic designed to associate a company, product, or service with a particular event, or to attract the attention of people attending the event, without payment being made for an official sponsorship. For example, a business affiliates itself with a particular athlete or sports team rather than paying to become an official Olympics sponsor. Successful ambush marketing diminishes the value of an official sponsorship. —Also called *parasitic marketing.*

> **CASE STUDY** There is no better place to spring an ambush marketing campaign than at the world's biggest sporting event. While the Super Bowl is the premiere sporting event in the United States, the World Cup sits at the pinnacle and attracts three times the television viewers of the annual U.S. football championship. Even U.S.-based companies such as Coca-Cola, Gillette, and Anheuser Busch each paid nearly $50 million to become one of the 15 official sponsors of the 2006 World Cup. Athletic clothing supplier Adidas has been a long-time official sponsor of World Cups, including the 2006 matches held in Germany. Adidas was also the official sponsor of several teams, including powerful Argentina. To the anguish of Adidas, competitor Nike always seems to develop a successful ambush-marketing campaign at world-class sporting events such as the Olympics and World Cup. Prior to the 2006 World Cup, Nike launched a social networking website for the world's soccer fans as part of its "Joga Bonito" (a beautiful game) marketing campaign. The company claimed that widespread interest in its website, along with sponsorship of the Brazilian soccer team, successfully competed with the higher costs of the official sponsorship by Adidas.

amended return A tax return that is filed to correct an error or omission in an earlier return. Individuals file Form 1040X to correct previously filed forms 1040, 1040A, or 1040EZ.

amendment A change or addition to a legal document that has the same legal standing as the original document.

amenity A feature that adds value or perceived value to something. For example, a swimming pool is an important amenity of many apartment complexes.

American Arbitration Association An organization that provides information, assistance, and expertise to individuals, groups, and businesses that desire to resolve conflicts without going to court. The association will assist with providing information, establishing hearings, and appointing mediators. It also offers rules for contracts that permit affected parties to request arbitration or mediation.

American Association of Individual Investors (AAII) An organization that sponsors publications, seminars, and other educational programs for individual investors. This group, established in 1979, has its headquarters in Chicago.

American currency quotation In foreign exchange trading, the value of a foreign currency in terms of the U.S. dollar. For example, if the euro is worth $1.30, the American currency quotation would be expressed as 1.30, meaning there are 1.3 dollars to the euro. —Compare EUROPEAN CURRENCY QUOTATION. —Also called *multiplier.*

American Depositary Receipt (ADR) The physical certificate that exchanges on a one-on-one basis for an American Depositary Share. American Depositary Shares trade electronically, but only American Depositary Receipts can be delivered to an investor. Although American Depositary Receipts and American Depositary Shares are different, the terms are frequently used interchangeably. —See also SPONSORED AMERICAN DEPOSITARY RECEIPT; UNSPONSORED AMERICAN DEPOSITARY RECEIPT.

American Federation of Labor–Congress of Industrial Organizations —See AFL-CIO.

American Institute of Certified Public Accountants (AICPA) A professional association for certified public accountants that provides guidance to members on accounting techniques and standards. The AICPA determines how financial data are calculated and reported to stockholders.

American Municipal Bond Assurance Corporation —See AMBAC ASSURANCE CORPORATION.

American National Standards Institute (ANSI) A private nonprofit organization founded in 1918 to administer and coordinate the U.S. voluntary standardization and conformity assessment system.

American option A put or call option that permits the owner to exercise the option at any time on or before the expiration date. —Compare ASIAN OPTION; EUROPEAN OPTION.

American Stock Exchange (AMEX, ASE) A large floor- and electronic-based securities exchange in New York City that provides facilities for trading stocks, bonds, index shares, and equity derivative securities. The AMEX, a leader in introducing new investment products such as exchange-traded funds, was acquired in 2008 by NYSE Euronext. —See also CURB EXCHANGE.

Americans with Disabilities Act (ADA) Federal civil rights legislation passed in 1990 that guarantees individuals with disabilities will have an equal opportunity to participate in activities, programs, and services. The law applies to accommodations, employment, public services, telecommunications, and transportation.

AMEX —See AMERICAN STOCK EXCHANGE.

amicus curiae A Latin term meaning "friend of the court" that refers to a person or organization that provides testimony in a lawsuit to which it is not a party. For example, the Sierra Club might offer testimony in support of someone involved in an environmental lawsuit.

amortization A gradual reduction in the value of an amount over time. For example, amortization of a loan is a gradual reduction in the amount owed when a series of equal payments are each credited against periodic interest and a portion of principal. —See also AMORTIZED LOAN.

amortization schedule A table that illustrates for each payment period of a loan the payment, interest expense, principal reduction, and loan balance over time.

amortize To write off gradually and systematically a given amount of money within a specific number of time periods. For example, an accountant amortizes the cost of a long-term asset by deducting a portion of that cost against income in each period.

amortized loan A loan in which periodic payments reduce principal as well as cover any periodic interest that is charged. A home mortgage that requires equal monthly payments over a specified number of years is an example of an amortized loan. Likewise, a car loan with equal monthly payments is an amortized loan. —Compare TERM LOAN. —Also called *constant payment loan.*

amount financed The amount of funds that are actually advanced to a borrower. Prepaid finance charges are subtracted from the loan's principal in determining the amount financed.

AMT —See ALTERNATIVE MINIMUM TAX.

analog Of or relating to data expressed in continuously variable physical quantities. For example, a phonograph record contains analog data that is continuous along the record's grooves. Transferring music from a record to a CD is an example of changing analog data to digital data. —Compare DIGITAL.

analysis An examination of the components of the entirety in an attempt to better understand the entirety and the relationships of the components. For example, a loan officer will do an analysis of a potential borrower's financial statements by examining income, assets, and liabilities.

analysis of variance Examination of the association between predictor variables and an outcome variable. For example, a financial analyst might examine the effect of changes in earnings per share, dividends, and cash flow on a stock's market price.

analyst A person who is skilled at evaluating data. —See also FINANCIAL ANALYST.

anchoring bias Basing a judgment on a familiar reference point that is incomplete or irrelevant to the problem being solved. For example, a consumer judges the relative value of a product on the basis of the cost in some previous period. An investor judges a stock price as overvalued or undervalued based on the stock's previous high price.

anchor tenant A major owner or lessee that increases traffic to a real estate development. Large and well-known department stores such as Dillard's and JCPenney are anchor tenants for many retail shopping malls. Large financial institutions are often anchor tenants in office buildings. —Also called *prime tenant.*

ancillary Of or relating to something that is available but not essential. For example, a study guide is one of several ancillary materials offered for many college textbooks.

ancillary probate Probate in a state that is different from the state in which a deceased person resided at the time of death.

angel investor A wealthy investor who provides capital for new business ventures.

annex To incorporate territory into an existing political entity. For example, a town council may vote to annex an adjacent parcel of land so that the land becomes part of the town.

annual cap The amount a variable-rate loan can increase during a calendar year. For example, an adjustable-rate loan may specify an annual cap for the amount the interest rate can be increased. Some states have instituted annual caps for property tax rates.

annual debt service The total amount of cash required by a business to pay interest plus the principal on maturing debt during the year.

annualized Of or relating to a variable that has been mathematically converted to a yearly rate. Inflation and interest rates are generally annualized since it is on this basis that these two variables are ordinarily stated and compared. As an example, disregarding the effects of compounding, the earning of a 3% return on an investment during a four-month period is equal to 9% (12/4 × 3%) on an annualized basis.

annual meeting The annual gathering of a corporation's directors, officers, and shareholders, during which new directors are elected, shareholder resolutions are passed or defeated, and operating and financial results of the past fiscal year are discussed.

annual mortgage constant Annual mortgage payments as a proportion of the initial principal amount of the mortgage.

annual mortgagor statement The annual report sent by a mortgage lender to a borrower describing the amount of interest and taxes paid during the previous year and the outstanding principal on the loan.

annual percentage rate (APR) The effective cost of credit on a consumer loan. The APR is calculated using interest, origination fees, and points. The APR must be disclosed to borrowers, who can utilize the information to compare rates being charged by different lenders. —See also EXACT INTEREST.

annual percentage yield (APY) The effective return, expressed as a percentage, earned on a deposit account. APY takes into account the effect of compounding and indicates the amount of interest a depositor will earn during a year assuming no withdrawals or additional deposits occur.

annual report A firm's annual statement of operating and financial results. The annual report contains an income statement, a balance sheet, a statement of changes in financial position, an auditor's report, and a summary of operations. Because many annual reports are prepared with public relations as a primary focus, serious investors should obtain a copy of a firm's 10–K in order to obtain detailed financial data.

annuitant The recipient of an annuity.

annuitize To convert a sum of money into a series of payments. For example, an investor may pay a sum of money in return for a lifetime series of monthly payments. The winner of a lottery may choose to have the monetary award annuitized.

annuity A stream of equal payments that occur at predetermined intervals (that is, monthly or annually). The payments may continue for a fixed period or for a contingent period, such as for the recipient's lifetime. Although annuities are most often associated with insurance companies and retirement programs, the payment of interest to a bondholder is also an example of an annuity. —See also ANNUITY CERTAIN; CONTINGENT ANNUITY; DEFERRED ANNUITY; FIXED ANNUITY; JOINT AND SURVIVOR ANNUITY; REFUND ANNUITY; STRAIGHT LIFE ANNUITY; TAX-SHELTERED ANNUITY; VARIABLE ANNUITY.

annuity bond —See CONSOL.

annuity certain An annuity that provides a fixed number of payments. If the annuitant dies prior to the completion of the contract, payments continue to the annuitant's designated beneficiary. —Also called *period certain annuity.*

annuity death benefit A guarantee in an annuity contract that the beneficiary will receive the value of the annuity in the event the annuity owner dies prior to the time benefit payments run out.

annuity due An annuity in which payments are made at the beginning of each period. —Compare ORDINARY ANNUITY.

ANSI —See AMERICAN NATIONAL STANDARDS INSTITUTE.

antedate To assign a date to a document that is earlier than the document's actual execution. For example, a contract executed on June 25 is dated June 23. —Also called *predate.*

anticipated holding period The time period during which a partnership expects to retain an asset.

anticipatory breach Declaration by one party to a contract that the terms of the contract will not be fulfilled. For example, a supplier may inform a customer that a product will not be delivered at the agreed-upon price.

antidilution clause A stipulation of virtually every convertible security that requires an adjustment to the conversion terms in the event of certain occurrences, such as stock splits, stock dividends, and new stock issues, that would dilute the value of the conversion privilege. As an example, a bond convertible into 40 shares of stock would have its terms changed to conversion into 120 shares if the stock split 3 for 1.

antidilutive Of or relating to the conversion of convertible securities into common stock when such conversion would result in an increase in diluted earnings per share or a decrease in diluted loss per share. For example, it is an antidilutive conversion if outstanding warrants are assumed to be exercised in order to acquire shares of common stock at a higher price than the market price of the stock. Such a conversion would result in an increase in diluted earnings per share. Conversions that would increase earnings per share or reduce loss per share are not generally used in calculating diluted earnings per share.

antidumping Of or relating to restrictions on the sale of imported goods at prices substantially lower than prices at which the same goods are sold in their home country. For example, a Chinese manufacturer of television sets would be prohibited from selling televisions in the United States at a price lower than the same sets were selling in China. —See also DUMPING 2.

antidumping duty A tax levied on imported goods that have been determined to be dumped, or sold below the home market price.

antigreenmail provision A provision in a firm's charter that prohibits management from purchasing a large shareholder's stock at a premium price without extending the same offer to other shareholders. —Compare GREENMAIL.

antilapse statute A law that permits descendents of an already deceased beneficiary to receive the beneficiary's share of an estate. An antilapse statute addresses the possibility that a beneficiary of a will may die prior to the death of the testator.

antiselection The tendency of people most likely to experience a loss to be more likely to buy or continue insurance coverage for such a loss. For example, people who continually experience illness are more likely than healthy people to buy or continue health insurance.

antitakeover measure An action by a firm's management to block or halt a takeover by another party. Examples of antitakeover measures include a fair-price amendment, staggered terms of office for directors, and a requirement for an increased number of affirmative votes from shareholders to approve a takeover.

antitakeover statute A state law that makes it easier for a firm based in that state to fend off a takeover hostile to the firm's management. Such a statute may actually penalize shareholders, because acquisition-minded firms or individuals may be less likely to make an offer for the firm's stock.

antitrust laws Federal and state statutes designed to promote competition among businesses. Antitrust laws in the United States originated from the laissez-faire excesses that took place in the early 1900s. Effectiveness of antitrust laws is heavily dependent on enforcement by the powers in charge—primarily the U.S. Justice Department. Thus, the success of antitrust laws has varied. —See also CELLER-KEFAUVER ANTIMERGER ACT; CLAYTON ACT; FEDERAL TRADE COMMISSION ACT OF 1914; SHERMAN ANTITRUST ACT.

> **CASE STUDY** Antitrust laws are often thought of as being directed toward competitors that meet in secret to devise a plan that will stifle competition and establish an artificially high price for their product. Or, perhaps, a company that attempts to drive its competitors out of business by temporarily reducing prices to a very low level. Giant forest-products company Weyerhaeuser successfully fought a $79 million jury award for antitrust violations related to paying too much for lumber, thereby driving smaller sawmills out of business. The plaintiff, Ross-Simmons Hardwood Lumber Co., had attempted to substantiate its case by claiming Weyerhaeuser was warehousing, rather than processing, much of the timber, thereby proving the firm was purchasing much more timber than required. Buying most of the timber resulted in Weyerhaeuser's competitors lacking raw materials and eventually going out of business.

any-and-all bid An offer to purchase all shares offered at a specified price until a predetermined date. A firm may make an any-and-all bid for the shares of a company it intends to acquire. —Compare TWO-TIER TENDER OFFER.

APB —See ACCOUNTING PRINCIPLES BOARD.

APB opinion A determination by the former Accounting Principles Board regarding the way a certain financial transaction is to be treated for reporting purposes. For example, APB Opinion 15 sets forth the ways in which convertible issues and common-stock equivalents are to be used in calculating earnings per share. In 1973 the Accounting Principles Board was superseded by the Financial Accounting Standards Board, thereby halting further APB opinions and initiating FASB statements.

APL Acronym for *A Programming Language*, a mathematical computer programming language that is best known for concise instructions that generate columns and rows of data.

apostille Document authentication for purposes of international acceptance in countries that subscribe to provisions of the 1961 Hague Convention. The convention designated a standardized apostille to simplify the certification and acceptance among countries of legal documents such as deeds and birth certificates.

apparent authority Responsibility of a principal when a third party has reason to believe that an agent of the principal has authority to bind the principal. For example, a customer (third party) may believe that a salesperson (agent) has the authority to quote a price that commits his employer (principal).

appeal bond In law, the guarantee as to payment of a legal judgment when the judgment is appealed to a higher court. The bond guarantees the original judgment will be paid in the event the appeal is unsuccessful.

appellant The party that appeals a judicial decision.

appellate court A higher court with the jurisdiction to review lower-court decisions when the losing party files an appeal.

appellee The winning party in a lawsuit whose verdict has been appealed to a higher court.

application A computer program written to accomplish a specific task. For example, Excel is a Microsoft application program that helps organize data into rows and columns.

application of funds statement —See STATEMENT OF CASH FLOWS.

applied economics The utilization of economic principles for solving real-world problems. For example, a corporate economist might use economic principles of supply and demand to make recommendations on how best to price a new product.

applied overhead Manufacturing costs other than direct labor and materials that are charged to a job or contract. Applied overhead includes expenses such as depreciation, insurance, and indirect labor.

applied research Research that is intended to resolve a specific problem or issue. For example, a home products company such as Procter & Gamble might conduct research for manufacturing a detergent with improved cleaning abilities.

apportionment The distribution of taxes among various states in which a multistate company has a presence.

appraisal An expert opinion on the value of an asset. An insurance company requires an appraisal of jewelry a person wishes to insure against theft or loss.

appraisal right The right of minority shareholders to obtain an independent valuation of their shares to determine a fair value in a two-tier tender offer. —See also FAIR PRICE AMENDMENT.

appraise 1. To estimate the value of an asset. 2. To consider something. For example, a marketing executive might appraise the potential of offering the firm's product in a foreign market.

appreciate To increase in value.

appreciation 1. An increase in value, as of an asset. 2. —Used to distinguish between securities that are likely to provide profits because of increases in price and those that provide dividend payments.

apprentice A person who is learning an occupation or trade, often as a member of a labor union. Working as an apprentice under supervision is often a requirement for subsequent work in an occupation.

appropriate 1. To take possession of the property of someone else. 2. To set aside funds for a specific purpose.

appropriated retained earnings Retained earnings that are unavailable for dividends. —Compare UNAPPROPRIATED RETAINED EARNINGS.

approved list —See LEGAL LIST.

appurtenant Something that is added or attached to something more important. For example, a property owner may have an easement that permits access via someone else's property. The easement is an appurtenant to the property.

APR —See ANNUAL PERCENTAGE RATE.

APY —See ANNUAL PERCENTAGE YIELD.

arb —See ARBITRAGEUR.

arbiter A person who has been chosen to settle a disputed issue. For example, the U.S. Tax Court is the arbiter of tax deficiencies determined by the Internal Revenue Service but disputed by the taxpayer.

arbitrage The simultaneous purchase and sale of substantially identical assets in order to profit from a price difference between the two assets. As a hypothetical example, if General Electric common stock trades at $35 on the New York Stock Exchange and at $34.75 on the Chicago Stock Exchange, an investor could guarantee a profit by purchasing the stock on the Chicago Stock Exchange and simultaneously selling the same amount of stock on the NYSE. —See also BASIS TRADING; RISK ARBITRAGE; TAX ARBITRAGE.

arbitrage bond A municipal bond issued for the purpose of investing the proceeds in securities with higher yields than those paid by the municipal bond. Generally, the arbitrage involves purchasing U.S. Treasury bonds that are used to prerefund an outstanding issue prior to the outstanding issue's call date.

arbitrage pricing theory A mathematical theory for explaining security values that holds that the return on an investment is a function of the investment's sensitivity to various common risk factors such as inflation and unemployment.

arbitrageur One who engages in arbitrage. —Also called *arb*.

arbitration A process for settling disputes between parties. For example, arbitration is often used between securities firms and their customers when the parties submit their differences to the judgment of an impartial third party or parties. Many brokerage firms require their customers to sign an agreement for binding arbitration to resolve disputes. —Compare MEDIATION. —See also AMERICAN ARBITRATION ASSOCIATION.

arbitration panel A group of individuals charged with resolving a dispute between individuals and/or organizations. Arbitration panels to resolve investment disputes are sponsored by self-regulatory organizations such as the National Association of Securities Dealers.

Archipelago An electronic communications network formed in 1996 as one of the four original ECNs approved by the SEC. In 2001 Archipelago received SEC approval to launch Archipelago Exchange (ArcaEx), an electronic stock market for New York Stock Exchange, American Stock Exchange, and Nasdaq securities. Archipelago merged with the New York Stock Exchange in 2006 to form NYSE Group.

arithmetic mean The result obtained from dividing a series of quantities by the number of quantities in the series. For example, the arithmetic mean of 6, 10, 16, and 20 is $(6+10+16+20)/4$, or 13. —Compare GEOMETRIC MEAN. —Also called *average; mean*.

ARM —See ADJUSTABLE-RATE MORTGAGE.

arm's length transaction A transfer of property between a willing buyer and a willing seller with no coercion or advantage being taken by either party. An arm's length transaction is most likely to result in a fair price to both the buyer and the seller.

arraignment The appearance in court of a defendant who is formally charged with a crime and asked to respond to the indictment or complaint.

arrangement fee The charge by a lender for setting up a loan. The fee is payable in advance and is generally applicable to mortgage loans.

array An orderly arrangement of something. For example, a spreadsheet can be used to produce an array of sales projections by month and year.

arrearage An overdue payment. —See also DIVIDENDS IN ARREARS.

articles of incorporation The document that a firm files with state authorities when establishing a corporation. This document contains the firm's name and address, the type and amount of stock to be authorized and issued, the type of business activity, a delineation of corporate powers, and other information. —Also called *charter*[1]; *corporate charter.*

artificial intelligence (AI) In computer science, machines responding to situations as if they were humans. For example, financial institutions utilize artificial intelligence in their computer systems to identify suspicious transactions. The ultimate in artificial intelligence was experienced by moviegoers who listened to Hal in *2001: A Space Odyssey.*

ASE —See AMERICAN STOCK EXCHANGE.

Asian currency Foreign currency–denominated deposits held in Asian financial institutions.

Asian option An option with a payoff that depends on the average price of the underlying asset during a period of time during the life of the option. —Compare AMERICAN OPTION; EUROPEAN OPTION.

as is Of or relating to an offer to sell an article in its existing condition. Potential buyers are free to inspect the article but have no recourse in the event a defect is discovered after purchase.

ask The price at which a security is offered for sale. —Compare BID 1. —Also called *offer.* —See also BEST ASK.

asking price The price at which something is offered for sale. The actual price paid may be different from the asking price, which is often negotiable.

assay A test to determine the purity of gold, silver, or other precious metals. Metals used for delivery of futures contracts must be assayed to verify that they meet standards established by the exchange on which the contracts trade.

assemblage In real estate, pulling together two or more properties to produce a larger parcel.

assembly language A computer programming language that permits a programmer to use words rather than the binary code of machine language. Assembly language is dependent on the hardware being utilized.

assembly line A production system in which an article moves from station to station, where repetitive operations are performed to efficiently convert inputs to a finished product. Assembly-line production standardizes operations in order to reduce costs and increase quality. Toyota Motor Corporation moved from a rigid assembly line, in which employees performed a specific task with dedicated equipment, to a more flexible production system in which workers were able to switch to different tasks.

assembly plant A building or collection of buildings where a series of parts are converted into a finished product.

assess 1. To impose a tax or fine on a person or organization. For example, a community may assess property owners for new sidewalks. 2. To establish a financial value for something. For example, an insurance adjuster assesses the cost of repairing the wrecked vehicle of a policyholder.

assessed value The designated value of an asset for purposes of levying a tax. —Also called *taxable value.*

assessment 1. The amount of money owed. For example, a taxpayer receives an assessment from the Internal Revenue Service for $2,000 in additional taxes. 2. Judgment of a situation. For example, a firm decides to forgo a merger because of the company president's negative assessment of the other firm's product mix.

assessment ratio The ratio of an asset's assessed valuation to the same asset's market valuation. If the assessment ratio is 40%, a home with a market value of $200,000 will be taxed at an assessed valuation of $80,000. Taxing authorities establish an assessment ratio in order to generate the appropriate amount of tax revenues.

assessor —See TAX ASSESSOR.

asset Something of monetary value that is owned by a firm or an individual. Assets are listed on a firm's balance sheet and include tangible items such as inventories, equipment, and real estate as well as intangible items such as property rights or goodwill. —Compare LIABILITY 1. —See also CURRENT ASSET; INTANGIBLE ASSET; TANGIBLE ASSET.

asset allocation The assignment of investment funds to broad categories of assets. For example, an individual investor decides to allocate a certain proportion of funds to bonds and a certain proportion to equities. Likewise, an investment manager may allocate clients' funds to common stocks representing various industries.

asset allocation fund An investment company that varies the proportion of its portfolio devoted to stocks, bonds, and money market securities in order to reduce the variability of returns and to take better advantage of different segments of the securities markets. An asset allocation fund is designed to save individual investors from being required to alter their investment mix in response to changes in market conditions.

asset-backed security A debt security collateralized by specific assets. Although the term applies to any debt backed by identified assets, it generally refers to securities backed by short-term collateral such as credit-card receivables, car loans, and home-equity loans. Because even the most financially strapped companies can hold valuable assets, it is possible for the credit quality of asset-backed securities to be substantially better than the general credit of the company issuing the securities.

asset class A category of investments, such as cash, near money, common equities, fixed income, international equities, and so forth.

asset depreciation range (ADR) The range of depreciable lives permitted by the Internal Revenue Service for specific classes of assets.

asset management account A comprehensive brokerage account that includes checking, a credit or debit card, margin loans, and the automatic sweep of cash balances into a savings account or money market fund. Examples of brokerage asset management accounts include Cash Management Account by Merrill Lynch (the first firm to offer this type account) and Financial Management Account by Smith Barney. Features and fees vary by firm. —Also called *central assets account; sweep account.*

asset play A stock with a market price considerably lower than the value of the firm's assets on a per-share basis. For example, a paper company may operate in an extremely competitive market and earn minimal profits. However, a financial analyst may believe investors are concentrating on poor earnings and are pricing the stock in a manner that does not consider extensive and valuable timber and real estate holdings and thus does not reflect the stock's current market price. Thus, the stock is an asset play.

asset redeployment The reallocation of underused assets in an attempt to make a firm more profitable. To effect asset redeployment, a company might sell a relatively unprofitable subsidiary and use the funds to strengthen another part of its business. Many corporate takeover attempts are based on the premise that assets will be redeployed once the acquisition has been completed.

asset stripping The sale of selected assets of an acquired company, generally for the purpose of raising money to pay off some of the debt incurred in financing the acquisition.

asset turnover —See TOTAL ASSET TURNOVER.

asset value —Used to refer to the stock of a company, especially a stock whose price does not necessarily reflect the full value of the firm's assets. This situation may occur when the assets are not producing much current income. —See also ASSET PLAY.

assign 1. To sign a document that transfers an asset or a right from one person to another. **2.** To decide which writer of an option or futures contract (the party that is short the security) will be required to perform the terms of the contract. Clearing corporations and brokerage companies usually assign this responsibility in a random manner when the holders of the contracts ask for delivery of the asset specified in the contract.

assigned dealer —See SPECIALIST.

assigned risk A substandard risk an insurance company would prefer to avoid but for which it is required by law to provide coverage. States frequently establish assigned-risk pools for motorists with poor driving records and homeowners who live in hurricane-prone locations.

assignee The person who is granted a contract or agreement. For example, a person will be the assignee of a deed following the purchase of property.

assignment 1. The transfer of an asset from one owner to another. The holder of a lease on an office building assigns the lease to another party. **2.** Notice to the writer of an option that that writer will be required to sell a security (call option) or buy a security (put option) from the option holder. **3.** Transfer of ownership rights to an annuity contract or a life insurance policy.

assignment of accounts receivable Using accounts receivable as collateral for a loan. An assignment can be general, in which case, if payments on the loan are not made, receivables held at the time will be collected to pay off the loan. If the assignment is specific, assigned receivables are collected with proceeds used to pay off the loan.

assignment of lease Transfer by a lessee to a third party a lease, with all its rights and obligations. Leases sometimes contain restrictions on assignments or subleases.

assignor The party that transfers a right, interest, or title to another party.

association plan A group insurance policy purchased by an organization or association that wishes to provide insurance coverage to its members.

Association to Advance Collegiate Schools of Business (AACSB) An international organization of educational institutions, businesses, foundations, nonprofit organizations, and professional associations that promotes business education, establishes standards for business educations, and accredits college and university business programs.

assumable mortgage A mortgage that permits the borrower to assign the balance of the loan, without penalty, to another person when the mortgaged asset is sold. Having a mortgage that is assumable can prove to be a major benefit to a borrower, especially when market rates of interest move above the level at which the assumable mortgage specifies. —See also SUBJECT TO MORTGAGE.

assumption fee The charge by a lender to a buyer who takes responsibility for an outstanding loan.

assumption of risk 1. Taking responsibility for a potential loss. For example, an individual who decides to forgo collision and comprehensive insurance on a vehicle assumes the risk of a loss from perils covered by these coverages. **2.** Contracting with another party to assume certain specified risks. For example, an individual may contract with an insurance company that assumes the risk there will be financial loss caused by a fire or strong winds.

asynchronous Of or describing events and/or objects that are not coordinated in terms of time. For example, computers transmit data one character at a time with uneven time periods between characters.

ATM —See AUTOMATED TELLER MACHINE.

at-risk rule A law that limits tax write-offs to the amount of money directly invested (and thus, at risk) in an asset. The purpose of an at-risk rule is to prohibit investors from deriving tax benefits that exceed the amount of money actually invested.

at sight Of or designating a negotiable instrument that is payable when presented to the drawee.

attachment 1. A court order that permits a party to take something of value from another party. For example, a person who is injured by another party may obtain a court order attaching certain property of the person at fault. **2.** An addition to an insurance policy.

attained age The current age of an insured person.

attained age conversion Conversion from one type of life insurance coverage to another type of coverage at the premium appropriate to the age of the insured person at the time of the conversion. For example, converting a term policy to a whole life policy will entail a premium rate based on the age of the insured person when the conversion occurs.

attest Affirm to be true or correct. In accounting, auditors attest to the accuracy of financial information.

at-the-close order A specialized order to a broker in which the customer specifies that execution take place at the closing price of the day. In practice, execution is permitted during the 30-to-60-second period before the closing bell.

at-the-market —See MARKET ORDER.

at-the-money Of or relating to a call or a put option that has a strike price equal to the price of the underlying asset. —Compare IN-THE-MONEY; OUT-OF-THE-MONEY.

at-the-opening order A specialized order to a broker in which the customer specifies that execution take place at the opening price of the day.

attorney-in-fact A person designated to act as an agent for someone else (the principal) under a written power of attorney. The authority of the attorney-in-fact depends on specific power included in the power of attorney.

attornment Agreement by a tenant to accept a new property owner as landlord.

attractive nuisance Something on a property that is tempting but naturally danger-ous, especially to children. A discarded refrigerator might attract a child who wants to hide, for example. The owner of an attractive nuisance must be concerned about a liability judgment in the event the nuisance is connected to an injury or death.

attribute sampling A statistical method that utilizes representative samples to analyze traits of a large body of data. For example, an auditor may select a sample of customer records in a financial institution to test whether each account includes a taxpayer identification number (TIN). The accounts either include a TIN or do not include a TIN.

attrition A gradual and natural reduction. A company may experience attrition in its workforce because of retirements and deaths. Many newspapers have experienced an attrition of subscribers as people look to the Internet for news.

at-will employment An employment arrangement that either the employer or em-ployee can terminate without cause except as spelled out by law. For example, dis-crimination on the basis of race, religion, or gender is prohibited.

auction market A market in which buyers and sellers gather to transact business through announced bid and ask prices. The organized securities exchanges are ex-amples of auction markets. —Compare DEALER MARKET; OPEN OUTCRY.

auction-rate security A type of floating-rate security for which interest or dividend payments are determined at periodic auctions conducted by the issuer rather than by short-term interest rates. A potential risk is that a lack of bidding may keep investors from being able to cash out. —Compare REMARKETED PREFERRED STOCK.

audience The part of the general public that may express an interest in a particular product or service. Advertising a denture adhesive on MTV is an example of targeting the wrong audience. —See also TARGET AUDIENCE.

audit 1. An examination of an organization's financial documents in order to deter-mine whether the records and reports are valid and the information is fairly present-ed. An independent audit is usually conducted by a certified public accountant who then issues an opinion as to whether the statements accurately and fairly represent the firm's operations and financial position. —See also EXTERNAL AUDIT; INTERNAL AU-DIT. **2.** An IRS or other tax agency examination to verify the accuracy of a corporate or individual tax return. An audit may take place at the taxpayer's place of business, at an agency office, or via correspondence. The burden of proof during an audit is on the taxpayer, who is often required to supply proof of deductions, expenses, and other items included in a tax return. —Also called *tax audit.*

audit committee A subcommittee of a corporation's board of directors that selects the firm's external auditors. The audit committee is responsible for hiring the audi-tors, resolving disputes with the auditors, and evaluating and disclosing the auditors' reports.

audited statement A financial statement that is prepared according to generally ac-cepted auditing standards. —Compare UNAUDITED STATEMENT.

auditing standards Guidelines to be followed by auditors who are examining financial statements. Appropriate guidelines to follow are established by professional organ-izations such as the American Institute of Certified Public Accountants. —See also GENERALLY ACCEPTED ACCOUNTING PRINCIPLES; GENERALLY ACCEPTED AUDITING STANDARDS.

auditor A person who examines an organization's financial records and reports. If the person is an employee of the organization being audited, he or she is known as an internal auditor. If the auditor is not an employee of the organization, he or she is called an external auditor.

auditor opinion —See OPINION 1.

audit trail A record of business transactions that can be used by an interested party to trace an organization's activities to original documents. Audit trails are used to verify account balances.

autarky The idea that a region or nation should pursue a policy of economic self-sufficiency. Where such a philosophy prevails, authorities decline to engage in trade outside their borders even at the expense of reducing the standard of living of their citizens. —See also CLOSED ECONOMY.

authenticate To prove that something is genuine. For example, a notary public may be required to authenticate a person's signature on a legal document.

authoritarian The personal trait of expecting absolute obedience.

authority 1. A government organization created to perform a certain function. A state or region, for example, may establish a public power authority to provide low-cost electricity to people living in a certain geographical area. **2.** A person, group, or organization that has the power to issue orders or make decisions. **3.** The power to make decisions or issue orders. For example, a firm's vice president for marketing has the authority to change advertising agencies.

authority bond A bond issued by an authority and having interest and principal payable from revenues generated by the authority. The quality of an authority bond is only as good as the quality of the projects sponsored by the authority. —Compare REVENUE BOND.

authorized capital stock The number of shares of capital stock a business may legally issue. Authorized capital stock is stated in a firm's articles of incorporation; changes in it may occur only if approved by the stockholders. The number of shares authorized often greatly exceeds the number actually issued. In this way, management can issue more shares to raise additional funds, or it can use the shares to make an acquisition. —Also called *shares authorized.*

autocorrelation —See SERIAL CORRELATION.

automated clearinghouse A computer-based clearing and settlement service for the interchange of electronic transactions among participating institutions. Electronic transactions are increasingly substituted for paper checks as individuals and businesses choose direct deposit and online payments.

automated stock trading The trading of securities without the direct assistance of a broker or specialist. Generally, automated stock trading involves investor trading of securities via computer. Security bid and ask prices are listed and are continually updated, with executions occurring automatically when the orders are entered.

automated teller machine (ATM) An unattended mechanical and electronic device that offers 24-hour banking services including cash withdrawals, deposits, and transfer of funds between accounts.

automatic checkoff —See CHECKOFF.

automatic dividend reinvestment —See DIVIDEND REINVESTMENT PLAN.

automatic premium loan A provision of life insurance policies that permits the insurance company to take out a loan against a policy's cash value in order to pay an overdue premium on the policy.

automatic reinvestment The automatic purchase of additional shares of an open-end investment company using any dividends and capital gains distributions that are made by the firm. This option (in lieu of actually receiving payments) permits a mutual fund shareholder to increase his or her holdings in the fund. Taxes must be paid on the amount reinvested, even though no funds are received directly. —See also DIVIDEND REINVESTMENT PLAN.

automatic stabilizers Government spending and taxation that automatically change to reduce variations in economic activity. For example, an increase in economic activity will result in individuals and businesses paying more taxes. These increased tax payments will leave consumers and businesses with less money to spend. Declining economic activity will be accompanied by increased unemployment benefits.

automatic stay In bankruptcy, temporary protection of a debtor from creditors, subject to the oversight of the bankruptcy judge. A stay protects the debtor against garnishments, foreclosure sales, repossessions, and lawsuits.

automatic withdrawal A feature of some mutual funds that allows a shareholder to specify that the fund remit fixed payments at periodic intervals. The payments are comprised of dividends, interest, and capital gains received by the fund, and, if these are insufficient, liquidation of some shares owned by the shareholder.

automation Operation of machinery that requires little or no human involvement. Automation is utilized to reduce the cost of producing and delivering, and/or to improve the quality, of a good or service.

available asset A person's or a firm's asset that is not being used as collateral for a loan and is therefore available for general use or for sale.

available credit The amount of credit that is available for new purchases. For credit cards, available credit is equal to a cardholder's credit limit less the outstanding balance. A cardholder with a credit limit of $9,000 and an outstanding balance of $3,500 has available credit of $5,500.

aval Third-party guarantee of a debt. For example, a business debt is guaranteed by the firm's bank.

average 1. —See ARITHMETIC MEAN. **2.** —See AVERAGES.

average age of inventory On average, the number of days between the acquisition of an inventory item and its sale. Average age of inventory is calculated by dividing the average inventory level (measured in dollars) by the firm's cost of goods sold. The result is multiplied by 365 days. An unusually high average age may indicate poor inventory management or a large amount of inventory that may be difficult to sell.

average collection period —See COLLECTION PERIOD.

average cost A cost amount calculated by dividing total cost by units of production. If a firm produces 10,000 units of output for a total cost of $25,000, the average cost of each unit is $25,000/10,000 units, or $2.50 per unit. Average cost is made up of fixed costs that remain unchanged throughout a range of output and costs that vary directly with output. Firms with the lowest average cost in an industry have a competitive advantage in the event of severe competition and price cutting.

average-cost method 1. A method of determining the value of an inventory by calculating unit cost; that is, the result obtained by dividing the total cost of goods available for sale by the number of units available for sale. —See also INVENTORY VALUATION. **2.** A method of valuing the cost basis of securities that are sold in order to determine the gain or loss for tax purposes. Average cost is calculated as total cost of shares owned divided by the number of shares owned. The average-cost method is particularly useful for shares acquired at varying prices in a reinvestment plan.

average cost of capital —See COST OF CAPITAL.

average daily balance The sum of the daily account balances during a given period divided by the number of days in the period. Financial institutions frequently use an account's average daily balance to calculate interest paid on savings accounts. Most credit card companies use average daily balance to calculate a cardholder's monthly finance charge.

average down To purchase shares of the same security at successively lower prices in order to reduce the average price at which the stock was acquired. If an investor buys 100 shares of Disney common stock at $40 per share and the price subsequently falls to $30 per share, the purchase of an additional 100 shares would average down the investor's cost to $35 per share. —Compare AVERAGE UP.

average life —See HALF-LIFE.

average maturity The average time to maturity of all the debt securities held in a portfolio. A relatively short average maturity results in smaller price fluctuations in response to changes in market rates of interest. A short average maturity subjects the owner of a debt portfolio to the risk that maturing debt will be replaced with debt carrying a lower interest rate. Average maturity is an important consideration for investors who hold bond and money market funds.

averages Stock price measures that are calculated and distributed by a number of organizations including Dow Jones, Standard & Poor's, and securities exchanges. The two major stock price measures are the Dow Jones Averages and the S&P 500. —Also called *average; market averages; market index; stock average.* —See also INDEX[1].

average tax rate Taxes paid as a proportion of income. Paying $10,000 in taxes on an income of $80,000 results in an average tax rate of $10,000/$80,000, or 12.5%. Financial decisions should be made based on a taxpayer's marginal tax rate rather than the average tax rate. —Also called *effective tax rate.*

average up To purchase shares of the same security at successively higher prices. When averaging up, the investor accumulates an increasingly larger position in a security while keeping the average cost of the position lower than the security's current market price. Such an investor will earn significant profits only if the stock price continues to rise. —Compare AVERAGE DOWN.

averaging —See DOLLAR-COST AVERAGING.

avoidance of contract Legal termination of a contract when an event renders it impossible or inequitable for one or both parties to successfully complete the terms of the contract. For example, a New Orleans wholesale supplier would almost certainly have been unable to fulfill delivery commitments in the days following hurricane Katrina.

away from the market —Used to refer to a security order at a price not immediately available. A limit order to buy 100 shares of Intel at $37 is away from the market if Intel stock is currently trading at $41 per share.

▪ B

B A low, speculative grade assigned to a debt obligation by a rating agency. Such a rating indicates there is considerable uncertainty as to the ability to pay interest and repay principal over a long period.

Ba —See BB.

Baa —See BBB.

Baby Bell One of several integrated-communications providers that were formerly part of AT&T but became independent in 1984 following AT&T's court-ordered divestiture. The seven original Baby Bells were once operating subsidiaries of AT&T that provided local and intrastate long-distance service. In 2006 the former parent was acquired by SBC, a reconfigured Baby Bell that adopted the AT&T name following the acquisition.

baby bond A bond that has a principal amount under $1,000. Baby bonds may be issued by firms hoping to attract investors who do not have funds to purchase bonds with $1,000 principal. Bonds of less than $1,000 principal are sometimes issued as part of a corporate reorganization.

baby boomer generation The 76 million people born in the United States between 1946 and 1964. The wants and needs of baby boomers have been endlessly studied by companies that want to market goods and services to this generally well-heeled generation.

bachelor of business administration (BBA) An undergraduate degree from a college or university with a concentration in general business or one of several business disciplines including accounting, business information systems, economics, finance, insurance, management, or marketing. BBA programs typically require approximately two years of nonbusiness courses such as English, math, and history plus two years of business-related courses. —See also ASSOCIATION TO ADVANCE COLLEGIATE SCHOOLS OF BUSINESS.

backdating 1. In stock option grants, pretending an option was granted on a date before the grant was awarded. Backdating allows a company to select a date on which the stock price was low, thereby giving the grantee an immediate boost in profits. Backdating can violate securities laws. 2. The practice of allowing a mutual fund shareholder to use previous purchases of the fund's shares so as to qualify for reduced commission charges on subsequent purchases. Backdating is used when a fund offers declining proportional sales charges on larger purchases. 3. —See ANTEDATE.

> **CASE STUDY** Backdating of stock options is not illegal so long as certain conditions are met. For example, the practice must be reported to shareholders and reflected in a firm's earnings and taxes. Unfortunately, backdating is sometimes conducted behind closed doors. Dozens of executives and directors have resigned or been fired as a result of investigations into the illegal granting of stock options. In 2007, Myron Olesnyckyj, former general counsel of Monster Worldwide, pleaded guilty to securities fraud and conspiracy to commit securities fraud, and agreed to forfeit $381,000 he claimed represented illegal gains. The Securities and Exchange Commission had charged Olesnyckyj with securities fraud for participating in a multiyear scheme to secretly backdate stock options granted to thousands of Monster officers, di-

rectors, and employees, including himself. The complaint alleged that, from 1997 through 2003, Olesnyckyj backdated stock option grants to coincide with the dates of low closing prices for the firm's stock. Certain officers and employees would select a low closing stock price, and Olesnyckyj, or others acting under his direction, prepared backdated documentation for the firm's compensation committee. The SEC complaint alleged the general counsel also misled the firm's outside auditors by granting undisclosed compensation to employees, failing to recognize the expense, and overstating net income by $340 million from 1997 through 2005.

backdoor borrowing Borrowing by a public authority without voter approval. Public authorities often use backdoor borrowing when voters reject proposed debt issues. Taxpayer funds are used to repay debt accumulated in backdoor borrowing.

backdoor listing Acquisition and merger with a listed company by an unlisted company in order to gain a listing on a securities exchange.

back-end load —See DEFERRED SALES CHARGE.

back-end value The amount paid to remaining shareholders in the last stage of a two-tier tender offer.

background checking Attempting to verify information provided by an applicant for employment. Background checks typically include verifying credentials, previous employment, and criminal history (or lack thereof).

backlog The accumulation of unfinished work or unfilled orders. A large backlog can indicate either inefficient management or a relatively prosperous future, at least until the backlog is worked off or unfilled orders are canceled.

back office The physical location within a business where records are kept and processed. In the case of a brokerage firm, the back office includes the section where individual account records are kept, checks are processed, and security certificates are sent. —Also called *operations department.*

back order A customer order that cannot be delivered on the scheduled date but will be delivered as soon as additional units are available for shipment.

back pay Wages that are owed from an earlier pay period.

back testing Using historical data to determine the relationship of specific variables. For example, a researcher might use historical data to determine if changes in the money supply have influenced changes in stock prices. This relationship, if positive, can be used to develop an investment policy.

back title letter A document describing the condition of a title as of a specified date given by a title insurance company to an attorney of the buyer or the seller. The attorney is expected to research the title from the date specified in the letter.

back-to-back loan —See PARALLEL LOAN.

back up 1. To make one or more additional copies of a computer file, program, or database. Financial institutions back up files of financial data in secure locations separate from the institutions. **2.** To arrange for an alternate method for providing a good or service in the event the primary method becomes inoperative. For example, a manufacturer may acquire a generator to back up service from the local utility.

backup withholding Compulsory withholding from payments to an investor in order to take care of a potential tax liability. Payments of interest, dividends, and proceeds from a sale of securities are subject to backup withholding when certain requirements are not met, including if the investor fails to provide a correct taxpayer identification number (TIN) or if dividends and interest have been underreported.

backwardation —See INVERTED MARKET.

backward-bending supply curve A curved line that depicts an unusual situation in which the supply of a good or service begins declining once price has reached a certain level. This is most frequently applied to labor on the theory that at some wage level the suppliers of labor will begin substituting leisure for work. For example, a person earning $100 per hour may already be earning enough to buy everything that is desired and decide to work fewer hours.

backward integration Acquisition by a business of one or more of its suppliers. For example, a vehicle manufacturer might acquire an electronics company or tire manufacturer in an attempt to reduce cost or improve quality. Backward integration is a type of vertical integration. —Compare FORWARD INTEGRATION.

bad check A written order of payment that is not honored by the paying institution because funds in the account on which the check is written are less than the amount of the check.

bad debt Money owed that the lender is unable to collect.

bad delivery The delivery of a security that fails to meet all the standards required to transfer title to the buyer. —Compare GOOD DELIVERY.

bad faith Intentionally misleading someone or undertaking an agreement without any intention of fulfilling its provisions. Concealing important facts from an insurance company on the filing of a claim is an example of bad faith. An insurance company's failure to pay a legitimate claim is also bad faith. —Also called *mala fides.*

bad title A title to property that offers questionable ownership and cannot be transferred to another party.

bail bond Funds posted by a bail bond company to guarantee a defendant will appear in court at the scheduled time. The judge may issue an arrest warrant and keep the bail bond in the event the defendant fails to appear.

bailee A person holding and responsible for an asset owned by someone else (bailor). For example, a bank is a bailee when it holds a borrower's securities as collateral for a loan.

bailment The act of a person (bailor) delivering personal property for safekeeping to someone else (bailee).

bailor A person who leaves personal property in the care of someone else (bailee). A borrower who provides a lender with securities as collateral for a loan is an example of a bailor.

bailout The financial rescue of a faltering business or other organization. Government guarantees for loans made in 1979 to Chrysler Corporation constituted a bailout.

CASE STUDY Following federal bailouts of Lockheed Corporation (1971) and New York City (1975) earlier in the decade, the U.S. government in 1979 came to the rescue of financially troubled Chrysler Corporation. Although the company's request for a federal bailout was criticized by both conservative and liberal members of Congress, political pressure by President Jimmy Carter and the economic importance of this smallest member of the Big Three resulted in passage of the Chrysler Corporation Loan Guarantee

Act of 1979. The federal guarantee of $1.2 billion in loans allowed Chrysler, unable to borrow on its own credit, to obtain the cash it needed to continue operating. In order to obtain the federal loan guarantee, Chrysler was required to gain concessions from existing lenders, who agreed to the conversion of nearly $700 million in debts into a special class of preferred stock that paid no dividends and could only be redeemed several years following issue. Chrysler was also required to pay a loan guarantee fee of 1% per year in addition to granting the government 14.4 million warrants to purchase the firm's stock. Chrysler quickly returned to profitability and was able to repay the guaranteed loans ahead of schedule. Years later it was purchased by Daimler Benz, which in 2007 suffered a huge loss when it sold Chrysler to a private equity firm.

bail out To sell an asset, generally at a loss, in anticipation of a further price decline. An investor who expects a major increase in market rates of interest may decide to bail out of long-term bonds.

bait and switch The unethical and illegal practice of a business promoting an item at an especially attractive price with the intention of convincing customers to buy something else that offers the business more profit. The business is likely to begin a bait and switch by telling customers who want to buy the promoted item that it is of inferior quality or is sold out and no longer available.

balance[1] **1.** The amount of funds available in an account. **2.** The amount of a loan remaining to be paid. For example, the balance on a $150,000 mortgage may be $135,000 after five years of payments. **3.** In accounting, the account difference between debits and credits.

balance[2] To reconcile a checking account register with the respective bank statement.

balanced budget A budget in which the expenditures incurred during a given period are matched by revenues.

balanced fund An investment company that spreads its investments among stocks and bonds. Essentially, a balanced fund is a middle-of-the-road fund made up of investments that will achieve both moderate income and moderate capital growth.

balance of payments The record of money payments between one country and other countries. Balance of payments is more inclusive than balance of trade because balance of payments comprises foreign investment, loans, and other cash flows as well as payments for goods and services. A country's balance of payments has a significant effect on its currency value in relation to other currencies. It is of particular interest to individuals who own foreign investments or who own domestic investments in companies dependent on exports. —See also CAPITAL ACCOUNT 2.

balance of trade A net figure calculated by subtracting a country's imports from its exports during a specific period. If a country sells more goods and services than it purchases, its balance of trade is said to be positive; that is, exports exceed imports. Such a balance is generally considered to be favorable. Conversely, a negative balance is said to be unfavorable. A country's balance-of-trade position has great impact on its economic activity and on the profits of companies operating within it. —Also called *trade balance.* —See also CURRENT ACCOUNT; TRADE DEFICIT; TRADE SURPLUS.

balance sheet The financial statement of a business or institution that lists the assets, debts, and owners' investment as of a specific date. Assets are ordered according to how soon they will be converted into cash, and debts according to how soon they must be paid. Because balance sheets do not list items at their current monetary value, they may greatly overstate or understate the real value of certain corporate assets and liabilities. —Also called *statement of financial condition; statement of financial position.* —See also CONSOLIDATED BALANCE SHEET.

balance-sheet loan A loan that the lender retains on its books rather than selling to another financial institution or to individual investors. Some borrowers prefer balance-sheet loans because they wish to deal with the original lender in the event a problem develops during the course of the loan.

Baldrige Award —See MALCOLM BALDRIGE NATIONAL QUALITY AWARD.

balloon interest A higher interest rate received on the longer-maturity bonds of a serial bond issue.

balloon payment A final loan payment that is significantly larger than the payments preceding it. For example, a bond issuer may redeem 3% of the original issue each year for 20 years and then retire the remaining 40% in the year of maturity. —See also BULLET LOAN.

BAN —See BOND ANTICIPATION NOTE.

bancassurance The sale of insurance products through the distribution channels of a commercial bank.

bangtail envelope A business reply envelope that includes an extra flap that can be easily torn off and inserted into the envelope. The flap can serve as an order form or information request form. Credit card companies often insert a business reply bangtail envelope with monthly bills, usually to solicit orders for inexpensive items being offered for sale.

bank A financial institution, generally chartered by a state or the federal government, that accepts deposits and uses these funds to make loans. Banks earn income on the difference between the interest they pay on deposits and the interest they receive on their loans and investments. Banks also generally offer many other services including selling U.S. savings bonds, issuing cashier's checks, certifying customer checks, and renting safe deposit boxes.

bank-discount basis A method of calculating the quoted yield on a debt security. In a bank-discount basis calculation, the amount of discount from face value is divided by the security's face value and the result is annualized. For example, a $10,000 face-amount bond due in two months and selling for $9,900 would be quoted at ($100/$10,000) x (360/60), or 6%. While this is a common way of quoting yields on certain securities such as Treasury bills and commercial paper, it actually understates the effective rate paid. —Also called *discount basis; discount yield.* —See also EQUIVALENT BOND YIELD.

bank draft A check drawn by a bank against its own funds on deposit in another bank. For example, Bank A writes a check on its account in Bank B made payable to a customer of Bank A.

banker's acceptance A short-term credit instrument created by a nonfinancial firm and guaranteed by a bank as to payment. Acceptances are traded at discounts from face value in the secondary market on the basis of the credit quality of the guaranteeing banks. —Also called *acceptance.*

banker's year A year with 12 months of 30 days each, or 360 days, to make interest calculations easier.

bank-grade —See INVESTMENT-GRADE.

bank holding company A corporation that owns the stock of one or more banks and thus exercises control over the bank or banks. —See also HOLDING COMPANY.

Banking Act of 1933 —See GLASS-STEAGALL ACT.

Bank Insurance Fund The federal fund administered by the Federal Deposit Insurance Corporation, which insures the deposits of individuals who invest at banks that are members of the Federal Reserve System. This includes all national banks and state banks that choose to join the Fed. The fund was created in 1989 in order to separate the insurance funds for commercial banks from those that insure thrift institutions.

bank line —See LINE OF CREDIT.

bank note Currency issued and guaranteed by a bank. The sole issuer of bank notes in the United States is the Federal Reserve Bank.

bankruptcy The financial status of a firm that has been legally judged either to have debts that exceed assets or to be unable to pay its bills. Formal bankruptcy may result in reorganization and continued operation of the firm, or it may require liquidation and distribution of the proceeds. In either case, most security owners, especially shareholders, are likely to suffer losses. —See also CHAPTER 7; CHAPTER 11; RECEIVERSHIP; REORGANIZATION.

bankruptcy court The federal district court in which bankruptcy petitions are filed and bankruptcy proceedings take place.

bankruptcy estate Legal property of a debtor in bankruptcy that is available to pay creditors. The bankruptcy estate includes the debtor's interest in jointly held property, but it excludes assets held in ERISA-qualified retirement plans and 401(k) plans.

bankruptcy petition The document filed by a debtor (voluntary bankruptcy) or by creditors (involuntary bankruptcy) that opens a bankruptcy case. —Also called *petition in bankruptcy.*

bankruptcy trustee An official appointed by the court to administer and/or liquidate assets of bankrupt individuals and organizations. Trustees have different duties depending on the type of bankruptcy. For example, trustees of Chapter 7 bankruptcies primarily liquidate assets for the benefit of creditors.

bank trust department The section of a bank that provides wealth management and fiduciary services that include administering trusts, settling estates, and providing agency services such as estate planning.

bank wire —See ELECTRONIC FUNDS TRANSFER.

banner ad Graphical advertising on an Internet website.

barbell portfolio A bond portfolio heavily weighted with long and short maturities but few intermediate maturities. Bonds with short maturities provide liquidity, and those with long maturities offer higher yields.

bar code A series of vertical bars of varying thickness and separation that provides information about the object to which it is attached. A bar code is read with a laser beam that is sensitive to reflected light that is converted into digital data. Bar codes are useful in improving the efficiency of sorting, inventory control, and checkout. —See also RADIO FREQUENCY IDENTIFICATION; UNIVERSAL PRODUCT CODE.

bargain basement **1.** The area of a department store, generally a basement, where goods are offered for sale at especially low prices. **2.** Of or referring to an especially low price for a good or service. For example, a car dealer may be offering last year's model vehicles at bargain-basement prices.

bargain hunter **1.** A consumer who spends considerable time and effort attempting to locate goods and services being sold at below-market prices. **2.** An investor who searches for undervalued stocks, bonds, real estate, or other investments.

bargaining agent A certified representative of an employee group that has the exclusive authority to act on the group's behalf with respect to certain matters. For example, the International Brotherhood of Teamsters might be the bargaining agent for all the drivers who work for a trucking company.

bargain purchase option The right of a lessee, at the end of a lease, to purchase the leased asset at a nominal price or renew the lease at a nominal rate.

bargain sale Transferring ownership of an asset for less than market value.

barometer An indicator of fluctuations. For example, the S&P 500 is a barometer for stock market movements. Likewise, long-term interest rates are a barometer of inflationary expectations.

barren money —See IDLE FUNDS.

barrier to entry An obstacle that makes it difficult for a new firm to enter and compete with companies that already operate in a particular business. In the case of cigarettes, for example, high advertising expenditures and resulting brand loyalty acts as a barrier to entry.

barter The exchange of goods and services without the use of money. Barter is sometimes used to hide income and reduce taxes. For example, an accountant might do the taxes of a dentist in return for free dental services. —See also COMPENSATORY TRADE.

base currency The currency to which another currency is compared. For example, the dollar is the base currency when the euro is quoted at .80 euros to the dollar. The euro becomes the base currency if the quotation is 1.25 dollars to the euro.

base pay Monetary compensation for a specific job exclusive of any overtime, commissions, bonuses, one-time payments, or benefits.

base period The time or period of time on which an index is based. Usually, the index is established at a value of 10 or 100 in the base year. The consumer price index of 220 in mid-2008 indicated that consumer prices were 120% higher than during the base period of 1982–84. The Standard & Poor's 500 Stock Index of 1275 in mid-2008 indicated that, on average, a portfolio of blue chip stocks with a market value of $10 during the period 1941–43 (the base period) had a market value of $1,275 in mid-2008. The portfolio of stocks making up the S&P 500 underwent substantial changes during the intervening years.

base rent The minimum fixed, periodic payment made by a tenant of a property to the owner of the property. A rental agreement may include provisions that cause the actual rent to be higher than the base rent. For example, a retailer leasing a commercial building may be required to pay the base rent plus a specified percentage of sales. Likewise, a rental agreement may include a provision under which the base rent is adjusted for inflation.

base stock The smallest amount of inventory that permits a firm to operate efficiently.

basic earnings per share Net income less preferred stock dividends during a given period, divided by the average number of shares of common stock outstanding during that period. —Compare DILUTED EARNINGS PER SHARE. —See also DUAL PRESENTATION.

basing point The physical location used to establish the selling price and freight expense for a product. Freight cost is based on the cost of shipping from the basing point to the delivery point, regardless of where the shipment actually originates. —See also PHANTOM FREIGHT.

basis 1. In futures trading, the difference between the futures price and the spot price. The basis will narrow as a contract moves closer to settlement. **2.** In taxation, the acquisition cost of an asset adjusted for depreciation or capital distributions (that is, stock dividends). An asset's basis is used in calculating gains and losses for tax purposes. —Also called *cost basis; tax basis.* —See also ADJUSTED BASIS. **3.** —See STEPPED-UP BASIS.

basis book A book of tables giving conversions to equivalent dollar prices for bond yields having given maturity lengths and coupon rates. —Also called *bond basis book.*

basis grade The specified grade for a commodity necessary for it to be acceptable for delivery on a futures contract.

basis point A value equaling one one-hundredth of a percent (0.01%). Basis point is used to measure yield differences among bonds and other types of debt. For example, there is a 30 basis-point difference between two bonds if one yields 5.3% and the other yields 5.6%.

basis price The price of a security quoted in terms of its yield rather than its dollar price. Bonds are often quoted on a basis price reflecting yield to maturity because such information is of greatest importance to an investor deciding to buy or sell.

basis trading An arbitrage operation in which an investor takes a long position in one type of security and a short position in a similar security in an attempt to profit from a change in the basis between the two securities. Basis trading is undertaken when the investor feels one security is priced too high or too low relative to the price of another security. Because of this, the profit on one side of the trade should more than cancel out the loss on the opposite side of the trade. —Compare PROGRAM TRADING.

basket A preassembled group of securities. Baskets allow individual investors to acquire a group of securities with a single trade while paying only one commission.

basket of currencies A collective unit that is calculated by weighting currencies from a designated group of countries.

batch processing Executing or processing a large number of accumulated orders or transactions at one time. For example, banks use batch processing for the monthly statements sent to customers. —Compare TRANSACTION PROCESSING.

batch trading A trading system for securities in which orders accumulate and then, at specified times, are executed all at once. Batch trading in the U.S. securities markets only is used on opening transactions when orders received after the previous day's close are executed all at one time. —Compare CONTINUOUS TRADING.

BB A grade assigned to a debt obligation by a rating agency to indicate significant speculative elements and a moderate ability to pay interest and repay principal. —Also called *Ba.*

BBA —See BACHELOR OF BUSINESS ADMINISTRATION.

BBB A medium grade assigned to a debt obligation by a rating agency to indicate an adequate ability to pay interest and repay principal. However, adverse developments are more likely to impair this ability than would be the case for bonds rated A and above. A BBB rating is the lowest rating a bond can have and still be considered investment-grade. —Also called *Baa*.

bear An investor who believes a security or some other asset or the security markets in general will follow a broad downward path. An investor can often be a bear on a particular asset but not on the general market and vice versa. For example, an investor may be generally upbeat on real estate, but a bear on real estate in a particular region. —Compare BULL.

bearer bond A debt instrument that does not have an owner name listed in the issuer's books or inscribed on the certificate. Because no record of ownership exists, bearer bonds are favored by investors who, illegally, want to avoid paying gift, estate, and local taxes. The issuance of new municipal bonds in bearer form was prohibited beginning in 1983. —Also called *coupon bond*. —See also COUPON CLIPPING 1.

bearer form —Used to refer to any security that, according to the books of the issuing organization, is not registered to an owner. Essentially, a person holding a security in bearer form is the owner of the security. —Compare REGISTERED SECURITY 1.

bearer stock Securities ownership certificates that are not registered in a name. As with other bearer securities, bearer stock is a negotiable certificate that can be transferred between owners without endorsement. Bearer stock is popular in Europe but not in the United States.

bear hug A buyout offer so favorable to stockholders of a company targeted for acquisition that there is little likelihood they will refuse it. Not only does a bear hug offer a price significantly above the market price of the target company's stock, but it is likely to offer cash payments as well. —See also TAKEOVER.

bearish Of or relating to the belief that a particular asset or the market as a whole is headed for a period of generally falling prices. —Compare BULLISH.

bear market An extended period of general price declines in an individual security or other asset, such as silver or real estate; a group of securities; or the securities market as a whole. Nevertheless, even during widespread bear markets, it is possible to have bull markets in particular stocks or groups of stocks. For example, stocks of gold-related companies often move against major trends in the security markets. —Compare BULL MARKET.

bear raid A concerted effort to drive down the price of a stock by selling many shares short. The bear raid was popular among speculators in the early 1900s. Such a raid would frequently be accompanied by unfavorable rumors and stories about the target firm that would be planted in business publications. The goal of the raid was to involve other investors in a selling stampede that would drive the stock's price down to a bargain level.

bear spread In futures and options trading, a strategy in which one contract is bought and a different contract is sold in such a manner that the person undertaking the spread makes a profit if the price of the underlying asset declines. Two contracts are used in order to limit the size of the potential loss. —Compare BULL SPREAD.

bear trap An accumulation of shares being sold short by bears trying to drive down the price of a stock. The bear trap occurs when the bears find they must repurchase the shares from an individual or a group at an artificial price determined by the seller.

beat the averages To obtain superior investment returns, generally on a risk-adjusted basis, compared with popular stock price averages such as the Dow Jones Industrial

Average or the S&P 500. Professional portfolio managers are generally judged by their ability to beat the averages, although many studies indicate that it is virtually impossible to do so consistently on a risk-adjusted basis.

bedroom community A community populated primarily by people who commute to work in a nearby city.

beggar thy neighbor A national policy of increasing domestic production and decreasing imports. This would include devaluing the domestic currency, imposing duties on imports, and establishing quotas.

beginning inventory Goods available for sale at the beginning of an accounting period. —Compare ENDING INVENTORY.

behavior modification The use of techniques that attempt to alter human behavior. For example, an employee is awarded a monetary bonus for being the top salesperson during the month.

Beige Book A Federal Reserve publication that includes an overview of the economy and a description of economic conditions in each of the twelve Federal Reserve districts. The Beige Book is published eight times per year and was first made public in 1983.

bell The device that sounds to mark the open and close of each trading day on an organized securities exchange.

bells and whistles Special features that are added to ordinary products to attract buyers' attention. For example, a vehicle may include an especially high-end music system. Bells and whistles also apply to investment assets. Some bonds include a put feature, while preferred stock may include floating dividends. —Also called *kickers; wrinkles.* —See also PLAIN-VANILLA.

bellwether A security that tends to lead the market and signal the general direction of future price movements. An increasing price for a bellwether stock is considered a bullish signal for the overall stock market.

belly up Of, relating to, or being in bankruptcy. —Used of a firm.

below market Of, or relating to, a price that is lower than would be expected. For example, a credit card company might temporarily offer a below-market interest rate on transferred balances as an enticement for customers to move balances from other loans.

below par Of or relating to a security that sells at less than face value or par value. For example, a $1,000 par bond with a market price of $850 is below par. Likewise, a $100 par preferred stock with a market price of $80 is below par. Fixed-income securities usually trade below par because market rates of interest are higher than they were when the securities were issued. —Compare ABOVE PAR. —See also DISCOUNT BOND.

below the line Of or relating to unconventional promotions such as celebrity endorsements, packaging inserts, and newspaper stories that do not use direct advertising. —Compare ABOVE THE LINE 2.

benchmark A standard by which something is measured. For example, bond yields are generally compared to benchmark yields on U.S. Treasury securities of similar maturity. Mutual fund performance is often compared to changes in the Standard & Poor's 500 Stock Index.

beneficial interest The right to benefit from a trust, contract, or other form of agreement. For example, each spouse has a beneficial interest in a bank account being held in joint name.

beneficial owner The owner of an asset that is registered in another name. For example, investors often leave securities in trust with their brokerage firms. Although the brokerage firm is shown on the issuer's books as the owner of record, the investor is the beneficial owner.

beneficiary A person, organization, or other entity that has received or is expected to receive a benefit of some type. For example, children may be beneficiaries of a parent's life insurance policy. —See also LEGATEE; PRIMARY BENEFICIARY; SECONDARY BENEFICIARY.

benefit **1.** An entitlement that is part of an employment contract. For example, employees at a firm may receive dental and health insurance as benefits. —Also called *employee benefit; fringe benefit.* —See also CERTIFIED EMPLOYEE BENEFIT SPECIALIST. **2.** Payment by an insurance company to an insured person or an insured person's beneficiary. A person who has health insurance and is hospitalized will receive benefits from his or her insurance company. —See also DEFINED-BENEFIT PENSION PLAN. **3.** Payment by a public assistance program.

benefit period The period of time during which benefits are to be received under a contractual agreement. A specified benefit period is a common part of health and disability insurance policies.

benefit principle The belief that individuals and organizations benefiting most from government expenditures should pay most of the taxes that finance the expenditures.

bequeath To leave personal property by means of a will. For example, a man might bequeath his restored 1957 Chevrolet convertible to his son or daughter.

bequest An asset that is transferred by means of a will.

Best, A. M. —See A. M. BEST COMPANY.

best ask The lowest quoted price at which an asset is offered for sale.

best bid The highest price that is being offered to purchase an asset.

best-efforts basis **1.** An agreement by an investment banker to do its best to oversee, while not guaranteeing, the sale of a security issue in the primary market. —See also UNDERWRITER 1. **2.** An investor's market order to buy or sell a security in which the brokerage firm agrees to obtain the best possible price.

best-execution requirement The obligation of broker-dealers and market makers to execute customer orders at the best available price.

best practice A method or technique that most frequently leads to the desired outcome. For example, a company may train its salespeople to use three important techniques in approaching potential customers.

beta **1.** A mathematical measure of the sensitivity of rates of return on a portfolio or a given stock compared with rates of return on the market as a whole. A high beta (greater than 1.0) indicates moderate or high price volatility. A beta of 1.5 forecasts a 1.5% change in the return on an asset for every 1% change in the return on the market. High-beta stocks are best to own in a strong bull market but are worst to own in a bear market. —See also ALPHA; CAPITAL-ASSET PRICING MODEL; PORTFOLIO BETA. **2.** A preliminary version of a software program that may have bugs and isn't ready for final release. Beta versions are distributed to users who understand they are testing a prerelease program.

betterment An improvement that increases the value of real property. For example, adding a deck to a home or installing solar heating to an office building.

better mousetrap A technically superior product that is expected to draw customers from similar products produced by competitors. A faster processor chip for personal computers is an example of a better mousetrap.

biannual —See SEMIANNUAL.

bias Indication offered by the Federal Reserve as to whether it is likely to increase or decrease the federal funds interest rate during its next meeting. A negative bias indicates the Fed is likely to lower the federal funds rate.

bid 1. The price that a potential buyer is willing to pay for a security. —Compare ASK. —See also BEST BID. 2. An offer to purchase something.

bid-ask spread —See SPREAD 4.

Big Blue A widely used reference to the firm International Business Machines Corporation. The term derives from the company's logo, usually appearing in blue.

Big Board A widely used reference to the New York Stock Exchange.

big-box Describing a very large retail store with floor space of 50,000 square feet or more. Wal-Mart, Target, and Costco are each considered big-box stores. Big-box stores generally emphasize volume rather than price markups.

big business Especially large commercial operations as measured by revenues, assets, units sold, or number of employees.

Big Four A widely used reference to the four largest public accounting firms that perform most of the external audits in the United States for large publicly owned corporations. The Big Four include PricewaterhouseCoopers, Deloitte Touche Tohmatsu, Ernst & Young, and KPMG.

bigger fool theory —See GREATER FOOL THEORY.

Big Three A widely used reference to the three major automobile manufacturers in the United States: Chrysler, Ford, and General Motors. The success of Japanese vehicle manufacturers, especially Toyota Motor Corporation, and the one-time foreign ownership of Chrysler have muddied the meaning of the reference.

big ticket Of, relating to, or being something that is relatively expensive. For example, a plasma television is a big-ticket item at an electronics store; a fully loaded luxury SUV is a big-ticket item at a car dealership.

bilateral contract An agreement in which each of two parties promises to do something. For example, a company promises to sell a building for $250,000, and another company promises to purchase the building for $250,000. —Compare UNILATERAL CONTRACT.

bilateral trade Commerce involving two entities. For example, the United States signs a bilateral trade agreement with Canada. —Compare MULTILATERAL TRADE.

bill 1. A statement of a liability by one party to another party following a transaction. 2. A Treasury bill. 3. A unit of paper money.

billing cycle The regular interval at which bills are sent. Most billing cycles are monthly.

billings The gross amount of revenue generated by a business during a specified period. For example, an advertising agency had billings of $500,000 during the month.

bill of exchange A written order by a person or business for payment of a specified amount by the recipient to a third party. A bill of exchange is negotiable and generally sells at a discount. —See also TRADE ACCEPTANCE.

bill of lading A written receipt provided by a carrier to a shipper of goods. The document acknowledges receipt of the goods described along with the provisions of transport. A bill of lading noting a deficiency, such as damaged merchandise, is described as *claused*. A bill of lading without a deficiency is *clean*. —See also ORDER BILL OF LADING; STRAIGHT BILL OF LADING.

bill of sale A document that legally transfers property or a business to another person, company, or organization.

binary system A numerical arrangement in which numbers are represented by the digits 0 and 1. For example, the decimal 12 has a binary equivalent of 1100. All input to computers is converted to binary form.

binder An agreement for temporary insurance coverage until a formal policy can be issued. A binder is frequently issued by an insurance company or its agent when a client purchases a new vehicle.

binding arbitration A noncourt process for resolving a dispute in which a neutral third party (the arbitrator) has the power to impose a settlement. The parties involved in the dispute sometimes agree in advance to limits that may be imposed by the arbitrator. —Also called *compulsory arbitration*.

bingo card A response card inserted in periodicals to be used by readers who wish to request information or samples. The name derives from the columns and rows of numbers or letters that correspond to advertisers offering literature or samples.

bird dog A junior salesperson who searches for potential customers that will be introduced to more senior salespersons.

bit An electronic signal that is either on (0) or off (1). A bit is the smallest unit of information utilized by a computer and derives its name from *b*inary dig*it*.

black Of or relating to the profitability of a firm or the operations of a firm. The term derives from the color of ink used to enter a profit figure on a financial statement. —Compare RED.

black box 1. A device that performs a task, with those using it not understanding how it works. For example, a computer is a black box to most users. 2. In computing, financial software that offers information without users being privy to the program's methodology.

black-box accounting Accounting methodology so complex that financial statements are nearly impossible to accurately interpret. Black-box accounting may be used to obscure unfavorable information.

Black Friday 1. The day after Thanksgiving, when consumers stand in line at retail stores, sometimes all night, to buy sale items, get free breakfasts, and generally make fools of themselves. The day is named to describe retailers' income statements that move from red ink (losses) to black ink (profits) in one of the biggest shopping days of the year. —See also CYBER MONDAY. 2. A widely used reference to September 24, 1869, the date on which stock market operator Jay Gould nearly cornered the gold market. Although eventually broken by government selling of the metal, the corner resulted in massive failures on Wall Street. Gould made considerable profits on the manipulation, but his brokers declared bankruptcy.

blacklist A directory of individuals, businesses, or organizations to avoid. For example, companies that have been found to cheat on government contracts may be placed on a blacklist to keep them from winning additional contracts.

blacklisting Refusal by a lender to make loans for properties of a particular class (for example, condominiums) or within a certain geographical region. For example, a bank may decide not to make mortgage loans in areas in which property values are expected to decline.

black market The market in which controlled or illegal goods and services are bought and sold without regulation by government authorities. Illegal drugs and child pornography are examples of goods that trade on the black market.

Black Monday A widely used reference to October 19, 1987, the day the Dow Jones Industrial Average dropped a record 508 points, or nearly 23%. Disarray in the financial markets resulted from a combination of trade deficits, budget deficits, and potential government regulation of mergers and issuance of junk bonds.

blackout period 1. The period prior to the release of financial information during which certain employees of a public company are prohibited from trading in the firm's stock. —See also WINDOW PERIOD. **2.** —See LOCKDOWN.

Black-Scholes Model A relatively complicated mathematical formula for valuing stock options. The Black- Scholes model is used in options pricing to determine whether a particular option should be selling at a price other than the one at which it currently trades.

Black Thursday A widely used reference to October 24, 1929, the date on which security prices plunged, producing one of the most memorable days in the history of the New York Stock Exchange.

Black Tuesday A widely used reference to October 29, 1929, the date of the greatest frenzy on the New York Stock Exchange during the Great Crash. Security prices plunged, volume surged to more than 16 million shares, and the ticker tape ran hours behind trading on the floor.

blank-check company A company that issues stock in order to finance its involvement in establishing a business in which principal operations have not yet commenced. The company either has no business plan, or plans to engage in a merger or acquisition with an unspecified business entity. Essentially, the company is given a blank check with regard to investors' money. Blank-check companies are required to provide certain information prior to and after the registration of securities. —Also called *special-purpose acquisition company.*

blank endorsement Endorsing or signing a negotiable instrument without indicating the person or organization to which the instrument is assigned. For example, signing the back of a check made out to you is a blank endorsement.

blanket advertising contract An agreement offering a discounted advertising rate to a company that promotes multiple products or uses more than one advertising agency.

blanket bond —See BLANKET FIDELITY BOND.

blanket fidelity bond A type of insurance that protects against losses from employee actions such as forgery or unauthorized trading. —Also called *blanket bond; fidelity bond.*

blanket insurance 1. Insurance coverage with a single limit for multiple properties at a single location or at several locations. **2.** Insurance for specified risks to all individuals in a single category. For example, a blanket health insurance policy may cover catastrophic or urgent health problems but not routine care or elective treatment.

blanket mortgage A single lien that covers two or more parcels of land. Developers who intend to subdivide property frequently utilize blanket mortgages.

blanket recommendation A recommendation to buy or sell a security that is sent by a brokerage firm to all its customers. Firms do not consider individual investors' objectives before sending out a blanket recommendation.

blank stock Stock for which voting powers, preferences, and rights are determined by the issuer's board of directors after the shares have been purchased by subscribers.

bleed To drain money or assets from an individual, company, or organization. For example, an unsuccessful business venture may bleed a company's cash reserves.

blended price The weighted average price paid to shareholders in a two-tier tender offer. If 60% of shares are purchased for $20 each and the remaining 40% of shares are acquired for $15 each, the blended price is (0.60 x $20) + (0.40 x $15), or $18.

blended rate An effective rate that is a composite of two or more rates. The blended rate of interest on a variable-rate certificate of deposit will be the weighted average of the rates in effect during the period the certificate is outstanding. Refinancing a loan may result in a blended rate of interest that is an average of the rate on the loan being refinanced and the current market rate.

blind ad An advertisement with limited contact information that fails to include the name of the party placing the ad. For example, a business may place a help-wanted advertisement that includes only job requirements and a box number for mailing applications.

blind pool An investment vehicle that raises capital from the public without telling investors how their funds will be utilized. These pools are sometimes used to acquire and convert private companies into public companies without going through a lengthy registration process. Blind pools are risky investments in which investors should pay particular attention to the background and knowledge of the promoters and officers.

blind trust A fiduciary-managed trust in which the beneficiaries do not have knowledge of the trust's assets. Blind trusts are frequently utilized by public officials who want to avoid the public perception of a conflict of interest.

block A large amount of a security, usually 10,000 shares or more.

blockage discount A reduction from fair market value because of an unusually large amount. For example, the price offered for a shareholder's stock may be below fair market value if the block of stock is so large it will be difficult to dispose of efficiently.

blockbuster A product or service that achieves enormous success. Movie studios, toy companies, publishers, and music producers are all looking for the next blockbuster.

blockbusting Frightening homeowners into selling at bargain prices by telling them that minorities have recently or will soon be moving into their neighborhood.

blocked account —See RESTRICTED ACCOUNT.

blocked market A market that is impossible to enter. For example, the U.S. government may prohibit trade with a particular country.

blockholder The owner of a large proportion of ownership shares of a company.

block house A brokerage firm that specializes in assisting with trades of blocks of securities. Block houses generally work with institutional clients such as mutual funds and pension funds that take large security positions.

block trade A trade of a block of shares that is most likely to occur between two institutions because of the large amount of money involved.

Bloomberg L.P. A leading provider of business news and data. Bloomberg utilizes radio, television, print, and the Internet to provide information to companies, news organizations, and individuals around the world.

blow-in card A printed card that is blown by machine between the pages of a periodical, where it remains loose until sliding out when pages are turned by a reader. Most blow-in cards are used to solicit subscriptions to the publications into which they are inserted.

blowout 1. The nearly immediate sale of a new security issue because of great investor demand. —See also HOT ISSUE. 2. The rapid sale of a product or products at an especially favorable price.

BLS —See BUREAU OF LABOR STATISTICS.

blue chip A very high-quality investment involving a lower-than-average risk of loss of principal or reduction in income. The term is generally used to refer to securities of companies having a long history of sustained earnings and dividend payments.

blue-collar Of or referring to wage earners who typically perform manual labor and wear work clothes. —Compare WHITE-COLLAR.

blue law A law that restricts specific activities, generally shopping, on Sundays. Blue laws originated in the Puritan colonies of New England for observing Sundays as a day of worship and rest.

blueprint A detailed action plan for accomplishing something. A newly hired corporate executive may have a blueprint for returning the company to profitability.

blue skying —Used to refer to the determination of whether a new issue of securities meets the requirements for distribution in the various states where it will be sold.

blue sky laws State regulations that cover the offering and sale of securities within state boundaries. Although the laws differ among states, most include provisions relating to fraudulent activities and the licensing of individuals who sell securities. The term derives from an effort to protect investors from unwittingly buying a piece of "blue sky."

board of directors The group of people responsible for supervising the affairs of a corporation. The board of directors generally sets broad corporate policy rather than participating in day-to-day managerial decisions, although selection of the chief executive officer is the board's responsibility. Members are elected by the firm's stockholders and may or may not be stockholders themselves. —Also called *directorate*. —See also CHAIRMAN; CLASSIFIED BOARD; INSIDE DIRECTOR; INTERLOCKING DIRECTORATES; OUTSIDE DIRECTOR; OVERBOARDING; STAGGERED TERMS.

board of governors 1. An elected body composed of members of a stock exchange that oversees the affairs of the exchange. 2. A group of people appointed by the President of the United States to the Federal Reserve to oversee the nation's money system. Decisions by the board have great impact on the securities markets. —See also FEDERAL OPEN MARKET COMMITTEE.

board of trustees Individuals selected to provide guidance to a nonstock organization such as a college or university.

board-out clause A provision that permits a firm's board of directors to decide whether to enforce a supermajority provision.

board room The room in which a firm's board of directors meets.

bogey An index whose performance an investment manager attempts to match. For example, the S&P 500 may be the bogey for the portfolio manager of an index fund.

boilerplate Standardized technical language used in a legal document such as a prospectus or a registration statement.

boiler room An area in a sales operation in which are located personnel who are engaged in contacting prospective buyers, usually by telephone, and in using high-pressure tactics to sell investments. These operations are associated with high commissions and unethical practices.

bona fide 1. Genuine. 2. Done in good faith. For example, a driver may have made a bona fide attempt to deliver supplies at the prescribed time.

bond 1. A long-term promissory note. Bonds vary widely in maturity, credit quality, and type of issuer, although most are sold in $1,000 denominations or, if a municipal bond, $5,000 denominations. 2. A written obligation that makes a person or an institution responsible for the actions of another.

bond anticipation note (BAN) A short-term municipal security that has its principal repaid from the proceeds of a long-term municipal bond issue that is sold at a later date. Essentially, BANs represent debt that is used until long-term funding is available.

bond basis book —See BASIS BOOK.

bond broker A broker who executes bond trades on an organized exchange or in the over-the-counter market.

Bond Buyer Index An index of yields for AA-rated and A-rated municipal bonds that is widely used by dealers to evaluate yields on new municipal bond issues. The index is published in the *Bond Buyer,* a daily publication specializing in fixed-income securities.

bond calendar —See CALENDAR.

bond conversion The exchange of a convertible bond for another asset, generally shares of common stock.

bond discount —See UNAMORTIZED BOND DISCOUNT.

bond dividend A type of liability dividend paid in the dividend payer's bonds.

bonded debt Liabilities of an organization that are represented by bonds the organization has issued.

bonded goods Goods being held in a bonded warehouse.

bonded warehouse A warehouse where goods subject to duties are stored until the appropriate duties are paid. For example, importers may store imported goods in bonded warehouses until buyers are located and funds to pay duties are available.

bond equivalent yield Annualized yield of a zero-coupon debt security purchased at a discount from face value. Bond equivalent yield is utilized to compare a short-term discount security such as a U.S. Treasury bill with other interest-bearing debt securities.

bond fund An investment company that invests in long-term debt securities. A bond fund may restrict its investments to certain categories of bonds, such as corporate, municipal, or foreign bonds, or it may hold many types of bonds. —See also CORPORATE BOND FUND; MUNICIPAL BOND FUND.

bondholder An individual or institution that owns bonds of a corporation or other organization.

bond indenture —See INDENTURE.

bond power A form, separate from a bond certificate, that permits the owner of the bond to transfer ownership to another investor without endorsing the bond certificate. —Compare STOCK POWER.

bond premium —See PREMIUM 3.

bond rating The grading of a debt security with respect to the issuer's ability to meet interest and principal requirements in a timely manner. The three major rating services—Fitch, Moody's, and Standard & Poor's—use AAA as their highest rating and grade down through Bs and Cs. (D is used only by Fitch.) Debts rated AAA, AA, A, and BBB are considered investment-grade. Higher-rated bonds provide lower returns, the price an investor pays for greater safety. —Compare STOCK RATING. —Also called *security rating.* —See also INTEREST COVERAGE.

bond ratio The proportion of a firm's long-term financing that is represented by long-term debt. A bond ratio is calculated by dividing a firm's total outstanding debt by its long-term debt and owners' equity. —Compare DEBT RATIO. —See also COMMON STOCK RATIO.

bond sinking fund —See SINKING FUND PROVISION.

bond swap The selling of one bond issue and concurrent buying of another issue in order to take advantage of differences in interest rates, maturity, risk, marketability, and other factors. In some instances, especially with municipals, bond swaps are undertaken in order to realize losses for tax purposes —See also REVERSE SWAP; SUBSTITUTION BOND SWAP; TAX SWAP.

bonus 1. Additional compensation that is paid as a reward for achieving specific goals or providing above-average performance. **2.** An additional good or service that is offered to potential customers in order to convince them to purchase a product. For example, an extended service contract may be offered to a company that purchases machinery.

book¹ 1. A securities exchange specialist's information on limit orders to buy and sell the security in which the specialist makes a market. The orders are from investors who wish to trade at a price that differs from the current market price. The book provides the specialist with an estimate of the demand for and supply of the stock in which he or she is a market maker. —Also called *specialist's book.* **2.** —See BOOK VALUE PER SHARE. **3.** An organization's written accounting record. **4.** An underwriting syndicate's record of activity for a new security issue.

book² In accounting, to recognize a transaction by recording an entry. For example, a financial institution books a loan when it lends money to a customer.

book closure The termination of announced benefits to new shareholders. For example, a company announces a specific date on which it will close the firm's books for shareholders to receive a dividend. —See also HOLDER OF RECORD.

book-entry security A security for which the purchaser receives a receipt rather than an engraved certificate. Although a certificate may exist in some instances, it is held in one location as ownership changes. The U.S. government, which issues Treasury bills only in book-entry form, uses this method as a way to reduce paperwork expenses. —See also DEPOSITORY TRUST COMPANY.

bookkeeper The person who records transactions and is in charge of keeping records for a business. A bookkeeper generally operates in a support position in a medium or large company but may enjoy substantial authority in a small firm.

book value

Does the accounting book value of a company provide any useful information for a firm's owners or creditors?

The information that book value conveys depends on the attribute of the asset being reported. As noted in the definition of book value, firms report many assets on an adjusted historical cost basis. Generally accepted accounting principles require market-based disclosure of certain assets, such as debt and equity security investments.

Book-value disclosures for assets reported at (adjusted) historical cost provide a conservative estimate of the net cash flows the firm expects them to generate. Firms lower the book value of these assets whenever they estimate that future cash flows will be less than their current carrying amount. They do not increase book value, however, when they expect cash to exceed the current carrying value. Consequently, the book value of a historical-cost asset provides the minimum cash recoverability of that investment. Conversely, the book value of assets reported at market value equals their economic worth as of the balance-sheet date.

Financial reporting is moving toward reporting assets at market (fair) value because it contains more relevant information than historical cost-based disclosures. As evidenced by market-based asset disclosures during the 2006–2008 housing crisis, however, market values are fluid and sometimes difficult to determine. Proponents of historical-cost reporting argue that these disclosures are more reliable than volatile market prices.

■ Peter M. Bergevin, PhD, Professor of Accounting, School of Business, University of Redlands, Redlands, CA

book loss —See UNREALIZED LOSS.

bookmark The name and web address of an Internet site that is maintained on a computer for easy reference of the site. For example, an investor may keep several bookmarks for Internet sites related to economics and finance.

book profit —See UNREALIZED GAIN.

bookrunner —See LEAD UNDERWRITER.

book-to-bill ratio The dollar amount of orders on the books compared to the dollar amount of orders filled. A high ratio indicates a backlog of orders that should produce revenues and profits in future periods. The book-to-bill ratio is often used to analyze the health of technology companies.

book transfer Transfer of ownership without physical movement of the item whose ownership is being changed. For example, ownership of a bond is generally transferred without movement of the actual bond certificate.

book value 1. The net dollar value at which an asset is carried on a firm's balance sheet. For example, a building that was purchased for $900,000 but that has depreciated $200,000 has a book value of $700,000. Book value, an accounting concept, often bears little relation to an asset's market value. —Also called *carrying value; depreciated cost; net asset value; unrecovered cost; written-down value.* 2. —See BOOK VALUE PER SHARE.

book value per share Common stockholders' equity determined on a per-share basis. Book value per share is calculated by subtracting liabilities and the par value of any outstanding preferred stock from assets and dividing the remainder by the number of outstanding shares of common stock. —Also called *book[1]; book value.* —See also MARKET TO BOOK.

boomerang method A sales ploy of turning around a potential customer's objection into a reason to buy now. For example, a couple considering the purchase of a condominium complain about the price, only to be told by the salesperson that they had better buy now before the price goes even higher.

boondoggle A useless or trivial task or project that consumes time and/or resources.

boot Cash or property included to equalize the values in an exchange of properties. For example, you might swap your home plus cash (the boot) with a neighbor whose home has a greater market value than yours.

bootstrap To assist a new business in getting off the ground.

borrower An individual or organization that owes money to another individual or organization that has served as a lender. The borrower is generally required to make periodic interest payments and, on a specified date, repay the outstanding principal.

borrowing power 1. A firm's ability to borrow significant amounts of money. This term is often applied to companies having valuable assets but few outstanding debts. 2. The amount of money that may be borrowed in a margin account.

Boston option —See DEFERRED PREMIUM OPTION.

Boston Stock Exchange (BSE) The third-oldest securities exchange in the United States. Founded in 1834, the Boston Stock Exchange suspended operations of its equities exchange in 2007 and was acquired by the Nasdaq Stock Market later the same year.

bottleneck A restriction on the amount of productive work that can be done or the amount of a product that can be produced. For example, a lack of available transmissions may prove to be a bottleneck in the production of vehicles.

bottom 1. The lowest price to which the economy, a stock, a market index, or another asset will sink. —Compare TOP. 2. The low point of an economic cycle.

bottom culling Periodically identifying and terminating an organization's weakest performers. For example, a CEO might institute a policy of annually laying off the 10% of staff that have been identified for underperformance of duties.

bottom fishing —Used to refer to the activity of investing in assets when it is believed that market values have reached bottom following a major decline.

bottom line 1. —See NET INCOME. 2. The end result of something. For example, the bottom line of rezoning property from agricultural to commercial is greater value for the owner.

bottom-up 1. In marketing, of or relating to establishing a promotion budget on the basis of what is expected to be required to meet sales and cost objectives. 2. In investing, of or relating to making investment decisions by first focusing on individual companies. Industry analysis and economic forecasts are considered after companies of interest have been identified. —Compare TOP-DOWN.

bought deal —See FIRM COMMITMENT.

bounce 1. Upward movement in the price of an asset following a period of price stability or price declines. For example, a stock might get a nice bounce because of a favorable comment from an influential analyst. 2. Return of an undeliverable email to its sender. 3. The return of a check to its maker by the bank, generally because of insufficient funds for payment. —Also called *rubber check*.

bounded rationality A model of management behavior that recognizes decisions must be made with constraints on information availability and on the ability of a person to consider every possibility. In general, individuals do the best they can with the information and decision-making ability that is available.

bourse The common name for a securities exchange located in Europe.

Bourse de Montreal, Inc. (Canadian Derivatives Exchange) The major Canadian exchange for trading derivative products, including options and futures contracts. The

---

brand loyalty

What are some actions my company can take to improve brand loyalty for our products?

If you are selling services, brand loyalty is built by bringing consistent value to your customer. If you bring new ideas to your customer, understand his or her marketplace as well as his or her specific business needs, and flawlessly execute on the services you provide, a customer will be much more likely to give you business in the future, as your company name will be associated with superior value.

■ E. Mace Lewis, Vice President, Business Development, QD Healthcare Group, Greenwich, CT

---

exchange has a history dating to 1874, and its current specialization derives from a 1999 agreement of the four principal Canadian exchanges to restructure into three specialized exchanges. —Formerly called *Montreal Stock Exchange.* —See also CANADIAN VENTURE EXCHANGE; TORONTO STOCK EXCHANGE.

boutique **1.** A small specialized retail store offering a limited product line that attracts a relatively small clientele. **2.** A small specialized service operation, sometimes within a larger organization. For example, a small hotel might cater to wealthy travelers. **3.** A relatively small, specialized brokerage company. —Also called *investment boutique.*

boycott To refuse to conduct business or deal with a particular organization. For example, members of a labor union may boycott a business that fails to recognize the union as a bargaining agent for the firm's employees. —See also HOT CARGO; PRIMARY BOYCOTT; SECONDARY BOYCOTT.

bracket creep The movement of a taxpayer into higher tax brackets as his or her taxable income increases over time. Bracket creep occurs because of the progressive nature of the federal income tax structure; that is, extra income is taxed at higher and higher rates. As a result of bracket creep, more and more individuals seek tax-advantaged investments.

bracketing The order in which underwriters' names appear in a securities offering. The names are generally listed in the order of importance in a particular offering. —See also TOMBSTONE.

brain drain The loss of skilled and educated people to other countries or geographic areas. A brain drain may occur for political reasons or because of better economic opportunities.

brainstorm An informal attempt, generally in a group setting, to generate spontaneous ideas in order to formulate policy or solve a problem. —See also AFFINITY DIAGRAM.

brand A name or symbol that identifies a good, service, or organization and differentiates it from similar offerings by competitors. —See also TRADEMARK.

brand association The extent to which a particular product or service is identified within its product or service category. For example, many restaurant customers may request Coca-Cola when they want a soft drink.

brand development A plan to improve the performance of a particular product or service. For example, as part of brand development a firm may initiate a new advertising campaign that includes free samples.

brand development index The extent to which a product or service is performing within an identified group of customers in comparison to its performance with all customers. Calculating a brand development index is useful in understanding specific market segments compared to the market as a whole.

brand equity The extent to which a brand adds value to a good or service by retaining existing customers and attracting additional customers.

brand extension Utilizing a well-known brand name to introduce new and modified products or services. Consumer-products companies frequently use brand extension in an attempt to gain shelf space and market share. Consider the variety of Total, Cheerios, and Special K cereals that are displayed on the shelves of grocery stores.

CASE STUDY Businesses have discovered that a new product linked by name with a brand familiar to consumers can serve as a low-cost method for gaining initial market acceptance. The possibility of a brand extension poaching sales from the existing product (buying Honey Nut Cheerios in place of regular Cheerios) can be an acceptable cost for additional shelf space and new customers that are likely to be attracted to a new but familiar brand with a different smell, shape, taste, or color. Not all brand extensions are successful, however. In 2004 and 2005 Swiss food company Nestlé introduced consumers in Great Britain to ten new flavors of its very successful KitKat candy bar. Unfortunately for Nestlé, consumers were so put off after their initial sampling of the new products, that demand faltered and the market became swamped with unsold KitKat bars that retailers began offering at steep discounts. The result was a decline in sales for the entire line. Nearly all of the KitKat extensions were soon discontinued, and the Nestlé executive who engineered the new products was reassigned and so resigned.

brand harvesting Reducing marketing expenditures on a brand in order to maximize cash flow and profits realized from purchases by loyal customers. Brand harvesting is generally applied to mature brands with declining popularity. The expectation is the brand will eventually be discontinued.

brand image The identity of a good or service as perceived by consumers. For example, Toyota vehicles are generally perceived as highly reliable. A brand may have multiple images of varying importance.

brand licensing Leasing a brand name to a company other than the owner of the brand. For example, a European beer company might lease its brand name to an American brewer.

brand loyalty The degree to which consumers prefer and continue to purchase the same brand within a product or service category. Brand loyalty results in improved sales volume and the ability to charge a premium price.

brand manager The person responsible for developing and executing marketing strategies that maximize a brand's profitability. The brand manager is involved in pricing, package design, and distribution of the brand. —Also called *product manager*.

brand name The commercial name for a concept, product, or service that a company wishes to differentiate from similar offerings of competitors. A brand name can apply to a single product or a line of products. Cheerios is a brand name, although the cereal is manufactured in several variations. The cholesterol drug Lipitor is Pfizer's brand name for atorvastatin.

brand share —See MARKET SHARE.

brand stretching Using an established brand name in order to introduce unrelated products. For example, a tobacco company may introduce nontobacco products in order to circumvent advertising restrictions.

breach 1. Failure to satisfactorily comply with a legal obligation. 2. Circumvention of a computer's security system.

breadth of market The underlying strength of stock market movements in an upward or a downward direction. Comparing the number of stocks that have advanced in price with the number of stocks that have declined in price is a popular method for measuring breadth of market. —Also called *market breadth*.

breadwinner The individual whose income provides the majority of financial support for dependents.

break¹ A sharp price decline in a particular security or in the market as a whole. A break usually occurs when unexpected negative information is made public and investors rush to sell. —See also PRICE BREAK.

break² 1. To dissolve an underwriting syndicate. 2. —See BUST.

breakeven 1. The level of output or sales necessary to cover fixed plus variable expenses. Companies in industries that have high fixed costs and, consequently, high breakevens, such as automobile and steel manufacturing, are likely to exhibit large fluctuations in earnings. 2. The price at which a security position can be closed out with no profit or loss. 3. In real estate, the occupancy level of a rental unit required to allow the owner to cover debt service and operating expense.

breakeven analysis A mathematical method for analyzing the relationships among a firm's fixed costs, profits, and variable costs. Financial analysts are particularly interested in how changes in output and sales will translate into changes in earnings.

breaking a buck A decline below $1 in the share price of a money market fund. A money market fund share price may break a dollar if a major decline occurs in the value of securities owned by the fund. For example, a borrower may default on commercial paper held by a fund.

breakpoint 1. The cumulative level of purchases of shares in a mutual fund that is required before an individual purchaser can qualify for a reduced sales commission. —Compare LETTER OF INTENT 2. —See also RIGHT OF ACCUMULATION. 2. The account balance at which the applicable interest rate changes. For example, a loan agreement might charge one interest rate on the first $1,000 and a somewhat lower interest rate on outstanding balances above $1,000.

breakup The division of a company into separate parts. One of America's most famous breakups was the 1984 division of AT&T (formerly, American Telephone & Telegraph Company). This breakup was intended to increase competition in the communications industry.

breakup fee A provision in a takeover agreement that requires a firm to pay the investment banker a large sum of money if another firm takes over the target company. A breakup fee tends to discourage other firms from making bids for the target. —See also TOPPER FEE.

breakup value The market value of all the individual parts of a firm if the firm were to be broken up and the individual parts operated independently. If the breakup value of a firm exceeds the market value at which its stock trades, the firm may be managed and operated inefficiently. In such a case, stockholder holdings would increase in value if parts of the firm were divested. Many takeovers originate when raiders spot firms with breakup values that exceed the prices at which those firms' stocks are traded.

Bretton Woods Agreement The 1944 accord that established a postwar international monetary system of convertible currencies, fixed currency exchange rates, and free trade. The New Hampshire meeting that was designed to provide economic aid for postwar Europe also established the International Monetary Fund and the World Bank.

bribe A promise, payment, or good offered or given in anticipation of receiving special treatment likely to be judged unethical.

bricks-and-mortar company A traditional business with a physical presence. For example, a local bank or corner drugstore is a bricks-and-mortar company. A bricks-and-mortar company stands in contrast to a company such as Amazon that conducts all of its retail business on the Internet. —Compare CLICKS-AND-MORTAR COMPANY.

bridge loan A short-term loan that is taken out until permanent financing can be arranged. —Also called *swing loan.*

broad-based Of or relating to an index or average that provides a good representation of the overall market. The S&P 500 and NYSE Composite are generally regarded as broad-based stock indexes, while the popular Dow Jones Industrial Average is biased toward blue chips and is not considered broad-based. —Compare NARROW-BASED.

broad tape An electronic newswire from Dow Jones, Reuters, or other financial services companies that offers current news and price information about the financial markets. —Also called *tape.* —See also TICKER TAPE.

broken lot Less than the standard amount in which merchandise is normally offered for sale. For example, a dining room set may be offered as a broken lot at a large discount because it includes five rather than six chairs.

broker 1. An individual or a firm that brings together buyers and sellers but does not take a position in the asset to be exchanged. —Compare DEALER 1. 2. —See REGISTERED REPRESENTATIVE.

brokerage 1. A business in which a fee is charged to bring together two or more parties in a transaction. 2. The fee charged by a broker to transact business.

broker call loan —See CALL LOAN.

broker-dealer A firm that functions both as a broker by bringing buyers and sellers together and as a dealer by taking positions of its own in selected securities. Many firms that are commonly called *brokers* or *brokerage firms* are actually broker-dealers.

brokered CD A certificate of deposit of a commercial bank or savings and loan that is sold through an intermediary (usually a brokerage firm) rather than directly by the savings institution itself. Small investors can frequently obtain rates paid on very large certificates through brokered CDs, which are generally sold in $1,000 units.

broker's loan Funds borrowed by a broker, mainly from banks, for various purposes, including a call loan for purchases of securities on margin, an underwriter's purchase of a new security issue for resale, or a specialist's inventory of securities. —Also called *general loan and collateral agreement.*

Brookings Institution A private nonprofit organization in which scholars analyze and make recommendations on a wide variety of public-policy issues. The institution is financed by an endowment and by the support of corporations, individuals, and philanthropic organizations.

BSE —See BOSTON STOCK EXCHANGE.

B2B e-commerce The conducting of commerce by companies, government agencies, and institutions with one another over the Internet.

B2C e-commerce The conducting of commerce by companies, government agencies, and institutions with consumers over the Internet. Amazon.com is typical of a company engaged in B2C e-commerce.

bubble A price level that is much higher than warranted by the fundamentals. Bubbles occur when prices continue to rise simply because enough investors believe investments bought at the current price can subsequently be sold at even higher prices. They can occur in virtually any commodity, including stocks, real estate, and even tulips.

bucket shop An illegal operation in which buy and sell orders are accepted, but no executions actually take place. Instead, the operators expect to profit when customers close out their positions at a loss. A bucket shop is similar in concept to a bookie who does not lay off bets and accepts the risk of a bettor winning.

buckslip A small, rectangular slip of paper with advertising on one or both sides that is included along with other material in a mailing. For example, the envelope with a credit card statement might include a buckslip to call attention to another service offered by the credit card issuer.

budget 1. An itemized projection of revenues and expenses for a specific period of time. Companies utilize a variety of budgets, including cash budgets that exclude noncash items such as depreciation and accruals. **2.** The amount of funds allocated for a specific purpose. For example, a company may establish a marketing budget or a family may set a budget for a vacation.

budget deficit The amount by which expenditures exceed revenues for a specific period. The term is generally applied to governments when expenditures exceed tax revenues and the difference must be made up with borrowing. Large budget deficits accompanied by major borrowing can result in higher market rates of interest. —Compare BUDGET SURPLUS.

budget surplus The amount by which revenues exceed expenditures for a specific period. A government can utilize a surplus to retire outstanding debt. A surplus by individuals and families can be used to pay down debt or accumulate savings. —Compare BUDGET DEFICIT.

buffer stock Reserve units of a good that are utilized to moderate price fluctuations. For example, the government may accumulate a commodity such as wheat during years of surplus production and low prices and sell from the stock during years of shortage and high prices.

buffer zone A defined area serving as a barrier that surrounds or separates a protected area. For example, a city zoning commission may require a buffer zone between a residential area and a commercial area.

building code A government ordinance that establishes minimum standards for the design, construction, and materials used in building.

building permit Written permission by government for the construction, alteration, or demolition of a building on a specified lot.

bulk mail Presorted mail including both first class and standard.

bulk sale The sale of an unusually large amount of inventory, merchandise, or equipment in a single transaction to a single buyer, generally at a lower-than-market price.

bulk sales law State law modeled on the Uniform Commercial Code that imposes certain conditions on the bulk transfer of a firm's assets such that creditors' claims are not devalued without their knowledge. For example, a financially troubled business might attempt to sell a substantial amount of its assets at a bargain price to another firm controlled by the same owner. The bulk sales law generally requires that the business owner inform the creditors and retain funds received from the sale for the creditors' benefit.

bull An investor who believes the price of a particular asset or asset class in general will follow a broad upward trend. An investor can often be a bull on a specific asset but not on the asset class, and vice versa. For example, an investor may be a bull on silver, but not on gold or other precious metals —Compare BEAR.

bullet bond A bond that is noncallable. Bullet bonds tend to offer lower yields than callable bonds that an investor may have to surrender prior to maturity.

bullet immunization The protection of a bond portfolio so as to fund a single liability.

Bulletin Board —See OTC BULLETIN BOARD.

bullet loan A loan with no amortization. A single payment of principal and interest is due at maturity. Bullet loans are generally made with the expectation of refinancing at maturity.

bullion Refined gold or silver in bulk (that is, ingots) rather than in the form of coins.

bullion coins Coins minted from precious metals, including silver and gold. Bullion coins are legal tender but are generally considerably more valuable for their content. Bullion coins include the American Gold Eagle and the South African Kruggerand.

bullish Of or relating to the belief that a particular asset or asset class is headed for a period of generally rising prices. —Compare BEARISH.

bull market An extended period of generally rising prices in an individual item, such as stock or gold; a group of items, such as commodities or oil stocks; or the market as a whole. Because asset prices are often subject to reversals, it is sometimes difficult to know whether there has been a temporary interruption in or a permanent end to a bull market. —Compare BEAR MARKET.

bull spread In futures and options trading, a strategy in which one contract is bought and a different contract is sold in such a manner that the person undertaking the spread makes a profit if the price of the underlying asset rises. Two contracts are used in order to limit the size of the potential loss. —Compare BEAR SPREAD.

bumping In labor contracts, the right of a senior employee to replace a less senior employee in a particular assignment or job for which both employees are qualified. For example, a municipal labor contract may specify that employees impacted by position cuts will have bumping rights within a job classification.

bunch To concentrate income or deductions within a tax year. For example, an individual may decide to itemize deductions every other year by bunching deductible expenses within the year. A taxpayer who bunches deductions uses the standard deduction in alternate years.

bundling Combining several products or services into a single package. For example, a brokerage company may bundle a brokerage account, checkwriting privileges, and a credit or debit card into a single account that requires a monthly or annual fee. —See also TYING CONTRACT.

buoyant Of or relating to a market in which prices have a tendency to move upward.

burden of proof The responsibility of providing convincing evidence that one particular version of a dispute is correct.

bureau A governmental administrative unit or department subdivision.

bureaucrat A career employee of an organization, usually associated with government. In a negative sense, a bureaucrat strictly follows procedures regardless of whether the procedures make sense or inconvenience the persons with whom the bureaucrat interacts.

Bureau of Labor Statistics (BLS) An agency of the U.S. Department of Labor that collects, processes, analyzes, and disseminates data involving the broad field of labor economics and statistics. BLS data includes consumer and producer prices, productivity, unemployment, and demographics.

burn and churn —See CHURN 1.

burnout Lack of energy, motivation, and enthusiasm to continue at a job or task. Burnout is likely to be accompanied by excessive absenteeism, a negative attitude, and a lack of productivity.

burn rate The speed with which a company consumes cash, generally stated on a monthly basis. A high burn rate indicates a firm will soon be out of business unless it can raise additional capital, dramatically increase cash sales, or reduce expenses. The burn rate was particularly high for dot-com companies that placed emphasis on capturing market share rather than on profitability.

business A commercial enterprise that attempts to earn a profit by providing services and/or manufacturing products that are offered for sale.

business activity code An Internal Revenue Service numerical system to classify a business on the basis of the type of activity in which it is engaged. For example, 112400 identifies goat and sheep farming. The code is used to facilitate the administration of the Internal Revenue Code.

business combination —See COMBINATION 1.

business conditions —See BUSINESS FUNDAMENTALS.

business cycle The somewhat irregular but recurring periods of change in economic activity over time. A business cycle is generally divided into four stages: expansion, prosperity, contraction, and recession. The stage in which an economy operates has a significant impact on a firm's profitability and prospects. This impact is especially severe with respect to firms that experience large swings in sales and profits.

business day 1. A day on which the securities markets are open. **2.** The hours each day during which most business are open to customers.

business ethics Accepted standards of conduct for business decision making. Operating in an ethical manner means knowing what is right and wrong and attempting to do what is right in dealing with stakeholders.

business expenses The cost of carrying on a business or trade. To be deductible for tax purposes, expenses must be ordinary (common and accepted in the business) and necessary (helpful and appropriate).

business fundamentals The general background within which an economy operates, including earnings, sales, wage rates, taxes, and inflation. —Also called *business conditions*.

business gift The voluntary transfer without compensation of a good to a customer, supplier, or some other person or organization associated with a business. A business is permitted to deduct up to $25 in business gifts per year to any one taxpayer.

business interruption insurance Insurance coverage that reimburses a business for lost income and at least a portion of the extra expenses involved in restoring a business to operation following a property loss. Coverage can be expanded to include a variety of other problems, including loss of income caused by a property loss at a major supplier or customer. —Also called *loss of income insurance.*

business liability insurance Commercial insurance coverage against claims for bodily injury, property damage, personal injury (libel or slander), and advertising injury. General liability insurance is often packaged with property coverage. —See also WORKERS' COMPENSATION INSURANCE.

business life insurance —See KEY PERSON INSURANCE.

business mix The combination of businesses in which a firm operates.

business office The location where an organization takes care of clerical and professional duties. For example, the business office of a college sells meal tickets, cashes personal checks, issues paychecks, and so forth. —See also PLACE OF BUSINESS.

business organization 1. An industrial or commercial establishment including all of its assets and employees. 2. The organizational structure of a business enterprise.

business owner's policy A comprehensive insurance policy offered to small- and medium-size businesses. Coverage includes general liability, property damage, and loss of business income resulting from insured perils.

business plan A written document that describes the objectives of a firm along with detailed projections on how the objectives will be realized. A business plan should include a company description, organizational structure, information about the product or service line, market analysis, historical and projected financials, and a summary of future plans.

business process reengineering The rethinking and extensive redesign of a business's procedures in an effort to reduce expenses, improve quality, and enhance efficiency. Business process reengineering is similar but more extensive than total quality management, which often brings change in small increments.

business risk The risk that a business will experience a period of poor earnings and resultant failure. Business risk is greatest for firms in cyclical or relatively new industries. Business risk affects both the lenders and owners of a business, since a firm may be unable to pay dividends and interest.

business segment —See SEGMENT.

bust To cancel an order after it has been filled. In most cases, cancellation occurs only under unusual circumstances, such as an error or a misunderstanding. —Also called *break².*

bust-up takeover The acquisition of a firm in which the acquiring company sells certain assets or segments of the target firm in order to raise funds and repay the acquisition debt. Such a takeover is most often undertaken when the target firm has a significant amount of undervalued assets and the acquiring company has little cash.

buy¹ A bargain-priced asset. For example, an investor may feel that political turmoil and expected inflation make gold and other precious metals a buy at their current prices.

buy² To purchase an asset. —Compare SELL.

buy-and-hold strategy The investment strategy of purchasing assets and holding them for extended periods. Investors using the buy-and-hold strategy select assets on the basis of their long-term outlook. Such investors are not influenced by short- or intermediate-term movements in the price of an asset.

buy-and-write strategy The investment strategy in which stock is purchased and call options on the stock are written. A buy-and-write strategy is a fairly conservative approach to generating maximum current income from a combination of option premiums and dividends.

buyback A company's repurchase of a portion of its own outstanding shares. The purpose of a buyback may be to acquire a block of stock from an investor who is unfriendly to the target firm's management and is considering taking over the firm. Conversely, a buyback may be an attempt to increase earnings per share by reducing the number of outstanding shares. Regardless of the purpose of a buyback, the result is increased risk for the firm because of reduced equity in the firm's capital structure. —Also called *stock buyback; stock repurchase plan.* —See also GREENMAIL; PARTIAL REDEMPTION; SELF-TENDER.

> **CASE STUDY** In summer 2006, Exxon Mobil Corporation reported quarterly net income of $10.36 billion, a 36% increase from the previous year's same quarter. On a per-share basis, a measure of more interest to the firm's shareholders, earnings increased from $1.20 to $1.72, or 43%. The larger increase in per-share earnings compared to overall earnings was primarily due to the decline in outstanding shares resulting from the company's continuing program of share buybacks. At the time of the earnings announcement, Exxon Mobil said it would spend $7 billion on additional share buybacks in the coming quarter, an increase from the $6 billion in share buybacks during the quarter of the earnings announcement. At a market price of about $70 per share, the $7 billion buyback would result in an additional reduction of 100 million shares outstanding. Buybacks benefit per-share earnings by spreading net income over fewer shares. In the case of Exxon Mobil, the firm had accumulated a stockpile of nearly $40 billion in cash, so expending funds to repurchase its own shares was not a problem.

buy back To repurchase an asset. For example, a company may decide to buy back shares of its own stock from an investor in order to reduce the possibility of a takeover.

buy-back agreement A contractual obligation for the seller of an asset to repurchase the asset under specified circumstances from the new owner, generally at the original sales price. Buy-back agreements are most frequently applied to real estate transactions.

buydown A mortgage-financing arrangement in which a real estate purchaser obtains reduced mortgage payments (sometimes temporarily) when the seller provides funds to the lender. Essentially a buydown means a seller subsidizes the buyer, who is then better able to qualify for a loan.

buy down To pay discount points on a loan in order to obtain a lower rate of interest on the loan.

buy down

I am interested in purchasing a home from a person who is anxious to sell. Is there any reason I should ask the seller to buy down the mortgage as opposed to simply lowering the price?

If interest rates are high or trending upward, it might make sense to try to get a lower rate by asking the seller to "buy down" the normal market rate you would get. To do this, the seller, at closing, would pay part of the sales price to your mortgage company in the form of discount points, which are prepaid interest. The advantage to you as the borrower is a lower fixed permanent interest rate, which of course lowers your monthly payment. If you plan to live in the home for a relatively long period of time, this can amount to substantial savings.

If rates are low or trending downward, you might be better off just having the seller reduce the sales price instead of buying down your mortgage. If you do not change the amount of your down payment, this would lower the amount of your mortgage, which of course would lower your monthly payment. If rates drop low enough, you can always refinance to get a better deal. If you plan to live in the home for a relatively short period of time (three years or less), the impact of having the seller buy down your interest rate is not as strong.

From the perspective of the seller, there isn't much difference between buying down the loan rate or just reducing the purchase price by the same amount—either way it means less money at closing.

▦ Scott Alderman, Broker and President, First Commercial Real Estate, Valdosta, GA

buyer An individual or organization that purchases a good or service.

buyer agent An agent, generally in the field of real estate, who works in the interest of the buyer rather than the seller. Most agents are employed by and work in the interest of a seller, not a buyer.

buyer behavior The decision-making processes of buyers in purchasing and using goods and services. Buyers may be either ultimate consumers or agents or dealers who purchase goods for resale to ultimate consumers. —See also CONSUMER BEHAVIOR.

buyer's market A market in which the supply of an asset swamps demand to the point that prices fall below the level expected under normal circumstances. For example, when a region with deteriorating economic activity loses population as people move to areas where jobs are more plentiful, a likely result is many houses being put up for sale, thus creating a buyer's market for housing. —Compare SELLER'S MARKET.

buyer's remorse Regret over a purchase. For example, a couple may have buyer's remorse after the purchase of an expensive home that will result in large monthly mortgage payments.

buying climax A period of very high volume and sharp upward movement in the stock market. A buying climax often signals the end of a bull market or, at the least, an overbought market that can be expected to fall. —Compare SELLING CLIMAX. —Also called *climax.*

buying panic A period of rapidly rising asset prices on very high volume as investors and speculators attempt to establish investment positions without regard to price. Buying panics occur when individuals and institutions believe they must buy a particular type of asset at once before prices rise further. —Compare SELLING PANIC.

buying power **1.** The amount of liquid funds available for investing. A large amount of buying power indicates that significant funds from investors are available to fuel a bull market. **2.** The funds in an investor's brokerage account that may be used for

---

bypass trust
Can you provide an example of a person that would benefit from establishing a bypass trust?
A bypass, or credit-shelter, trust is often used by married couples whose combined assets exceed the amount sheltered by the U.S. applicable estate tax credit ($2,000,000 in 2008, scheduled to be $3,500,000 in 2009), but are not so large that the surviving spouse will not need access to all of the couple's combined assets. Consider, for example, spouses who have combined assets of $3,000,000 (when the applicable estate tax credit shelters $2,000,000): if the surviving spouse inherits the combined assets outright and dies with $3,000,000, currently a federal estate tax will be due on the assets in excess of $2,000,000. If, instead, the predeceased spouse had left $1,000,000 to a bypass trust in which the surviving spouse had liberal rights in income and principal (but had no interest in the trust which would cause the trust property to be included in the surviving spouse's gross estate for estate tax purposes), and the assets owned by the surviving spouse did not exceed $2,000,000 at death, no federal estate tax (under the estate tax law in effect in 2008) would be payable. The savings in federal estate tax at 2008 rates is $450,000. State estate tax savings may also result.

▪ Stephen F. Lappert, Partner, Trusts and Estates Department, Carter Ledyard & Milburn LLP, New York, NY

---

purchasing securities. An investor's buying power includes cash balances plus the loan value on securities held in the account.

Buying Power Index A popular indicator of a geographical area's relative consumer buying power. The index is calculated using weighted data for income, retail sales, and population in the area being evaluated. The index might be used by a retailer considering new store locations.

buy on margin To buy securities by putting up only a part, or a margin, of the purchase price and borrowing the remainder. The loan is usually arranged for by the investor's broker. The securities must be kept in the account. —See also INITIAL MARGIN REQUIREMENT; MAINTENANCE MARGIN REQUIREMENT.

buyout 1. The purchase of all the stock of a company or controlling interest in a company. —See also LEVERAGED BUYOUT. 2. The purchase of all the stock of a company owned by a single investor or by a group of investors.

buy out 1. To purchase all the stock of a company or all the stock of a company owned by one investor or by a group of investors. For example, corporate management may decide to buy out an investor in order to halt a potential takeover. 2. To terminate a contract before its scheduled termination date by reaching a monetary agreement satisfactory to the parties involved.

buy-sell agreement A written agreement in which the owners of a business agree to buy the interest of one or more of the owners under certain circumstances. For example, a buy-sell agreement may include a predetermined price or formula for buying the interest of an owner who dies.

buy signal An indication provided by a technical tool, such as a chart or trading volume, that a particular security or securities in general should be purchased. For example, the achievement by a stock of a new high price on heavy trading volume is often interpreted as a buy signal. —Compare SELL SIGNAL.

buzz words Trendy words used to impress and/or to obscure meaning. Examples of buzz words used in business include *brainstorm, empowerment,* and *greenmail.*

bylaws Stockholder-approved rules governing the conduct of a business. Bylaws typically include rules concerning election of directors, selection of auditors, and amendment of existing bylaws.

bypass trust An irrevocable estate-planning device that transfers assets in such a way as to take full advantage of estate tax exemptions while providing maximum income to a surviving spouse. Assets held in a bypass trust pay the spouse a lifetime income and pass free of taxation to the designated beneficiary at the death of the spouse.

by-product Production process output that is in addition to the main product. For example, production from a gold mine might result in low volumes of the ore of other metals. A by-product generally has a relatively low market value compared to the main product.

byte Computer memory required to store eight bits, or one character of data. One kilobyte (1KB) is equal to 1,024 bytes.

 C

Caa —See CCC.

CAC 40 A market-capitalization-weighted index of the 40 most actively traded stocks on the Paris Bourse. CAC is short for Cotation Assiste en Continu.

cache 1. A secret place for storage of money or valuables. **2.** High-speed memory held in a storage device or a reserved section of a computer's main memory. A cache stores recently used data so that it can be accessed rapidly.

cadastre A public record of land ownership, quantity, and valuation that is used for tax purposes.

cafeteria plan An arrangement offered by some employers that permits employees to choose their own benefit package from a variety of options that may include disability insurance, medical insurance, dependent care insurance, term life insurance, adoption assistance, vacation pay, and cash. Flexible benefits offered in a cafeteria plan allow employees to get the most for their money.

calendar A list of upcoming bond issues. A full calendar indicating a large number of issues may force issuers to increase interest rates in order to compete for buyers. —Also called *bond calendar.*

calendar effects The impact a particular day, week, or month an asset is owned has on rates of return. For example, studies indicate tax selling produces downward pressure on stock prices during the end of the calendar year, followed by upward price pressure in January. —See also JANUARY EFFECT.

calendar spread In options and futures trading, the purchase of one contract and the sale of another contract that differs from the first only by its delivery or expiration date. An example of calendar spread would be the purchase of a December call with a strike price of $20 and the sale of a June call with the same strike price. An investor would use a calendar spread in order to profit from a change in the price difference as the securities move closer to maturity. —Also called *horizontal spread; time spread.*

calendar year A year that begins on January 1 and ends on December 31. —Compare FISCAL YEAR.

call[1] 1. An option that permits its holder to purchase a specific asset at a predetermined price until a certain date. For example, an investor may purchase a call option on General Electric stock that confers the right to buy 100 shares at $35 per share until October 17. Calls are sold for a fee by other investors, who incur an obligation. —Compare PUT[1] 1. —Also called *call option.* **2.** An issuer's right to repurchase an issue of bonds at a predetermined price before maturity. The feature is used when interest rates fall, so that the bonds can be repurchased and a new, lower-rate issue sold. A call feature is normal for nearly all long-term bond issues, and it operates to the detriment of bond owners. —See also CALL PRICE; CLEANUP CALL; EXTRAORDINARY CALL; OPTIONAL CALL; SINKING FUND CALL. **3.** Redemption of an issue of bonds before maturity by forcing the bondholders to sell at the call price.

call² **1.** To force an option writer to sell shares of stock at a price stipulated in a contract. Stocks usually are called just before the expiration of the options. **2.** To redeem bonds prior to the scheduled maturity. **3.** To redeem shares of preferred stock. **4.** To demand repayment of a bank loan.

callable bond A bond that is subject to redemption by its issuer before maturity.

callable CD A certificate of deposit that can be redeemed prior to the scheduled maturity. Many retail brokerage firms broker callable CDs issued by insured financial institutions. These CDs, often with long maturities, are traded in the secondary market and can fluctuate in value with changes in market rates of interest. —Also called *deposit note.*

callable common stock Common stock of a subsidiary that is sold by the parent company and is subject to a stock purchase option agreement. The exercise price of the call generally steps up over time. —Compare PUTTABLE COMMON STOCK.

callable preferred stock An issue of preferred stock that may be repurchased by the issuer at a specific price, usually par value or slightly above. The option to repurchase such stock is held by the issuer, not the investor. Calls can be expected when market rates of interest have fallen significantly below the yield on the preferred stock at the time the stock was issued.

call date The date on which a security can be repurchased by the issuer at a predetermined price. The issuer establishes the call date at the time a security is issued.

called away —Used to refer to the forced sale of a security by an investor because of the action of another party. For example, the writer of a call option has the underlying stock called away when the call owner exercises the option. Likewise, a bondholder may have bonds called away by the issuer if interest rates decline and the issuer decides to redeem a portion of the issue before maturity. In nearly all cases, a call works to the disadvantage of the owner of the security.

call feature —See CALL PROVISION.

call loan A loan that may be terminated at any time by either party. For investors, a call loan means bank loans to stockbrokers for the purpose of carrying customer margin borrowing, using securities as collateral. The rate of interest, similar to that on other high-quality short-term loans, varies over time. —Also called *broker call loan.* —See also BROKER'S LOAN.

call market A market in which trading in individual securities occurs at specific times as opposed to continuously. In a call market, all orders to buy and sell a particular security are assembled at one time in order to determine a price at which most of the orders can be executed. The participants then move on to a different security. Call markets are frequently used in situations in which there are few securities and participants.

call option —See CALL¹ 1.

call premium The difference between the principal amount of a security and the price at which the security can be called by the issuer. Call premiums often gradually decline over the life of the security until they reach zero at maturity. Calls for sinking fund requirements are usually made at par rather than at a premium. —Also called *redemption premium.*

call price The price at which an issuer may, at its option, repurchase a security for redemption before the security's maturity. For bonds, the call price often declines over the life of the security until it reaches par value at maturity. —Also called *redemption price.* —See also EXTRAORDINARY CALL; OPTIONAL CALL; SINKING FUND CALL.

call protection The prohibition against an issuer's calling a bond from an investor during the early years of the security's life. A longer period of call protection is advantageous to the investor because calls nearly always occur during periods of reduced interest rates. —Also called *cushion.* —See also NONCALLABLE; NONREFUNDABLE 1.

call provision The stipulation in most bond indentures that permits the issuer to repurchase securities at a fixed price or at a series of prices before maturity. This provision operates to the detriment of investors because calls on high-interest bonds usually occur during periods of reduced interest rates. Thus, an investor whose bond is called must find another investment, often one that provides a lower return. Certain preferred stock issues are also subject to call. —Also called *call feature.* —See also MAKE-WHOLE CALL PROVISION.

call risk —See PREPAYMENT RISK.

Calvo Doctrine A foreign-policy principle holding that a dispute involving an international investment is subject to the jurisdiction of the country in which the investment is located.

camera-ready copy The final layout of a page exactly as it will appear in publication.

Canadian Derivatives Exchange —See BOURSE DE MONTREAL, INC.

Canadian Venture Exchange (CDNX) The Canadian marketplace for trading securities of emerging companies. The exchange specializes in trading small- and medium-cap equity issues, while the Toronto Stock Exchange serves as the Canadian exchange for large-cap issues. The Canadian Venture Exchange is headquartered in Calgary with trading facilities in Vancouver.

cancel 1. To mark a check so that it cannot be used again. **2.** To offset something. For example, a decrease in an asset's value may offset, or cancel, an earlier gain.

cancellation clause The clause in a contract that describes the conditions under which each party can cancel the agreement. For example, an apartment owner may have the right to cancel a lease in the event a tenant causes physical damage or disturbs other tenants.

canned program Computer software that can be purchased.

cannibalize To suffer a sales loss in a product or outlet because of the introduction of a similar product or the opening of a new outlet. For example, a new Wal-Mart will experience some sales that are cannibalized from other, nearby Wal-Mart stores that lose sales to the new store. The introduction of a new flavor of a soft drink will almost certainly cannibalize sales from other flavors of the same brand already being offered.

cap 1. An upper limit on the interest rate or the adjustment to interest rates to be paid on a floating-rate note. A loan may have an annual cap and a lifetime cap. **2.** —See CAPITALIZATION.

capacity 1. The maximum output that can be expected from a person, a plant, a company, or the economy during a specified period. For example, an automobile plant may have a capacity of 1,000 vehicles per day. **2.** The maximum quantity that something can hold. For example, an underground oil tank may have a capacity of 25,000 gallons. **3.** The dollar amount of exposure (or proportion of surplus) an insurer is willing to place at risk. **4.** —See DEBT CAPACITY.

capacity utilization rate The proportion of an economy's plant and equipment capacity that is being used to produce goods and services. A high capacity utilization rate is a characteristic of a strong economy, when manufacturers find it relatively easy to increase prices. A low capacity utilization rate is often accompanied by price cutting in an attempt to increase sales.

capital 1. Money or property owned by a person or a business. **2.** In economics, assets that can be used in the production of goods and services.

capital account 1. In accounting, a general ledger account of contributions by owners of the business. Retained earnings is included, along with common stock and paid-in capital in excess of par value. **2.** In economics, a country's international movements of financial assets including stocks, bonds, and short-term money market instruments such as Treasury bills. The purchase of foreign investments by U.S. investors is considered a capital outflow of the United States. —Compare CURRENT ACCOUNT.

capital appreciation An increase in the market value of an asset.

capital appreciation bond —See ZERO-COUPON BOND.

capital asset 1. An asset that has an expected life of more than one year and that is not bought and sold in the usual course of business. Buildings and machinery are examples of capital assets. **2.** In taxation, an asset such as shares of stock held for investment purposes. Gains and losses realized from the sale of capital assets are subject to special tax rules.

capital-asset pricing model (CAPM) A mathematical model for asset pricing in which the relative riskiness of an asset is combined with the return on risk-free assets. This model, which uses beta, the widely used measure of risk, has been criticized; nevertheless, it is considered a very important element of modern investment and portfolio theory. —See also CAPITAL MARKET LINE.

capital budgeting Corporate evaluation of long-term investment proposals, generally by means of discounting estimated future cash flows.

capital consumption allowance The expenditures a country must make in order to maintain its productivity. Capital consumption allowance for a nation is analogous to depreciation expense for a business. Gross domestic product less the capital consumption allowance equals net domestic product.

capital contributed in excess of par value —See ADDITIONAL PAID-IN CAPITAL.

capital controls Restrictions on the movement of capital among countries. For example, a country may enact legislation that prohibits citizens from sending funds out of the country.

capital dividend A dividend considered to be drawn from paid-in capital rather than from current earnings or retained earnings. Capital dividends are generally not taxable to a stockholder when paid; rather, they are used to adjust the basis of the security downward such that a larger capital gain or a smaller capital loss will result at the time the security is sold. —Also called *return of capital.*

capital expenditure Funds used to acquire a long-term asset. A capital expenditure results in depreciation deductions over the life of the acquired asset. —Also called *capital outlay.*

capital flight The shifting of funds out of a country to avoid confiscation, controls, or depreciation. Capital flight results in further deterioration of a currency's exchange rate.

capital formation The creation of productive assets that expand an economy's capacity to produce goods and services. Private savings facilitates capital formation by allowing resources to be diverted to corporate investment rather than individual consumption.

capital gain The amount by which proceeds from the sale of a capital asset exceed the cost basis.

capital gains distribution Payments to investment company shareholders based on gains from securities in the firm's portfolio that have been sold. These gains are passed through to the shareholders and are taxed to the shareholders. Distributions usually occur once each year.

capital gains tax The tax applicable to gains realized from the sale of capital assets, including stocks and bonds. The capital gains tax rate and holding period requirements are periodically changed by Congress. A favorable tax rate is generally applied to realized gains on assets that are sold following a holding period of over one year. Realized capital gains on assets held a year or less do not generally receive favorable tax treatment.

capital goods Assets that are used in the production of goods and services. Machinery to manufacture cars and equipment to produce memory chips are each an example of a capital good. —Compare CONSUMER GOODS.

capital improvement Enhancement to property, plant, or equipment that improves productivity or increases the life. An addition to a factory or remodeling an office building is an example of a capital improvement. Capital improvements are depreciated rather than expensed for tax purposes.

capital intensive Of or relating to a firm or industry that requires large amounts of fixed assets and/or cash to operate. Steel, automobile manufacturing, and mining are capital-intensive industries.

capitalism An economic system that is based on private ownership of the means of production and distribution. Prices for goods and services are determined by the free market, and businesses are operated for the economic gain of the owners.

capitalization The amounts and types of long-term financing used by a firm. Types of financing include common stock, preferred stock, retained earnings, and long-term debt. A firm with capitalization including little or no long-term debt is considered to be financed very conservatively. —Also called *cap; capital structure; financial structure; total capitalization.* —See also COMPLEX CAPITAL STRUCTURE; LARGE-CAP; MARKET CAPITALIZATION; RECAPITALIZATION; SMALL-CAP.

capitalization rate The rate used to convert an income or cash stream into a present-value lump sum. For example, a capitalization rate of 10% and a permanent income stream of $2,000 annually provide a present value of $2,000/0.1, or $20,000. The capitalization rate for a particular flow of income is a function of the rate of interest on Treasury bills (the risk-free rate) and the risk associated with the flow of income. A riskier investment has a higher capitalization rate and, therefore, a lower present value. —Also called *cap rate.*

capitalize 1. To calculate the current value of a future stream of earnings or cash flows. For example, to calculate the current price at which rental property should sell, a financial analyst must capitalize the interest payments and principal repayment that will be made to the investor. **2.** To issue securities in return for investment capital. **3.** To take advantage of something. For example, a farmer near a city may capitalize on urban growth by selling farmland to developers for a high price.

capitalized value The current value of a future stream of earnings or cash flow. The capitalized value of a rental property is the discounted value of all future cash flows, including rental income, tax benefits, and so forth. The capitalized value of an asset is heavily dependent on the rate at which the projected cash flow stream is discounted.

capital lease The long-term lease of a capital asset. To the lessee, a capital lease is the same as owning the asset. Accounting rules require that the leased asset and the present value of the lease payments be recorded on the lessee's balance sheet. —Also called *financial lease.*

capital loss The amount by which the cost basis of a capital asset exceeds the proceeds from its sale.

capital market The market for long-term funds where securities such as common stock, preferred stock, and bonds are traded. Both the primary market for new issues and the secondary market for existing securities are part of the capital market.

capital market line The line used in the capital-asset pricing model to present the rates of return for efficient portfolios. These rates will vary depending on the risk-free rate of return and the level of risk (as measured by beta) for a particular portfolio. The capital market line shows a positive linear relationship between returns and portfolio betas. —Also called *market line.* —See also ALPHA; BETA 1; SYSTEMATIC RISK.

capital outlay —See CAPITAL EXPENDITURE.

capital rationing A limitation on the amount of money a company is able to spend on capital projects. Capital rationing causes a company to choose among available investment projects, even when all the investments meet the firm's minimum return requirement.

capital requirement 1. Long-term financing required for ongoing operations by a business. **2.** Funds required for a proposed investment. **3.** The required minimum level of liquid assets to be held by broker/dealers and banks.

capital resources 1. Assets used in the production of goods and services **2.** Financing sources for a business. For example, venture capital firms are a capital resource for small businesses.

capital spending Spending for long-term assets such as factories, equipment, machinery, and buildings that permits the production of more goods and services in future years.

capital stock Any of various shares of ownership in a business. These shares include common stock of various classes and any preferred stock that is outstanding. If a firm has only a single class of capital stock outstanding, the terms *common stock* and *capital stock* are often used interchangeably. —See also AUTHORIZED CAPITAL STOCK; OUT-STANDING CAPITAL STOCK; STOCK CLASS.

capital structure —See CAPITALIZATION.

capital surplus —See ADDITIONAL PAID-IN CAPITAL.

capital turnover A measure indicating how effectively investment capital is used to produce revenues. Capital turnover is expressed as a ratio of annual sales to invested capital.

capitation A fixed fee or payment per person. For example, a health maintenance organization pays a physician a fixed monthly fee for each patient included in the program regardless of the services provided.

CAPM —See CAPITAL-ASSET PRICING MODEL.

capped-style option An option with an established price (the cap price) at which the option will be automatically exercised. The cap price is equal to the strike price plus a predetermined interval for a call option and the strike price less a predetermined interval for a put option.

cap rate —See CAPITALIZATION RATE.

CAPS —See CONVERTIBLE ADJUSTABLE PREFERRED STOCK.

captive agent In insurance, an agent that represents only a single company.

captive finance company A subsidiary that raises capital and makes loans in order to benefit the parent company. For example, automobile manufacturers have long owned captive finance companies that loaned money to facilitate dealer inventories or customer purchases.

captive product A product that is manufactured for use with another product. Software games that work only with a particular game console are captive products. Likewise, specialized razor blades may fit only a particular type of razor. Captive products are often sold at high prices because they become a necessary part of the other product.

card check A method for determining whether employees feel a union should be recognized by their employer as their collective bargaining agent. Favorable sentiment for recognition is defined by a majority of the employees signing cards expressing support for the union during an established period. Card check is an alternative to a secret-ballot election. Employers are not legally required to recognize a union, no matter how much support a card check indicates.

CARDS —See CERTIFICATES FOR AMORTIZING REVOLVING DEBTS.

cargo Goods or commodities transported on a train, ship, truck, or other vehicle.

cargo insurance Financial protection for losses resulting from transport of goods or commodities.

carload 1. The minimum weight or quantity to qualify for a reduced shipping rate. **2.** In commodities trading, a railroad car or truckload of grain that ranges from 1,400 to 2,500 bushels.

carpetbagger A newcomer or outsider who seeks influence or other personal gain. Carpetbaggers are often resented by others and may be perceived to lack long-term commitment. For example, an investor or group of investors acquire an initial stake in a business in an effort to overhaul the firm's finances and operations before selling the stake to others at a profit. The term originated during the Civil War when Northerners moved to the South in order to profit from reconstruction.

carriage trade Wealthy individuals and families that are subject to special rules and treatment: *The small investment house catered to the carriage trade.*

carrier 1. An insurance company that underwrites (carries the risk) and issues an insurance policy **2.** —See COMMON CARRIER.

carrier's lien The right of a common carrier to retain possession of a cargo until all freight charges have been paid.

carrot and stick A combination offer of a reward along with a threat of punishment if the carrot isn't earned. For example, a construction company may be offered a bonus if a building is completed by a specified date, but be penalized if the target date isn't met.

carryback A business operating loss that, for tax purposes, may be deducted for a certain number of prior years, usually no more than three. A business uses a carryback to recover taxes paid on income earned in prior years. For example, if a firm experiences a year of large losses following a period of profitable operations, it may use the losses to cancel out profits from preceding years on which taxes have been paid. When the taxes a company paid on profits are canceled because of a carryback, the firm is issued a refund by the Internal Revenue Service. —Also called *carryover; tax loss carryback.*

carryforward 1. A business operating loss that, for tax purposes, may be claimed a certain number of years in the future, often up to 15 years. Thus, a loss in one year would be carried forward to a future year and used to offset profits up to the amount of the carryforward. Carryforwards are especially useful to firms operating in cyclical industries such as transportation. —Also called *tax loss carryforward.* **2.** In taxation of individuals, net capital losses exceeding the annual limit of $3,000 that may be carried to succeeding years so as to offset capital gains or ordinary income. There is no limit on the amount of capital losses that may be used to offset capital gains in any one year, only on the amount of losses in excess of gains that may be used to offset income. —Also called *carryover.*

carrying charge 1. The cost of owning and storing a commodity during a period of time. This cost influences the difference between the futures price and the expected future spot price. **2.** The cost of holding real estate prior to development. For example, spending $100,000 for land that is unlikely to be developed for ten years involves substantial annual costs for interest (if funds for the purchase are borrowed) and taxes. **3.** Interest charged on the balance of an installment loan. **4.** —See COST OF CARRY.

carrying value —See BOOK VALUE 1.

carryover 1. —See CARRYBACK. **2.** —See CARRYFORWARD 2.

carryover basis 1. The cost basis for tax purposes of an asset that has been received as a gift. In general, the carryover basis of assets received as a gift is the same as the basis of the giver. **2.** The tax basis of property received in a like-kind exchange. The tax basis of relinquished property carries over to the replacement property. —Also called *substituted basis.*

carry trade An investment strategy of borrowing funds in a market with low interest rates and investing in debt securities or other assets in a different market. For example, an investor might borrow money in a country in which interest rates are low and invest the borrowed funds in a different country in which interest rates are high. Likewise, an investor could borrow at low short-term rates and invest the funds at higher long-term rates. Changes in relative interest rates or economic conditions can result in this strategy producing substantial losses.

> **CASE STUDY** Large flows of money in the carry trade can move interest rates, investment values, and currency exchange rates. Years of weak economic growth caused Japan's central bank to maintain a short-term benchmark interest rate of zero. The carry trade took advantage of the low rates by borrowing funds in Japan, converting yen to dollars, euros, and other curren-

cies, and investing in the United States, Europe, and other countries with higher interest rates or promising investment opportunities. For example, a large investor such as a hedge fund might borrow in Japan, convert yen to dollars, and invest in high-yielding bonds in the United States. The flow of cash out of Japan caused the yen to decline versus the dollar and other currencies, until in early 2007 the yen had hit an all-time low versus the euro and was generally considered the world's weakest major currency. In early 2005, 100 yen were worth approximately $0.98 U.S. dollars, while two years later the same 100 yen were worth only about $0.82. The falling value of the yen resulted in even greater profits for the carry trade, because the currencies into which yen had been converted were worth even more yen when the trades were eventually reversed. Investors became worried about overvalued stock markets and real estate values by spring 2007 and started converting dollars back into yen, thereby causing the dollar to decline in value versus the yen.

CARS —See CERTIFICATE FOR AUTOMOBILE RECEIVABLES.

cartage Transporting goods over a short distance. For example, a commercial carrier transports a customer's products from the factory to the airport.

carte blanche Complete freedom to act. For example, a board of directors may offer a new chief executive officer carte blanche, or complete discretion, in restructuring the firm's operations.

cartel A group of companies or countries acting together to control the supply and price of certain goods or services. Cartels are formed to produce higher profits than would ordinarily be earned.

carve-out 1. In medical insurance, services that are separated from a contract and paid under a different arrangement. **2.** —See EQUITY CARVE-OUT.

case law Legal doctrine established by previous court decisions. For example, case law indicates contingent-fee contracts are speculative future income and not includable as marital property in divorce proceedings.

cash¹ Coins and currency on hand and in checking account balances. Because cash is a nonearning asset, firms usually attempt to keep their cash balances to the minimum level required to sustain operations.

cash² To exchange a negotiable instrument, generally a check, for money.

cash account A brokerage account requiring that cash payments on purchases and deliveries on sales be made promptly. (Settlement is officially three business days after the transaction date.) The cash account is the most popular type of brokerage account even though it does not permit investor borrowing (that is, buying on margin). Certain accounts, such as Individual Retirement Accounts, must be cash accounts. —Compare MARGIN ACCOUNT. —Also called *special cash account.*

cash advance 1. A loan on a personal line of credit, generally by means of a credit card that is presented at a bank or used in an automated teller machine. **2.** —See ADVANCE 1.

cash and equivalents The sum of cash and short-term assets that can be easily converted to cash. This measure of corporate liquidity indicates a firm's ability to meet its short-term obligations.

cash balance plan A qualified employer pension plan in which the employer guarantees a contribution level and minimum rate of return.

cash basis accounting A method of accounting in which the receipt and payment of cash are the basis for recording transactions. Thus it is not the date on which goods and services are received that matters, as in accrual accounting, but the dates on which the cash changes hands for the transactions. Cash basis accounting is typically used for tax purposes by individuals but not by corporations. —Compare AC-CRUAL ACCOUNTING.

cashbook An accounting record of cash receipts and cash disbursements. A cashbook is used to maintain a record of a firm's cash position.

cash budget An important planning tool that details projected cash receipts and payments in order to forecast cash balances. The cash budget permits management to become aware of potential cash shortages and take corrective measures.

cash commodity —See ACTUAL.

cash contract A fairly unusual security transaction in which settlement with payment and security delivery are to occur on the same day as the trade date. This type of trade often occurs during the last week of a calendar year, when sellers wish to settle early in order to realize a gain for tax purposes. —Compare REGULAR-WAY CONTRACT. —Also called *cash trade.*

cash conversion cycle The length of time between when a company pays for purchases of inventory and when it receives cash from its own customers who purchase the inventory. For example, a retailer orders goods on January 4 with payment due on January 14. The goods are sold on January 10 with payment received from customers on January 31. The cash conversion cycle is 17 days, the difference between January 14, when the company pays its suppliers, and January 31, when the company receives payment from its own customers. A short cash conversion cycle allows a business to quickly acquire cash that can be used for additional purchases or debt repayment. —See also OPERATING CYCLE.

> **CASE STUDY** The cash conversion cycle measures the length of time between when cash flows out to suppliers and when it is later replenished with payments from customers. A shorter time between cash outflows and inflows means less required financing and more profits. Businesses attempt to shorten the cash conversion cycle by speeding payments from customers and slowing payments to suppliers. This isn't always easy to accomplish, because most businesses are attempting to do the same thing. A firm's suppliers want to get paid more quickly at the same time its customers are attempting to pay more slowly. The perfect business is one in which cash comes in before it goes out. This "negative" cash conversion cycle is a major advantage of the business model developed by Internet bookseller Amazon. Although Amazon warehouses some of the books it sells, many titles are not ordered from publishers until orders are received from customers. Amazon charges customers' credit cards as soon as books are shipped and typically receives payment within two days. At the same time, the Internet bookseller doesn't pay publishers for, on average, nearly a month and a half. As the company states in its annual report: "We generally have payment terms with our vendors that extend beyond the amount of time necessary to collect proceeds from our customers." Thus, Amazon is able to pay its suppliers with its customers' money, and then only after having the funds available to help cover the firm's overhead for more than a month.

cash cow A business or a segment of a business that produces significantly more cash than it consumes. As an example, a firm may sell a product that requires minimal advertising and promotional expenditures but continues to generate revenues year after year. Firms sometimes use cash cows to provide cash for financing other segments of their business. —See also HARVEST STRATEGY.

cash disbursement Payment of money, generally by means of cash or writing a check.

cash discount The reduction in price for payment of a bill prior to a specified date.

cash dividend A dividend paid in cash (that is, by check) to holders of a firm's stock. Although the amount is usually based on profitability, it may temporarily exceed net income. Certain legal and contractual restrictions may limit a firm's ability to pay cash dividends.

cash earnings Cash revenues less cash expenses. Cash earnings does not account for noncash expenses (depreciation, purchases on credit) or noncash receipts (sales on credit) and so differs from reported earnings.

cash equivalent 1. An asset, such as property or stock, that has a realizable cash value equivalent to a specific sum of money. 2. An asset that is so easily and quickly convertible to cash that holding it is essentially equivalent to holding cash. A Treasury bill is considered a cash equivalent.

cash flow The amount of net cash generated by an investment or a business during a specific period. One measure of cash flow is earnings before interest, taxes, depreciation, and amortization. Because cash is the fuel that drives a business, many analysts consider cash flow to be a company's most important financial statistic. Firms with large cash flows are frequently takeover targets because acquiring firms know that the cash can be used to help pay off the costs of the acquisitions. —See also FREE CASH FLOW.

cash flow per share A value calculated by dividing a firm's cash flow by the average number of shares of capital stock that are outstanding. Cash flow per share is frequently used in valuing a firm's stock by analysts who believe the amount of net cash a firm produces is a more valid measure of its value than its reported earnings per share.

cashier 1. A person who is in charge of collecting payments for goods and/or services. 2. A bank officer responsible for the organization's assets.

cashier's check A check drawn by a bank on itself. A cashier's check is made out to a designated institution or person and must be paid for before it is issued. —See also CERTIFIED CHECK.

cash item A check presented to a bank that authorizes immediate credit to the depositor's account.

cash management Administration of working capital in an attempt to maximize the return earned on current assets and minimize the cost of current liabilities. For example, the financial manager of a retailer might attempt to reduce the time it takes the firm to collect receivables.

cash management bill A very short-term security (typically one having 10 to 20 days from date of issue until maturity) that is issued by the U.S. Treasury in order to manage its cash balances. A cash management bill is issued in minimum denominations of $1 million and is bought by institutional investors.

cash market The market in which trades are made for the immediate sale or purchase of a particular item. Cash market is commonly used in commodities trading to differentiate transactions involving immediate or nearly immediate delivery from transactions requiring delivery at a future time. —Also called *spot market.*

cash matching strategy A method of assembling a bond portfolio so that cash receipts from coupon and principal payments exactly meet future cash needs.

cash-on-cash return The rate of return based on annual cash income in relation to the amount of cash invested. This measure of return is used most frequently for investments such as real estate in which a large portion of the purchase price is borrowed.

cash on delivery (COD) **1.** Describing a transaction in which payment in full, either by cash or certified check, is required at the point of delivery. **2.** —See DELIVERY VERSUS PAYMENT.

cash-out refinancing Refinancing a mortgage when the principal amount of the new mortgage is greater than the remaining principal of the mortgage being refinanced, and the difference is taken in cash. —Compare NO CASH-OUT REFINANCING.

cash position **1.** The amount of short-term liquid assets held by a firm in relation to the firm's size. **2.** Proportion of a mutual fund's assets that are held in short-term liquid securities such as U.S. Treasury bills.

cash price A price quotation in a cash market. In securities trading, a cash price distinguishes a transaction as being other than a regular three-day delivery, a difference that may be sought for tax or dividend reasons. In commodities trading, a cash price implies immediate or nearly immediate delivery as opposed to settlement in a specified future month. —Also called *spot price.*

cash ratio A type of current ratio measure that compares a firm's cash and cash equivalents with its current liabilities. A firm's cash ratio is a demanding test of its liquidity. —Compare QUICK RATIO.

cash register A machine that records and maintains a record of transactions, and that includes a money drawer.

cash reserves Investment funds that are held in short-term assets such as Treasury bills and certificates of deposit until more permanent investment opportunities are available. A large amount of cash reserves offer flexibility and safety but generally hinder profitability.

cash settlement Settlement of a futures contract in cash rather than in the asset underlying the contract. For example, stock index futures call for cash settlement because it is not feasible actually to deliver an index or the securities constituting an index.

cash shortage/overage The extent to which physical cash is less/more than cash that should be on hand according to the record of receipts and disbursements.

cash surrender value The money paid by an insurance company to a policyholder who cancels an annuity or cash-value life insurance policy. Cash value accumulates when premiums and interest on any previous cash value exceed the cost of insurance. Generally, the cash value a policyholder receives on cancellation is not taxable unless it exceeds the sum of the premiums paid. —Also called *surrender value.*

cash trade —See CASH CONTRACT.

cash-value life insurance A type of life insurance in which part of the premium is used to provide death benefits and the remainder is available to earn interest. Thus, cash-value life insurance is both a protection plan and a savings plan. This insurance entails a significantly higher premium than protection-only insurance and, depending on the issuer and the policy, may pay a relatively small return on savings compared with other investments. —Compare TERM INSURANCE. —Also called *permanent insurance; whole life insurance.*

casual labor Work that is occasional or irregular and not in the normal course of an employer's trade or business: *The retailer hired casual labor to move inventory to the new store location.*

casualty insurance Broad coverage to protect against financial loss from property damage and liability caused by sudden and unexpected events. Casualty insurance includes worker's compensation, malpractice, liability for death, injury, or disability of a human being, and a range of other potential hazards. —See also DUAL-TRIGGER INSURANCE.

casualty loss A financial loss resulting from a sudden and unexpected event such as a fire, storm, or accident. A casualty loss in excess of insurance reimbursement is allowed as a deduction in calculating taxable income.

catastrophe bond A debt security with a payoff tied to the relative severity of a natural disaster such as a hurricane or earthquake. Bondholders are paid with insurance premiums but may have to accept reduced principal repayment in the event the specified disaster occurs during the life of the bond.

catastrophe call Redemption of a bond because of a disaster. For example, a bond issue collateralized by an airplane may be called if the plane crashes.

catastrophe insurance Insurance coverage for exceptionally large financial losses. An example would be a major medical policy with very high limits and, generally, a large deductible. Catastrophe insurance is also available for property losses from earthquakes and terrorism.

cats and dogs Speculative assets.

cause of action The set of facts or allegations that serve as the basis of a legal claim.

caveat emptor Latin for "let the buyer beware." For example, a consumer who purchases a vehicle "as is" from a private seller assumes the possibility of costly mechanical problems.

caveat venditor Latin for "let the seller beware." For example, a manufacturer that decides to sell on credit to a company that is heavily in debt and financially shaky must consider the possibility of not being paid.

CBOE —See CHICAGO BOARD OPTIONS EXCHANGE.

CBOT —See CHICAGO BOARD OF TRADE.

CCC A very speculative grade assigned to a debt obligation by a rating agency. Such a rating indicates default or considerable doubt that interest will be paid or principal repaid. —Also called *Caa.*

CCH A leading provider of tax and business law information and software. CCH was purchased by Wolters Kluwer in 1995.

C corporation A corporation with profits taxed separately from its owners'. The name derives from subchapter C of the Internal Revenue Code. A C corporation differs from an S corporation, whose profits are passed through to shareholders and taxed at the personal rates of the shareholders.

CD —See CERTIFICATE OF DEPOSIT.

CDNX —See CANADIAN VENTURE EXCHANGE.

CDO —See COLLATERALIZED DEBT OBLIGATION.

cede In insurance, to relinquish a portion of an insurer's business to a reinsurance company.

Celler-Kefauver Antimerger Act A 1950 federal antitrust law that updated the Clayton Act by severely restricting anticompetitive mergers resulting from acquisition of assets.

censure Official disapproval by a government agency or professional organization. For example, a state bar association may censure an attorney whose behavior is in conflict with the association's rules of professional conduct.

central assets account —See ASSET MANAGEMENT ACCOUNT.

central bank A bank administered by a national government. A central bank issues money and carries out the country's monetary policy. The Federal Reserve System is the central bank of the United States. —Also called *national bank.*

central bank intervention The buying and selling of domestic or foreign currencies by a central bank in an effort to influence interest rates or currency exchange rates. For example, the Federal Reserve might intervene in the foreign exchange market in order to dampen rapid fluctuations or signal the markets that recent exchange rate movements do not indicate a fundamental trend. —See also FOREIGN EXCHANGE DESK 2.

central buying Combining purchases through a central authority. For example, a retail grocery chain with hundreds of stores is likely to make many purchasing decisions at headquarters for all the stores.

central tendency In statistics, the center or middle of a distribution as measured by the mean, median, and mode. For example, a study might find the majority of grocery retailers earn between 2% and 3% on sales.

CEO —See CHIEF EXECUTIVE OFFICER.

certainty equivalent The minimum sum of money a person would accept to forgo the opportunity to participate in an event for which the outcome, and therefore his or her receipt of a reward, is uncertain. For example, suppose you are told to draw one card from a full deck of cards. If you draw a red card you win $100, and if you draw a black card you win nothing. If you would accept $40 to forgo the selection and the possibility of winning, $40 is the certainty equivalent of the outcome of the event. Certainty equivalents are used in evaluating risk.

certificate 1. Evidence of ownership of a bond or shares of stock. A certificate contains detailed information relating to the issuer and the owner, including the issuer's name, particulars of the issue, the number of shares or the principal amount of the bonds, and the name and address of the owner. —Also called *stock certificate.* —See also BOOK-ENTRY SECURITY. **2.** A document attesting to or verifying something. For example, a certificate may indicate the completion of a course of study.

certificate for automobile receivables (CARS) A short-term debt security backed by automobile loans and originating when lenders package and resell the automobile loans to the public. CARS provide lenders with more funds to use in additional lending and provide investors with relatively safe securities that pay short-term interest rates slightly above Treasury securities of similar maturity.

certificate of deposit (CD) A receipt, issued by a financial institution for a deposit of funds, that permits the holder to receive interest plus the deposit at maturity. Federal law requires a nominal penalty for early withdrawal of CDs, but financial institutions often impose more costly penalties. —See also ADD-ON; CALLABLE CD; EARLY-WITHDRAWAL

PENALTY; JUMBO CERTIFICATE OF DEPOSIT; NEGOTIABLE CERTIFICATE OF DEPOSIT; TERM CERTIFI-
CATE; ZERO-COUPON CERTIFICATE OF DEPOSIT.

certificate of incorporation A certificate issued by a state that approves a corporation's articles of incorporation and proves the corporation's existence.

certificate of indebtedness A U.S. Treasury debt obligation with an original maturity of one year or less and a fixed coupon rate of interest. A certificate of indebtedness differs from a Treasury bill, which is sold at a discount from face value and has no coupon.

certificate of participation (COP) Entitlement to a participation, or share, in the lease payments from a particular project. The lessor generally assigns lease payments to a trustee that distributes the payments to certificate holders.

certificate of title 1. A state-issued document for a motor vehicle that includes the registered owner's name and address, type of vehicle, vehicle identification number, and the name of any lienholder. 2. In real estate, a written statement of a title company or attorney regarding the status of a property title.

Certificates for Amortizing Revolving Debts (CARDS) A special type of asset-backed debt security collateralized by credit card balances.

certification Official or professional validation of something. For example, a teacher may have state certification to teach grades one through three; a diamond may have certification that it meets a certain quality grade.

certified check A check that a financial institution draws on an individual's account and then certifies to indicate that sufficient funds are available to cover the amount of the check when cashed.

certified employee benefit specialist A professional benefit specialist who has successfully completed an eight-course program covering all aspects of compensation. Separate specialty designations are awarded in retirement planning, group benefits, and compensation management. The program is jointly sponsored by the Wharton School of the University of Pennsylvania and the International Society of Certified Employee Benefit Specialists.

certified financial planner (CFP) A professional financial planner who has completed a series of correspondence courses and has passed examinations in subject areas such as insurance, securities, and taxes. The designation is awarded by the Institute of Certified Financial Planners. —Compare CHARTERED FINANCIAL CONSULTANT.

certified financial statement A financial statement that has been reviewed and approved by a certified public accountant.

Certified in Financial Management (CFM) A professional designation awarded by the Institute of Management Accountants to members who demonstrate knowledge of financial management principles by passing a series of examinations. Members must meet a work-experience requirement and provide evidence of continuing education.

Certified in Management Accounting (CMA) A professional designation awarded by the Institute of Management Accountants to members who demonstrate knowledge of management accounting by successfully passing a series of four computer-based examinations. Candidates for the designation must have two years of professional experience in management accounting, and individuals who earn the designation are required to present evidence of continuing education.

Certified Lenders Program A program of the Small Business Administration that provides expedited service on loan applications submitted by lenders with a satisfactory lending history that have demonstrated an understanding of the SBA program. Loans submitted by certified lenders are reviewed but do not have to go through a second analysis by the SBA.

certified mail First-class or priority mail for which the sender is provided a mailing receipt. A return receipt and restricted delivery are available at extra cost.

certified public accountant (CPA) An accountant who has met certain state requirements as to age, education, experience, residence, and accounting knowledge, the latter measured by the successful completion of an extensive series of examinations. In most instances, only CPAs are permitted to render opinions on the fairness of financial statements. —See also CERTIFIED FINANCIAL STATEMENT.

CFA —See CHARTERED FINANCIAL ANALYST.

CFM —See CERTIFIED IN FINANCIAL MANAGEMENT.

CFO —See CHIEF FINANCIAL OFFICER.

CFP —See CERTIFIED FINANCIAL PLANNER.

CFTC —See COMMODITY FUTURES TRADING COMMISSION.

chain of command An organizational structure in which authority passes down from the top and each person in the chain is directly responsible to the person above.

chain of title A chronological history of ownership transfers for a tract of real property. A chain of title includes legal judgments, deaths of joint property owners, foreclosures, and other actions relevant to the property's ownership. —See also ABSTRACT OF TITLE.

chain store One of a large number of stores offering similar merchandise and operating under the same central management.

chairman The highest-ranking executive in a corporation. The chairman leads the board of directors in setting broad corporate goals and determining if managers are, in fact, pursuing and achieving those goals. In large corporations the chairman is not ordinarily involved in day-to-day operational activities, although it is likely that he or she was the chief executive officer before attaining the position of chairman. In some corporations, the chairman also serves as the president and the chief executive officer. —Also called *chairman of the board.* —See also DIRECTOR.

chairman of the board —See CHAIRMAN.

champerty An agreement in which a party (generally, an attorney) agrees to finance a lawsuit in return for entitlement to a proportion of the plaintiff's recovery.

champion A person who actively supports and promotes a particular person, project, or idea. For example, a corporate executive is a champion for instituting a wellness program.

chancery Of or describing a court of equity as opposed to a court of common law. A court of equity operates under a system of fairness and flexibility rather than strict law.

change —See NET CHANGE.

change in accounting principle Converting from one accounting principle to another. For example, a firm may change inventory valuation from first-in, first-out, to last-in, first-out when accounting for cost of goods sold.

change in control provision A stipulation in a contract or corporate charter that permits certain actions in the event that there is a change in control of the organization. For example, benefits in an executive compensation plan may accelerate in the event of a change in control. Some bond indentures allow bondholders to redeem their bonds at a premium in the event the issuer is acquired and the bonds are downgraded.

CASE STUDY Bondholders are generally at the mercy of corporate management, which tends to place maximum emphasis on pleasing stockholders. For example, a company might issue substantial amounts of additional debt in an effort to improve stockholder returns, even though the added liabilities increase the risk for all of the firm's existing creditors, including its bondholders. Stockholders are also at greater risk, but at least they expect to benefit from a higher return on their investment. Existing bondholders shoulder greater risk without any accompanying benefits. Following a number of high-profile buyouts involving substantial amounts of debt and credit downgrades, uniform maker Cintas Corporation issued $250 million of investment-grade debt that included a change in control covenant. The covenant offered protection to buyers of the bonds by allowing them to redeem the debt early in the event the company was taken over. In early 2007, Alcoa issued $2 billion of new bonds with a change in control provision. Alcoa's debt was to be used to reduce outstanding commercial paper and fund a buyback of short-term notes. The Alcoa debt was oversubscribed, in large part because the issue included the provision to protect bondholders in the event of a takeover that would almost certainly be financed with additional debt.

change management The systematic process of dealing with changing the traditional methods by which organizations and individuals perform.

Change to Win A labor federation formed in 2005 when five former unions affiliated with the AFL-CIO joined with the Teamsters and United Food and Commercial Workers. The breakaway unions felt the AFL-CIO concentrated too much on politics and devoted too little effort to organizing workers. Members of Change to Win are concentrated in the construction, health care, hospitality, and trucking industries.

channel of distribution The network of organizations and individuals that connect the manufacturer of a product with ultimate consumers. For example, a soft drink may move from the manufacturer to a regional distributor to a retailer to the consumer. —Also called *distribution channel.*

channel stuffing Artificially inflating current sales and earnings by shipping more goods than would normally be ordered. For example, an appliance manufacturer may inflate revenues and earnings in the current accounting period by shipping to retail stores more refrigerators, stoves, and dishwashers than the stores are likely to sell. The practice of channel stuffing borrows revenues and earnings from the future because overstocked customers will reduce orders in future periods.

Chapter 7 A bankruptcy option in which a bankrupt firm is liquidated after the courts have determined that reorganization is not worthwhile. A trustee is charged with liquidating all assets and distributing the proceeds to satisfy claims in their order of priority. In Chapter 7 bankruptcies, the creditors often receive a fraction of the value of their claims and the stockholders receive nothing. —See also EXEMPT PROPERTY; NO-ASSET CASE; NONEXEMPT PROPERTY.

Chapter 9 The section of the Bankruptcy Code dealing with the reorganization of municipalities, including taxing districts, utilities, and school districts.

Chapter 11 A bankruptcy option in which a trustee is appointed to reorganize the bankrupt firm. Although the existing claims of security holders are likely to be reduced or replaced with different claims, it is expected that the firm will continue operating. Both creditors and owners must vote approval of the plan before the reorganization can be confirmed by court action and become effective. —See also PREPACKAGED BANKRUPTCY; REORGANIZATION PLAN.

> **CASE STUDY** Once the supermarket industry's most profitable company, Jacksonville, Florida–based Winn-Dixie Stores filed for Chapter 11 bankruptcy protection on February 21, 2005. At the time of the filing, Winn-Dixie was the country's eighth largest food and drug store chain and ranked number 182 on Fortune's 500 listing of America's largest corporations. Unfortunately, Winn-Dixie was being squeezed between the low prices of Wal-Mart's Supercenters and the upscale service and stores of Florida-based Publix Super Markets. On the filing date, Winn-Dixie listed $2.23 billion of assets and $1.87 billion of debts. The company indicated that it expected to close a third of its 913 stores and reduce its workforce by 22,000 employees. It would cease operations in North Carolina, South Carolina, Tennessee, and Virginia. Twenty-one months after filing for Chapter 11, Winn-Dixie emerged as a new company, with 522 stores and 55,000 employees. In the interim, the firm had closed stores and sold warehouses and manufacturing plants. Its old common stock was canceled, and 54.5 million shares of stock of the new company were issued to the bankrupt company's unsecured creditors. The company operated stores in only five states following its emergence from Chapter 11 bankruptcy.

Chapter 13 Personal bankruptcy in which an individual may retain personal property but must partially or completely repay debts over a period of three to five years. Minimum repayment depends on the amount of disposable income less reasonable expenses. —Also called *Wage Earner Plan.*

charge **1.** The price charged for a good or service. **2.** Demand for payment. **3.** Purchase of a good or service with a promise of payment on a later date. **4.** Instructions to a jury at the end of a case. **5.** An accusation against a person or organization. For example, a person may be charged with theft.

chargeback **1.** A fee charged to a retailer by a credit card company when a disputed charge is won by a cardholder. **2.** A penalty by a customer against a supplier whose goods do not meet the terms of the sales agreement.

charge card —See CREDIT CARD.

charge off —See WRITE OFF.

charitable contribution deduction An itemized income-tax deduction for donations of assets to Internal Revenue Service–designated organizations. Certain qualifications on this deduction apply, such as a contribution limit of 50% of a taxpayer's adjusted gross income.

charitable lead trust A trust that pays an income to a charity for a specific length of time, then leaves the remainder of the trust to designated beneficiaries, usually family members. The purpose of the charitable lead trust is to reduce taxes on the estate of the deceased while maintaining the family's control of the estate's assets. —Compare CHARITABLE REMAINDER TRUST.

charitable trust

What type of person is most likely to benefit from establishing a charitable trust?

Wholly charitable trusts (trusts that distribute only to charity) may benefit the donor by creating an income, gift, or estate tax charitable deduction for the property transferred to the trust while allowing the donor to control the disposition (by the terms of the trust or, possibly, as trustee) of the trust property for charitable purposes. [See also PRIVATE FOUNDATION.] Thus, for example, an individual with charitable intentions who has significant income this year and who could benefit from a charitable deduction could establish and fund a wholly charitable trust during the year and, in future years, direct the income and principal of the trust to public charities. Such trusts are typically exempt organizations for income tax purposes and subject to significant regulation under the federal tax laws and may also be regulated by state agencies supervising charitable activities.

Some trusts that have charitable beneficiaries also have noncharitable beneficiaries. The common forms of these are the charitable remainder annuity trust, the charitable remainder unitrust, the charitable lead annuity trust, and the charitable lead unitrust, and each has provisions prescribed by the Internal Revenue Code, federal tax regulations, and IRS publications. These trusts permit a donor a means to provide for both charity and individual beneficiaries, and the value of the charitable interest will also qualify for the gift and estate tax charitable deduction, and may also provide the donor with an income tax charitable deduction. Charitable remainder trusts are exempt from income tax and allow income tax planning for the disposition of highly appreciated assets.

▪ Stephen F. Lappert, Partner, Trusts and Estates Department, Carter Ledyard & Milburn LLP, New York, NY

charitable remainder trust A trust that pays an income to one or more individuals for a specified length of time, then leaves the remainder of the trust to a designated charity. A charitable remainder trust can produce substantial tax benefits and is particularly suitable for use by a married couple with no children. —Compare CHARITABLE LEAD TRUST.

charitable trust A legal arrangement whereby real or personal property is placed in trust for the benefit of a charity. A charitable trust can produce substantial tax benefits for an individual and his or her estate.

charity —See QUALIFIED CHARITY.

chart Data displayed in a diagrammatic manner, often to show relationships between different sets of numbers. Charts are used to observe the historical values of variables and, frequently, to spot trends that may provide insights for use in projecting future values. —Also called *graph*.

charter¹ 1. Of or relating to a business offering transportation for hire. For example, a sports team might contract with a charter bus company. 2. —See ARTICLES OF INCORPORATION.

charter² 1. To temporarily hire transportation for passengers or cargo. 2. To temporarily lease a means of transportation to a person or group.

chartered financial analyst (CFA) A financial analyst who has met certain standards of experience, knowledge, and conduct as determined by the Association for Investment Management and Research. The successful candidate must pass examinations covering economics, security analysis, portfolio management, financial accounting, and standards of conduct.

chartered financial consultant (ChFC) A professional financial planner who has completed a series of courses and examinations in subject areas such as economics, insurance, real estate, and tax shelters. The designation is awarded by the American College in Bryn Mawr, Pennsylvania. —Compare CERTIFIED FINANCIAL PLANNER.

chartered life underwriter (CLU) A life insurance professional who has successfully completed formal training in a course of study in life insurance and personal insurance offered by the American College in Bryn Mawr, Pennsylvania. The course of study includes estate planning, insurance law, business and professional planning, and a series of elective topics.

chartered property casualty underwriter (CPCU) An insurance professional who has successfully completed a course of study in property-casualty and risk management offered by the American Institute for CPCU and the Insurance Institute of America. Individuals who achieve the designation are subject to a code of professional ethics.

chart formation A series of graphed stock prices or other market variables that form a recognizable pattern that may be used to determine future movements of the charted variable. Chart formations are not always as clearly defined as their users would like; thus the ability to recognize and use charted data varies among technicians. —Also called *formation; pattern.*

charting The graphing of market variables, especially of stock prices and market averages. Technicians also chart other variables, including commodity prices, interest rates, and trading volume, in an attempt to determine trends and project future values.

chart of accounts A coded list of accounts in the general ledger that can be used to properly classify, record, and report for purposes of constructing financial statements.

chase a stock To attempt to buy a stock that is rising in price by placing orders at increasingly higher prices.

chattel Personal property such as automobiles, paintings, inventories, domestic animals, or real estate leases, but not real estate ownership.

chattel mortgage A mortgage loan using personal property rather than real estate as security.

cheap 1. Of, relating to, or being an asset that sells at a market price below what is expected given fundamental factors such as income-producing potential and resale value. Determining whether an asset is cheap is a subjective judgment. —Compare EXPENSIVE. **2.** Of, relating to, or being a good or service that sells at a price below the price being charged for similar goods or services. **3.** Of or describing a good of inferior quality.

cheap money —See EASY MONEY.

check A written order for a bank to pay a specified amount of money from deposited funds of the maker. —See also CASHIER'S CHECK; CERTIFIED CHECK.

check digit A digit attached to a data item to help with error detection. For example, the last digit of a check's bank routing number is a check digit. A check digit is calculated from a formula using other digits in the number. Entry of the number causes the computer to recalculate the check digit to determine if the number has been entered correctly.

> **CASE** The last digit of each UPC number is a check digit used to verify that
> **STUDY** the UPC for a particular product is correct. The verification process
> for each 12-digit UPC code works like this: (1) the 6 digits in odd positions

are added and the sum is multiplied by 3; (2) the first 5 digits in even positions are added; (3) the sums calculated in steps 1 and 2 are added; (4) the last digit (the check digit) is added to the result in step 3, and the result should equal a multiple of 10. For example, the UPC for an 18-ounce jar of Jif peanut butter is 051500241356.

Step 1: $0 + 1 + 0 + 2 + 1 + 5 = 9$; $9 \times 3 = 27$
Step 2: $5 + 5 + 0 + 4 + 3 = 17$
Step 3: $27 + 17 = 44$
Step 4: The check digit of 6 is added to step 3 to equal 50, a multiple of 10.

check kiting —See KITING 1.

checkoff Authorized deduction of union dues from member wages. —Also called *automatic checkoff; dues checkoff.*

check register A written record of each check written along with the check number and name of the payee.

check truncation Removing the original paper checks from the collection or return process. Financial institutions do not return canceled checks to an account holder, who can obtain a microfilmed copy if the need arises. Check truncation is designed to improve the efficiency of the nation's payments system. —Also called *truncation.* —See also SUBSTITUTE CHECK.

checkwriting privilege The privilege of writing checks against shares held in a mutual fund. This option, which provides greater liquidity for the investor, is generally offered free of charge. The dollar amount of each check is usually subject to a minimum value—often $250 or $500—depending on the policy of the fund.

ChFC —See CHARTERED FINANCIAL CONSULTANT.

Chicago Board of Trade (CBOT) A derivatives exchange established in 1848 to trade forward contracts in agricultural commodities, including wheat, corn, and oats. The exchange introduced electronic trading in 1994 after 145 years of using open outcry. The Chicago Board of Trade was purchased in 2007 by the Chicago Mercantile Exchange to form CME Group, Inc.

Chicago Board Options Exchange (CBOE) A securities exchange established in 1973 as the nation's first organized floor for trading standardized options. Although its success spawned option trading on a number of other exchanges, the CBOE remains the most active options exchange in the country. Unlike most exchanges that use a specialist system of trading, the CBOE uses market makers who compete among themselves for trades.

Chicago Mercantile Exchange (CME) A leading commodities exchange established in 1919 as a marketplace for agricultural futures contracts. In 2000 the *Merc* became the first U.S. financial exchange to demutualize and become a shareholder-owned corporation. The Chicago Mercantile Exchange acquired the Chicago Board of Trade in 2007 to form CME Group, Inc. —Also called *Merc.*

Chicago Stock Exchange (CHX) A regional securities exchange that provides a fully automated matching system for equities. The CHX first opened for business in 1882 and later merged with exchanges in Cleveland, Minneapolis, and St. Louis to form the Midwest Stock Exchange. The exchange reclaimed its prior name in 1993. The CHX currently trades over 3,500 stocks, including many issues also listed on the NYSE, AMEX, and Nasdaq.

chief executive officer (CEO) The person responsible to a company's board of directors for carrying out its policies. Essentially, the CEO is the highest-ranking executive managing the firm on a day-to-day basis. —See also CHAIRMAN.

chief financial officer (CFO) The corporate executive responsible for financial planning, approving appropriations, raising capital, and financial oversight. The CFO is frequently the second-highest-ranking executive in a firm.

chief operating officer (COO) The person responsible for a firm's day-to-day activities. The COO generally reports to the chief executive officer.

child and dependent care credit A federal tax credit available to working taxpayers or taxpayers seeking work who pay someone else to take care of children or dependents. The credit is calculated as a percentage of spending on child and dependent care, with the percentage a function of a taxpayer's adjusted gross income. —Also called *dependent care credit.*

child support 1. The legal obligation of parents to provide financial support for their children. The obligation ends when a child reaches 19 years of age, unless he or she is disabled or a student. **2.** Court-ordered payments by one parent to another who has custody of the couple's child.

Chinese wall An imaginary separation placed between a brokerage firm's investment banking business and its trading and retail business. A Chinese wall prevents investment bankers, who frequently are privy to information that could substantially influence the price of a client's securities, from leaking that information to the firm's traders and sales personnel. The exchange of such information is legally prohibited.

chi-square test A statistical tool that is used to determine the probability of obtaining an observed result by chance. For example, a chi-square test might be used to determine if the people in a group are distributed across categories (male/female, minority/nonminority, bald/not bald, etc.) as would be expected by chance.

churn 1. Active trading in a brokerage account in order to increase brokerage commissions rather than customer profits. Brokers may be tempted to churn accounts because their income is directly related to the volume of trading undertaken by customers. Churning is illegal and unethical. —Also called *burn and churn; overtrade.* **2.** Turnover of customers. For example, a wireless phone company may experience high churn as customers seek the lowest rate. —See also CUSTOMER LIFETIME VALUE.

CHX —See CHICAGO STOCK EXCHANGE.

CIF —See COST, INSURANCE, AND FREIGHT.

cipher A message written in code.

circuit breaker The automatic response, usually a halt or slowdown, in activity at an exchange in response to certain occurrences in trading. Circuit breakers are designed to reduce market volatility and were instituted following the large market breaks in October 1987 and October 1989. —See also SUSPENDED TRADING.

circuit court A court that sits in different locations within a specified territory known as the circuit. The term derives from the time when judges and lawyers (including Abraham Lincoln) traveled the circuit.

circular file A wastebasket.

civilian labor force All employed and unemployed individuals 16 years of age and older who are not institutionalized and not in the U.S. armed forces.

civil law A system of laws based on written legal code that govern disputes between individuals. Civil law is applied to issues involving property and contracts, as opposed to criminal acts.

civil recovery Legal means by which a business may attempt to reclaim losses and costs directly from a wrongdoer without the expense of using the court system. For example, a merchant may utilize civil recovery in relation to a person who is caught with unpaid merchandise. The person accused of theft may make restitution or choose to have the matter tried in civil court. —See also MERCHANT'S PRIVILEGE.

claim A demand made by the insured or a beneficiary of the insured for payment of insurance policy benefits. —Also called *insurance claim.*

claims-made policy An insurance policy in which the insurer agrees to pay claims only during the term of the policy or within a specified period after expiration of the policy. The insurer is protected against other future claims.

claims-occurrence policy An insurance policy in which the insurer is responsible for claims made because of events that take place during the period the policy is in force. A claim can be filed after a policy is no longer in force.

class 1.—See STOCK CLASS 1. **2.** Option contracts of the same type (put or call) and style (American or European) on the same security and expiring on the same expiration date. **3.** Individuals who meet certain established criteria. For example, individuals who have suffered health ills after taking a particular type of drug may qualify as plaintiffs in a class action lawsuit.

class action lawsuit A lawsuit in which one party or a limited number of parties sue on behalf of a larger group to which the parties belong. For example, investors may bring a class action lawsuit against a brokerage firm that has actively promoted a tax shelter without having adequately disclosed the attendant risks. —See also SHAREHOLDER DERIVATIVE SUIT.

class beneficiary designation A designation of life insurance beneficiaries that names a group of people rather than individuals by name.

classified board A corporate board of directors whose members are elected to terms that expire in different years. A classified board makes it more difficult for a new owner to assume control in a takeover. —See also STAGGERED TERMS.

classified stock —See STOCK CLASS 1.

class life The recovery period of an asset for depreciation purposes using the Modified Accelerated Cost Recovery System. —Compare USEFUL LIFE.

class struggle Group conflict based on social or economic class.

clause A section of a legal document. For example, a life insurance policy may include an incontestability clause that prevents the insurer from denying coverage after a specified period because of misstatements by the insured.

claused bill of lading —See BILL OF LADING.

clawback 1. A provision in an incentive stock option that requires an employee to reimburse the company for any gains realized from exercising options in the event the employee goes to work for a direct competitor within a specified number of months of the exercise. **2.** Excessive management share of profits that must be refunded to investors of a venture capital fund. A clawback is required when managers of a venture capital fund take a contractual share of early investment gains that are subsequently reduced by losses.

Clayton Act A 1914 federal antitrust law designed to promote competition by prohibiting or severely restricting practices such as the acquisition of competitors, price discrimination, secret rebates, and interlocking directorates.

clean balance sheet A balance sheet with only a small amount of debt in relation to assets.

clean float Currency exchange rates that are free from central bank intervention and subject only to free market forces.

clean hands 1. Lack of past misconduct related to the subject matter for the plaintiff of a legal claim. 2. Of or relating to someone who is considered honest because their past is free of misconduct.

clean opinion The opinion of a firm's auditors that its financial statements are fairly presented in accordance with generally accepted accounting principles. A clean opinion does not necessarily mean that the firm is financially strong or that its future is favorable, since even financially weak firms generally receive clean opinions. —Compare ADVERSE OPINION; DISCLAIMER OF OPINION; QUALIFIED OPINION. —Also called *standard opinion; unqualified opinion.* —See also SUBJECT TO OPINION.

clean price The price of a bond without accrued interest. —Compare DIRTY PRICE.

clean title —See CLEAR TITLE.

cleanup call Early redemption of the entire balance of a debt issue when a relatively small amount of the original issue remains outstanding. For example, mortgage-backed securities are gradually paid down as mortgages backing the bonds are paid off by homeowners. At some point the issuer of the mortgage-backed securities may decide to reduce its own administrative expenses by calling the balance of the issue.

clean-up fund Life insurance coverage necessary to pay the debts and burial expenses of the deceased.

cleanup merger A merger in which an acquired firm is consolidated into the acquiring firm. —Also called *take-out merger.*

cleanup requirement The requirement that a borrower reduce the balance on a renewable line of credit to zero for a specified period of time during the year. The requirement is to make certain the borrower is not using the line of credit for permanent financing.

clear[1] 1. To pay for securities delivered into an account and accept funds for securities delivered out of an account. 2. To collect funds on which a check is drawn and make payment of the funds to the person who presented the check. 3. To make a profit after all expenses are considered. For example, a person might sell a piece of real estate and clear $50,000 after realtor fees.

clear[2] Of or relating to a trade in which the seller delivers securities and the buyer delivers funds in the prescribed manner and on time. —Compare FAIL[1]. —See also GOOD DELIVERY.

clearance sale A special sale to reduce inventory. For example, an automobile dealership might have a clearance sale just prior to receiving new models.

clear and convincing proof The standard of proof that must ordinarily be offered to win a case in civil lawsuits and regulatory hearings.

clearinghouse 1. A corporation established by an exchange in order to facilitate the execution of trades by transferring funds, assigning deliveries, and guaranteeing the performance of all obligations. 2. In banking, a cooperative funds transfer system for interbank clearing of checks and electronic entries.

clear title Ownership of an asset whose title is free of liens and legal questions by others. —Compare TITLE DEFECT. —Also called *clean title; good title.* —See also TITLE REPORT.

clerk 1. A salesperson. 2. An employee who keeps and/or files records.

clicks-and-mortar company A traditional business with a physical presence that also utilizes the Internet. For example, clothing retailer Clearwater Creek operates numerous stores but also conducts a major portion of its business via the Internet. "Clicks and mortar" is a play on the term *bricks and mortar,* which refers to an old-economy company with only a physical presence. —Compare BRICKS-AND-MORTAR COMPANY.

click-through rate The response to an Internet ad as measured by the percentage of people viewing the ad who actually click on and follow the link to the destination page. The click-through rate is used to measure the effectiveness of an Internet ad.

client 1. A computer system that utilizes the services of another computer system. 2. A customer. 3. A person or organization that uses the services of a professional. For example, someone who seeks advice from an attorney or financial services consultant is a client.

clientele effect The tendency of different securities to attract different types of investors, depending on the dividend policy of the issuer. For example, certain investors are attracted to stocks (for example, electric utility stocks) with high dividend yields while other investors prefer stocks with lower dividend yields but more capital gains potential.

Clifford trust A temporary trust (established to last at least ten years and one day, or until the death of the beneficiary) in which assets are irrevocably transferred to the trust and income from the trust is given to the beneficiary. When the trust is terminated, the principal passes back to the creator. Clifford trusts are used almost exclusively by people with dependent children or dependent parents. Income from trusts created after March 1, 1986, is taxed at the donor's rate even after the minority child has reached 14 years of age.

climax 1. —See BUYING CLIMAX. 2. —See SELLING CLIMAX.

clincher An inducement offered by a salesperson to a potential customer in order to complete a sale. For example, a timeshare salesperson may offer an extra discount or free membership in a vacation club if an agreement is signed on the same day as the sales presentation.

clip To detach the interest coupons from a bearer bond. These coupons must be presented to a bank, a brokerage house, or the issuer's agent in order for the holder of the bearer bond to receive interest payments.

clipping service A business that monitors media sources and collects stories and citations relevant to clients. For example, a book publisher employs a clipping service to monitor media outlets for reviews or mentions of the publisher's books. —Also called *press clipping service.*

clone To produce a copy or near copy of something. For example, a computer software company might attempt to clone a successful software application developed by another firm.

clone fund A mutual fund started by another mutual fund as a result of the parent fund's large growth and management's assessment that the parent is limited as to the investments it can make. For example, a very large fund would generally be unable to establish investment positions in small or new corporations. Thus, a new, smaller fund with the same goals as the older, bigger fund is started. Although the parent fund and clone fund have the same investment objectives, they purchase different securities and generally operate under different managements.

close 1. In the securities business, the end of a session of trading. 2. The last price at which a security trades during a trading session. The last price is reported in the financial media and is of particular importance to the valuation of investment portfolios. —Also called *closing price; last.* 3. To finalize a transaction. 4. In accounting, transferring revenue and expense accounts in order to prepare a trial balance at the end of a period. 5. To terminate operations.

close a position To eliminate an investment position. The most common way to close a position is to sell a security that is owned. An investor might also close a position by purchasing stock to replace shares borrowed for a short sale.

close corporation —See CLOSELY HELD COMPANY.

closed account 1. A bank account, credit card account, or securities account that has been formally terminated. 2. In accounting, a revenue or expense account balance that has been set to zero in preparation for a new accounting period.

closed dating Use of packing numbers placed on products by manufacturers. Closed dating provides information for the manufacturer and retailers for use in stock rotation and product recalls. This method of product identification is generally unintelligible to consumers.—Compare OPEN DATING. —Also called *coded dating.*

closed economy An economy that attempts to be self-sufficient and does not participate in international trade. —Compare OPEN ECONOMY. —See also AUTARKY.

closed-end credit A loan for a specific amount of money that requires full repayment of principal and interest by a predetermined date. Automobile loans, home improvement loans, and mortgages are examples of closed-end credit. —Compare LINE OF CREDIT.

closed-end investment company An investment company that issues a limited number of shares and does not redeem those that are outstanding. Shares of closed-end investment companies trade on the exchanges or in the over-the-counter market. Thus, like stock of other publicly traded companies, share prices are determined by the pressures of supply and demand rather than by the value of underlying assets. —Compare MUTUAL FUND. —Also called *publicly traded fund.* —See also REGULATED INVESTMENT COMPANY.

closed-end mortgage A mortgage with a prohibition against additional borrowing using the same lien. The prohibition against additional borrowing protects the existing creditors from having the security diluted. —Compare OPEN-END MORTGAGE.

closed fund A mutual fund that no longer issues shares to nonshareholders, but that may continue to sell shares to existing shareholders. A fund usually closes because its management has decided the fund has grown too large to be managed effectively.

closed promotion A promotion that makes a good or service available to a limited group of potential consumers. For example, a pizza restaurant advertises in a school newspaper with a discount coupon that can be redeemed only when accompanied by a student ID.

closed shop A company or other organization in which new hires must be, or agree to become, members of a union. —Compare OPEN SHOP. —See also UNION SHOP.

closed stock Items that are sold only as part of a set. For example, stainless steel eating utensils are often sold only as a set. —Compare OPEN STOCK.

closely held company A firm whose shares of common stock are owned by relatively few individuals and are generally unavailable to outsiders. —Also called *closed corporation.*

close market A narrow spread between the bid price and ask price of a security. A close market in a security is facilitated by active trading and multiple market makers.

closeout A special sale in which prices are reduced in order to sell all of a product that remains in stock. Closeouts often occur near the end of a model year.

closet index fund An investment company that claims to actively manage its portfolio but in reality emulates a market index such as the S&P 500. Closet index funds generally charge sales fees and annual expenses that are typical for an actively managed fund.

closet indexing An investment method in which an individual develops a widely diversified portfolio of securities that achieves a performance level nearly identical to that of a broad-based market average, yet claims the performance is the result of active management based on market expertise.

closing 1. The final step in a real estate transaction, when payment is made and ownership is transferred. —Also called *loan closing; real estate closing; settlement.* **2.** Termination of operations.

closing agreement An agreement that finalizes a dispute between a taxing authority and a taxpayer. The dispute may be in regard to a tax liability or a related issue such as whether certain charitable contributions are deductible in calculating a tax liability.

closing costs Expenses paid by the buyer and seller that are associated with finalizing a real estate transaction. Closing costs are likely to include appraisals, attorney fees, credit reports, discount points, homeowner's insurance, title insurance, and deed filing. —See also CLOSING STATEMENT.

closing entry In accounting, a final entry made at the end of an accounting period to close an account and transfer the balance to the balance sheet.

closing inventory The value and quantity of inventory on hand at the end of an accounting period.

closing price —See CLOSE 2.

closing purchase —See CLOSING TRANSACTION 2.

closing quote The final bid and ask price for a security as stated by the market maker or specialist at the end of a trading session.

closing range In futures trading, the range of prices at which transactions occur during the close of the market.

closing sale —See CLOSING TRANSACTION 2.

closing statement In a real estate transaction, a final accounting and separate listing of each of the expenses paid by both the buyer and the seller. The closing statement itemizes fees, commissions, and other expenses resulting from the transaction. —Also called *settlement sheet.*

closing transaction 1. The final transaction for a particular security during a trading day. —Compare OPENING TRANSACTION 1. **2.** An option order that eliminates or decreases the size of an existing option position. An investor who repurchases three options that have been sold short is entering into a closing transaction. —Compare OPENING TRANSACTION 2. —Also called *closing purchase; closing sale.* —See also CLOSE A POSITION.

cloud on title A real or probable claim on a property title that is likely to make ownership difficult to transfer. A typical problem is failure to record repayment of a debt that used the property as collateral.

CLU —See CHARTERED LIFE UNDERWRITER.

cluster analysis A statistical tool in which variables (people, events, etc.) are sorted into homogeneous groups, or clusters, such that, for certain criteria, members within a group exhibit more similarities than do members between groups. For example, a study of retailers might cluster companies according to geographic area.

clutter **1.** Advertisements, public announcements, and other interruptions to radio and television programming. **2.** Multiple advertisements clustered together such that a viewer or listener experiences difficulty remembering any particular ad: *Advertisers are constantly attempting to break through the clutter.*

CMA —See CERTIFIED IN MANAGEMENT ACCOUNTING.

CME —See CHICAGO MERCANTILE EXCHANGE.

CME Group, Inc. A large floor- and electronic-based securities exchange formed in the 2007 merger of the Chicago Board of Trade and the Chicago Mercantile Exchange. CME Group is a for-profit exchange that specializes in derivative products based on interest rates, equity indexes, foreign exchange, agricultural and industrial commodities, and energy.

CMO —See COLLATERALIZED MORTGAGE OBLIGATION.

COBRA (Consolidated Omnibus Budget Reconciliation Act) A U.S. government act that requires employers to offer continuing group health coverage for covered persons who lose health or dental coverage due to specified reasons, including job termination, marriage, divorce, death of a covered spouse, and birth.

CoCo bond —See CONTINGENT CONVERTIBLE BOND.

COD —See CASH ON DELIVERY.

Code —See INTERNAL REVENUE CODE.

coded dating —See CLOSED DATING.

code of ethics A collection of rules of conduct to be used in guiding ethical behavior.

codicil A legal change made to a will.

coding of accounts Identification of accounts in a financial statement with a series of numbers. Accounts and their identifying numbers are listed in a chart of accounts.

coefficient of determination In statistics, a measure of the correlation between a dependent variable and an independent variable. Essentially the coefficient of determination indicates the degree to which two sets of numbers vary together; for example, the proportion of the variation in a retailer's sales that is explained by the weather. The coefficient of determination is the square of the correlation coefficient and is often referred to as r^2.

Coffee, Sugar and Cocoa Exchange (CSCE) An organized exchange, established in 1882, that in 2004 merged with the New York Cotton Exchange to form the New York Board of Trade.

cognitive behavior The activity of mental processes: awareness and the ability to think, learn, and judge.

cohabitation agreement

Is a cohabitation agreement considered legally binding in all legal jurisdictions? Are there any particular issues to consider in drawing up one of these agreements?

The legal consequences of cohabitation vary. Although cohabitation may not, by itself, give a party rights in the other cohabitant's property, one party may assert the existence of an agreement regarding the ownership of property or promised compensation which the other party disputes. The legal effect of cohabitation agreements has not been tested in every jurisdiction. However, a cohabitation agreement which would be respected as contract under local law and is supported by valid consideration should be enforceable. (Valid consideration would be, for example, the parties' mutual promises relating to property rights or the provision of services, but not their agreement to maintain a sexual relation.) It is important to recognize that the cohabitation agreement may not be self-effectuating with respect to the rights the parties wish to confer on each other. For example, if a party wishes the other to have the right to make medical decisions for him or her, the party should execute the health care proxy or other document recognized in the jurisdiction.

■ Stephen F. Lappert, Partner, Trusts and Estates Department, Carter Ledyard & Milburn LLP, New York, NY

cohabitation agreement A written contract governing the rights and obligations of unmarried individuals who live together. Cohabitation agreements typically address issues such as how property will be distributed in the event of a death or breakup, the manner in which debts will be paid, any rights to make medical decisions, and custody and support for minors. Cohabitation agreements are particularly important because unmarried partners do not share many of the legal rights and protections provided by marriage. —See also PRENUPTIAL AGREEMENT.

coincidental survey A survey of radio listeners or television viewers conducted during the time the subject program is on the air. A coincidental survey has the advantage of providing relatively accurate data because there is no reliance on memory. —Also called *simultaneous survey.*

coincident indicator An economic variable, such as personal income, that varies directly with the business cycle. Coincident indicators are utilized to assess the current condition of the economy.

coinsurance In property insurance, the percentage of the market value of a property the policyholder is required to insure. For example, with a coinsurance clause of 80%, a $200,000 house must be insured for at least $160,000. Insurance coverage of less than this results in a reduced reimbursement in the event of a claim. —See also COPAY.

> **CASE STUDY** The coinsurance clause included in property insurance policies can result in an unpleasant surprise for a homeowner who files a substantial claim. Unlike coinsurance, or copay, in health insurance, in which the insured and insurer each agree to pay a predetermined portion of any claim, coinsurance applied to property insurance is the percentage of value a policyholder is required to insure. For example, a home with a value of $300,000 and an 80% coinsurance clause must be insured for at least $240,000. Coverage of less than the required amount will result in the insurance company paying a reduced amount for a claim, even if the claim is less than the amount of coverage. Suppose the homeowner in the above example carries $200,000

of coverage, $40,000 less than required by the coinsurance clause. A fire causing damage of $150,000 will result in an insurance reimbursement equal to the proportion of actual coverage compared to the required coverage times the amount of the claim. In this case, reimbursement is ($200,000/$240,000) x $150,000, or $125,000, less any deductible. Nearly all property insurance policies contain a coinsurance clause.

COLA —See COST-OF-LIVING ADJUSTMENT.

cold call A telephone call or personal visit by a salesperson to a heretofore-unknown person, during which the salesperson tries to enlist that person as a customer. Cold calling is often a necessary evil for many new salespeople.

collapsible corporation A company that is formed with the intention to liquidate assets before a substantial amount of taxable income has been earned.

collar **1.** In options, buying a put and selling short a call so as to limit the potential profit and loss from an investment position. **2.** The level at which an index triggers a circuit breaker to temporarily stop trading. **3.** In an acquisition, an upper and lower limit that will be paid for shares of the company to be acquired. **4.** In a new issue, a limit on the price or interest rate that is acceptable. —See also ZERO-COST COLLAR.

collate To assemble in correct sequence. For example, copied pages of an assembly manual must be collated so the reader will do things in the proper order.

collateral Assets pledged as security for a loan. In the event that the borrower defaults on the terms of the loan, the collateral may be sold, with the proceeds used to satisfy any remaining obligations. High-quality collateral reduces risk to the lender and results in a lower rate of interest on the loan.

collateral assignment **1.** Duties and responsibilities of an executive or employee that are in addition to the person's primary duties and responsibilities. For example, an employee may be assigned to serve as head of a labor relations committee. **2.** Assignment of an asset to a lender as security for a loan. For example, an ownership of an annuity or the cash surrender value of a life insurance policy may be transferred from one person to another to serve as collateral for a debt.

collateralize To pledge an asset as security for a loan.

collateralized debt obligation (CDO) A debt security collateralized by a variety of debt obligations, including bonds and loans of different maturities and credit quality.

collateralized mortgage obligation (CMO) A security collateralized with mortgage loans and issued by Freddie Mac. Although collateralized in a manner similar to a Freddie Mac pass-through, a CMO provides interest and principal payments in a more predictable manner. CMOs are classed according to expected maturity ranges at the time of issue. The greater certainty of payment size is offset by slightly lower yields compared with an ordinary pass-through.

collateral trust bond A long-term debt obligation with a claim against securities rather than against physical assets. This type of bond is issued primarily by holding companies that own mainly securities of subsidiaries. —Also called *trust certificate*.

collect **1.** To receive payment for a debt. **2.** To obtain payment on a check. For example, banks often form associations in order to speed the process of collecting checks drawn on other members.

collectible An asset of limited supply that is sought for a variety of reasons, including, it is hoped, an increase in value. Stamps, antiques, coins, and works of art are among the many things usually classified as collectibles. Collectibles are often regarded by investors as hedges against inflation, since their value tends to appreciate most when general prices are rising.

collection period The number of days, on average, that a firm requires for collection of a credit sale. The length of the collection period indicates the effectiveness with which a firm's management grants credit and collects from customers. A short period is desirable because the firm obtains cash more quickly for reinvestment or for paying its own bills. The collection period is calculated by dividing accounts receivable by average daily credit sales. —Also called *average collection period.*

collective bargaining Negotiations between an employer and an organized group of employees. Collective bargaining generally results in agreements regarding rates of pay, hours of employment, benefits, and other conditions of employment.

collective good —See PUBLIC GOOD.

college-savings plan A plan that allows individuals to set aside money in a special account designed to pay for future college expenses. Funds in the account grow tax deferred, and withdrawals used for college expenses are exempt from federal income taxes. Parents are permitted to change from one state plan to another once a year with no penalty. Many states also offer tax incentives for these plans. —Also called *529 plan.*

collusion A secret agreement for a fraudulent or deceitful purpose. For example, several companies may reach a secret agreement, or collude, before bidding on a government contract.

combination **1.** A union of two or more entities, either by merging one or more of the entities into another of the entities or by consolidating the entities into a new entity. —Also called *business combination.* **2.** In statistics, the number of ways objects can be arranged or selected.

combination security A security that combines the attributes of two or more individual securities. An example of a combination security is a convertible bond that is part debt and part common stock.

combined financial statement A financial statement that merges the financial statements of two or more entities.

COMEX —See NEW YORK MERCANTILE EXCHANGE.

comfort letter **1.** A statement issued by a certified public accountant declaring no indication of false or misleading information in the financial statements being used in connection with a securities offering. **2.** A written commitment of one party to another. For example, a company considering the purchase of property might seek assurance from the Environmental Protection Agency that the firm will not be held responsible for contamination resulting from previous use.

comity In law, an informal agreement among legal jurisdictions to recognize the decisions or laws of one another. For example, most marriages that take place under the laws of one state are recognized by each of the other 49 states.

command economy An economy in which a central authority controls supply and prices. Government rather than market forces drive a command economy. —Also called *controlled economy; managed economy; planned economy.*

commencement of coverage The date on which insurance coverage will become effective.

Commerce Clearing House —See CCH.

commercial 1. An advertising message presented through a media outlet such as radio, television, or a theater. 2. Of or pertaining to an organization engaged in commerce.

commercial bank A federally or state-chartered financial institution that makes loans, accepts deposits, and offers an array of related services that are likely to include issuing letters of credit, renting safe deposit boxes, and selling travelers checks, and buying and selling foreign currency. —Compare INVESTMENT BANK.

commercial blanket bond A bond that provides an employer with a single amount of insurance coverage for losses from employee dishonesty, regardless of the number of employees involved.

commercial credit insurance —See CREDIT INSURANCE 2.

commercial frustration An uncontrollable event that makes it impossible to satisfy the terms of an existing contract. For example, inventory scheduled for shipment to a buyer is lost or damaged beyond repair by a hurricane. Commercial frustration is grounds for rescinding a contract without penalty.

commercial law The collection of laws applicable to commercial transactions. Commercial law in the United States has been formalized in the Uniform Commercial Code. —Also called *mercantile law*.

commercial loan A short-term loan used to finance a firm's working capital needs, including inventories and accounts receivable.

commercial paper A short-term unsecured promissory note issued by a finance company or a relatively large industrial firm. The notes are issued in large denominations ($25,000 minimum) and generally sold at a discount from face value with maturities ranging from 30 to 270 days. Commercial paper is a popular investment for money market mutual funds. Used interchangeably with the term *paper*. —See also PRIME PAPER.

commercial property Real estate used for business purposes. Examples of commercial property include manufacturing plants, shopping centers, warehouses, and motels.

commercial unit A unit of goods, either a single unit or a quantity, offered for typical commercial usage. Division of a commercial unit is likely to result in an impairment of the value of the contents. For example, a barrel is the commercial unit for petroleum, and a bolt is a commercial unit of finished cloth.

commingled fund An investment fund that consists of assets of several individual accounts. A commingled fund is established to reduce the cost and effort required to manage accounts separately.

commingling 1. Combining personal funds of a fiduciary with those of a client. Commingling by a fiduciary is generally illegal. 2. Combining the assets of several clients into a single fund.

commissary 1. A grocery store that sells provisions to active and retired military personnel and their families. 2. A commercial enterprise that sells food and equipment to the general public.

commission 1. The fee levied by an agent for services provided on behalf of a customer. For example, an investor will pay a commission to a broker in order to buy or sell shares of stock. Commissions can be a fixed amount or a percentage of the value of a transaction. —See also CONTINGENT COMMISSION; FACTORAGE. 2. An appointed or elected group that has been granted authority to consider certain issues or make certain decisions. For example, a state public service commission may have the authority to set electric rates for businesses and residential consumers.

commission broker An employee of a member firm of an organized securities exchange who transacts orders for the firm or its customers on the exchange floor. Orders flow to the commission broker from the firm's trading desk or from its registered representatives.

commission house A firm whose primary business is the execution of its customers' orders to buy and sell securities, activities for which it earns a fee. Commission houses earn the name from acting as brokers rather than as dealers.

commission override —See OVERRIDE 1.

commitment 1. A pledge to do something. For example, an appliance manufacturer makes a commitment to have 10,000 toasters available for purchase by a certain date. **2.** A legal obligation. A contractor makes a commitment to complete a building by January 12.

commitment fee Payment by a potential borrower to a lender for a legal promise to make credit available on a specified future date or for a line of credit. —Also called *standby fee.*

commitment letter Written notice from a lender to a potential borrower that a loan application as been approved. The commitment letter states the loan amount, interest rate, term, and any conditions attached to the loan.

committee 1. In government, a group of elected officials who are appointed to consider legislation, investigate something, or take on other assigned duties. **2.** A group appointed to consider and make recommendations on a special matter.

Committee on Foreign Investment in the United States A federal interagency committee established in 1975 to monitor and evaluate the impact of foreign investment in the United States. A major charge of the committee relates to evaluating national security concerns posed by foreign acquisition of U.S. companies. The secretary of the treasury heads the committee.

Committee on Uniform Securities Identification Procedures (CUSIP) An appointed board that assigns standard identification (CUSIP) numbers for all stock certificates and registered bonds issued in the United States. —See also CUSIP NUMBER.

commodities exchange A facility for the organized trading of commodities contracts. The New York Mercantile Exchange is a commodities exchange that specializes in trading futures contracts for metals and energy products.

commodities futures —See FUTURES CONTRACT.

commodity 1. A generic, largely unprocessed good that can be processed and resold. Commodities traded in the financial markets for immediate or future delivery are grains, metals, and minerals. They are generally traded in very large quantities. —Also called *physical commodity.* —See also FUTURES CONTRACT. **2.** A product that is difficult or impossible to differentiate from similar products from competitors. Pencils, computer memory chips, and light bulbs are examples of commodity products.

commodity-backed bond A rare bond that has its interest payments and/or principal repayment tied to the price of a commodity such as silver or oil. Although such a bond carries a relatively low interest rate at the time of issue, it gives the investor a hedge against inflation. Firms having a major stake in a commodity (for example, a firm engaged in gold or silver mining) are most likely to issue these bonds. —Also called *gold bond.*

commodity brokerage firm —See FUTURES COMMISSION MERCHANT.

Commodity Futures Trading Commission (CFTC) A federal agency, established in 1974, that regulates and supervises the trading of commodity futures and commodity options. Additional regulation is effected by the exchanges on which the contracts are traded.

commodity option An option either to buy or to sell a commodity futures contract at a fixed price until a specified date. —See also CALL[1] 1; PUT[1] 1.

common carrier A business that transports persons, goods, or messages at any time and to any location in its operating area. —Compare CONTRACT CARRIER. —Also called *carrier.*

common counts A legal claim for payment of multiple debts that have been consolidated into a single pleading in order to prevent the defendant from successfully escaping the claim because of a technical fault in one of the counts.

common equity The dollar amount of common shareholders' investment in a company, including common stock, retained earnings, and additional paid-in capital.

common law Unwritten law derived from custom and prior judicial decisions rather than legislative statutes.

Common Market —See EUROPEAN ECONOMIC COMMUNITY.

common-size statement A financial statement that has variables expressed in percentages rather than in dollar amounts. For example, items on an income statement are shown as a percentage of revenue or sales, and balance sheet entries are displayed as a percentage of total assets. Common-size statements are used primarily for comparative purposes so that firms of various sizes can be equated. —Also called *one hundred percent statement.*

common stock A class of capital stock that has no preference to dividends or any distribution of assets. Common stock usually conveys voting rights and is often termed *capital stock* if it is the only class of stock that a firm has outstanding (that is, the firm has neither preferred stock nor multiple classes of common stock). Common stockholders are the residual owners of a corporation in that they have a claim to what remains after every other party has been paid. The value of their claim depends on the success of the firm. —See also CALLABLE COMMON STOCK; COMMON STOCK EQUIVALENT; PUTTABLE COMMON STOCK.

common stock equivalent A security viewed as basically the same as common stock, generally because the equivalent security may be exchanged for shares of common stock. Common stock equivalents include convertible bonds, convertible preferred stock, options, and warrants. Common stock equivalents are used in calculating earnings per share even though the calculation overstates the actual number of shares outstanding.

common stock fund A mutual fund that limits its investments to shares of common stock. Common stock funds vary in risk from relatively low to quite high, depending on the types of stocks in which the funds invest.

common stock ratio The portion of a firm's capitalization that represents owner(s) equity. A relatively high common stock ratio is the mark of a conservatively financed company.

communism An economic system in which property is under collective ownership and labor is organized for the benefit of all members. In effect, the state plans and controls the economy.

community property

I live in a community property state and am planning to remarry. Are there any special precautions I need to consider?

States which follow the community property regime have different rules as to what will constitute community property and how it will be divided or distributed in the event of divorce or death. Generally, property acquired by a spouse before the marriage, as well as property acquired by gift or inheritance, will be treated as the spouse's separate property and not community property. However, income from separate property received during the marriage is treated as community property in some jurisdictions. In the event of divorce or upon death, community property is divided between the spouses, but state laws vary as to how this is done. Preserving the identity of separate property is critical and may be difficult. If one spouse contributes separate property to the purchase of property during the marriage, such as the family home, the division of the property or its proceeds in the event of divorce may be difficult. A business owned by one spouse prior to the marriage and continued during the marriage may also be community property in part. Retirement assets owned prior to and during the marriage may also be affected. A prenuptial agreement and the careful segregation of separate property through, for example, the use of a revocable trust to which a party contributes his or her separate property and does not thereafter contribute additions from sources that could be community property, can preserve the separate status of the property.

▪ Stephen F. Lappert, Partner, Trusts and Estates Department, Carter Ledyard & Milburn LLP, New York, NY

community association —See HOMEOWNERS' ASSOCIATION.

community property Property that is owned jointly by spouses. The legal concept in community property states that, with the exception of gifts and inheritance, all property acquired during a marriage is equally owned by each spouse. The community property statute is very important in the event that the marriage is dissolved or one spouse dies. In some locales, the concept of community property extends to individuals participating in unions other than marriage.

Community Reinvestment Act A 1977 Congressional act encouraging depositary institutions to meet the needs of the communities in which they operate. Emphasis is on serving the needs of middle- and low-income neighborhoods. Periodic evaluations of each institution's record are considered when the institution is seeking approval for mergers or expanded facilities.

commutation right The right of the beneficiary of a life insurance policy to receive a lump-sum settlement in place of the remaining payments of an installment option. The lump sum to be received is equal to the discounted present value of the remaining payments.

commuter tax A tax levied on people who work in a place in which they do not live. For example, in 1966 the New York legislature authorized New York City to impose a tax on people who worked, but did not live, in the city.

co-mortgagor A person whose name is on a loan application along with the mortgagor. Income, assets, and debts of the co-mortgagor are combined with those of the mortgagor for purposes of loan analysis.

companion bond In a collateralized mortgage obligation, a class of bonds most likely to be retired early from mortgage prepayments. Companion bonds entail more payment risk and generally offer higher returns compared to other bonds from a CMO.

company An enterprise engaged in business. A company can be organized as a proprietorship, partnership, or corporation.

company car A vehicle driven by an employee but owned or leased by the employer.

company risk The risk that certain factors affecting a specific company may cause its stock to change in price in a way different from stocks as a whole. For example, the profits and stock price of a firm selling an unusually large portion of its output to foreign customers are subject to certain factors, such as changes in foreign exchange rates, that are less important to other companies.

company union A labor union, generally comprised of employees of a single company, that is strongly influenced by management. —Compare INDEPENDENT UNION.

comparables Substantially equivalent properties used in establishing a value for real estate. Real estate agents and appraisers examine recent sales of comparable properties when appraising the value of a property.

comparable worth The economic and social theory that jobs of equal value should entail equal compensation. The term "comparable worth" emerged following passage of the Civil Rights Act of 1964 and was applied to both racial and sexual discrimination.

comparative advantage In economics, the benefit to regions and countries of producing goods and services at which they are most efficient, even though the same goods and services can be produced more efficiently elsewhere. The theory of comparative advantage is the basis for justifying the economic benefits of free trade. —Compare ABSOLUTE ADVANTAGE. —See also ACQUIRED ADVANTAGE.

comparative advertising A promotion in which a firm's service or product is directly compared with competing services or products from other companies. For example, a soft drink company advertises a blind taste test with a soft drink manufactured by its biggest competitor.

comparative financial statements Financial statements—the current statement and the statement from the previous accounting period—presented together for comparative purposes.

comparative market analysis An informal evaluation of a property's market value by researching the prices at which similar properties sold within the last year. A comparative market analysis is generally undertaken in order to establish a price at which to list the property for sale. —Also called *market comparison appraisal.*

comparative negligence The assigned degree of fault for injuries that are suffered when both parties contribute to an accident. For example, a person who slips on a wet floor exhibits comparative negligence if a "wet floor" sign is clearly visible. A monetary award is adjusted if a plaintiff is found to have comparative negligence. —See also CONTRIBUTORY NEGLIGENCE.

comparative shopping Gathering price and quality information from several sources prior to making a purchase. For example, someone interested in purchasing a new shirt might do comparative shopping by visiting several stores. Comparative shopping results in getting better value at the cost of spending additional time.

compensating balance The funds that a corporate borrower is required to keep on deposit in a financial institution in order to satisfy the terms of a loan agreement. The deposit may be in a checking account, savings account, or certificate of deposit, depending on the nature of the agreement. The net effect of a compensating balance requirement is an increase in the effective cost of the loan, because the borrower is unable to use all the funds on which interest is paid.

compensation Monetary and nonmonetary payment given or accepted in return for a service or a loss.

compensatory damages Money awarded as compensation for the actual loss or injury suffered by a plaintiff. Compensatory damages could be awarded to compensate loss of wages, permanent disability, medical bills, repair or replacement of property, emotional distress, and pain and suffering. —See also PUNITIVE DAMAGES.

compensatory stock option A stock option given by an employer to an employee as partial compensation for the employee's services. In general, the value of a compensatory stock option is considered an expense for the employer and taxable income to the employee.

compensatory time Time off given in place of overtime pay. Compensatory time is generally awarded at a rate of 1.5 hours for each hour worked beyond 40 during any workweek. Under this system, an employee who worked 44 hours would be awarded 6 hours (4 hours of overtime x 1.5) of compensatory time. —Also called *comp time.*

compensatory trade The sale of goods and services with payment in the form of goods rather than cash. For example, the sale of manufacturing equipment by a U.S. firm to several Asian businesses that promise payment in the form of goods to be produced by the equipment.

competition 1. A rivalry of two or more businesses that target the same customers. Business competition tends to result in increased efficiency as firms attempt to reduce expenses. On the negative side, competition may result in duplication of efforts. 2. A testing of the intelligence, strength, speed, or some other ability of two or more people.

competitive bidding 1. A method in which a corporation or government organization wishing to sell securities in the primary market chooses an investment banker for the sale on the basis of the best price submitted by interested investment bankers. Municipal governments and public utilities are often required to ask for competitive bids on new security issues. —See also NEGOTIATED OFFERING. 2. The bidding on U.S. Treasury securities in which an investor stipulates a particular price or yield. 3. A method by which a contractor submits a sealed bid to a purchaser. The bid includes the price and terms, such as a payment schedule.

competitive strategy A plan for how a firm will compete, formulated after evaluating how its strengths and weaknesses compare to those of its competitors. For example, a small meatpacking firm may decide to concentrate on a special niche product offered in limited areas after determining it cannot compete on price with major competitors.

competitor 1. A rival that offers a competitive product or service in a firm's marketing area. 2. An aggressive and hard-working person. 3. A business that works hard to compete with rivals.

compilation A presentation of financial information without an accountant's guarantee of conformity with generally accepted accounting principles.

complaint 1. The first pleading of a plaintiff in a civil action. 2. A formal charge of a crime. 3. A criticism. For example, a customer who feels she was treated rudely may file a complaint with the manager.

complementary goods Goods that go together such that increased demand for one is generally accompanied by increased demand for the other. Computers and software are complementary goods. —Compare SUBSTITUTE GOODS. —See also JOINT DEMAND.

completed-contract method A method of recognizing revenues and costs from a long-term project in which profit is recorded only when the project has been completed. Even if payments are received while the project is in progress, no revenues are recorded until its completion. The completed-contract method is a conservative way of accounting for long-term undertakings and is used for certain types of construction projects. —Compare PERCENTAGE-OF-COMPLETION METHOD.

completion bond A bond issued by an insurance company guaranteeing a lender that a construction project will be satisfactorily completed by a specific date.

complex capital structure A corporate capital structure that contains financing other than straight debt and stock. Thus, a firm that has securities outstanding, such as convertible bonds, convertible preferred stocks, options, rights, or warrants, is said to have a complex capital structure. Potential dilution of earnings resulting from a complex capital structure occurs in firms that report earnings per share on a primary and a fully diluted basis.

complex trust A trust that is permitted to accumulate income and make charitable gifts. An income tax deduction is permitted for the charitable gifts. —Compare SIMPLE TRUST.

compliance audit A special audit to offer an opinion on whether a contractual agreement is being adhered to. For example, an annual compliance audit may be used to determine if a school district is sending appropriate student test scores to a state agency. Likewise, a compliance audit may be used to determine if a borrower is adhering to covenants in a loan agreement.

component depreciation Depreciation of the individual components of an asset rather than depreciation of the asset as a whole. Component depreciation recognizes that an asset has individual parts that each have a different useful life compared to the whole asset. For example, a building shell might have a useful life of 40 years, while plumbing, wiring, and elevators are assigned a life of 15 years.

composite depreciation Application of a single depreciation rate to an asset even though the asset is comprised of multiple components, each with different useful lives. The composite depreciation rate is calculated by dividing the sum of each component's annual depreciation by the sum of the cost assigned to each component.

composite tape A security price-reporting service that includes all transactions in a security on each of the exchanges and in the over-the-counter market. A composite tape is structured to provide a complete picture of a security's price and volume activity rather than limiting the information to that which occurs on a single exchange.

compound growth rate The percentage rate, generally stated on an annual basis, at which a variable grows, adjusted for compounding. For example, a 7% compound growth rate for ten years results in $100 growing to slightly less than $200. Without compounding, the $100 would earn $7 per year and grow to only $170.

compounding period The interval at which interest is paid or is added to principal. For example, a quarterly compounding period indicates interest is paid or is calculated at three-month intervals.

compound interest Interest paid both on principal and on interest earned during previous compounding periods. Essentially, compounding involves adding interest to the sum of principal and any previous interest in order to calculate interest in the next period. —Compare SIMPLE INTEREST. —See also FREQUENCY OF COMPOUNDING.

compound option An option to purchase an option. Examples include a call on a call option or a call on a put option. A fee must be paid to buy a compound option, and a second payment must be made to the owner of the option in the event the compound option is exercised. —Also called *split-fee option.*

compound return The annual rate of return earned on an investment in which earnings or appreciation in each year are reinvested at the same annual rate of return.

compradore An agent who serves as a commercial facilitator for foreign-based companies. For example, a small U.S. manufacturer may employ a compradore to assist with sales of its products in China.

comprehensive annual financial report The official annual financial report of a governmental entity. The report includes a balance sheet, a statement of changes in financial position, and a statement of revenues and expenses.

comprehensive general liability insurance Broad commercial insurance coverage for all liability exposures that are not specifically excluded. For example, a policy may exclude pollution coverage that is available through endorsements or separate policies.

comprehensive health insurance All-inclusive health insurance that covers both doctor and hospital expenses, subject to a deductible and coinsurance payments. These policies are designed to cover general medical expenses such as blood work or visits to a doctor's office and health catastrophes such as heart attacks and cancer.

comprehensive insurance 1. Insurance providing broad coverage. For example, comprehensive health insurance offers a wide range of coverage for most expenses caused by illness or accidents. **2.** Vehicle insurance to cover financial loss from theft or vehicle damage other than collision. For example, damage from a hailstorm is covered by comprehensive insurance, subject to a deductible.

comps 1. In real estate, slang for comparable properties, that is, properties referenced when doing an appraisal that are similar to the subject property. **2.** In business, especially relating to casinos, slang for free goods or services. For example, a heavy gambler may receive a room and meals from a casino as comps.

comp time —See COMPENSATORY TIME.

comptroller —See CONTROLLER.

Comptroller of the Currency 1. A bureau of the U.S. Treasury that charters, regulates, and examines national banks. The bureau supervises a nationwide staff of over 2,300 bank examiners. —Also called *Office of the Comptroller of the Currency.* **2.** The administrator who disseminates and oversees the execution of laws relating to national banks.

compulsory arbitration —See BINDING ARBITRATION.

compulsory insurance Insurance coverage required by law. For example, most states require auto liability insurance before a vehicle can be registered for legal operation. The minimum required coverage is generally low, and there is doubt about the effectiveness of the laws in reducing the number of uninsured drivers.

compulsory retirement —See MANDATORY RETIREMENT.

computer security The prevention of unauthorized computer access and destruction or alteration of computer information.

con artist A person who uses persuasive powers to swindle others. —See also CONFI-DENCE GAME.

concealment Intentional withholding of a fact or circumstance. For example, it is il-legal to conceal assets from an officer of the court during a bankruptcy proceeding.

concentration account A central bank account into which funds are transferred from regional accounts. A concentration account allows a business to gain quicker access to funds received from customer payments in different locations.

concentration ratio The share of business in a market that is controlled by a limited number of firms. For example, two supermarkets may command 85% of a commu-nity's grocery business. A high concentration ratio is generally positively correlated to the price consumers pay (few firms result in high prices) and is a consideration of the Federal Trade Commission in deciding whether to challenge merger proposals.

concept company A firm that attracts investors more on the basis of the type of busi-ness it is in, or by the direction in which its management says it is moving, than on its current earnings or dividends. For example, a company involved in sophisticated biomedical research that might eventually achieve a major scientific breakthrough and large profits could qualify as a concept company. Concept companies might in-clude firms engaged in computer software development, Internet commerce, genetic engineering, and medical technology.

concept test An evaluation of people's reaction to a description of a new concept or product, done in order to predict success in the marketplace prior to introduction. Concept tests are commonly used in evaluating proposals for advertising campaigns.

concession **1.** The dollar discount from a security's retail selling price received by members of an underwriting syndicate. For example, a syndicate member paying $995 for a bond to be sold at par (that is, at $1,000) is receiving a $5 concession. —Also called *selling concession.* **2.** A discount or rebate from a contracted price. **3.** A contract to operate a subsidiary business. For example, the local civic club has a concession to operate a restaurant at the county fair. **4.** A government grant to use property for a specific purpose. For example, a private business has a concession to operate all nine lodges in Yellowstone National Park.

conciliation Dispute resolution in which the parties in dispute are not in the same room. A conciliator meets with each party separately in an attempt to narrow the dif-ferences and convince the parties to agree to a general meeting. Conciliation differs from mediation, in which the parties in dispute meet directly with a neutral third party.

conciliator A person who attempts to resolve a dispute.

concurrent mortgage sale An exchange of like mortgages (similar terms and quality) between two lenders.

condemnation **1.** The judicial process of exercising eminent domain by paying fair market value and taking private property for public use. **2.** Declaring a structure unfit for occupancy because of physical defects or other difficulties.

condemnation award Money or other assets given as just compensation for property condemned by a government authority.

conditional contract A binding agreement that includes conditions that must be satis-fied before any of the parties become obligated. For example, a contract to purchase a home may be conditional on the buyer being able to obtain financing.

conditional rating —See PROVISIONAL RATING.

conditional sale 1. A sale in which the buyer takes possession of an asset but receives title only after performance of some condition, normally full payment. 2. Acquisition of an asset along with an agreement to resell under certain conditions.

condition precedent A condition that must be met before a contract is binding. For example, a contract to purchase real estate may not become effective until a professional inspection of the property results in an evaluation that is acceptable to the buyer.

condition subsequent A condition in a contract that results in the contract becoming invalid if a specified event occurs. For example, a real estate contract becomes valid when signed, but can later become invalid if an attorney raises an issue that is not addressed within a specified period.

condominium 1. A building comprised of multiple living units that are individually owned, while the building itself and the land on which it stands is owned in common. 2. A unit that is individually owned in a multiunit structure.

conduit A financial vehicle that holds asset-backed debt such as mortgages, vehicle loans, and credit card receivables, all financed with short-term loans (generally commercial paper) that use the asset-backed debt as collateral. The profitability of a conduit depends on the ability to roll over maturing short-term debt at a cost that is lower than the returns earned from asset-backed securities held in the portfolio. Financial institutions establish and operate conduits in order to generate fee income without booking assets that require reserves. Short-term lenders to a conduit are generally protected with backup credit lines from the financial institutions. —See also STRUCTURED INVESTMENT VEHICLE.

conduit IRA A special IRA established to accept rollovers from other tax-deferred plans such as a 401(k) or 403(b). Funds rolled into a conduit IRA can be rolled back into a 401(k) or 403(b) so long as the funds have not been commingled with other IRA funds. A conduit IRA is useful for someone who is changing jobs and wishes to transfer retirement funds between employer-sponsored plans.

conduit theory The theory that states that because regulated investment companies merely act as conduits for the passage of dividends, interest, and capital gains to stockholders, these income items should not be taxed once to a company and again to the company's stockholders. If an investment company complies with certain federal regulations, the income is taxed only to the stockholders receiving the distributions. —Also called *pipeline theory.*

conference call A single call with three or more participants, each at a different location.

confidence game A swindle in which a dishonest person or persons attempt to gain someone's confidence in order to take their money or property.

confidence indicator A measure of investors' faith in the economy and the securities market. A low or deteriorating level of confidence is considered a bearish sign.

confidence interval In statistics, the range of values with a specified probability of a parameter falling within the range. The larger the confidence interval, the less the power of a study to detect differences between groups.

confidence level The probability associated with a confidence interval. For example, suppose a statistical study indicates that 70% of people who sample a new peanut butter cookie will choose to purchase at least one package. If the study indicates a

95% probability to the confidence interval of 70% ± 3%, the researcher is relatively certain that between 67% and 73% of tasters will buy the cookies.

confidence limits The upper and lower boundaries of a confidence interval.

configure To arrange something for a particular purpose. For example, a computer is configured to run a particular software program.

confirmation 1. Acknowledgment of a transaction that generally lists important details such as date, size of the transaction, price, commission, taxes, and amount of money involved. **2.** In security analysis, the reaction of one technical indicator (such as the movement of a stock price average) that strengthens a signal given by another indicator. **3.** In accounting, a written reply to an auditor's request for verification of accounts receivable or payable.

conflict of interest A situation in which a person has competing personal and professional interests. For example, a corporate executive who is part owner of a company that does business with the firm at which the executive is employed.

conformed copy In law, an exact copy of an original document.

conforming loan 1. A loan application that meets a lender's specified standards. For example, a lender might require that a borrower have a good credit record, job stability, a minimum ratio of debt to income, and make a substantial down payment. **2.** A conventional mortgage that conforms to standards established by Fannie Mae or Freddie Mac.

conglomerate A company engaged in varied business operations, many of which seem unrelated. A conglomerate is designed to have reduced risk, since its various operations are affected differently by business conditions over time. In addition, it is possible for a conglomerate to redistribute its corporate assets depending on which operations show the most promise. Conglomerates were popular among investors during the 1960s, but investors' interest in them faded during the 1970s and the 1980s. By the turn of the century, many companies were selling or spinning off parts of their businesses in order to become more specialized.

conquesting Placing advertisements adjacent to reviews or editorial material about rival organizations, products, or services. For example, AT&T arranges to locate a newspaper advertisement next to a story about competing wireless provider Verizon.

consensus estimate The average of multiple analyst earnings estimates for a particular stock. For example, if three analysts estimate next year's earnings per share for a company at $3.00, $3.20, and $2.70, the consensus estimate is ($3.00 + $3.20 + $2.70)/3, or $2.97. Reporting earnings per share different from the consensus estimate is likely to affect the stock's market price.

consent decree A judicial announcement that a voluntary agreement has been reached by parties in a dispute. For example, a pharmaceutical company and the Food and Drug Administration might enter into a consent decree on a decision to halt the sale of a drug.

consent dividend The retained earnings that are credited to paid-in surplus by a personal holding company. The consent dividend is taxed to stockholders as an ordinary dividend; however, this tax liability is partially offset by the stockholders' increase in the cost basis of the stock by the same amount.

conservative 1. Of or relating to accounting methods that lessen reported income by reducing revenue and increasing expenses. For example, a firm might recognize expenses that could be deferred to the following year. **2.** In managing, describing the choice to make safe decisions. For example, a firm chooses to finance expansion by issuing shares of stock rather than borrowing. Likewise, a firm's directors might be slow to expand capacity for fear demand for its product might slow.

conservator A court-appointed individual who oversees the affairs of a minor or someone who is incapacitated. A conservator's duties may be limited to financial affairs or may also include regular daily activities.

consideration 1. Something of value provided by one party to another. For example, a person might provide an idea or labor to a business in exchange for shares of ownership. **2.** Payments made to an insurance company for the purchase of an annuity.

consignee The person or company whose name is on a bill of lading as the recipient of a shipment.

consignment 1. One or more pieces tendered by a shipper at one time from a single address to be shipped to one consignee at a single destination. **2.** Placing goods with another party without surrendering ownership rights. For example, a distributor ships products to a retailer but does not surrender ownership or get paid until the retailer sells the products to its customers. Consignment reduces risk and increases profitability of a retailer by requiring the manufacturer or distributor to finance the retailer's inventory.

consignment shop A retail establishment that offers for sale goods that are owned by others. Consignment shops earn a profit by retaining a portion of the purchase price of the goods that are sold. —Compare THRIFT SHOP.

consignor —See SHIPPER.

consistency 1. Using the same accounting methods over time. **2.** Using accounting methods that satisfy generally accepted accounting principles or other applicable professional standards.

consol A debt instrument having no scheduled return of principal, and therefore perpetual interest payments and no maturity. Consols fluctuate widely in price with changes in long-term interest rates. They have never been popular in the United States. —Also called *annuity bond; perpetual bond.* —See also PERPETUITY.

consolidated balance sheet A balance sheet in which assets and liabilities of a parent company and its controlled subsidiaries are combined, thereby presenting balance sheet items for the parent and its subsidiaries as if they were a single firm.

consolidated bond A single bond issue used to replace two or more outstanding issues.

consolidated income statement An income statement that combines the income statements of two or more organizations. As with other consolidated statements, a consolidated income statement eliminates any funds owed to or due from firms within the same group.

consolidated mortgage A mortgage made to replace two or more outstanding mortgages.

Consolidated Omnibus Budget Reconciliation Act —See COBRA.

Consolidated Quotation System (CQS) An electronic system for disseminating the bid, ask, and size for a security in each market in which the security is traded. CQS was developed in 1978 by the National Association of Securities Dealers and the organized exchanges.

consolidation loan

How can I decide if it is wise to use a consolidation loan to pay off my outstanding debts?

Most debt consolidation loans will have fees you must pay. In order to reduce your monthly payments, a consolidation loan must have a lower average interest rate than your existing debt, or it must have a longer payout period, or both. It may be to your benefit to consolidate your debt if the total interest plus fees you pay over the life of the new loan is less than interest and fees on your existing loans. You won't come out ahead if you incur new debt and have an overall increased debt burden after your debt consolidation. Also, extending the time to pay off the debt might create problems for you in the future.

Consider an alternative strategy of paying off your current debt that has the highest interest rate. After it is paid off, start on the next one. It is difficult to come out ahead with a debt consolidation loan.

▪ Michael W. Butler, PhD, Professor of Economics, Angelo State University, San Angelo, Texas

consolidated tape An integrated reporting system of price and volume data for trades in listed securities in all markets in which the securities trade. Thus, the consolidated tape would report trades in General Motors stock not only from its principal market on the New York Stock Exchange, but also from all the other markets in which it trades.

consolidated tax return A tax return that combines the reports of all affiliated companies that are at least 80% owned by the parent.

consolidation A combination of two or more firms into a completely new company. Assets and liabilities of the firms are absorbed by the new company. —Compare MERGER.

consolidation loan A loan that pays off and replaces several existing loans. Most consolidation loans reduce monthly payments to creditors, although this is often the result of a longer payment period.

consolidator 1. A business that assembles carload shipments from smaller lots in order to benefit from lower shipping costs. 2. A company that buys airline tickets in bulk, normally at significant discounts, and resells the tickets to individuals.

consortium A group of organizations that participate in a joint venture. For example, several libraries may join to form a consortium in order to secure expensive electronic information services and offer patrons a greater variety of materials.

constant dollar plan A formula plan for investing in which a constant dollar amount is kept in stocks, with other investments in bonds or short-term securities. Essentially, this plan forces the investor to sell stocks in rising markets and purchase them in falling markets.

constant dollars Dollars reported in unchanged value compared with the value reported on a previous date. For example, a company may have raised its dividends on each share of common stock from $2.00 in 1999 to $5.00 in 2009. However, after investors have adjusted for consumer price increases during the ten-year period, the 2009 dividend amounts to only $3.90 in constant dollars. In this case, the 2009 dollars are constant in terms of their 1999 purchasing power.

constant payment loan —See AMORTIZED LOAN.

constant ratio plan A formula plan for investing in which the market value of all stocks in an investor's portfolio is kept at a predetermined percentage, with other investments making up the remainder of the portfolio. Thus, stocks must be sold if they rise in value more rapidly than other investments, and bought if they fall in value more rapidly than other investments in the portfolio. As an example, an investor may decide on a portfolio of 70% stocks and 30% bonds.

construction loan A short-term mortgage taken to finance the construction of a real estate project before permanent long-term financing is obtained. Because of its relatively high return, some real estate investment trusts specialize in this type of loan. Construction loans are often more risky than long-term mortgages.

constructive dividend A corporate payment to a stockholder that is characterized by the Internal Revenue Service as a dividend distribution even though the corporation calls it something else. For example, a small firm may pay an employee who is also a stockholder an excessive salary so that the payment can be used as a tax-deductible expense rather than as an aftertax dividend payment. The IRS may determine that part of the payment is a constructive dividend and disallow it as a tax-deductible expense.

constructive possession In legal theory, the ability and intention to control an asset without having actual physical contact. For example, a key to a safe deposit box is constructive possession of the contents of the box. Likewise, a key to a car is constructive possession of the car even when the car is in someone else's driveway.

constructive receipt Receipt of items considered to be income for a given tax period even though payment is not received until later. For example, a dividend paid and mailed on December 30, 2009, but not received by stockholders until after the first of the following year is considered taxable income for 2009 because the stockholders are considered to have constructive receipt of the dividend.

constructive stock ownership Effective control of stock that is registered in the name of someone else. For example, the Internal Revenue Service considers an individual to own stock when the stock is directly or indirectly owned by or for his or her family.

consultant An individual or organization that provides expert or professional advice or services for a fee.

consumed-income tax A tax levied against only the part of income that is spent. Proponents of this type of taxation contend that exempting the portion of income that is saved will encourage savings, provide funds for investment, and make the economy more productive.

consumer An individual or organization that purchases goods and services for personal use rather than for resale or manufacturing.

consumer behavior Consumer decision-making processes in purchasing and using goods and services. —See also BUYER BEHAVIOR.

Consumer Confidence Index A measure of consumer views regarding the current economic situation and consumer expectations for the future. Information for the index is compiled and released on the last Tuesday of each month by the Conference Board, an independent not-for-profit research group. Consumer views of the economy affect consumer spending, which makes up two thirds of the U.S. economy.

consumer credit Short-term loans to individuals for purchasing goods and services for personal and household use. Credit card debt, vehicle leases, and installment loans are examples of consumer credit.

Consumer Credit Protection Act of 1968 Federal legislation designed to protect individual borrowers with respect to garnishment of wages and availability of information relative to loans. One section of the act limits the amount of earnings that may be garnished and prohibits dismissing an employee because of garnishment of any one debt. Another section requires that creditors make certain written disclosures concerning finance charges and related aspects of credit transactions. —Also called *Truth in Lending Act.* —See also REGULATION Z; RIGHT OF RESCISSION.

consumer durables —See DURABLE GOODS.

consumer finance company A business that makes loans to individuals who would normally have difficulty obtaining a loan at a commercial bank.

consumer goods Goods such as television sets, clothing, and furniture that are purchased and consumed by households. —Compare CAPITAL GOODS.

consumerism 1. A movement to promote consumer interests, including improved safety standards, better dissemination of information, and greater value. **2.** The economic theory that increased consumption of goods and services is good for the economy.

consumer price index (CPI) A measure of consumer price level changes relative to a base period (currently 1982–84). The CPI can be a misleading indicator of the impact of inflation on an individual because it is based on the spending patterns of families living in urban areas. —Compare PRODUCER PRICE INDEX. —Also called *price index.* —See also GDP DEFLATOR.

CASE STUDY The consumer price index (CPI) is not intended to be a comprehensive gauge of the cost of living that applies equally to everyone. It is reported in two separate measures, calculated to reflect the spending patterns of two groups: (1) all urban consumers and (2) urban wage earners and clerical workers. The first measure represents nearly 90% of the entire U.S. population and is the one reported in most media reports about inflation. The CPI does not accurately reflect expenditure patterns of the elderly, who tend to spend a larger than average proportion of their income on health care, and it does not reflect the spending patterns of people who live in rural areas. In addition, the CPI omits any consideration of quality of life issues such as health, safety, and the environment. For example, the CPI is unaffected if manufacturers choose to keep the cost of their products from rising by dumping large amounts of pollutants in the water and air. Some critics claim the CPI understates inflation. Producers sometimes choose to reduce service or size rather than raise prices. For example, has the real price of a hammer, ladder, or bicycle increased if shoppers have difficulty locating an employee who can provide knowledgeable assistance? Does spending more time in the checkout lane in a store that has cut back on the number of cashiers increase the real cost of goods purchased? The cost of housing is calculated as owners' equivalent rent, a measure that is unlikely to accurately reflect this important component of the cost of living for someone searching for a home to purchase. In short, the CPI has shortcomings that should be considered when inflation numbers are reported.

consumer protection Actions taken that protect consumers from misleading advertising and defective or dangerous goods and services. For example, many states have enacted "lemon laws" that offer assistance to individuals who purchase trouble-prone vehicles.

consumer research Marketing studies that attempt to determine the preferences and needs of individuals. For example, a firm might evaluate consumer perceptions of several possible packaging designs for a new candy bar.

consumer surplus In economics, the excess between the price a consumer is willing to pay for something compared to the price that must actually be paid. For example, the consumer surplus of $4,000 results if you can buy a Mazda RX-8 for $24,000 when you would be willing to pay $28,000.

consumption function In economics, the positive relationship between consumption and disposable income. The relationship between consumption and disposable income was a building block for the macroeconomic theories of famous economist John Maynard Keynes.

consumption tax A tax levied on individual commodities or services and included as part of the retail price of those commodities or services paid by consumers. For example, a 25¢ tax levied on a pack of cigarettes is a consumption tax. Many people advocate consumption taxes as an inducement to increase savings in the economy. —Compare EXCISE TAX; VALUE-ADDED TAX.

contango In futures or options trading, a market in which longer-term contracts carry a higher price than near-term contracts. The premium accorded to longer maturities is a normal condition of the market and reflects the cost of carrying the commodity for future delivery. —Compare INVERTED MARKET.

contempt of court An intentional failure to show respect or obey a court's order. For example, a newspaper reporter may be held in contempt of court for failing to reveal sources of information to a federal grand jury.

contestable market A market dominated by few firms but with nominal barriers to entry, such that potential competition causes existing firms to operate on a competitive basis. Rising profits would be likely to result in new entries in a contestable market.

contestable period The length of time during which an insurance company may deny payment of a claim because of suicide or misrepresentation on an insurance application.

contingency fee The cost of legal representation when payment to an attorney is based on a percentage of what a client receives in a settlement or judgment. Personal injury cases often entail contingency fees.

contingency fund Funds set aside for unexpected needs.

contingency table In statistics, a cross-classification of data in which one variable is indicated in rows (across) and a second variable is indicated in columns (down). For example, a contingency table may illustrate differences in portfolio composition (equities/bonds/cash) by age group.

contingent annuity A series of payments scheduled to begin at the time of a specified event. For example, an individual's death may set in motion an annuity payable to a designated person or organization.

contingent commission A fee paid to a broker only when a standard is met or a specified event occurs. For example, a broker is paid a commission contingent on steering a minimum amount of business to the insurance company.

| **CASE STUDY** The attorney general of Connecticut announced in December 2006 that insurance giant Chubb Corporation had agreed to pay $17 mil-

lion and adopt certain business reforms to settle allegations the firm had paid contingent commissions to agents and brokers who steered business to Chubb. In one instance, Chubb solicited agents and brokers to become part owners in an offshore reinsurance company the firm had created. Chubb paid the offshore company (and its owners) a fee to reinsure a portion of claims resulting from policies steered by the agents and brokers to Chubb. In other instances, the firm paid salaries to individuals who claimed to be independent agents, but who actually sold only Chubb policies. An internal investigation by Chubb indicated the firm paid contingent commissions of nearly $850 million between 1999 and 2002. The state claimed these costs resulted in higher premiums for consumers. Insurance companies ACE, AIG, St Paul Travelers Companies, and Zurich American Insurance Company had previously reached settlements that prohibited them from paying contingent commissions in specified lines of insurance.

contingent convertible bond A bond convertible into shares of stock only if the share price achieves a specified level. —Also called *CoCo bond.*

contingent deferred sales charge A mutual fund redemption fee that is reduced or eliminated for specified holding periods. For example, a fund might charge a 6% redemption fee for a holding period of less than one year, a 5% fee for a holding period of one to two years, and so forth. Mutual funds with a contingent deferred sales charge also generally levy an annual 12b–1 fee.

contingent financing clause —See FINANCE CONTINGENCY CLAUSE.

contingent interest 1. An ownership arrangement in real property that becomes effective only in the event of a particular incident or circumstance. For example, a child assumes ownership of an office building only if an older sibling is no longer living. **2.** Interest on a loan that is paid only under certain circumstances. For example, a loan specifies an additional 3% annual interest in the event a firm's cash flow exceeds a specified level.

contingent issue An issue of securities that is to be distributed only when a specified event has occurred or when a given standard has been met. For example, the poison-pill defense against hostile takeovers involves issuance of additional securities in the event that the raider acquires a certain percentage of the takeover target's outstanding stock.

contingent liability 1. An obligation that may result but is not likely to result, because the event causing the obligation is improbable. For example, the award from a lawsuit against a firm is a contingent liability of the defendant if there is little likelihood the plaintiff will recover the award. **2.** Liability of a corporation or partnership for accidents caused by people other than employees for whose acts the partnership or corporation is responsible.

contingent order A special type of security order that instructs the broker to take some action only in the event that something else has occurred. An example would be an order to sell call options on Google common stock only after shares of Google have been purchased at a specified limit price.

contingent voting rights The entitlement to vote in a corporate election in the event of certain prescribed events. For example, owners of preferred stock may obtain the right to vote for a firm's directors in the event that preferred dividends are not paid.

continuation coverage Temporary continuation of health insurance benefits on a voluntary basis when plan coverage would ordinarily terminate. For example, a terminated employee might wish to temporarily continue benefits until he or she has found a new job. An employee who chooses continuation coverage must normally pay the full premium. —See also COBRA.

continuing education A course or instructional program that attempts to improve knowledge or skills in a particular area but does not count as credit toward a degree.

continuing operations The parts of a business that are expected to be maintained as an ongoing segment of an overall business operation. Income and losses from continuing operations are reported separately if any segments have been discontinued during the accounting period. —Also called *going lines.*

continuity program **1.** An ongoing promotion to attract and retain customers. Airline frequent flier programs are an example of a continuity program designed to influence travelers to book travel on a single airline. **2.** A retail campaign designed to convince customers to purchase a series of related items one at a time. For example, a supermarket may offer its customers a set of dishware, one item per week, over a period of months.

continuous audit Audit-related activities that are provided on a continuous or real-time basis. Continuous audit contrasts with the traditional audit, in which a period of time passes between the field work and issuance of an audit report. A continuous audit can identify suspicious transactions when they occur rather than weeks or months later.

continuous compounding Compounding of interest using the shortest possible interval of time. Although continuous compounding sounds impressive, in practice it results in virtually the same effective yield as daily compounding.

continuous reinforcement Rewarding or punishing certain behavior each time it occurs in order to encourage a desired response. For example, the office manager of a retail outlet sends a congratulatory note to each employee who persuades three customers to apply for a company charge card.

continuous trading A trading system for securities in which transactions take place whenever a sell limit order equals or is less than a buy order, or a buy limit order equals or is more than a sell order. Essentially, continuous trading occurs when dealers and brokers attempt to execute orders as soon as they have been received. Except for opening transactions, continuous trading is the way securities are bought and sold in the United States. —Compare BATCH TRADING.

contra account In accounting, a balance sheet account with a balance that is opposite normal accounts. For example, allowance for doubtful accounts is a contra account. The net value of accounts receivable is equal to accounts receivable less allowance for doubtful accounts.

contraband Goods legally forbidden for import, export, or ownership. For example, a large amount of cigarettes purchased in a low-tax state like Kentucky for illegal delivery to a high-tax state like New York.

contra broker The broker on the opposite side of a transaction. To a broker acting as an agent to buy, the contra broker is the selling broker. Conversely, to a broker on the sell side, the contra broker is the broker on the buy side.

contract **1.** A binding agreement between two or more parties that become obligated to do or not do something. —See also ORAL CONTRACT; PAROL CONTRACT. **2.** In futures trading, an agreement between two parties to make and take delivery of a specified commodity on a given date at a predetermined location. **3.** In options trading, an agreement by the writer either to buy (if a put) or to sell (if a call) a given asset at a predetermined price until a certain date. The holder of the option is under no obligation to act.

contract carrier A transportation company that provides shipping services on a select basis. For example, a contract carrier may provide transportation services to a single company or a small group of companies with which it has contracts. —Compare COMMON CARRIER.

contract for deed An installment sale of real estate in which the buyer may utilize the property, but the seller retains title until the contract is paid in full. —Also called *installment land contract; land contract.*

contract grades In commodities trading, the standards that a commodity must meet in order to be used for delivery on a futures contract. For example, the Chicago Board of Trade requires silver deliveries to take place with 1,000- or 1,100-ounce bars assaying at a fineness of not less than 0.999.

contraction 1. A period of reduced business activity in the overall economy or a particular sector of the economy. **2.** Intentional reduction in the size of a company. For example, managers may decide to close a portion of the firm's manufacturing facilities.

contract month The month in which a futures contract requires delivery of the commodity. Most contracts are offset or closed before this time, so that no delivery is necessary.

contract of indemnity An insurance contract that reimburses the insured party for financial loss.

contractor 1. A business or person who builds things for others. **2.** A person who works under contract for others. For example, an individual may contract to set up computer systems for homeowners and businesses.

contract size In futures and options, the size or amount of an asset to be delivered. For example, stock options nearly always specify 100 shares, while a silver futures contract on the Chicago Mercantile Exchange stipulates 5,000 troy ounces.

contractual plan A program in which an investor in a mutual fund agrees to invest a fixed amount of money at regular intervals in accumulating shares. For example, an individual may contract to invest $100 per month with a selected fund regardless of what the market does or at what price the fund's shares sell throughout the period. —See also DOLLAR-COST AVERAGING; LOAD SPREAD OPTION.

contrarian An investor who decides which securities to buy and sell by going against the crowd. For example, a contrarian would tend to purchase the stock of steel companies when steel stock prices are depressed and most investment counselors are advising against them. Contrarians operate on the premise that when stocks are very popular they are overbought, and when they are very unpopular they are oversold.

contributed capital Funds or property transferred to a company by its stockholders. The contribution may be made in return for stock, in which case the payment is recorded as paid-in capital, or it may be a donation, in which case it is recorded as donated capital.

contribution margin The price at which a firm sells its product less the variable cost of producing the product. A company with a large contribution margin is likely to experience substantial profit increases during an economic upswing. —Also called *net contribution.*

contributory negligence Negligence on the part of a plaintiff that contributes to the cause of the injury and prevents a recovery of damages. Most states have replaced the contributory negligence test with comparative negligence, which permits partial recovery.

contributory pension plan A pension plan in which the participating employees are required to support the plan with contributions. —Compare NONCONTRIBUTORY PENSION PLAN.

control The ability to manage or direct an organization.

control account A summary account in the general ledger with totals from a subsidiary ledger.

controlled account —See DISCRETIONARY ACCOUNT.

controlled circulation Delivery of a publication limited to a specific group of qualified individuals, groups, or businesses. For example, *CFO* is a free, controlled-circulation monthly publication targeted at senior financial executives.

controlled corporation A corporation that is majority owned and effectively controlled by another corporation. For example, Ford Motor Credit Company is a controlled company of Ford Motor Company.

controlled economy —See COMMAND ECONOMY.

controlled group **1.** One or more chains of corporations that are connected through stock ownership with a common parent when 80% of the stock of each corporation is owned by one or more corporations in the group and the parent owns at least 80% of one other corporation. **2.** A group of two or more corporations in which five or fewer common owners (individuals, trusts, or an estate) own directly or indirectly a controlling interest (generally 80% or more of the stock) of each group and have effective control.

controller An organization's chief accounting officer, who is responsible for establishing and maintaining the organization's accounting system. —Also called *comptroller.*

controlling interest The ownership of a quantity of outstanding corporate stock sufficient to control the actions of the firm. Controlling interest often involves ownership of significantly less than 51% of a firm's outstanding stock because many owners fail to participate in decision making.

control person —See AFFILIATED PERSON.

control premium The additional value of a block of shares that allows an investor to gain control of a business. A person or company owning 35% of a business is likely to pay a premium for additional shares that will lead to control of the firm. Control premium is particularly applicable to closely held companies in which there are few owners. —Compare MINORITY DISCOUNT.

control stock —See SUPERVOTING STOCK.

control value The value of shares in a firm when the number of shares available is sufficient to control the firm. If one person or a group owns 60% of a firm's outstanding stock, the shares in the controlling 60% are worth more on a per-share basis than the remaining 40% of outstanding shares.

convenience good A widely distributed and inexpensive article that is easily purchased, generally for immediate use. Candy, cigarettes, and soft drinks are examples of convenience goods.

convenience sampling In statistics, a sampling technique in which a sample is selected on the basis of convenience and ease. The problem is, the sample is likely to be unrepresentative of the population as a whole. For example, a study of the age and sex of shoppers at a mall might entail surveying mall shoppers for three hours during a weekday morning. The sample drawn is likely to be unrepresentative of all mall shoppers because of the lack of representation of working adults, who are most likely at work, and school-age children, who should be in school.

convenience store A retail business with a primary emphasis on providing customers with a convenient location and a wide array of quickly purchased goods and services. Traditional convenience stores are about 2,400 to 2,500 square feet in size, with hours that are extended compared to average retailers.

conventional mortgage A fixed-rate residential mortgage that is not insured by the Veterans Administration or the Federal Housing Administration.

conventional option A put or call option contract negotiated independently of the organized option exchanges. Before 1973 and the opening of the Chicago Board Option Exchange, all options originated through private negotiations. The disadvantage of conventional options is their lack of liquidity due to a limited secondary market.

convergence The process by which the futures price and the cash price of an underlying asset approach one another as delivery date nears. The futures and cash prices should be equal on the delivery date.

conversion equivalent The price at which common stock would have to sell in order to make a convertible security worth its market price in common stock value alone. The equivalent is calculated by dividing the conversion ratio into a convertible security's market price. A $1,000 face amount bond trading at $1,200 and convertible into 40 shares of stock has a conversion equivalent of $1,200/40 shares, or $30 per share.

conversion option A clause of some adjustable-rate mortgages that permits the borrower to switch to a fixed-rate mortgage at stipulated intervals.

conversion parity The condition of a convertible security when it sells at a price equal to the value of the underlying asset for which it may be exchanged.

conversion period The time during which a convertible security may be exchanged for other assets. Most conversion periods extend for the lives of the convertible securities (until maturity for bonds), although some periods are limited. An issuer will occasionally extend a conversion period.

conversion premium The excess at which a convertible security sells above its conversion value. The conversion premium usually declines as a convertible security rises in market price. A bond trading at $1,400 and convertible into 50 shares of common stock with a current market price of $22 each sells at a conversion premium of $1,400 − (50 × $22), or $300.

conversion price The price per share at which common stock will be exchanged for a convertible security. The principal amount of a convertible security divided by the conversion price equals the number of shares that will be received upon exchange. The conversion price is usually adjusted downward for events such as stock splits and dividends. —See also ADJUSTMENT IN CONVERSION TERMS.

conversion privilege —See EXCHANGE PRIVILEGE.

conversion ratio The number of shares of stock into which a convertible security may be exchanged. The ratio for a convertible bond is calculated by dividing the principal amount of the bond by the conversion price.

conversion value The market value of the underlying asset(s) into which a convertible security may be exchanged. Generally, conversion value is calculated by multiplying the number of shares that can be obtained by the market price per share. Thus, a bond that can be converted into 30 shares of stock with a market price of $20 each has a conversion value of $600.

convert **1.** To exchange one security for a different security. For example, the owner of a convertible bond can choose to submit the bond to the issuer for conversion into a specified number of shares of stock. **2.** To switch life insurance coverage from term insurance to permanent insurance. **3.** To change a building from rental units to condominiums. Building owners operating under restrictions of rent control find condo conversion particularly appealing. **4.** —See SWITCH 2.

convertible —See CONVERTIBLE SECURITY.

convertible adjustable preferred stock (CAPS) Preferred stock with a dividend tied to rates paid by U.S. Treasury securities. CAPS can be converted to cash or shares of stock when the following period's dividend is announced, a feature that adds liquidity and protects principal.

convertible ARM An adjustable-rate mortgage that permits the borrower to convert to a fixed-rate mortgage under specified conditions.

convertible floating-rate note A floating-rate note that gives the holder the option of exchanging it for a longer-term debt security with a specified coupon. Unlike a regular floating-rate note, the convertible feature protects investors against declining interest rates.

convertible security A security that, at the option of the holder, may be exchanged for another asset, generally a fixed number of shares of common stock. Convertible issues frequently are fixed-income securities such as debentures and preferred stock. Their prices are influenced by changes in interest rates and the values of the assets into which they may be exchanged. Convertible securities vary in price to a greater degree than straight debt, but to a lesser degree than the underlying asset. —Also called *convertible.* —See also BOND CONVERSION; CONVERSION PREMIUM; CONVERSION PRICE; CONVERSION RATIO; CONVERSION VALUE; MANDATORY CONVERTIBLE SECURITY.

CASE STUDY In 2006, giant real estate investment trust Equity Office Properties Trust issued $1.5 billion in debt convertible into the firm's common stock. The issue was unusual not only because of its large amount of borrowing, but also because of the purpose of the issue—raising cash that would be used to repurchase the firm's own common stock. The company was issuing a security convertible into common stock in order to raise funds to reduce the number of shares of common stock. The issue carried a 4% coupon and was convertible into common stock at a price of $43 per share. The proceeds of the issue were used to repurchase 17.2 million shares at the current market price of $36.21. Essentially the company was able to acquire stock for debt that would eventually be converted into stock at a price more advantageous to the company. The downside was the firm incurred an additional $1.5 billion of debt and was obligated to pay $60 million more in annual interest expense.

A private equity company acquired the firm for over $50 per share the following year.

convertible term insurance Term life insurance that can be exchanged, at the option of the policyholder, for whole life insurance or universal life insurance. Proof of insurability of the policyholder is not required for the exchange.

convexity A mathematical measure of the sensitivity of a bond's price to changing interest rates. A high convexity indicates a greater responsiveness of a bond's price to interest rate changes.

convey In law, to transfer in writing a title to real property.

conveyance An instrument that transfers title of real property for one person or group to another person or group.

COO —See CHIEF OPERATING OFFICER.

cookie A small file stored on a client computer by a web browser. A cookie is referenced to identify previous visitors and allows a server to store its own information about a user on the user's own computer.

cookie jar accounting Smoothing reported earnings by taking reserves against losses during especially profitable periods and utilizing the reserves during unprofitable periods.

cook the books To distort a firm's financial statements. For example, a manager may intentionally overstate sales or understate expenses in order to create high net income.

cooling-off period 1. The required waiting period between a firm's filing a registration statement for a new security issue with the SEC and the time the securities actually can be issued. The cooling-off period is usually 20 days, although the SEC may alter it for individual issues. —Also called *twenty-day period; waiting period.* —See also EFFECTIVE DATE 2. **2.** A formal waiting period during which parties in a dispute can continue a dialogue. This is often applied to a labor conflict in which a union and employer are required to continue bargaining rather than strike or initiate a lockout.

co-op 1. A business that is jointly owned and controlled by the people who use its services. —See also PRODUCER COOPERATIVE. **2.** A relationship among a student, an educational institution, and an organization in which the student combines academic study with periods of paid work experience. **3.** Retailer advertisement that includes mention of a particular product or company that reimburses the retailer in part or whole. **4.** A housing community that is jointly owned and managed by the residents. —Also called *cooperative.* —See also LIMITED EQUITY COOPERATIVE.

cooperative —See CO-OP 4.

co-op mailing A promotional mailing that includes material from two or more advertisers in the same envelope. Co-op mailings allow companies to share the cost of advertising noncompeting products.

COP —See CERTIFICATE OF PARTICIPATION.

copay The payment required of a health plan participant for a covered good or service. For example, a health insurance policy might require a $10 copay for the purchase of a generic drug.

copyright Legal protection given to authors, artists, composers, or playwrights for exclusive rights to distribute or to transfer the rights to distribute their work.

core competencies The unique set of skills, knowledge, and expertise that allows an organization to remain competitive and provide value to customers. For example, household-products giant Procter & Gamble has core competencies in product marketing, science-based product development, quality assurance, and distribution.

core earnings A measure of a firm's earnings in which adjustments have been made to reported earnings in order to provide a more accurate measure of the profitability of the firm's ongoing operations. Developed by Standard & Poor's Corporation, core earnings excludes pension plan income, gains or losses from asset sales, and litigation settlements. Core earnings does include merger and acquisition expenses, employee stock options, and restructuring charges from ongoing operations.

core holding An investment expected to be part of a portfolio over a long period of time. For example, an investor may consider shares of Intel, Procter & Gamble, and General Electric as core holdings, to be supplemented by other investments with short- and intermediate-term holding periods.

core inflation A measure of consumer price increases that excludes volatile components such as energy and food. Core inflation is generally considered more accurate than changes in the consumer price index in representing the economy's underlying inflationary pressures.

corner¹ Control over a sufficient portion of a particular security such that it is possible to control the security's price. Others wishing to purchase the security, especially to cover short positions, are forced to buy it at an artificially high price. Corners were popular in the early 1900s, when the securities markets were virtually unregulated.

corner² To acquire a large enough position in a particular security or commodity such that control over its price and supply is achieved.

corporate 1. Of or relating to a bond issued by a corporation, as opposed to a bond issued by the U.S. Treasury or a municipality. **2.** Of or relating to top management at a corporation's headquarters.

corporate amnesia Loss of an organization's knowledge or procedures due to lack of organization or a turnover of personnel. For example, an extensive review of a firm's employment procedures must be repeated because an earlier study is misplaced or key participants retire and are replaced by new employees.

corporate bond fund An investment company that invests in long-term corporate bonds and passes the income from these securities to its stockholders. Although these funds vary in value with changes in long-term interest rates, they usually provide a current return in excess of money market funds. Corporate bond funds are of interest primarily to investors seeking high current income or to those betting on a substantial fall in long-term interest rates.

corporate charter —See ARTICLES OF INCORPORATION.

corporate culture The operating environment of a business, including its values, norms, and the behavioral patterns of its employees.

corporate indicator An identifying word or abbreviation included as part of a corporate name to indicate a business is a corporation. Appropriate corporate indicators vary by state, but most states accept the following: company, corporation, incorporated, or limited.

corporate raider —See RAIDER.

corporate reorganization —See REORGANIZATION 2.

corporate structure The formal interrelationships of businesses and departments within a company.

corporate veil Protection of individual wealth and actions by the limited liability accorded to corporations. —See also PIERCING THE VEIL.

corporate venturing A large company taking a minority ownership position in a smaller firm engaged in a related business. The small firm benefits from financial and other resources it might otherwise have difficulty obtaining. The large firm may gain a foothold in a new technology being developed by a business that has greater flexibility and focus.

corporation An organized body, especially a business, that has been granted a state charter recognizing it as a separate legal entity having its own rights, privileges, and liabilities distinct from those of the individuals within the entity. A corporation can acquire assets, enter into contracts, sue or be sued, and pay taxes in its own name. Corporations issue shares of stock to individuals supplying ownership capital and issue bonds to individuals lending money to the business. The corporation is a desirable organization for a business entity for a variety of reasons, including the increased capability such an entity has to raise capital. Most large firms, especially those engaged in manufacturing, are organized as corporations. —Compare PARTNERSHIP; PROPRIETORSHIP. —See also INCORPORATE; LIMITED LIABILITY; UNLIMITED LIABILITY.

corpus 1. The principal of a bond. For example, securities dealers create zero-coupon Treasury receipts by purchasing a regular Treasury bond and separating the interest coupons from the corpus. —See also COUPON STRIPPING. **2.** The principal amount of an estate or trust.

correction A sharp, relatively short price decline that temporarily interrupts a persistent upward trend in the value of an asset or a class of assets: *Analysts were forecasting a correction in technology stocks.*

correlation The relationship between two variables over a period, especially one that shows a close match between the variables' movements. For example, all utility stocks tend to have a high degree of correlation because the same forces influence their share prices. Conversely, gold stock price movements are not closely correlated with utility stock price movements because the two are influenced by very different factors. —See also SERIAL CORRELATION.

correlation coefficient In statistics, a measurement of the degree to which two things vary together. The maximum value for a correlation coefficient is 1.00, which occurs when two variables have a perfect positive correlation. A negative correlation coefficient indicates two variables that have an indirect relationship.

correspondence audit An IRS query of a tax matter that is conducted through the mail. Correspondence audits cover less complex issues and generally address only one or two matters.

correspondent 1. A financial organization such as a securities firm or a bank that regularly performs services for another firm that does not have the requisite facilities or the access to perform the services directly. For example, a member of a securities exchange may execute a trade for a nonmember firm. **2.** A person who is paid to provide articles or news stories to a media outlet.

cosign To sign a loan agreement or lease and commit to be responsible for the obligation in the event the primary debtor does not pay.

cost The expenditure of funds or use of property to acquire or produce a product or service. —See also AVERAGE COST; FIXED COST; HISTORICAL COST; MARGINAL COST; REPLACEMENT COST; VARIABLE COST.

cost accounting The field of accounting that measures, classifies, and records costs. A cost accountant, for example, might be required to establish a system for identifying and segmenting various production costs so as to assist a firm's management in making prudent operating decisions. —See also MANAGEMENT ACCOUNTANT.

cost approach In real estate, appraising a property as equal to the land value plus the cost to reproduce any improvements net of depreciation.

cost basis —See BASIS 2.

cost-benefit analysis The comparison of benefits and costs in decision making. Dollar values are assigned to benefits and costs in most cost-benefit analyses.

cost center A segment of a business or other organization in which costs can be segregated, with the head of that segment being held accountable for expenses. Cost centers are established in large organizations to identify responsibility and to control costs.

cost containment Reducing expenditures or the rate of growth of expenditures. For example, a company may attempt cost containment of health insurance expenses by increasing the size of deductibles that employees must absorb.

cost depletion Depletion calculated as a percentage of the original cost of a natural resource that is consumed during a period. —See also PERCENTAGE DEPLETION.

cost effectiveness A comparison of the added costs with the added benefits of a course of action. For example, a retailer might investigate the cost effectiveness of hiring more security personnel in an attempt to reduce theft of merchandise. Hiring more personnel would be cost effective if the added cost of additional staff was less than the savings from a reduction in stolen goods.

cost, insurance, and freight (CIF) A sale in which the contract price includes the cost of the good, the cost of transportation, and the cost of insurance.

cost of capital The overall percentage cost of the funds used to finance a firm's assets. Cost of capital is a composite cost of the individual sources of funds, including common stock, debt, preferred stock, and retained earnings. The overall cost of capital depends on the cost of each source and the proportion that source represents of all capital used by the firm. The goal of an individual or business is to limit investment to assets that provide a return that is higher than the cost of the capital that was used to finance those assets. —Also called *average cost of capital.*

cost of carry Direct costs to maintain an investment position. For example, an individual purchasing securities on margin must pay interest expenses on borrowed funds. —Also called *carrying charge.*

cost of funds The interest cost of borrowing money expressed as a percentage. Cost of funds is sometimes calculated as the weighted average interest rate on all outstanding loans. For example, a bank's cost of funds is the weighted interest rate paid on checking accounts, money market accounts, savings accounts, and certificates of deposit.

cost of goods sold The cost of purchasing materials and preparing goods for sale during a specific accounting period. Costs include labor, materials, overhead, and depreciation.

cost-of-living adjustment (COLA) An adjustment of wages to compensate for changes in the cost of living. The adjustments are generally based on the consumer price index as published by the U.S. Department of Commerce. COLAs are included in many union contracts and government pensions, including Social Security.

cost overrun The excess of expenditures incurred or expected to be incurred compared to the initial project cost estimate.

cost-plus Of or relating to a contract that stipulates the buyer will pay an amount equal to the actual cost of production plus an agreed-upon fee or percentage profit. Cost-plus contracts offer the possibility the contracting party will have little incentive to minimize expenses.

cost-push inflation Rising consumer prices caused by businesses passing along increases in their own costs for labor and materials. Cost-push inflation does not necessarily result in rising corporate profits, because businesses may be unable to pass through all of their cost increases. —Compare DEMAND-PULL INFLATION.

cotenancy —See JOINT OWNERSHIP.

cottage industry A small-scale production facility, generally in a home and operated by family members or neighbors. For example, several neighbors may quilt and offer their finished quilts for sale.

Council of Economic Advisers A group of three economists appointed by the President of the United States to advise the executive branch on domestic and foreign economic issues. The influence of the council has varied widely depending on the views of the President in office and the use he wishes to make of its advice.

counsel 1. An attorney who offers legal advice and representation in court. **2.** Guidance and advice. For example, a divorcee may receive counsel from a friend.

counterclaim A claim by a defendant against the plaintiff. Counterclaims are often filed to counteract a plaintiff's claim, especially with regard to public opinion.

countercyclical economic policy Government fiscal and monetary policy intended to moderate changes in economic activity. For example, government spending on highways is increased (fiscal policy) during a recession and interest rates are increased (monetary policy) during an economic boom.

countercyclical stock A stock that tends to increase in price during recessions and decrease in price during economic expansions. The stocks of companies with relatively stable sales and profits are generally considered countercyclical. —Compare CYCLICAL STOCK.

counterfeit A copy or imitation of something, often employed in a deception.

counter offer An alternate offer with different terms made in response to an offer that has been rejected. For example, a person with property for sale rejects a $7,000 per acre offer from a potential buyer and responds with a counter offer of $7,500 per acre.

counterparty risk The risk that a party to a transaction will fail to fulfill its obligations. The term is often applied specifically to swap agreements in which no clearinghouse guarantees the performance of the contract.

countervailing duties Duties imposed by a country on imported goods that are subsidized by the government of the exporting country. Countervailing duties are designed to keep imported goods from being sold at less than fair market value and damaging domestic producers.

coupon 1. The annual interest paid on a debt security. A coupon is usually stated in terms of the rate paid on a bond's face value. For example, a 6% coupon, $1,000 principal amount bond would pay its owner $60 in interest annually. A coupon is set at the time a security is issued and, for most bonds, stays the same until maturity. **2.** The detachable part of a coupon bond that must be presented for payment every six months in order to receive interest. —See also CLIP; COUPON CLIPPING 1. **3.** A cents-off voucher in a newspaper or magazine that can be detached and presented to a merchant for a price reduction when buying the advertised item. —See also COUPON CLIPPING 2.

coupon bond —See BEARER BOND.

coupon clipping 1. The removal of interest coupons attached to a bearer bond in order that they might be taken to a bank or sent to a paying agent for redemption. Coupon clipping is necessary because owners of bearer bonds do not automatically receive interest checks in the mail every six months. **2.** The removal of cents-off coupons from newspapers and magazines.

coupon-equivalent rate An alternative measure of yield that is used to make securities usually quoted on a discount basis comparable with those quoted on the more usual return on the amount invested. Stating interest at the coupon-equivalent rate is useful for securities, such as Treasury bills and commercial paper, sold at discounts from face value. As an example, a $10,000, 91-day Treasury bill selling for $9,750 is usually quoted at:

$$[(\$10,000 - \$9,750) \div \$10,000] \times (360 \text{ days} \div 91 \text{ days}) = 9.89\%$$

However, the coupon-equivalent rate calculated on the amount of money invested is:

$$[(\$10,000 - \$9,750) \div \$9,750] \times (360 \text{ days} \div 91 \text{ days}) = 10.14\%$$

—See also BANK-DISCOUNT BASIS.

coupon-equivalent yield The stated rate of return on bonds without accounting for any compounding. Because bonds nearly always pay interest twice a year, the coupon-equivalent yield must be compounded semiannually to produce the effective annual yield, a measure used by many banks in advertising certificates of deposit. For example, a 12% coupon, $1,000 principal amount bond pays $60 in interest each six months, resulting in an effective yield of 12.36%, because the first $60 payment each year can be reinvested to earn an additional $3.60 during the latter half of the year.

coupon stripping The purchase of ordinary bonds (usually, U.S. Treasury bonds) that are then repackaged such that the receipts to interest and corpus payments are sold separately. The effect is to transform a security paying regular interest into zero-coupon receipts of varying maturities. —Also called *stripping.* —See also SEPARATE TRADING OF REGISTERED INTEREST AND PRINCIPAL OF SECURITIES.

covariance A statistical measure of the extent to which two variables move together. Covariance is used by financial analysts to determine the degree to which returns on two securities are related. In general, a high covariance indicates similar movements and lack of diversification. —Compare VARIANCE 1. —See also RISK.

covenant 1. A written promise or contract by two or more parties who each promise to do something or not do something. **2.** A clause in a loan agreement written to protect the lender's claim by keeping the borrower's financial position approximately the same as it was at the time the loan agreement was made. Essentially, covenants spell out what the borrower may do and must do in order to satisfy the terms of the loan.

—Also called *protective covenant; restrictive covenant.* —See also NEGATIVE COVENANT; POSITIVE COVENANT.

cover **1.** To meet fixed expenses. For example, a company reports earnings that, before interest and taxes, exceed, or cover, interest expense for the period. **2.** —See SHORT COVER.

coverage In insurance, a guarantee to pay for specified financial losses.

coverage ratio A measure of a corporation's ability to meet a certain type of expense. In general, a high coverage ratio indicates a better ability to meet the expense in question. —See also DIVIDEND COVERAGE; FIXED-CHARGE COVERAGE; INTEREST COVERAGE; PREFERRED DIVIDEND COVERAGE.

cover bid The second-highest bid in a competitive sale.

Coverdell Education Savings Account A special individual retirement account opened on behalf of a child under age 18. Annual contributions may be made by anyone who meets specified income limits. Contributions are not tax-deductible, but earnings grow tax-deferred until withdrawn. Money withdrawn prior to the child turning age 30 to pay for elementary, secondary, or postsecondary education expenses after high school is not subject to federal income tax. —Formerly called *Education IRA.*

covered call option A call option sold short by an investor owning the underlying stock. If the option is later exercised against the short seller of the option, the seller is covered by the stock that is owned. —Compare NAKED OPTION.

covered put option A put option sold short by an investor who is short the underlying stock. If the put is later exercised, the investor will be required to purchase the underlying stock from the holder of the put. The stock will then be used to cover the short position in the stock.

covered writer The seller or writer of a call option who owns the underlying asset that may be required for delivery. Covered writers are usually conservative investors seeking extra current income. —See also BUY-AND-WRITE STRATEGY.

CPA —See CERTIFIED PUBLIC ACCOUNTANT.

CPCU —See CHARTERED PROPERTY CASUALTY UNDERWRITER.

CPI —See CONSUMER PRICE INDEX.

CQS —See CONSOLIDATED QUOTATION SYSTEM.

craft union A labor union whose members are all in the same occupation or trade. The United Brotherhood of Carpenters and Joiners of America is an example of a craft union. —Compare INDUSTRIAL UNION. —Also called *horizontal union.*

cram down Relating to a business deal in which a group of investors or lenders is forced to accept an undesirable arrangement. For example, minority shareholders of a company being bought out may have to accept less than what they consider a fair price for their stock.

crash A protracted major decline in asset values.

crawler —See ROBOT 2.

creative A person who is hired to come up with original concepts. For example, an advertising agency may employee creatives for copywriting and art direction.

creative accounting The use of aggressive and/or questionable accounting techniques in order to produce a desired result, generally high earnings per share. Creative accounting may include selling assets with a low cost basis, shipping unusually large

covered call option

My broker suggested that I write covered call options. Is this a good idea, or is she just trying to generate extra commission income for herself?

In general, writing covered calls is a good idea for those looking to reduce risk and generate extra cash flow. Selling calls provides a bit of downside protection (equal to the option premium received). The option writer also enjoys increased cash flow, as the option premium is received when the option is sold and can be used however the writer wishes—it can be spent, reinvested, etc. Writing calls is a very sound investment technique; however, there are issues to consider. Calls are best written on shares the investor is willing to sell and at a strike price the investor is comfortable with. In addition, investors should be cognizant of the potential tax ramifications of their option strategies. Selling calls against very low-basis stock can result in large taxable gains if the option is exercised. Also, certain covered calls—depending on strike price and time until expiration—can alter the holding period of the underlying common shares. Similarly, certain calls can eliminate the tax benefits of qualified dividends received on the underlying shares.

■ Noah L. Myers, CFP®, Principal and Chief Investment Officer, MiddleCove Capital, Centerbrook, CT

quantities of product near the end of the year, and failure to write down inventories that have declined in value.

creative financing Unusual financing, often with minimal if any down payment and deferred repayment of principal. Creative financing is most often associated with real estate and includes seller financing and interest-only loans.

credit 1. The ability to borrow or to purchase goods and services with payment delayed beyond delivery. **2.** An accounting entry resulting in an increase in liabilities or owners' equity or in a decrease in assets. —Compare DEBIT. **3.** The balance in an account. **4.** An adjustment in favor of a customer. For example, a business may receive credit for damaged merchandise delivered by a manufacturer.

credit analyst 1. A person who analyzes financial statements and makes financial projections in order to judge the credit quality of debt instruments. **2.** An individual who reviews and makes recommendations on loan applications.

credit bureau A privately owned business that collects and sells the credit histories of individuals. —See also CREDIT SCORE.

credit card A plastic card that can be used to purchase goods and services or obtain cash advances on a revolving line of credit. —Also called *charge card.*

credit crunch A period during which borrowed funds are difficult to obtain and, even if funds can be found, interest rates are very high. Credit crunches were particularly severe before 1980, when the ceilings on interest rates that financial institutions could pay resulted in a drying up of deposits.

credit-default swap A contract in which one party agrees to pay the other party a fixed periodic payment, while the other party agrees to compensate the first party in the event of certain credit events, generally bankruptcy, default, or credit restructuring. A credit-default swap is essentially an insurance contract in which a lender transfers risk to another party, who is compensated by a series of agreed-upon payments.

credit enhancement An addition to a bond issue that improves the issue's safety of principal and interest. For example, the purchase of insurance guaranteeing payments on a bond issue is credit enhancement.

credit insurance 1. Insurance required of a borrower that pays the remaining balance of a loan in the event the borrower dies or becomes disabled. A lender is required to disclose to borrowers the terms and cost of credit insurance. **2.** Insurance coverage purchased by a manufacturer or service company that reimburses the insured for unpaid bills by its customers. —Also called *commercial credit insurance.*

credit limit 1. The maximum outstanding balance permitted on a revolving line of credit. **2.** The maximum credit a lender will extend to a potential borrower.

credit line —See LINE OF CREDIT.

creditor One to whom funds are owed. Holders of bonds and debentures are creditors to whom funds are owed by the issuers. —Compare DEBTOR. —Also called *lender.* —See also SECURED CREDITOR; UNSECURED CREDITOR.

credit order A customer order received without payment.

creditors' committee A group of lenders who seek to protect their interests in connection with a borrower that experiences financial difficulties.

credit policy Guidelines addressing how a company evaluates potential customers who wish to buy on credit. Guidelines include credit terms that specify discounts, interest rates, and credit limits.

credit rating A grading of a borrower's ability to meet financial obligations in a timely manner. Credit ratings are established by lenders and by independent agents for companies, individuals, and specific debt issues. —See also BOND RATING.

Credit Rating Agency Reform Act of 2006 Federal legislation intended to encourage competition in the business of rating government and business credit quality. The act facilitated the entry of new credit rating organizations by allowing eligible firms to register with the SEC as nationally recognized statistical rating organizations. It also abolished the ability of the SEC to designate nationally recognized rating agencies. Standard & Poor's and Moody's dominated the industry at the time the bill was signed into law on September 29, 2006.

credit rationing A partial or complete limitation on borrowing, even when a borrower is willing to accept the terms of the lender.

credit risk The risk that a borrower will be unable to make payment of interest or principal in a timely manner.

credit score A number calculated from information in a person's credit report that indicates how likely that person is to pay his or her bills. The higher the score (the range is generally 300 to 850), the better a person's credit history. A credit score affects a person's ability to get credit, and it affects the interest rate that is charged when credit is made available.

credit squeeze Restricted bank lending that is accompanied by rising short-term interest rates and a decline in economic growth. Credit squeezes are generally attributed to policy actions of the Federal Reserve.

credit union A nonprofit cooperative financial institution that provides credit to its members. Credit unions often pay slightly higher rates of interest on passbook-type savings accounts and charge lower rates on consumer loans.

credit watch The reevaluation of the credit quality of a firm's debt obligations by a rating agency. Being the object of a credit watch generally indicates the credit quality of a firm's debt has deteriorated and may be downgraded.

creditworthy Of or relating to a person or organization that enjoys an acceptable credit rating.

creeping inflation Modest increases in consumer prices that may prove troublesome over a long period, especially if the increases gradually begin to move higher..

creeping tender offer The purchase of a target firm's stock at varying prices in the open market rather than through a formal tender offer. Most shares are often acquired in large blocks from arbitrageurs, frequently resulting in the exclusion of small stockholders from the offer. The purpose of a creeping tender offer is to gain control of a firm's stock more cheaply and quickly than an ordinary tender offer permits. —See also WILLIAMS ACT.

crime insurance Property insurance coverage for losses caused by theft, robbery, and burglary.

crisis management Preparing for and responding to a major emergency in order to keep the problem from growing worse.

critical path management A technique for identifying, analyzing, and controlling a series of dependent activities along a critical path that leads to completion of a project.

critical region In statistics, the set of values in which the null hypothesis of a hypothesis test is rejected.

cross-docking Unloading goods from a railcar, ship, or trailer, and quickly reloading the same goods in a similar or alternative source of transportation. Cross-docking eliminates the need for warehousing and typically takes place at a transportation hub where goods are unloaded, sorted, and reloaded.

crossed market A situation in which one market maker's ask price for a security is lower than another market maker's bid price for the same security.

cross elasticity The degree of change in the demand for one product as a response to a change in the price of a different product. For example, an increase in the price of petroleum is likely to have a negative impact on the demand for gas-guzzling vehicles and a positive impact on the demand for fuel-efficient vehicles. The cross elasticity for substitutes is generally positive, in that a price increase for one product will result in an increase in demand for a substitute.

cross hedge In futures trading, an offsetting position in a futures contract for an existing position in a related commodity in the cash market. An example would be the sale of a contract on wheat for delivery in two months in order to offset an existing cash position in oats.

cross holding The holding of securities in one another by two or more corporations. For example, firm A owns equity in firm B at the same time that firm B holds equity in firm A.

crossover credit Of or relating to a bond that straddles the gap between investment-grade and speculative. Crossover credits are generally rated low investment-grade by one rating agency and upper-grade speculative by another rating agency. —See also SPLIT RATING.

cross rate The rate at which two currencies exchange, based on exchange rates using a third currency. For example, the cross rate of euros for yen might be based on the rate of euros for dollars and dollars for yen.

cross selling Promoting goods or services that are related to the product a customer has expressed an interest in buying. For example, a waiter or waitress might ask if a customer would like an appetizer with a dinner order.

cross training Teaching an employee to perform two or more job responsibilities. For example, a hotel may cross train front-desk personnel as reservation agents. At the supervisory level, a department head might cross train in a different department. Cross training results in greater job flexibility and may improve employee motivation.

crowding out The borrowing of large amounts of money by the federal government—a process that soaks up lendable funds, drives up interest rates, and eliminates from the credit markets many private firms wishing to borrow money from those markets. The government is able to crowd out private borrowers because its credit rating is so high and because it is willing to pay the interest rate demanded by the market. Small firms and companies with poor credit ratings are those most adversely affected by crowding out.

crown jewel 1. A company's prize asset. For example, a diversified company might have one division that is very profitable. 2. —Used to refer to a part of a business that is sought by another firm or an investor in a takeover attempt that is hostile to the target firm's management. —Compare SCORCHED EARTH.

crown jewel lockup agreement —See LOCKUP AGREEMENT.

Crummy trust A special type of irrevocable trust used to transfer assets to a minor. Gifted assets qualify for the gift-tax exclusion, while control is maintained by a trustee as long as the minor is given a temporary time (usually 30 days) to withdraw newly contributed assets.

CSCE —See COFFEE, SUGAR AND COCOA EXCHANGE.

C type reorganization A reorganization in which a host company issues voting shares to a target company in exchange for substantially all of the target's assets.

cubes —See QQQQ.

cum dividend —Used to refer to a stock trading such that buyers qualify to receive the next dividend payment. Stocks trade cum dividend until the third business day before the record date. —Compare EX-DIVIDEND.

cum rights —See RIGHTS ON.

cumulative Of or relating to preferred stock and income bonds on which dividends must be paid in full before any payment of dividends is made to common stockholders. Thus, any dividends that are passed eventually must be brought up to date before common stockholders may receive payments. Nearly all issues of preferred stock are cumulative. —Compare NONCUMULATIVE. —See also DIVIDENDS IN ARREARS.

cumulative voting A type of corporate voting right in which a stockholder receives one vote per owned share times the number of directors' positions up for election. The stockholder may allocate votes among the different positions as he or she wishes. For example, an owner of 200 shares is permitted a total of 1,200 votes if six positions are to be voted on. These 1,200 votes may be cast for a single director, may be split between two directors, or may be allocated equally among all six directors. Cumulative voting, making it easier for smaller interest groups to be represented, is required by some states. —Compare MAJORITY VOTING.

curable depreciation Physical deterioration or obsolescence of an asset that is repairable or replaceable at reasonable cost. Curable depreciation in a rental property might include worn carpet, faded paint, and nonworking appliances. The deduction required for curable depreciation is generally the cost of the needed repairs.

Curb Exchange An early name for what is now the American Stock Exchange. The term derived from the market's beginnings on a street in downtown New York.

currency Money used as a medium of exchange. In most instances the term is used to refer only to paper money. —See also BANK NOTE.

currency futures A contract for the future delivery of a specified amount of a major currency. Currency futures were developed in response to the substantial volatility of currency trading rates that occurred following the 1971 shift from fixed to flexible currency exchange rates.

currency futures option An option that gives the owner the right to buy (call) or to sell (put) a currency futures contract.

currency union A group of countries that agree to coordinate monetary policies and peg their currency exchange rates.

current account A country's international transactions in goods and services including such items as cars, computers, and return on investments. Surpluses/deficits in a country's current account must be offset by deficits/surpluses in the country's capital account. —Compare CAPITAL ACCOUNT 2.

current asset Cash or an asset expected to be converted into cash within one year. In addition to cash, current assets include marketable securities, accounts receivable, inventories, and prepaid expenses. Current assets are typically not very profitable, but tend to add liquidity and safety to a firm's operation. —Also called *gross working capital.*

current coupon Of or relating to a bond with an interest coupon very close to the coupons being carried on new issues of the same maturity. Therefore the bond must be selling at a price close to its par value. —Also called *full coupon.*

current dollars The inflation-adjusted price of something valued in a previous time period. For example, a 50% overall inflation since milk was purchased in 1998 for $2.00 a gallon results in a price of $3.00 in current dollars.

current income Investment income earned from interest, dividends, rent, premiums from option writing, and similar sources as opposed to that derived from increases in asset value.

current issue The most recently issued Treasury security of a particular type. For 13-week Treasury bills that are auctioned each Monday, the current issue is the bill issued on the most recent Monday.

current liability A debt due within a year. Current liabilities include accounts payable, short-term loans from financial institutions, current maturities of long-term debt, dividends declared but not paid, and expenses incurred but not paid. Current liabilities are generally met using current assets.

current market value The value of an asset that is appraised at its current market price.

current maturity The length of time before a security matures. For example, a bond issued 15 years ago that had an original maturity of 20 years, has a current maturity of 5 years. The current maturity, rather than the original maturity, is important in valuing a bond.

---

current ratio

Is the current ratio always a good measure of a firm's liquidity? Can a firm have a current ratio that is too high?

The answers are no and yes, respectively. While a high current ratio connotes that the firm can meet its maturing obligations, a high current ratio means that the firm may be tying up too many dollars in non-value-added resources. In such instances, the entity pays too much to finance its current operations. Moreover, it could improve profitability by shifting some of its current investments into longer-term, and more productive, resources.

Industry leaders, such as Dell, Coca-Cola, and Wal-Mart, usually have lower current ratios than those of their competitors. Sometimes these firms maintain such an aggressive short-term liquidity position that their current ratio falls below one (i.e., current liabilities exceed current assets). Their efficiencies allow them to meet maturing obligations while their vendors finance current operations.

■ Peter M. Bergevin, PhD, Professor of Accounting, School of Business, University of Redlands, Redlands, CA

---

current ratio A measure of a firm's ability to meet its short-term obligations. The current ratio is calculated by dividing current assets by current liabilities. Both variables are shown on the balance sheet. A relatively high current ratio compared with those of other firms in the same business indicates high liquidity and generally conservative management, although it may tend to result in reduced profitability. —See also CASH RATIO; QUICK RATIO.

current value accounting The preparation of financial reports utilizing the current value rather than the historical cost of assets.

current yield The annual rate of return received from an investment, based on the income received during a year compared with the investment's current market price. For example, a bond selling at $800 and paying an annual interest of $80 provides a current yield of $80/$800, or 10%. —Also called *rate of return; running yield.*

curriculum vitae A detailed written description of a person's educational and employment history. —Also called *CV; resumé.*

curtesy A widower's portion of his wife's assets that were acquired during the course of their marriage. Curtesy usually amounts to one third of the assets. —Compare DOWER.

cushion —See CALL PROTECTION.

cushion bond A high-coupon bond that sells at a price only slightly above par because of a call provision permitting the issuer to repurchase the security near its current price. A cushion bond has an unusually high current yield, little chance for a price rise, and considerable protection against falling prices caused by increased interest rates.

CUSIP —See COMMITTEE ON UNIFORM SECURITIES IDENTIFICATION PROCEDURES.

CUSIP number A unique identification number that is assigned to stock and bond certificates in an effort to improve the efficiency of clearing operations.

custodial account An account controlled by a custodian rather than the owner of the assets. Custodian accounts are often used for minors or other individuals who are unable or unwilling to handle their own assets.

custodial fee The fee charged by a financial institution that holds securities in safekeeping for an investor.

custodian An organization, typically a commercial bank, that holds in custody and safekeeping someone else's assets. These assets may be cash, securities, or virtually anything of value.

custody A safekeeping service that a financial institution provides for a customer's securities. For a fee, the institution collects dividends, interest, and proceeds from security sales and disburses funds according to the customer's written instructions.

customer A person or organization that purchases goods or services.

customer-centric Describing an organization that is operated from a customer's point of view. Rather than developing new products and attempting to convince consumers to purchase them (the iPhone?), a customer-centric firm develops products and services their customers need (for example, a fully staffed and knowledgeable service department).

customer lifetime value In marketing, the economic value of a customer during the life of the customer's association with a business. An estimate of customer lifetime value allows a business to determine the amount of money that can be spent on acquiring and retaining a customer. For example, a high customer lifetime value may convince a credit card company to offer expensive incentives to attract new clients. —Also called *lifetime customer value.*

customer profile Characteristics of a customer group. For example, the customer profile for a particular radio station might include average age, median income, weekly spending, sex, and so forth. A firm's customer profile is particularly useful in targeting advertising.

customer service An organization's ability to satisfy its customers' needs.

customer service representative An employee who serves as the main intermediary between a business and its customers. Responsibilities vary by employer, but generally include providing assistance to customers who contact the firm with questions or problems.

customs **1.** Duties paid on imported goods. **2.** Location where federal agents inspect baggage and goods being brought into the country. **3.** The federal agency responsible for collecting duties and inspecting imported goods.

customs court A federal court that hears appeals relating to duties and classification of merchandise.

cut-case display A merchandise exhibit consisting of the product being offered presented in an open shipping carton. For example, a hardware store may use a cut-case display for a popular weekend sale item.

CV —See CURRICULUM VITAE.

cyber Monday The Monday following Thanksgiving, which is one of the year's biggest online shopping days. Critics say cyber Monday is overhyped and not nearly as important to online retailers as proponents claim. —See also BLACK FRIDAY 1.

cyberspace The global computer networks that facilitate communications among individuals and organizations.

cycle billing Billing a portion of one's customers each business day so that all customers are billed within a predetermined period, generally one month. Cycle billing is utilized by many utilities.

cyclical Of or relating to a variable, such as housing starts, car sales, or demand for electricity, that is subject to regular or irregular up-and-down movements. —See also BUSINESS CYCLE.

cyclical stock Common stock of a firm whose profits are heavily influenced by cyclic changes in general economic activity. As investors anticipate changes in profits, cyclical stocks often reach their high and low levels before the respective highs and lows in the economy. —Compare COUNTERCYCLICAL STOCK.

cyclical unemployment Unemployment that results from reduced demand for goods and services and varies inversely with economic activity. —Compare STRUCTURAL UN-EMPLOYMENT.

D

daily trading limit In commodities, the range of prices within which trades may take place during a day. The limit is usually determined on the basis of the previous day's settlement price.

daisy chain Manipulative trading among a small group of individuals or institutions that is intended to give the impression of heavy volume. As outsiders see the unusual trading activity and are drawn into the chain, the traders who started the daisy chain then sell their positions, leaving the new investors with overpriced securities.

damages Money awarded to a plaintiff in a lawsuit based on loss or injury caused by the defendant. —See also COMPENSATORY DAMAGES.

D&B A major source of information for businesses on credit, risk management, supply management, and sales and marketing. The firm maintains a corporate database for use by clients. —Formerly called *Dun & Bradstreet.* —See also D-U-N-S NUMBER.

D&O coverage —See DIRECTORS' AND OFFICERS' LIABILITY INSURANCE.

database A structured collection of information that can be easily accessed and managed. For example, a library is likely to have a database for its book collection that allows individuals to call up books by title, author, or subject.

database management Creating, updating, managing, and utilizing a database.

database marketing Targeting prospective and current customers using information that has been accumulated in a database. For example, a company uses a database of customer purchasing history to target advertising for a new project.

data encryption —See ENCRYPTION.

data mining Analyzing a large database in an effort to identify relationships that can be used to develop predictive models with commercial applications. For example, a credit card company analyzes years of data for credit transactions in an attempt to identify customers most likely to default.

dated date The date on which a newly issued bond begins to accrue interest. The buyer of a bond in the primary market must pay the issuer interest accruing between the dated date and the settlement date in addition to the principal amount of bonds purchased. This additional interest is returned to the buyer when the issuer makes the first interest payment. —Also called *issue date.*

date of acquisition For accounting and tax purposes, the effective purchase date of an asset.

date of issue The date on which a security is issued and begins trading.

date of record —See RECORD DATE.

dating Extending the period during which a customer can pay an account.

DAX The leading German index of equity prices based on the 30 most heavily traded stocks on the Frankfurt Stock Exchange.

day loan A one-day loan made by a bank to a broker for the purchase of securities. The loan is used until delivery allows a regular call loan to be arranged.

day order A customer order to buy or sell a security that will expire automatically at the end of the trading day on which it is entered. A day order is used when a customer prefers to reconsider an order that is not executed on the day it was placed. —See also GOOD-TILL-CANCELED ORDER.

day trade A trade opened and closed on the same trading day. A purchase and sale of the same security on the same day is an example of a day trade. Likewise, a short sale followed by a covering purchase on the same day is a day trade.

day trader A speculator who buys and sells securities on the basis of small short-term price movements. Day traders are thought to add a measure of liquidity to the market.

DBA 1. —See DOING BUSINESS AS. 2. —See DOCTOR OF BUSINESS ADMINISTRATION.

deadbeat 1. A person who fails to meet a financial obligation. 2. Someone who exhibits little effort.

dead cat bounce A sharp, and likely temporary, rise in the market price of a stock following an extensive decline.

dead-end job Employment with little prospect of development or advancement. Manual labor in a chicken-processing plant is an example of an unpleasant dead-end job.

dead hand poison pill A special type of poison-pill antitakeover defense in which only ousted directors can rescind the poison pill. Poison-pill plans are put in place in order to make a hostile takeover prohibitively expensive by issuing a huge number of new shares.

deadhead A commercial vehicle traveling without passengers or cargo. For example, a truck may drive empty to Florida in order to pick up a load of oranges.

dead letter An undeliverable letter that cannot be returned to the sender.

deadline The last date on which some action must be taken. For example, a bill must be paid or a project must be completed.

dealer 1. An individual or a firm that buys securities for and sells securities from its own portfolio as opposed to bringing buyers and sellers together. In practice, many firms operate as broker-dealers and perform both services, depending on the market conditions and on the size, type, and security involved in a particular transaction. —Compare BROKER 1. 2. A person or organization that buys for and sells from its own account. For example, an art dealer buys paintings for resale. 3. A business that maintains an inventory of goods offered for resale. For example, an appliance dealer stocks major appliances it offers for sale to the public.

dealer bank A commercial bank that buys and sells municipal securities and/or U.S. government and agency securities.

dealer loan A short-term, secured bank loan to a security dealer for the purpose of financing inventory.

dealer market A market in which securities are bought and sold through a network of dealers who buy, sell, and take positions in various security issues. —Compare AUCTION MARKET; OPEN OUTCRY.

dealer paper Commercial paper that is sold by original issuers through dealers who wholesale the paper to its ultimate buyers. Individual investors are usually excluded from trading in dealer paper because of the size of the investment required, usually a minimum of $250,000. —Compare DIRECT PAPER.

death benefit Funds payable to beneficiaries of a deceased person's life insurance policy or pension. —See also ADVANCE DEATH BENEFIT.

death spiral 1. The deteriorating financial condition and associated stock price of a cash-starved company that can raise capital only under the most onerous of terms. Restrictions and high interest charges on new capital cause the company to end up in an even worse financial position. **2.** The deteriorating financial condition of an insurance plan caused by changes in the plan's covered population. For example, a health insurance plan with few restrictions for applicants is likely to attract poor risks at the same time that healthy individuals look elsewhere. **3.** The financial condition of a debtor who must borrow additional funds in order to meet interest obligations on existing debt.

death tax 1. —See ESTATE TAX. **2.** —See INHERITANCE TAX.

debenture A corporate bond that is not secured by specific property. In the event that the issuer is liquidated, the holder of a debenture becomes a general creditor and therefore is less likely than the secured creditors to recover in full. Because of their high risk factor, debentures pay higher rates of interest than secured debt of the same issuer. —See also SUBORDINATED DEBENTURE.

debit An accounting entry that results in an increase in assets or a decrease in liabilities or owners' equity. —Compare CREDIT 2.

debit card A plastic card that may be used for purchasing goods and services or for obtaining cash advances for which payment is made from existing funds in a bank account. Debit cards are handier than writing checks, and can be used either for PIN-based online transactions or offline transactions requiring a signature. From a consumer's standpoint, a debit card is generally a less desirable method of payment than a credit card, which offers longer float and better rewards.

> **CASE STUDY** Debit cards, often called "check cards," have rapidly replaced checks and cash as a means of paying for consumer purchases. The popularity is due in large part to banks heavily promoting a very profitable product. Use of a debit card allows the issuing bank to earn a fee from the accepting merchant without being required to process a check or wait on payment. Debit cardholders often don't realize they face more risk than holders of credit cards. Unauthorized use can produce substantial losses when a debit card is lost or stolen, because liability is limited to $50 only if the cardholder notifies the issuing bank within two days of learning of fraudulent use. The liability can be $500 or more after two days and up to the amount of the fraudulent use in some instances. In comparison, consumer liability for credit card fraud is limited to $50. If fraudulent use involves use of the credit card number but not a loss of the card itself, there is no liability for unauthorized use. In addition, credit card users are permitted to dispute a charge and withhold payment pending an investigation of the disputed transaction by the issuer. Purchases with a debit card come directly from the cardholder's bank account, so payment will already have taken place if the cardholder wishes to question the transaction. Thus, the cardholder must battle with the

issuing bank for the return of the money. In the meantime, fraudulent use of the card that drains an account may result in bounced checks and accompanying fees levied by the issuing bank. Consumers should also keep in mind that rental car companies generally will not accept a debit card payment as a security deposit for a rental vehicle.

debt —See LIABILITY 1.

debt-based asset An investment in the debt of another party. Savings accounts, bonds, annuities, and certificates of deposit are all debt-based assets, because they represent debt of the issuer. Debt-based assets are generally conservative investments that pay a fairly predictable rate of return.

debt capacity The extent to which an individual or organization can use borrowed funds and maintain an ability to meet debt-service requirements. —Also called *capacity.*

debt coverage —See DEBT MANAGEMENT RATIO.

debt-discharge income Income attributed to a borrower resulting from debt forgiveness by a lender. For example, when a lender forgives a third of the balance on an outstanding debt of $15,000, the borrower has debt-discharge income of $5,000. Debt-discharge income is generally, but not always, taxable, and the borrower should receive a Form 1099-C from the lender.

debt financing The acquisition of funds by borrowing. For example, a business may use debt financing to raise funds for building a new factory. Corporations find debt financing attractive because the interest paid on borrowed funds is a tax-deductible expense. —Compare EQUITY FINANCING.

debt limit The statutory maximum amount of debt that a municipality may have outstanding.

debt management The regulation of the size and handling of the structure of the public debt. Actions taken to manage the debt have significant effects on the financial markets because government securities compete with private securities for limited funds in the capital market.

debt management ratio A measure of the extent to which a firm uses borrowed funds to finance its operations. Owners and creditors are interested in debt management ratios because the ratios indicate the riskiness of the firm's position. —Also called *debt coverage.* —See also DEBT RATIO; DEBT-TO-EQUITY RATIO; FIXED-CHARGE COVERAGE.

debtor An individual or organization that owes a debt or has an obligation to another party. —Compare CREDITOR.

debtor in possession A company that continues to operate while in Chapter 11 bankruptcy.

debtor in possession financing Financing arranged during the time a company is in Chapter 11 bankruptcy.

debt ratio The proportion of a firm's total assets that is being financed with borrowed funds. The debt ratio is calculated by dividing total long-term and short-term liabilities by total assets. For example, a firm with assets of $1,000,000 and $150,000 in short-term debts and $300,000 in long-term debts has a debt ratio of $450,000/$1,000,000, or 45%. A low debt ratio indicates conservative financing with an opportunity to borrow in the future at no significant risk. —Compare BOND RATIO.

debt restructuring An exchange of one or more new debt issues for outstanding debt issues that can be made when the new issues have interest rates and/or maturities that differ from those of the outstanding issues. For example, a firm might offer holders of 9% coupon bonds with 5 years to maturity a new bond with a higher coupon rate and a 25-year maturity. Creditors having difficulty making interest and/or principal payments often restructure their debt to reduce the size of the interest payments and to extend debt maturity. —Compare RESTRUCTURING. —Also called *troubled debt restructuring.*

debt retirement Reduction in the principal amount of a debt.

debt security A security representing borrowed funds that must be repaid. Examples of debt securities include bonds, certificates of deposit, commercial paper, and debentures.

debt service Funds required to meet interest expenses, principal payments, and sinking fund requirements during a specific period. A firm's ability to service its debt is estimated by comparing cash flow with debt service.

debt-to-equity ratio The relationship between long-term funds provided by creditors and funds provided by owners. A firm's debt-to-equity ratio is calculated by dividing long-term debt by owners' equity. A high debt-to-equity ratio, which indicates very aggressive financing or a history of large losses, results in very volatile earnings. A low debt-to-equity ratio indicates conservative financing and low risk.

debt warrant A security that allows the holder to buy additional bonds from the issuer at the same price and yield as the initial bond.

decedent A person who has died.

December effect The tendency of stock prices to move upward during the last month of the year. Historical statistics indicate December is the strongest month of the year for stock prices.

decentralization Distributing power and decision making among different people, departments, or locations within an organization. For example, a national retail chain may allow its store managers to make decisions on the merchandise that will be carried in their particular stores.

deceptive advertising Material representation, omission, or practice that is likely to mislead consumers who act rationally. The Federal Trade Commission has primary responsibility for regulating advertising in the United States.

decertification Revocation of the right of an individual or organization to pursue some activity or to represent some group. For example, workers who wished to be represented by a rival union might submit a petition for decertification to the Agricultural Labor Relations Board.

decision matrix A chart comparing options and criteria that is designed to help identify an optimal solution. For example, a business considering the introduction of several new products (the options) identifies and weights various considerations (the criteria, including projected sales, costs, legal difficulties, etc.) that are important in evaluating the various alternatives. Relative weights are often assigned to each of the criteria.

decision support system An interactive computer-based system that supports and improves the process of decision making.

decision tree A graphical representation of sequential decisions and their potential outcomes. A decision tree is used to evaluate the likely consequences of several different courses of action.

declaration date The date on which a firm's directors meet to announce the date and amount of the next dividend. Following the declaration, dividends become a legal liability of the firm. —See also EX-DIVIDEND DATE; INTEREST DATES; RECORD DATE.

declaration of estimated tax The return that must be filed by a taxpayer whose amount of tax withheld is less than his or her estimated tax liability for the year.

declaration of trust A written document creating and setting the terms of a trust, including the purpose, creators, trustee, trustee's powers, and beneficiaries.

declaratory judgment A civil court decision informing the parties of their rights and responsibilities, but without requiring any action or awarding damages to the plaintiff. For example, an insurance company may seek a declaratory judgment to a defense to coverage.

declare 1. To authorize a dividend formally. A declared dividend becomes a liability of the business until it is paid. **2.** To state to customs officials articles that are being brought into the country. **3.** To state income when completing a tax return.

declared dividend A dividend authorized by a firm's board of directors. At the time a dividend is declared, the firm creates a liability for the dividend's payment.

decline A decrease in the value of an asset or some other variable. For example, a recession represents a decline in economic activity.

declining-balance method A system for calculating depreciation in which a constant percentage is applied to the undepreciated (book) value of an asset. For example, an asset with a life of five years is depreciated at a rate of 20% (one fifth) of the undepreciated value each year.

decree A judgment or sentence of the court.

dedication —See PORTFOLIO DEDICATION.

deductible 1. The amount of claims that must be paid by the insured before any payments will be made by the insurance company. —See also DISAPPEARING DEDUCTIBLE. **2.** An expense that may be used to reduce taxable income.

deduction An expenditure that may legally be used to reduce an individual's income-tax liability. Potential deductions include charitable contributions, mortgage interest expense, state and local income taxes, and property taxes. —Also called *itemized deduction; tax deduction; tax shield.* —See also CHARITABLE CONTRIBUTION DEDUCTION; STANDARD DEDUCTION.

deed A written document for transferring real property. —See also QUITCLAIM DEED.

deed in lieu A deed given by a borrower to a lender, generally in exchange for forgoing foreclosure. A lender accepting a deed in lieu of foreclosure becomes the new owner and is responsible for any other outstanding liens on the property.

deed of gift A document transferring property without monetary compensation. —Also called *gift deed.*

deed of trust An official document recorded in land records that transfers title to real property to a trustee that holds the deed as security for a loan. The deed of trust describes what constitutes a default, in which case the trustee can sell the property in order to pay the lender. The deed is transferred to the borrower when the loan is repaid. —Also called *trust deed.*

---

deed restriction

How do I find out about possible deed restrictions that are applicable to a home I am interested in buying?

Reviewing the text of the deed to the property will alert you to any restrictions that apply to your next home. Deeds can be accessed online in most jurisdictions and you may also search the title manually by visiting your local county registry of deeds office. Before purchasing the house, it would be wise to check the title abstract, which will show details of deeds going back at least 50 years, to make sure that restrictions placed on the property 20 years ago, for example, were not omitted from the current deed.

■ Joan A. Koffman, Esq., Real Estate Attorney, Koffman & Dreyer, Newton, MA

---

deed restriction A clause in a deed that limits the use of real property. For example, a deed restriction may require that any home built on a property be of a minimum size or larger. Deed restrictions are common in subdivisions.

deep-discount bond 1. A long-term debt security that, because of a low coupon rate of interest compared with current rates of interest, sells at a substantial discount from face value. —See also MUNICIPAL CONVERTIBLE; ZERO-COUPON BOND. **2.** —See ORIGINAL-ISSUE DISCOUNT BOND.

deep-in-the-money —Used to describe a call (put) option that has a strike price considerably less (more) than the market price of the underlying stock. A deep-in-the-money option is almost certain to be exercised on or before its expiration.

deep market A market for a security in which there are numerous sizable bids and offers. A deep market for a security provides an investor in that security with more liquidity. —Compare THIN MARKET; TIGHT MARKET 2.

deep-out-of-the-money 1. —Used to describe a call option with a strike price significantly above the market price of the underlying asset. A deep-out-of-the-money call option sells at a low price because in all likelihood it will expire without value. **2.** —Used to describe a put option with a strike price significantly below the market price of the underlying asset. A deep-out-of-the-money put option sells at a low price because in all likelihood it will expire without value.

deep pockets Describing an organization that enjoys substantial financial resources. A lawsuit brought against a small company may include other large organizations as defendants because their deep pockets offer the possibility of a large recovery.

de facto Latin for "in fact." For example, a company may offer such a widely used product that the product becomes the de facto standard of the industry. The product is not officially recognized as the standard, but in practice the product is the standard. —Compare DE JURE.

defalcation Misappropriation of trust funds or funds held in any fiduciary capacity. Defalcation includes innocent as well as intentional or negligent misappropriation. Thus, a fiduciary may be guilty of defalcation without having intent to defraud.

default The failure to live up to the terms of a contract. Generally, default is used to indicate the inability of a borrower to pay the interest or principal on a debt when it is due. —See also TECHNICAL DEFAULT.

default judgment A decision awarded to a plaintiff in a case that is uncontested by the defendant within the time set by law. The defendant in a default judgment must show a valid excuse when requesting that the judgment be set aside.

default risk The possibility that a borrower will be unable to meet interest and/or principal repayment obligations on a loan agreement. Default risk has a significant effect on the value of a bond: if a borrower's ability to repay debt is impaired, default risk is higher and the value of the bond will decline.

defeasance The extinguishment of debt. While defeasance technically refers to extinguishment by any method (for example, by payment to the creditor), in practice it is generally used to mean discharging debt by presenting a portfolio of securities (usually Treasury obligations) to a trustee who will use the cash flow to service the old debt. This procedure permits the firm to wipe the debt off its financial statements and to show extra income equal to the difference between the old debt and the smaller new debt. —Also called *in-substance debt defeasance.*

defeasible title A title to real property that under certain conditions may be voided. For example, a title to a house may be conveyed to a child with the condition that if the child moves out of the house before age 40, the title will be conveyed to a different person.

defective title A title that, because of a flaw, fails to transfer ownership. The title may have a faulty property description or lack an element necessary for a good title.

defendant —See RESPONDENT 1.

defense of property A claim by a defendant that he or she should not be held liable because the action was taken in defense of the defendant's premises or personal property. For example, a homeowner who has suffered several robberies sets a trap inside the home that injures someone who has entered the home illegally. The homeowner is sued and claims defense of property.

defensive acquisition A firm or an asset purchased by a potential target of a takeover in order to make itself less desirable to raiders. For example, a target company might purchase another firm engaged in the same business as the raider in order to create an antitrust problem for the raider. —See also RAIDER; TARGET COMPANY.

CASE STUDY In late 2006, French electronic equipment manufacturer Schneider Electric agreed to pay $6.1 billion for American Power Conversion, a U.S. manufacturer of power supplies for electronic gear. Schneider's CEO said the acquisition was part of the firm's strategic plan, but many investors believed Schneider Electric paid too high a price for the U.S. firm. At $31 per share, the purchase price was 30% above APC's market price immediately prior to the offer and nearly double its price of two months earlier. It turned out that several months before the agreement to purchase APC, three private equity firms had expressed an interest in acquiring Schneider. Thus, while Schneider's acquisition of American Power Conversion may have been part of the firm's strategic plan, it was also a defensive acquisition that made it less likely Schneider itself would become the target of another firm.

defensive stock A stock that is resistant to general stock market declines. Stocks of electric utilities, gold and silver producers, and some consumer goods companies are considered defensive. Although defensive stocks resist downturns, they generally move up more slowly than other stocks during bull markets.

deferment period The period following the issue of a security during which it cannot be called by the issuer. —Also called *deferred call period; preferred call period.* —See also CALL PROTECTION.

---

deferred annuity

I've been told that deferred annuities often impose high fees and tend to be poor investments. Who might benefit from buying one of these?

Fees associated with deferred annuities can be high. The front-end cost, and any annual fees, must be weighed against the long-term benefit of the annuity. Typically, deferred annuities do not require that you pay taxes on accumulated income until you take the money out of the annuity. If you are trying to minimize taxes, a deferred annuity might be to your advantage. If you want a guaranteed income after retirement, or if you want to provide a guaranteed income for a loved one, the feeling of safety and assurance might be considered against the costs associated with buying the annuity.

■ Michael W. Butler, PhD, Professor of Economics, Angelo State University, San Angelo, Texas

---

deferral of taxes —See TAX DEFERRAL.

deferred account An account that defers taxes to a future time. An IRA is an example of a deferred account.

deferred annuity An annuity that is not scheduled to begin payments until a given date. These annuities may be purchased with a single payment or, as is more often the case, with a series of periodic payments. Deferred annuities are most commonly purchased by individuals who make periodic payments during their working lives in order to receive monthly or annual income payments from the annuities during their retirement. —Compare IMMEDIATE ANNUITY. —Also called *deferred-payment annuity.* —See also LONGEVITY INSURANCE; PERIODIC PURCHASE DEFERRED CONTRACT; SINGLE-PREMIUM DEFERRED ANNUITY.

deferred billing Delaying an invoice to a credit customer, generally until the good or service has been received.

deferred call period —See DEFERMENT PERIOD.

deferred charge An expenditure treated as an asset because it is expected to produce benefits in future periods. For example, expenses in establishing a business are treated as an asset and amortized over several years.

deferred compensation Compensation that is being earned but not received, a process that defers the taxes on the compensation until it is actually received. Deferred compensation includes various plans, some being pensions, profit-sharing, and stock options.

deferred contracts Futures contracts that settle in months beyond the closest current trading month.

deferred credit —See DEFERRED INCOME.

deferred gain A realized gain on which tax is deferred to a future period. Prior to May 7, 1997, realized gains on the sale of a personal residence could be deferred if the next house bought was more expensive than the house that was sold.

deferred group annuity A retirement plan in which a single-payment deferred annuity is purchased for each member of a group, so that each member will receive a lifetime income beginning on a specified date.

deferred income Income received by a business but not yet reported as earned. For example, a business may receive payment for a service or a product that has not yet been delivered. Deferred income is treated as a liability until reported as income earned. —Also called *deferred credit.*

deferred income tax A liability created by income recognized for accounting purposes but not for tax purposes. The liability recognizes future taxes due when earned income is later reported for tax purposes. The use of accelerated depreciation for reporting to the Internal Revenue Service and straight-line depreciation for reporting to stockholders is one of the major reasons a firm includes deferred income taxes as a liability on its balance sheet.

deferred-interest bond A bond that does not pay interest for a specified period, typically three to ten years. At the end of the initial period, the interest payments on the bond begin in accordance with its coupon rate. Deferred-interest bonds generally sell at steep discounts to par during a period of deferred interest.

deferred liability A liability that usually would have been paid but is now past due.

deferred maintenance Repairs or upgrades that are deferred to a future budget period or until funding becomes available.

deferred-payment annuity —See DEFERRED ANNUITY.

deferred premium option An option requiring payment of the premium at maturity rather than on the purchase date. The premium is paid whether or not the option is exercised. —Also called *Boston option.*

deferred-prosecution agreement A voluntary alternative to adjudication in which a prosecutor agrees to grand amnesty in return for the defendant abiding by certain requirements. For example, a case of corporate fraud may be settled using a deferred-prosecution agreement in which the defendant agrees to pay fines, enact corporate reforms, and fully cooperate with the investigation. Fulfilling the requirements will result in dismissal of the charges.

CASE STUDY In August 2005, accounting firm KPMG admitted that it had engaged in selling improper tax shelters that generated $11 billion in illegal tax losses and cost the U.S. government over $2.5 billion in lost tax revenues. The firm also admitted its employees took steps to conceal the existence of the shelters by failing to register them with the IRS. As part of an agreement with the U.S. Department of Justice, KPMG was required to pay a $456 million fine, terminate some its operations, implement a compliance and ethics program, install an independent monitor, and fully cooperate with a criminal investigation of the firm's practices. KPMG's agreement was part of a deferred-prosecution agreement in which the government's criminal charge was deferred until the end of the following year if the specified conditions were met. KPMG was desperate to avoid a criminal indictment that was likely to result in a business collapse similar to the one that befell Arthur Anderson in the wake of the Enron Corporation failure. A federal judge agreed in January 2007 to dismiss the deferred criminal charge against the company, although 17 of its former executives had been criminally charged. A federal judge dismissed charges against 13 former employees in July 2007 because the government had violated the defendants' rights by forcing KPMG into not paying their legal fees.

deferred retirement Continuing employment with the same employer beyond the earliest retirement date.

deferred sales charge A fee levied by some open-end investment companies on shareholder redemptions and by many insurance companies on annuities. The charge, of up to 5% of the value of the shares being redeemed, frequently varies inversely with the period of time the shares have been owned. A deferred sales charge is indicated in mutual fund transaction tables in newspapers by the symbol *r.* —Also called *back-end load; exit fee; redemption fee.* —See also CONTINGENT DEFERRED SALES CHARGE.

deficiency 1. The amount by which an individual's or an organization's tax liability as computed by the Internal Revenue Service exceeds the tax liability reported by the taxpayer. **2.** The amount by which a firm's liabilities exceed assets.

deficiency judgment A court order authorizing a lender to collect the portion of a debt that has not been satisfied by the sale of collateral. For example, a bank may sell a car that has been repossessed because the borrower defaulted on the loan. If the sale price is less than the remaining balance on the loan, the bank will obtain a deficiency judgment for the difference.

deficiency letter A letter from the SEC indicating disapproval of one or more aspects of a security issuer's registration statement.

deficit 1. A negative retained earnings balance. A deficit results when the accumulated losses and dividend payments of a business exceed its earnings. **2.** An excess of government spending compared to revenues. **3.** An excess of the value of a country's imports compared to the value of its exports. **4.** A shortage in something. For example, harsh weather may cause an oil company to suffer a production deficit. **5.** —See OPERATING LOSS.

deficit financing The sale of debt securities in order to finance expenditures that are in excess of income. Generally, deficit financing is applied to government finance because income, represented by tax revenues and fees, is often unavailable to pay expenses. As with monetizing the debt, deficit financing puts upward pressure on interest rates, because government debt securities compete with private securities for limited capital.

deficit net worth —See NEGATIVE NET WORTH.

deficit spending Expenditures that are in excess of revenues during a given period. Deficit spending is generally applied to governmental units, but the concept is equally applicable to private businesses.

defined-asset fund An investment trust with a fixed portfolio of assets that generally has a defined lifetime, at the end of which the trust assets are liquidated.

defined-benefit pension plan A pension plan in which retirement benefits rather than contributions into the plan are specified. Thus, a retired employee who has reached a certain age with a given number of years of service and has earned a certain income is entitled to a specific monthly pension payment.

> **CASE STUDY** The defined-benefit pension plan is a retirement program in rapid decline as businesses shift the risk of adequate employee retirement from themselves to their workers. According to *CFO* magazine, the percentage of full-time employees of large and midsize firms that participate in defined-benefit plans declined from 80% in 1985 to 33% by the end of 2003. Businesses shifted their employees to defined-contribution plans without guaranteed retirement benefits or dropped retirement plans altogether. Two events

in 2006 accelerated the move to drop defined-benefit pension plans. The Financial Accounting Standards Board issued rules that require plan sponsors to include pension assets and liabilities in the body of their financial statements rather than as footnotes. This change increases the transparency of future pension liabilities. In addition, the Pension Protection Act of 2006 requires stiffer funding requirements and high premiums for government pension insurance.

defined-contribution pension plan A pension plan in which an employer's periodic payments into the plan, rather than eventual retirement benefits to employees, are specified. For example, a defined-contribution pension plan may require an employer to contribute 5% of its employees' gross pay into a fund, with contributions earmarked for each employee upon retirement.

deflation A reduction in consumer or wholesale prices. The term generally applies to more than just a temporary decline. —Compare INFLATION. —See also DISINFLATION.

deflationary gap The amount by which the economy's aggregate demand is below full employment output. A substantial deflationary gap is likely to spur the Federal Reserve to reduce interest rates in an attempt to stimulate the economy.

deflator A statistical measure used to adjust prices for inflation. For example, the GDP deflator adjusts the current level of gross domestic product for changes in purchasing power subsequent to a base year.

defunct Describing a business or other organization that no longer exists. Surprisingly, the stocks of defunct companies sometimes trade in public markets.

deindustrialization A shift in an economy from producing goods to producing services. Such a shift is most likely to occur in mature economies such as that of the United States. This shift has considerable impact on investors' views of the attractiveness of various industries.

de jure A Latin term for "of the law." —Used to indicate something is correct according to the law. —Compare DE FACTO.

delayed convertible A security with a conversion feature that does not come into effect until a specified date.

delayed opening An intentional delay in the opening transaction of a particular security. Generally the delay occurs when unexpected developments before the opening make it difficult for the specialist to match buy and sell orders.

delayed settlement The transfer of a security or cash at a date beyond the usual settlement date. A seller may prefer delayed settlement in order to be listed on a firm's books on the record date for a dividend.

del credere risk The possibility a buyer or guarantor will be unable or unwilling to make payment.

delegate 1. To authorize someone as a representative. 2. To assign a task.

deleverage A reduction in the use of fixed-cost financing, generally in an effort to reduce risk. For example, a company repays debt with proceeds from the sale of a subsidiary. —Compare LEVERAGE.

delinquency Failure of a borrower to make a scheduled payment on a loan.

delinquency rate The dollar amount of loans past due as a percentage of the dollar amount of loans in a portfolio. The delinquency rate is sometimes calculated on the basis of the number of loans delinquent rather than the dollar amount of loans past due. The delinquency rate is a measure of the proportion of a loan portfolio that is at risk.

delinquent Describing a loan on which payment is overdue.

delist To drop a security from trading on an organized exchange. Delisting may occur for a number of reasons, including failure to meet an exchange's standards or placement of a new listing on another exchange. —Compare LIST 1.

deliver To relinquish possession of an asset for transfer to another party.

delivery 1. The transfer of a security to an investor's broker in order to satisfy an executed sell order. Delivery is required by the settlement date. **2.** The transfer of a specified commodity in order to meet the requirements of a commodity contract that has been sold. **3.** The transfer of property from one party to another party.

delivery day 1. In futures trading, the day on which delivery of the asset is to be made according to the quantity, quality, and location specified in the contract. **2.** The date on which something is to be delivered by the seller to the buyer.

delivery notice 1. In futures trading, a notice that the party having sold (short) a contract intends to make delivery of the commodity in settlement of its terms. The quantity, quality, and point of delivery are designated by the exchange. —Also called *transfer notice.* **2.** Notice by a seller to a buyer that delivery has taken place or will take place on a specified date.

delivery versus payment (DVP) In securities trading, a settlement procedure in which a customer instructs that he or she will make immediate payment upon delivery of the purchased security. —Compare RECEIVE VERSUS PAYMENT. —Also called *cash on delivery.*

Delphi technique A forecasting procedure in which a series of questions and the resulting feedback are used to reach a group consensus. For example, each person in a group is asked to submit an estimate of the next year's inflation rate. The results are tallied and conveyed to participants who are then asked to submit another estimate. The process continues until a general consensus results.

demand The desire and ability to purchase a good or service at a particular price during a specified period. —Compare SUPPLY[1]. —See also LATENT DEMAND.

demand curve A graphical representation of the quantity demanded of a good or service at various prices. The demand curve generally slopes downward, indicating fewer units being demanded at higher prices. —Compare SUPPLY CURVE.

demand density The extent to which demand for a good or service is concentrated within a particular zip code, area code, or some other geographic region.

demand deposit A checking account balance held at a financial institution. Because demand deposits constitute one of the most important segments of the nation's money supply, the financial community closely monitors their size. —Compare TIME DEPOSIT. —See also M1.

demand loan A loan due at any time the lender decides to request payment. —Also called *demand note.*

demand note —See DEMAND LOAN.

demand-pull inflation Rising consumer prices resulting from the demand for goods and services exceeding supply. Demand-pull inflation is likely to enhance corporate profits because businesses are able to increase the prices they charge without incurring corresponding increases in their costs. —Compare COST-PUSH INFLATION.

demarketing The attempt to discourage demand for a product or service. Demarketing may target overall demand or demand from a specific market segment. For example, a governmental authority in a region experiencing a drought utilizes public service announcements in an attempt to convince residents to conserve water.

demerit good A good or service that policymakers feel is likely to be overconsumed and should be taxed or restricted in some manner. For example, tobacco products are generally considered demerit goods, justifying a host of taxes that reduce consumption. —Compare MERIT GOOD.

Deming Cycle A continuous quality-improvement model developed by W. Edwards Deming in which a sequence of the four repetitive steps (plan, do, check, and act) comprise a feedback loop that allows a business manager to identify and correct deficiencies.

de minimis Latin for "of trifling importance." In practice, something so inconsequential that no corrective action will be taken. For example, an individual may underpay taxes by such a small amount the tax authority doesn't follow up with a notice of taxes due.

demographics Statistical analysis of the characteristics and behavior of population groups. For example, a retailer will consider the demographics of a particular city or county in deciding whether to build a new store.

demonetization Abandonment of something as legal tender. Gold was demonetized in the United States in 1971.

demurrage 1. Detainment of a cargo transport beyond its scheduled departure. 2. Compensation for detaining cargo transport beyond its scheduled departure.

demurrer In law, a court request that a lawsuit have no legal claim and that it be dismissed. For example, a neighbor might dislike you having a dog in your backyard and sue in court. If there is no law against keeping dogs, you would file a demurrer and request a hearing.

denomination 1. The face value of a security. For bonds, it is usually $1,000 ($5,000 for municipals) or multiples thereof, and for stock it is the par value. 2. The face value of currency.

density zoning An ordinance that restricts the number of dwelling units that can be constructed on an acre of land.

department 1. A specialized unit of an organization. 2. A department store area that focuses on a particular line of products. For example, the electronics department sells televisions, computers, DVD players, and so forth.

departmentalize 1. To assign specific tasks or knowledge to separate individuals or groups of individuals. An organization may attempt to improve security by departmentalizing segments of an ongoing project. 2. To divide an organization into separate units. For example, a company may have a finance department, marketing department, and so forth.

Department of the Treasury, U.S. The federal agency charged with overseeing the U.S. economy and financial markets. The department advises the President on economic and financial issues, promotes the administration's growth agenda, and attempts to enhance corporate governance in financial institutions. —Also called *Treasury Department*.

department store A large retail store, generally part of a large chain, whose floor space is organized by categories of merchandise or services.

dependent A person who relies on another for support. For tax purposes, the IRS requires that a dependent meet specific standards in order to be classified as a qualifying child or qualifying relative.

dependent care credit —See CHILD AND DEPENDENT CARE CREDIT.

dependent coverage Medical and dental insurance protection provided to qualifying dependents of the insured. Dependent coverage is generally available only at extra cost to the insured.

dependent variable A variable affected by another variable or by a certain event. For example, a stock's price is a dependent variable affected by dividend payments, earnings projections, interest rates, and many other things. —Compare INDEPENDENT VARIABLE.

depletion The periodic cost assigned for a reduction in the quantity and indicated value of a natural resource such as a mineral deposit or timber. Thus, depletion indicates an activity such as harvesting or mining a natural resource. —See also COST DEPLETION; DEPRECIATION 1; PERCENTAGE DEPLETION.

deposit 1. Payment as part of an obligation. **2.** Funds placed in an account at a financial institution. **3.** Money offered as a guarantee. For example, a new homeowner may be required to provide a deposit with the electric company before service is turned on. **4.** Accumulation of a mineral. For example, a mining company may discover a deposit of gold.

depositary receipt A negotiable certificate that represents a company's publicly traded debt or equity. Depositary receipts are created when a company's shares or bonds are delivered to a depositary's custodian bank, which instructs the depositary to issue the receipts. Depositary receipts facilitate trading of foreign securities. —See also AMERICAN DEPOSITARY RECEIPT.

deposit insurance 1. —See FEDERAL DEPOSIT INSURANCE CORPORATION. **2.** —See SECURITIES INVESTOR PROTECTION CORPORATION.

deposition Sworn testimony of a witness prior to a trial. Depositions are taken out of court and without the presence of a judge.

deposit note —See CALLABLE CD.

depository —See SECURITY DEPOSITORY.

depository institution A financial institution that makes loans and obtains most of its funds from deposits made by the public. Examples include commercial banks, credit unions, savings banks, and savings and loan associations.

Depository Trust Company (DTC) A national depository for security certificates that records, maintains, and transfers securities for member firms. The DTC seeks to reduce the movement of certificates by arranging for computerized transfers.

depreciable Of, relating to, or being a long-term tangible asset that is subject to depreciation.

depreciable life In taxation, the period during which the cost of an asset may be recovered through depreciation. For example, personal property such as appliances and automobiles are considered to have a depreciable life of five years.

depreciate To reduce the value of a long-term tangible asset.

depreciated cost —See BOOK VALUE 1.

depreciation 1. The periodic cost assigned for the reduction in usefulness and value of a long-term tangible asset. Because firms can use several types of depreciation, the amount of depreciation recorded on corporate financial statements may or may not be a good indication of an asset's reduction in value. Depreciation not only affects the asset's value as stated on the balance sheet, it also affects the amount of reported earnings. —Also called *expense*. —See also ACCELERATED COST RECOVERY SYSTEM; ACCELERATED DEPRECIATION; ACCUMULATED DEPRECIATION; RECAPTURE OF DEPRECIATION 1; STRAIGHT-LINE DEPRECIATION. 2. A decline in the value of a currency in relation to other currencies. For example, the dollar may suffer depreciation against the euro, meaning that more dollars are required to purchase a given amount of euros.

depreciation recapture —See RECAPTURE OF DEPRECIATION 1.

depreciation reserve —See ACCUMULATED DEPRECIATION.

depressed Of or relating to a security, product, or market in which demand is weak and price continues to decline.

depression A sharp and extended period of declining economic activity, generally characterized by high levels of unemployment and relatively stable or declining price levels.

deregulate To reduce or eliminate control. One of the major forces in the financial markets in the 1970s and 1980s was the federal government's decision to deregulate interest rates. The commissions charged to investors on security trades were deregulated in 1975.

deregulation The act of removing controls from some sector of the economy. In nearly all cases, deregulation of a given industry has both positive and negative implications for investors. Typically, firms in a strong financial position benefit from deregulation, while firms in a weak financial position suffer.

derivative An asset that derives its value from another asset. For example, a call option on the stock of Coca-Cola is a derivative security that obtains value from the shares of Coca-Cola that can be purchased with the call option. Call options, put options, convertible bonds, futures contracts, and convertible preferred stock are examples of derivatives. A derivative can be either a risky or low-risk investment, depending on the type of derivative and how it is used. —See also UNDERLYING ASSET 2.

derivative suit —See STOCKHOLDER DERIVATIVE SUIT.

derived demand The demand for a good or service that results from the demand for another good or service. For example, the demand for pine trees is derived, in part, from the demand for newsprint. —Compare PRIMARY DEMAND 1.

descent Acquisition of property by means of inheritance.

descent and distribution statute State law that stipulates how estate assets are to be distributed when the deceased has no will. Distribution is typically based on the relationship to the deceased. —Also called *intestacy law*. —See also INTESTATE SUCCESSION.

> **CASE STUDY** Not having a valid will may result in a person's estate being distributed in a manner other than which the person desires. Without a will, the descent and distribution statute in the deceased's state of residence determines how the estate's assets are distributed. Ohio law stipulates intestate estates be distributed entirely to a surviving spouse, even when there are surviving children or surviving descendants of deceased children. Illinois law requires that a surviving spouse receive only half the estate when there are

surviving children of the decedent. The remaining half is distributed to the deceased's children, regardless of the number of children. A surviving widow and children of the deceased also share fifty-fifty in South Carolina. The various statutes become more complicated when surviving heirs are more distant from the immediate family. For example, in Illinois, if there is no surviving spouse, descendant, parent, sister, brother, descendant of a brother or sister, grandparent, or descendant of a grandparent, the estate is split between the survivors of the descendant's maternal great-grandparents and paternal great-grandparents.

descriptive statistics The branch of statistics that describes the basic features of a set of data. For example, suppose a researcher has collected a large amount of historical data on the stock market. A descriptive statistic might be that over the last 20 years stocks have offered investors an average annual return of 10%. The statistic is easy to understand, but may be misleading. —Compare INFERENTIAL STATISTICS.

desk —See TRADING DESK.

destination store A retail establishment with unique products or such a wide assortment of offerings that it attracts consumers who are willing to make a special trip from throughout a wide geographic area. The L.L. Bean store in Freeport, Maine, is an example of a destination store.

detachable warrant A warrant issued in conjunction with another security (nearly always a bond) that can trade or be exercised separately following the issue date.

detailed audit A thorough and complete examination of all or a selected portion of an organization's books. In a detailed audit, as opposed to a normal audit, systems of internal control, the details of all the transactions, books of account, subsidiary records, and supporting documentation may be examined for accuracy, use of generally accepted accounting principles, total accountability, and legality.

deterministic Describing a variable or a system's output that can be predicted with certainty. In a deterministic system a change in one variable will have a predictable effect on another variable. —Compare STOCHASTIC.

devaluation A reduction in the value of one currency in relation to other currencies. For example, when Mexico devalued the peso, more pesos were required to obtain a given amount of a foreign currency. Devaluation is generally undertaken by a government in order to make its country's products more competitive in world markets. —Compare REVALUATION.

developer 1. A person who plans and supervises the development of land for commercial or residential use. 2. A person who determines how a website will function and writes the programming code to make it do so.

development 1. Improvements to make a tract of land more useful, generally made by a single developer. 2. In computers, a software engineering project. For example, a software company may be engaged in project development for three-dimensional mapping.

deviation policy An organization's guidelines for handling unexpected conduct or activities. For example, the comptroller of the currency requires that it receive at least 60 days' written notice of a bank's intent to change from its business plan.

devise To pass real estate by means of a will.

devisee An individual who receives real estate by means of a will.

DIA —See DIAMONDS.

Diamonds (DIA) Registered name for interest in a trust that holds all 30 stocks included in the Dow Jones Industrial Average. Ownership of a Diamond allows an investor to track the DJIA with a single investment.

dicker To bargain or negotiate, generally over small differences.

differential In commodities trading, the premium or discount in the futures contract price caused by delivering a commodity that does not exactly meet the standards fixed by the exchange. Allowances for these differentials are included in the contract specifications.

differential advantage **1.** A unique quality of a good or service that gives it an advantage over competitors. **2.** The benefit enjoyed by a company or production facility as a result of the economic environment in which it operates. For example, a manufacturing plant enjoys a differential advantage because of a high education level and work ethic of the local population.

differentiated oligopoly An industry in which production of a similar but not identical product is concentrated in a few firms. Firms operating in a differentiated oligopoly attempt to differentiate their products in order to be able to charge consumers a higher price. Cigarette manufacturing is an example of a differentiated oligopoly. —Compare HOMOGENEOUS OLIGOPOLY.

differentiation Unique qualities, perceived or real, of a good or service that distinguish it from a competing good or service. For example, a consumer products company may develop a razor with an additional blade and advertise that it produces a closer shave. Companies use differentiation in order to improve sales and/or charge a higher price. —Also called *product differentiation.*

digital Of or relating to data that is recorded, stored, or played in numerical form. Unlike analog data that is continuous, digital data is discrete. —Compare ANALOG.

digitize To convert to digital form. Scanning a photo converts an image into digital form.

diluted earnings per share An earnings measure calculated by dividing net income less preferred stock dividends for a period by the average number of shares of common stock that would be outstanding if all convertible securities were converted into shares of common stock. Net income is adjusted for any changes that would occur because of the conversions. Diluted earnings per share is a particularly effective method of presenting earnings-per-share data for companies with complex capital structures. —Compare BASIC EARNINGS PER SHARE. —See also DUAL PRESENTATION.

dilution A decrease in the equity position of a share of stock because of the issuance of additional shares. Dilution is usually detrimental to the position of existing shareholders because it weakens their proportional claim on earnings and assets. —See also POTENTIAL DILUTION.

diminishing marginal utility The reduction in satisfaction that results from successive units of a good or service. For example, ice cream has diminishing marginal utility because the second dish provides less satisfaction than the first dish.

diminishing returns Successively smaller increases in output that result from adding additional units of input. Adding a third cashier to the checkout section of a store is likely to be less productive than was the addition of the second cashier. Adding a fourth cashier is likely to produce even smaller gains in revenue. —Also called *law of diminishing returns.*

dink An acronym for "dual-income, no kids," a two-career couple that is likely to enjoy substantial amounts of disposable income to spend on vehicles, clothes, restaurant meals, and vacations.

dip A small, short decline in a variable, such as the price of a security or interest rates. A broker may advise a customer to accumulate a particular stock on dips. It is often difficult to know if a decline is just a dip, or if it is the initial step in a more substantial reduction.

direct cost A cost that can be directly related to producing specific goods or performing a specific service. For example, the wages of an employee engaged in producing a product can be attributed directly to the cost of manufacturing that product. Certain other costs, such as depreciation and administrative expenses, are more difficult to assign and are not considered direct costs. —Compare INDIRECT COST.

direct deposit Electronic deposit of funds into a savings account or checking account. Direct deposit reduces the expense of making payments and the time required to credit payments to an account.

directed verdict A ruling by a judge that a jury return a specific verdict, generally after the judge has determined the plaintiff did not present sufficient evidence to prove the case. A criminal case can result in a directed verdict for acquittal but not for guilt.

direct (federal) government obligation A debt that is backed by the full taxing power of the U.S. government. Direct obligations include Treasury bills, Treasury bonds, and U.S. savings bonds. These investments are generally considered to be of the very highest quality. —See also FEDERAL AGENCY SECURITY.

direct financing The raising of funds without using an intermediary. For example, a firm may decide to save an underwriter's fee by offering new securities directly to investors.

direct financing lease A nonleveraged capital lease in which the lessor is not a manufacturer or dealer. —Compare LEVERAGED LEASE.

direct investment 1. Purchase of equity by a lender. For example, a bank takes an ownership position in a company. 2. Purchase of securities directly from the issuer. Investing through dividend reinvestment plans (DRIPS) is generally considered direct investment, even though investment bankers administer most of these plans. —See also DIRECT STOCK PURCHASE PLAN 3. —See FOREIGN DIRECT INVESTMENT.

direct liability A legal obligation imposed on an individual who is directly responsible for negligence that results in property damage or bodily injury. For example, an executive who destroys evidence relative to a lawsuit brought by an employee is held liable. —Compare INDIRECT LIABILITY.

direct mail Mail promoting products or services that is sent by sellers to potential customers. —See also JUNK MAIL.

direct marketing An advertising campaign in which a seller attempts to directly contact a select group of potential customers. Direct marketing typically utilizes a list of potential customers that are contacted via mail, telephone, or computer. —See also ACTION DEVICE.

director A member of a firm's board of directors. A director also may hold a management position within the firm. —See also INSIDE DIRECTOR; OUTSIDE DIRECTOR.

directorate —See BOARD OF DIRECTORS.

directors' and officers' liability insurance A type of insurance taken to protect a firm's directors and officers against lawsuits—mainly suits instituted by unhappy shareholders of the firm. Directors' and officers' liability insurance became very expensive and difficult to obtain during the late 1990s and early 2000s as the number of shareholder lawsuits increased dramatically. Companies find it very difficult to recruit outside directors unless the candidates are supplied with liability insurance. —Also called *D&O coverage.*

> **CASE STUDY** Although unusual, a company's directors are sometimes held personally liable for misconduct even when the firm carries directors' and officer's liability insurance. In 2006 and 2007 five outside directors of bankrupt shoe retailer Just for Feet paid $41.5 million to settle a lawsuit brought by a court-appointed trustee charged with recovering money for creditors. A 2001 Alabama lawsuit had charged the directors with conflict of interest and breach of fiduciary duty. Although directors' and officers' insurance generally provides coverage for these types of judgments, the firm's officers had pleaded guilty and subsequently consumed nearly all the firm's liability insurance coverage in settling an earlier class action lawsuit filed by shareholders. Only $100,000 in coverage remained for the outside directors. It was unclear whether a third-party source, such as an employer, covered the settlement by the outside directors. For example, companies can purchase special liability insurance designed to protect and benefit individuals as opposed to the business entity. Coverage would have been more likely if the directors' employers had encouraged them to serve on the board of Just for Feet.

direct paper Commercial paper sold directly by issuers to individual investors without the use of an intermediary. This method is most often used by finance companies such as General Motors Acceptance Corporation. —Compare DEALER PAPER.

direct participation program An investment program in which tax consequences and cash flows pass directly from the investment to the investors. The purpose of a direct investment program is to permit investors to enjoy certain benefits (for example, depreciation deductions) usually available to a corporation.

direct placement The sale of a new security issue to a limited number of large buyers rather than to the general public. Direct placement generally involves less expense to the issuer, although the buyer may be able to negotiate a more favorable price.

direct play A firm or the stock of a firm that concentrates its operations in a specific industry. An investor expecting favorable opportunities from a particular line of business may seek a direct play in the business itself rather than invest in the stock of a company engaged not only in that business but also in a variety of other businesses. —Also called *play.*

direct premium **1.** A free item or other incentive offered to a consumer at the time of a purchase. For example, a consumer who purchases a particular brand of perfume may be offered a free tote bag. **2.** The premium collected by an insurance company prior to any premiums paid to a reinsurance company.

direct purchase To buy shares of a mutual fund directly from the fund rather than from an intermediary such as a broker or financial planner. Mutual funds that sell directly to investors do not have sales personnel and generally charge no sales fee or a relatively small sales fee.

direct reduction mortgage An amortized loan with periodic payments that cover interest and a portion of principal. Each period's interest is calculated on the remaining loan balance, which declines over the life of the mortgage.

direct response advertising A marketing effort to a target group that encourages members of the group to respond directly to the advertiser. For example, a company may offer classic rock CDs to viewers of a late-night 1950s television show. The offer will be accompanied by a toll-free telephone number for viewers who decide to order the music.

direct selling Selling goods or services person-to-person outside a fixed retail location. Direct selling includes door-to-door solicitation, home parties, and contacting potential customers via the telephone.

direct stock purchase plan A plan initiated by some firms that permits investors to purchase stock directly from the issuer (thereby avoiding brokerage commissions). Although generally open only to employees and current shareholders, an increasing number of companies allow nonstockholders to make direct purchases.

direct tax A tax paid by the individual or organization on which it is levied. For example, the personal income tax is levied on individuals, who end up bearing the entire burden of the tax. A direct tax cannot be shifted from the entity on which it is levied. —Compare INDIRECT TAX.

dirty float A system of floating currency exchange rates in which government central banks occasionally intervene in order to influence the relative values of the currencies. —Also called *managed float*.

dirty price The price of a bond including accrued interest. —Compare CLEAN PRICE.

dirty stock A security that is not in deliverable form for transfer. For example, a certificate may not be endorsed properly.

disabilities Restrictions or special handling requirements that are placed on an individual's brokerage account. For example, an employee of a financial institution involved in the securities business must have special permission from the employer in order to have a margin account.

disability benefits Money available from private insurance or Social Security to individuals who meet established medical guidelines for disability. Benefits from private insurance are generally based on a percentage of income, while Social Security benefits are similar to retirement benefits. —See also TOTAL DISABILITY.

disability income insurance Insurance coverage for a portion of lost income when a wage earner is unable to work because of an illness or accident. —Also called *loss of income insurance*.

disaffirm To refuse to confirm. For example, a minor is generally permitted to disaffirm, or renounce, a contract and all of its legal obligations.

disappearing deductible The portion of any loss or expense normally required of a policyholder that is reduced or eliminated under certain conditions. For example, the deductible in an extended automobile warranty is eliminated if repairs are performed at the dealership issuing the warranty.

disbursement A payment in cash or by check.

discharge 1. To dismiss from employment. 2. To comply with the terms of a debt or other obligation.

discharge in bankruptcy Release of a debtor from certain debts set forth in the Bankruptcy Code. Creditors of discharged debt are prohibited from taking any actions against the debtor to collect the debts.

discharge of lien Removal of a legal claim against real property after the claim has been satisfied.

disclaimer Denial of responsibility. For example, a book on personal finance may offer a disclaimer that the author is not engaged in providing professional investment advice.

disclaimer of opinion The statement of a certified public accountant that an audit opinion cannot be rendered because of limitations on the extent of the examinations. —Compare CLEAN OPINION.

disclosure The submission of facts and details concerning an asset, a situation, or a business operation. For example, the seller of a home may be required to provide disclosure to potential buyers of any defects. Likewise, a lender must offer borrowers full disclosure of the terms of a loan. In general, security exchanges and the SEC require firms to disclose to the investment community the facts concerning issues that will affect the firms' stock prices. Disclosure is also required when firms file for public offerings. —See also FULL DISCLOSURE.

discontinued operation A segment of a business that has been abandoned or sold, or for which plans for one or another of these actions have been approved. —See also CONTINUING OPERATIONS.

discount¹ 1. The amount by which a bond sells below face value. —See also BELOW PAR; DISCOUNT BOND. 2. A reduction in the price at which merchandise is being sold. For example, an appliance sale may allow customers to purchase refrigerators at a discount of 25% off the regular retail price. 3. A reduction in the price paid for a shipment of goods if payment is made by a specified date. 4. The relationship in valuation between two assets. For example, a stock may sell at a discount to book value.

discount² 1. To adjust the value of an asset on the basis of information rather than activity or events. For example, investors may already have discounted a firm's stock price because of the anticipation of weak earnings. 2. To deduct the charge for making a loan from the loan's principal before distributing funds to the borrower.

discount basis —See BANK-DISCOUNT BASIS.

discount bond A bond selling at a price that is less than its par value. In addition to semiannual interest payments, a discount bond offers investors additional appreciation if the security is held until maturity.

discount brokerage firm A brokerage firm that discounts commissions for individuals to trade securities. Most discount brokerage firms offer limited advice, but reduce their fees by 50% or more compared with full-service brokerage firms.

discounted cash flow A method of estimating an investment's current value based on the discounting of projected future revenues and costs. The answer derived from the technique is only as accurate as the estimates used, which, in many cases, are far from certain.

discounted payback period The time required for an investment's discounted cash flows to cover the initial outlay required. The shorter the discounted payback period, the more desirable the investment.

discounting the news Adjusting an asset's price so that it already reflects some anticipated event or series of events. For example, a stock price may be unaffected by a favorable earnings report because the report was expected. Likewise, home prices in a town might not increase much in price following an official announcement of a new company coming to town, because the news was anticipated.

discount points A fee paid by a borrower to a lender in return for reducing the interest rate on a loan. A point is equal to 1% of the amount borrowed, and points are generally paid when a loan closes. Points increase the effective rate on a loan above the stated rate.

discount rate 1. The interest rate charged by the Federal Reserve on loans to its member banks. A change in this rate is viewed as a strong indicator of Fed policy with respect to future changes in the money supply and market interest rates. Generally, a rise in the discount rate signals increasing interest rates in the money and capital markets. —Also called *rediscount rate.* **2.** The rate at which an investment's revenues and costs are discounted in order to calculate its present value.

discount security 1. Any security that is issued at less than face value. —See also ORIGINAL-ISSUE DISCOUNT. **2.** A money market security, such as a Treasury bill or commercial paper, that is issued at a discount but that matures at face value. The only income received by the investor is the difference between the price paid and the proceeds received at maturity or on the sale of the security. —See also BANK-DISCOUNT BASIS.

discount store A retail store that sells most items at reduced prices compared to prices suggested by the manufacturers.

discount window The lending facility of the Federal Reserve through which commercial banks borrow reserves. Federal Reserve policy toward supplying banks with reserves has a major effect on credit conditions and interest rates. —Also called *window.*

discount yield —See BANK-DISCOUNT BASIS.

discovery In law, the pretrial investigation used by the plaintiff and the defendant to uncover pertinent evidence of the opposition's case. Discovery typically includes submitting a list of questions that must be answered and asking oral questions of the other party or the witnesses.

discrete manufacturing The production of distinct items such as lawnmowers, glasses, and flashlights. —Compare PROCESS MANUFACTURING.

discretionary account A brokerage account in which the customer permits the broker to act on the customer's behalf in buying and selling securities. The broker may make decisions regarding securities, prices, and timing—subject to any limitations specified in the agreement. —Compare ADVISORY ACCOUNT. —Also called *controlled account.*

discretionary expense A nonessential expenditure that is subject to management or individual control. Advertising is an example of an expense that can be increased or decreased at the discretion of management. Governmental discretionary expenses include expenditures on highways and defense.

discretionary fiscal policy Elective changes in government spending and taxation in response to changes in economic activity. For example, in a period of recession, the government might increase highway spending in order to stimulate aggregate demand. Discretionary fiscal policy is not automatic and is not mandated by law.

discretionary income Individual income that is not allocated to expenditures for necessities such as food and shelter. Increasing amounts of discretionary income are especially favorable for the prospects of firms that sell luxury or leisure items and services.

discretionary order In securities transactions, a customer order to a broker giving the broker discretion in the buying and selling of securities. Depending on the customer's instructions, the amount of discretion may vary from very limited (that is, price only) to nearly complete.

discretionary trust A trust in which the trustee may use his or her discretion in distributing assets to beneficiaries. For example, a discretionary trust for a minor may allow a distribution that the trustee feels is reasonable. —Compare NONDISCRETIONARY TRUST.

discrimination Behavior that differentiates treatment among groups on the basis of race, gender, religion, or some other social or physical factor.

diseconomies 1. Inefficiencies and bottlenecks in manufacturing processes that cause unit costs to rise as output increases. A manufacturing plant may grow so large that it becomes difficult to manage and, as a result, less efficient. —Compare ECONOMIES OF SCALE. **2.** Costs that are not borne directly by a manufacturer. For example, a coal-fired electric power plant may emit particulate matter and sulfur oxides that cause damage to vegetation and human health.

disguised unemployment Potential workers who are not employed but who do not count officially as unemployed because they are not considered part of the civilian labor force. For example, a person able to work but who fails to look for employment or apply for unemployment benefits is considered as part of disguised unemployment.

dishonor To refuse payment on a negotiable instrument such as a check.

disinflation A slowdown in the rate of inflation. A drop in the inflation rate from 3% in one year to 2% in the next year is an example of disinflation. On an overall basis, disinflation is good for security prices, but it can be painful for individual companies that have made investment and borrowing decisions based on a belief that a high rate of inflation would continue. —See also INFLATION.

disintermediation 1. The withdrawal of funds from financial intermediaries such as banks, thrifts, and life insurance companies in order to invest directly with ultimate users. Deregulation of financial intermediaries was intended to dampen the periodic swings toward disintermediation. —Compare INTERMEDIATION. **2.** In product distribution, avoiding a middleman by utilizing an alternative delivery channel. For example, a manufacturer circumvents retailers by selling directly to consumers.

disinvestment Divestiture, liquidation, or sale of a segment of a firm. Disinvestment may occur for a number of reasons, including a poor outlook for a particular line of business or a firm's need to raise additional capital for other more promising segments of its business.

dismiss 1. To remove someone from employment: *The directors dismissed the CEO after several years of poor earnings.* **2.** To terminate a civil case at the request of the defendant. **3.** To cease consideration of something: *The CEO dismissed the proposal to change advertising firms.* **4.** To instruct someone to leave.

disposable income Aftertax income, calculated quarterly, that consumers have available for spending or saving. Economists view changes in disposable income as an important indicator of the present and future health of the economy. —See also PERSONAL INCOME.

dispossess To deprive a person of real property. For example, a landlord sends a dispossess notice to a tenant who has not paid rent.

disqualifying disposition The sale, gift, or exchange of stock acquired through an employee stock purchase plan within two years of enrollment or one year of the purchase date. A disqualifying disposition results in ordinary income for tax purposes.

dissenters' rights The right of shareholders who are opposed to certain fundamental corporate actions to receive a cash payment for the fair value of their shares. For example, state law may convey dissenters' rights when a merger has been approved by corporate directors.

> **CASE STUDY** The comptroller of the currency in June 2002 approved a share exchange involving the First National Bank of Midland (Texas). The bank was proposing to undertake an ownership restructuring in which a share exchange would result in the bank becoming a subsidiary of a holding company. Under the proposal, stockholders of the bank would exchange their shares for shares of the holding company. An exception would be made for out-of-state residents, who would receive $2.75 in cash for each bank share. The differing compensation for out-of-state shareholders allowed the holding company to avoid costs associated with registering its stock under the Securities Act of 1933. One of the standards applied by the comptroller of the currency for approval of the proposal was dissenters' rights for all shareholders involved in the exchange. With dissenters' rights, any shareholder of the bank was permitted to opt out of the exchange by requesting the fair market value in cash for the stock he or she surrendered.

dissident director A director who wishes to change a firm's policies and generally acts in opposition to the wishes of the other directors.

dissident shareholders Shareholders who oppose a firm's management or management policy. For example, dissident shareholders of Hewlett-Packard opposed that firm's offer to purchase Compaq Computer.

dissolution 1. Termination of a corporation's legal existence. 2. Termination of a contract.

distraint Seizure of property to serve as security for an unpaid claim. A taxing authority normally has the power of distraint to help ensure collections from individuals who are negligent or refuse to pay taxes.

distressed debt Debt with low junk status and a market price substantially below par value, often pennies on the dollar. Investors sometimes buy distressed debt on the possibility that management can renegotiate loan agreements and keep the issuer out of bankruptcy. Alternatively, distressed debt may offer potential value in the event the issuer is liquidated or successfully reorganized.

distressed property Developed real property that is in poor physical condition (residential) or poor financial condition (commercial) because of high vacancies.

distress sale A forced sale of something, generally at a below-market price. For example, a bank may sell a home it has obtained through foreclosure.

distribution 1. —See PUBLIC OFFERING. 2. An investment company payment to its shareholders of capital gains realized from the sale of securities. Investment company shareholders, not the investment company, pay taxes on a distribution. **3.** Dispensing assets to beneficiaries according to the terms of a will.

distribution channel —See CHANNEL OF DISTRIBUTION.

distribution fee —See 12B–1 FEE.

distribution in kind Distribution of additional shares of stock or some other real property to the owners of a business.

distributive share Allocation to a partner of income or loss from a trade or business carried on by a partnership.

distributor **1.** A firm that markets and delivers merchandise to retailers. For example, a company may have the exclusive right to sell and deliver a soft drink to retailers in a specific region. **2.** A business that buys shares from a mutual fund for resale to investors.

district court A federal court that tries and decides federal civil cases in one of 94 districts. The President of the United States appoints federal district court judges for life.

diversifiable risk —See UNSYSTEMATIC RISK.

diversification The acquisition of a group of assets in which returns on the assets are not directly related over time. An investor seeking diversification for a securities portfolio would purchase securities of firms that are not similarly affected by the same variables. A company can diversify by operating in different industries or having operations in different countries. Proper diversification is intended to reduce the risk inherent in particular products, services, or geographic regions. Diversification is just as important to companies as it is to investors. —See also UNSYSTEMATIC RISK.

diversified company A company engaged in varied business operations not directly related to one another. A diversified company is less likely to suffer either a collapse or a spectacular gain in earnings compared with a firm concentrating its operations in a single business.

diversified management company An investment company with a minimum of 75% of its assets as cash, government securities, securities of other investment companies, and other securities subject to a limitation of no more than 5% of the diversified management company's assets or 10% of the voting securities of the issuing company. Most investment companies, including mutual funds and closed-end investment companies, are diversified management companies. —Compare NONDIVERSIFIED MANAGEMENT COMPANY.

diversify To acquire a variety of assets that do not tend to change in value at the same time. To diversify a securities portfolio is to purchase different types of securities in different companies in unrelated industries.

divestiture The sale, liquidation, or spinoff of a division or subsidiary. For example, a firm may decide to divest itself of a division in order to concentrate its managerial efforts on more promising segments of its business.

CASE STUDY British confectionary and beverage company Cadbury Schweppes announced in March 2007 that it planned the divestiture of its American beverage unit from its candy business. The announcement followed pressure from shareholders, including one investor who had acquired nearly 3% of the firm's outstanding shares, for the company to concentrate on its core confectionary business. The U.S. beverage business included 7 Up, Dr.

Pepper, Sunkist, Schweppes, Hawaiian Punch, Canada Dry, and Snapple. At the time of the announcement, financial analysts estimated the beverage unit value at between $13 billion and $15 billion, somewhat less than the likely value of the firm's better-known confectionary business. If the divestiture took place by means of a spinoff, it was anticipated investors owning one share of Cadbury Schweppes prior to the split would own one share in each of the two companies following the split. Analysts also thought it possible that one or more private equity firms would offer to purchase the beverage unit. In either case, it was anticipated the divestiture would result in a gain for shareholders. The announcement was accompanied by a 2% increase in the price of the firm's shares that were traded as American Depositary Receipts on the New York Stock Exchange.

dividend A share of a company's net profits distributed by the company to a class of its stockholders. The dividend is paid in a fixed amount for each share of stock held. Although most companies make quarterly payments in cash (checks), dividends also may be in the form of property, scrip, or stock. Unlike interest on a debt, a company's directors must vote to approve each dividend payment. —Also called *payout.* —See also CAPITAL DIVIDEND; CASH DIVIDEND; CONSENT DIVIDEND; CONSTRUCTIVE DIVIDEND; DEC-LARATION DATE; DECLARED DIVIDEND; EX-DIVIDEND DATE; FINAL DIVIDEND; ILLEGAL DIVIDEND; INTERIM DIVIDEND; LIABILITY DIVIDEND; LIQUIDATING DIVIDEND; OPTIONAL DIVIDEND; STOCK DIVIDEND.

CASE STUDY Stockholders are required to wrestle with four relevant dates for each dividend a company pays. These are:

Announcement or declaration date: The date a firm's directors tell shareholders and the investment community the size of the next dividend, when the dividend will be paid, and when an investor must be recorded as an owner in order to receive the payment.

Ex-dividend date: The first day when a new purchaser of the stock *will not* receive the declared dividend. If an investor buys the stock on or after the ex-dividend date, he or she will not receive the upcoming dividend payment.

Stockholder-of-record or record date: The date by which an investor must be registered on the firm's books as a shareholder in order to receive the declared dividend.

Payment date: The date on which the declared dividend is scheduled for payment.

Of these four dates, the ex-dividend date is most important to investors. Shares must be purchased at least one business day prior to the ex-dividend date for the buyer to claim a dividend that has been announced but not yet paid. Buy shares of stock on the ex-dividend date, and the seller, not the buyer, will receive the upcoming dividend. The ex-dividend date is two business days prior to the record date, because three days are required for regular settlement of a stock transaction. Buy stock on Tuesday, and an investor will be listed as the owner of record on Friday, the day that payment is required for the stock purchase. If a firm's directors have declared that a dividend will be paid to stockholders of record on Friday, the stock must be purchased by Tuesday in order to have a right to the dividend. In this case the ex-dividend date is

Wednesday, two days prior to the record date. Relevant dates for the common stock of home products giant Procter & Gamble for 2006–07 are illustrated below.

	Quarter 1	Quarter 2	Quarter 3	Quarter 4
Announcement date	Mar 13	July 11	Oct 10	Jan 9
Ex-dividend date	April 19	July 19	Oct 18	Jan 17
Record date	April 21	July 21	Oct 20	Jan 19
Payment date	May 15	August 15	Nov 15	Feb 15

Notice that the record date for each quarterly dividend follows the ex-dividend date by two business days. In the first quarter an investor must have purchased the stock by April 18 to be listed as a stockholder on April 21 and receive the dividend paid on May 15. An investor purchasing the stock on April 19 would not have been listed as a stockholder of record until April 22, one day beyond when the company determined who was to receive the dividend. A weekend or holiday between the ex-dividend and record dates lengthens the time difference to four days or three days, respectively. The schedule for Procter & Gamble indicates owners of the stock on the day prior to the ex-dividend date must wait nearly a month for actual payment of the dividend.

dividend addition A distribution to an owner of a participating life insurance policy that can be used to purchase additional life insurance coverage.

dividend capture The trading of a stock in order to be the holder of record for dividend payment purposes. Once the right to receive the dividend payment has been earned, the stock is sold. Dividend capture is practiced chiefly by corporations; they are permitted to exclude from their taxable income 80% of dividends received. Certain specific tax rules apply to dividend capture.

dividend coverage The extent to which a firm's net income supports the company's total dividend payments. For example, a utility earning $5.00 per share and paying a dividend of $4.79 per share has relatively weak dividend coverage. Poor coverage allows a firm's management less flexibility to raise dividends or to maintain them at the same level in the event that earnings decline. —See also PREFERRED DIVIDEND COVERAGE.

dividend discount model A model used to determine the price at which a security should sell based on the discounted value of estimated future dividend payments. Dividend discount models are used to determine if a security is a good buy, such as one that sells at a lower current price than the model would indicate, or a bad buy, such as one that sells at a higher current price than the model would indicate.

dividend equivalent right In incentive stock options, the right to a credit for additional shares for the value of dividends a firm pays on its shares.

dividend exclusion For corporate stockholders, the dividends received that are exempt from taxation. A corporation that owns less than 20% of the stock in another company can exclude 70% of the dividends received from taxable income. When between 20% and 79% of the stock of another company is owned, 75% of the dividends received from that firm can be excluded from taxation. When 80% or more of another company's stock is owned, all of the dividends received from that firm can be excluded from taxation. Dividend exclusion is not applicable to individual investors.

dividend payable A dividend that has been declared by directors but not paid to stockholders. A dividend that is declared becomes a general liability of the company until paid to shareholders.

dividend payment date The date on which an issuer's paying agent will send dividend payments to stockholders. —See also EX-DIVIDEND DATE; PAYMENT DATE 2.

dividend payout ratio —See PAYOUT RATIO.

dividend recapitalization Issuing debt and using the proceeds to pay a special dividend to stockholders. Dividend recapitalizations are used by private equity firms that wish to extract cash from businesses they have acquired. For example, in 2006 two private equity firms purchased Travelport for $1 billion plus $3.3 billion of debt. Less than a year later, the new owners undertook a dividend recapitalization by issuing $1.1 billion in new debt and using the proceeds to pay themselves a dividend.

dividend reinvestment plan (DRIP) A plan that allows stockholders to automatically reinvest dividend payments in additional shares of the company's stock. Instead of receiving the usual dividend checks, participating stockholders will receive quarterly notification of shares purchased and shares held in their accounts. Dividend reinvestment is usually an inexpensive way of purchasing additional shares of stock, because the fees are low or are completely absorbed by the company. In addition, some companies offer stock at a discount from the existing market price. Reinvested dividends are fully taxable even though no cash is received by the stockholder. —Also called *automatic dividend reinvestment; reinvestment plan.* —See also SUPER DRIP.

dividend requirement Total annual preferred dividends to be paid by a company.

dividends in arrears Dividend payments on cumulative preferred stock that have been passed by a firm's directors. These dividends must be brought up to date before any payments are made to common stockholders. Any payments of dividends in arrears go to the current holders of the preferred stock regardless of who held the stock when the dividend was passed. —Also called *accumulated dividend.*

dividend test A provision in some borrowing agreements that restricts the borrower's ability to pay dividends to stockholders. This provision is supposed to protect the position of creditors against a drawdown on assets by dividend payments.

dividend yield The annual dividends from a common or preferred stock divided by that stock's market price per share. If a common stock trades at a price of $50 per share, its $.92 dividend provides a dividend yield of $.92/$50, or 1.84%. This figure measures the current return on a particular stock but does not take into account potential gains and losses in the security's value.

divider —See EUROPEAN CURRENCY QUOTATION.

division A major administrative unit of a business, often large enough to operate independently. In 2005 Microsoft Corporation announced a realignment of the company into three divisions: Microsoft Platform Products and Services; Microsoft Business Products, and Microsoft Entertainment and Devices.

division of labor The separation of a major task into smaller tasks in which participants specialize. For example, an automobile service center may have an employee who performs alignments, another who does oil and filter changes, and yet another who works on exhaust systems.

DJA —See DOW JONES AVERAGES.

DJIA —See DOW JONES INDUSTRIAL AVERAGE.

dividend yield

I tend to favor stocks that have a high dividend yield. Is this a smart investment strategy?

There are many reasons, both good and bad, that a stock would have a high dividend yield. A company could be experiencing business problems causing the stock price to fall and the dividend yield to rise and a dividend cut to be in its future. I would be concerned if a company's dividend yield were out of line with that of other companies in its industry group. On the other hand, a high dividend yield could indicate a mature company with strong free cash flow and a strong balance sheet that is simply distributing profits to its shareholders. As long as you do your due diligence on the financial strength of the company, purchasing stocks with a high dividend yield can be a smart investment strategy.

▪ Richard S. Campbell, CIMA®, Senior Vice President, Wealth Management, Portfolio Management Director, Smith Barney, Valdosta, GA

dock To penalize an employee through a reduction of wages, generally for being late or not showing up for work.

Doctor of Business Administration (DBA) A terminal degree that concentrates on real business and managerial issues. Many doctorate-granting business schools offer a DBA, with concentrations in various areas of business such as finance, management, and marketing.

documentary evidence Printed evidence, including photographs, maps, letters, and notebook pages, that is presented in a trial. —Compare ORAL EVIDENCE.

documentation 1. The process of collecting, organizing, and recording printed material. **2.** Reference material for operating and maintaining computer software and hardware.

dog 1. A product with low market share in a slow-growing market. **2.** An investment that has experienced poor performance. For example, a rental property with extended vacancies at the same time it has required extensive maintenance expenditures.

Dogs of the Dow The investment strategy of purchasing the ten stocks in the Dow Jones Industrial Average that offer the highest current dividend yield. The ten-stock portfolio is continuously rebalanced as stock prices and dividends change. The theory is that Dow stocks offering the highest dividend yield are solid investments that are temporarily undervalued.

doing business as (DBA) Operating a business under a name that is different from the real name of the person or company. Often abbreviated in official notices and contracts as *DBA*.

dollar bond A bond that is traded and quoted on the basis of its dollar price rather than on its yield. Dollar quotations are fairly unusual, except in the case of municipal revenue bonds. Price quotes may or may not include any dealer fees, therefore it is important for an investor to determine which is the case.

dollar-cost averaging Investment of a fixed amount of money at regular intervals, usually each month. This process results in the purchase of extra shares during market downturns and fewer shares during market upturns. Dollar-cost averaging is based on the belief that the market, or a particular stock, will rise in price over the long term, and that it is not worthwhile (or even possible) to identify intermediate highs and lows. —Also called *averaging*.

dollar price The price of a bond quoted as a dollar percentage of par value rather than yield. For example, a bond selling at par would be quoted at 100.

dollar-value LIFO A method of inventory valuation that attempts to differentiate changes in inventory value caused by inflation from changes in value caused by a different inventory mix. Inventory changes are measured in terms of equivalent base-year dollars as opposed to changes in quantity.

domestic corporation A firm incorporated under the laws of the country or state in which it does business. For example, a firm incorporated in the United States is considered a domestic corporation in the United States, but a foreign corporation elsewhere. —Compare FOREIGN CORPORATION.

domicile 1. An individual's principal place of residence. The location of a domicile is especially important with regard to taxation and other legal matters. **2.** The headquarters location of a business.

dominant tenement Real estate with the right to use a portion or all of an adjacent or nearby property. For example, a homeowner near a lake may have the right to gain access to the lake by a walking path through a nearby property.

donated capital Funds or property given as a gift to a corporation. The donation may be from individuals or organizations not affiliated with the corporation. —See also CONTRIBUTED CAPITAL.

donated stock Stock given by a shareholder to the issuing corporation, generally in return for consideration.

donee An individual or organization that receives a gift.

donor An individual or organization that bestows a gift.

door-to-door 1. Selling to or canvassing residences. **2.** Delivering goods from the manufacturer or retailer directly to the residence or place of business of the buyer.

dot-com 1. Of or relating to a company or the stock of a company engaged primarily in a business associated with the Internet. Amazon.com is the most obvious example of a dot-com company. **2.** —See INTERNET STOCK.

double auction market A market in which multiple buyers compete to purchase many items that are simultaneously offered for sale. Sales are made to buyers willing to offer the highest price by sellers who are willing to offer the lowest price. The New York Stock Exchange is an example of a double auction market.

double-breasted In labor relations, an employer that runs both a unionized and non-unionized operation. For example, a unionized trucking company may start a subsidiary operation that is not unionized.

double-declining-balance depreciation A depreciation method that records large depreciation expenses in the early years of an asset's life and reduced depreciation expenses in the later years of an asset's life. The acceleration of depreciation is designed to reduce taxable income and tax payments so that extra cash will be available for reinvestment. According to this method, depreciation is calculated by multiplying twice the straight-line depreciation rate by the asset's book value each year. —See also MODIFIED ACCELERATED COST RECOVERY SYSTEM.

double-digit inflation An annual inflation rate of 10% or above.

double dipping Working for wages while receiving pension benefits from the same organization. Military personnel often double dip by working for the federal government following retirement from the military.

double-dip recession An extended decline in economic activity following an aborted recovery from a previous recession. A relatively weak economic recovery sometimes causes investors to worry about the economy entering another recession.

double-entry bookkeeping In accounting, recording at least two offsetting entries, including at least one debit and one credit, for every transaction. Double-entry bookkeeping results in a balanced ledger of debits and credits.

double-exempt fund A mutual fund that limits its investments to tax-free bonds of issuers from a single state. Thus, a double-exempt fund pays investors residing in the same state as the issuers of the bonds with income free of federal and state income taxes. Double-exempt funds have been particularly popular in the populous, high-tax states of California and New York. If an investor lives in a city with an income tax, these funds are exempt from three taxes. —Also called *single state municipal bond fund.* —See also TRIPLE TAX EXEMPT.

double precision In computing, the additional accuracy realized when a computer utilizes twice as much storage location to hold floating point numbers.

double taxation Taxation of the same income twice by the same taxing authority. It is generally used to refer to the taxation of dividends that are taxed once at the corporate level (as income before dividends are declared) and again at the personal level (when the dividends are received).

double time Twice the normal rate of pay, generally for working overtime or during holidays. —See also TIME-AND-A-HALF.

doubling option A provision in some indentures that allows the borrower, at its option, to retire twice as many bonds as stipulated under a sinking fund requirement. The additional retirements take place at or near par, so that the option is used during periods of low interest rates and is to the disadvantage of investors. —Compare SINKING FUND PROVISION. —See also CALL PROVISION.

Dow —See DOW JONES INDUSTRIAL AVERAGE.

dower A widow's portion of her husband's assets that were acquired during the course of their marriage. The dower, usually amounting to one third, applies even if the deceased husband wills her a portion less than this. —Compare CURTESY.

Dow Jones & Company, Inc. A major publisher of financial data and business news. Although best known as the publisher of *The Wall Street Journal* and compiler of the Dow Jones Averages, Dow Jones also publishes a magazine, produces a radio show and a television show, and provides an electronic news service to the financial community. Dow Jones is a subsidiary of News Corporation.

Dow Jones Averages (DJA) A trademark for an index of the relative prices of selected industrial, transportation, and utility stocks based on a formula developed and periodically revised by Dow Jones & Company, Inc.

Dow Jones Industrial Average (DJIA) A trademark for one of the oldest and most widely quoted measures of stock market price movements. The average is calculated by adding the share prices of 30 large, seasoned firms, such as Intel, ExxonMobil, General Electric, and GM, and dividing the sum by a figure that is adjusted for such things as stock splits and substitutions. Dow Jones also publishes other averages, including one for transportation and one for utilities. —Also called [the] *Dow.*

downgrading A reduction in the quality rating of a security issue, generally a bond. A downgrading may occur for various reasons, including a period of losses, or increased debt service required by restructuring a firm's capital to include more debt and less equity. For example, takeover targets that engage in stock buybacks to prop up the price of their shares are subject to debt issue downgrading by the rating agencies. —Compare UPGRADING 1.

down payment Funds advanced as partial payment when buying an asset. For example, a lender may require a down payment of 10% for new car loans.

downscale 1. Describing a retailer that offers inexpensive products purchased mostly by consumers of modest means. **2.** Inexpensive products similar in function to more costly products. For example, a discount store may offer downscale versions of fashion clothing.

downside protection An investment position that seeks to reduce losses resulting from the decline of a stock or a fall in the overall market. For example, put options provide downside protection against a decline in the price of the underlying stock. Likewise, writing covered call options can provide partial downside protection against price declines.

downside risk The potential losses that may occur if a particular investment position is taken. For example, the downside risk from holding Treasury bills is quite small. The downside risk from investing in collectibles can be quite high, especially for a novice investor. —Compare UPSIDE POTENTIAL.

downsize 1. To reduce the size of a company, often by closing, selling, or spinning off one or more divisions. Management may decide to downsize a firm in an effort to improve efficiency and to increase the returns to shareholders. Downsizing can cause a firm to grow smaller and more valuable at the same time. **2.** To move to smaller accommodations. For example, a couple may downsize, or move to a smaller home, after their children are grown.

downstream Of or relating to earnings or operations at a firm that are near or at the final stage of consumption. For example, marketing and transportation are downstream operations for a large, integrated oil company. —Compare UPSTREAM.

> **CASE STUDY** Major integrated oil companies such as BP, ExxonMobil, Royal Dutch Shell, and ConocoPhillips are vertically integrated, with upstream operations in oil exploration and production and downstream operations in refining and distribution. Being vertically integrated provides a degree of diversification and stability, but it can also result in disappointing overall results, even when some segments of the business are operating on all cylinders. In October 2007 ConocoPhillips announced that its third-quarter results to be reported later that month would be penalized by downstream operations. Although the price of gasoline and heating oil had been rising, the increase was not sufficient to offset the much larger increases in crude oil prices. The result was a significant narrowing refining margin: the difference between the price of oil representing the upstream portion of the business, and the price of refined products representing the downstream business. The firm's negative report resulted in reduced earnings estimates and a decline of nearly 2% in its stock price.

downstream merger A type of merger in which a parent firm is absorbed into one of its subsidiaries.

downtick A downward price movement for a security transaction compared with the preceding transaction of the same security. —Compare UPTICK. —Also called *minus tick*.

downtime A period of time during which operations are halted. For example, a production line might be shut down in order to perform scheduled maintenance on machinery. Downtime may be planned or unplanned. —Compare UPTIME.

downtrend A series of price declines in a security or the general market. Many analysts feel that investors should avoid securities in a downtrend until the pattern is broken. —Compare UPTREND.

downturn A decline in security prices or economic activity following a period of rising or stable prices or activity. Even strong bull markets are subject to occasional downturns.

downzone To rezone a designated area such that the permitted density and/or height of structures is reduced. Downzoning often occurs in response to concern about rapid development in a particular area of a town.

dowry Money, personal property, or other assets given to a groom by a bride or the bride's family.

Dow theory A technical trading theory that holds that stock market price trends can be forecast based on price movements of the Dow Jones Averages (industrials and transportation). The theory classifies price movements into individual components of primary, secondary, and daily. Only when both averages reach new highs or lows (one average confirms the other) is a major trend in progress.

draft 1. A written order by one party for a second party to make payment to a third party. A check is an example of a draft drawn by a depositor (first party) on a financial institution (second party) and payable to an individual or organization (third party). —See also OVERDRAFT; SIGHT DRAFT; TIME DRAFT. **2.** An initial version of a document.

drag-along rights The right of majority shareholders to force minority shareholders to join in a sale of a company. These rights allow majority shareholders to complete a sale in the event a buyer wants to own 100% of the firm.

draining reserves Action taken by the Federal Reserve to reduce bank reserves in an effort to restrain lending and reduce the rate of economic growth. The primary method for reducing bank reserves is to sell bonds to dealers, who must reduce bank balances to pay for the bonds. The Fed can also increase the reserve requirement that determines the reserves banks must hold against deposits, or it can raise the discount rate at which reserves are loaned to banks.

draw 1. To write a preliminary draft of a legal document, such as a will. **2.** To withdraw funds from a depository institution. **3.** To receive an advance payment against funds that are or will be owed. **4.** To take funds (as an owner) from one's own business.

drawback Taxes or duties on imported goods that are repaid by government when the goods are reexported or used in the manufacture of exported goods.

drawee The person or entity on which an order for payment is drawn.

drawer The person or entity that issues an order for the drawee to make payment to another party.

drawing account In accounting, a general ledger account used to maintain a record of funds withdrawn from a business.

dressing up a portfolio —See PORTFOLIO DRESSING.

DRIP —See DIVIDEND REINVESTMENT PLAN.

drive-by deal A short-term investment by a venture capitalist in a start-up company.

drive-in A section of a retail establishment accessible by customers in vehicles. For example, a bank drive-in permits customers to conduct business while remaining in their SUV. —Also called *drive-through*.

drive-through —See DRIVE-IN.

drop dead date The last possible date on which something must be completed. For example, a bid must be delivered by a specified date (the drop dead date) to be considered.

droplock bond A floating-rate bond that automatically converts to a fixed-rate bond if the interest rate used to peg the floating rate falls to a predetermined level. The new fixed rate stays in place until the droplock bond reaches maturity.

drop ship Delivering a product directly from the manufacturer to the buyer. Drop shipping relieves an intermediary such as a retailer from maintaining an inventory.

dry goods —See SOFT GOODS.

DTC —See DEPOSITORY TRUST COMPANY.

dual agent In real estate, an agent who represents both the buyer and the seller. The potential conflict of interest inherent in representing both a buyer and seller has resulted in this practice being illegal in some states. In states where it is legal, both the buyer and seller must normally sign a written agreement.

dual banking A system in which both the federal and state governments charter and supervise banks.

dual-class recapitalization The issue of a second class of common stock, generally with reduced voting power, in exchange for already outstanding shares of common stock. This type of recapitalization typically results in the entrenchment of management that enjoys increased control over corporate affairs.

dual-class stock —See STOCK CLASS 1.

dual contract In real estate, a second and inflated purchase agreement submitted by a borrower to a lender in an attempt to qualify for a larger loan.

dual coupon bond —See STEPPED COUPON BOND.

dual-currency bond A debt security that pays coupon interest in one currency and the principal in a different currency. Several variations of dual-currency bonds are issued, including some that specify the exchange rate at which currencies are converted for payments.

dual distribution Utilizing two channels of distribution to get a product into the hands of a customers. For example, a clothing manufacturer may distribute through retail stores at the same time it offers products through its own website.

dual fund —See DUAL PURPOSE FUND.

dual listing The listing of a security on more than one exchange. Many stocks are traded on the New York or the American stock exchanges and on one or more of the regional exchanges. For example, the common stock of General Motors is listed on the New York Stock Exchange, but it also enjoys a large amount of activity on the Chicago Stock Exchange.

dual presentation The presentation of a firm's earnings per share on a basic and a diluted basis. Dual presentation of earnings per share is required only for firms with complex capital structures.

dual purpose fund A special-purpose, unusual type of closed-end investment company offering two classes of stock in approximately equal amounts. One class, called income shares, is entitled to all the portfolio's dividend and interest income, while the second, called capital shares, is entitled to appreciation in investments in the firm's portfolio. At the time a dual purpose fund is established, a date is set on which the fund will be liquidated. At that time, income shareholders receive preference up to the par value of their shares, and capital shareholders receive any excess. —Also called *dual fund; leveraged investment company.*

dual-trigger insurance An insurance policy that pays benefits only when two specified events occur. For example, an electric utility might purchase a policy for coverage in the event of a specified loss in generating power and an increase in the price of spot electricity above a given level. Dual-trigger insurance offers lower premiums because of the reduced likelihood of two triggering events occurring at the same time.

due Of or relating to an obligation or receivable that is outstanding and payable.

due bill **1.** A written document signifying indebtedness. **2.** A document indicating a seller's obligation to deliver securities to a buyer. **3.** A written agreement to provide certain goods or services in return for something. For example, a radio station may barter advertising time in exchange for hotel accommodations.

due care Care that a reasonable person would provide under normal circumstances. For example, the AICPA Code of Professional Conduct requires that CPAs exercise due care in discharging their professional responsibilities with competence and diligence. Whether a person exercised due care is frequently an issue in legal proceedings.

due date The date on which a payment must be received.

due diligence Performing in a reasonable and responsible manner. For example, a financial consultant exercises due diligence in investigating securities and their issuers before making recommendations to clients.

due-diligence meeting A meeting between officials of the organization that will be issuing securities and members of the syndicate that will be distributing the securities. A due-diligence meeting is held for the purpose of discussing the terms of the issue, preparing a final prospectus, and negotiating a final agreement between the issuer and syndicate members.

due-on-sale clause An inclusion in some loan agreements that requires full payment of unpaid principal and accrued interest in the event the borrower sells or transfers ownership of the asset being used as collateral for the loan. A loan with a due-on-sale clause cannot be assumed by the new owner without permission of the lender. —Also called *alienation clause.*

dues checkoff —See CHECKOFF.

dumb terminal A monitor and keyboard that communicates only with a host computer. A dumb terminal does not have its own processing capabilities (as does a PC), and sends and receives data to a central server.

dummy director The director of a firm who acts and votes according to the wishes of another party who is not a member of the board.

dummy stockholder An individual or firm holding stock in its own name when the stock is really owned by another party.

dumping 1. The selling of large amounts of a stock, or stocks in general, at whatever market prices are in effect. For example, investors might dump stocks on hearing of an outbreak of fighting in some part of the world. **2.** The selling of a product in one market at an unusually low price while selling the same product at a significantly higher price in another market. For example, a firm may sell a product in its home market at a price covering all costs, and then sell the product in a foreign market at a significantly lower price, covering only variable costs. —See also ANTIDUMPING.

dun To repeatedly demand payment for an overdue debt.

Dun & Bradstreet —See D&B.

Dun's Market Identifier —See D-U-N-S NUMBER.

D-U-N-S Number A nine-digit number assigned by D&B to identify businesses, and published along with information such as finances and management personnel. —Also called *Dun's Market Identifier.*

duopoly A market structure dominated by two suppliers. For example, a community is served by two competing companies offering cable television service.

duplex 1. An apartment with rooms on two floors. **2.** Two dwelling units, each with its own entrance, sharing a single building.

durable goods Merchandise, such as appliances and automobiles, having a useful life over a number of periods. Firms that produce durable goods are often subject to wide fluctuations in sales and profits. —Also called *consumer durables.*

durable power of attorney A legal document conveying authority to an individual to carry out legal affairs on another person's behalf.

duration The number of years required to receive the present value of future payments, both interest and principal, from a bond. Duration is determined by calculating the present value of the principal and each coupon, and then multiplying each result by the period of time before payment is to occur. The concept of duration is used to relate the sensitivity of bond price changes to changes in interest rates. —Also called *mean term.*

duration of benefits The length of time during which benefits will be paid. For example, disability benefits may be payable for a specific number of years or until the insured reaches age 65.

Dutch auction An auction in which the seller reduces the offering price until a level can be found that clears the market. This is the price at which all sales will take place. The auction for Treasury bills is similar to this, except that the Treasury accepts the highest bids first and works through progressively lower bids until an issue is completely sold. Thus, in a Treasury bill auction, various prices are accepted.

duty 1. A professional obligation. For example, a certified financial planner has a duty to exercise reasonable and prudent judgment in providing professional services. **2.** —See TARIFF 1.

duty to warn The legal obligation to warn others of a known danger. For example, a product supplier who has reason to believe that use of the product for its intended purpose may entail danger has an obligation to provide adequate warning to those who can be expected to use or be affected by the product.

DVP —See DELIVERY VERSUS PAYMENT.

durable power of attorney

When is it wise to give another person a durable power of attorney over my affairs?

A power of attorney is "durable" if the agent's authority continues notwithstanding that the person granting the power of attorney (the "principal") has become incapacitated (legally unable to manage his or her affairs). Powers of attorney can authorize specific acts (for example, acting for the principal in a particular transaction) or can broadly authorize the agent to act for the principal. If a person becomes incapacitated and has not granted a durable power of attorney, it may be necessary to have a guardian appointed to manage his or her property, which is often cumbersome and expensive. For this reason, spouses often grant each other durable powers of attorney granting broad powers, and older persons often give a trusted person a durable power of attorney to manage their affairs. Broad powers of attorney can be abused and should be granted carefully.

■ Stephen F. Lappert, Partner, Trusts and Estates Department, Carter Ledyard & Milburn LLP, New York, NY

dwelling A structure, such as a house, apartment, or mobile home, where someone is living.

dwell time The time spent waiting. For example, the time spent by a boxcar waiting to be unloaded in a railyard. Likewise, dwell time describes the time spent by a customer waiting in line for service.

 # E

eager beaver A hard-working individual who does more than is required and volunteers for additional duties.

early retirement 1. Full repayment of a loan ahead of schedule. 2. Leaving employment prior to the normal retirement age or the number of years of employment normally required. Early retirement generally results in reduced benefits and in some cases a tax penalty.

early settlement The transfer of a security or cash on a date prior to the usual settlement date. A buyer of stock may prefer an early settlement in order to be listed on a firm's books on the record date for a dividend. The buyer of a municipal bond may desire an early settlement in order to begin earning tax-free interest on an earlier date.

early-withdrawal penalty The fee assessed when a saver withdraws funds from a fixed-term investment prior to the scheduled maturity. The charge for early withdrawal is permitted as an adjustment in calculating taxable income.

earned income Individual income, such as commissions, salaries, and bonuses, that is derived as compensation for personal services. —Compare UNEARNED INCOME 1.

earned income credit A tax credit or cash supplement available to certain low-income working individuals and families even if no tax has been withheld from wages. The U.S. Congress created the earned income credit in 1975 to help offset the Social Security payroll tax on low-income individuals and families.

earned premium In insurance, the portion of a premium that has been used by the insurance company to provide coverage. Premiums are typically paid ahead of coverage, so that the earned portion increases gradually over the life of a premium. —Compare UNEARNED PREMIUM.

earned surplus —See RETAINED EARNINGS.

earnest money Money advanced by a buyer to a seller as proof that an agreed-upon purchase will be completed. Earnest money is generally subject to forfeiture in the event the buyer withdraws from the transaction. —See also GOOD FAITH DEPOSIT 1.

earning power 1. Earnings that an asset could produce under optimal conditions. For example, AT&T may currently be earning $2.50 per share, but under optimal conditions each share could have earnings of $3.75. 2. The expected yield on a security.

earnings The income of a business. Earnings usually refers to aftertax income, but may occasionally be used synonymously with pretax income or even revenues.

earnings before interest and taxes (EBIT) —See OPERATING INCOME.

earnings before interest, taxes, depreciation, and amortization (EBITDA) One popular measure of cash generated from the operation of a company. Financial analysts frequently use EBITDA to evaluate the ability of a company to service its debt obligations. EBITDA is also used as a measure of profitability in valuing a company and in comparing a company's financial performance with other firms. Critics contend EBITDA can be a misleading financial tool, in part because companies have wide discretion in determining the dollar amount of the components used in calculating EBITDA. In addition, EBITDA does not consider the funds a company is likely to require for capital investments. —See also CASH FLOW; FREE CASH FLOW.

earnings before taxes —See PRETAX INCOME.

earnings capitalization rate —See EARNINGS-PRICE RATIO.

earnings momentum An increase of earnings per share at an increasing rate. For example, a company is said to have earnings momentum if its reported earnings per share increases 10%, 15%, and 25% in successive years.

earnings multiple —See PRICE-EARNINGS RATIO.

earnings per share (EPS) An earnings measure calculated by subtracting the dividends paid to holders of preferred stock from the net income for a period and dividing that result by the average number of common shares outstanding during that period. EPS is the amount of reported income, on a per-share basis, that a firm has available to pay dividends to common stockholders or to reinvest in itself. As with other financial measures, EPS can vary with differing accounting techniques; therefore, reported EPS may give a very misleading signal as to how the firm is really doing. —Also called *income per share; net income per share.* —See also BASIC EARNINGS PER SHARE; DILUTED EARNINGS PER SHARE.

earnings-price ratio (E/P ratio) A measure indicating the rate at which investors will capitalize a firm's expected earnings in the coming period. This ratio is calculated by dividing the projected earnings per share by the current market price of the stock. A relatively low E/P ratio anticipates higher-than-average growth in earnings. Earnings-price ratio is the inverse of the price-earnings ratio. —Also called *earnings capitalization rate; earnings yield.*

earnings quality The extent to which a firm's reported earnings accurately reflect income for that period. Firms using conservative accounting practices tend to penalize current earnings and are said to have high earnings quality. At least over the short run, the earnings reported by a firm are as much a function of its accounting methods as they are a measure of its business success. —Also called *quality of earnings.* —See also INVENTORY PROFIT.

earnings report —See INCOME STATEMENT.

earnings retention ratio —See RETENTION RATE.

earnings statement —See INCOME STATEMENT.

earnings surprise Earnings reported by a company that are different from the earnings that had been expected by the investment community. An earnings surprise often produces a sharp increase or decrease in the market price of a stock.

earnings yield —See EARNINGS-PRICE RATIO.

earnout A contingency component of an acquisition agreement in which the acquiring company consents to additional payments in the event certain performance-based goals are achieved. For example, owners put a promising but money-losing technology company up for sale. A buyer with substantial capital agrees to pay a fairly low price and assume the firm's debt. As part of the sale agreement, the buyer agrees to share with the sellers a portion of future earnings in the event the venture is successful. The earnout reduces the risk to the buyer, who benefits from a low acquisition price, at the same time it allows the sellers to participate in future success of the enterprise they were unable to fund.

easement The right of limited access to another person's property. For example, a utility may have an easement to run electric lines over or under property it does not own.

easy money A condition of the money supply in which the Federal Reserve permits substantial funds to accrue in the banking system, thereby cutting interest rates and facilitating the acquisition of loans. A policy of easy money is pursued during periods of economic weakness when the Federal Reserve desires more economic growth. —Compare TIGHT MONEY. —Also called *cheap money.*

EBIT —See EARNINGS BEFORE INTEREST AND TAXES.

EBITDA —See EARNINGS BEFORE INTEREST, TAXES, DEPRECIATION, AND AMORTIZATION.

e check —See ELECTRONIC CHECK.

echelon The level of a person's responsibility in an organization. A new hire for a management training position would be considered a lower-echelon employee.

ECN —See ELECTRONIC COMMUNICATIONS NETWORK.

e-commerce The buying and selling of goods and services over the Internet. Ebay is a company that has taken advantage of e-commerce.

econometrics The development and application of mathematical techniques to study economic relationships.

economic activity The production and distribution of goods and services at all levels. Economic activity and expected future levels of it have an important influence on corporate profits, inflation, interest rates, and other variables. One frequently used measure of economic activity is gross domestic product.

economic base The type of businesses that provide employment and pay taxes in a specific town or region. For example, coal mining is the economic base of Gillette, Wyoming.

Economic Census A statistical portrait of the U.S. economy taken every five years by the U.S. Census Bureau. Decades of data at fixed intervals are compiled by industry, geographic area, and product line.

economic depreciation A loss in the market value of an asset caused by factors other than the physical condition of the property. For example, a drug store may decline in value because of a change in the composition of the neighborhood population.

economic efficiency Utilizing resources in a manner that results in the greatest value of output. A system is characterized by economic efficiency if goods, services, and resources flow to those who will pay the highest prices. Taxes, subsidies, quotas, and regulations result in reduced economic efficiency.

economic exposure The potential deterioration in a firm's valuation caused by unanticipated changes in currency exchange rates. Currency exchange rate fluctuations affect a firm's competitive position, the value of its assets, and its operating cash flows.

economic freedom The right of individuals and organizations to pursue their own interests through voluntary exchange of goods and services under the rule of law.

economic growth An increase in the production levels of goods and services. If measured in monetary terms, the increases must occur after adjustments for inflation have been made.

economic indicator A variable such as the unemployment rate or volume of help-wanted advertising that indicates the direction of the economy.

economic life The period of time during which a fixed asset competitively produces a good or service of value. The economic life of an asset may be particularly short in a rapidly changing field such as electronics, where new developments often render an asset obsolete shortly after it is purchased. Companies sometimes continue to carry assets with expired economic lives on their balance sheets because they do not wish to penalize their earnings by writing off the assets. —See also PHYSICAL LIFE.

economic loss 1. Current and future expenses expected to be incurred as a result of an injury or death. Economic loss for a person hit by a vehicle includes lost wages, legal fees, medical expenses, attorney fees, and so forth. 2. The amount by which total expenses, including opportunity cost, exceed total revenues.

economic order quantity (EOQ) The order quantity for inventory that minimizes the combination of processing and storage costs. Larger orders decrease ordering costs and increase storage costs. Smaller orders increase ordering costs and decrease storage costs.

economic rent The difference between the cost of a factor of production and the amount that would have to be paid for continued availability of the factor. For example, an NBA center of modest talent earns $7 million per year when he would gladly do the same job for $500,000. His economic rent is $6.5 million. —Also called *rent*.

economics The study of societal and individual uses of scarce resources in satisfying wants.

economic sanctions Economic penalties imposed on companies or countries in an attempt to force a change in policies. For example, the United States might prohibit the import of products from a country that supports terrorist organizations.

economic shock An external and unexpected event that impacts an economy. For example, a natural disaster such as an earthquake or hurricane can have a major impact on an economy.

economies of scale The increase in production efficiencies realized as output increases. For example, a manufacturer may be able to produce 100 units at $40 per unit and 150 units at $35 per unit. Economies of scale result in big companies having lower unit costs and enjoying an economic advantage over smaller companies. —Compare DISECONOMIES 1.

economies of scope The reduction in costs that results from having two or more enterprises or processes utilize the same resources. For example, a media conglomerate enjoys economies of scope by having a single newsgathering organization provide content to its newspapers, Internet site, television stations, and radio stations.

ECU —See EUROPEAN CURRENCY UNIT.

EDGAR (Electronic Data Gathering, Analysis, and Retrieval) A Securities and Exchange Commission computer database utilized by companies to electronically transmit required SEC filings for securities offerings and disclosure statements.

Edge Act corporation A corporation established under the 1919 Edge Act to undertake activities in international banking and investing. The act gives U.S. firms more flexibility in competing effectively with foreign firms. Corporations established under the Edge Act are often organized in order to finance foreign trade or to own foreign securities. —Also called *agreement corporation.*

edict An official decision entered on the court record.

Education IRA —See COVERDELL EDUCATION SAVINGS ACCOUNT.

EEC —See EUROPEAN ECONOMIC COMMUNITY.

effective date 1. The date an agreement takes effect. For example, FAS 152 by the Financial Accounting Standards Board became effective for financial statements for fiscal years beginning after June 15, 2005. **2.** The date on which underwriters may sell a new offering registered with the SEC. There is usually a 20-day cooling-off period between the filing of a registration and the effective date.

effective debt Total liabilities of a company, including the capitalized value of lease obligations.

effective net worth The book value of assets less all liabilities other than subordinated debt. Effective net worth is a measure of the financial security enjoyed by senior creditors.

effective rate of interest The rate of interest that incorporates compounding in the calculation used to determine the amount of interest to be credited to an account. For amounts invested during an entire year, the annual effective rate of interest multiplied by the principal will equal the amount of earned interest.

effective tax rate —See AVERAGE TAX RATE.

efficiency A measure of productivity that compares output to inputs. In automobile manufacturing one measure of efficiency is the number of labor hours required to produce a vehicle.

efficiency engineer An individual whose job it is to improve the efficiency of a process or organization. For example, a specialized efficiency engineer may have a job promoting energy efficiency in buildings and appliances.

efficient market A market in which asset prices reflect all available information and adjust instantly to any new information. If the security markets are truly efficient, it is not possible for an investor consistently to outperform stock market averages such as the S&P 500 except by acquiring more risky securities. —Also called *market efficiency.* —See also RANDOM-WALK HYPOTHESIS.

efficient portfolio A combination of investments that offer either the highest possible yield at a given risk level or the lowest possible risk at a given yield level. Although

---

ejectment

I currently rent a nice apartment with a location near my work. I have heard the owner is in the process of selling the building to a group of investors. What rights do I have as a tenant? For example, can I be forced to move before my lease is up?

It depends on the language in your lease. Most residential leases allow (by implication) the tenant to remain in the property for the stated term, even if the property is sold. Whoever buys the property is also buying the lease, and must honor its terms as the new landlord. The exception would be if the property were sold through the foreclosure of the previous owner's loan. In almost all of these cases, the new buyer can force the tenant to move immediately. Some leases specifically state that if the property is sold, the new landlord will have the option to force the tenant to move, although usually there is a reasonable notice period involved. If your original lease has expired, or if you never had a written lease, state laws will determine how quickly the current or new landlord can force you to move; typically this period is 60 days.

In most leases for commercial property, there is language that gives the tenant the right to remain in the property after it is sold, and the new owner must honor all terms of the lease as the new landlord. In the case of foreclosure, the language in the lease will prevail. This is one of many reasons why the preparation of commercial leases usually requires legal counsel in order to enumerate and protect the rights of both landlord and tenant—particularly to protect a tenant's rights to remain in the property and conduct their business if the property is sold.

■ Scott Alderman, Broker and President, First Commercial Real Estate, Valdosta, GA

---

the concept of an efficient portfolio is important to understand, in practice it is more academic than practical.

EFT —See ELECTRONIC FUNDS TRANSFER.

8–K A report filed with the SEC by any firm seeking to provide information on a material event that affects its financial condition. Any firm with shares traded on a national exchange or in the over-the-counter market must file the report. The SEC makes 8–Ks available to the public. —Also called *Form 8–K.*

80/20 rule —See PARETO'S LAW.

ejectment Legal action to remove someone who is occupying real property. A landlord who sells a rental property and can't convince a tenant to leave will obtain an order of ejectment to be served by a marshal.

elastic Of or relating to the demand for a good or service when the quantity purchased varies significantly in response to price changes in the good or service. For example, the demand for a product with many close substitutes is elastic because a small price rise will cause consumers to switch to competing brands. —Compare INELASTIC. —See also UNITARY ELASTICITY.

elasticity The responsiveness of the quantity of an item purchased to changes in the item's price. If the quantity purchased changes proportionately more than the price, the demand is elastic. If the quantity purchased changes proportionately less than the price, the demand is inelastic. For example, price increases by cigarette manufacturers have a relatively small effect on cigarette consumption, thus, the demand for cigarettes is inelastic. —Compare INELASTICITY. —Also called *price elasticity.* —See also ADVERTISING ELASTICITY; CROSS ELASTICITY; UNITARY ELASTICITY.

elderly or disabled tax credit A federal credit for individuals who are either 65 years of age or older, or under 65 years of age but retired on permanent and total disability. The credit is available only to U.S. citizens and residents who have adjusted gross income and nontaxable Social Security and pensions that are less than a specified amount.

election cycle —See PRESIDENTIAL ELECTION CYCLE.

elective share The proportion of an estate that may be claimed by a surviving husband or wife in place of what is provided by the deceased spouse. Elective share varies by state but usually ranges from 33% to 50% of estate property.

> **CASE** In 1999 the Florida legislature enacted a major change in the state's
> **STUDY** elective share statute. Prior to the legislation that became effective in
> October 2001, a surviving spouse could elect to take 30% of the decedent's
> probate estate property. Not only was the percentage share among the small-
> est of any state in the country, but the base was narrowly defined to include
> only probate estate property (assets in the decedent's name alone). The lim-
> ited base allowed insurance policies, assets in a living trust, and assets held
> jointly with someone other than the surviving spouse to pass outside probate
> and escape the elective share. Under the law it was fairly easy for someone to
> completely disinherit a spouse. The definition of elective share was broadened
> to include probate property plus other assets such as the decedent's ownership
> interest in property, jointly titled bank accounts and securities, retirement
> and pension plans, and the cash surrender value of life insurance policies.
> While the legislation helped offset some of the unfairness of the old law, it also
> created new problems for some Florida residents, including those who had
> been married several times with children from prior marriages.

electronic check An electronic file that substitutes for and contains all of the relevant information of a paper check. Merchants are permitted to use a paper check as a source of information to make one-time electronic payments from a customer's account. —Also called *e check*.

electronic communications network (ECN) A computerized trading network that matches buy and sell orders entered electronically by customers. Orders that cannot be immediately matched are posted for viewing by investors who may wish to take an offsetting position. Instinet became the first ECN when it started business in 1969. Archipelago and Island became two other large electronic communications networks.

Electronic Data Gathering, Analysis, and Retrieval —See EDGAR.

electronic filing Submitting tax return data via the Internet to the Internal Revenue Service. In 2005 the IRS started its "Free File" program that allows individuals to prepare and file their tax returns without charge on the IRS website.

electronic funds transfer (EFT) The transfer of funds, as from one account to another or from buyer to seller, by telephone or computer. The use of EFT results in the instantaneous movement of money. The additional time that the funds are available to earn income can more than offset the fees charged by institutions for this service. —Also called *bank wire; wire transfer*.

Electronic Return Originator (ERO) A professional tax preparer who is authorized by the Internal Revenue Service to transmit tax return information to the IRS.

electronic trading Buying and selling securities using the Internet. Individual investors typically use electronic trading to transmit orders to brokerage firms that provide the executions. Member firms have direct access to markets using electronic trading.

elephant An institutional investor that controls a substantial amount of funds and that makes investment decisions that can have a major impact on a security's market price.

elevator pitch A logical and concise overview of a product, service, or business that can be delivered quickly (the time of an average elevator ride).

eligibility requirements Minimum standards for acceptability. For example, an individual must meet a minimum age standard and have 40 quarters of coverage to qualify for Social Security retirement benefits. Employers nearly always have eligibility requirements for employees to qualify for medical and retirement benefits.

eligible margin Collateral that is specified by a firm or an exchange as acceptable for satisfying margin requirements. For example, certain low-priced stocks may not be acceptable as margin.

eligible paper Negotiable instruments, including commercial paper and banker's acceptances, that the Federal Reserve will accept from commercial banks for rediscount.

emancipation A legal procedure that frees children from control by their parents or guardians prior to the age of majority. Being emancipated means a minor has the right to take certain actions, such as applying for work and enrolling in a school or college.

embargo Prohibition of a category of trade that is applicable to either an export or an import. For example, concern about disease may cause France to place an embargo on beef imports from the United States.

embedded option A provision within a security giving either the issuer or the security holder the right to take a specified action against the other. For example, a call provision is an embedded option in a bond that gives the issuer the right to redeem the bond prior to the scheduled maturity.

embezzle To take illegally something of value being held in custody for someone else.

emblement The right to crops, or cash received from crops already planted, legally belonging to the tenant of agricultural land who supplied the labor.

emerging growth stock The common stock of a relatively young firm that is operating in an industry that has very good growth prospects. Although this kind of stock offers unusually large returns, it is very risky because the expected growth may not occur or the firm may be swamped by the competition.

emerging markets Security markets in countries such as Mexico and Malaysia that are still developing their industrial base. Investments in emerging markets entail substantial risk along with the potential for above-average returns.

eminent domain The legal right of government to take private property for the public purpose without consent of the property owner. Just compensation must be paid for property taken.

CASE STUDY The U.S. Supreme Court's 2005 decision allowing a Connecticut city to seize private property for economic development by another private entity created a public firestorm, especially among conservatives. Essentially, the nation's highest court ruled that a private citizen does not have a constitutional right to resist government's taking of property via eminent domain, regardless of the reason. Rather, property owners must rely on state law for regulating the taking of private property for public purposes. The Supreme Court decision resulted in the introduction in several states of ballot measures intended to limit the use of eminent domain. Several states also took up the issue of the extent to which governments could restrict the use of land.

emolument Compensation received from employment or holding an office.

employee A person who receives compensation for performing services subject to the will and control of an employer with regard to what shall be done and how it shall be done.

employee assistance program A worksite-based program that identifies and attempts to resolve problems associated with employees impaired by personal concerns. Employee assistance programs may deal with substance abuse, financial issues, marital programs, or a host of other matters.

employee benefit —See BENEFIT 1.

employee contribution An employee's required payment for a portion of the total cost of a benefit offered by an employer. For example, an employee may be required to contribute $100 per month for health insurance coverage.

employee profit sharing —See PROFIT-SHARING PLAN.

Employee Retirement Income Security Act (ERISA) A 1974 act that protects the retirement income of pension fund participants by setting standards for eligibility, performance, investment selection, funding, and vesting. The act was designed to curb abuses by pension fund managers so as to ensure that retirement funds would actually be available at the time of the workers' retirement.

employee stock option —See INCENTIVE STOCK OPTION.

Employee Stock Ownership Plan (ESOP) A qualified retirement plan in which employees receive shares of the common stock of the company for which they work and the company receives an investment tax credit. The purpose of this type of plan is to give employees a vested interest in the company, thereby providing them with an additional incentive toward greater productivity. —See also LEVERAGED ESOP.

CASE STUDY An ESOP allows the owners of a small company to gain a tax benefit and diversify their personal investment portfolio while the firm's employees become owners. ESOPs were first offered in the 1950s on the theory that employees who become part owners will work harder, thereby creating a more productive and profitable company. The owners of the business who initiate an ESOP receive tax benefits at the same time they gain more loyal and productive employees. Depending on the size of the business, the firm might borrow several million dollars that it then lends to the ESOP. The ESOP uses the borrowed money to purchase shares from the owners (or the company). Special tax breaks applicable to ESOPs allow the company to deduct both interest and principal payments on the loan. The disadvantage to the employees is the lack of diversification of their retirement plan, which is subject to many of the same risks as their current employment. If the firm encounters financial difficulties, the employees are subject to losing both their jobs and their retirement nest eggs.

employee withholding allowance certificate The IRS form provided by employers to employees who claim exemptions and allowances for income tax withholding purposes. —Also called *Form W-4*.

employer An individual or organization that hires and pays wages to others.

employer identification number An IRS-issued nine-digit number for taxpayer identification of corporations, partnerships, estates, and trusts.

employers' liability acts Federal and state legislation that defines the extent to which an employer will be held liable for damages for injuries to employees during the course of their work.

employment agency An organization that assists individuals in locating jobs and assists businesses and other organizations in locating employees.

employment certificate —See WORKING PAPERS 2.

employment contract An agreement between an employee and an employer that specifies the terms of employment and can include compensation, sick pay policy, dismissal requirements, hours of work, and so forth. —See also YELLOW-DOG CONTRACT.

employment cost index A closely watched economic report by the Bureau of Labor Statistics that indicates the total cost of employing a civilian worker. A larger-than-expected increase in the index is likely to place downward pressure on security prices.

emporium A large retail marketplace. An emporium can be organized into numerous departments and operate as a department store, or it can specialize in a particular line, such as vehicles, furniture, or appliances.

empowerment Having the information, resources, and authority to make meaningful choices. A corporate head who delegates authority provides empowerment to division and department heads.

empty nester A parent whose children have all grown up and left home.

enabling clause A provision in a law that specifies the individuals or officials who have the power of implementation and enforcement.

encroachment Extension of a structure or portion of a structure onto someone else's property without permission. For example, someone might construct a fence that encroaches on his neighbor's yard.

encryption The manipulation of data to prevent accurate interpretation by all but those for whom the data is intended. Financial institutions use encryption to increase the security of data transmitted via the Internet. —Also called *data encryption*.

encumbrance **1.** A liability on real property. For example, a mortgage encumbers title to real estate because the lender has an interest in the property. —Compare UNENCUMBERED. **2.** A commitment within an organization to use funds for a specific purpose. Thus, a college may encumber funds for later payment to cover expenses associated with a faculty member's trip to recruit new professors.

ending inventory Goods available for sale at the end of an accounting period. —Compare BEGINNING INVENTORY.

end-of-month (EOM) dating A billing provision that the credit period for goods received begins on the first day of the following month. A billing of 3/10 net 30 EOM for goods shipped February 20 requires full payment by March 30, or payment by March 10 to benefit from the 3% discount.

endorse **1.** To sign a negotiable instrument in order to transfer it to another party. For example, investors holding securities must endorse the certificates before delivery to the broker. **2.** To give support to a product, service, person, or cause. For example, a professional athlete may endorse a line of clothing. —Also called *testimonial.*

endorsement **1.** An owner's signature that serves to transfer the legal rights to a negotiable certificate to another party. **2.** An addition to a contract. For example, an insurance agent might suggest that a client add an endorsement to their homeowner's insurance contract for coverage of a valuable coin collection.

endorsement in blank An endorsement of a negotiable instrument by the owner without any transferee being named. Such an endorsement is risky, because anyone coming into possession of the negotiable instrument may become its new owner.

endowment A capital fund designed to provide a permanent source of income. A university may have an endowment to pay for student scholarships.

endowment life insurance A life insurance policy that provides benefits for a specified period (for example, 20 years or until age 65) and that may be redeemed at face value if the insured is alive at the end of the specified period. Thus, payment is made regardless of whether the insured lives or dies, although the cost of the policy is quite high compared with other types of life insurance.

end user The ultimate consumer of a product.

Engel's Law Observation by German statistician Ernst Engel that expenditures on food consume a smaller proportion of rising incomes. Poorer families spend a larger proportion of income on food than do wealthier families.

enjoin **1.** To prohibit. **2.** To give direction in an authoritative manner.

enrolled agent A licensed professional who is authorized to appear before the Internal Revenue Service in place of a taxpayer. Enrolled agents specialize in taxation and must either pass a two-day examination or have at least five years' experience working for the IRS.

enrollment period The period of time during which an employee can sign up for an employer-sponsored benefit such as health insurance.

enterprise value The market value of all of a firm's debt and equity. For example, if a company has $2 million of outstanding debt currently valued at 90% of face value and 100,000 shares of common stock trading for $50 per share, the enterprise value is (0.9 x $2 million) + (100,000 shares x $50), or $6.8 million.

enterprise zone A designated geographical area in which businesses receive special tax benefits, advantageous financing, or other incentives.

entitlement program A government program that offers benefits to individuals or organizations that meet specified standards. Social Security, Medicare, and unemployment benefits are examples of entitlement programs.

entity A person or organization that is considered separate and distinct for legal purposes. A corporation is an entity that pays taxes, enters into contracts, and can sue or be sued.

entrapment Inducing someone to commit a crime that the person had no previous intention to commit. For example, government agents talk someone into selling drugs. A claim of entrapment is a valid defense to prosecution.

entrepot 1. A temporary storage facility. For example, a state might attempt to stimulate employment by establishing an entrepot where goods could be imported and exported without duties being paid. **2.** A financial center. London is a major entrepot where funds are collected and distributed to users.

entrepreneur A risk taker who has the skills and initiative to establish a business. —See also INTRAPRENEURSHIP.

entry-level Describing employment that is available to individuals without experience.

environmental assessment A concise record of environmental issues and concerns relevant to a proposed project, alternative means of accomplishing the project, and the environmental effects of each alternative.

environmental impact statement A study required of anyone proposing action on public lands, including the building of structures or roads. The statement describes the project, offers reasonable alternatives, and addresses environmental consequences. An environmental impact statement is similar to, but more comprehensive than, an environmental assessment.

Environmental Protection Agency (EPA) The federal agency charged with protecting human health and the environment. Established in 1970, the EPA develops and enforces environmental regulations, performs environmental research, and provides financial support for state and educational research on the environment.

EOM —See END-OF-MONTH DATING.

EOQ —See ECONOMIC ORDER QUANTITY.

EPA —See ENVIRONMENTAL PROTECTION AGENCY.

E/P ratio —See EARNINGS-PRICE RATIO.

EPS —See EARNINGS PER SHARE.

Equal Credit Opportunity Act Federal legislation that prohibits discrimination against individuals or businesses in the granting of credit. Creditors are prohibited from considering an applicant's sex, race, religion, marital status, or national origin. Age may be considered in certain circumstances. The Federal Trade Commission enforces the act.

Equal Employment Opportunity Commission The federal agency created in 1964 to end discrimination in employment based on race, sex, religion, or national origin. The agency later became responsible for ending employment discrimination based on disability or age.

equalization board A government board that attempts to make certain that taxes are administered fairly. Initially established to assure the fairness of property tax assessments, the work of many equalization boards has been expanded to cover other areas of taxation and to administer revenues collected from these taxes.

equalizing dividend A dividend payment that is intended to compensate for a change in regular dividend dates. For example, a firm may move back its dividend payment dates by one month and compensate its shareholders with a one-time equalizing dividend to account for the four-month, instead of the normal three-month, interval before the first payment under the new schedule.

equal opportunity employer An employer that agrees to promote affirmative action and avoid discrimination in accordance with applicable state and federal laws.

equilibrium A state of balance in a variable. For example, equilibrium price occurs when the quantity supplied of a good or service equals the quantity demanded and no surplus or shortage exists.

equipment Fixed assets that are acquired as additions or supplements to more permanent assets. Equipment includes lighting fixtures in a building, for example. Equipment, unlike real estate, is generally moveable.

equipment lease —See LEASE.

equipment leasing limited partnership A partnership in which investors' funds are used to acquire equipment that is leased to businesses. Lease payments are passed through to partners, with much of the income sheltered from taxation by depreciation and interest expense. At the termination of a lease, the equipment is sold and a cash distribution is made to the partners.

equipment trust certificate An intermediate- to long-term security that pays a fixed return based on payments received from the lease of equipment. These certificates are frequently used by railroads and airlines to finance rolling stock and aircraft, respectively.

equitable distribution 1. A fair apportionment of something. For example, a judge attempts to reach an equitable distribution of assets among creditors in a bankruptcy proceeding. **2.** In divorce, a fair division of assets and earnings acquired during marriage.

equitable owner The beneficiary of assets being held in trust.

equitable title A title to property in which a party has a beneficial interest and will eventually acquire legal title. For example, the beneficiary of a trust has an equitable title in assets held in the trust.

equity 1. In a brokerage account, the market value of securities minus the amount borrowed. Equity is particularly important for margin accounts, for which minimum standards must be met. **2.** Stock, both common and preferred. For example, an investor may prefer investing in equities instead of in bonds. —Also called *equity security.* **3.** In accounting, funds contributed by stockholders through direct payment and through retained earnings. —See also OWNERS' EQUITY. **4.** The market value of real estate less the balance on any financing. A home with a market value of $400,000 and a remaining loan balance of $275,000 has equity of $400,000 less $275,000, or $125,000.

equity arbitrage —See RISK ARBITRAGE.

equity buildup The increasing ownership value of an asset as payments reduce the outstanding balance on an amortized loan.

equity carve-out The initial sale of common stock by a corporation of one of its business units. The initial public offering generally involves less than the entire amount of the stock in the unit, so the parent company retains an equity stake in the subsidiary. An equity carve-out is sometimes followed by a distribution of the remaining shares to the parent's stockholders. —Also called *carve-out; splitoff IPO.*

> **CASE STUDY** Equity carve-outs—initial public offerings of subsidiaries—are not unusual. The Limited, Inc. carved out 18% of Abercrombie & Fitch Co. in a 1996 IPO. Two years later DuPont raised $4.4 billion by undertaking an equity carve-out equal to 30% of its oil subsidiary Conoco. Later the same year, CBS raised $3 billion in a carve-out of 16% of subsidiary Infinity Broad-

casting. In August 1998 Cincinnati Bell sold 15 million shares in an initial public offering of subsidiary Convergys. Later that year Cincinnati Bell distributed to its shareholders the remaining 137 million Convergys shares. Equity carve-outs can offer several advantages to a company and its shareholders. In general, management of the parent firm believes the market value of the separated companies will be greater than the market value of the combined firm prior to the carve-out. Perhaps the investment community has been overlooking the real value of the subsidiary that produces good financial results but is overshadowed by the other parts of the firm. Another plus derives from a separately traded stock allowing the former subsidiary to use its own stock as a currency for acquisitions and management incentives. The new publicly traded company will have access to the equity markets that can provide capital for expansion.

equity commitment note Corporate debt that eventually will be repaid by issuing stock.

equity financing The acquisition of funds by issuing shares of common or preferred stock. Firms usually use equity financing when they are unable to raise sufficient funds through retained earnings, or when they have to raise additional equity capital to offset debt. —Compare DEBT FINANCING.

equity-indexed annuity A contract with an insurance company that promises periodic payments keyed in a specified manner to a stock market index. Unlike variable annuities, equity-indexed annuities specify a guaranteed minimum return that is typically 3%. These contracts may also specify an upper limit (cap) on the return that is paid. Indexing methods vary, and surrender charges often apply to early withdrawals.

equity-indexed life insurance —See INDEXED LIFE INSURANCE.

equity interest Part ownership of an asset or group or business. For example, a common stockholder of General Electric has an equity interest in the business. Equity interest contrasts with a creditor's position as a lender.

equity kicker An addition to a fixed-income security that permits the investor to participate in increases in the value of equity ownership. Two common types of equity kickers are a convertible feature on some bonds that allows the bonds to be exchanged for shares of stock, and warrants to purchase stock that are sold in combination with some new bond issues.

equity method A method of accounting for an investment in another company in which the book value of the investment reflects a share of the acquired firm's increases in retained earnings. Thus, if Firm A purchases 20% of Firm B's stock and Firm B earns $3 million after taxes during the next year, Firm A will increase the carrying value of its investment by 20% of $3 million, or $600,000. If Firm B pays half its earnings in dividends, Firm A will increase its investment by $300,000.

equity note Intermediate-term debt that is automatically converted into common stock at maturity.

equity of redemption The right of a borrower to reclaim title to property once the terms of a mortgage have been satisfied.

equity option An option for which the underlying asset is stock. —Compare NONEQUITY OPTION.

equivalent taxable yield

My broker has advised me that I should consider investing in municipal bonds. How can I decide if municipal bonds are right for me?

Municipal bonds are exempt from federal income taxes (and in some cases from state income taxes) and, therefore, would have a lower interest rate than taxable bonds with the same risk, liquidity, and maturity. Use the formula at **equivalent taxable yield** to calculate the after-tax equivalent yield of the municipal bond you are considering and compare it to the yield of a taxable bond with the same risk, liquidity, and maturity. If the municipal bond has a higher yield than the bond with taxable interest, other things equal, then it may be right for you.

▪ Michael W. Butler, PhD, Professor of Economics, Angelo State University, San Angelo, Texas

equity participation loan A loan in which the lender obtains, or has the right to obtain, an ownership interest in the project being financed.

equity REIT A real estate investment trust that purchases property with investors' money. Investors in an equity REIT earn dividend income from rental income earned by the REIT on property it owns. The investors also participate in increases in value of the owned real estate. —Compare MORTGAGE REIT.

equity risk premium The extra return expected from investments in common stocks compared to the return from U.S. Treasury securities.

equity security —See EQUITY 2.

equity warrant —See WARRANT.

equivalent bond yield The annual yield on a short-term security that is usually quoted on a bank-discount basis to make the yield comparable with quotations on other interest-bearing debt.

equivalent taxable yield The taxable return that must be achieved in order to equal, on an aftertax basis, a given tax-exempt return. Equivalent taxable yield is calculated by dividing the available tax-exempt yield by one minus the investor's marginal tax rate. For example, a tax-exempt return of 4% for an investor in a 40% marginal tax bracket would require a taxable return of 0.4/0.6, or 6.67%, to produce the same aftertax equivalent.

ergonomics 1. The study of workers and their environment. 2. The science of designing equipment and arranging the work environment so as to improve worker comfort and productivity.

ERISA —See EMPLOYEE RETIREMENT INCOME SECURITY ACT.

ERO —See ELECTRONIC RETURN ORIGINATOR.

erosion 1. A reduction or decline in a variable. A financial analyst may report erosion in the quality of a firm's reported earnings. 2. A wearing away of land through the forces of nature.

errors and omissions insurance Liability coverage for client claims that something done on their behalf was done incorrectly and caused them harm. This type of coverage is designed for someone such as a software designer, teacher, consultant, or financial planner who offers advice. —Also called *professional liability insurance.*

escalator clause A contract provision that stipulates payment increases under certain circumstances. For example, a lease may call for increased payments to cover increases in energy costs or taxes. Escalator clauses are often included in union contracts for adjusting wages according to some identified index.

escape clause A contract provision specifying conditions under which the parties can avoid liability for nonperformance. For example, a venture capital firm that has signed a contract to provide funding for a new business might include an escape clause that releases them in the event the business does not achieve identified goals by specific dates.

escheat The right of the state to claim a deceased person's property when there are no individuals legally qualified to inherit it or to make a claim to it. This occurrence is fairly unusual, even when the deceased leaves no will.

escrow The holding of assets, including legal documents or cash, by a third party. For example, the owner of real property may be required to leave a deed in custody of a third party until a loan is completely repaid.—See also TRUST ACCOUNT.

escrow account —See IMPOUND ACCOUNT.

escrowed to maturity —Used to describe a bond that has been prerefunded to the degree that cash flows will match the debt obligation to the retirement date.

ESOP —See EMPLOYEE STOCK OWNERSHIP PLAN.

espionage —See INDUSTRIAL ESPIONAGE.

essential function bond A bond issued by a municipality when funds from the bond issue are used for traditional government purposes such as government office buildings, libraries, parks, prisons, roads, and schools. The interest on municipal essential function bonds is exempt from federal income tax and is not subject to the alternative minimum tax. —Compare PRIVATE ACTIVITY BOND. —See also MUNICIPAL BOND.

essential industry A domestic industry judged to be critical to meeting the economic and wartime needs of a country. Aircraft manufacturing is an example of an essential industry in the United States.

estate 1. The assets owned by a person, generally at the time of death. —See also GROSS ESTATE; RESIDUARY ESTATE. **2.** A large tract of real estate owned by a person or family.

estate in reversion An estate that reverts to the grantor following temporary ownership by another party named by the grantor. For example, a daughter gives a home to her parents with the stipulation that the home will be returned to the daughter at the death of both the parents.

estate in severalty An estate being held by a single individual.

estate planning The preparation for the orderly administration and disbursement of a person's estate. The preparation includes taking actions that will minimize taxes and distribute assets to the appropriate heirs.

estate tax A tax on the estate of the deceased before any distribution is made to the heirs. A federal unified gift and estate tax provides an exemption before any tax is paid. Although some states also levy an estate tax, it is generally at a much lower rate than the federal tax. —Compare INHERITANCE TAX. —Also called *death tax; federal estate tax.*

estimated tax The estimated tax liability on income that is not subject to withholding. Individuals with even moderate investment income are generally expected to file a declaration of estimated tax and to pay quarterly installments on the estimated tax liability.

estoppel A restriction from saying or doing something. For example, in court a person is restricted from denying an allegation that has already been admitted.

estoppel certificate A document with specifics about a party's interest in a piece of real estate. For example an estoppel certificate may include the terms of a lease agreement that would be of interest to a potential purchaser of the property.

ETF —See EXCHANGE-TRADED FUND.

Ethernet A standard for communication developed by Xerox Corporation and used primarily on local area networks.

ethical Performed in a manner that is consistent with accepted standards of conduct.

ethical fund A mutual fund that limits investment alternatives to securities of firms meeting certain social standards. For example, an ethical fund might exclude securities of companies that are known to practice discrimination, that operate in certain countries, or that produce specific products (for example, those having to do with nuclear weapons or nuclear power plants). —See also SOCIAL INVESTING.

ethical investing —See SOCIAL INVESTING.

ETN —See EXCHANGE-TRADED NOTE.

e-trade To buy or sell a security via computer. Brokerage firms route computer-generated customer orders to appropriate dealers and exchange specialists.

euro A common currency used by many European countries. The euro was established in 1999 when 11 European countries adopted a common currency in order to facilitate global trade and encourage the integration of markets across national borders. Euro banknotes and coins began circulating in January 2002.

Eurobond A type of foreign bond issued and traded in countries other than the one in which the bond is denominated. A dollar-denominated bond sold in Europe by a U.S. firm is a Eurobond.

Euro CD A certificate of deposit issued primarily in London by a foreign bank or a foreign branch of a U.S. bank.

Euroclear The world's largest settlement system for international and domestic bond and equity transactions. Euroclear provides a variety of financial services, including securities lending, settlement, and clearing.

Eurocurrency Funds deposited in a bank when those funds are denominated in a currency differing from the bank's own domestic currency. Eurocurrency applies to any currency and to banks in any country. Thus, if a Japanese company deposits yen in a Canadian bank, the yen will be considered Eurocurrency.

Eurodollar A dollar-denominated deposit made in foreign banks or foreign branches of U.S. banks. Depositors sometimes transfer their funds to European banks in order to take advantage of higher interest rates. The Eurodollar is one type of Eurocurrency.

Eurodollar bond A dollar-denominated bond sold to investors outside the United States. These securities allow buyers to benefit, or lose, from variations in currency exchange rates. A Eurodollar bond is an example of a Eurobond.

Eurodollar CD A certificate of deposit denominated in U.S. dollars and issued by a financial institution outside the United States.

Euronext N.V. An integrated European securities exchange that was formed from a merger of local exchanges in Paris, Brussels, and Amsterdam. This group later purchased a London derivatives exchange and merged with a Portuguese exchange. Euronext N.V. merged in 2007 with the NYSE Group, Inc. to form NYSE Euronext.

European Central Bank The central bank that has been responsible for monetary policy in the euro area since 1999. Located in Frankfurt, Germany, the bank's main mission is to maintain price stability and the euro's value in the 15 European countries comprising the euro area.

European currency quotation In foreign exchange trading, the value of a dollar in terms of a foreign currency. For example, if the euro is worth $1.25, the European currency quotation would be expressed as 0.80, meaning that there are 0.80 euros to the dollar. —Compare AMERICAN CURRENCY QUOTATION. —Also called *divider.*

European Currency Unit (ECU) A weighted index of the currencies of European Economic Community members used prior to the 1999 introduction of the euro.

European Economic Community (EEC) A group of Western European countries that have joined together to promote trade and economic and political cooperation. Essentially, the EEC represents an attempt to combine a group of countries into a single economic unit. —Also called *Common Market.*

European option An option that can be exercised only on its expiration date, in contrast to the option available in the United States whereby the owner may exercise an option at any time up to and including the expiration date. —Compare AMERICAN OPTION.

evaluator An expert who appraises and assigns a worth to assets for which it is difficult to determine market value.

even lot —See ROUND LOT.

event risk The risk that some unexpected event will cause a substantial decline in the market value of a security. For example, a leveraged buyout that entails huge amounts of new debt will cause a decline in the market value of the target company's outstanding debt.

eviction Removing a tenant from property rented from a landlord. An eviction can be considered *constructive* when a tenant is forced to move because of the condition of the property. A *partial* eviction occurs when a portion of the rented property is unavailable to the tenant.

evidence of title A document such as a deed or car title that proves ownership of property.

ex —Used in combination to refer to a security that trades without something, such as a dividend, warrant, or some other distribution. For example, when a stock trades ex-dividend, it trades without the right to receive the next dividend payment.

exact interest Interest calculated on the basis of a 365-day year as opposed to a 360-day year. —Compare ORDINARY INTEREST.

examination of title —See TITLE SEARCH.

Excelsior list A register of eligible employees' names and addresses submitted by an employer to a union after a union election has been directed by the National Labor Relations Board.

exception An auditor's qualification of a financial report that indicates disagreement with an item in the report or limitations to the extent of the audit.

excess contribution The amount by which a contribution to a retirement program such as an IRA or 403(b) plan exceeds the allowable limit. Without correction, an excess contribution results in an IRS penalty.

excess depreciation The amount by which accumulated depreciation using an accelerated method exceeds accumulated depreciation using the straight-line method. The excess occurs when a firm uses accelerated depreciation for tax purposes (additional depreciation expense results in lower taxes) and straight-line depreciation for financial reporting purposes. Excess depreciation results in ordinary income when an asset is sold.

excessive trading The act of churning.

excess margin The dollar amount of equity in an investor's brokerage margin account that is in excess of what is necessary for meeting either initial margin or maintenance margin requirements. Excess margin may be withdrawn or used to purchase more securities.

excess profits tax A temporary tax levied on business profits during a period of national emergency. For example, the federal government may levy an additional corporate income tax during wartime to generate extra government revenues.

excess reserves The reserves held by banks and thrifts in excess of what is required by the Federal Reserve. Large excess reserves indicate a potential for credit expansion and reduced interest rates that could prove beneficial to the securities markets. Conversely, small excess reserves indicate reduced possibilities for credit expansion and a relatively tight monetary policy by the Federal Reserve. —Compare REQUIRED RESERVES.

excess return The return on an asset or a portfolio in excess of the risk-free return. If short-term corporate debt provides a return of 4½% while U.S. Treasury bills are yielding 3½%, excess return on the corporate debt is 1%. Excess return is usually correlated with the risk of an investment.

exchange¹ —See SECURITIES EXCHANGE.

exchange² —See SWAP².

exchangeable bond A special type of convertible security that permits the holder to exchange the bond for shares of a company in which the issuer has an ownership position. An exchangeable bond differs from an ordinary convertible bond in that a convertible permits the holder to convert it into shares of stock of the issuer.

exchange controls Government restrictions on the purchase of foreign currencies by its own residents and of the domestic currency by nonresidents.

exchange offer An offer by a firm to exchange its own securities for those of another firm or for a different series of the same firm's securities. For example, a firm may offer a new bond issue in exchange for an older series currently outstanding. Depending on the type of securities included in the offer, the security holder may be taxed for the exchange.

exchange privilege The right to exchange shares in one mutual fund for shares in another fund managed by the same firm. The rate at which shares are exchanged is determined by differences in relative values. There is usually a nominal charge for each transfer. This privilege is designed to allow investors to move their money among funds without incurring additional sales fees as their investment goals change. —Also called *conversion privilege*.

exchange rate The price of one currency expressed in terms of another currency. For example, if the U.S. dollar buys 1.20 Canadian dollars, the exchange rate is 1.2 to 1. Changes in exchange rates have significant effects on the profits of multinational corporations. Exchange rate changes also affect the value of foreign investments held by individual investors. For a U.S. investor owning Japanese securities, a strengthening of the U.S. dollar relative to the yen tends to reduce the value of the Japanese securities because the yen value of the securities is worth fewer dollars. —Also called *foreign exchange rate.* —See also DEVALUATION; FIXED EXCHANGE RATE; FLOATING EXCHANGE RATE; FOREIGN EXCHANGE RISK.

exchange rate risk —See FOREIGN EXCHANGE RISK.

exchange-traded fund (ETF) An investment company whose shares trade on a securities exchange, generally at or very near net asset value per share. Unlike ordinary mutual funds that continually issue and redeem their own shares, exchange-traded funds are similar to closed-end investment companies, whose shares trade among investors. ETF shares are initially issued in very large blocks called "creation units" that are split up and sold on the secondary market as individual shares. The share price is maintained at or near net asset value because of the ability of large investors to convert creation units to the underlying stocks or to trade underlying stocks for creation units of the ETF. ETFs generally have low annual operating expenses in comparison to mutual funds.

> **CASE STUDY** Exchange-traded funds (ETFs) enjoyed rapidly increasing popularity following the 1993 introduction of the first of these hybrid investment vehicles. Part mutual fund and part stock, ETFs offer low expenses (little management oversight is required), continuous pricing (mutual funds are priced only at the end of each day), tax efficiency (infrequent trading produces few realized gains to distribute), and a financial asset that can be purchased on margin (like most stocks, but unlike mutual funds). EFTs were initially designed to track popular market indices, including the Standard & Poor's 500 and the Dow Jones Industrial Average. Soon after the turn of the century, investment firms began introducing more specialized ETFs that allow individual investors (wisely or not) to invest in narrow segments of the market, including particular industries, single countries, or groups of stocks with certain similarities such as a high dividend yield or low price-earnings ratio. Although EFTs tend to have low operating expenses, investors must still pay a brokerage commission to buy and sell the shares.

exchange-traded note (ETN) An unsecured debt security guaranteed by its issuer to track the value of a particular asset or index. For example, in November 2007 the New York Stock Exchange listed a Goldman Sachs–sponsored ETN that tracks a broad-based commodity index. ETNs have a maturity date but do not pay periodic interest.

exchange-traded security —See LISTED SECURITY.

excise tax A tax on the manufacture, purchase, or sale of a good or service. The tax may be based on the number of units or on value. —Compare CONSUMPTION TAX.

exclusion 1. In insurance, the lack of coverage for certain risks, properties, or persons. For example, valuable jewelry may be excluded from coverage under a homeowner's policy. **2.** Income that must be reported but is not taxed. For example, proceeds of up to $500,000 from the sale of a residence are permitted as an exclusion by married couples.

exclusionary rule The principle that information obtained in violation of the defendant's constitutional rights cannot be used in prosecuting a criminal case.

exclusionary tender offer An offer to purchase shares of a firm's stock on a pro rata basis while excluding the offer from one or more specific shareholders. The SEC prohibits exclusionary tender offers.

exclusive distribution Offering a product for sale only in one outlet or the outlets of a single company. For example, Kodak announced in early 2007 that the firm's new line of EasyShare printers would be available only in Best Buy stores for the first three months.

exclusive listing A real estate contract that specifies a limited time during which an agent has the sole right to sell a property. —Compare NONEXCLUSIVE LISTING.

exclusive provider organization A managed-care program in which participants will be reimbursed only when care is received from approved providers.

exclusive right to sell listing An exclusive listing in which the broker receives the full commission regardless of whether the property is sold by the broker, another broker, or the owner.

exculpatory 1. Of or relating to a clause in a contract that relieves one party of liability in the event of wrongdoing. **2.** In law, of or relating to evidence that clears a person of wrongdoing.

ex-distribution Of or relating to a stock, such as a spinoff of a subsidiary's stock, that no longer carries the right to a specific distribution.

ex-distribution date The first day of trading when the seller, rather than the buyer, of a stock will be entitled to a recently announced distribution of an asset. The price of the stock can be expected to fall by approximately the value of the distribution on this date, because the stock no longer carries the right to the distribution.

ex-dividend—Used to refer to a stock no longer carrying the right to the next dividend payment because the settlement date occurs after the record date. If, for example, a common stock goes ex-dividend on May 31, an investor purchasing the stock on or after that date will not receive the next dividend check. —Compare CUM DIVIDEND.

ex-dividend date The first day of trading when the seller, rather than the buyer, of a stock will be entitled to the most recently announced dividend payment. The length of time ensuing between the ex-dividend date and the date of actual payment may be up to a month.

execution 1. The consummation of a security trade. **2.** The completion and delivery of a legal document. **3.** Successfully completing a task.

executive A key employee who has major managerial and administrative authority.

executive MBA A graduate program in business administration developed especially for executives and managers who wish to earn a graduate degree without interrupting their careers. Executive MBA programs generally require more extensive managerial experience for entrance and build delivery around concentrated campus meetings (weekends or several full days once a month, for example) and communications via the Internet.

executive secretary A secretary who works under the supervision of an executive and is accorded a high level of responsibility.

executor or executrix The person or institution that administers and disburses the assets of an estate. The executor is charged with various duties, including identifying assets, paying taxes, taking care of debts, and distributing the balance to appropriate individuals and organizations. Executor is masculine and executrix is feminine. —See also ADMINISTRATOR 2; INDEPENDENT EXECUTOR OR EXECUTRIX.

executory Of or pertaining to something that has not been completed. An executory contract is one in which performance remains due by one or both parties. An example would be an unexpired software license under which both the licensee (making payments to the licensor) and the licensor (providing service to the licensee) have an obligation remaining.

exempt employee A person who is exempt from the overtime pay provisions or the child labor provisions of the Fair Labor Standards Act. Common exemptions include commissioned-sales employees, farm workers on small farms, salespeople, executives, and professionals. —Compare NONEXEMPT EMPLOYEE.

exemption 1. An annual deduction permitted a taxpayer and each dependent for use in computing taxable income. An extra exemption is allowed for being blind or for being 65 years of age or older. The size of the annual exemption is altered each year according to the level of inflation. —Also called *personal exemption.* 2. The amount of income that can be subtracted from adjusted gross income when calculating the alternative minimum tax. 3. —See HOMESTEAD EXEMPTION.

exempt organization An organization, corporation, association, or other legal entity that has been determined by the Internal Revenue Service to be exempt from taxation under federal law. Examples include cemeteries, charitable organizations, churches, fraternal societies, and labor unions. Not all nonprofit organizations are exempt organizations. —Also called *not for profit; tax-exempt organization.*

exempt property Property that may be retained in a Chapter 7 bankruptcy or when a judgment is won by a creditor. Most states permit individuals to keep clothing, an inexpensive vehicle, household furnishings, and, in some states, a home. —Compare NONEXEMPT PROPERTY.

exempt security A security that is exempt from registration under the Security Act of 1933 or from margin requirements of the Securities Exchange Act of 1934. Examples of exempt securities are small issues, intrastate issues, and direct placements. U.S. government and agency securities are also exempt.

exercise To require the delivery (for example, a call option) or to force the purchase (for example, a put option) of the option's underlying asset. Many options expire without being exercised because the strike price stated in the option is unfavorable to the holder.

exercise loan A loan from an employer to an employee to pay for the exercise of incentive stock options. Exercise loans are sometimes forgiven in the event that specified performance goals are met.

exercise price The dollar price at which the owner of a warrant or an option can force the writer to sell an asset (in the case of a call option or warrant) or to buy an asset (in the case of a put option). The exercise price is set at the time the option is issued and, except for unusual instances that include warrants, remains constant until the option expires. A market price of an asset that is above, or is expected to be above, an option's exercise price gives the option value. —See also STEP-UP.

exit fee —See DEFERRED SALES CHARGE.

exit interview A meeting between an employer and a departing employee. An exit interview allows an employer to gain an assessment of the organization from an employee who has no reason to bias his or her comments.

exit strategy The method by which an investor plans to cash out of an investment. For example, a venture capitalist may intend to utilize an initial public offering to liquidate an investment in a closely held company.

ex-legal Of or relating to a municipal bond that is traded without the benefit of the legal opinion of a bond counsel. The trading of ex-legal municipal bonds is permitted as long as the buyers are informed about the lack of legal opinion.

ex officio Of or relating to a right deriving from the office or position that is held. For example, a firm's chief executive officer may be an ex officio member of several committees without the need of formal appointments.

exonerate **1.** To free from a task or responsibility. **2.** To declare not guilty of a crime: *An internal investigation exonerated the executive of backdating options.*

exotic option An option with a nonstandard feature. A lookback option that allows the owner flexibility in selecting an exercise price is an example of an exotic option. Exotic options are traded in the over-the-counter market.

expansion **1.** An increase in a firm's capacity to provide products or services. For example, a software company may acquire additional office space in order to hire employees that will work on a new project. **2.** A period during which there is an increase in economic activity.

expectancy theory of motivation The theory that motivation is a function of three variables: the perceived likelihood of success, the association between success and realizing a goal, and the value of achieving a goal. All three factors are interdependent and necessary for proper motivation.

expectations hypothesis The explanation that the slope of the yield curve is attributable to expectations of changes in short-term interest rates. The yield curve relates bond yields and maturity lengths.

expected rate of return The rate of return expected on an asset or a portfolio. The expected rate of return on a single asset is equal to the sum of each possible rate of return multiplied by the respective probability of earning on each return. For example, if a security has a 20% probability of providing a 10% rate of return, a 50% probability of providing a 12% rate of return, and a 25% probability of providing a 14% rate of return, the expected rate of return is: $(0.20 \times 0.10) + (0.50 \times 0.12) + (0.25 \times 0.14) = 0.12$, or 12%.

expected value The sum of all possible outcomes times the probability of each outcome.

expediter A person who ensures goods are delivered quickly and efficiently to the intended location. For example, in the building trades an expediter makes certain the correct materials are delivered on time to a job site.

expense **1.** Spending on goods and services used in the normal course of business. **2.** —See DEPRECIATION 1.

expense account **1.** An account in which expenditures are recorded. —Compare INCOME ACCOUNT. **2.** A fund for reimbursement by an employer for employee expenses incurred in the course of carrying out duties of employment.

expense budget Anticipated costs during a specified period.

expense ratio 1. The proportion of assets required to pay annual operating expenses and management fees of a mutual fund. If a fund charges an annual fee of $.50 per $100 of net assets, the expense ratio will be 0.5%. **2.** —See OPERATING EXPENSE RATIO.

expense report A list of expenses incurred during performance of a job. An expense report for a salesperson might include gasoline, meals, lodging, and associated expenditures.

expensive Of, relating to, or being an asset that sells or is offered for sale at a price above what is expected based on fundamental factors of valuation such as location or earnings potential. Deciding whether an asset is expensive is a subjective judgment. —Compare CHEAP 1.

experience rating In insurance, analyzing losses incurred for a particular type of coverage in order to determine the appropriate premium that should be charged to cover expenses, losses, and a fair profit.

experience refund The return of a portion of premiums to a class of policyholders when insured losses have been less than anticipated.

expert witness A person having special experience, skills, or knowledge who testifies in court.

expiration The relinquishment of the rights of an options contract by permitting the contract to terminate on the expiration date. —Also called *abandonment.*

expiration date 1. The last day on which an option holder may exercise an option. This date is stated in the contract at the time the option is written. —Also called *expiry date.* **2.** The end of an agreement or contract period. **3.** The last date on which a product should be used. For example, pharmaceutical products have an expiry date.

expiration Friday The Friday once each quarter when stock index futures, index options, and stock options simultaneously expire. Investors tend to close out positions in futures, options, and stocks on expiration Friday, with the result being extremely volatile prices on this day. —See also TRIPLE WITCHING HOUR.

expiration notice Written notification of the termination date of insurance coverage sent by an insurance company to an insured.

expired cost An expense incurred during a period when benefits were received. For example, depreciation expense for an asset used in the production process expires when goods are sold. —Compare UNEXPIRED COST.

expiry date —See EXPIRATION DATE 1.

exploration cost The cost of searching for and drilling exploratory gas and oil wells.

exponential smoothing A statistical technique for forecasting in which future outcomes are estimated on the basis of a weighted average of observations from past periods. More recent observations are thought to be better predictors and are given heavier weighting.

export A good or service that is produced in one country and then sold to and consumed in another country. Because many companies are heavily dependent on exports for sales, any factors such as government policies or exchange rates that affect exports can have significant impact on corporate profits. —Compare IMPORT. —See also BALANCE OF TRADE.

export credit A loan or loan guarantee designed to stimulate a country's exports. Typically this involves a direct loan to a foreign buyer of domestic goods and services, or a guarantee for a private loan to a domestic exporter. The loan essentially guarantees that the domestic exporter will be paid.

Export-Import Bank The official export credit agency of the United States, whose mission is to facilitate the financing of U.S. goods and services for export. In general, the bank assumes credit risks and country risks that other institutions are unable or unwilling to accept.

export quota A restriction imposed by a country on the quantity or value of a particular class of exports. An export quota is designed to support world prices (for example, OPEC's petroleum export quotas) or protect domestic consumers against shortages and price increases.

ex post facto Latin for "after the fact," generally used to refer to adopting laws making acts a crime after the acts have already been committed.

exposure 1. Vulnerability to loss. For example, a company with valuable facilities in a foreign country has exposure to political unrest and currency exchange risk. 2. The opportunity for potential customers to learn about a product or service.

exposure draft A proposal seeking comments concerning the revision of standards of financial accounting and reporting by the Financial Accounting Standards Board. Exposure drafts include proposed standards, an effective date of application, and a method of transition.

express contract An agreement in which all terms are clearly stated. —Compare IMPLIED CONTRACT.

Express Mail The most rapid delivery service for letters, documents, or merchandise offered by the U.S. Postal Service. Next-day delivery by noon or 3 p.m. is offered for many destinations.

expropriation Official government seizure of private property, generally for appropriate compensation.

expungement The erasure of a record or a portion of a record. For example, a court allows for the expungement, or deletion, of the criminal record of a minor who reaches a specified age without committing any other criminal offenses.

ex-rights —Used to describe a stock that trades without giving the stockholder the privilege to receive rights to buy shares of a new stock issue. Because new shares are sold at below-market price to rights holders, the rights have value. Thus, a stock trading ex-rights is worth less than the same stock with rights attached. —Compare RIGHTS ON. —Also called *rights off*. —See also RIGHTS OFFERING.

ex-rights date The first day of trading on which new buyers of a firm's stock will not be entitled to receive recently declared rights to buy shares in a new security issue.

extendable bond A long-term debt security that permits the owner to extend the maturity such that interest payments continue and the principal repayment is delayed beyond the original date. This relatively rare type of bond works to the advantage of investors during periods of declining interest rates.

extended coverage An endorsement to an insurance policy that provides coverage for risks not offered in a basic policy.

extended-hours trading The trading of securities when the exchanges are closed. Extended-hours trading often refers to trading a listed security in the over-the-counter market or on an electronic communications network either before or after the exchanges are open for trading. This fairly common practice is not illegal. —Also called *after-hours trading*.

extended term insurance option A nonforfeiture option attached to an ordinary life insurance policy in which the net cash value is used as a single premium to purchase paid-up term insurance with coverage equal to the original policy. The length of coverage of the term policy depends on the life expectancy of the insured and the amount of cash value available for the premium.

extension 1. Additional time for filing an income tax return. 2. Delaying the date on which parties are to satisfy the terms of a contract.

extension swap The exchange of a bond or note for another virtually identical security having a longer maturity.

external audit An examination of a company's records and reports by an outside party. —Compare INTERNAL AUDIT. —Also called *independent audit; outside audit.*

external funds The funds that are raised from sources outside a firm. The monies that are received from the sale of stock and bonds are external funds. Firms seek external funds when they are unable to finance expenditures with money generated from operations. External funds are particularly important for a young, fast-growing company that has capital requirements that greatly outstrip its ability to generate funds internally. —Compare INTERNAL FUNDS.

externality The impact of the action of one or more parties on an unrelated party or on society. For example, air pollution is an externality of generating electricity by means of a coal-fired power plant. Externalities can be either negative (as per the coal-fired power plant) or positive. —Also called *spillover.*

extra —See EXTRA DIVIDEND.

extra dividend A nonrecurring additional payment to stockholders that is brought about by special circumstances. An extra dividend may be issued when a firm in a cyclical industry has an especially profitable period and wishes to distribute some extra funds to its stockholders. —Also called *extra; special dividend.*

> **CASE STUDY** Phelps Dodge Corporation, a large domestic copper producer, announced in October 2005 that the directors had approved a shareholder capital return program of $1.5 billion. The program consisted of share repurchases and special dividends that were in addition to regular quarterly dividends. The announcement followed an extended rise in copper prices accompanied by large increases in the firm's profits. The extra dividends consisted of $5 per common share paid in December 2005 and $4 per common share paid in March 2006. The special dividends were in addition to regular quarterly dividends of 18.75¢ per share. In April 2006, Phelps Dodge announced that it would increase the program to an overall level of $2 billion and pay a third special dividend of $2 per common share in June. The $2 extra dividend was in addition to the regular quarterly dividend, which was increased to 20¢ per share. Later that year, Phelps Dodge became the target of a successful takeover by another copper producer.

extraordinary call Redemption of a debt security due to unusual circumstances. For example, some bond issues can be redeemed prior to the scheduled maturity because of the destruction of the facility that was financed by the bonds. Extraordinary calls are most frequently used to retire single-family mortgage revenue bonds when homeowners refinance their mortgages. Extraordinary calls, generally made at par, nearly always work to the disadvantage of bondholders. —Also called *extraordinary redemption; special call.* —See also OPTIONAL CALL.

extraordinary gain Income from an unusual, infrequently occurring event or transaction. For example, a firm might sell a subsidiary at a price significantly higher than the value at which that subsidiary's assets are carried on the firm's balance sheet. An extraordinary gain is reported separately from regular income to emphasize the fact that it is nonrecurring.

extraordinary item An infrequently occurring transaction or event that, if material, is reported separately from continuing operations.

extraordinary loss A loss caused by an unusual, infrequently occurring event or transaction. For example, a firm might sell a money-losing business at a price lower than the value at which the business is carried on its balance sheet.

extraordinary redemption —See EXTRAORDINARY CALL.

extrapolate To estimate a value or values on the basis of collected data. For example, a firm may forecast annual sales during the next five years from historical data of actual sales and sales growth during the most recent ten years.

 F

face amount The dollar amount of life insurance that will be paid to beneficiaries in the event of death of the insured. For example, an individual may have $500,000 face amount of life insurance coverage.

face-amount certificate Debt issued by a face amount certificate company obligating the issuer to redeem the certificate at face value at maturity. The buyer makes installment payments that earn interest over the life of the certificate.

face value —See PAR VALUE 1.

facilitator An individual who assists in the management of an exchange of ideas, information, and opinions. A facilitator is expected to offer guidance along the way to making decisions rather than provide expertise on a particular subject relevant to the decisions.

facsimile **1.** An exact copy. **2.** A telegraphy machine that transmits images. —Also called *fax.*

factor[1] **1.** A firm that purchases accounts receivable from another firm at a discount. The purchasing firm then attempts to collect the receivables. **2.** An input in the production of a good or service. For example, labor is an important factor in most service industries. Factors of production include labor, materials, capital goods, and capital. **3.** A businessperson who receives a commission while acting for someone else.

factor[2] To sell accounts receivable to another party at a discount from face value. Thus, a firm in need of cash to pay down short-term debt may decide to factor its accounts receivable to another firm.

factorage The fee or commission paid for the services of an agent or broker.

factor analysis A statistical technique to analyze a large volume of measurements and search for their interrelationships. A restaurant chain might gather and conduct factor analysis for a large volume of data on consumer preferences in order to determine the relative importance of portion size, pricing, and perceived quality.

factory outlet —See OUTLET STORE.

factory overhead Manufacturing expenses other than direct labor and direct materials.

fad A product, service, or activity that becomes very popular but is not long-lived. For example, diets and clothing fashions are subject to frequent fads.

fail[1] Of or relating to a trade in which the seller does not deliver securities or the buyer does not deliver funds in the prescribed manner at the prescribed time, usually on the settlement date. —Compare CLEAR[2].

fail[2] To go out of business. A retail chain is likely to fail if it can't offer competitive prices or superior service.

failure of consideration Refusal or inability to deliver the goods or services promised in a contract. Failure of consideration may be partial (a building isn't completed) or total (promised goods are not delivered).

Fair Access to Insurance Requirements (FAIR) Plan Guaranteed insurance coverage for businesses and individuals who live in high-risk areas. Originally established in the 1960s by the Federal Housing and Urban Development Act to provide coverage in riot-prone areas, the concept was adapted by states that began offering their own FAIR plans. For example, California developed a FAIR plan in 1968 for homeowners who live in high-risk fire areas.

Fair Credit Billing Act Federal legislation that provides settlement procedures for billing disputes regarding open-end credit arrangements, including credit card and revolving charge accounts. For example, a borrower's responsibility for unauthorized charges is limited to $50. The act does not apply to installment credit.

Fair Credit Reporting Act Federal legislation passed in 1970 that protects consumers with respect to their credit record. The legislation specifies that consumers are to be treated fairly by credit reporting agencies. For example, consumers must be given access to their credit report and supplied with the name and address of any credit bureau that has supplied information resulting in a denial of credit.

> **CASE STUDY** Insurance companies frequently make use of credit reports when evaluating applicants for coverage. The industry justifies use of the reports by claiming that poor credit histories tend to be associated with poor drivers. Thus, a low credit score, as calculated by the insurance company evaluating a report, is likely to lead to a higher insurance premium or the rejection of coverage. The Fair Credit Reporting Act requires that firms notify consumers when taking adverse action because of information in a credit report. For example, an applicant must be notified if coverage is denied or premiums are increased because of information obtained in the applicant's credit report. The Supreme Court ruled during summer 2007 that insurance companies are not required to notify consumers when a credit report is used in evaluating an applicant and the applicant is not offered the lowest available rate. In the case considered by the court, insurance company Geico claimed the firm offered the consumer the same rate as if the applicant's credit report had not been seen, even though the rate was not its lowest available rate. The Supreme Court indicated that notification is required only when information in a report results in a higher rate than would apply if information in the report were not considered.

Fair Housing Act Federal legislation that prohibits discrimination in the financing, sale, or rental of dwellings.

Fair Labor Standards Act Federal legislation from 1938 that established minimum wage, overtime pay, recordkeeping, and child labor standards affecting full-time and part-time workers in the private sector, and in federal, state, and local governments. Passage of the act was designed to improve the living conditions of working families.

fair market purchase option In leasing, the opportunity of the lessee to acquire leased property at the termination of a lease at the then fair market value. The lessor cannot retain title to the leased asset in the event the lessee exercises the purchase option.

fair market rent U.S. Department of Housing and Urban Development rent estimates used to determine the eligibility of rental housing units for housing assistance payments. The estimates are designed to be high enough to ensure an adequate supply of rental units, but low enough to serve as many families as possible.

fair market value The price at which a buyer and a seller willingly consummate a trade.

fair market value lease —See TRUE LEASE.

fairness opinion An independent opinion characterizing the fair value of a firm's stock. A fairness opinion is frequently obtained by a majority owner of a company that is attempting to buy out the interests of minority shareholders. For example, Royal Dutch Petroleum, the 70% owner of Shell Oil, sought a fairness opinion from Morgan Stanley in an attempt to set a price on the shares it wished to purchase from Shell's minority stockholders. —See also SQUEEZE-OUT.

fair price amendment An addition to a company's bylaws that prevents an acquiring firm or investor from offering different prices for the shares held by different stockholders during a takeover attempt. The amendment tends to discourage takeover attempts by making them more expensive. —See also APPRAISAL RIGHT.

fair trade **1.** Abiding by established standards for the treatment of labor and the environment in the production of goods involved in international trade. **2.** An agreement between retailers and a manufacturer that a product will be sold at a manufacturer-specified price or higher.

fair use In copyright law, the legal reproduction of copyrighted material without permission of the copyright holder and without paying a fee. Fair use is not clearly defined but is generally considered to include reviews, scholarly research, and news reports.

> **CASE STUDY** A San Francisco federal jury ruled in 2006 that the *San Jose Mercury News* did not violate copyright law in using a photograph from *The Life You Save May Be Your Own: An American Pilgrimage* in the newspaper's review of the book. Photographer Christopher Harris, whose photograph had appeared with his permission in author Paul Elie's book, sued the newspaper for copyright infringement and sought damages of $205,000. The April 2003 newspaper review included four of the book's photographs. The photographer claimed the newspaper was not paying a royalty for the photo simply in order to save money, while the newspaper argued that including the photo with the book review was an example of fair use under the applicable copyright law. The jury sided with the newspaper. Interestingly, the same photographer had won a similar 2001 lawsuit for a book review that appeared in the New Orleans *Times-Picayune*.

fair value 1. In accounting, the price at which an asset can be bought or sold in a current transaction. **2.** In futures trading, the equilibrium price for a futures contract. **3.** The price at which an asset should trade based on all relevant factors. —See also EFFICIENT MARKET.

fallback option An alternate plan in the event the current plan must be discarded. For example, news reports indicated database giant Oracle was considering a fallback option of acquiring Siebel in the event its bid for PeopleSoft failed. As it turned out, Oracle acquired Siebel one year after its 2005 acquisition of PeopleSoft.

fallen angel A once-popular security that has lost investor favor and has declined in value. For example, a high-growth company may hit a period of heavy competition or saturated markets such that its stock declines in price and becomes a fallen angel.

false advertising Advertising that misrepresents the nature, characteristics, and qualities of goods, services, or commercial activities.

Family and Medical Leave Act Federal legislation that required covered employers to grant an eligible employee up to 12 workweeks of unpaid leave for any of the following reasons: birth and care of a newborn child of the employee, placement of a son or daughter for adoption or foster care, care of a family member with a serious illness, or medical leave when the employee is unable to work because of a serious health problem.

family brand A common brand name used for different products. Cosmetics companies often use the same brand name on a variety of products. Family branding is a marketing strategy that uses a familiar and respected name to increase the appeal of other products.

family limited partnership A limited partnership restricted to family members, generally with parents as general partners who retain full control over assets that have been contributed to and are held by the partnership. These partnerships are designed to reduce estate and gift taxes, and at the same time they permit parents to continue to control the assets until their death.

family of funds A group of mutual funds operated by the same investment management company. Investors are often able to transfer money between mutual funds within a particular family of funds at only a nominal charge. Thus, an investor with shares in a growth fund could move funds out of the growth fund and into a money market fund or a bond fund without paying a new sales charge if a single investment firm manages each of these funds. —Also called *fund group; group of funds.* —See also FUND SWITCHING.

family trust A trust established for the purpose of passing assets to children or other heirs rather than to a surviving spouse. —See also SPRINKLING TRUST.

Fannie Mae 1. A private, shareholder-owned company created by Congress in 1938 to bolster the housing industry during the depression. Fannie Mae facilitates homeownership by adding liquidity to the mortgage market when it purchases loans from lenders who use the funds received to make additional loans. Fannie Mae finances mortgage purchases by issuing its own bonds or by selling mortgages it already owns to financial institutions. —Formerly called *Federal National Mortgage Association.* —See also QUASI-PUBLIC CORPORATION. **2.** A security issued by this company that is backed by insured and conventional mortgages. Monthly returns to holders of Fannie Mae securities consist of interest and principal payments made by homeowners on their mortgages.

FAQ An acronym for *f*requently *a*sked *q*uestions.

Farmer Mac (Federal Agricultural Mortgage Corporation) A federally chartered and government-sponsored corporation with a mission to increase the availability of mortgage financing to farmers and ranchers by providing a secondary market for agricultural real estate and rural housing mortgage loans. Farmer Mac purchases qualified loans from agricultural mortgage lenders, thereby increasing funds available for further agricultural lending.

far month In futures and options, the longest settlement or expiration month of a currently traded contract.

FASB —See FINANCIAL ACCOUNTING STANDARDS BOARD.

FASB statement A standard set by the Financial Accounting Standards Board regarding a financial accounting and reporting method. Essentially, FASB statements determine the acceptable accounting practices that certified public accountants use in reporting corporate financial information to stockholders, the SEC, and the general public. —See also APB OPINION.

fast track **1.** Rapid advancement in an organization's management structure that is sometimes offered to employees considered to have special promise. **2.** The legislative procedure in which Congress is required to vote without offering amendments on foreign trade agreements submitted by the President. For example, the North America Free Trade Agreement was passed as fast-track legislation.

fax —See FACSIMILE 2.

FCM —See FUTURES COMMISSION MERCHANT.

FDA —See FOOD AND DRUG ADMINISTRATION.

FDIC —See FEDERAL DEPOSIT INSURANCE CORPORATION.

feasibility study A detailed analysis of a proposal with respect to its anticipated cost, potential problems, and possible outcomes in order to determine if the proposal should be implemented. A feasibility study for a small business might include: an assessment of the market; an estimate of fixed costs, variable costs, revenues, and breakeven; identification of potential problems; and an evaluation of the firm's management quality.

featherbedding A requirement to use more employees than are necessary to perform a job. For example, a union agreement with a company may not permit employee layoffs even during periods of declining sales and output.

feather one's nest To take advantage of one's position or situation in order to gain money or power. For example, a firm's directors may vote themselves a lucrative retirement program.

Fed —See FEDERAL RESERVE SYSTEM.

federal agency security A debt obligation of government-owned agencies such as the Export-Import Bank and Ginnie Mae. Federal agency securities offer higher yields than direct Treasury obligations even though, with the exception of U.S. Postal Service and Tennessee Valley Authority issues, they are guaranteed by the U.S. government. Certain issues are exempt from state and local taxes. —Compare FEDERALLY SPONSORED CORPORATE SECURITY. —Also called *indirect government obligation.*

Federal Agricultural Mortgage Corporation —See FARMER MAC.

Federal Deposit Insurance Corporation (FDIC) The independent agency of the United States government that insures deposits at commercial banks and savings and loan associations to a limit of $100,000 per depositor, or combination of depositors, at each insured institution. Self-directed retirement accounts, including IRAs, are insured to a maximum of $250,000. The insurance fund is financed by a small fee paid by the banks based on the amount of their insured deposits. —Also called *deposit insurance.*

federal estate tax —See ESTATE TAX.

Federal Farm Credit Bank A federally sponsored financing organization intended to consolidate operations of the Banks for Cooperatives, the Federal Intermediate Credit Banks, and the Federal Land Banks. The Federal Farm Credit Bank issues short-term securities to raise funds that are used by local associations for loans to farmers, ranchers, and rural home buyers.

federal funds Reserve balances that are maintained by commercial banks in the Federal Reserve System at amounts above what is required. These excess reserves are available for lending to other banks in need of reserves. Although the loans are usually made on a single-day basis, they may be renewed. The availability of and the rate paid for federal funds are important indicators of Federal Reserve policy; hence, both are watched closely by financial analysts in order to forecast changes in the credit markets. —Also called *fed funds.*

federal funds rate The rate of interest on overnight loans of excess reserves made among commercial banks. Because the Federal Reserve has significant control over the availability of federal funds, the rate is considered an important indicator of Federal Reserve monetary policy and the future direction of other interest rates. A declining federal funds rate may indicate that the Federal Reserve has decided to stimulate the economy by releasing reserves into the banking system. —Also called *funds rate.*

Federal Home Loan Bank System (FHLBS) A government-sponsored enterprise established in 1932 to improve the supply of funds to lenders, including credit unions, thrifts, banks, and insurance companies, that finance loans for home mortgages. With an AAA credit rating, the system is able to borrow funds at relatively low cost and pass the savings through to borrowers in the housing market. The Federal Housing Finance Board regulates the 12 Federal Home Loan Banks.

Federal Home Loan Mortgage Corporation —See FREDDIE MAC 1.

Federal Housing Administration (FHA) A government-sponsored organization insuring mortgage loans made by private lenders.

Federal Insurance Contributions Act (FICA) The federal law requiring that employers withhold a specified portion of employee pay for contribution to Social Security and Medicare. The contributions are used to help finance retirement, disability, and survivor benefits.

Federal Intermediate Credit Banks Privately owned, government-sponsored organizations that provide short-term loans to the agricultural sector. Federal Intermediate Credit Banks obtain funds from debt issues of the Federal Farm Credit Bank.

Federal Land Banks Privately owned, government-sponsored organizations that make funds available for farm-related activities. Federal Land Banks secure funds from the Federal Farm Credit Bank, which issues debt securities.

federally sponsored corporate security A security issued by a privately owned, government-sponsored firm such as Fannie Mae or the Federal Land Banks. These securities, primarily debt obligations, are not guaranteed by the U.S. government but are generally considered relatively safe. —Compare FEDERAL AGENCY SECURITY.

Federal National Mortgage Association —See FANNIE MAE 1.

Federal Open Market Committee (FOMC) A policy-making committee within the Federal Reserve that has the responsibility for establishing and carrying out open-market operations. Policies and decisions of the committee have a substantial impact on interest rates and the securities markets. The FOMC is composed of the 7 members of the Board of Governors of the Federal Reserve System and presidents from 5 of the 12 Federal Reserve Banks. —Also called *Open Market Committee.*

Federal Register The official daily publication for rules, proposed rules, notices of federal agencies and organizations, and presidential orders and documents. The Federal Register is published by the National Archives and Records Administration and is available free to the public on the Internet.

Federal Reserve Bank One of 12 regional banks plus 25 branches of the Federal Reserve System. The banks operate a nationwide payments system, supervise and regulate member banks, and provide services for the U.S. Treasury.

Federal Reserve Board The seven governing members of the Federal Reserve System who are appointed by the President for 14-year terms. Board members play an important role in determining the country's monetary policy, which in turn strongly influences economic activity. —See also BEIGE BOOK.

Federal Reserve note Paper currency issued by the Federal Reserve. Federal Reserve notes serve as legal tender for all debts and make up nearly all the circulating currency in the United States.

Federal Reserve System The independent central bank that influences the supply of money and credit in the United States through its control of bank reserves. Federal Reserve actions have great impact on security prices. For example, restriction of bank reserves and lending ability in an attempt to restrain inflation tends to drive up interest rates and drive down security prices over the short run. —Also called *Fed.* —See also FEDERAL OPEN MARKET COMMITTEE.

federal savings and loan association —See SAVINGS AND LOAN ASSOCIATION.

federal tax lien A lien of the United States government against the assets of a delinquent taxpayer.

Federal Trade Commission (FTC) A federal agency responsible for maintaining the competitive markets, thereby discouraging restraint of trade and monopoly. The clout and aggressiveness of the FTC vary greatly depending on its membership and the incumbent presidential administration.

Federal Trade Commission Act of 1914 The federal law that established the Federal Trade Commission and provided it with limited power to investigate corporate conduct, hold hearings, and issue cease-and-desist orders. In a 1938 amendment, the FTC was given expanded powers in halting merger activities. —See also CLAYTON ACT; SHERMAN ANTITRUST ACT.

Federal Unemployment Tax Act Federal legislation that authorizes the Internal Revenue Service to collect a federal employer tax used for payments of unemployment compensation to workers who have lost their jobs. The federal tax is equal to 6.2% of the first $7,000 paid in wages to each employee during a calendar year. Employers who pay a state unemployment tax receive an offset credit of up to 5.4%.

fed funds —See FEDERAL FUNDS.

Fedwire A high-speed communications system for transferring funds and ownership of book-entry securities between banks. The Fedwire is used to move bank reserves and to make credit available without delay.

fee 1. A charge for services. For example, a landlord may charge a cleaning fee when a tenant moves out. **2.** An inherited estate of land.

feedback Information gained by an individual or business in response to some type of interaction, such as the sale of a product or service. Positive feedback indicates satisfaction by the respondent, while negative feedback signifies dissatisfaction and a need for improvement.

fee for service The traditional system of reimbursement under health insurance and Medicare. Health care providers bill patients for services supplied, and costs are shared according to a contractual agreement between the patient and insurance company. A fee-for-service system allows patients maximum flexibility in the choice of providers and services.

fee simple Ownership of an asset by a single individual, who has the right to determine how the asset is used or transferred. —Also called *fee simple absolute.*

FGIC —See FINANCIAL GUARANTY INSURANCE CORPORATION.

FHA —See FEDERAL HOUSING ADMINISTRATION.

FHA loan A real estate loan guaranteed by the Federal Housing Administration. The FHA insures variable-rate loans, fixed-rate loans, and loans to add energy-efficient features to a home. Most FHA loans require an annual premium plus an initial fee at the loan closing.

FHLBS —See FEDERAL HOME LOAN BANK SYSTEM.

fiat money Money used as a medium of exchange but with no inherent value. Paper money is an example of fiat money used as a medium of exchange because of the willingness of the public to accept it in exchange for goods and services.

FICA —See FEDERAL INSURANCE CONTRIBUTIONS ACT.

fidelity bond —See BLANKET FIDELITY BOND.

fiduciary A person, such as an investment manager or the executor of an estate, or an organization, such as a bank, entrusted with the property of another party and in whose best interests the fiduciary is expected to act when holding, investing, or otherwise using that party's property.

fiduciary bond An insurance bond that guarantees the honest and faithful performance of executors, trustees, and other fiduciaries. A fiduciary bond is often required by statute in order to protect the interests of those for whom the fiduciary acts. —Also called *probate bond.*

FIFO —See FIRST-IN, FIRST-OUT.

fighting brand A low-cost product similar to another, higher-end product from the same company. Fighting brands are intended to contend with similar low-priced products from competitors. For example, a household products company with an existing name-brand shampoo may release a new low-priced shampoo to compete with house brands offered by retailers. The fighting brand allows the manufacturer to retain the premium price charged for its existing shampoo without conceding market share to competitors.

fight the tape To trade securities against the trend. For example, a trader fights the tape if he or she continues to buy stock in a declining market or sell stock in a rising market. One of the axioms of stock market trading is to not fight the tape.

file¹ 1. To organize and store material in an orderly manner that facilitates subsequent access. 2. To submit one or more documents. For example, most individuals are required to file a tax return each April.

file² A set of stored records.

filing status The category in which an individual files an income tax return. The five categories of filing status are: single, married filing jointly, married filing separately, head of household, and qualifying widow(er) with dependent child. A taxpayer's filing status determines the rates at which income is taxed.

fill To complete a customer's order. For example, a mail-order firm fills a customer order for five vegetable gizmos that were offered on a late-night television advertisement.

fill-or-kill order An order sent to the floor of an exchange, demanding that it either be filled immediately and in full or be canceled.

fill rate The proportion of orders that can be immediately met by available inventory. Increased customer satisfaction associated with a high fill rate must be weighed against the higher expense of maintaining a greater depth and breadth of inventory. —See also JUST-IN-TIME INVENTORY.

filtering down The process by which a neighborhood deteriorates with age as individuals and families move to newer and more elaborate dwellings and the neighborhood is occupied by individuals and families of lesser wealth and lower social status.

final assembly The completion of a manufacturing process, when the finished product is put together and readied for delivery to the final buyer.

final dividend 1. The concluding dividend payment from a firm that is liquidating. 2. The last dividend of a firm's fiscal year. The final dividend is declared when management is able to estimate rather accurately the firm's earnings and its dividend-paying ability. —Compare INTERIM DIVIDEND. —Also called *year-end dividend.*

final good —See FINISHED GOOD.

finance 1. To raise funds for. For example, a company may need to finance a new project. 2. To supply funds for. For example, a couple may finance most of their child's college education.

finance charge The cost of obtaining credit, including interest and any fees, including points and required insurance premiums.

finance company A financial intermediary that makes loans to individuals and businesses, but does not accept deposits.

finance contingency clause A clause in a contract that specifies the buyer can back out of the agreement if reasonable financing is unavailable to the buyer. For example, a person signs an agreement to purchase a home, but only if a loan commitment can be obtained by a particular date. —Also called *contingent financing clause.*

financial accounting The area of accounting involved with the collection of financial information for use in constructing and reporting an organization's financial results to external parties, including stockholders and government agencies.

finance contingency clause

A finance contingency clause seems to add risk for the seller. Do most contracts include this clause?

While a finance contingency clause *does* add risk for the seller, most buyers will not sign a contract to purchase a home without one. Buyers are willing to move forward with a purchase and pay their deposit into escrow as a sign of good faith. However, if they apply for a mortgage loan and cannot secure financing, they will expect their deposit to be returned. Sellers can protect themselves at the outset by requiring the buyer to prove his or her creditworthiness *before* signing a contract. Buyers can easily obtain a mortgage prequalification letter or preapproval letter to show that they are a good risk. This letter should provide the seller with some degree of comfort in going forward with the deal.

■ Joan A. Koffman, Esq., Real Estate Attorney, Koffman & Dreyer, Newton, MA

Financial Accounting Standards Board (FASB) The independent accounting organization that determines the standards for financial accounting and reporting. The rules set by the FASB play a large role in determining the numbers that companies show the financial analysts and stockholders. —See also EXPOSURE DRAFT; FASB STATEMENT; GOVERNMENT ACCOUNTING STANDARDS BOARD.

financial adviser Someone trained in offering counsel in financial investments, including stocks, bonds, and insurance. Some financial advisers serve as financial planners and offer advice on a wide range of financial issues, including retirement and taxes. Other financial advisers have a more narrow interest and concentrate on particular types of investments, such as securities, insurance, or real estate.

financial analysis Examining the financial condition and prospects of an organization.

financial analyst A person with expertise in evaluating financial investments. Financial analysts, who serve as investment advisers and portfolio managers, use their training and experience to investigate risk and return characteristics of securities. —Also called *securities analyst.* —See also ANALYST; CHARTERED FINANCIAL ANALYST.

financial asset A financial claim on an asset that is usually documented by some type of legal representation. Examples include bonds and shares of stock, but not tangible assets such as real estate or gold. —Compare REAL ASSET.

financial condition —See FINANCIAL POSITION.

financial contagion A financial problem that spreads among companies or regions. For example, Russia's 1998 default triggered sharp declines in the market values of debt issued by emerging countries.

financial futures Obligations to buy or sell particular positions in financial instruments. The features of financial futures are identical to those of any futures contract, except that the asset for delivery is of a financial nature. Financial futures are traded on certificates of deposit, commercial paper, Ginnie Mae certificates, foreign currencies, Treasury bills, and Treasury bonds. —See also FUTURES MARKET.

Financial Guaranty Insurance Corporation (FGIC) A private insurer of interest and principal payments on municipal bond issues. As it would with other insurers, the municipality issuing the bond pays the required premium to FGIC in order to obtain a higher rating on the issue. In this way, the bonds can be sold at a lower interest rate.

financial highlights The section of a corporate report providing investors with an overview of the firm's performance during the period covered by the report. For example, a report's highlights may note a major acquisition made by the firm during the period, and it may discuss the implications of the acquisition relative to future sales and corporate earnings.

financial institution An organization that invests chiefly in financial assets such as loans and securities rather than in tangible assets. Financial institutions include banks, trust companies, consumer finance companies, savings and loans, credit unions, pension funds, insurance companies, and mutual funds.

Financial Institutions Reform, Recovery, and Enforcement Act of 1989 (FIRREA) Federal legislation that revamped regulation and insurance of depository financial institutions in response to the savings and loan crisis. The act created several new organizations, including the Resolution Trust Corporation, which closed and merged troubled institutions, and the Bank Insurance Fund, which replaced the Federal Savings and Loan Insurance Corporation as the insurer of thrift deposits.

financial intermediary A financial institution such as a commercial bank or thrift that facilitates the flow of funds from savers to borrowers. Financial intermediaries profit from the spread between the amount they pay for the funds and the rate they charge for the funds. —Also called *intermediary.* —See also INTERMEDIATION.

financial lease —See CAPITAL LEASE.

financial leverage The extent to which interest on debt magnifies changes in operating income into even greater proportionate changes in earnings after taxes. Financial leverage magnifies increases in earnings per share during periods of rising operating income, but adds significant risks for stockholders and creditors because of added interest obligations. —Compare OPERATING LEVERAGE. —See also DEBT MANAGEMENT RATIO; DEBT-TO-EQUITY RATIO.

financial market A system that facilitates the exchange of money for financial assets. A security market such as the New York Stock Exchange is an example of a financial market.

financial planner A person who counsels individuals and corporations with respect to evaluating financial status, identifying goals, and determining ways in which the goals can be met. Although many people call themselves financial planners, a large number are primarily interested in selling a limited selection of products they represent. A full-time professional planner, including a certified financial planner, an investment manager, or a tax attorney, may be better able to provide unbiased advice to the investor. —See also CERTIFIED FINANCIAL PLANNER; CHARTERED FINANCIAL CONSULTANT.

financial position The state of and the relationships among the various financial data found on a firm's balance sheet. For example, a company with fairly valued and relatively liquid assets, combined with a small amount of debt compared to owner's equity, is generally described as being in a strong financial position. —Also called *financial condition.*

financial pyramid —See PYRAMID¹.

financial ratio —See RATIO.

financial risk The risk that a firm will be unable to meet its financial obligations. This risk is primarily a function of the relative amount of debt that the firm uses to finance its assets. A higher proportion of debt increases the likelihood that at some point the firm will be unable to make the required interest and principal payments.

financial statement A report providing financial statistics relative to a given part of an organization's operations or status. The two most common financial statements are the balance sheet and the income statement. —See also COMPARATIVE FINANCIAL STATEMENTS.

financial structure —See CAPITALIZATION.

financial supermarket A financial services company that offers customers a wide variety of financial products, generally including insurance, stocks, bonds, real estate services, and annuities. Financial supermarkets are convenient, but may not offer the best deals on each of the financial products they sell.

finder A person who puts deals together. For example, a finder may locate funds for a corporation seeking capital, bring together firms for a merger, or find a takeover target for a company seeking an acquisition.

finder's fee The charge levied by a person or firm for putting together a deal. For example, a finder may receive a fee equal to 3% of the principal amount paid for a corporate acquisition.

> **CASE STUDY** In late 2002 the SEC filed a complaint alleging that Frank Walsh, a director of Tyco who served on the firm's compensation committee, recommended that Tyco acquire CIT. Following a meeting between the two firms' CEOs that had been arranged by Walsh, Tyco CEO Dennis Kozlowski proposed to pay Walsh a substantial finder's fee if the deal was consummated. Walsh subsequently voted in favor of the transaction, but did not disclose to other members of Tyco's board that he would receive a large fee if the transaction was consummated. Following the transaction, Kozlowski caused Tyco to pay Walsh a $20 million finder's fee consisting of $10 million in cash and $10 million as a contribution to the charity of Walsh's choosing. Walsh did not admit or deny the SEC allegations, but consented to a final judgment that permanently barred him from acting as an officer or director of a publicly held company. In addition, he was ordered to pay restitution of $20 million.

fineness A measure of the purity of a precious metal. Fineness is quoted in parts per thousand, with 1,000 fine being equivalent to 24-karat gold, and 583.3 fine being equivalent to 14-karat gold.

finished good A good that is consumed or used in its final form rather than used in the production of additional goods or services. Clothing is an example of a finished good. —Also called *final good*.

fire To dismiss a person from employment.

fire insurance Insurance coverage for financial loss to property caused by fire or lightning. Fire insurance is generally part of a homeowner's policy or multiple-peril commercial policy.

firewall A software program that protects a computer or a computer network from unwanted access by outsiders, especially hackers.

firm A business entity.

firm commitment In securities offerings, a commitment by the underwriter to purchase securities from the issuer for resale to the public. With a firm commitment, the risk of being unable to sell an entire issue at the offering price is transferred from the issuer to the underwriter. —Also called *bought deal*.

firm offer An offer to do something that cannot be withdrawn for a specified length of time. Acceptance of the offer by the specified date results in a binding contract.

firm order 1. An investor's order to buy or sell that is not conditional on any additional instruction. 2. An order placed on behalf of a broker-dealer firm rather than on behalf of the firm's client. 3. An unconditional offer to purchase goods or services.

firm quote A quotation from a market maker to buy and sell a security at firm bid and ask prices. —Compare NOMINAL QUOTE.

FIRREA —See FINANCIAL INSTITUTIONS REFORM, RECOVERY, AND ENFORCEMENT ACT OF 1989.

First Call The best-known segment of Thomson Financial, a major provider of financial information. First Call provides current and historical data on broker recommendations, insider transactions, financial ratios, and earnings estimates. Consensus earnings estimates from First Call are often utilized for comparison purposes by the financial press when corporations report quarterly earnings.

first call date The earliest date on which a security may be redeemed by the issuer. The first call date is likely to be either five years or ten years after the date of issue; however, the timing varies by bond issue. Bonds selling at a premium are often quoted at the yield to first call. —See also YIELD TO CALL.

first-in, first-out (FIFO) An accounting procedure for identifying the order in which items are used or sold. With FIFO, the oldest remaining items are assumed to have been sold first. During a period of inflation, this procedure tends to keep costs low for accounting purposes; it results in higher reported profits and a greater tax liability, however. —Compare LAST-IN, FIRST-OUT.

first lien A legal claim that has a priority to proceeds from the sale of an asset being used as collateral for a loan.

first-line manager An individual who works under the supervision of a middle manager and is responsible for managing the daily activities of a group of workers.

first mortgage A real estate loan with the right to payment in full before payments to other lenders are made. First mortgages are generally considered low-risk investments, although the quality of real estate pledged as collateral is of crucial importance in determining the riskiness of the mortgage.

first-mover's advantage The competitive advantage gained by early entry into a market. For example, a soft-drink company accepts initial losses in order to be the first entry into a developing country. —Compare FOLLOWER'S ADVANTAGE.

first preferred stock A class of preferred stock with a preferential claim over common stock and other preferred stock from the same issuer with respect to dividends and assets.

first stage capital In venture financing, initial funds provided to an entrepreneur to start marketing and commercial production of an existing product. —Compare SECOND STAGE CAPITAL.

fiscal agent The organization responsible for paying the interest and principal of another organization's debt. For example, Valdosta State Bank may be fiscal agent for, and make interest and principal payments on, debt incurred by Scott Motors Corporation.

fiscal drag The tendency of tax revenues to rise as a share of GNP during economic expansions, thereby slowing the growth of demand for goods and services. Fiscal drag results from progressive tax rates that rake off higher percentages of income as the economy expands.

fiscal neutrality A combination of government spending and taxing that produces no net impact on aggregate demand. For example, a balanced budget or an increase in government spending matched by an equal increase in taxation can be viewed as fiscally neutral.

fiscal period The period covered by financial reports. For example, an annual report covers a fiscal period of one year, but a quarterly report includes accounting data for three months. —Also called *accounting period.*

fiscal policy The existing policy the government has for spending and taxing. Fiscal policy directly affects economic variables such as tax rates, interest rates, and government programs that influence security prices. —See also MONETARY POLICY.

fiscal year (FY) The 12-month accounting period for an organization. Because many firms end their accounting year on a date other than December 31, the fiscal year often differs from the calendar year. —Compare CALENDAR YEAR.

Fisher effect The direct relationship between inflation and interest rates. Increasing inflationary expectations result in increasing interest rates.

fit A condition in which a product fulfills a consumer's needs. For example, an investor may select a new municipal bond because that bond's maturity makes it a good fit in the investor's portfolio. Along other lines, a relatively small two-bedroom home is a good fit for a retired couple.

Fitch Ratings An international rating agency for financial institutions, insurance companies, and corporate, sovereign, and municipal debt.

529 plan —See COLLEGE-SAVINGS PLAN.

five whys A problem-solving technique of asking five times why a particular problem occurred. For example, why does machinery continually break down? The assumption behind this technique is that an average of five whys is required to get at the root of a problem. Of course, five whys is only a rule of thumb, and a solution to a problem may require more or less than five whys. —See also SIX SIGMA.

fix To set the price of a commodity. For example, commodity traders in London fix the price of gold on a daily basis.

fixed annuity A stream of unchanging payments for a specific period or for an individual's lifetime, depending on the terms of the annuity contract. Insurance companies sell fixed annuities to people who desire a fixed income. —Compare VARIABLE ANNUITY. —Also called *guaranteed-dollar annuity.* —See also HYBRID ANNUITY.

fixed asset An asset not readily convertible to cash that is used in the normal course of business. Examples of fixed assets include machinery, buildings, and fixtures. A firm whose total assets are made up primarily of fixed assets is in a less liquid financial position, thus entailing greater risk of a big tumble in profits if its revenues fall.

fixed asset turnover A financial ratio that indicates a firm's ability to generate sales based on its long-term assets. Fixed asset turnover is calculated by dividing annual sales by the dollar amount of fixed assets. A high fixed asset turnover indicates management's effective use of the firm's fixed assets.

fixed-charge coverage The number of times that a firm's operating income exceeds its fixed payments. Fixed-charge coverage is a measure of a firm's ability to meet contractually fixed payments, with high coverage indicating significant flexibility for making payments in the event that business conditions deteriorate and earnings decline. Expenses used in calculating fixed-charge coverage usually include interest, lease payments, preferred dividends, and principal payments on debt. —Compare INTEREST COVERAGE. —Also called *times fixed charges.*

fixed cost A cost that remains unchanged even with variations in output. An airline with 20 airplanes has the fixed costs of depreciation and interest (if the planes are partially financed with debt), regardless of the number of times the planes fly or the number of seats filled on each flight. Firms with high fixed costs tend to engage in price wars and cutthroat competition because extra revenues incur little extra expense. These firms tend to experience wide swings in profits. —Compare VARIABLE COST.

fixed exchange rate An exchange rate between currencies that is set by the governments involved rather than allowed to fluctuate freely with market forces. In order to keep currencies trading at the prescribed levels, government monetary authorities actively enter the currency markets to buy and sell according to variations in supply and demand. —Compare FLOATING EXCHANGE RATE. —See also DEVALUATION.

fixed fee A guaranteed price for completion of a task. For example, a contractor may charge a fixed fee for remodeling a bathroom based on the requirements of the homeowner.

fixed income Periodic income that remains unchanged over time. Owners of bonds, preferred stock, and many pensions and insurance annuities receive fixed incomes that are subject to declining purchasing power during periods of inflation.

fixed-income security A security, such as a bond or preferred stock, that pays a constant income each period. Price changes in a fixed-income security are caused primarily by changes in long-term interest rates.

fixed price —See OFFERING PRICE.

fixed-price contract An agreement for delivery of a good or service at a certain price, specified at the time the agreement is negotiated. The party that agrees to make delivery is subject to the risk that costs will be higher than anticipated at the time delivery is required.

fixed-rate loan A loan with an interest rate that does not fluctuate during the term of the loan. For example, a family might purchase a home with proceeds from a 15-year fixed-rate loan. Choosing a loan with a fixed rate protects a borrower from rising payments or a longer term. —Compare ADJUSTABLE-RATE MORTGAGE.

fixed trust 1. —See NONDISCRETIONARY TRUST. **2.** —See UNIT INVESTMENT TRUST.

fixture In real estate, something that is permanently attached to real property such that its removal would negatively impact the value of the property. —See also TENANT FIXTURES.

flanker brand —See LINE EXTENSION.

flat[1] Of, relating to, or being a bond that trades without accrued interest. For example, bonds of a company in bankruptcy proceedings trade flat.

flat[2] A single-level apartment.

flat loan A loan without interest to the lender.

flat market A securities market in which there has been no tendency either to rise or to fall significantly. —Also called *sideways market.*

flat rate 1. Describing a product or service price that remains the same regardless of quantity. For example, most local telephone service requires the same monthly rate regardless of the number or length of local calls. **2.** In advertising, a pricing schedule that does not include discounts for time or for quantity of space.

flat scale A municipal bond offering in which similar yields are available at all the various maturities.

flat tax An income tax that has a single rate of taxation. For example, a taxing authority may levy a flat tax of 3% against gross income. —Also called *proportional tax.* —See also GRADUATED FLAT TAX.

flat yield curve At a particular time, similar yields on bonds of similar risk at all maturity lengths. During a period of a flat yield curve, an investor would receive approximately the same yield on a long-term bond as would be earned on a short-term bond. Likewise, a homebuyer would pay approximately the same rate of interest on a 15-year mortgage as on a 30-year mortgage.

flea market A market, generally outdoors, at which vendors rent spaces in order to sell new and used merchandise to the general public.

flexible benefits An employer plan that allows employees to choose among available taxable benefits such as cash, and nontaxable benefits such as health insurance, child care, and retirement plans.

flexible budget A projection of costs and revenues at various levels of output or sales. —Compare STATIC BUDGET.

flexible exchange rate —See FLOATING EXCHANGE RATE.

flexible manufacturing A manufacturing process that utilizes computers to automatically adjust production equipment for different kinds of output.

flexible pricing 1. A pricing policy in which consumers negotiate a price rather than pay a fixed price established by the seller. **2.** —See VARIABLE PRICING.

flexible spending account An employer-sponsored plan in which employee salaries are reduced through contributions to accounts that can be used to pay for dependent care or medical reimbursements. The accounts allow employees to pay medical and dependent care expenses with before-tax dollars. —See also HEALTH REIMBURSEMENT ARRANGEMENT; HEALTH SAVINGS ACCOUNT.

flextime A system of employment in which employees are permitted to choose the hours during which they will work, subject to certain limitations set by the employer. For example, employees may be permitted to work a 40-hour week as either 10 hours per day for four days or 8 hours per day for five days. Alternatively, employees may be permitted to choose whether to start their 8-hour days at any time between 6:00 a.m. and 9:00 a.m.

flight to quality A movement by investors to purchase higher-quality securities. For example, an investor might sell bonds rated lower than BBB and invest the proceeds in bonds rated AA or AAA. A flight to quality occurs when investors expect a deterioration in political stability or in economic activity.

flip-in pill A type of poison pill in which shareholders of a company that has become the target of a takeover are permitted to purchase additional shares of the target firm at a steep discount. The effect is to increase the per-share cost and decrease the likelihood of a hostile takeover.

flip-over pill An entitlement granted by a firm's management to its stockholders giving them the right to purchase shares of an acquiring company's stock at a bargain price in the event of a merger. The flip-over pill is a variation of the poison pill.

flipper A trader who attempts to make a small profit by very quick in-and-out buying and selling. For example, a flipper might try to take advantage of a hot real estate market by purchasing new homes from contractors and quickly selling them at a profit.

flipping The rapid buying and selling of assets such as real estate or stocks.

float¹ 1. Funds that, because of inefficiencies in the collection system, are on deposit at two institutions at the same time. This situation permits a person or firm to earn extra income, because both institutions are paying interest on the same funds. As an example, a person writes a check on a money market fund in order to make a deposit in a local financial institution. Until that check gets back to the bank on which it was written (a transit often entailing two or three days), the investor receives interest on his or her funds from both institutions. **2.** Premiums an insurance company has collected but has not yet used for payment of claims. Insurance companies use float for investing until the funds are required to pay claims. **3.** The number of shares in public hands and available for trading. —Also called *floating supply*.

float² To permit a country's currency to change freely in value against foreign currencies.

float an issue To sell a security issue in the primary market. For example, a firm may decide that it needs to expand its manufacturing facilities and float a new issue of common stock to pay for the expansion. Issuers generally employ an investment banker to assist in floating an issue.

floater 1. Insurance coverage for movable property such as jewelry and musical instruments. A floater is generally an attachment to a homeowner's policy. —Also called *personal property floater*. **2.** —See FLOATING-RATE NOTE.

floating debt Short-term debt that is subject to continual re-funding by the issuer.

floating exchange rate An exchange rate between two currencies that is allowed to fluctuate with the market forces of supply and demand. Floating exchange rates tend to result in uncertainty as to the future rate at which currencies will exchange. This uncertainty is responsible for the increased popularity of forward, futures, and option contracts on foreign currencies. —Compare FIXED EXCHANGE RATE. —Also called *flexible exchange rate*.

floating-rate note An unsecured debt issue with an interest rate that is reset at specified intervals (usually every six months) according to a predetermined formula. Floating-rate notes usually can be redeemed at face value on certain dates at the holder's option. Floating-rate notes pay short-term interest and generally sell in the secondary market at nearly par value. —Also called *floater; variable-rate note.* —See also CONVERTIBLE FLOATING-RATE NOTE; DROPLOCK BOND; VARIABLE-RATE DEMAND OBLIGATION.

floating-rate preferred stock A special and unusual type of preferred stock with a dividend that is reset at specified intervals according to a predetermined formula. Floating-rate preferred stock contrasts with most preferred stock issues that pay a fixed quarterly dividend. Floating-rate preferred stock issues do not generally fluctuate much in price, because the dividend is automatically adjusted to keep the shares selling near to par. —Also called *adjustable-rate preferred stock; variable-rate preferred stock*.

floating supply —See FLOAT¹ 3.

flood insurance Coverage for property damage from flooding caused by an excess of water on land that is normally dry. Homeowner, renter, and business owner insurance policies do not cover losses from flood damage, and a separate flood insurance policy is needed to obtain this coverage.

floodplain A relatively flat land area adjacent to a river or stream that is subject to recurring flooding.

floor The area of an organized exchange where securities are traded. Customer orders are transferred to the floor, where they are executed by members of the exchange.

floor broker A member of a securities exchange who executes orders on the exchange floor. A commission broker is an example of a floor broker.

floor plan 1. A two-dimensional scale drawing for each floor of a building. 2. A funding system used to finance a merchant's inventory. For example, most automobile dealerships use floor-plan financing to acquire their inventory of vehicles.

floor plan insurance Insurance coverage purchased by a lender to protect its security interest in high-value merchandise being held by a merchant.

floor trader An independent trader on a securities exchange who trades primarily for his or her own account. Floor traders add liquidity to the market, as they attempt to profit from short-term price swings. —Also called *registered trader.* —See also REGISTERED COMPETITIVE MARKET MAKER.

flotation cost The expense involved in selling a new security issue. This expense includes items such as registration of the issue and payment to the investment banker. Flotation costs depend on the size and riskiness of an issue as well as on the type of security to be sold.

flowchart A graphical representation of a process as it is intended to progress from start to finish. Flowcharts use symbols such as ovals, rectangles, and arrows to indicate inputs, decision points, and flow direction.

flow of funds In economics, flow of capital among issuers, investors, and intermediaries that buy and sell securities in the capital markets. Flow of funds accounts are used to examine economic trends such as the growth of debt by certain sectors of the economy.

flow of funds statement 1. For municipal bond issues, a listing of priorities for municipal revenues, including the relative position of debt service and sinking fund requirements. 2. —See STATEMENT OF CASH FLOWS.

fly-by-night Of or relating to a person or business that is thought to be unreliable. People going door to door offering to do home improvements often fit the description of being fly-by-night operators.

FNMA —See FANNIE MAE 1.

FOB —See FREE ON BOARD.

focused factory A manufacturing facility that concentrates on a narrow range of products for a limited number of markets. The goal of a focused factory is to operate more efficiently.

focus group A representative group selected from a population. Focus groups are used by businesses, politicians, and others to evaluate products and concepts. For example, an advertising agency assembles a focus group to help develop an effective promotion for a new product.

folio A personalized collection of stocks an investor can assemble or purchase as a preselected basket. Investors can sell and replace individual stocks in a folio, generally as often as desired, for a single monthly or annual fee. Being able to choose when to replace stocks allows an investor substantial control over the tax consequences of owning folios compared to owning mutual funds.

follower's advantage The reduced likelihood of failure when a company isn't the first to market or use a new good or service. For example, an electric utility doesn't adopt a new pollution-control system until it has been proven successful by another utility. A follower is able to learn what works and what doesn't work before committing its own resources to something. —Compare FIRST-MOVER'S ADVANTAGE.

follow-on offering A stock issue that follows an initial public stock offering from a firm. The follow-on offering can consist of primary and/or secondary shares. Companies will sometimes authorize additional shares that are issued at a higher price following a successful initial public offering. —Also called *add-on financing; piggyback.*

FOMC —See FEDERAL OPEN MARKET COMMITTEE.

Food and Drug Administration (FDA) An agency of the U.S. Department of Health and Human Services charged with protecting the public health by regulating the quality and safety of medical devices, foodstuffs, pharmaceuticals, and cosmetics.

footnote A detailed explanation of an item in a financial statement. Footnotes are nearly always located at the end of a statement. For example, a company is likely to attach footnotes to its annual report to expand on the depreciation and inventory valuation methods used by its accountants. Many financial analysts consider footnotes the most important information in an annual report. —Also called *note.*

Footsie —See FTSE 100 INDEX.

forbearance Delay in seeking a remedy to a claim. For example, a borrower may ask a creditor for forbearance with regard to payments on a loan.

Forbes 500 The annual listing of the 500 largest publicly traded firms published by *Forbes* magazine. The Forbes 500, a compilation of separate lists categorized by assets, market value of shares, profits, and sales, is constructed somewhat differently from the Fortune 500, which lists firms on the basis of industry segment and amount of assets owned.

forced conversion The call for redemption of a convertible security at a price lower than the market value of the underlying asset into which the convertible may be exchanged. The investor finds it more favorable to exchange the convertible for the underlying asset than to give up the security for cash at the call price.

forced sale The required sale of property, often by a sheriff who has taken possession because of an unpaid obligation.

forced saving An involuntary reduction in consumption. A government requirement for mandatory retirement contributions is an example of forced saving. Forced saving may also result when price controls limit the amount of goods that are available for sale.

force majeure A clause in a contract that exempts one or both parties from liability in the event the terms of the contract cannot be satisfied because of unforeseen events. For example, a supplier may be unable to deliver promised goods because of a natural disaster.

foreclosure The legal seizure of property by a creditor from a borrower who has failed to make the required payments on a loan. The most likely outcome is for the lender to sell the property and use the proceeds to satisfy the outstanding balance on the loan.

foreign bond A debt security issued by a borrower from outside the country in whose currency the bond is denominated and in which the bond is sold. For example, a bond denominated in U.S. dollars that is issued in the United States by the government of Canada is a foreign bond. A foreign bond allows an investor a measure of international diversification without subjection to the risk of changes in relative currency values. —See also EUROBOND.

foreign corporation A firm that conducts business in states or countries other than the state or country in which it is incorporated. For example, a firm incorporated in Canada but conducting business throughout North America is considered a foreign corporation in the United States. —Also called *alien corporation.* —Compare DOMESTIC CORPORATION.

Foreign Corrupt Practices Act A 1977 amendment to the Securities Exchange Act that sets penalties for those engaging in bribery of foreign government officials or foreign personnel, and that requires adequate records and internal controls in all publicly held companies.

foreign currency future A contract for the delivery of a specified amount of a foreign currency. For example, a U.S. business selling products in Germany may decide to sell futures contracts on the euro in order to guarantee an exchange rate of the euro to dollars on a specific date.

foreign currency option The right to buy (a call option) or to sell (a put option) a foreign currency futures contract at a fixed price until a specified date.

foreign currency translation —See TRANSLATION.

foreign direct investment Investment by a company or government of one country in production facilities in a different country. The direct investment may be by means of purchasing a foreign company or constructing production facilities as part of an existing business. For example, in 2001 Swiss-based Nestlé paid $10 billion to acquire U.S. pet food maker Ralston Purina. —Also called *direct investment.*

foreign exchange 1. Foreign currency and financial instruments that can be used to make payments in foreign countries. **2.** The purchase or sale of foreign currencies.

foreign exchange controls Restrictions that are imposed by a nation on the free exchange and convertibility of its own currency. Foreign exchange controls are most often instituted by countries whose currencies are weak and whose citizens prefer to hold and use the currencies of other nations. Institution of foreign exchange controls hinders foreign investors who wish to extricate their funds.

foreign exchange desk 1. The area at a financial institution where foreign currencies are traded. **2.** The desk at the New York Federal Reserve Bank where the Federal Reserve undertakes operations as an agent for the U.S. Treasury and foreign banks.

foreign exchange rate —See EXCHANGE RATE.

foreign exchange risk The risk that the exchange rate on a foreign currency will move against the position held by an investor such that the value of the investment is reduced. For example, if an investor residing in the United States purchases a bond denominated in Japanese yen, a deterioration in the rate at which the yen exchanges for dollars will reduce the investor's rate of return, since he or she must eventually exchange the yen for dollars. —Also called *exchange rate risk.*

foreign investment The acquisition by individuals, businesses, and governments of financial and real assets in a foreign country. General Motors building a vehicle-manufacturing plant in Mexico is an example of foreign investment. Countries often rely on foreign investment to develop their resources and provide their citizens with employment and a higher standard of living. —See also FOREIGN DIRECT INVESTMENT.

foreign person For federal tax purposes, a nonresident alien individual, foreign corporation, foreign partnership, foreign trust, foreign estate, and any other individual who is not a United States person. —Compare UNITED STATES PERSON.

foreign sales agent A company or individual that serves as a foreign representative for a domestic company. Small companies often contract with foreign sales agents to represent their products in foreign countries.

foreign sales corporation An offshore corporation in a U.S. possession or in certain foreign countries that have an exchange of information agreement with the United States. Regulations apply to directors, number of shareholders, and capitalization of a foreign sales corporation. Foreign sales corporations are eligible for a reduction of U.S. federal income taxes on export-related income such as selling or leasing export property or supplying export-related services.

foreign tax credit The reduction in a U.S. tax liability because of taxes accrued or paid to a foreign government during the same taxable year.

forensic accounting Accounting examinations arrived at in a scientific fashion with a high level of detail and thoroughness that will successfully withstand judicial review.

forfeitable Subject to surrender. For example, an employee's vacation leave may be forfeitable unless the leave is used during the calendar year.

forfeiture The loss of property because of a violation of the law. For example, a truck being used to bring illegal aliens across the border from Mexico is subject to forfeiture. Likewise, profits and assets acquired with profits from an investment scam are subject to forfeiture.

forgery Altering or counterfeiting an instrument with the intent to defraud.

formation —See CHART FORMATION.

Form 8–K —See 8–K.

Form SB–1 An SEC form used by small businesses to register offerings of up to $10 million of securities, provided the company has not registered over $10 million in securities offerings during the preceding 12 months.

Form 1040 —See 1040.

Form 10–K —See 10–K.

Form 10–Q —See 10–Q.

Form W-2 —See WAGE AND TAX STATEMENT.

Form W-4 —See EMPLOYEE WITHHOLDING ALLOWANCE CERTIFICATE.

Form W-9 —See TAXPAYER IDENTIFICATION NUMBER.

formula plan The buying and/or selling of securities according to a predetermined formula. This approach to investment decisions is intended to eliminate the investor's emotions and instead follow a mechanical set of rules. A huge number of formula plans have been developed over the years.

form utility The elements of the composition and appearance of a product that make it desirable. Successful companies are constantly looking for ways to stimulate sales by improving a product's form utility. For example, a household products company might improve the packaging of toothpaste.

for-profit Describing an entity that is formed and operated with the intention of earning a profit. For example, General Electric is a for-profit corporation. In contrast, the American Red Cross is a nonprofit organization. —Compare NONPROFIT ORGANIZATION.

fortuitous event An unplanned and unexpected occurrence. Insurance coverage is only available for fortuitous events.

Fortune 500 A trademark for a well-known, widely quoted annual listing by *Fortune* magazine of the largest industrial corporations in the United States. Firms are listed along with their assets, sales, and profits. Subsequent issues include the largest retailers, utilities, financial institutions, transportation companies, foreign corporations, and the second 500 largest industrial firms.

for valuation only (FVO) —See FOR YOUR INFORMATION 2.

forward contract An agreement between two parties to the sale and purchase of a particular commodity at a specific future time. Although forward contracts are similar to futures, they are not liquid because they are not easily transferred or canceled.

forward integration Acquisition by a business of one or more other business that are between the acquiring firm and its customers. For example, a manufacturer purchases a distributor. Forward integration is a type of vertical integration. —Compare BACKWARD INTEGRATION.

> **CASE STUDY** Natural health care products company Comvita purchased its Hong Kong distributor GreenLife Ltd. for NZ\$9.03 million in 2007. The New Zealand–based company paid \$2.2 million in cash and the balance in stock in an effort to enhance growth into China and neighboring Asian countries. Comvita's chairman indicated the forward integration with GreenLife's retail stores, sales staff, and in-store promoters would allow the firm to quickly and effectively launch new products into the Asian market. Comvita had undertaken a similar acquisition in the United Kingdom two years earlier in order to expand into the European Union.

forward-looking statement A projected financial statement based on management expectations. A forward-looking statement involves risks with regard to the accuracy of assumptions underlying the projections. Discussions of these statements typically include words such as *estimate, anticipate, project,* and *believe.*

forward P/E The price-earnings ratio of a firm's common stock calculated as the current stock price divided by estimated earnings per share for the coming year. —Compare TRAILING P/E.

forward pricing The pricing of mutual fund shares on the basis of the next net asset valuation following receipt of a customer's order to buy or sell. While the price is based on net asset value, this value is adjusted for any applicable redemption or sales fee. The SEC requires forward pricing.

forward rate 1. The expected yield on a given fixed-income security at a particular time in the future. For example, if the yield on six-month Treasury bills is expected to be 10.5% in a year, this yield is the forward rate on six-month bills. 2. The rate at which a particular currency or commodity may be purchased on a forward contract.

forward stock In retailing, merchandise displayed on the selling floor as opposed to that held in a stockroom.

for your information (FYI) 1. An addition to a note or memorandum that alerts the reader that no action or response is required. 2. Of or relating to a market maker's quotation for trading purposes when the price is not firm. For example, a market maker might supply an FYI quote for valuation purposes. —Also called *for valuation only.*

---

four P's

Does the relative importance of each of the four P's vary with the type of business being evaluated?

There are definitely times when price will be a customer's number-one concern. If you are selling a commodity or a service in a highly competitive environment, a customer may simply be looking for the best price he or she can get and will always take the lowest bid. If, however, you have a good track record with a customer and have brought value to him or her through superior ideas and execution, price often becomes less of a focus.

▪ E. Mace Lewis, Vice President, Business Development, QD Healthcare Group, Greenwich, CT

---

foul bill of lading A receipt from a carrier to a shipper noting a shortage and/or that some or all of the goods were received in damaged condition.

401(k) plan —See SALARY REDUCTION PLAN.

403(b) plan —See TAX-SHELTERED ANNUITY.

four P's The four fundamental components of successful marketing: product, place, price, and promotion. The four P's involve marketing the appropriate good or service to the desired customer base at a satisfactory price.

fourth market The market for securities in which large investors bypass exchanges and dealers in order to trade directly among themselves. —Compare SECONDARY MARKET; THIRD MARKET.

fractional currency Paper money with a denomination of less than a country's standard monetary unit. In the United States, fractional currency would be any paper money with a denomination of less than a dollar. During the Civil War, the U.S. government issued more than $368 million in fractional currency, consisting of 3- to 50-cent denominations.

fractional interest Partial ownership of real property. For example, a family may purchase a one-twelfth interest in an expensive vacation home.

fractional share Less than one share of stock; that is, one-third or one-half a share. Fractional shares are generally created from dividend reinvestment plans or stock dividends. For example, if a firm's directors declare a 2% stock dividend, an owner of 70 shares would be entitled to 1.4 additional shares. Because corporations do not issue certificates including fractional shares, the stockholder would receive one share and the cash equivalent for the fractional share. Fractional shares are credited to dividend reinvestment plans.

fragmentation The lack of full interconnection of the various securities markets. Fragmentation can result in customer orders being sent to markets that do not offer the best available price. Critics claim the inefficiencies of fragmentation can be cured with a central order book that includes orders from all markets.

franchise 1. An agreement between a firm and another party in which the firm provides the other party with the right to use the firm's name and to sell or rent its products. Selling franchise rights is a method of expanding a business quickly with a minimum of capital. —See also FRANCHISEE; FRANCHISOR. **2.** A right granted to another party by a government to engage in certain types of business. For example, a firm may obtain a government franchise to supply certain public services within a limited geographic region. **3.** A geographical area within which an individual or firm has the right to market a company's product or service. For example, a soft drink distributor may have the southern half of the state as its franchise.

franchisee An individual or a company that has the right to sell or rent another firm's products and to use its name. —Compare FRANCHISOR.

franchise tax A tax on the right of a firm to do business within a certain geographic region.

franchisor A firm that sells to others the right to sell or rent its products and to use its name. —Compare FRANCHISEE.

frank A mark that exempts mail from postage fees.

Frankfurt Stock Exchange One of the world's largest securities exchanges that provides both floor and electronic trading facilities. The Frankfurt Stock Exchange was founded in 1585 and is operated by Deutsche Börse AG.

fraud Deception carried out for the purpose of achieving personal gain while causing injury to another party. For example, selling a new security issue while intentionally concealing important facts related to the issue is fraud.

Freddie Mac 1. A stockholder-owned corporation chartered by Congress in 1970 to help supply funds to mortgage lenders such as commercial banks, mortgage bankers, savings institutions, and credit unions that in turn make funds available to homeowners and multifamily investors. Freddie Mac purchases mortgages from lenders and then packages the mortgages into guaranteed securities that are sold to investors. —Formerly called *Federal Home Loan Mortgage Corporation.* **2.** A security that is issued by this corporation and is secured by pools of conventional home mortgages. Holders of Freddie Macs receive a share of the interest and principal payments made by the homeowner-borrowers.

free alongside ship A clause in a sales contract that identifies the seller's obligation to assume the risk and pay the expenses for transportation from the seller's place of business to the embarkation point where the buyer or buyer's agent will accept the goods.

free and clear Of or referring to real property against which there are no claims. For example, land without a lien or outstanding legal judgment is free and clear.

free cash flow The cash flow that remains after taking into account all cash flows including fixed-asset acquisitions, asset sales, and working-capital expenditures. The definition of free cash flow varies depending on the purpose of the analysis for which it is being used.

free credit balance Cash held in a brokerage account that may be withdrawn or used to acquire additional securities. Free credit balances generally originate from dividends, interest payments, and security sales.

free domicile A purchase agreement in which the shipper pays transportation costs and any duties.

Freedom of Information Act The federal statute that provides access to federal agency records, except to the extent that records are protected from disclosure by specific exemptions. Anyone is eligible to make a request, which must be in writing. Federal agencies are expected to respond to a request within 20 business days.

free enterprise An economic system where business is carried out without government intervention. Proponents contend that free enterprise maximizes consumer wealth by promoting the most efficient allocation of resources.

free list A directory of items not subject to import duties or related licensing requirements in an individual country.

free look period The period during which the buyer of an annuity can cancel the contract without penalty.

free lunch Getting something for nothing. Some economists contend "there's no such thing as a free lunch," but this is not universally accepted, especially among people who accumulate frequent-flyer points.

free market A marketplace in which government plays a minor role.

free on board (FOB) —Used in commodities contracts to indicate the geographical point to which delivery is included in the price. After this point, the buyer is responsible for all risks and delivery costs. The FOB point is only important to someone who sells or buys a futures contract with the intention of making or taking delivery of the specific commodity.

free port —See FREE TRADE ZONE.

freeriding The purchase and sale of a security in a short period of time without putting up any money. Freeriding by investors is prohibited by the Federal Reserve Board's Regulation T. —Compare FROZEN ACCOUNT 2.

free trade agreement A trading arrangement in which goods and services pass without restrictions between or among countries included in the agreement.

free trade zone A geographic area, often near a port or airport, where goods can be imported, stored, improved, and exported without duties. Duties are required only if and when goods in the free trade zone enter into commerce in the host country. —Also called *free port*. —See also TRANSIT ZONE.

free transferability of interest The right to sell an ownership interest without obtaining the permission of another party. For example, shareholders of an S corporation have the right to sell their interest without obtaining the approval of the other shareholders.

freeze-out provision A clause in a corporate charter that permits an acquiring firm to buy the shares of noncontrolling stockholders at a fair price after a specified period, generally two to five years. —See also DISSENTERS' RIGHTS.

freight forwarder A company that arranges commercial transportation for the cargo of other firms. The freight forwarder generally assumes responsibility for shipments until they reach their destinations.

frequency of compounding The number of times interest is calculated and added to the sum of the principal and any interest added during a particular period (nearly always one year). More frequent compounding results in a more rapid buildup of funds. For example, $1,000 deposited at 12% interest compounded twice a year equals: $1,000(1.06 × 1.06), or $1,123.60 at the end of one year; while compounding four times a year results in: $1,000(1.03 × 1.03 × 1.03 × 1.03), or $1,125.51.

frictional unemployment Unemployment that results from people moving between jobs. For example, a person who is searching for the right job after quitting or being laid off is considered to be part of frictional unemployment.

friendly fire A fire that burns as intended and remains within expected bounds. Loss from friendly fire is generally not covered by insurance. For example, wood burned in a fireplace is friendly fire. —Compare HOSTILE FIRE.

friendly suit A lawsuit agreed to by both parties in an attempt to gain a court order that will offer an opinion on a legal question.

friendly takeover The acquisition of a firm with approval of the acquired firm's board of directors. —Compare UNFRIENDLY TAKEOVER.

friends and family stock The shares of an initial public offering that are allocated to individuals designated by executives of the firm being taken public.

fringe benefit —See BENEFIT 1.

frontage In real estate, the distance over which a property borders a road, river, or body of water.

front-end load —See LOAD.

front foot In real estate, a linear foot along a street or road.

frontier markets Securities markets in the least developed of the emerging markets. For example, Mexico and Taiwan are generally considered emerging markets, while Zimbabwe, Jamaica, and Kenya are considered frontier markets. Political factors are especially important to the trading and valuation of securities traded in frontier markets.

fronting In insurance, issuing a policy and immediately passing the entire risk to another firm that pays the issuing company a commission. This is similar in nature to lenders making and then reselling loans.

front man —See STRAW MAN 1.

front money 1. Funds paid in advance. 2. Funds required to begin a project or a business.

front office 1. The revenue-generating section of a financial services company. For example, the area housing financial consultants of a brokerage firm. Front-office personnel generally deal directly with customers. 2. The area of an office where policymakers reside.

front running Entering into a trade while taking advantage of advance knowledge of pending orders from other investors. For example, an exchange specialist may step in front and buy stock for slightly more than the price offered by other investors. —Also called *pennying; stepping in front.*

frozen account 1. A bank account in which activity by the owner is prohibited. For example, an account holder is barred from making withdrawals because of a dispute about ownership of the account. 2. A brokerage account in which a customer must pay in full before securities are bought, and must deliver certificates before securities are sold. An account is frozen when a customer fails to maintain the proper margin required by Regulation T. —Compare FREERIDING.

frozen asset An asset that may not be liquidated.

frozen collateral Collateral that the lender is unable to seize in order to satisfy repayment of a debt. For example, a lender may find that there is a legal question as to who actually owns the asset pledged as collateral.

FTC —See FEDERAL TRADE COMMISSION.

F test In statistics, a comparison of the variances of two samples from normal distributions.

FTSE 100 Index A market-weighted index of the 100 leading companies traded in Great Britain on the London Stock Exchange. The *Financial Times* calculates several other indexes, although financial commentators typically refer to the FTSE 100 when they say "Footsie." The full name is Financial Times–Stock Exchange 100 Share Index.

fulfillment Successfully completing something. For example, fulfillment of a college's curriculum and credit-hour requirements will lead to a bachelor's degree. "Fulfillment" is the designation frequently applied to mail-order companies that contract to fill customer orders.

full coupon —See CURRENT COUPON.

full coverage Insurance coverage against all types of losses. For example, a vehicle owner is covered for personal injury, liability, property damage, collision, comprehensive, uninsured motorist, etc. Full coverage may indeed provide coverage against all types of losses, but it may not cover a loss fully because of deductibles or coinsurance.

full disclosure The disclosure of all relevant financial and operating information. For example, the SEC requires public corporations to make full disclosure when they issue securities.

full employment In theory, the situation of everyone who wants a job being employed. In practice, economists generally consider an unemployment rate of approximately 4% to represent full employment.

full-faith-and-credit bond —See GENERAL OBLIGATION BOND.

full-faith-and-credit pledge In a municipal obligation, a pledge of the full financial resources and taxing power of the issuer. A full-faith-and-credit pledge is an important element of general obligation bonds. —See also SPECIAL ASSESSMENT BOND.

full payout lease A lease in which required lease payments allow the lessor to recover all expenses plus an acceptable return, exclusive of any residual value of the leased asset at the termination of the lease.

full position In print advertising, preferred placement of an advertisement that is likely to benefit from increased notice by readers. —Compare RUN OF PAPER.

full price Fair price as applied to a security or an acquisition. For example, if a firm's stock is selling at close to full price, the firm is less likely to be a candidate for a takeover.

full retirement age The age at which a person can retire and draw full benefits under Social Security. The age for full retirement benefits is scheduled to gradually increase to 67 for individuals born in 1960 and after. Individuals born prior to 1960 will earn full retirement benefits at a slightly younger age than 67.

fully amortized loan A loan with equal periodic payments that result in an outstanding balance of zero at maturity. Each loan payment is part interest and part principal. Many vehicle loans and home loans are examples of fully amortized loans.

fully depreciated Of or relating to a fixed asset that has been depreciated to a book value of zero. An asset can be fully depreciated and still be used.

fully invested To have committed nearly all available funds to assets other than short-term investments such as savings and money market accounts. Fully invested is generally used in reference to institutional investors such as mutual funds or trust departments and indicates that these investors are very bullish.

fully valued Of or relating to an asset that is selling at a price knowledgeable investors believe fully reflects the asset's value and earnings potential. A fully valued asset is likely to have limited appreciation potential.

functional currency The currency of the primary economic environment in which an entity operates. For example, the U.S. dollar is the functional currency for U.S. taxpayers, except for qualified business units that are separate and identifiable entities of a trade or business that maintains separate books and records.

functional obsolescence A decrease in the value of a product or service caused by wear and tear or modified preferences of users. For example, homes built 30 years ago often have floor plans that don't appeal to younger homebuyers. Likewise, vehicles 10 or 12 years old are worth considerably less than newer models in part because of higher maintenance costs. —Compare TECHNICAL OBSOLESCENCE.

functional organization An organization structured according to specialty. For example, a pension committee may include active members, nonactive members, and independent members. The functional organization includes the manner in which members are elected or appointed, how they are trained, and a description of their duties.

fund 1. Money available for a specific use or general purposes. 2. —See MUTUAL FUND. 3. An accounting entity with self-balancing accounts for recording assets, liabilities, and fund balances.

fund accounting The accounting system utilized by not-for-profit organizations in which resources are classified for accounting and reporting purposes in accordance with donor objectives and governing board guidelines.

fundamental analysis Analysis of security values grounded in basic factors such as earnings, balance sheet variables, and management quality. Fundamental analysis attempts to determine the true value of a security, and, if the market price of the stock deviates from this value, to take advantage of the difference by acquiring or selling the stock. —Compare TECHNICAL ANALYSIS.

fundamentals The basic economic, financial, and operating factors that influence the success of a business or the value of an asset.

funded debt Long-term interest-bearing debt, such as that for bonds and debentures.

funded pension plan A trustee-managed retirement plan in which an employer makes financial contributions for the benefit of employees. —See also DEFINED-BENEFIT PENSION PLAN; DEFINED-CONTRIBUTION PENSION PLAN.

fund group —See FAMILY OF FUNDS.

funding 1. Refinancing a debt. 2. Placing money or other assets into an account that is to serve as a source of future benefits. For example, a company may devote a substantial portion of its current revenue to funding its employee retirement program. 3. Allocating money to an endeavor. For example, a petroleum company may budget $300 million toward funding the development of a new oil field.

fund manager The supervisor of a pool of investment capital such as that held by a mutual fund, pension fund, or closed-end investment company. The fund manager is charged with making investment decisions that adhere to stated investment objectives.

fund raising Solicitation of donations for a particular cause or organization.

funds from operations A measure of cash generated by a real estate investment trust. Funds from operations is equal to net income plus depreciation or amortization, minus gains on sales of properties. The adjustments to net income are designed to provide a better measure of a trust's real performance.

funds rate —See FEDERAL FUNDS RATE.

funds statement —See STATEMENT OF CASH FLOWS.

fund switching An investment activity in which shares in one mutual fund are sold and the proceeds from the sale are reinvested in another mutual fund. Fund switching results from an investor's changed perception of investment opportunities. High sales charges involved in purchasing some funds make switching practical only if no-load funds are used or if the investor switches within a family of funds.

fungible Of or relating to assets that are identical in quality and are interchangeable. Commodities, options, and securities are fungible assets. For example, an investor's shares of General Electric left in custody at a brokerage firm are freely mixed with other customers' General Electric shares. Likewise, stock options are freely interchangeable among investors, and wheat stored in a grain elevator is not specifically identified as to its ownership.

funnel sinking fund A special type of bond retirement system in which an issuer has the option to make all its outstanding bonds subject to one annual sinking fund requirement. Thus, the issuer may take the annual sinking fund requirements for all outstanding issues and concentrate them into retiring an unusually large amount of a high-coupon issue.

furlough 1. A leave of absence for a specified reason. 2. A temporary layoff from employment.

future interest The right to an ownership interest in real property on some specific date in the future. For example, a woman might leave her valuable jewelry to her granddaughter, but only after the death of her daughter. The granddaughter has a future interest in the jewelry.

futures commission firm —See FUTURES COMMISSION MERCHANT.

futures commission merchant (FCM) A firm that carries out futures transactions for another party. Essentially, futures commission merchants are to futures trading what ordinary brokerage firms are to stock and bond trading. Some futures commission merchants are full-line brokerage firms in which futures trades make up only a small part of their business. —Also called *commodity brokerage firm; futures commission firm.*

futures contract An agreement to take (that is, by the buyer) or make (that is, by the seller) delivery of a specific commodity on a particular date. The commodities and contracts are standardized in order that an active resale market will exist. Futures contracts are available for a variety of items, including grains, metals, and foreign currencies.

futures market A market in which futures contracts are bought and sold. The various organized futures exchanges specialize in certain types of contracts. For example, the Chicago Board of Trade trades futures contracts on agricultural products, U.S. Treasury securities, gold and silver, and the Dow Jones Industrial Average. The New York Mercantile Exchange handles futures contracts in energy and metals.

futures option A put or call option on a futures contract. Because of the price volatility of futures contracts, options on these contracts are high-risk investments.

future value The amount to which a specific sum or series of sums will grow on a given date in the future. The sums are assumed to earn an annual return that is related to the market rate of interest. For example, $1,000 has a future value of $1,120 in one year, assuming an annual return of 12%. —Compare PRESENT VALUE.

FVO —See FOR VALUATION ONLY.

FY —See FISCAL YEAR.

FYI —See FOR YOUR INFORMATION.

G

G8 The world's eight largest industrial countries, including Canada, France, Germany, Great Britain, Italy, Japan, Russia, and the United States. G8 finance ministers meet annually to evaluate and coordinate economic policy.

GAAP —See GENERALLY ACCEPTED ACCOUNTING PRINCIPLES.

GAAS —See GENERALLY ACCEPTED AUDITING STANDARDS.

gain The excess of the amount received as opposed to the amount expended in a transaction. For example, receipt of $4,500 from the sale of an asset with a book value of $3,000 results in a gain of $1,500. —Compare LOSS. —See also REALIZED GAIN; UNREALIZED GAIN.

gainful employment Employment that is beneficial both to the employer and the employee.

gain sharing An employment arrangement in which an employee benefits from his or her contribution to improved performance of the organization. For example, a hospital might offer physicians a share of any cost reductions in patient care attributable to actions taken by physicians. Gain sharing attempts to motivate employees through financial rewards.

> **CASE** The Government Travel Savings Program is a gain-sharing arrange-
> **STUDY** ment that rewards federal government employees who save money
> while on official travel. In general, the cash awards equal 50% of the savings
> on lodging expenses and/or contract carrier airfare. For example, government
> employees who stay with relatives or friends and avoid lodging expenses while
> on official travel receive one-half of the allowed maximum lodging rate. Employees who obtain a free coach-class ticket using their own frequent flyer
> benefits are also eligible for a reward based on the government contract rate
> or, if no contract rate is in effect, the lowest available nonrestricted coach fare.
> Rewards earned under the program are subject to federal, state, and local
> taxation.

gaming 1. In business, modeling in which two or more parties compete to win something. For example, several defense contractors compete to win a contract to build a new tank by making decisions based partly on expectations regarding their competitors' bids. Too high a bid will result in losing the contract to a competitor, and too low a bid will win the contract but without a reasonable profit. **2.** The gambling industry.

Gantt Chart A horizontal bar chart that presents a graphical representation of a production schedule. The bar is labeled with dates for each stage, from a preliminary investigation to the final report.

GAO —See GOVERNMENT ACCOUNTABILITY OFFICE.

gap analysis An assessment of where an organization needs to be compared to where it actually is. For example, a household products company might use gap analysis

garnishment

Under what conditions is garnishment permitted? Are there restrictions on the part of the party seeking garnishment?

A judgment creditor ("creditor") may seek a wage deduction order known as a creditor garnishment (or garnishment for ordinary debt) to seek repayment of a debt from another individual. Garnishments can be taken for any type of debt but must be executed pursuant to the specific conditions and procedures expressly authorized by the relevant federal and state statutes.

A creditor is restricted with regard to the amount of an employee's earnings that may be garnished. Title III of the federal Consumer Credit Protection Act (CCPA) sets the maximum amount that may be garnished in any one pay period, regardless of the number of garnishment orders received by the employer. The maximum amount that may be garnished is the lesser of 25% of disposable earnings (wages left after legally required deductions have been taken) or the amount by which disposable earnings are greater than 30 times the federal minimum hourly wage. CCPA does allow a higher percentage of an employee's disposable earnings to be garnished for child support or alimony, and exempts for tax levies.

Creditors may be further restricted under state garnishment laws. States are allowed to enact their own garnishment laws and if a state garnishment law differs from the CCPA, the law resulting in the *smaller* garnishment is followed as long as garnishment orders issued under federal authority take effect. Under this authority, states such as South Carolina and Texas limit wage garnishment for debts related to taxes, child support, federally guaranteed student loans, and court-ordered fines or restitution for a crime the debtor committed. Florida offers a significant "head of family" exemption, where the wages of a person who provides more than half the support for a child or other dependent are exempt from garnishment. In North Carolina and Pennsylvania, wages may not be garnished to pay for what the states refer to as "consumer" debt.

Another constraint for creditors is the order of priority. When a state allows wage garnishments for ordinary debt, the general rule is that they are given priority on a first-in-time basis. However, the rules for priority are actually quite complex and determined by federal and state laws. When priority garnishments such as for child support or tax levies are received by the employer, they take precedence over creditor garnishments. In short, an employer is required to deduct for child support or tax levy before a garnishment for ordinary debt. If any one of these priority deductions exceeds CCPA restrictions, the employer can't withhold wages for the creditor garnishment.

Wage garnishment for ordinary debt is generally determined by the laws of the state in which the debtor resides. As indicated by this answer, these laws vary greatly from state to state. An overview of each state's garnishment laws is provided at: http://www.fair-debt-collection.com/state-wage-garnishments.

■ Helen M. Kemp, Division Counsel and Assistant Director,
Retirement and Benefit Services, Office of the State Comptroller, State of Connecticut

to evaluate its market penetration for a particular product. Gap analysis is used to initiate policy changes that will close any gap that is identified. The household products company might decide to change its marketing mix in order to improve market penetration.

gap financing Temporary borrowing to provide needed funds between the termination of one loan and the beginning of permanent financing. For example, a developer might obtain gap financing to provide funds for the period between the end of a construction loan and when permanent financing becomes available.

garbage in, garbage out (GIGO) The principle that faulty inputs into a process will produce flawed results.

garnish To withhold wages under legal order to satisfy an obligation. For example, a person may have wages garnished for child support.

garnishment A legal order that takes property to satisfy a person's debt. For example, a court may order that an employer withhold a portion of an employee's wages in order to satisfy a creditor's claim.

GASB —See GOVERNMENT ACCOUNTING STANDARDS BOARD.

gatefold One or more large pages that are inserted and folded to fit the page size of a publication. The gatefold must be opened or unfolded in order to read the content. Vehicle manufacturers often use gatefolds in automobile magazines to advertise new models.

gatekeeper Someone who controls access. For example, a primary care physician monitors a patient's health care and serves as gatekeeper for HMO services. Similarly, an executive secretary serves as a gatekeeper for information flow to the executive.

GATT —See GENERAL AGREEMENT ON TARIFFS AND TRADE.

GDP —See GROSS DOMESTIC PRODUCT.

GDP deflator A price index used to adjust gross domestic product for changes in prices of goods and services included in the GDP. The GDP deflator is a more broadly based and, many economists argue, a better measure of inflation than the consumer price index or the producer price index. —Also called *gross domestic product deflator.*

GDR —See GLOBAL DEPOSITARY RECEIPT.

general account —See MARGIN ACCOUNT.

General Agreement on Tariffs and Trade (GATT) A 1947 multilateral trade agreement designed to establish rules, reduce tariffs, and provide a setting for a solution to international trade problems. GATT agreements are of particular importance to industries and firms heavily involved in international trade.

general contractor A person or firm that oversees a construction or development project. A general contractor may utilize his or her own employees or use the services of other firms, called subcontractors. —Also called *primary contractor.*

general creditor A lender with an uncollateralized loan. In the event that a borrower goes bankrupt, its general creditors are likely to recover a smaller proportion of what is owed them than secured creditors will.

general fund In governmental and nonprofit accounting, the account that covers all receipts, appropriations, and expenditures other than those that specifically require separate funds. The general fund accounts for most of an entity's revenues and expenditures.

general journal The primary record of transactions, which includes a date, account to receive a debit entry, account to receive a credit entry, and a description of the transaction.

general liability insurance Coverage that protects a business for claims of bodily injury or property damage involving the products, operations, or premises of the insured.

general lien The right of a lender to seize all of a borrower's personal property.

general loan and collateral agreement —See BROKER'S LOAN.

generally accepted accounting principles (GAAP) Guidelines and rules for use by accountants in preparing financial statements. These principles, which evolved over a period of years, are designed to help ensure that financial data are presented fairly

general power of appointment

Should restrictions be attached to a general power of appointment?

The "general" power of appointment is distinguished from the "special (or limited)" power of appointment by its tax consequence. A power of appointment is general if it grants the holder the ability to appoint (that is, to give) the property subject to the power to any one or more of (1) the holder, (2) his or her creditors, (3) his or her estate, or (4) the creditors of his or her estate. A power which includes any one of these four classes, and permits the holder to appoint to anyone else as well, is a general power of appointment. By contrast, a power which excludes the four classes but permits the holder to give the property to anyone else in the world is still "limited" for U.S. estate and gift tax purposes.

The tax effect of the general, as opposed to the special or limited, power is that the property subject to the power is treated as owned by the power holder for gift and estate tax purposes; that is, the holder's exercise or release of a general power (and, subject to certain limitations, the holder's permitting the power to lapse) is a gift for federal gift tax purposes, and property subject to a general power at the holder's death is included in the holder's estate for federal estate tax purposes. As a result, a general power typically is conferred with the express intention to produce these tax consequences and otherwise is carefully avoided. Indeed, because a power which is "limited" for tax purposes still permits appointment among a very large class, there is rarely a non-tax reason to confer a general power. The creditors of the holder of a general power who has the current right to appoint to himself or his creditors may be able to reach the property subject to the power. Thus, if the conferral of a general power is desired, it may be preferable to restrict the provision which causes the power to be general to the ability to appoint to the holder's estate.

■ Stephen F. Lappert, Partner, Trusts and Estates Department, Carter Ledyard & Milburn LLP, New York, NY

and are comparable from firm to firm and from industry to industry. In expressing an opinion on financial statements, certified public accountants are required to stipulate whether their statements have been prepared according to generally accepted accounting principles.

generally accepted auditing standards (GAAS) Guidelines established by the American Institute of Certified Public Accountants for use by public accountants when conducting external audits of financial statements. —See also AUDITED STATEMENT; UNAUDITED STATEMENT.

general obligation bond (GO) A municipal debt obligation on which interest and principal are guaranteed by the full financial resources and taxing power of the issuer. This broad promise makes a general obligation bond of higher quality than issues secured by a particular project or a more limited guarantee. —Also called *full-faith-and-credit bond.* —See also REVENUE BOND.

general partnership A partnership in which each of the partners is liable for all of the firm's debts, and the actions of one partner are binding on each of the other partners. —Compare LIMITED PARTNERSHIP.

general power of appointment The legal authority granted to a person to distribute to anyone the grantor's property. For example, a person may grant to her attorney a general power of appointment to distribute her household and personal items. The attorney then has the authority to distribute the items to the grantor's children, the grantor's creditors, or to anyone else, including herself. —Compare SPECIAL POWER OF APPOINTMENT. —Also called *power of appointment.*

general power of attorney A legal document that allows another to act on behalf of the principal in all matters. A general power of attorney is often authorized when individuals become concerned about the possibility of becoming incapacitated and unable to make their own decisions.

general price level accounting —See INFLATION ACCOUNTING.

General Securities Registered Representative Examination —See SERIES 7.

general warranty deed A deed in which the owner guarantees a clear title and the right to transfer the property.

generational accounting Estimating the effects of government policy by age. For example, a transportation plan that includes an increase in the federal gasoline tax to fund renewable energy sources is evaluated with regard to the benefits and costs to different generations of citizens. Generational accounting may indicate the proposal would result in current generations paying for benefits that would be received by future generations.

generation-skipping transfer tax A federal tax designed to ensure that family property will be subject to taxation at least once each generation. For example, property given to a grandchild is subject to the generation-skipping transfer tax that is intended to result in a tax that is the same as if the property had been given first to a child and had been given subsequently to the grandchild.

generic Of, relating to, or being a product that is identified as part of a class rather than as a brand. For example, a clothing manufacturer sells pants without a brand name to discount stores. Grocery stores frequently sell generic canned goods at lower prices.

generic mark A word or symbol that identifies a class of products or services rather than the product or service of a particular provider. For example, "corn flakes," while once a trademarked product, now identifies a particular type of cereal, but not that of a particular manufacturer. Generic marks are not subject to trademark protection.

genetic engineering A process that alters the structure of an organism's genes, generally in an attempt to improve some aspect of the organism. Scientists have successfully used genetic engineering to protect some plants from particular kinds of viruses.

gentrification Revitalization of a neighborhood, district, or town when middle- and high-income individuals and families replace lower-income residents.

geodemography The processing and analysis of census data to profile the demographic and economic characteristics of the population in a limited geographical area. A mail-order firm may utilize geodemography to target marketing of its products.

geometric mean A measure of central tendency that is frequently used when changes in a variable are relative. The geometric mean is calculated by taking the nth root of the product of n variables. For example, you wish to calculate the mean return when the stock market has produced annual returns during the last three years of 25%, -10%, and 18%. In this case the geometric mean is calculated by taking the cube root of 1.25 x 0.90 x 1.18. —Compare ARITHMETIC MEAN. —Also called *mean*.

ghost stock Stock that has been sold short, but that has not been borrowed and therefore cannot be delivered to the buyer.

GIC —See GUARANTEED INVESTMENT CONTRACT.

gift A voluntary transfer of property without receiving anything in return.

gift causa mortis A gift made in contemplation of the impending death of the donor. The gift is revoked in the event the death does not occur.

gift deed —See DEED OF GIFT.

gift inter vivos Transfer of property without consideration during a donor's lifetime.

gift splitting A gift of property by one spouse of a marriage that is treated as being gifted equally by both spouses. For example, a married woman can give $18,000 to a grandchild and elect to have the gift treated as $9,000 each from her and her husband.

gift tax A federal tax that is imposed on the giver and determined on the basis of a unified gift and estate tax schedule. Annual gifts above a specified amount per recipient are deducted from a lifetime exemption. This exemption applies jointly to accumulated gifts and to the taxable estate left at death. In most cases, only relatively large gifts incur a tax. —See also UNIFIED CREDIT.

gift tax exclusion The maximum dollar value of gifts per recipient that a donor is permitted each year without incurring a federal gift tax.

GIGO —See GARBAGE IN, GARBAGE OUT.

Gilded Age The years between the Civil War and World War I, when institutions undertook financial manipulations that went virtually unchecked by government. This era produced many infamous activities in the securities markets.

gilt-edged security Any high-quality security in which the chance of default or failure is quite slim.

Ginnie Mae A wholly owned government association that operates the mortgage-backed securities program designed to facilitate the flow of capital into the housing industry. Ginnie Mae–approved private institutions issue mortgage-backed securities with payments that are guaranteed even if borrowers or issuers default on their obligations. Ginnie Mae was created in 1968 when the Federal National Mortgage Association was partitioned into two parts. —Formerly called *Government National Mortgage Association.* —See also GINNIE MAE PASS THROUGH; MOBILE HOME CERTIFICATE.

Ginnie Mae pass through A security backed by the Federal Housing Administration, Veterans Administration, and the Farmers Home Administration mortgages that is guaranteed by Ginnie Mae. The issuers of the securities service the mortgages and pass through interest and principal payments to the security holders. During periods of declining interest rates, holders of Ginnie Mae pass throughs are likely to receive extra principal payments as mortgages are refinanced and paid off early. —See also GINNIE MAE.

giveback The relinquishment by employees of certain existing benefits or contract provisions. For example, many companies engaged in manufacturing have asked for employee givebacks on the premise that lower costs are needed in order for the companies to be more competitive with foreign producers.

glamour stock A widely held stock that receives a considerable amount of favorable publicity in the financial press. Glamour stocks typically represent firms with strong earnings growth and bright futures. Glamour stocks, which tend to sell at relatively high price-earnings ratios, are found in most institutional portfolios.

glass ceiling The invisible barrier (discrimination) that makes it difficult for females and minorities to advance in an organization.

Glass-Steagall Act A 1933 act that prohibited commercial banks from undertaking investment banking activities such as underwriting the securities of private corporations. The legislation was passed to keep banks from entering into nonfinancial businesses (for example, owning corporate stock) and more risky activities. The Glass-Steagall Act was repealed in 1999. —Also called *Banking Act of 1933.*

glitch A malfunction or temporary problem.

Global Depositary Receipt (GDR) A receipt on shares of a foreign company when funds are simultaneously raised in two or more markets.

global fund A mutual fund that includes at least 25% foreign securities in its portfolio. The value of the fund depends on the health of foreign economies and exchange rate movements. A global fund permits an investor to diversify internationally. —Compare INTERNATIONAL FUND. —Also called *world fund.*

global shares Stock that trades in multiple currencies. For example, shares of DaimlerChrysler, considered by many to be the first truly global shares, were traded in dollars in the United States, euros in Germany, yen in Japan, and in the home currencies of several other countries. (DaimlerChrysler sold the Chrysler operation to a private equity firm in 2007.) Global shares are uncommon and are different from American Depositary Shares, which are claims on a firm's ordinary shares.

glut An overabundance of a good or service. A glut generally results in a falling price. For example, a glut in memory chips allowed computer manufacturers to purchase the chips at very low prices compared to last year.

GNMA —See GINNIE MAE.

GO —See GENERAL OBLIGATION BOND.

goal An objective or target to be achieved, generally by a specific date. For example, corporate management may set a goal of doubling revenues in five years.

goal congruence Aligning the goals of two or more groups. Corporations often justify giving management generous stock options on the basis of aligning management goals with those of the firm's stockholders.

goal programming In management, a system for determining the best solution when multiple goals exist. For example, a company may want to build a new production facility where taxes are low, customers are nearby, land is cheap, and potential employees are educated and well-trained.

going concern A business expected to continue to operate in the foreseeable future. A going concern is valued differently from a firm for which liquidation is expected.

going-concern statement An auditor's statement that there is concern about whether the company being audited can remain in business. A going-concern statement indicates equity investors are at substantial risk.

going lines —See CONTINUING OPERATIONS.

going long Buying an investment.

going private The process by which a publicly held company has its outstanding shares purchased by an individual or by a small group of individuals who wish to obtain complete ownership and control. The group wishing to take the firm private may feel that the market is undervaluing the company. In addition, the purchaser(s) may not wish to meet the various requirements imposed on a publicly held company. —Also called *management buyout.*

CASE STUDY San Diego–based PETCO Animal Supplies announced in July 2006 that its board of directors had approved a $1.68 billion acquisition offer for the company by two private-equity firms. The offer of $29 per share was nearly 50% above PETCO's prior day's closing stock price of $19.45. The buyers also agreed to assume $120 million of PETCO debt. PETCO Animal Supplies was the nation's second largest pet supply retail chain and among several large specialty retailers to go private. More unusual was the fact that PETCO had been taken private once before, in 2000, before going public again in 2002. In both instances, a relatively low stock price attracted the investors who took the firm private.

going public The process by which a privately held company sells a portion of its ownership to the general public through a stock offering. Owners generally take their firms public because they need additional large sums of equity funding that they are unable or unwilling to contribute themselves.

going short Selling an investment asset that is not owned. An example of such an asset would be shares of stock you borrowed through your broker. Going short means you owe and must eventually replace what you have sold.

gold bond —See COMMODITY-BACKED BOND.

goldbrick A person who attempts to avoid work and responsibility.

gold bug An individual who thinks that investors should keep all or part of their assets in the form of gold. The tendency to recommend gold nearly always stems from the gold bug's expectation of rapid or uncontrolled growth of the money supply accompanied by high rates of inflation. Some gold bugs also predict economic collapse, with gold becoming the standard of payment.

golden boot A lucrative financial package offered an employee who is being involuntarily terminated.

golden handcuffs A lucrative incentive offered to a firm's executive in order either to keep him or her from moving to a job at another company, or to buy the executive's longer-term cooperation after departure.

golden handshake A substantial severance payment to a departing employee, often as an incentive for early retirement.

golden hello A substantial bonus offered as an employment inducement. For example, Hewlett-Packard offered NCR head Mark Hurd a $2 million signing bonus, a $2.75 million relocation allowance, 1.15 million stock options, 400,000 restricted HP shares, and one year of free housing to become chief executive of HP. This golden hello was in addition to Hurd's annual salary, long-term incentive payments, and annual bonus.

golden parachute An employment agreement that provides a firm's key executives with lucrative severance benefits in the event that control of the firm changes hands and that shifts in management subsequently occur. A golden parachute benefits management more than the stockholders. —Also called *golden umbrella*. —See also SILVER PARACHUTE.

CASE STUDY After six years at the helm of Atlanta-based The Home Depot, CEO Robert Nardelli abruptly resigned in January 2007 with a $210 million golden parachute. The former General Electric executive had instituted a top-down management style that helped produce higher revenues and profits at The Home Depot, but a stagnant stock price. Unhappy stockholders felt that Nardelli's lucrative compensation (he received over $30 million in compensation and stock options the previous year) was overly generous in view the stock's poor performance. They were also angered by Nardelli's actions during the firm's spring annual meeting when he had been unwilling to answer shareholder questions. He was the only member of the board of directors who had bothered to attend the meeting. The outsized golden parachute was comprised of $20 million in cash, $44 million in previously earned and vested deferred stock, $32 million of retirement benefits, acceleration of unvested stock options valued at $77 million, plus additional benefits. The price of The Home Depot common stock increased 91¢ per share on the day the resignation was announced.

golden umbrella —See GOLDEN PARACHUTE.

gold fix The setting of the price of gold by dealers so as to establish values for gold bullion, gold products, and gold-related products. The price of gold is fixed twice a day in each of the world's gold centers. —See also FIX.

gold fund An investment company with all or a major part of its assets in gold or gold-related securities. A gold fund's price, which is closely related to the value of gold, frequently moves opposite the prices of other securities and stock market indexes.

goldilocks economy An economy that is growing at a sustainable pace without worrisome inflationary pressures.

gold standard A monetary system under which a country's money is defined in terms of gold and is convertible into a fixed quantity of gold. A gold standard effectively takes monetary policy out of the hands of government policymakers. While use of the gold standard reduces the likelihood of inflation, the accompanying inability to pursue other economic goals, such as full employment or reduced interest rates, has resulted in the gold standard's fall from favor. —See also SILVER STANDARD.

good delivery Delivery of a security that meets all the standards required to transfer title to the buyer. Thus, a certificate must be delivered on time with proper denomination, endorsements, and endorsement guarantee. —Compare BAD DELIVERY.

good faith deposit **1.** Funds advanced as a guarantee that a contract or promise will be fulfilled. —See also EARNEST MONEY. **2.** A sum of money required of an investor who is placing an order when that investor is not known to the brokerage firm. A good faith deposit ensures that the customer will follow through with proper payment for a buy order or with delivery of securities for a sell order. **3.** A sum of money deposited by competing underwriters of a new municipal bond issue. The deposit is a relatively small proportion (usually under 5%) of the value of the issue being underwritten.

good money **1.** In commercial banking, federal funds that clear and are available for use on the same day. In contrast, clearinghouse funds that result from the deposit of personal and business checks might not be available for several days. **2.** In economics, money that has the greatest intrinsic value. For example, gold coins have substantial intrinsic value while paper money does not. —See also GRESHAM'S LAW.

goodness of fit A statistical test that examines the degree to which the variability of data is explained by a fit. The result indicates the agreement between an actual distribution (the data) and a theoretical distribution (the fit).

goods in process —See WORK IN PROCESS.

good-till-canceled order (GTC) An order either to buy or to sell a security that remains in effect until it is canceled by the customer or until it is executed by the broker. In practice, most brokerage firms impose a time limit on unexecuted orders. —Also called *open order.*

good title —See CLEAR TITLE.

goodwill 1. The amount above the fair net book value (adjusted for assumed debt) paid for an acquisition. Goodwill appears as an asset on the balance sheet of the acquiring firm and must be reduced in the event the value is impaired. **2.** The discounted value of a larger-than-normal return on tangible assets. For example, a business may build goodwill over time as loyalty builds among its customer base.

Government Accountability Office (GAO) The nonpartisan federal agency that evaluates federal programs, audits federal expenditures, and issues legal opinions. The GAO advises Congress and executive branch heads on how to make government more efficient and effective. —Formerly called *Government Accounting Office.*

Government Accounting Standards Board (GASB) The independent, private-sector organization that establishes the financial accounting and reporting standards for U.S. state and local governments. The GASB was established in 1984 and is funded by publication sales, contributions from state and local governments, and voluntary assessment fees from municipal bond issues. —See also FINANCIAL ACCOUNTING STANDARDS BOARD.

government enterprise A government-sponsored business. For example, the Intermountain Power Agency, a political subdivision of the state of Utah, includes in its membership 23 Utah municipalities that own electric utilities.

Government National Mortgage Association (GNMA) —See GINNIE MAE.

governments All bonds issued by the U.S. Treasury or other agencies of the U.S. government. —Also called *United States government securities.* —See also FEDERAL AGENCY SECURITY; SAVINGS BOND; TREASURIES.

grace period 1. The period of time a payment can be late without resulting in a penalty or cancellation. For example, an insurance policy may stipulate a one-month grace period before the policy is canceled. **2.** The period during which the issuer of a bond is not required to make interest payments. For example, a bond issued this year might start paying interest only five years from now. Bonds with grace periods are sometimes issued during a corporate restructuring.

graduated flat tax An income tax having a minimal number of progressively higher rates. For example, a taxing authority may levy a tax of 10% on all income up to $15,000, 15% on income from $15,000 to $25,000, and 20% on all income above $25,000. The graduated flat tax is a compromise between a flat tax and a progressive tax.

graduated lease A lease agreement that allows for or stipulates changes in the payment depending on certain variables (e.g., inflation) or the passage of time. —Also called *step-payment lease.*

graduated payment mortgage A mortgage with monthly payments that start low and gradually increase over time. These loans allow individuals to more easily qualify for a mortgage on the assumption that their incomes will increase over time to enable them to meet the later higher required monthly payments.

graft Using one's position or offering something of value in a dishonest attempt to gain a profit or an advantage.

---

grantor trust

Can you provide an example of when a grantor trust may be desirable? Is there a downside to these trusts?

"Grantor trust" is an income tax classification for a trust that is, wholly or in part, disregarded for income tax purposes; in other words, the property transferred by the grantor to the trust is treated to some extent as still being owned by the grantor for income tax purposes. The portion of the trust property that is treated this way is determined by the grantor's interest in or control over the trust. For example, a grantor's interest in trust income may cause the trust to be a grantor trust as to ordinary income (interest and dividends), but the grantor may not have sufficient power over trust principal to cause the trust to be a grantor trust as to capital gains (which result from the sale of principal). The grantor's retained powers or interests that cause the trust to be treated as a grantor trust for income tax purposes may also cause the trust property to be treated as owned by the grantor for gift and estate tax purposes. If this occurs, trust property is included in the grantor's gross estate for the federal estate tax. This is not always the case, and grantor trusts ("defective grantor trusts") are often intentionally drafted that cause the trust property to be treated as owned by the grantor for income tax purposes, but not owned by the grantor for federal gift and estate tax purposes. This distinction can allow the grantor to pay the income tax on trust income enjoyed by the trust beneficiaries and, under current federal income and gift tax laws, avoid having the payment of that income tax being treated as a gift by the grantor.

The consequence of grantor trust status, that the income of the trust assets is taxed in the grantor's income tax return, can be undesirable if the tax would have been less if the income had been taxed in the trust or taxed to the beneficiaries receiving distributions. However, because the marginal brackets applicable to trusts are quite compressed (in 2008, a trust's taxable income in excess of $10,700 was taxed at the 35% bracket), accumulated income of trusts of even moderate size will often be taxed at the highest income tax bracket, and there will be no effective tax disadvantage of using a grantor trust.

■ Stephen F. Lappert, Partner, Trusts and Estates Department, Carter Ledyard & Milburn LLP, New York, NY

Graham and Dodd Authors of *Security Analysis,* one of the more well known and durable works dealing with investment philosophy. Graham and Dodd stressed the importance of value investing; that is, buying shares of companies with undervalued assets and low price-earnings ratios.

Graham-Rudman-Hollings Balanced Budget and Emergency Deficit Control Act of 1985 Federal legislation that attempted to reduce federal budget deficits by imposing spending limits.

grandfathering When rules are changed, allowing actions taken before a certain date to remain subject to the old rules. For example, Congress may change the law by stipulating that certain types of municipal bonds no longer pay tax-free interest, while at the same time grandfathering the municipal bonds issued before the date on which the new law is to take effect.

grant 1. Monetary assistance, generally for a specific purpose. For example, a student may receive a government or other grant for attending a college or university. **2.** In law, a transfer of property.

grantee The recipient of a grant.

grantor 1. An investor who sells short a call option or a put option. The grantor of a call option agrees to sell stock at a fixed price, and the grantor of a put option agrees to buy stock at a fixed price. **2.** A person who establishes a trust. —Also called *settlor*. **3.** A person who grants or transfers something.

grantor trust A trust in which the person who establishes the trust—the grantor—retains an interest and control, and because of this, is required to pay taxes on trust income.

grapevine The path along which informal communications spread.

graph —See CHART.

gratis Given without anything expected in return.

gratuity Extra money or other compensation given in exchange for good service. —Also called *tip*.

graveyard market A declining market with low prices that discourage investors from selling and with little interest among investors for buying.

graveyard shift Late-night and early-morning work schedule.

gray market The sale of products by merchants who have not received authorization to sell them from the products' manufacturers. For example, a company may import and sell vehicles without the authorization of the vehicle manufacturer. The buyer of a gray-market product may have difficulty getting the manufacturer to honor the product warranty.

Great Crash The major declines in economic activity and stock prices that occurred in 1929 and the early 1930s.

greater fool theory The theory that no matter what price a person pays for something, someone else with less sense will be willing to buy it later. The greater fool theory reaches its height of popularity near the end stage of a speculative bubble. —Also called *bigger fool theory*.

greenback U.S. paper currency.

green card A federally issued immigrant registration card indicating the cardholder has been granted permanent residence status.

green investing Choosing to invest in companies that have a positive environmental record. Green investing is a special category of social investing.

> **CASE STUDY** Green Century Capital Management, the administrator of Green Century Funds, was founded in 1991 by several nonprofit environmental advocacy organizations. All of the fees received for managing the funds are used to fund environmental and public interest advocacy work. Green Century Funds include a balanced fund with stocks and bonds of environmentally responsible corporations. The firm's equity fund attempts to achieve a long-term total return that matches the performance of the Domini 400 Social Index, which excludes the stocks of companies that manufacture tobacco products or engage in the production of nuclear energy or weapons. It also excludes companies that derive more than 2% of their revenue from military weapons, or companies that produce firearms or alcohol, or earn revenue from gambling facilities. The five largest holdings of the equity fund as of the end of 2007 were Microsoft, AT&T, Johnson & Johnson, Apple, and Cisco Systems. According to the firm's brochure, the Green Century Equity Fund had underperformed the S&P 500 Index during the ten-year period ending in 2007 by approximately 1.8% annually.

greenmail A defensive maneuver aimed at thwarting a potential takeover in which the target firm purchases shares of its own stock from a raider at a price above that available to other stockholders, who are ordinarily excluded from the transaction. —Compare ANTIGREENMAIL PROVISION. —Also called *negotiated share repurchase.* —See also FAIR PRICE AMENDMENT.

Gresham's Law The economic theory of Thomas Gresham that bad money drives out good money. In other words, if good money (for example, gold coins) and bad money (paper money) are both used as a medium of exchange, consumers will hoard the gold coins and spend the paper money so that only paper money circulates. The paper money drives gold coins out of circulation.

grievance A disagreement that is considered grounds for a formal complaint. The term is generally used in relation to workplace relationships, conditions, or practices.

gross 1. A quantity of 12 dozen (144). **2.** The largest measure of a variable, prior to any reductions. For example, gross sales is total sales, prior to reductions for discounts and expected returns.

gross domestic product (GDP) The dollar output of final goods and services in the economy during a given period (usually one year). GDP is one measure of the economic vitality of a country and provides some indication of the health of near-term corporate income. —See also ECONOMIC ACTIVITY; NET DOMESTIC PRODUCT.

gross domestic product deflator —See GDP DEFLATOR.

gross earnings An individual's salary or wages prior to any reductions for benefits, income taxes, and Social Security.

gross estate The total dollar value of all the assets in an estate before paying debts and taxes.

gross income 1. For a business, its total revenues exclusive of any expenses. **2.** For an individual, all income except as specifically exempted by the Internal Revenue Code. For example, an inheritance is specifically excluded from gross income.

gross leasable area The floor space available for lease or rent, expressed in square feet, in a retail center such as a shopping mall.

gross lease A lease in which the costs of maintaining the leased asset, including its insurance and taxes, are paid by the lessor. —Compare NET LEASE.

gross margin —See GROSS PROFIT MARGIN.

gross profit Total revenue of a business minus the cost of goods it sold. Gross profit does not include income from incidental sources and also excludes selling and administrative expenses. —Compare NET INCOME.

gross profit margin A measure calculated by dividing gross profit by net sales. Gross profit margin is an indication of a firm's ability to turn a dollar of sales into profit after the cost of goods sold has been accounted for. —Compare NET PROFIT MARGIN. —Also called *gross margin; margin of profit.* —See also RETURN ON SALES.

gross profit method A method of estimating ending inventory. Purchases are added to ending inventory in order to calculate goods available for sale. The estimated gross profit margin is multiplied by sales and the result subtracted from net sales to estimate cost of goods sold. Cost of goods sold is subtracted from cost of goods available for sale to determine the cost of ending inventory. The gross profit method is suitable for interim reports, but not for annual financial statements.

gross profit ratio A method of calculating gains to be reported for tax purposes when real estate is disposed of through an installment sale. The ratio is equal to gross profit (selling price less adjusted basis) divided by the contract price (selling price less any assumed debt). The ratio is multiplied by periodic lease payments to determine the amount of taxable gain that must be reported.

gross rent multiplier The sale price of a rental property divided by gross monthly rental income assuming all available rental units are occupied. Gross rent multiplier is used to estimate the value of rental properties when financial information is available for sales of similar properties in the same market. —Also called *multiplier.*

gross sales Total sales for a period before discounts, returns, and freight expenses have been deducted. —Compare NET SALES.

gross weight 1. The weight of a package or container including packaging. **2.** The weight of a vehicle including occupants and cargo.

gross working capital —See CURRENT ASSET.

ground lease A lease applied only to land. Any improvements by the lessee revert to the owner at the end of the lease. —Also called *land lease.*

ground rent Rent paid for the use of land, but not for any improvements on the land.

group disability insurance Insurance coverage for an organization's employees or members who are unable to work and earn a paycheck because of injury or illness. Benefits are generally a function of earnings prior to the disability or illness and are limited to payments for a maximum number of months.

group dynamics The interaction of individuals within a relatively small group.

group health insurance Insurance coverage for an organization's employees or members who through injury or illness incur hospital, doctor, and other medical expenses. Most group health insurance includes deductibles and copays and is likely to require additional employee premiums to cover dependents.

group interview 1. An interview in which an employer holds a discussion with several candidates at one time. **2.** A meeting in which several people interview a potential employee.

group life insurance Life insurance coverage for an organization's employees or members. Group life insurance is generally term insurance with no cash buildup.

group of funds —See FAMILY OF FUNDS.

Group of Ten The 11 industrial countries (the name remained unchanged when Switzerland became the 11th member) that consult and coordinate economic and financial policy. Members include Belgium, Canada, France, Germany, Italy, Japan, the Netherlands, Sweden, Switzerland, the United Kingdom, and the United States.

group rotation —See SECTOR ROTATION.

groupthink Faulty decision making caused by group members' desire for conformity and a failure to adequately consider alternatives. Some studies indicate groups with initial dissent are more likely to make a correct decision. Groupthink is less likely when dissent is encouraged and members have diverse viewpoints.

growing-equity mortgage A mortgage loan with a fixed interest rate and payments that are scheduled to periodically increase in order to retire the principal more rapidly.

growth and income fund An investment company that invests in the common stock of growing companies that have a history of paying dividends. This type of fund is a compromise between a growth fund that concentrates on capital gains and an income fund that concentrates on maximizing current income.

growth fund An investment company whose major objective is long-term capital growth. Growth funds offer substantial potential gains over time, but vary significantly in price during bull and bear markets. This type of fund is most appropriate for someone who will not need to withdraw funds in the near future.

growth rate The annual rate at which a variable, such as gross domestic product or a firm's earnings, has been or is expected to grow. One common method of estimating future growth rate is simply to measure a variable's past growth rate and then project a continuation of the trend.

growth recession An economy in which the output of goods and services slowly expands but unemployment remains high or grows.

growth stock The stock of a firm that is expected to have above-average increases in revenues and earnings. These firms usually retain most earnings for reinvestment and therefore pay small dividends. The stock, often selling at relatively high price-earnings ratios, is subject to wide swings in price. Examples include Google, Amazon, and Apple.

GTC —See GOOD-TILL-CANCELED ORDER.

g-type reorganization A court-approved reorganization in which assets are sold and the debtor in bankruptcy is liquidated.

guaranteed bond A bond that is issued by one firm and guaranteed as to interest and principal by one or more other firms. Such bonds, often resulting from joint ventures, are particularly common among railroads that lease tracks to and from each another.

guaranteed-dollar annuity —See FIXED ANNUITY.

guaranteed insurability A life insurance policy option that permits the insured to purchase additional coverage at predetermined times without proof of insurability.

guaranteed investment contract (GIC) An investment product sold by life insurance companies that guarantees a return for a specific length of time on a large, lump-sum premium. Most GICs are funded by transfers from some other pension plan. The return of principal is dependent on the insurance company's ability to satisfy its obligation.

guaranteed mortgage A mortgage with payments guaranteed by a third party. For example, the Veterans Administration guarantees VA loans.

guaranteed mortgage certificate A pass through issued by Freddie Mac in which conventional mortgages purchased by Freddie Mac are resold to investors in $100,000, $500,000, and $1,000,000 principal amounts. Interest is paid semiannually and principal repayments are made annually. —See also PASS-THROUGH SECURITY.

guaranteed payments to partners Priority distributions by a partnership to a partner for services or for the use of capital. The payments are made regardless of whether the partnership is profitable.

guaranteed stock Preferred stock that is issued by one company and guaranteed as to dividends by one or more other companies. Guaranteed stock issues, like guaranteed bonds, are most prevalent among railroads.

guarantee of signature A certificate that verifies the authenticity of the signature of the registered owner of a bond or stock. The guarantee of signature is attached to the assignment of a bond or stock certificate.

guarantor A person or entity that endorses or guarantees something. For example, a person or company may become a guarantor of a debt and be required to fulfill its terms in the event the primary debtor defaults.

guaranty A promise to assume someone else's debt or other obligation in the event they fail to keep their promise.

guardian 1. A person or entity expected to protect someone or something **2.** A court-appointed adult who is legally responsible for protecting the interests of a minor or an incompetent adult.

guerilla marketing Unconventional promotions that attempt to gain maximum exposure with a limited budget.

> **CASE STUDY** Guerilla marketing is often untried and edgy, which means it may prove unsuccessful, or even worse, backfire. Chaos resulted in early 2007 after a Boston advertising firm hired two men to distribute 40 blinking boxes on bridges and other public places in the city to promote a late-night program on Turner Broadcasting System's Cartoon Network. City officials called out the explosive unit after a suspicious commuter found one of the packages in an overhang at a subway station. The city closed highways and subways while law enforcement officials searched for additional devices. It turned out that similar boxes had been planted in other major cities, including Atlanta, Philadelphia, and San Francisco. Both TBS and the advertising agency drew harsh criticism from city officials, marketing educators, and marketing professionals.

guild An association of individuals with similar interests or employment. For example, the Writers Guild of America, West represents thousands of writers of television shows, movies, and news programs in their contracts with film and television producers.

gun jumping 1. Trading in a security before inside information has been released to the public. **2.** Solicitation of orders for a new security underwriting before the SEC has approved the registration statement.

H

habendum The section of a deed that describes the ownership rights of the transferee.

half-life The length of time before half the principal on a debt is expected to be repaid through amortization or sinking fund payments. For example, a 25-year bond issue may require the issuer to retire 5% of the beginning principal commencing 5 years after the issue date. Thus, the bond issue has a half-life of 5 years plus the number of years required to retire half the issue, or 15 years. Mortgage-backed securities often have a relatively short half-life because many homeowners pay off or refinance their mortgages early. —Also called *average life*.

handyman special

I've read that a person can make a lot of money buying handyman specials and fixing them up to sell at a big profit. Is it really this easy?

Buying low, renovating, and selling higher can be done, but I don't think it's a very easy way to make money. You must first have the cash or qualify for a mortgage to buy the house. You must also have some way to pay for the renovations before you get any money from a buyer. Finally, even if the house looks great, it may not sell now, or for several months, or ever. Buyers of "handyman specials" should have a "plan B" to carry the renovated house until it is sold. Otherwise, the "easy" profit, and more, could be eaten up by the carrying costs until resale.

■ Joan A. Koffman, Esq., Real Estate Attorney, Koffman & Dreyer, Newton, MA

half-year convention The assumption for tax purposes that a newly acquired asset is placed in service halfway through the year regardless of when the asset is actually acquired and placed in service. The half-year convention affects annual depreciation, taxation, and earnings calculations.

halo effect The phenomenon whereby an overall positive impression, or "glow," is gained from limited exposure. The halo effect can make it difficult for observers to be entirely objective. For example, a major increase in a company's stock price may create a halo effect over the firm's management, even if the stock price increase was mostly caused by external factors such as falling interest rates or an expanding economy.

hammering the market The heavy selling of securities, which drives down prices. Unexpected bad news, such as disclosure of corporate fraud, a terrorist attack, or the outbreak of armed hostilities, can cause a hammering of the market.

handling allowance A rebate or discounted price by a manufacturer to compensate a distributor or retailer for handling a product. For example, a government agency may offer an automobile dealership a handling allowance of $150 per vehicle for delivery and fuel.

handyman special In real estate, a property that requires substantial repairs in order to bring it up to standard.

Hang Seng Index A market-weighted index of 33 stocks making up approximately 70% of the market value of all stocks traded on the Stock Exchange of Hong Kong. HSI Services Limited, a subsidiary of Hang Seng Bank, calculates the index.

hard asset —See TANGIBLE ASSET.

hard cash Currency and coins as opposed to checks, credit cards, and debit cards.

hard-core unemployed Individuals who do not have full-time jobs because they lack the skills, knowledge, or work ethic necessary for employment.

hard currency A currency that enjoys investor confidence. A hard currency is typically issued by a country that has a strong economy, an acceptable rate of inflation, and a responsible fiscal policy. The euro and the dollar are examples of hard currencies. —Compare SOFT CURRENCY. —Also called *hard money.*

hard dollars Cash payment to a brokerage firm for goods or services provided by the firm. Thus, individual investors are usually required to pay cash for a market letter. —Compare SOFT DOLLARS.

hard goods Durable items including appliances, dinnerware, and tools. The term is often used to describe an area of a department store where these good are sold. —Compare SOFT GOODS.

hard money —See HARD CURRENCY.

hard-money loan A risky loan, usually short-term, that entails a very high rate of interest. Hard-money loans are generally secured by real estate and made to borrowers with poor credit records. For example, a person with a poor credit record obtains a hard-money loan for real estate development after being turned down by several financial institutions.

hardship distribution Withdrawal of pretax contributions to a 401(k) savings plan because of an immediate and severe financial need of the employee. Paying medical bills is sufficient for a hardship distribution. Hardship distributions are limited and the IRS requires documentation.

harvest strategy Extracting, or harvesting, cash from a business by limiting the amount of new money that is committed. For example, a cereal manufacturer may limit advertising for a particular brand that appears to offer little opportunity for sales growth. Rather, the firm harvests cash from the brand, termed a "cash cow," in order to have funds available for more promising brands.

> **CASE STUDY** Companies typically choose a harvest strategy for mature products that remain profitable but offer little potential for growth. Rather than pour additional funds into research and marketing, the firms choose to continue selling these products and harvest the cash they generate for supplementing the budgets of more promising products. A harvest strategy was chosen by Kodak for what had historically been its most profitable product, film. As businesses and consumers moved from film to digital photography, Kodak's major products faced a bleak future with deteriorating revenues. To meet this challenge, Kodak management chose to make a major push into digital photography. The firm announced that it would no longer sell film-based cameras in the United States, Western Europe, and Canada. Later the company said it would stop promoting film, although this former flagship product would continue to be sold. Reflecting Kodak's new direction, research and development spending by the firm's Film & Photofinishing Systems Group declined from $155 million in 2004 to $40 million in 2006. During the same period, R&D spending by the Consumer Digital Imaging Group increased from $164 million to $171 million.

hash total Adding numbers associated with a set of records to validate the integrity of the data. A summation is compared to a prior total to determine if any data has been lost or erroneously entered.

hatchet man An individual who agrees to carry out unpleasant assignments. For example, a person in the personnel department may be assigned to inform employees they are being terminated.

Hawthorne Effect The theory that employees will perform at a higher level when they are consulted and are aware of being observed by their supervisors.

hazard —See PERIL.

hazard insurance Insurance coverage for financial losses from real and personal property damage caused by storms, fire, and vandalism.

headhunter An individual or company that locates and recruits managers for businesses and government clients.

head of household A federal tax filing category for an unmarried taxpayer who paid more than half the cost of maintaining a household that includes at least one dependent. A dependent parent does not have to live in the same household as the taxpayer. Filing as head of household results in a reduced tax liability compared to filing as a single individual.

health care power of attorney —See POWER OF ATTORNEY FOR HEALTH CARE.

health maintenance organization (HMO) A health care system that provides comprehensive medical services to a voluntarily enrolled group, generally in a particular geographic region, for a fixed prepaid fee.

Health Reimbursement Arrangement (HRA) An employer-sponsored and -funded health insurance plan that reimburses employees for qualified medical expenses, including health insurance premiums. These arrangements are preferred by many employers, who can limit their own cost of health care by establishing a limit on the contributions they will make for employees, who are forced to seek individual health insurance. Funds contributed to an HRA are the property of the employer, and unused contributions cannot be moved when an employee moves to a new employer.

Health Savings Account (HSA) An account for accumulating funds that can be utilized to pay nonreimbursed medical expenses (excluding health insurance premiums) for an individual who works for a small business and is covered by a high-deductible medical plan. The account is funded with tax-deductible contributions by the individual and/or the employer. Amounts contributed to an HSA grow tax-free through investment income, are the property of the account holder, and are portable. HSAs were created in 2003 as an incentive for individuals to save for qualified medical and retiree health expenses on a tax-advantaged basis. Funds withdrawn from the account are not taxable if used for qualified medical expenses. Unused funds may be rolled forward without penalty.

hearing 1. In law, a legal proceeding in which evidence is presented before a judge in order to determine an issue of fact. A hearing typically occurs when there exists a dispute about a legal issue prior to a trial. **2.** A meeting of a legislative or administrative body in order to gather information about some topic. **3.** Reconsideration of a claim for Social Security disability benefits after the initial claim has been rejected a second time. The request for a hearing results in the case being sent to an administrative law judge.

hearsay 1. Secondhand information. **2.** In law, testimony of a witness who testifies about something someone else said or saw.

heavy industry An industry that requires substantial investment in fixed assets. Examples include automobile manufacturing, coal mining, and steel manufacturing. —Compare LIGHT INDUSTRY.

heavy market A declining market.

hedge A transaction that reduces the risk on an already existing investment position. An example is the purchase of a put option in order to offset at least partially the potential losses from owned stock. Another example is the purchase of tangible assets such as diamonds or gold as a hedge against the possibility of inflation. —See also PERFECT HEDGE; RISK HEDGE; SHORT HEDGE.

hedge clause A statement in an advertisement, a market letter, or a security report indicating that the information therein is believed to be accurate and that it has been obtained from usually reliable sources, with nothing, however, guaranteed. Essentially, a hedge clause indicates to readers that the writer believes the information is accurate and that reasonable care has been taken to ensure its accuracy.

hedge fund A very specialized, volatile, open-end investment company that permits the manager to use a variety of investment techniques usually prohibited in other types of funds. These techniques include borrowing money, selling short, and using options. Hedge funds offer investors the possibility of extraordinary gains with above-average risk.

heir A person who by will or statutory law receives or is scheduled to receive a portion or all of the assets of an estate. —See also PRETERMITTED HEIR.

hemline theory The theory that holds that stock prices tend to move in the same direction as the length of hemlines on dresses. Thus, rising hemlines are a bullish sign and falling hemlines are a bearish sign.

hidden agenda An undisclosed strategy. For example, a politician may oppose a rezoning request by claiming it will result in urban sprawl, when the real reason (the hidden agenda) is that a successful rezoning will result in new businesses that compete with the businesses owned by the politician's friends and campaign contributors.

hidden assets Items of value that are owned by a firm but do not appear on its balance sheet. For example, a trademark or patent may be a firm's most valuable owned asset, yet it would not appear as such on its balance sheet.

hidden inflation Decreases in quantity and/or quality without an accompanying decline in price. The decreasing size of candy bars without a decline in price is an example of hidden inflation.

hidden load A mutual fund sales fee that is not readily apparent to investors. The term generally applies to an annual 12b-1 fee that is charged by many mutual funds.

hidden persuader A promotional message that is not readily apparent as an advertisement. Product placement in a movie or television show is an example.

hidden tax A tax that is difficult for taxpayers to detect. For example, the price paid by consumers for alcoholic beverages includes a substantial hidden tax. A hidden tax often creates little public criticism because many taxpayers do not realize the extent to which they are being taxed. —Also called *stealth tax.*

hierarchy The structure of an organization based on the chain of authority from top to bottom.

high credit The total amount of credit allowed by a lender for a single borrower or customer.

highest and best use Appraisal of real estate at its highest present value based on the probable and legal use that produces the greatest net return. For example, an older home on property that is zoned commercial would be appraised as commercial property, not residential property, assuming the commercial valuation is higher.

high flyer A heavily traded stock that sells at a high price-earnings ratio. High flyers go through a period of rapidly rising prices when something about the firms or the industries in which they operate catches the investing public's fancy.

high-grade Of, relating to, or being a bond with little risk of default on the part of the issuer. High-grade is usually reserved for bonds rated AAA or AA by the rating services. —Compare INVESTMENT-GRADE.

historic district

I was told that purchasing a home located in a historic district may be accompanied by tax benefits. Is this true? Are there any disadvantages to owning property in a historic district?

Properties in historic districts may have advantages and disadvantages that result from such designation. If the property is within a *national* historic district (as designated by the National Historic Preservation Act), certain federal tax credits are available for building renovations. These credits can be a significant offset to the substantial costs involved in renovating old buildings. (A tax credit is a direct reduction against tax liabilities, as compared to the less-impactful tax deduction, which is only a reduction in taxable income. Before making any purchase decisions, a buyer should always consult with a tax expert in this field.) Another advantage is market-based: If enough momentum has been created by enough historic renovation projects in a certain market, profit opportunities can be created and exploited by the knowledgeable and savvy developer-investor who is willing to take an above-average risk and earn a commensurate return.

The primary disadvantages are: (1) Ownership of such a property implies contending with an additional and significant layer of governmental and bureaucratic regulations that restrict the property's use and renovation. Attendant costs can be offset by the federal tax credits referenced above. However, many cities have their own local historic districts that severely restrict the renovation or demolition of properties within. And if the properties are not in a national historic district, they are not eligible for federal tax credits. Some states might have their own tax-credit historic renovation programs, but they offer less relief than a federal tax credit. (2) Construction costs for the renovation of an old building can be higher than the costs of a new building. This is due mostly to a relative lack of supply of craftsmen skilled in such work, and to the time involved in complying with what can often be a myriad of conflicting and arbitrary set of rules and regulations imposed by the federal, state, and local historic jurisdictions and their enforcement personnel.

■ Scott Alderman, Broker and President, First Commercial Real Estate, Valdosta, GA

highly confident letter An investment bank's statement that it can raise the necessary capital to complete a deal based on current market conditions and its analysis of the deal. Highly confident letters are useful for companies that want to convince the investment community they can raise the necessary capital to finance an acquisition.

highly leveraged Of or referring to an investment, business, or other entity that is financed with a large amount of debt and little equity. Highly leveraged investments and businesses tend to be risky and produce either high returns or large losses.

high rise A building with many stories and an elevator. Buildings qualify as high rises relative to their locations. For example, a high rise in Lincoln, Nebraska, is unlikely to qualify as a high rise in New York City.

high-technology stock The stock of a company that is involved in sophisticated technology, such as electronics, computer software, robotics, or life sciences companies. A high-technology stock often offers large potential gains, but tends to be quite risky because of intense competition and uncertain success.

high-yield bond —See JUNK BOND.

high-yield financing —See JUNK FINANCING.

histogram A graph with vertical rectangles representing frequency data. For example, a histogram might display the population of a city each year for the last decade. Ten vertical blocks, each indicating population for a given year, would be side by side along the horizontal axis.

historical cost The amount of money that was originally used to pay for an asset. A company records assets on a balance sheet at historical cost, which often bears little relation to the market value of the assets after they have been owned several years. —Also called *original cost.*

historical yield The yield that a mutual fund has provided during a specified period. Investors frequently compare historical yields when selecting a fund to purchase.

historic district A designated area in which buildings and improvements enjoy a historical significance that may not be reflected in their market values. Historic-district designation may result in federal benefits and in restrictions on building modifications and treatments.

historic preservation easement A legal agreement that protects a significant historic, archaeological, or cultural resource by providing assurance the property's intrinsic value will be preserved through subsequent ownership. Tax benefits are available for owners of properties that qualify for preservation easements.

> **CASE STUDY** A charitable tax deduction for a historic preservation easement is justified by an assumed reduction in a property's market value following the donation. The deduction can also include related appraisal and attorney's fees incurred by the owner. For example, a historic home located in an area zoned for commercial development may lose substantial market value when the owner agrees to a historic preservation easement that includes a prohibition against using the property as an office building. Abuses, including exaggerated estimates of declining property values resulting from donations of historic easements, resulted in federal reform legislation in 2006. Among other provisions, the legislation disallowed deductions for easements that permit changes incompatible with a building's historic character. In addition, the legislation required that the owner provide the Internal Revenue Service with detailed substantiation justifying the value of the easement donation. It also imposed tougher qualification standards for appraisals and appraisers, and reduced thresholds for overvaluation penalties.

hit[1] A successful product, service, or business. For example, a new sugary cereal may be a hit with children.

hit[2] **1.** To sell a security at a bid price quoted by a dealer. For example, a trader will hit a bid. **2.** To suffer a loss of money on a trade. For example, a dealer may take a hit on the holdings of Moore's Fried Foods' common stock. **3.** To access a webpage.

hit the bricks To go on strike.

HMO —See HEALTH MAINTENANCE ORGANIZATION.

hoard[1] A secret store of something valuable, such as cash.

hoard[2] To accumulate a large quantity of something for potential future use. For example, a business may hoard cash if its CEO is concerned about the possibility of a strike.

hobby An activity pursued without the expectation of making a profit. Losses experienced from a hobby are generally deductible only to the extent they can be used as an offset to hobby income. In other words, hobby losses cannot be deducted from other income. The IRS assumes an activity is profit driven only if it results in a taxable profit in three of the last five years.

holdback **1.** In real estate, a portion of the purchase price or loan proceeds withheld until a specified event takes place. For example, a commercial lender might withhold part of a loan on an office building because a major tenant is continuing to work on improvements. The remainder of the loan will be released when the improvements are completed and the tenant has moved in. **2.** A manufacturer's financial incentive for dealers of new vehicles. The holdback is designed to compensate for a dealer's interest expense on loans used to keep new vehicles on the lot and available for sale.

holder in due course The holder of a negotiable instrument such as a check or note that has been received in good faith for providing something of value. For example, a company that purchases loans from the original lender becomes the holder in due course. Likewise, a person or business becomes the holder in due course when they accept an endorsed check. —See also PAYMENT IN DUE COURSE.

holder of record A security holder listed in a firm's books as having ownership of the security on the record date. This list is used in determining who will receive dividends, interest, proxies, financial reports, and so on. —Also called *owner of record; shareholder of record; stockholder of record.* —See also RECORD DATE.

hold harmless agreement An arrangement between parties in which one party assumes the liability and agrees to hold the other party blameless. For example, an aircraft owner may agree to hold a maintenance company blameless for any problems that may develop from service on the aircraft.

holding Assets owned by an investor or business. For example, an investor may have a holding of 4,000 shares of General Electric common stock.

holding company A type of parent company that exists primarily to exercise control over other firms. The control is exercised through ownership of a majority of the controlled firm's shares. Earnings of the holding company are derived from earnings of the controlled firms, which pay dividends on the shares. —Compare SUBSIDIARY. —See also OPERATING UNIT.

holding period The length of time during which an investment is owned.

holding period return (HPR) The return achieved from an investment, including current income and any change in value during an investor's holding period. This measure proves useful in comparing expected returns from different investments. —Also called *holding period yield.*

holdover tenant A tenant who continues to occupy leased property after the expiration of a lease.

holiday effect The unusually good performance by stocks on the day prior to market-closing holidays.

home equity conversion Conversion of the equity in a home (market value of the home less any remaining balance on an outstanding loan) into a cash payment or a stream of income. The loan representing the conversion is generally not repayable until the homeowner dies or moves out of the home.

home equity loan A loan or open-end line of credit secured by a second mortgage on the borrower's home.

home office **1.** A company's headquarters or the location of the headquarters. **2.** An area of a home that is utilized as a business office. For example, a writer might convert a bedroom into a home office that includes a desk, computer, file cabinets, and so forth.

homeowners' association An organization of property owners that oversees the common interests of a neighborhood, planned development, or condominium. A homeowners' association generally collects dues, takes care of certain maintenance, and enforces any covenants or property restrictions. —Also called *community association.*

homeowner's insurance Wide-ranging insurance coverage for financial losses suffered from damage to a residence or personal property from common disasters including fire, wind, lightning, and vandalism. A homeowner's policy also includes personal liability insurance, although many individuals decide to purchase additional liability coverage. —See also INFLATION ENDORSEMENT.

homeowner warranty program (HOW) A program offered by some homebuilders that provides buyers of new homes with a guarantee on materials, workmanship, and structural integrity.

home run A product or investment that produces a large return within a short period. For example, an investor might purchase shares in an initial public offering that moves sharply upward in subsequent trading in the secondary market.

homeshoring Transferring to employees' homes work that is typically done in an office or factory. For example, a hotel chain might decide to reduce office expenses by homeshoring its reservation agents.

homesourcing Paying people to work from their residences rather than from a facility provided by the employer. For example, a software company offers customer technical support via employees who work in their homes. Homesourcing can allow a business to save on overhead at the same time it offers a convenient workplace for labor. —See also OUTSOURCING.

homestead **1.** A dwelling plus adjoining land and buildings. State laws often protect a homestead from creditor claims. **2.** Land granted to settlers by the government.

homestead exemption The amount of a home's assessed valuation that is protected from property taxes. —Also called *exemption.*

homogeneous oligopoly An industry in which production of an identical product is concentrated in a few firms. Price differences among the firms are typically quite small. Examples are pencils and sheet metal. —Compare DIFFERENTIATED OLIGOPOLY.

honor To accept for payment. For example, a business may honor most national credit cards.

honorarium A one-time payment to a nonemployee as a show of appreciation for a special service. For example, a well-known professional receives an honorarium for a speech.

Hope Scholarship Tax Credit A federal tax credit available for qualified tuition and related expenses of students in their first or second year of postsecondary education. The credit is available for each qualifying dependent. —Also called *tuition tax credit.*

horizon —See TIME HORIZON.

horizontal analysis A comparison of financial statements or specific items in a financial statement that covers two or more periods. —Compare VERTICAL ANALYSIS.

horizontal equity The principle that individuals in the same income group should be taxed equally. The concept of equals receiving equal treatment is also a principle of property taxation. —Compare VERTICAL EQUITY.

horizontal expansion

Is horizontal expansion bad for consumers? It seems to me that fewer firms in an industry mean less competition and higher prices.

Horizontal expansion tends to cut costs because the new products can be sold through the same distribution pipe or channels the company already has. GE is a master of this. While famous for a few major acquisitions, they actually do best when "filling in gaps," such as with line extensions or horizontal expansion. Colgate-Palmolive did this in the health and beauty aids business when they bought Tom's of Maine. What is the impact on pricing? Lower costs mean lower sales prices. Tom's toothpaste is now available on promotions at 25% to 35% less than when owned by Tom's, though the company is still run by the original Tom's people.

■ Deaver Brown, Publisher, Simplysoftwarecd.com, Lincoln, MA

horizontal expansion Corporate growth through the development or acquisition of business in the same line of products or services. For example, a cola company expands its product line by acquiring another soft-drink manufacturer.

horizontal marketing Promoting a product or service to potential customers that share common characteristics that are spread among a wide range of industries. For example, a software company targets human resource departments at companies with fewer than 500 employees. —Compare VERTICAL MARKETING.

horizontal merger A merger between firms that provide similar products or services. Merging one steel manufacturer into another steel manufacturer is an example of a horizontal merger. Horizontal mergers permit the surviving firm to control a greater share of the market and, it is hoped, gain economies of scale. —Compare VERTICAL MERGER.

horizontal specialization Managerial organization such that a group of managers at the same level of authority are given specialized tasks based on their skill and knowledge. For example, a firm's marketing department may be specialized by product. —Compare VERTICAL SPECIALIZATION 1.

horizontal spread —See CALENDAR SPREAD.

horizontal union —See CRAFT UNION.

hospitalization insurance Insurance reimbursement for all or a portion of expenses incurred during a hospital stay because of injury or illness.

hostile fire In property insurance, a fire that becomes uncontrollable or breaks out from where it was intended to burn. Property damage must generally result from hostile fire in order for coverage to be provided under a homeowner's insurance policy. —Compare FRIENDLY FIRE.

hostile leveraged buyout The purchase of a firm, against the wishes of the acquired firm's managers, in which a small group of investors finances the purchase primarily by borrowing. Although leveraged buyouts have become quite common, hostile leveraged buyouts are unusual because lenders financing takeovers generally prefer that the acquired firms' managements remain, albeit under new ownership.

hostile takeover —See UNFRIENDLY TAKEOVER.

hostile tender offer An offer to purchase shares from a firm's stockholders when directors of the target firm have recommended that stockholders not sell their stock. Hostile tender offers sometimes cause the directors of the target company to seek a better offer from another party. —Compare TENDER OFFER. —See also UNFRIENDLY TAKEOVER.

hot cargo Merchandise shipped from a plant subject to a labor dispute or by an employer that has been placed on a union boycott list.

hot issue A new security issue for which investor demand exceeds securities available in the issue. National Association of Securities Dealers rules forbid members from taking advantage of the likelihood that these securities will rise in price immediately after issue.

hot money Funds that are controlled by investors who seek high short-term yields when the funds are likely to be reinvested somewhere else at any time. Some financial institutions attract hot money by offering above-average yields on certificates of deposit. However, if the rate is lowered, the funds are likely to be lost to another institution or investment.

> **CASE STUDY** Although an improbable target for currency speculators, tiny Iceland (population approximately 300,000) gained fame as a world depository for hot money shortly after the country lifted currency exchange controls in the late 1990s. Funds seeking the krona's high interest rates flooded into the island country from around the world, much of it representing borrowed money obtained in low-interest Japan. The inflows helped produce a booming economy with a strong currency, soaring stock market, and skyrocketing housing prices. The economic boom was accompanied by inflation, causing the central bank to raise interest rates to 11.5% by mid-2006. The increase in interest rates also resulted from the government's concern that hot money would begin flowing back out of Iceland as interest rates started rising in Europe, Japan, and the United States. A rapid outflow of hot money would depress the country's currency, increase the cost of imported goods, and cause a downward spiral in asset values.

hot stock A stock that has large price movements on very heavy volume. Hot stocks often run in cycles dependent on the investing public's interest in particular industries or particular concepts. Hot stocks are usually quite risky and are suitable for speculators involved in short-term trading.

house 1. An organization that acts as a broker-dealer or an underwriter. 2. A freestanding residence. 3. Certain commercial establishments, including casinos and theaters. For example, a gambler who wins the first several hands of blackjack is playing with the house's money.

house account A brokerage account considered sufficiently important that it is handled by one of the firm's executives or at the firm's main office.

household worker A person hired to perform household tasks such as gardening, cleaning, cooking, or babysitting. Persons employing a household worker 18 years of age and older may be responsible for reporting wages and paying Social Security taxes.

house maintenance requirement The minimum equity that must be kept in a customer's margin account as determined by the firm holding the account. A house maintenance requirement is imposed when a brokerage firm desires a more strict maintenance margin requirement than the one required by an exchange or by the National Association of Securities Dealers.

house of issue —See LEAD UNDERWRITER.

house organ An in-house publication targeted at employees and customers. A house organ is designed to build loyalty and promote an organization and its products or services by communicating with interested individuals and groups.

housing affordability index A measure of the percentage of homes sold in a metropolitan area that a median-income family living in that area can afford. The index is used as an indication of the degree to which homes are reasonably priced, with a higher index indicating greater affordability.

Housing and Urban Development Department (HUD) The cabinet-level U.S. agency created in 1965 with a mission to increase home ownership, support community development, and increase access to affordable housing free from discrimination.

housing code Local, state, or federal government minimum standards for sanitation and safety of residential buildings.

housing starts The number of single- or multiple-family dwellings on which construction has commenced during a stated period. Data on housing starts is released monthly by the U.S. Department of Commerce.

HOW —See HOMEOWNER WARRANTY PROGRAM.

HPR —See HOLDING PERIOD RETURN.

HRA —See HEALTH REIMBURSEMENT ARRANGEMENT.

HSA —See HEALTH SAVINGS ACCOUNT.

HUD —See HOUSING AND URBAN DEVELOPMENT DEPARTMENT.

human capital The accumulated skills, knowledge, and expertise of a person or a workforce. Spending on education and training is considered an investment in human capital.

human relations The understanding and enhancement of how individuals work together to achieve success and fulfillment.

human resource accounting The identification, measurement, and reporting of employee contributions to an organization. The goal is to make an organization more efficient by identifying and evaluating the costs and benefits of human resources.

human resources **1.** The individuals and their associated skills and knowledge that are available to a business or other entity. —Also called *personnel.* **2.** In economics, labor that is used as a factor of production.

hurdle rate In long-term investment decisions, the minimum acceptable rate of return that is expected in order to commit funds. A potential investment should be rejected if the expected rate of return is below the hurdle rate. An appropriate hurdle rate is subjective and differs among firms and among investments with different risks within the same firm.

hush money Funds paid or offered to someone in return for their silence. For example, an employer may pay an employee not to report a safety violation.

hybrid annuity A single annuity in which a part of an investor's payments purchase units of a variable annuity and the remaining funds purchase units of a fixed annuity.

hybrid mortgage —See TWO-STEP MORTGAGE.

hybrid security A security that has features characteristic of two or more securities. A convertible bond, for example, is a hybrid security in that it has the features (that is, interest, maturity, and principal) of an ordinary bond but is heavily influenced by the price movements of the stock into which it is convertible.

hygiene factors Factors in the workplace that tend to cause dissatisfaction among employees. Important hygiene factors include relationships with other employees, salary, supervision, and company policies. Surprisingly, a different set of factors was found to result in employee satisfaction.

hype To use extensive publicity to promote something. For example, a household products company may hype a new toothpaste by spending large sums of money on print, radio, television, and Internet advertising.

hyperinflation A very high level of inflation that tends to result in the breakdown of the monetary system, the hoarding of goods, and difficulty in achieving real economic growth. The classic case of hyperinflation occurred in Germany during the 1920s. Hyperinflation, which tends to motivate people to own real goods, adversely affects security prices.

hypothecate To pledge securities as collateral for a loan without giving up ownership of the securities. —See also REHYPOTHECATE.

hypothecation agreement A written agreement between a customer opening a margin account and a brokerage firm that pledges stock in the account as collateral for margin loans. The brokerage firm is permitted to sell the stock in the event that equity in the account falls below a stipulated level.

hypothesis A provisional explanation for a set of facts or observations. For example, a firm's marketing department may have more than one hypothesis about why a new product met with failure in the marketplace. Each hypothesis may later be examined more thoroughly to test its validity.

hypothesis testing Collecting and evaluating sample data to prove or disprove the validity of one or more claims.

IASB —See INTERNATIONAL ACCOUNTING STANDARDS BOARD.

iceberg principle The theory that, as with an iceberg, only a small proportion of many things is clearly evident. For example, a person's personality is mainly hidden from view. Likewise, most problems are much deeper than they at first appear.

ICI —See INVESTMENT COMPANY INSTITUTE.

icon A highly regarded and well-known person who is closely associated with something. For example, Warren Buffett is an icon among investors.

identify shares To distinguish which shares among those that are owned are to be sold. An investor may buy shares of a company or mutual fund at many different prices over a period of years. If a portion of those shares is to be sold, the investor may identify shares so as to control the profits or losses that are realized. An investor who identifies shares having the highest cost basis often can minimize the taxes associated with such a sale.

identity theft The unauthorized use of an individual's personal identifying information such as a Social Security number or credit card number to create fraud. For example, someone may engage in identity theft by opening a credit card account using the name and personal information of another person. Someone who is a victim of

illegal dividend

How can a dividend be illegal? Can you cite an example?

Corporate law does not allow dividend payments that jeopardize the entity's ability to make its creditors whole. Illegal dividends often entail treasury stock transactions, whereby stock is repurchased by the issuing company, reducing the entity's legal capital and potentially exposing creditors to greater risk.

For example, assume that a firm had the following balance sheet: $100 of assets = $60 of liabilities + $40 of shareholders' equity. Its equity consisted of $15 of common stock and $25 of retained earnings. Further assume that the firm bought back most of its stock in a secondary market for $20. This transaction would reduce assets and shareholders' equity by $20, resulting in a revised balance sheet of $80 = $60 + $20. (The $20 of equity consists of $15 common stock + $25 retained earnings − $20 treasury stock). An illegal dividend would occur if the firm then paid a dividend equal to its $25 retained earnings. Such a transaction would reduce assets (cash) and shareholders' equity (in the form of retained earnings) by $25. The dividend, in other words, would bankrupt the firm. It would have only $55 of assets remaining to meet $60 of liabilities. The illegal dividend would result in a negative $5 of equity ($15 of issued common stock + 0 retained earnings − $20 of treasury stock). The illegal dividend yields an untenable balance sheet: $55 of assets = $60 of liabilities − $5 of equity.

■ Peter M. Bergevin, PhD, Professor of Accounting, School of Business, University of Redlands, Redlands, CA

---

identity theft should file an ID Theft Complaint with the Federal Trade Commission and an Identity Theft Report with the police.

idle capacity Floor space or production facilities that remain unused because of a lack of business or a lack of labor or resources. Domestic vehicle manufacturers have suffered substantial idle capacity of their production facilities because of a lack of demand for the vehicles they make.

idle funds Money, as the funds in a checking account, that is not invested and therefore earns no income. Investors and businesses wishing to increase their income try to keep idle funds to a minimum. —Also called *barren money.*

idle time Nonproductive time during which an employee is on the job but not working. For example, a problem with machinery is likely to create idle time for a number of employees. Idle time may also result from management scheduling more employees than are needed for the work available.

illegal alien A person who lives in a county without its official permission or citizenship.

illegal dividend A declared dividend that violates the corporate charter or the laws of the state in which the firm is incorporated.

illegal income Income from illegal activities such as operating as a bookie (taking bets) or selling moonshine. Despite being earned from an illegal activity, illegal income is taxable and must be reported.

illegal strike Employees refusing to work in violation of the law. U.S. President Ronald Reagan fired air traffic controllers in 1981 when they declared an illegal strike.

illiquid 1. Of or relating to an asset that is difficult to buy or sell within a short period without its price being affected. For example, collectibles, including stamps, coins, and art, are often difficult to sell quickly at a fair price. —Compare LIQUID 1. **2.** Of, relating to, or being an investment position in which a low proportion of assets is in cash or near-cash, thereby creating difficulty for the investor who is trying to raise funds for another purpose.

illusionary contract An agreement that is so vague it does not bind either party and cannot be enforced in court. For example, a customer tells the owner of an appliance store he may return and purchase the dishwasher later that day.

IMA —See INSTITUTE OF MANAGEMENT ACCOUNTANTS.

image advertising Promotion that attempts to influence public perception of a company, a brand, or a product. For example, a petroleum company may place advertisements touting all of the actions being undertaken by the firm to maintain a clean environment. These advertisements are designed to enhance the image of the company. —Also called *institutional advertising*.

imbalance of orders —See ORDER IMBALANCE.

IMF —See INTERNATIONAL MONETARY FUND.

immaterial Of so little importance or relevance as to have no significant impact on an outcome. For example, a firm may be engaged in a lawsuit involving such an insignificant amount of money that the lawsuit's outcome will not appreciably affect the firm. Thus, the lawsuit and its potential results are immaterial to the preparation of the firm's financial statements. —Compare MATERIAL[1].

immediate annuity An annuity that is purchased with a lump sum and that begins making payments one period after the purchase. Immediate annuities are most commonly purchased by people who have accumulated a sum of money and are ready for retirement. —Compare DEFERRED ANNUITY. —See also LONGEVITY INSURANCE.

immediate relative In immigration law, a spouse, parent, widow(er), or unmarried child under the age of 21 of a U.S. citizen. For parents of a U.S. citizen, the petitioning child must be at least 21 years old.

immunization A technique of investing in bonds such that the portfolio's target return is protected against interest rate fluctuations. Changes in returns at which cash flows can be reinvested are offset by changes in the value of the securities in the portfolio. —See also BULLET IMMUNIZATION.

impairment **1.** In accounting, the situation that exists when the carrying value of a long-term asset or asset group is larger than fair market value. **2.** Reduction in a firm's capital as a result of distributions or losses.

> **CASE STUDY** Ohio-based hamburger chain Wendy's International purchased fast-casual restaurant chain Baja Fresh Mexican Grill for $275 million in 2002. Shortly thereafter, Wendy's acquired two additional restaurant chains, Café Express and Pasta Pomodoro. Baja Fresh failed to meet Wendy's expectations and, despite several new CEOs, experienced a decrease in same-store sales of 4.6% in 2003, 6.3% in 2004 and 3.7% in 2005. At the same time, the new developing-brands division, of which Baja Fresh was the major component, suffered operating losses of over $60 million during 2004 and 2005. Wendy's bit the bullet in 2006, taking a $122.5 million pretax impairment charge (writing down goodwill that resulted from buying the Mexican-food chain for more than book value) related to Baja Fresh and selling the chain to private investors for $31 million, $244 million less than it had paid four years earlier. The prior year Wendy's had taken a $25 million impairment charge for its Tim Hortons doughnut chain, which it had spun off to its own shareholders.

imperfect market **1.** A market in which individual suppliers or consumers have an impact on supply or demand. For example, a market characterized by a monopoly or oligopoly is imperfect. **2.** A market in which information is incomplete. Participants in an imperfect market are more likely to make poor decisions than they would be if information were more readily available.

imperialism Domination of a small country or countries by a more powerful country. For example, European countries practiced imperialism by establishing overseas colonies.

implied agency An agreement by words or actions rather than by a document.

implied contract An agreement in which the terms are assumed but not explicitly stated. An example of an implied contract is the implied warranty accompanying the purchase of a product that the product should perform as a reasonable buyer would expect. For example, a lawnmower is sold with an implied contract that it will cut grass. —Compare EXPRESS CONTRACT.

implied easement An easement created when interested parties act as if one exists even though there is no formal document. For example, if land is divided, one section used for the benefit of another section is likely to include an implied easement.

implied warranty The unwritten assurance that a product will perform its specified purpose. —Also called *warranty of merchantability.* —See also IMPLIED CONTRACT.

import A good or service brought into a country from another country and offered for sale. While some imported items originate in foreign subsidiaries of domestic companies, large increases in imports tend to hurt sales and profits of many firms located in the importing country. —Compare EXPORT. —See also BALANCE OF TRADE; QUOTA.

impost A tax or duty, especially with regard to imported goods.

impound To confiscate and take control of something. For example, police may impound vehicles and their contents during a drug bust.

impound account An account established for future needs. For example, a lender may set up an impound account into which a homebuyer prepays recurring expenses such as insurance and taxes. —Also called *escrow account.*

imprest fund A designed level of funds that are used to cover relatively small expenses for supplies and other operating necessities. —Also called *petty cash fund.*

improvement An increase in the value of real estate achieved by changing its configuration or by adding to it. —Also called *land improvement.*

imputed cost 1. In accounting, the expense of unreimbursed goods and services provided by one entity to another entity. **2.** An expense that is borne indirectly. For example, paying cash for a car avoids the direct cost of interest payments to a lender, but it entails the imputed cost of lost income from having funds invested in the car rather than a more productive asset.

imputed income Benefits that accrue even though no money is received. For example, an employee receives imputed income when an employer offers free health insurance and life insurance coverage. Some types of imputed income must be reported to the IRS.

imputed interest Interest on an investment that is assumed for certain purposes to be paid, even though no interest payment is actually transferred to the investor. For example, the Internal Revenue Service considers annual accretion on a zero-coupon corporate or a zero-coupon Treasury bond to be imputed interest for tax purposes, even though investors holding these bonds receive no periodic interest payments from the issuers.

imputed interest rate A minimum market rate of interest assumed by the government for tax purposes regardless of the actual rate charged on a loan. The imputing of interest is an attempt to stop tax avoidance by people making loans at artificially low interest rates.

inactive account A brokerage or bank account in which few transactions take place. Some financial institutions levy a fee on accounts that have no activity during a specified time.

inactive security A security that has a relatively low trading volume. A particularly inactive security may not trade for days or weeks at a time, although bid and ask quotations for it are generally available.

in camera In private. In law, describing a meeting in the judge's chambers that excludes members of the jury or public.

incapacity 1. Inability of an employee to adequately perform his or her assigned duties. **2.** Reduced mental and physical abilities that make it difficult to manage financial and personal affairs. —See also LEGAL INCAPACITY.

incentive fee —See PERFORMANCE FEE.

incentive pay A wage or salary arrangement in which additional compensation is awarded for performance that exceeds an established benchmark. For example, employees of a company may be rewarded with a proportion of the firm's profits that exceed a specific amount.

incentive stock option An option that permits an employee to purchase shares of the employer's stock at a predetermined price. No tax is due on any gain until the time of sale if the sale date is at least one year subsequent to the date on which the option was granted. —Compare NONQUALIFYING STOCK OPTION. —Also called *employee stock option; option; qualifying stock option; stock option.* —See also RELOAD.

incidence of tax —See TAX INCIDENCE.

incident of ownership Evidence of control over an asset. For example, a person may add a child's name to a savings account but still retain control over the account.

inclusionary zoning Land use regulation that requires developers of a new tract of land to offer housing units affordable by a wide range of household incomes. For example, a developer is required to set aside a portion of housing units for low- and moderate-income households. Developers may be offered an incentive, such as an increase in density, as an offset to the added expense of inclusionary zoning.

income Financial gain during a specified period. —See also ADJUSTED GROSS INCOME; GROSS PROFIT; NET INCOME; TAXABLE INCOME.

income account In accounting, one or more accounts used to record various types of revenue, including sales, interest income, and income from the sale of assets. —Compare EXPENSE ACCOUNT 1.

income approach Estimating the market value of commercial and investment real estate by dividing anticipated annual income (rental income less operating expenses) by a capitalization rate reflecting returns that are available on investments of comparable risk. For example, a rental property with annual income of $12,000 and a capitalization rate of 12% has a market value of $12,000/0.12, or $100,000.

income beneficiary A person who receives income from a trust.

income bond A long-term debt security in which the issuer is required to pay interest only when interest is earned. This rare security, issued principally as part of a corporate reorganization, offers an investor a relatively weak promise of payment. Some issues require that unpaid interest be accumulated and made up in periods that earnings permit. —Also called *adjustment bond.*

income dividend A distribution of dividends, interest, and short-term capital gains by an investment company to its shareholders. —See also CAPITAL GAINS DISTRIBUTION.

income effect The effect on personal consumption of a change in the price of a good or service. For example, an increase in the price of gasoline results in consumers having less real purchasing power and reducing their consumption expenditures.

income elasticity of demand The proportional change in the quantity demanded of a good or service as a result of a change in income. Luxury goods and services tend to have a high income elasticity of demand, while cigarettes and necessities such as groceries have a low income elasticity of demand. In other words, an increase in income is likely to produce a substantial increase in the demand for luxury goods and very little increase in demand for cigarettes.

income-equity fund An investment company that invests primarily in the equities of companies with good records of paying dividends so as to produce a high level of current income for shareholders.

income fund An investment company whose main objective is to achieve current income for its owners. Thus, it tends to select securities such as bonds, preferred stocks, and common stocks that pay relatively high current returns. This type of fund is most appropriate for someone seeking high current income rather than growth of principal. —Also called *income-mixed fund.*

income in respect of a decedent Income to which a decedent was entitled but that was not properly included in the decedent's gross income in the year of death. The fair market value of income in respect of a decedent must be included in the tax return of the beneficiary.

income-mixed fund —See INCOME FUND.

income per share —See EARNINGS PER SHARE.

income property Real estate that produces current income, typically from rental payments. Apartments, office buildings, and rental homes are considered income property.

income redistribution Changing the manner in which income is distributed to members of an economy. For example, imposing tariffs and quotas on foreign-made goods would likely result in an income redistribution as domestic manufacturers experience greater demand for their products and find it necessary to pay higher wages to attract additional employees.

income replacement Income provided by a disability income insurance policy designed to replace a portion of wages or salary that are lost because of illness or injury.

income shifting Transferring income from one person to another person, who pays taxes at a lower rate. For example, a parent might transfer income-earning assets to a child who is taxed at a lower rate than the parent. —Also called *income splitting.*

income splitting 1. Married couples filing a joint return with wide brackets that assume assets and income are split between the spouses. The wide tax brackets applicable to joint returns were designed to mitigate the effects of a progressive tax on married couples. 2. —See INCOME SHIFTING.

income statement A business financial statement that lists revenues, expenses, and net income throughout a given period. Because of the various methods used to record transactions, the dollar values shown on an income statement often can be misleading. —Also called *earnings report; earnings statement; operating statement; profit and loss statement.* —See also CONSOLIDATED INCOME STATEMENT.

income stock A stock that has a relatively high dividend yield. The stock's issuer is typically a firm having stable earnings and dividends and operating in a mature industry. The price of an income stock is heavily influenced by changes in interest rates.

income tax A tax levied on the annual earnings of an individual or a corporation. Income taxes are levied by the federal government and by a number of state and local governments. One set of rules applies to individual income and another to corporate income.

incompetent In law, someone found by the legal system as unable to handle their financial and personal affairs.

incontestable clause In a life insurance contract, a provision that prohibits the issuing company from contesting a claim because of fraud or misrepresentation by the insured in the application for insurance. Most life insurance policies become incontestable after two years from the date of issue.

incorporate To obtain a state charter establishing a corporation. Owners of proprietorships and partnerships incorporate in order to obtain limited liability for themselves and for potential investors. The limited liability makes it easier for the firm to raise additional equity capital.

incorporeal property Intangible property, including patents, leases, copyrights, and mortgages.

incremental analysis —See MARGINAL ANALYSIS.

incremental cost —See MARGINAL COST.

incubator An organization designed to assist start-up companies, generally with respect to providing knowledge and technical assistance.

incurable depreciation Obsolescence or physical deterioration of an asset so extensive that repair is not economically feasible.

indemnify 1. To insure against loss or damage. For example, an individual may purchase liability insurance to indemnify himself against claims arising from negligence. **2.** To pay another's expenses. For example, a company may reimburse, or indemnify, its directors for legal expenses they incur in performance of their duties for the company.

indemnity 1. An agreement to compensate someone for a loss or damages they incur. **2.** An exemption from liability.

indenture A legal contract between a bond issuer and its lenders that specifies the terms of the issue. Typical provisions are the amount and dates of interest payments, name of the trustee, maturity date, collateral, restrictions on dividends or other borrowing, and specifics of a sinking fund or potential calls. —Also called *bond indenture; trust deed.* —See also COVENANT.

independent adjuster A person or company that acts on behalf of an insurer in investigating and adjusting claims arising under insurance contracts issued by the insurer. An independent adjuster would be employed by several insurance companies that do not write enough policies in a particular area to be able to afford internal adjusters.

independent audit —See EXTERNAL AUDIT.

independent contractor A person or company that offers its services under a temporary agreement in which the independent contractor is not an employee and is subject to lesser control by the entity purchasing its services. Unlike employees, independent contractors often assume the risk of losing money during the term of an agreement.

independent director A corporate director who has no material relationship with the company in which he or she serves as director. For example, an independent director cannot be employed or have a family member employed by the company.

independent executor or executrix An executor who is permitted to administer an estate free from control of the court. For example, an independent executor can avoid the red tape of seeking court approval to sell estate assets. In most states an independent executor must be designated in the will of the deceased.

independent union A labor organization that is not dominated by an employer and is not affiliated with the AFL-CIO. —Compare COMPANY UNION.

independent variable A variable that is not affected by any other variables with which it is compared. For example, in comparing the price of an electric utility stock with interest rates, the interest rates are an independent variable because they are not affected by utility stock prices. —Compare DEPENDENT VARIABLE.

index[1] The relative value of a variable in comparison with itself on a different date. Many security price indicators such as the Standard & Poor's series and the New York Stock Exchange series are constructed as indexes. —See also BASE PERIOD.

index[2] To adjust a variable by a selected measure of relative value. For example, some individuals have proposed that an investor's cost basis on a security be indexed for changes in consumer prices so that only real increases in value will be taxed. —See also SUBINDEX.

index arbitrage An investment strategy that takes advantage of the price discrepancies between an asset or group of assets and an index futures contract on the asset. For example, a money manager might attempt to earn a profit for shareholders by selling an overpriced stock index futures index and buying the underlying stock.

indexed life insurance Life insurance products with nonguaranteed additional credited interest tied to an index outside the contract. For example, the contract value of a policy may be tied to the performance of the S&P 500. —Also called *equity-indexed life insurance.*

indexed loan A loan, generally long-term, with its maturity, interest, principal, or payments subject to change based on some variable, such as the consumer price index. For example, the interest rate charged on a loan may be a function of the prime rate.

index fund A mutual fund that keeps a portfolio of securities designed to match the performance of the market as a whole. The market is represented by a market index such as the S&P 500. An index fund has low administrative expenses and appeals to investors who believe it is difficult or impossible for investment managers to beat the market.

index futures Futures contracts on stock indexes such as the S&P 500. Index futures are settled in cash.

indexing 1. A strategy for choosing securities so that a portfolio mimics the market as represented by some chosen market index. Most stock index funds attempt to mimic

index fund

With so many different index funds available, how are individuals to decide which ones best fit their needs?

For those investors who believe that investment managers offer no value, an index fund is a good option for participating in the equity markets. The best index funds have a low expense ratio and a low tracking error (the difference between the return of a portfolio and the return of a benchmark index). Investors should also properly diversify according to their asset allocation plan.

■ Richard S. Campbell, CIMA®, Senior Vice President, Wealth Management,
Portfolio Management Director, Smith Barney, Valdosta, GA

the S&P 500. **2.** Adjusting a variable such as wages or a contract price to a specific index. For example, Social Security payments are tied to a cost-of-living index.

index lease A lease agreement that includes periodic adjustments to payments according to some specified variable such as a cost of living index.

index of industrial production —See INDUSTRIAL PRODUCTION.

index of leading economic indicators An index that is compiled by the Conference Board, a private-sector consulting firm. The index is designed to indicate the future direction of economic activity. A rising index signals that economic activity can be expected to increase in the near future. Stock market price movements are considered as a separate leading indicator.

index option A call option or put option with a specific index as the underlying asset. For example, a call option on the S&P 500 gives the option buyer the right to purchase the value of the index at a fixed price until a predetermined date. Index options provide a means to leverage a bet on the future direction of the market or of a particular industry segment without purchasing all the individual securities.

indicator A variable used to forecast the value or change in the value of another variable. For example, changes in the producer price index are used to forecast subsequent changes in the consumer price index. Likewise, some financial analysts believe a change in the money supply is an indicator of the direction of the stock market. —See also TECHNICAL INDICATOR.

indicia An identifying sign or mark. For example, a postal mailing permit account allows a direct mailer to imprint a postage-paid indicia on the upper right corner of a return envelope. Institutions such as universities claim all rights to indicia such as mascots, service marks, and trademarks.

indirect cost A cost that is not directly related to the production of a specific good or service, but that is indirectly related to a variety of goods or services. For example, the cost of administering a large company is an indirect cost that must be spread over a number of products or services. —Compare DIRECT COST. —Also called *overhead.*

indirect government obligation —See FEDERAL AGENCY SECURITY.

indirect labor Wages, salaries, and associated expenses of employees in a manufacturing plant that are general in nature and cannot be assigned to a specific product. Expenses associated with employing security personnel in a plant that manufactures several products are an example.

indirect liability A legal obligation resulting from damages awarded to an injured party because of the negligent act of someone else. For example, a hospital may be held accountable because of the negligent behavior of one of its employees. —Compare DIRECT LIABILITY.

indirect tax A tax paid by an entity other than the one on which it is levied. For example, a retail sales tax is collected and remitted to the government by a business, even though consumers ultimately pay the tax. —Compare DIRECT TAX.

individual account An account opened in the name of one person. For example, a husband and wife may each decide to maintain individual checking accounts. —Compare JOINT ACCOUNT.

individual retirement account —See IRA.

Individual Taxpayer Identification Number (ITIN) A tax-processing number issued by the Internal Revenue Service to individuals who are required to have a U.S. taxpayer identification number but are not eligible to obtain a Social Security number. ITINs are issued regardless of immigration status because both resident and nonresident aliens may have U.S. tax return responsibilities. Each ITIN is a nine-digit number that begins with 9 and includes either a 7 or 8 as the fourth digit.

industrial Of or related to companies engaged in the manufacture of products. The word also can refer to firms only marginally engaged in what is generally thought of as industrial. For example, Microsoft is classified as an industrial company for purposes of calculating the Dow Jones Averages.

industrial advertising Promotional efforts by a business to influence decision makers at other businesses. For example, a tire company advertises in a periodical read by automobile manufacturers.

industrial bond A long-term debt security issued by a corporation engaged in industrial activities such as manufacturing or refining.

industrial development bond A type of municipal revenue bond in which interest and principal payments are secured by the credit of a private firm rather than by the municipality. —Also called *industrial revenue bond.* —See also PRIVATE ACTIVITY BOND.

industrial engineer A systems integrator who attempts to make things work better by improving productivity and quality. Industrial engineers work in both manufacturing and service industries to reduce waste in energy, materials, and money.

industrial espionage Attempts at gathering commercial secrets about competitors. Legal activities include investigating relevant publications and industry reports. Bribing a competitor's employees is an example of illegal industrial espionage. —Also called *espionage.*

industrial goods Intermediary goods and services purchased for use in the production of additional goods and services. Examples include screws, tools, and machinery.

industrialist A person who owns, manages, or provides major financing for an industrial company. Andrew Carnegie of U.S. Steel and Alfred Sloan of General Motors are famous American industrialists.

industrial park A land area designated for manufacturers and distributors, who often receive tax benefits and favorable lease arrangements.

industrial production A measure of the country's economic health judged by its output from manufacturing, mining, and utility industries. Industrial production is calculated by the Federal Reserve, which publishes a monthly index of industrial production. —Also called *index of industrial production.*

industrial psychology Applied psychology that addresses varied business problems, including employee job satisfaction and performance.

industrial relations The interaction between an organization and its employees or members. For example, it could describe relations between a company and a union, a union and its members, or a government agency and its employees.

industrial revenue bond —See INDUSTRIAL DEVELOPMENT BOND.

industrial revolution The development and adoption of new and improved production methods that changed America and much of Europe from agrarian to industrial economies. The industrial revolution began in England in the late 18th century.

industrial union A labor union that includes all the members of a particular industry, regardless of their occupation or trade. For example, all the employees in a particular factory, regardless of their job, may belong to an industrial union. The United Auto Workers is an example of an industrial union. —Compare CRAFT UNION.—Also called *vertical union.*

industry 1. A business segment. For example, the airline industry. **2.** A manufacturing facility.

industry life cycle The stages of evolution through which an industry progresses as it moves from conception to stabilization and stagnation. The stage in which a particular industry (and thus, a firm within the industry) currently exists plays a major role in the way investors view its future.

industry segment An identifiable component of a business. This may be a company's product line, geographic region, division, or other divisible part of the company. Firms often evaluate performance on a segment basis. Segments also may be sold as the firm reevaluates its product lines or territories.

industry standard A voluntary industry-accepted benchmark for products or practices. For example, industry standards for computer hardware and software allow consumers to purchase software programs that run satisfactorily on any computer.

inelastic Of or relating to the demand for a good or service when the quantity purchased varies little in response to price changes in the good or service. For example, the demand for medicines and medical services is generally inelastic because the quantity purchased by consumers is unresponsive to price changes. Producers of products and services facing inelastic demand curves find it relatively easy to increase prices. —Compare ELASTIC. —See also UNITARY ELASTICITY.

inelasticity The lack of responsiveness of the quantity purchased of an item to changes in the item's price. If the quantity purchased changes proportionately less than the price, the demand is inelastic. For example, price increases for relatively inexpensive foods such as sugar and flour tend to produce small changes in the quantity demanded. —Compare ELASTICITY. —Also called *price inelasticity.*

infant industry An emerging area of business or commerce. For example, a country may be in the early development stage of automobile manufacturing. Some people argue that infant industries need protection in the form of quotas or tariffs in order to grow and be competitive.

inferential statistics A branch of statistics that uses sample data to make a judgment about a population of data. For example, suppose a researcher has compiled years of data for stock prices and dividends. Inferential statistics might compare the risk-adjusted historical returns of different categories of stocks in order to provide guidance for the best types of stocks to own. —Compare DESCRIPTIVE STATISTICS.

inferior good A good that consumers buy less of as they grow wealthier and can afford something better. Generic canned vegetables are an inferior good that consumers tend to avoid buying as they grow wealthier and can afford fresh or branded goods. —Compare SUPERIOR GOOD.

inflation A general increase in the price level of goods and services. Unexpected inflation tends to be detrimental to financial assets, primarily because it is accompanied by rising interest rates. A point to keep in mind is that a certain amount of inflation is already embodied in most asset values. —Compare DEFLATION. —See also CONSUMER PRICE INDEX; CORE INFLATION; COST-PUSH INFLATION; DEMAND-PULL INFLATION; GDP DEFLATOR; PRODUCER PRICE INDEX; PURCHASING POWER RISK.

inflation accounting Alteration of a firm's financial statements to account for changes in the purchasing power of money. With inflation accounting, gains and losses from holding monetary items during periods of changing prices are recognized. Likewise, long-term assets and liabilities are adjusted for changing price levels. Inflation accounting is used to supplement regular financial statements in order to illustrate how changing price levels can affect a firm. —Also called *general price level accounting.*

inflationary psychology Consumers' belief that prices will inevitably rise, a belief that drives them to speed up purchases, especially of real assets (that is, gold, diamonds, and real estate), and avoid investment in financial assets (that is, stocks and bonds). As a result, the consumers themselves can cause the inflation that they fear will occur.

inflationary spiral Inflation that grows stronger as price increases feed on themselves. Consumer prices rise, causing workers to demand higher wages. Higher wages cause higher expenses for businesses, which raise prices yet again.

inflation endorsement In real estate, an addition to title insurance or property insurance that provides for an automatic increase in coverage in order to keep up with inflation.

inflation hedge An investment with a value directly related to the level of general price changes. Tangible investments, including real estate and collectibles, tend to be inflation hedges. Among securities, the common stock of natural resource companies (such as gold, timber, and oil) is often considered an inflation hedge because the value of the companies' assets should rise during a period of inflation.

inflation-indexed security A security with a rate of return linked to some specified measure of inflation. For example, Series I U.S. savings bonds pay holders a specified fixed rate adjusted for changes in the consumer price index.

inflation premium The portion of an investment's return that compensates for expected increases in the general price level of goods and services. The expectation of rising inflation results in higher long-term interest rates as lenders and borrowers build in an increased inflation premium.

inflation rate The percentage change in the price of goods and services, generally on an annual basis. —See also CONSUMER PRICE INDEX; GDP DEFLATOR; PRODUCER PRICE INDEX.

information overload A state in which the amount of available information is so overwhelming a person is unable to effectively process and utilize it. For example, a person interested in franchise opportunities may be inundated with hundreds of proposals.

informative advertising

How does informative advertising generate sales?

The main goal of informative advertising is to help consumers make their own informed decisions. For example, nonbranded advertisements in the pharmaceutical industry—particularly those used on television—that do not mention a specific product but, rather, focus on a disease state or condition, raise interest and awareness, and, in turn, generate sales.

■ E. Mace Lewis, Vice President, Business Development, QD Healthcare Group, Greenwich, CT

information return Communication with the Internal Revenue Service or another taxing authority that provides information but does not include an actual tax return or payment.

information superhighway A term coined by Vice President Al Gore to identify the communications network that carries voice, data, and images around the world at lightning speed.

information system An integrated communications network of people and machines that assembles, processes, and distributes data.

informative advertising A promotional effort at generating interest in a good, service, or organization by providing consumers with information. For example, a petroleum company undertakes an advertising campaign to inform citizens about the firm's environmental efforts. Similarly, an automobile manufacturer might undertake informative advertising about vehicle care or safe driving.

infrastructure 1. In economics, the capital assets that allow the citizens of a country to travel, communicate, work, and live. This includes roads, communications networks, bridges, utilities, and so forth. **2.** In information technology, the hardware that connects computers and users.

infringement A violation of someone else's rights, generally with regard to a patent, trademark, or copyright. Unauthorized copying of the "expression" of a copyrighted work is considered an infringement. —Also called *patent infringement.*

ingot A bar or block of metal, generally of a standardized size and shape for ease in handling and storage.

inherit To receive property from the estate of a deceased person.

inheritance Assets that are received by an heir of a deceased.

inheritance tax A state tax levied on the recipient of an estate rather than on the estate itself. The tax varies by state, and its severity in a given state usually depends on the kinship between the deceased and the heir. Some states levy a tax on the estate instead of a tax on the amount inherited. —Compare ESTATE TAX. —Also called *death tax.*

in-house Of or referring to something that takes place within an organization. For example, a company may develop its promotional material in-house rather than use an outside advertising firm.

initial margin requirement The minimum portion of a new security purchase that an investor must pay for in cash. For example, with an initial margin requirement of 60%, the most an investor can borrow is $2,000 on a $5,000 purchase. The Federal Reserve Board determines the initial margin requirement. —Also called *margin requirement.*

initial public offering (IPO) A company's first sale of stock to the public. Securities offered in an IPO are often, but not always, those of young, small companies seeking outside equity capital and a public market for their stock. Investors purchasing stock in IPOs generally assume very large risks for the possibility of large gains. —See also PRE-IPO.

injunction A court order to bring a specified activity under control. For example, Company A might ask for an injunction to prevent Company B from using advertising that includes Company A's name or trademark. A court will sometimes issue a preliminary injunction that remains effective until additional evaluation of the issue can lead to the possibility of a permanent injunction.

in-kind pay Compensation in the form of goods or services rather than money. For example, as part of compensation an employee receives goods that he or she helps produce.

inland carrier A railroad, barge line, trucker, or airline that transports cargo inland from a port.

inner city The central portion of a metropolitan area that is generally older and heavily populated by low-income minority families.

innocent purchaser An individual who buys real property without knowledge of a title flaw. For example, someone who purchases a television for $350 from an appliance store cannot be charged if it is later shown the television had previously been stolen.

innovation Creative use of a good, service, or idea that is already available. Ebay's development of a competitive marketplace on the Internet is an example of innovation.

in play Of or relating to a company that has been, or is widely rumored to be, the target of a takeover attempt. After a firm is in play, additional offers may be forthcoming.

in perpetuity Forever. For example, a memorial fund may be established to fund a charitable project in perpetuity. —See also PERPETUITY.

in personam A lawsuit or judgment against a specific person or organization. —Compare IN REM.

in rem A lawsuit or judgment against a thing (e.g., personal property) as opposed to a person. —Compare IN PERSONAM.

inside buildup The cash value increases in a life insurance policy. Inside buildup is free of income taxation during the period of buildup, thus making cash-value insurance a more desirable investment vehicle for people in high income-tax brackets.

inside director A member of a firm's board of directors who is also employed in another capacity by that firm. An example is a chief executive officer who also sits on the board. —Compare OUTSIDE DIRECTOR.

inside information Details of a company's affairs that are known by its directors and officers but are not yet released to the public. For example, initial data on a giant oil field that has not been publicized is inside information.

insider **1.** A person who, because of his or her position within a firm, has access to proprietary information unavailable to the general public. Although the term obviously includes corporate officers, it also may extend to relatives of these officers or to employees of other firms having a special relationship with the firm in question. —See also 10b5-1 PLAN **2.** Officially, an officer, a director, or the owner of 10% or more of a firm's securities.

insider trading The illegal buying or selling of securities on the basis of information that is generally unavailable to the public. An example is the purchase by a director of shares of his or her firm's stock just before the release of surprisingly good earnings information.

> **CASE STUDY** On February 8, 2008, a Credit Suisse banker was found guilty of 28 counts of insider trading related to a TXU buyout and other major deals. The prior year the Securities and Exchange Commission had filed a complaint with the U.S. District Court in Chicago alleging that unknown buyers purchased 8,000 call option contracts (rights to buy stock at a fixed price) for TXU common stock in advance of a buyout announcement. TXU, a giant Texas utility, had received the buyout offer from a consortium of private equity firms. According to the SEC complaint, the call options had been purchased through foreign accounts, although the trades were cleared through domestic brokerage firms with purchase orders on the Chicago Board Options Exchange. The SEC claimed the trades were made on the basis of buyers being in possession of material, nonpublic information ahead of the announcement. The firm's common stock price had surged during the two trading days prior to the announcement of the buyout.

insolvency clause A clause in a reinsurance contract that states the reinsurance company will remain responsible for its share of claims even if the primary insurer is insolvent at the time the claims are made.

insolvent Unable to meet debts or discharge liabilities. —Compare SOLVENT 1.

installment A partial payment on a financial obligation. For example, an annual or monthly payment to the seller of an asset, such as a farm, on a long-term contract is an installment. Installments are comprised partly of principal and partly of interest. If all the installments are of equal size, each subsequent payment incorporates an increasing amount of principal and a decreasing amount of interest.

installment contract An agreement in which the delivery of money, goods, or services is to occur in segments over a specified period. An automobile loan is an example of an installment contract that stipulates equal monthly payments until the principal on the loan is repaid.

installment land contract —See CONTRACT FOR DEED.

installment method The accounting method of treating revenue from the sale of an asset on installments such that profits are recognized in proportion to the percentage of the sale price collected in a given accounting period. For example, if an asset with a book value of $12,000 is sold for $15,000 and payment is to occur in 5 equal installments of $3,000 each, the seller would record annual profits of ($15,000 − $12,000)/5, or $600. The installment method is a conservative way of treating an installment sale because profit is not recognized until receipt of payment.

installment sale A sale in which the buyer is scheduled to make a series of payments over a period of time. An installment sale can offer certain tax advantages; however, the seller may have a lengthy wait before receiving the entire proceeds. Virtually any asset, including securities and real estate, may be disposed of through an installment sale.

Institute of Management Accountants (IMA) A professional organization for individuals employed in management accounting and financial management. IMA provides educational resources, establishes a set of ethical standards, and awards professional certification to members who pass a series of examinations and provide proof of continuing education. —See also CERTIFIED IN FINANCIAL MANAGEMENT; CERTIFIED IN MANAGEMENT ACCOUNTING.

institutional advertising —See IMAGE ADVERTISING.

institutional broker A broker specializing in security trades for institutions such as banks and pension funds. Institutions usually trade in large blocks that require special handling.

institutional investor An entity such as an insurance company, an investment company, a pension fund, or a trust department that invests large sums in the securities markets. Institutional investing has had an increasing impact on securities trading: as the institutions buy and sell huge blocks of the same securities during short periods of time, large security fluctuations ensue.

institutional lender A financial institution such as a commercial bank, pension fund, or life insurance company that invests its funds in loans.

institutional ownership The ownership of a company's stock by mutual funds, pension funds, and other institutional investors, generally expressed as a percentage of outstanding shares. A high proportion of institutional ownership may result in relatively large changes in a stock's price, as institutions tend to buy and sell the same stocks at the same time.

Institutional Shareholder Services (ISS) A private organization that provides proxy voting and corporate governance services to institutional investors. The firm evaluates proxy proposals and makes voting recommendations to its clients.

instrument A legal document, such as a check, security, or will.

in-substance debt defeasance —See DEFEASANCE.

insurability The conditions under which an insurance company is willing and able to write a policy for coverage of a financial risk. For example, a person with a terminal illness does not meet the requirements for insurability for most health insurance providers.

insurable interest Having a financial interest in an individual or a thing. To have an insurable interest, an individual must be in a position to suffer an assessable financial loss if a person should die or a thing is damaged, destroyed, or lost.

insurable risk A financial risk that can be transferred to an insurance company. For a risk to be insurable it must be random, definable, and measurable. In addition, an insurance company must be able to charge a sufficient but reasonable premium in order to offer coverage.

insurable value Generally the market value of an insured item. For real estate, insurable value is generally the market value or replacement cost of the structure and contents. Land is not part of the insurable value, because it is considered indestructible.

insurance Transferring the risk of financial loss in return for periodic premium payments to the entity that accepts the risk.

insurance agent A representative of one or more insurance companies who sells the firms' products. An independent agent represents several insurance companies, while a captive agent offers insurance products from a single company. State Farm agents are examples of captive agents. Both independent and captive agents increasingly offer financial planning services and sell an assortment of financial products, including mutual funds and annuities.

insurance broker A person or business that represents purchasers of insurance products. Insurance brokers evaluate offerings of different insurance companies in an effort to locate the best coverage at the best price for their customers.

insurance claim —See CLAIM.

insurance company A business that accepts certain risks for which it receives payments. Insurance companies are organized either as mutual companies owned by policyholders or stock companies owned by stockholders who expect to earn a return on their investment. Insurance companies are regulated by the states in which they do business.

insurance contract A written agreement in which an insurance company agrees to accept specified risks in return for receiving premium payments from the policyholder.

insurance coverage The types and amounts of risk that have been transferred to an insurance company. For example, a family may have $250,000 of coverage on a homeowner's insurance policy that covers financial loss from fire, wind, and so forth.

insurance dividend A payment by a life insurance company to the holder of a participating whole life insurance policy. Insurance dividends are generally paid annually and depend on the insurance company's investment returns and expenses. Policyholders are generally allowed to choose whether to take a dividend in cash or use it to purchase additional coverage.

insurance premium A payment to an insurance company to purchase a policy or to keep a policy in force.

insurance, property —See PROPERTY INSURANCE.

insured account A personal or business account at a financial institution that is a member of a state or national insurance organization. For example, the Securities Investor Protection Corporation insures assets in brokerage accounts. The insurance of brokerage and bank accounts protects losses from a failure of the financial institution, but not losses caused by declining asset values.

insured bond A municipal debt obligation for which interest and principal are guaranteed by a private insurance company. Municipal issuers pay a premium to purchase the insurance in order to obtain a higher credit quality rating and a lower rate of interest on the debt.

insured mail A letter or package sent via the U.S. Postal Service that has been insured for damage or loss by the sender. Insurance requires a fee that is in addition to the cost of postage.

intangible asset An asset such as a patent, goodwill, or a mining claim that has no physical properties. Since intangible assets are often difficult to value accurately, such assets when included on a corporate balance sheet may have a true value significantly different from the dollar amounts indicated there. —Compare TANGIBLE ASSET.

intangible drilling costs Expenses incurred while exploring for gas, geothermal, or oil reserves. These items may be expensed in the year incurred, or they may be capitalized and deducted throughout a period of years. Intangible drilling costs are an effective means of reducing taxes because they can be used to offset income in a single year, even though the costs were incurred in order to produce or develop a capital asset (energy reserves) that will in turn generate income for many years. Costs for fuel, preparation of a site, and wages are examples of intangible drilling costs.

intangible tax A tax imposed by some states or local governments on the market value of intangible assets such as stocks, bonds, money market funds, and bank account balances.

> **CASE** The intangible tax, once a popular means for raising tax revenues **STUDY** from wealthy individuals, has slowly disappeared, in part because many individuals either discovered ways to legally avoid or simply did not pay the tax. Many states decided the tax was not worth the expense and aggravation of trying to collect it. Florida imposed an intangible personal property tax in 1931 that was based on the market value of intangible property owned by Florida individual residents, Florida entities, and non-Florida businesses with tax situs in Florida. The Florida tax was levied against the market value of corporate stocks and bonds, loans, accounts receivable, leases, mutual funds, money market funds, limited partnership interests, and beneficial interests in any trusts as of January 1. The Florida tax excluded cash, savings accounts, checking accounts, direct bond issues of the federal government, and bonds issued by the State of Florida. The tax rate varied over the years, and in 2006 was 5 mills (0.0005, or $50 on $100,000 of taxable intangibles), with an exemption of $250,000 per resident. In 2006 the Florida legislature voted overwhelmingly to repeal the tax effective January 1, 2007.

integrate **1.** To open an entity to individuals of all races and ethnic groups. **2.** To combine parts, units, or activities into a whole. For example, a company may attempt to improve efficiency and communications by integrating the front- and back-office computer network. —See also BACKWARD INTEGRATION; FORWARD INTEGRATION; VERTICAL MERGER.

integrated pension plan A retirement plan with benefits that are adjusted downward for Social Security retirement benefits. For example, a retiree's monthly pension check from her employer is reduced by a portion or all of the benefits received from Social Security. —Compare NONINTEGRATED PENSION PLAN.

intellectual capital Accumulated skills and knowledge of a person or organization that have been gained through education, training, and experience. For example, a business gains intellectual capital by scheduling periodic meetings with its customers.

intellectual property Creation by wit including music, drawings, photographs, films, paintings, novels, inventions, and so forth. Copyrights, trademarks, and patents provide legal protection for intellectual property.

intensive distribution Maximizing a product's availability by having it offered through as many outlets as possible.

interbank rate —See LONDON INTERBANK OFFERED RATE.

interchange fee The transaction fee on credit card and debit card purchases charged by the banks that issue the cards. The interchange fee is designed to compensate for risk (the card user might not pay) and for the costs of processing a transaction. It is paid by the merchants who accept the cards for payment. An interchange fee typically comprises a fixed charge per transaction plus a percentage of the amount charged.

CASE STUDY Interchange fees are a major expense for merchants that accept credit and debit cards as payment for goods and services. Each credit card transaction includes four parties: the merchant accepting the card, the merchant's bank, the bank that issued the card, and the card user. Suppose a consumer uses a credit card for a $100 purchase. The merchant may sell the transaction to its bank for $98.00. That bank, in turn, sells the transaction to the issuing bank for $98.50. The cardholder is subsequently billed for the full $100 purchase. The card issuer's share of this transaction, in this case $1.50, is the interchange fee. Interchange fees are a function of several variables, including the quantity of transactions a merchant processes, the processing procedure followed by the merchant (in-person transactions incur a smaller fee than mail-order transactions), whether the card is swiped or entered manually (swiped is less expensive), and the type of card that is used in the transaction (premium cards that offer rewards are more expensive). The increasing use of credit cards and the substantial costs borne by merchants that accept the cards has resulted in an increasing number of legal battles between merchants and issuers.

intercompany transaction A business deal completed between two units of the same company. For example, the syrup unit of a soft drink company sells its product to the company-owned bottling unit.

interest 1. Payment for the use of borrowed money. 2. Partial ownership of an asset. For example, a part owner of a restaurant has an interest in the business. 3. Income earned from lending money to others. For example, the owner of a certificate of deposit or a corporate bond earns interest.

interest coverage A measure of a firm's ability to meet required interest obligations. A high coverage ratio indicates enhanced ability to make timely interest payments. Interest coverage is calculated by dividing the firm's operating income by its required interest payments. —Compare FIXED-CHARGE COVERAGE. —Also called *times interest earned.* —See also DEBT MANAGEMENT RATIO.

interest dates The dates on which interest is paid to bondholders, nearly always involving two payments per year. Interest dates are set at the time of issue and remain unchanged throughout the life of the bond. —See also PAYMENT DATE 2.

interest deduction The reduction in taxable income from the payment of interest on borrowed funds that may be declared on tax returns. Individuals are permitted to deduct mortgage interest and interest on funds used for investment purposes, but only when deductions are itemized. Interest on consumer loans is not permitted as a deduction. Businesses are permitted to deduct nearly all interest expenses.

interest group Individuals who have come together because of a common interest or agenda, such as a public policy issue.

interest-only Of or describing a loan with required periodic payments of interest but no payment of principal until the scheduled maturity date.

interest rate The percentage rate for borrowing or lending money, generally stated on an annualized basis. —Also called *rate.*

interest rate future A contract on the future delivery of interest-bearing securities, primarily U.S. Treasury bills or Treasury bonds, although contracts on certificates of deposit, Ginnie Mae certificates, and Treasury notes are also available. As with other futures contracts, interest rate futures permit a buyer and a seller to lock in the price of an asset (in this case, a specified package of securities) for future delivery.

interest rate option An option contract on interest-bearing securities or on a futures contract on interest-bearing securities. These options are generally used as a means to manage the risk of a bond portfolio.

interest rate parity The interrelationship between currency exchange forward rates and spot rates that result from interest rate differentials. If interest rates are higher in the United States than in a foreign country, the forward dollar value of the foreign currency will exceed the spot dollar value of the foreign currency.

interest rate risk The risk that interest rates will rise and reduce the market value of an investment. Long-term fixed-income securities, such as bonds and preferred stock, subject their owners to the greatest amount of interest rate risk. Interest rate movements are much less important in influencing the values of short-term securities such as Treasury bills. Changes in interest rates can have a major impact on real estate values.

interest rate swap —See SWAP[1].

interest-sensitive life insurance Whole life insurance with a level premium, guaranteed death benefit, guaranteed minimum cash value, and accumulations in cash value that fluctuate with market rates of interest.

interim audit Examination of financial records during the course of a fiscal year, generally to reduce the amount of work required for the end-of-year audit.

interim dividend A dividend declared before a firm's annual earnings and dividend-paying ability are accurately known by its management. An interim dividend is ordinarily paid in each of the first three quarters of the fiscal year. These payments are followed by a final dividend at the time that earnings can be accurately determined. —Compare FINAL DIVIDEND 2.

interim financing The financing that supports a transaction until permanent financing can be arranged.

interim report A financial statement that has a date other than that of the end of a fiscal year. Interim reports, generally unaudited, are intended to indicate the level of a firm's performance, usually during quarterly intervals of the fiscal year.

interlocking directorates Boards of directors of different firms that have one or more of the same people serving as directors. Interlocking directorates are illegal among competing firms.

interlocutory decree A transitional judicial ruling that remains in force until the judge gathers additional information and is able to determine if the ruling is effective and should be made permanent.

Intermarket Trading System (ITS) An interconnection of security-trading venues that allows brokers and market makers to trade securities in additional markets. The system is intended to allow customers to obtain the most favorable price available.

intermediary 1. A person or entity that serves as a link between two or more persons or groups. For example, an insurance broker serves as an intermediary between insurance companies and insurance buyers. **2.** —See FINANCIAL INTERMEDIARY.

intermediate bond A debt security with a maturity of 7 to 15 years. —Also called *medium-term bond.* —See also LONG BOND; SHORT BOND.

intermediate good A product of one process that becomes the input of another process. For example, lumber is an intermediate good produced from timber and used for building.

intermediate-term Of or relating to an investment with an expected holding period somewhere between short-term and long-term. For bonds, collectibles, and real estate, intermediate-term usually refers to a holding period that ranges between one and seven years. For stocks, intermediate-term indicates a somewhat shorter period of six months to several years.

intermediation The flow of funds through financial intermediaries (such as banks and thrifts) on its way to borrowers. The depositing of money at financial institutions that make the money available to corporate borrowers is an example of intermediation. This process tends to facilitate saving and investing in sophisticated financial systems. —Compare DISINTERMEDIATION 1.

internal audit The examination of a company's records and reports by its employees. Internal audits are usually intended to prevent fraud and to ensure compliance with board directives and management policies. In contrast, the financial statements presented to stockholders are typically prepared by outside parties to ensure absolute objectivity. —Compare EXTERNAL AUDIT.

internal control The process by which management checks the effectiveness and efficiency of an organization's operations and assesses the reliability of its reporting.

internal financing The financing of asset purchases with funds generated in the usual course of operations rather than funds that are borrowed or raised from the issuance of stock.

internal funds Funds that are raised within a firm. For example, income after taxes and noncash expenses, such as depreciation, provide a firm with funds to use in the acquisition of investments. Companies that are able to finance expenditures with internal funds do not have to rely on borrowing or on the sale of additional shares of stock. —Compare EXTERNAL FUNDS.

internalize To send a customer order from a brokerage firm to the firm's own specialist or market maker. Internalizing an order allows a broker to share in the profit (spread between the bid and ask) of executing the order.

internal rate of return (IRR) The rate of discount on an investment that equates the present value of the investment's cash outflows with the present value of the investment's cash inflows. Internal rate of return is analogous to yield to maturity for a bond.

Internal Revenue Code The tax law of the United States.

Internal Revenue Service (IRS) The agency of the U.S. Treasury Department that administers the Internal Revenue Code.

International Accounting Standards Board (IASB) A privately funded, London-based organization whose goal is to establish a single set of enforceable global financial reporting standards. The IASB was originally formed in 1973 as the International Accounting Standards Committee.

International Bank for Reconstruction and Development —See WORLD BANK.

international banking facility A department of a depository institution with segregated assets and liabilities restricted to foreign deposits and loans. International banking facilities are designed to be competitive with foreign banks in large part because they

international fund

Should most individual investors own shares in an international fund, or is it enough to invest in domestic companies with substantial foreign business operations?

I believe that investors should own an international fund so that they can get full exposure to the region in which they are interested in investing. Large U.S. companies that derive significant international revenues offer some exposure, but not as much as country- and region-specific funds.

■ Richard S. Campbell, CIMA®, Senior Vice President, Wealth Management,
Portfolio Management Director, Smith Barney, Valdosta, GA

are not required to abide by U.S. reserve requirements and interest rate restrictions that apply to domestic institutions.

International Development Association —See WORLD BANK.

international fund A mutual fund that invests in the equity securities of companies located outside the country in which the fund is located. —Compare GLOBAL FUND.

international law Legal principles applicable to relationships among nations. Rather than a single body of law, international law is a compilation of a multitude of laws, treaties, principles, and customs.

International Monetary Fund (IMF) An international financial agency that is affiliated with the United Nations and has as goals the stabilization of foreign exchange rates, the lowering of trade barriers, and the correction of trade imbalances among countries. The IMF, which was established in 1944, works with countries much as a credit counselor works with individuals having financial difficulties.

International Securities Exchange (ISE) An SEC-registered securities exchange that commenced operation in 2000 for electronic trading of options. The exchange has ten designated trading areas, each staffed by market makers who make orderly markets, including firm bid and ask prices for designated options. The ISE was funded by a consortium of broker-dealers and is based in New York City. The exchange issued shares to the public in a 2005 IPO.

International Trade Commission, U.S. An independent federal agency charged with administering U.S. trade remedy laws, maintaining an appropriate U.S. tariff schedule, and reporting tariff and trade analysis to the U.S. President and Congress. For example, the commission adjudicates complaints regarding the infringement of U.S. intellectual property rights.

Internet service provider (ISP) A local or regional business that provides businesses and individuals with Internet access. ISPs generally charge a fixed monthly fee and often offer to create and maintain customer websites.

Internet stock The equity security of a company engaged primarily in a business associated with the Internet. —Also called *dot-com.*

interperiod income tax allocation Accounting for a deferred tax liability or asset caused by temporary difference in a corporation's pretax financial income and taxable income. Corporations typically report revenues and expenses in one period for financial reporting purposes and in another period for tax purposes. For example, a company may use straight-line depreciation for financial reporting purposes and accelerated depreciated for income-tax purposes.

interpleader A legal action in which a plaintiff files a lawsuit that requires two or more parties to litigate competing claims to an asset. For example, two parties claim the right to collect a loan from a borrower who is unsure which party to pay. The borrower files an interpleader action, deposits the disputed funds with the court, and allows the creditors to argue their respective claims.

> **CASE STUDY** Computer company CCI had held the domain name "CLUE.COM" for several years when it was informed by Network Solutions, administrator of Internet domain names, that CCI would have to produce a trademark certification for "CLUE" or accept the assignment of a new domain name. The demand resulted from a claim by game and toy maker Hasbro that CCI's use of the domain name infringed on Hasbro's registered trademark of CLUE, the name of one of the firm's most popular games. Hasbro had already obtained several domain names by this method. Network Solutions was then sued by CCI, which claimed that Hasbro sought to obtain an asset belonging to someone else without paying for it. CCI also sought a restraining order on transfer of the domain name. In an effort to force CCI and Hasbro into litigation against each other, Network Solutions filed an interpleader complaint with the U.S. District Court that, if successful, would permit Network Solutions to step out of the way while Hasbro and CCI fought it out in court. The interpleader complaint proved unsuccessful when the U.S. District Judge dismissed the case.

interpolate To estimate a value that is between two known values. For example, suppose a financial institution advertises interest rates it is paying for 3-month, 6-month, and 12-month savings instruments. A potential saver wanting to invest in a 9-month certificate might estimate the rate that will be paid by interpolating between the 6-month rate and the 12-month rate.

interrogatory Written questions to witnesses and a party to a lawsuit submitted as part of pretrial discovery by the opposing party.

interstate commerce The movement of goods, services, and money from one state to another, or within a state if it affects commerce in another state.

interview A formal discussion in which one or more participants attempt to gain information and guidance from another participant. For example, members of a company's marketing department may schedule an interview for a prospective employee.

interviewer bias Intentional or unintentional partiality of an interviewer that affects the response of the person being interviewed. For example, the tone of an interviewer's voice or the look on the interviewer's face may influence a response.

inter vivos transfer A gift of property during the lifetime of the person making the gift.

inter vivos trust —See LIVING TRUST.

intestacy law —See DESCENT AND DISTRIBUTION STATUTE.

intestate Of, relating to, or being an individual who has died without leaving a valid will. In such a case, the estate of the deceased is distributed according to the laws of the state in which he or she resided. —Compare TESTATE. —See also DESCENT AND DISTRIBUTION STATUTE.

intestate

Are there any instances when having a valid will isn't really important?

A will is not necessary if all of a deceased person's assets are held jointly with other persons or pass to others by beneficiary designation or are held in an inter-vivos trust (a "revocable" or "living" trust) whose terms dispose of the property on the grantor's death. However, life makes this result difficult to assure; some items of property cannot be jointly owned or pass by designation, and property can be acquired shortly before death without time to transfer to the owner's trust. Therefore, most people who intend their property to pass by beneficiary designation, joint ownership, or the terms of an inter-vivos trust also have a will that disposes of any other property they own at death.

The intestacy law of the state in which the deceased person lived specifies how the property of a person who dies without a will is distributed. This law is intended to distribute property in the way most people would have wanted if they had thought about it. However, the administration of the estate of someone who dies intestate is often more cumbersome and more expensive than if that person had a will. For example, an individual who is survived by children, and wishes to leave all of his or her property to the children equally, will not, in most jurisdictions, need a will to accomplish that result. However, the children may not agree on which of them should act as administrator of the intestate estate, a controversy which could have been avoided if the individual had designated an executor in a will. Further, an administrator's powers to deal with estate property may be more limited than those which are granted an executor by law or would typically be granted by the terms of a will, which can result in greater court supervision of the administration of the intestate estate and increased cost.

■ Stephen F. Lappert, Partner, Trusts and Estates Department, Carter Ledyard & Milburn LLP, New York, NY

intestate succession The sequence in which assets of an estate are distributed when the deceased dies without a will. The sequence is determined by a state's descent and distribution statutes.

in-the-money —Used to describe a call (put) option that has a strike price that is less (more) than the price of the underlying asset. If Convergys common stock is trading at $25 per share, a call option on Convergys with a strike price of $23 is in-the-money. —Compare AT-THE-MONEY; OUT-OF-THE-MONEY.

in the tank —Used to describe a particular investment, or the entire class of assets that includes the investment, during or following a period of large price declines.

intranet A private network within a single enterprise used mainly to share information and resources among the organization's employees.

intraperiod tax allocation Distributing a period's total tax expense or benefit among components of total income. For example, a firm allocates total tax expense among continuing operations, discontinued operations, and extraordinary gains.

intrapreneurship The use of entrepreneurial skills such as innovation, persistence, and risk taking while working as an employee of a large company. For example, a company searches for a new leader with entrepreneurial skills to bring major changes to an underperforming division.

intrastate offering A security offering in which the issue is offered and sold only to persons within the state in which the issuer is incorporated. Intrastate offerings are exempt from registration under the Securities Act of 1933.

inventory control

How can a business reach an acceptable compromise between having too little and too much inventory?

There are trade-offs between simple solutions to inventory control and more complex solutions. The simple solutions (such as ABC or EOQ) will not balance availability and cost control for the large variety of inventory items that many companies have. The more complex solutions (MRP and JIT) can be costly and still may not be optimal. The ABC system is a simple classification of inventory items into three groups (A is most critical and C least critical). The bulk of control efforts go to the A items. The EOQ (economic order quantity) is a mathematical formula that can be applied to each separate item to determine at what level of stock the item should be reordered. MRP (materials requirement planning) and JIT (just in time) systems require sophisticated information systems to support inventory management. Generally, the fewer resources available, the simpler the system. Whatever the system, accurate estimation of costs associated with inventory is critical to success.

> ■ Phyllis G. Holland, PhD, Professor and Head, Department of Management,
> Langdale College of Business, Valdosta State University, Valdosta, GA

intrinsic value The value of an asset as justified by the facts. For example, the intrinsic value of a security is justified by factors such as the issuing company's assets, dividends, earnings, and management quality. Intrinsic value is at the core of fundamental analysis, since it is used in an attempt to calculate the value for an asset and then compare it with the market price.

introductory rate —See TEASER RATE.

inure To benefit or vest with someone. For example, assets in an irrevocable trust inure to the benefit of the trust's beneficiaries.

invasion powers A provision in a trust that permits the trustee to use the principal of the trust if its income is insufficient to fulfill the requirements of the beneficiary. However, trustees are usually prohibited from exercising this power without prior authorization.

inventory 1. The amount of raw materials, work in process, and finished goods being held for sale at a given time. Diamonds held by a jeweler, engines owned by General Motors, and canned and frozen foods in a grocery store chain's warehouse are examples of inventory. —See also BEGINNING INVENTORY; ENDING INVENTORY. **2.** Assets owned by an individual or family. For example, a family makes an inventory of household items for insurance purposes in the event their home is damaged by fire.

inventory certificate A written and signed document attesting to the inventory a business or organization has on hand.

inventory control Supervision of the delivery, availability, and utilization of an organization's inventory in an attempt to ensure adequate supplies and at the same time minimize expenses caused by theft, spoilage, or excessive stock.

inventory profit Profit that results from the increase in value that assets undergo during the time they are held in inventory. Inventory profit, ordinarily due to general inflation, is not considered to be of high quality, because it is incidental to the firm's primary business. —See also FIRST-IN, FIRST-OUT; LAST-IN, FIRST-OUT.

inventory remarketing Negotiating the sale of unused stock of a new product prior to the product's introduction. Inventory remarketing reduces the financial risk of introducing a new product by guaranteeing its sale regardless of the product's acceptance by buyers. For example, a company brings out a new brand of toothbrush that generates poor sales. An inventory-remarketing agreement would allow the manufacturer to sell all the remaining units at a previously agreed upon price.

inventory shortage The amount by which a physical count of inventory is less than the amount recorded on the company's books. An inventory shortage may be the result of theft or of incorrect records listing deliveries and usage.

inventory turnover A measure indicating the number of times a firm sells and replaces its inventory during a given period, calculated by dividing the cost of goods sold by the average inventory level. A relatively low inventory turnover may be the result of ineffective inventory management (that is, carrying too large an inventory) or carrying out-of-date inventory to avoid writing off inventory losses against income. —Also called *stock turnover*.

inventory valuation The cost assigned to inventory for the purpose of establishing its current value. Inventory valuation is determined according to the basis by which a firm assumes inventory units are sold. If the first units acquired are assumed to be the first units sold (first-in, first-out), costs of the last units purchased are used for valuing inventory remaining in stock. Conversely, if the last units acquired are assumed to be the first units sold (last-in, first-out), the costs of the first units purchased are used for valuing the inventory remaining in stock.

inverse condemnation Legal action to gain compensation for a reduction in asset value caused by government action or activity. For example, the government's pumping water out of a property results in sinkholes in an adjacent property. The owner of the property with sinkholes files suit against the government, claiming inverse condemnation.

inverted market In futures or options trading, a market with nearby contracts having a price that is higher than more distant contracts. This unusual situation may occur when the underlying asset is heavily in demand. —Compare CONTANGO. —Also called *backwardation*.

inverted scale An issue of serial bonds having yields on short-term securities that exceed yields on long-term securities. An inverted scale is generally caused when investors judge interest rates to be unusually high and expect them to fall.

inverted yield curve —See NEGATIVE YIELD CURVE.

invest To commit funds in the expectation of earning a profit through current income, a gain in value, or both.

invested capital An investment measure calculated by adding an investor's net worth and long-term liabilities.

investment **1.** Property acquired for the purpose of producing income for its owner. Just as factories and equipment are investments for manufacturers, stocks, bonds, and rental real estate are investments for individuals. **2.** Expenditures made for income-producing assets.

investment adviser A person who offers professional investment advice. Investment advisers are required to register with the SEC.

Investment Advisers Act of 1940 A federal act that defines what an investment adviser is, requires such advisers to register with the SEC, and sets standards for advertising,

investment climate

I've heard that an investor should sell stocks when the investment climate is very good and buy stocks when the investment climate is very bad. Does this make sense?

It makes sense in the same way that the admonition to "buy low and sell high" does. In reality, you can't predict turning points in the market with any degree of accuracy. The investment climate may be good for business investment spending in some industries, but not others. This may or may not translate into increasing stock prices. Most individual investors need to take a long-run view in their buying and selling decisions rather than attempting to time the highs and lows of the market.

■ Michael W. Butler, PhD, Professor of Economics, Angelo State University, San Angelo, Texas

disclosure, fees, liability, and recordkeeping. The act was passed to offer protection to investors. —Also called *Advisers Act.*

investment advisory service A business that offers investment recommendations. Investment advisers are required to abide by regulations in the Investment Advisers Act of 1940.

investment bank A firm that functions as an intermediary between organizations that need additional funds and individuals and organizations having surplus funds to invest. An investment banker, an expert in the financial markets, sells its expertise to organizations wishing to raise funds. —Compare COMMERCIAL BANK. —See also PRIMARY DISTRIBUTION; STANDBY UNDERWRITING.

investment boutique —See BOUTIQUE 3.

investment climate The overall environment for investments. A favorable investment climate is likely to include low inflation, falling interest rates, growing corporate earnings, political stability, and a high degree of consumer confidence.

investment club A group of people who meet regularly and pool their funds to invest in securities. In many instances, a club is formed as much for social and educational reasons as for making profits. Since most investment clubs are formed as partnerships, their dividends, realized capital gains, and losses are passed through for tax reporting by the individual members.

investment company A firm in which investors pool their funds to allow for diversification and professional management. Because individual firms often specialize in particular types of investments, the potential returns and risks vary considerably among firms. Charges to investors—both to acquire shares in a firm and to pay management for operating the company—vary significantly from firm to firm. —Also called *management company.* —See also CLOSED-END INVESTMENT COMPANY; CONDUIT THEORY; MANAGEMENT FEE 1; MUTUAL FUND; PERFORMANCE FEE; REGULATED INVESTMENT COMPANY.

Investment Company Act A 1940 act that regulates the management of investment companies in relation to items such as financial statements, stated investment goals, personnel, debt issuance, and directors. The goal of the act was to provide adequate disclosure and to curb the management abuses prevalent during the 1920s and 1930s.

Investment Company Institute (ICI) A national association for mutual funds, closed-end investment companies, and unit investment trusts. ICI, established in 1940, collects and publishes industry data, represents its members in matters of regulation and taxation, and promotes the interests of the industry and its shareholders.

investment-grade Of, relating to, or being a bond suitable for purchase by institutions under the prudent man rule. Investment-grade is restricted to those bonds graded BBB and above by Standard & Poor's and graded Baa3 and above by Moody's. —Compare HIGH-GRADE. —Also called *bank-grade*.

investment income Earnings such as interest, dividends, rent, and gains in asset values that result from the ownership of investment assets.

investment management The selection and administration of financial assets including cash, stocks, bonds, and mutual funds. —See also PROPERTY MANAGEMENT.

investment objective The financial goal or goals of an investor. An investor may wish to maximize current income, maximize capital gains, or set a middle course of current income with some appreciation of capital. Defining investment objectives helps to determine the investments an individual should select.

investment philosophy The investment ideology practiced by a professional money manager. For example, a portfolio manager may seek maximum capital gains at the expense of volatile and uncertain returns. An individual investor should choose a money manager with an investment philosophy that coincides with the individual's investment objectives.

investment portfolio —See PORTFOLIO 1.

investment strategy An investor's plan for allocating funds among different investments based on the investor's investment outlook, financial goals, risk tolerance, tax liabilities, and so forth.

investment vehicle A specific investment having attributes that are intended to accomplish certain goals. Examples of investment vehicles include common stock, preferred stock, bonds, options, futures, annuities, and collectibles.

investor A person who purchases income-producing assets. An investor—as opposed to a speculator—usually considers safety of principal to be of primary importance. In addition, investors frequently purchase assets with the expectation of holding them for a longer period of time than speculators.

investor relations department The unit of a business that is responsible for providing current and prospective investors with an accurate portrayal of the firm's performance and prospects.

invisible hand Free-market economic forces that guide scarce resources to their most productive uses. This term is credited to economist Adam Smith, who believed a capitalistic system with people free to act in their own self-interest would produce the greatest public good.

invoice A seller's listing and pricing of goods and services delivered to a buyer.

involuntary bankruptcy Bankruptcy that is forced by creditors instead of being initiated by the firm or individual. —Compare VOLUNTARY BANKRUPTCY. —See also CHAPTER 7; CHAPTER 11.

involuntary conversion The forced exchange of property for another asset (often cash) that serves as compensation for seizure, theft, condemnation, or destruction of the property being exchanged. For example, a wrecked vehicle may be considered a total loss by the insurance company, resulting in a forced conversion of the vehicle for a cash settlement. Any gain from an involuntary conversion is generally considered taxable.

involuntary lien A lien placed on an asset without consent of the asset's owner. For example, a lien may be placed on real property for nonpayment of taxes.

Inwood capitalization Using an annuity table factor to calculate the present value of a level stream of income. For example, the present value of $500 per year for 10 years, discounted at an annual rate of 6%, is equal to $500 x 7.360, or $3,680.

IOU An abbreviation for "I owe you," and an informal notice of a debt being owed.

IPO —See INITIAL PUBLIC OFFERING.

IRA A custodial account or trust in which individuals may set aside earned income in a tax-deferred retirement plan. For individuals who earn under a specified amount or who are not in an employer-sponsored retirement plan, contributions to an IRA (subject to an annual maximum) are deferred along with any income the contributions earn. Withdrawals at retirement are fully taxable. For individuals in an employer-sponsored plan and having an adjusted gross income above a specified amount, all or part of the contribution may be taxable, although any income earned in the IRA is tax deferred. IRA investment opportunities include certificates of deposit, mutual funds, and securities purchased through brokerage accounts. —Also called *individual retirement account.* —See also COVERDELL EDUCATION SAVINGS ACCOUNT; KEOGH PLAN; ROTH IRA; SELF-DIRECTED IRA; SIMPLIFIED EMPLOYEE PENSION PLAN.

IRA rollover Reinvestment of a lump-sum distribution from an IRA when physical receipt of funds has been taken by the investor. The lump-sum distribution must be deposited in an IRA rollover account within 60 days of receipt to escape taxation. —Compare IRA TRANSFER. —See also CONDUIT IRA.

IRA transfer The direct transfer of assets in an individual retirement account from one trustee to another. With an IRA transfer, the investor does not take physical possession of the IRA assets; thus, there are no tax consequences to the movement of the funds. A direct transfer may result in some lost income to the investor, since the funds could remain in transit for a number of days. —Compare IRA ROLLOVER.

iron law of wages The classical economic theory that wages will tend to be at or near subsistence level. Increases above subsistence will result in population growth that produces more workers and a resulting decline in wages. —Also called *subsistence theory of wages.*

IRR —See INTERNAL RATE OF RETURN.

irregular coupon A bond interest payment for more or less than six-months' interest. The first coupon on many bonds is irregular because payment is other than six months from the dated date. —Also called *odd coupon.*

irregular goods Flawed merchandise that is generally sold at a cut-rate price.

irreparable damage Harm that cannot be reversed and cannot be offset with monetary compensation. A plaintiff in a patent infringement suit may claim irreparable harm if an injunction is not issued.

irrevocable Of or referring to something that cannot be reversed or undone. For example, a company that processes Internet transactions has a policy that buyer payments are irrevocable and cannot be reversed.

irrevocable trust A trust in which the grantor gives up any right to amendments or termination. Income from an irrevocable trust is taxable to the beneficiary if disbursed, or to the trust if not disbursed. —Compare REVOCABLE TRUST.

IRS —See INTERNAL REVENUE SERVICE.

ISE —See INTERNATIONAL SECURITIES EXCHANGE.

iShares Exchange-traded funds with portfolios based on a series of stock indexes, including the S&P indexes, the Dow Jones indexes, and the Russell indexes. Shares of each fund represent proportional ownership of individual stocks that make up the index on which the fund is based.

island display A merchandise exhibit with two sides on a main aisle and no adjoining units.

ISP —See INTERNET SERVICE PROVIDER.

ISS —See INSTITUTIONAL SHAREHOLDER SERVICES.

issue¹ 1. A particular grouping of an organization's securities. For example, General Motors has a number of different issues of preferred stock listed on the New York Stock Exchange. **2.** A fact or disputed matter in a legal proceeding.

issue² To sell securities in the primary market. For example, in late 1996, Florida Panthers Holdings, Inc., owner of the NHL hockey team, issued 2,700,000 Class A shares of common stock at a price of $10 per share.

issue date —See DATED DATE.

issued capital stock Capital stock that has been authorized and issued, but that may have been reacquired in part. Issued capital stock reacquired as Treasury stock or stock that has been retired is not included in earnings-per-share calculations. —See also OUTSTANDING CAPITAL STOCK.

issuer An organization that is selling or has sold its securities to the public.

itemized deduction —See DEDUCTION.

ITIN —See INDIVIDUAL TAXPAYER IDENTIFICATION NUMBER.

itinerant worker A laborer who moves from region to region in search of employment. —Also called *transient worker.*

ITS —See INTERMARKET TRADING SYSTEM.

January effect The tendency of stocks to perform better in January than at any other time of the year. Some analysts speculate that the stock market tends to become oversold in December, when investors sell to establish losses for tax purposes or to obtain money for holiday spending.

January indicator The tendency of stock market movement in January to set the market trend for the entire year. Thus, if a market average is higher at the end of January than it is at the beginning of January, chances are that the year will produce a rising market.

jawbone To attempt to persuade a person or group. For example, the chairman of the Federal Reserve may jawbone members of the banking system to improve the credit quality of their loan portfolios.

J curve In economics, continuing deterioration before a variable begins to improve following some policy change. For example, a trade deficit continues to get worse before it reverses and grows smaller following a currency devaluation. The dip and subsequent recovery follow the shape of the letter J.

job 1. Regular activities undertaken in return for compensation. **2.** A particular project that is in progress. For example, a painter drives to the job site each morning.

job action A collective employee activity other than striking that is designed to pressure an employer. For example, airline pilots may engage in a slowdown in order to pressure management to make safety changes.

job analysis The duties and responsibilities of a particular job and the qualifications required of an applicant.

job bank A listing of employment opportunities posted by an employer or an employment agency.

jobber A middleman who buys in large lots from an importer or manufacturer and resells to businesses rather than final consumers.

job description The purpose, responsibilities, and expected activities of a particular job.

job enrichment Assigning different tasks and permitting greater worker involvement and participation.

job evaluation An attempt to judge the relative value and responsibilities of a job within an organization. For example, all jobs within a company might be ranked against one another.

job hopper An individual who changes jobs frequently.

job lot **1.** A specified quantity of goods to be sold in a single lot. **2.** In commodities trading, the quantity of a commodity that is smaller than what is specified in a standard contract.

job placement Locating employment opportunities that are consistent with an individual's training and abilities.

job security Confidence an employee will continue to work for the same employer as long as the employee is able and willing to provide the required services.

job sharing Dividing the responsibilities of a single job among two or more people. For example, clerical workers may split up the days each works during the week. Job sharing is sometimes employed by businesses that are downsizing so employees don't have to be dismissed.

joint account An account at a financial institution in which two or more individuals hold joint interests. Joint accounts may be established in a number of different forms that produce very different results. —Compare INDIVIDUAL ACCOUNT. —See also PARTNERSHIP ACCOUNT.

joint and several liability Liability in full for a debt or legal judgment by each responsible party. For example, if three parties are responsible and one cannot pay, the remaining two must make up the difference.

joint and survivor annuity An annuity that pays a lifetime income to the annuitant and to another person, generally a spouse. The payments may be scheduled to decrease at the death of either recipient. —Also called *joint life annuity.* —Compare SINGLE-LIFE ANNUITY.

joint demand The demand for a good or service that is dependent on the demand for another good or service. For example, the demand for certain software is directly related to the demand for computers. Joint demand occurs when two or more products are used together. —See also COMPLEMENTARY GOODS; JOINT SUPPLY.

Joint Economic Committee The congressional committee of U.S. House and U.S. Senate members whose job it is to review economic conditions and recommend improvements in economic policy. The committee is comprised of ten House members and ten Senate members.

joint life annuity —See JOINT AND SURVIVOR ANNUITY.

joint ownership Ownership of an asset, such as property, by two or more parties. Joint ownership of property has advantages and disadvantages compared with individual ownership. For example, the property automatically passes to the co-owners on the death of one of the other owners. Also, with one type of joint ownership, one owner can sell the property without the permission of the other owners. —Also called *cotenancy.* —See also JOINT TENANCY WITH RIGHT OF SURVIVORSHIP; TENANCY BY THE ENTIRETY; TENANCY IN COMMON.

joint product cost In accounting, the cost assigned to a product that originates from a production process that results in several products. For example, crude oil is refined into several different products, including gasoline, heating oil, and kerosene. Joint products from the same process must be apportioned product costs in order to calculate profitability and tax consequences.

joint rate A single rate for a freight shipment that will be carried on two or more carriers.

joint return A single income-tax return filed commonly by a husband and wife. In a joint return, the tax liability is calculated on the premise that each spouse has contributed equally to the reported income. A joint return is especially advantageous for couples in which one spouse has considerably more taxable income than the other spouse. —Compare SEPARATE RETURN.

joint-stock company A rare type of business organization characterized by some features of a partnership and some features of a corporation. Shares are transferable and the company is assessed taxes according to corporate tax rates. However, the liability of each owner is unlimited. Joint-stock companies are established primarily because of the ease with which they are formed.

joint supply Two or more goods that derive from a single product or process. For example, dairy cattle can provide milk, hides, and meat. High demand for one of the three goods might result in an increase in the breeding of dairy cattle and reduce prices for the other two products.

joint tenancy with right of survivorship (JTWROS) Asset ownership for two or more persons in which each owner holds an equal share and may give away or sell that share without the permission of the other owner(s). In the event of death, an owner's share is divided equally among the surviving co-owners. —Compare TENANCY IN COMMON. —Also called *right of survivorship.* —See also TENANCY BY THE ENTIRETY.

joint venture A business undertaken by two or more individuals or companies in an effort to share risk and use differences in expertise. For example, oil companies often enter into joint ventures on particularly expensive projects carrying a high risk of failure. —See also CONSORTIUM.

journal In accounting, a book that includes all transactions and their appropriate accounts.

journal entry The recording of a business transaction and its monetary value in the accounting journal. Each entry results in both a debit and a credit, and is generally accompanied by a receipt or invoice.

journeyman **1.** An experienced worker who performs adequately, but not at the highest level. For example, a journeyman in baseball can often play several positions and fill in when a starter is injured or needs a rest. **2.** A skilled craftsman who has completed an apprenticeship but has not yet met requirements as a master.

JTWROS —See JOINT TENANCY WITH RIGHT OF SURVIVORSHIP.

judgment In law, a decree in the form of a sentence or determination by a court following evaluation of evidence.

judgment creditor A person who has obtained a favorable court order for collection of a debt. A judgment creditor is generally responsible for locating assets of the debtor that are subject to seizure.

judgment debtor A person a court has held liable for payment of a debt.

judgment lien A legal claim for a creditor on the property of a debtor.

judgment-proof Describing a person who, because of legal statutes or insolvency, is insulated from legal judgments.

judgment sample Selection of a sample on the basis of personal experience and knowledge rather than scientific principles. For example, a market researcher might draw a sample based on his or her personal knowledge of the subject.

judicial bond A bond filed with the court as a guarantee. For example, a party to a court action may post a judicial bond to guarantee payment of a verdict while an appeal is being considered. Judicial bond is a broad category that includes a variety of specialized bonds such as a fiduciary bond, a removal bond, and an appeal bond.

judicial dissolution Court-ordered disbandment of a corporation or partnership. For example, a court may dissolve a corporation if it finds that the articles of incorporation were obtained through fraud.

judicial foreclosure A court judgment that orders the sale of real property to satisfy the terms of a loan. A creditor generally pursues a judicial foreclosure in order to obtain a deficiency judgment for any amounts that may be owed following sale of the asset. —Compare STATUTORY FORECLOSURE.

juice —See VIGORISH.

jumble display A mixture of similarly priced products included in a single sales display. For example, a hardware store may have a jumble display of various tools and home improvement products near the entrance.

jumbo certificate of deposit A certificate of deposit with a principal of $100,000 or more. Jumbo certificates of deposit are negotiable and ordinarily carry slightly higher interest rates than smaller certificates.

junior debt A class of debt that is subordinate to another class of debt issued by the same party. Junior debt is more risky for an investor to own, but it pays a higher rate of interest than debt with greater security. Debentures are junior debt. —Compare SENIOR DEBT.

junior partner A person of lower rank or experience who has limited authority for making decisions.

junior security A security having a subordinate claim to assets and income with respect to another class of security. For example, preferred stock is a junior security compared with a debenture, and a debenture is a junior security compared with a mortgage bond. In general, a junior security entails greater risk but offers higher potential yields than securities with greater seniority.

junk bond A high-risk, high-yield debt security that, if rated at all, is graded less than BBB by Standard & Poor's or BBB3 by Moody's. These securities are most appropriate for risk-oriented investors. —Also called *high-yield bond.*

junk financing The raising of funds by issuing unsecured high-yield securities, as, for example, during takeover attempts in which the acquiring firm has little cash and must issue unsecured debt to finance the acquisition. —Also called *high-yield financing.*

junk mail Unsolicited mail generally sent in huge quantities to "occupant" or "resident" using standard mail.

jurat 1. A sworn officer of the court. 2. Official certification of a sworn document with regard to the signature, place, and date. For example, a notary public's certification of an affidavit.

jurisdiction The authority of a court or judge to hear or act on a petition or action.

just compensation 1. Equitable pay for work that is performed. 2. Fair reimbursement for a loss. For example, government is expected to pay full value for property that is taken for a public purpose.

just-in-time inventory Maintaining a very low inventory level by coordinating production schedules with suppliers who deliver materials as they are required. Just-in-time inventory reduces a manufacturer's costs of production, but increases the risk that an interruption in the supply of materials will cause production to grind to a halt. —See also ZERO INVENTORY.

▪ K

K —Used frequently in the financial literature as a symbol for 1,000.

Kansas City Board of Trade A commodities exchange chartered in 1876 that is primarily known for trading futures and options on hard red winter wheat, the primary ingredient in bread. The exchange also trades stock index futures and options on the Value Line Index.

karat A measure of the purity of gold. Pure gold is indicated by the label 24 karat. —See also FINENESS.

Keogh plan A federally approved retirement program that permits self-employed individuals to set aside savings up to a specified amount. All contributions and income earned by the account are tax deferred until withdrawals are made during retirement. Investment opportunities include certificates of deposit, mutual funds, and self-directed brokerage accounts. —Also called *self-employment retirement plan.*

Keynesian economics A segment of economic thinking that emphasizes the importance of aggregate demand (spending by consumers, business, and government) and considers government fiscal policy (spending and taxing) to be the major factor in maintaining a vibrant economy. Keynesians believe changes in total spending have their greatest short-term impact on real output and not prices.

key person insurance Life insurance coverage on one or more of an organization's essential employees, with premiums paid by the organization, which is also the beneficiary. A key person might be a chief executive officer, chief financial officer, or sales manager whose loss would have serious negative consequences for an organization. —Also called *business life insurance.*

key rate The interest rate that is most influential in determining the cost of credit to borrowers.

keystone markup Pricing a product at double its cost. For example, a retailer purchasing a brand of shampoo for $1.50 per bottle would establish a retail price of $3.00 per bottle.

kickback Something of value offered in secret for a favorable decision. For example, a sales representative may offer cash to a purchasing agent who places a large order.

kickers —See BELLS AND WHISTLES.

kiddie tax A federal income tax levied on the investment income of children 18 years of age and under, or under age 24 if the child is a full-time student. Income above a specified amount is taxed at the parent's top, or marginal, tax rate. The kiddie tax is designed to make it less advantageous for parents to shift income to their children.

kill To halt a business deal or security trade.

killer bee An individual or organization that assists a firm in repelling a takeover attempt, especially by devising defensive strategies.

killing A substantial profit earned from an investment.

kiosk A small structure from which information or merchandise is offered. For example, a kiosk in a shopping mall may offer a selection of sunglasses or cell phone accessories.

kiting 1. Writing a check for more than the balance in an account in order to take advantage of the lag in time before funds will be collected. For example, you write a check for the rent knowing your account does not have sufficient funds for payment, however, you expect to make a deposit in your account before said check is presented to the bank for payment. —Also called *check kiting.* **2.** Altering a check by fraudulently increasing the amount of the check.

knocked down Describing a product that is delivered in an unassembled or partially unassembled state. For example, large machinery may be imported in an unassembled state in order to reduce the cost of shipping.

knockoff An inexpensive imitation of a branded product, nearly always produced without permission. Knockoffs of well-known and expensive purses and watches are sometimes illegally offered on street corners of major cities.

knock off To reduce the price of something: *The merchant agreed to knock off $5 from the listed price.*

knock-out option An option that loses its entire value in the event the underlying asset crosses a predetermined price level.

know-how The wisdom and ability to perform a task.

knowledge-based pay Compensation that is a function of an employee's skill and knowledge as well as the job being performed. For example, public school systems typically pay teachers based on their educational level as well as number of years of service. Organizations offering knowledge-based pay often absorb the expense of additional training.

knowledge management The process of gathering, storing, organizing, analyzing, and sharing information among colleagues within an organization.

know-your-customer rule A requirement that brokers understand the financial needs and circumstances of a customer before providing investment advice.

Kondratieff Wave The theory that economic behavior in capitalistic countries leads to 50-year boom-and-bust business cycles. The theory is named for its originator, Russian economist Nickolai Kondratieff.

Krugerrand A gold coin minted in South Africa.

■ L

labor 1. The class of people who work for wages. 2. A type of work.

labor agreement A contract between management and employees that addresses wages, benefits, working conditions, and other relevant issues.

labor force All persons 16 years of age and older who are employed or who are unemployed and searching for employment.

labor-intensive Of or relating to a process or an industry that requires substantial labor relative to capital. Most service industries are labor-intensive, while manufacturing industries tend to be capital-intensive. —Also called *people-intensive.*

Labor Management Reporting and Disclosure Act —See LANDRUM-GRIFFIN ACT.

labor mobility The willingness and ability of workers to move or change jobs. Mobility is hindered by numerous factors, including limited skills, friends, expenses involved in moving, school-age children, and employment commitments of a spouse.

labor pool The group of workers with applicable skills and knowledge who are available for employment. A rural area is likely to have difficulty recruiting a large manufacturer because of the area's small labor pool.

labor theory of value The economic theory that the value of any good or service is proportional to the amount of labor consumed in its production and delivery. The labor theory of value was a central feature of economic analysis by Adam Smith and, later, Karl Marx.

labor union An organization of workers that promotes the members' interests with respect to wages, benefits, and working conditions. —Also called *trade union.*

laches The legal doctrine that neglect in asserting a right for an unreasonable time may serve as a disadvantage and offer a defense to another party.

laddering An investment strategy in which bonds or certificates of deposit that have different maturities are assembled for a portfolio. For example, an investor with $50,000 might invest $10,000 in bonds with a two-year maturity, $10,000 in bonds with a four-year maturity, $10,000 in bonds with a six-year maturity, and so forth. Principal from matured bonds or CDs is either spent or reinvested in additional bonds or CDs with longer maturities at the top of the ladder. —Also called *liquidity diversification; staggering maturities.*

laddering a stock Price manipulation in which a stock is purchased at escalating price levels in order to push the price even higher.

lading Cargo transported by a large carrier. —See also BILL OF LADING.

Laffer curve Graphical representation of economist Robert Laffer's theory about the effect of rising tax rates on tax revenues. The curve is shaped like a mound and depicts rising tax rates initially resulting in rising revenues, but at some point additional rate increases cause a decline in revenues. If the curve depicts reality, a taxing authority can increase tax revenues by reducing high (but not low) tax rates.

labor mobility

I don't want to get stuck in my current job because I don't have any other options. What actions can I take to improve my mobility?

Being stuck in a job is a function of both occupational conditions (lack of training, experience) and personal conditions (inability to sell a house, family ties to an area, and so forth). The occupational conditions are more readily addressed. Take advantage of all company-sponsored training and development opportunities. Allocate personal resources to training and development as well. This may mean going to school at night or attending meetings or conferences at personal expense. Finally, take advantage of networking opportunities. Start with your own organization (meet people in other parts of your company), reach out to industry contacts including customers and suppliers, and also move to meet people outside your industry in organizations such as the Chamber of Commerce. Networking is also accomplished by volunteering in community organizations that provide potential employers an opportunity to see your organizational skills, your people skills, and possibly your technical competence. Just be sure that you follow through with any commitment you make to volunteer organizations.

Always have your business card handy and keep your resume up to date. Check with your company's human resources department for postings of internal openings and have in mind someone who could take your job or be trained to take it if you are transferred or promoted within the company.

■ Phyllis G. Holland, PhD, Professor and Head, Department of Management, Langdale College of Business, Valdosta State University, Valdosta, GA

lagging economic indicator An economic or financial variable, the movements of which tend to follow the movement of overall economic activity. Thus, a lagging economic indicator would reach a peak after a peak in economic activity and would hit bottom after a bottom in economic activity. —Compare LEADING ECONOMIC INDICATOR.

laissez-faire 1. Of, relating to, or being an economy devoid of government interference. 2. Describing an organizational structure with decision-making authority in the hands of lower-level managers.

LAN —See LOCAL AREA NETWORK.

land 1. Real estate, including all that is above and below the surface. 2. A firm's dollar investment in real estate.

land contract —See CONTRACT FOR DEED.

land improvement —See IMPROVEMENT.

land lease —See GROUND LEASE.

landlocked 1. Of or referring to a country without direct access to the sea. Landlocked countries are at a significant economic disadvantage, although Switzerland seems to have adjusted nicely. 2. Describing a tract of land without direct access to a public road.

landlord An owner of real property who rents it under a lease agreement to another party.

landmark In real estate, a well-known or easily observable object or structure that serves as a point from which other places of interest can be located or measured.

Landrum-Griffin Act Federal legislation passed in 1959 that deals with the relationship between unions and their members. The act established a bill of rights for union members and requires that unions follow democratic procedures. The official name is the Labor Management Reporting and Disclosure Act.

land tenure The rights and duties associated with real property. Land tenure may (or may not) include the right to transfer property, the right to exclude others from using property, and the right to derive income from property. It may also include the duty to protect property from harm. —Also called *tenure in land.*

land trust 1. An organization that purchases and holds real estate under the terms of the organization's charter. For example, a conservation land trust might purchase property adjacent to a national park to hold until the government designates funds for its acquisition. **2.** A legal agreement in which real property is managed for the benefit of beneficiaries.

land-use planning A formalized assessment of land and water resources with a goal of developing options that are most beneficial to users while at the same time preserving environmental values. Local zoning commissions are involved in land-use planning.

Lanham Act Federal legislation passed in 1946 that governs the registration and protection of trademarks and service marks.

lapse In insurance, termination of coverage resulting from failure of a policyholder to pay premiums.

lapsed option An option that remains unexercised after its expiration. A lapsed option has no value.

large-cap 1. Of or relating to the common stock of a big corporation that has considerable retained earnings and a large amount of common stock outstanding. Large-cap stocks, which are generally well known, include the ones listed in the Dow Jones Averages. —See also MID-CAP 1. **2.** Of or relating to a mutual fund that chooses to hold a portfolio of large-cap stocks. Large-cap funds tend to have a more stable net asset value than either microcap or mid-cap funds.

last —See CLOSE 2.

last-in, first-out (LIFO) An accounting method for identifying the order in which items are used or sold. With last-in, first-out, the most recently acquired items are assumed to be sold first. During a period of inflation, last-in, first-out accounting tends to result in high costs that reduce reported profits. The reduced profits result in a lower income-tax liability. —Compare FIRST-IN, FIRST-OUT.

last sale The most recent transaction in a particular security.

last trading day 1. The day on which a trader must liquidate a futures position or else be required to receive (if long) or make delivery (if short). Following this day, the particular contract will cease trading. **2.** The last day on which a particular option is traded. Currently, this day is the third Friday of the expiration month.

late charge A fee assessed a borrower by a lender who receives payment after the due date.

latent defect A flaw in a product or structure that would not be discovered at the time of delivery or prior to the sale. For example, a product may have a defect that could result in harm to an unsuspecting buyer, who would have no way to know about the problem. Likewise, a home may have a structural defect that a buyer would be unlikely to discover until later.

latent demand A desire that is not currently being satisfied because no satisfactory good or service can be located. For example, there is a latent demand for a low-calorie, creamy, and excellent-tasting ice cream.

launch 1. To start a new company. **2.** To release a new product. For example, a household products company launches a new brand of toothpaste.

launder To convert money obtained from illegal activities into funds that appear to have been acquired legally. For example, illegally obtained funds are used to purchase chips at a casino. Winnings would then be pocketed as legitimate.

lavish or extravagant expense An expense that is unreasonable and cannot be deducted for tax purposes.

law of diminishing returns —See DIMINISHING RETURNS.

law of large numbers In statistics, the theorem that larger samples lead to more accurate forecasts. For example, an insurance company that substantially increases the number of life insurance policies in force improves the likelihood the firm will correctly forecast the mortality rate of its policyholders.

law of one price —See PURCHASING POWER PARITY.

law of supply and demand The economic theorem that in a free market supply and demand will establish an equilibrium for price and quantity. Increases in price tend to increase quantity supplied and decrease quantity demanded. Decreases in price have the opposite effect. Increases in supply or decreases in demand tend to reduce price, while decreases in supply or increases in demand tend to increase price.

layoff 1. An employer-initiated reduction in the number of employees. For example, in 2006 a major electronics company announced a layoff of over 10,000 employees. **2.** The allocation of unsold shares to syndicate members from a new issue rights offering by the managing underwriter.

lay off To terminate employees.

LBO —See LEVERAGED BUYOUT.

LDC —See LESS DEVELOPED COUNTRY.

lead A potential customer. For example, time-share salespersons often obtain leads from existing customers, who are offered incentives for providing the names of friends. —See also QUALIFIED LEAD.

leader 1. A company or product that is one of the most important in its market. For example, Toyota is a leader in vehicle manufacturing. **2.** An active stock that tends to lead the general market in price movements. For example, strength and activity may have made a stock a leader in a recent upward market movement.

leader pricing Establishing a low price for a very popular product in an attempt to attract customers who are likely to purchase other products at regular price. For example, grocery stores often use milk, sugar, and eggs for leader pricing.

leadership 1. Upper-level management in a company. **2.** The influence of a person or group over others. **3.** —See MARKET LEADERSHIP.

leading economic indicator An economic or financial variable that tends to move ahead of and in the same direction as general economic activity. —Compare LAGGING ECONOMIC INDICATOR. —See also INDEX OF LEADING ECONOMIC INDICATORS.

lead time 1. The time between order placement and delivery. **2.** The time between when a project begins and ends. For example, planning for a new housing development requires substantial lead time because of the many permits that are required.

lead underwriter The main underwriter of a new security issue. The lead underwriter forms a distribution system to sell the security issue and is generally responsible for the largest part of the offering. —Also called *bookrunner; house of issue; managing underwriter.*

lead user An early adopter of a new product or technology that is expected to eventually receive widespread use. For example, Wal-Mart was a lead user of computerized inventory systems.

leakage 1. Disclosure of confidential information. **2.** —See SHRINKAGE.

LEAPS —See LONG-TERM EQUITY ANTICIPATION SECURITIES.

learning curve The graphical representation of the skill or knowledge gained in doing something and the time spent doing it. A learning curve illustrates that the time to complete a task is reduced as the task is repeated over and over. It also illustrates that improvements in time become successively smaller.

lease An agreement that permits one party (the lessee) to use property owned by another party (the lessor). The lease, which may be written either for a short term or for a long term, often results in tax benefits to both parties. —Also called *equipment lease.* —See also CAPITAL LEASE; GRADUATED LEASE; GROSS LEASE; LEVERAGED LEASE; NET LEASE; OPEN-END LEASE; OPERATING LEASE; PUT[1] 3; SUBVENTED LEASE.

leaseback —See SALE AND LEASEBACK.

lease bonus Consideration paid to a lessor as an incentive to sign a mineral lease.

leased fee An interest in real property encumbered by a lease. A leased-fee interest allows the lessor to receive rent payments for the length of a lease and to have the property returned at the end of the lease.

lease fund An investment company that invests the shareholders' money in lease obligations. A lease fund is very similar to a bond fund, except that the maturities of its investments are shorter. Because leases do not have an active secondary market, the fund manager must secure outside agreements to buy the leases in case the shareholders redeem their shares.

leasehold The right to use property and the obligation to pay rent during the term of a lease.

leasehold cost The expense of acquiring and maintaining a lease. The capitalized leasehold cost is often not much less than the cost of an outright purchase.

leasehold improvement An improvement of a leased asset that increases the asset's value. The expense of a leasehold improvement is carried as an asset that declines in value over time as the value is depreciated over the life of the lease or the improvement.

leasehold insurance Coverage against a lessee's loss of value from losing a favorable lease (a lease with relatively low payments) because of an insured loss. For example, a tenant with a favorable long-term lease on a building that recently incurred substantial fire damage must move to a new location that involves a much higher lease payment. Leasehold insurance is designed to cover the loss suffered from cancellation of the favorable lease.

leasehold mortgage A loan by a tenant to obtain or help finance a leasehold interest in a property. For example, an individual might obtain a leasehold mortgage to finance the construction of a building on leased land.

lease purchase option A lease agreement that allows the lessee to purchase the leased asset under stipulated circumstances. For example, a business may sign a lease for a building with an option to purchase the building at an agreed-upon price at any time during the term of the lease. A lease purchase option gives a lessee time to use and evaluate an asset with little upfront money.

lease-rental bond A long-term state or municipal obligation, the proceeds of which are used to finance public-purpose projects such as police stations and public office buildings. Debt service, along with maintenance and operational expenses, is covered by rental or lease payments from the facilities, although some bonds are also general obligations of the respective issuers.

leave of absence An employer-approved extended absence from work without loss of employment standing. A company may offer leaves of absence for a variety of reasons, including medical conditions, conducting research, completing education programs, or undertaking charitable activities. Leaves may be with full pay, partial pay, or no pay.

ledger In accounting, the book in which financial transactions are classified and summarized for use in preparing an entity's financial statements.

legacy **1.** Assets bequeathed by will. **2.** Of, describing, or being an antiquated computer or software system that continues to be utilized because of the expense of replacement.

legacy cost The financial expense of supporting retiree benefits, including pensions, heath care, and insurance. Legacy cost is especially burdensome for mature and once vibrant companies that suffer declining markets and a shrinking labor force.

legal —See LEGAL INVESTMENT.

legal age The age at which a person legally becomes an adult and assumes all the rights and responsibilities thereof. This includes the right to enter into a contract and the responsibility to live up to its conditions. —Also called *majority*.

legal assistant —See PARALEGAL.

legal capital Capital that by law or resolution must remain within a firm and that is restricted for purposes of dividends or other distributions. Legal capital is generally equal to the par or stated value of all outstanding stock. —Also called *stated capital.*

legal description A geographical description of a real estate parcel in sufficient detail that it can be used for legal transactions. The description must include any existing easements.

legal entity A person, business, trust, or organization that has the legal standing to enter into a contract, take on an obligation, and assume responsibility for its actions. A legal entity such as a corporation has an identity separate from its owners.

legalese Language used by lawyers and in legal documents that ordinary people have difficulty understanding.

Legal Exchange Information Service (LEXIS) —See LEXISNEXIS.

legal expense insurance Insurance coverage that provides legal services or reimbursement for specified legal expenses incurred in defending or pursuing civil actions.

legal incapacity Legal declaration that an individual is unable to properly manage his or her affairs.

legal investment An investment that is eligible for purchase by a fiduciary. —Also called *legal; statutory investment.*

legal list The list of securities designated eligible as investments by institutions such as life insurance companies, restricted trust funds, and commercial banks. Such lists are generally limited to relatively high-grade securities of issuers exhibiting little chance of default. —Also called *approved list.*

legal list state A state with laws that restrict investment of certain funds to only those securities included in a legal list.

legal monopoly A person, firm, or organization that has a government-approved right to offer a service or product within a particular geographical area. For example, a patent gives the holder the exclusive right to distribute a particular product. Likewise, an electric utility generally holds a legal monopoly within a specified territory.

legal opinion 1. Explanation by a judge or group of judges of a decision rendered by the court. **2.** An official statement by an attorney with regard to what is legal. **3.** The statement of a bond counsel that a municipal bond issue is legal under the laws and restrictions of the issuing jurisdiction, and which indicates whether interest on the bonds is exempt from federal income taxes. A legal opinion is generally necessary to bring an issue to market. —See also EX-LEGAL.

legal representative A person with official standing to act on behalf of an entity or another person. For example, an adult child may have a power of attorney and serve as the legal representative of an elderly parent.

legal reserves —See RESERVES 2.

legal tender The coins and currency of a country that are legally acceptable for the payment of debts and as a medium of exchange. —Also called *tender¹.*

legal title Ownership of an asset that is legally recognized.

legal transfer 1. An asset assignment that is recognized by law. **2.** The transfer of a registered security when more than an endorsed bond or stock power is required for legal change of ownership. For example, transfer of securities registered to a deceased person usually requires submission of a death certificate.

legatee A person who receives property by means of a will.

lemon A poorly performing product or investment. Many technology stocks became lemons during the 2000 and 2001 bear market.

lender —See CREDITOR.

lender liability The legal obligation of a financial institution to make available funds that have been promised to a loan applicant and, once funds have been made available, to abide by the terms of a loan agreement. Failure to abide by the promise of funds or the terms of a loan opens the creditor to legal action by the borrower.

less developed country (LDC) A country with relatively low per capita income and little industrialization.

lessee A party using under lease an asset owned by another party. —Compare LESSOR.

lessor The owner of an asset who permits another party to use the asset under a lease. —Compare LESSEE.

less than carload Of or referring to a shipment that does not meet the minimize size to qualify for favorable freight rates applicable to carload lots. The term has historically applied to railroad freight, although it is sometimes used for any type of transportation, including trucks.

let To lease or rent. For example, a homeowner near a college campus may let rooms to students.

letter bond —See RESTRICTED SECURITY.

letter of credit (LOC) A promise of payment in the event that certain requirements are met. A letter of credit essentially substitutes the credit of a third party (usually a large bank) for that of a borrower.

letter of guarantee A letter from a bank stating that a customer owns a particular security and that the bank will guarantee delivery of the security. A letter of guarantee is used by an investor who is writing call options when the underlying stock is not in his or her brokerage account.

letter of intent 1. Written notice of an interest in entering into a contract or merger. For example, a pharmaceutical company issues a letter of intent confirming an exclusive licensing agreement with another firm. A letter of intent may or may not be binding, depending on its content and wording. **2.** An agreement by a mutual fund shareholder to invest a specific sum over a defined period in order to qualify for reduced sales fees. The reduced fee may apply to an individual fund or to all the funds operated by an investment management group. —Compare BREAKPOINT 1. —See also RIGHT OF ACCUMULATION.

letter ruling —See REVENUE RULING.

letter security —See RESTRICTED SECURITY.

lettershop A business that personalizes and prepares mailings according to U.S. Postal Service regulations. A lettershop typically performs services such as personalized printing, labeling, folding, sealing, sorting, and delivery to the appropriate transportation service.

letter stock —See RESTRICTED SECURITY.

level-load fund A mutual fund that charges a relatively high 12b–1 fee.

level-payment mortgage A self-amortizing real estate loan with fixed periodic payments. A portion of each payment covers interest, and the remainder reduces the outstanding principal of the loan.

level playing field An environment in which all participants operate under the same rules.

level-premium insurance A life insurance policy with fixed premium payments during the duration of the contract. Whole life policies that build cash values have level premiums. Term insurance typically has premiums that increase over time, although some policies guarantee level premiums for limited periods.

leverage The use of fixed costs in order to increase the rate of return from an investment. One example of leverage is a company using debt financing to pay for an expansion of its operations. Even greater leverage is created when a company issues debt in order to raise funds that are used to repurchase stock. While leverage can operate to increase rates of return, it also increases the amount of risk inherent in an investment, for both individuals and businesses. —Compare DELEVERAGE. —See also FINANCIAL LEVERAGE; OPERATING LEVERAGE.

> **CASE STUDY** Corporate managers sometimes decide owners would benefit financially if borrowed funds were used to repurchase shares of the company's stock. Substituting debt for equity increases leverage and results in more risk to both borrowers and owners. On the positive side, the increased leverage may increase the return the firm is able to earn on the shareholders' investment. International Business Machines (IBM) announced in April 2007 that it would increase its dividend by 33% and repurchase $15 billion of its

own stock. With over 1.5 billion shares outstanding, the quarterly dividend alone would amount to over $600 million. The $15 billion stock repurchase was in addition to another $1.4 billion that remained from an earlier repurchase authorization. The firm planned to finance much of the stock buyback with borrowing because at the time of the announcement IBM had only $10.8 billion in cash, much less than required for both the dividend and authorized stock repurchase. The stock buyback was expected to increase the firm's earnings per share, but Fitch Ratings said the increased leverage would cause them to place IBM debt on "Watch Negative," indicating the possibility of a future downgrading of the firm's debt. Thus, increased leverage resulting from the stock buyback financed largely with debt financing appeared to benefit the firm's shareholders but harm its existing creditors, who would experience a deterioration in their claims against the firm.

leveraged Of, relating to, or being an investment situation for which borrowed funds are used. A highly leveraged investor or firm is in a relatively risky position if interest rates rise or if the investment yields are disappointingly low.

leveraged buyout (LBO) The use of a target company's asset value to finance most or all of the debt incurred in acquiring the company. This strategy enables a takeover to be accomplished with little capital; however, it can result in considerably more risk to owners and creditors. —See also HOSTILE LEVERAGED BUYOUT; REVERSE LEVERAGED BUYOUT.

leveraged company A company that uses borrowed money to help finance its assets. Leveraged companies often have more volatile earnings than firms that rely solely on equity financing. This volatility is offset, however, by the possibility of a higher return to stockholders if the firm is able to earn more on its assets than the cost of the money used to finance those assets.

leveraged ESOP An employee stock ownership plan that borrows funds to purchase securities of the employer.

leveraged investment company **1.** An investment company that uses borrowed money to acquire securities. Leveraged investment companies produce more volatile returns for their shareholders than do investment companies not using debt financing. **2.** —See DUAL PURPOSE FUND.

leveraged lease A long-term lease in which a major part of the purchase price of the to-be-leased asset is financed by a third party. Thus, the lessor uses a combination of its own funds and borrowed money in order to purchase the asset that is then leased to another party. —Compare DIRECT FINANCING LEASE.

leveraged loan Credit extended to a less-than-investment-grade borrower. For example, a bank provides a short-term loan to temporarily finance a corporate buyout, with repayment of the loan to take place when permanent financing is in place. Leveraged loans are relatively risky for the lender, who is compensated with a higher interest rate.

leveraged recapitalization A corporate reorganization in which borrowed funds are used to pay a large one-time dividend to shareholders. The result is a company with greater financial risk because of increased debt and reduced equity. In some instances the dividend is paid in shares of stock rather than cash to inside shareholders, who increase their proportional ownership and control.

leverage up To increase the portion of debt in a firm's capital structure by issuing debt and using the proceeds to repurchase stock, or by financing any new expansion through debt. Firms generally decide to leverage up in an attempt to improve the market price of their stock, thereby fending off takeover attempts.

levy¹ An assessment or charge.

levy² To assess. For example, the city commission voted to levy a tax on pets.

LexisNexis An online subscription service for legal research (Lexis) combined with an extensive database of news and business information (Nexis).

liability 1. An obligation to pay to another party an amount in money, goods, or services. The balance sheet of a business lists its liabilities. —Compare ASSET. —Also called *debt*. —See also CONTINGENT LIABILITY; CURRENT LIABILITY. **2.** An obligation or duty to perform some act. For example, a new employee has a liability to his or her employer.

liability dividend A dividend paid with a type of debt, such as a bond. Liability dividends are usually paid when a firm is short of cash. —Compare SCRIP DIVIDEND. —See also BOND DIVIDEND.

liability insurance Insurance coverage for what someone is legally obligated to pay as a result of causing property damage or personal injury to someone else. Liability coverage is included as a component of homeowner's policies and automobile policies, although many individuals choose to purchase additional coverage. Liability insurance is also available to businesses. —See also UMBRELLA LIABILITY INSURANCE.

liable Legally responsible or obligated.

libel False and malicious material that is published or broadcast and damages a person's reputation. —See also SLANDER.

LIBOR —See LONDON INTERBANK OFFERED RATE.

library rate A special mailing rate offered by the U.S. Postal Service for qualifying institutions such as libraries, universities, zoos, and research institutions mailing educational and research materials. —See also MEDIA RATE.

license An official document that allows a person to own something or perform some act. For example, a person must have a state-issued driver's license and a state-issued license plate in order to legally drive a vehicle on a public road.

license bond A document that guarantees a person or business will comply with all government requirements. For example, a contractor license bond guarantees the contractor has all required licenses and will meet any government-mandated requirements.

licensed appraiser An appraiser who is certified by a state licensing agency. States often offer licensing at different levels or for different specialties.

licensing A contractual arrangement in which the legal owner grants another permission to use intellectual property such as a brand. For example, a well-known regional real estate firm may reach a licensing agreement for another company to use the firm's brand name in a different region of the country.

lien The legal right of a creditor to sell mortgaged assets when the debtor is unable or unwilling to meet requirements of a loan agreement. A lien makes a lender's claim more secure.

lienholder A person or other entity that holds a legal claim on real property owned by someone else who owes a debt to the lienholder.

lien-theory state A state in which the buyer of property holds the deed, and the mortgage held by the lender becomes a lien that is removed when the loan is fully repaid. —Compare TITLE-THEORY STATE.

life annuity A stream of payments intended to continue during the annuitant's lifetime and to cease automatically at the annuitant's death.

life beneficiary A person named by a will or trust to receive benefits for the person's lifetime.

life cycle The progression of a business or product as it moves through successive stages from origin to eventual decline. Stages of a life cycle typically include conception, rapid growth, expansion, maturity, and decline. —Also called *product life cycle.*

lifecycle fund A mutual fund holding a portfolio of other mutual fund shares managed according to a specified target date. A lifecycle fund moves toward a more conservative mix (a larger proportion of bonds and smaller proportion of stocks) as the target date is approached. These funds are designed to appeal to individuals who wish to invest for retirement and have some idea of when the retirement will occur. Mutual fund families generally offer a number of lifecycle funds with target dates in five-year intervals. —Also called *target fund; target-retirement fund.*

CASE STUDY A lifecycle fund holds the shares of other mutual funds and is sometimes described as a fund of funds. Rather than purchase shares of General Motors, Intel, and Google, a lifecycle fund purchases shares of stock and bond mutual funds. The appropriate portfolio composition of fund shares is determined by the fund's target date, which represents the year near when most of its shareholders expect to retire. A lifecycle fund with a distant target date can experience large fluctuations in share value because it holds a portfolio that is heavily weighted with stocks. The portfolio of a lifecycle fund is managed to gradually become more conservative (more heavily weighted with bonds) and less volatile as the target date grows closer. A lifecycle fund can be viewed as a kind of "one-stop" investment vehicle for a person's retirement needs because the composition of the portfolio gradually evolves as the stockholder grows older and nearer retirement. A look at the portfolios of three lifecycle funds operated by TIAA-CREF illustrates how the portfolio composition varies according to target date.

	Years to Target Date of Lifecycle Fund		
	Less than 5 Years	Approximately 10 Years	Approximately 30 Years
Underlying Fund Class			
Domestic equity	41.1%	53.1%	67.5%
International equity	13.7	17.7	22.5
Long-term fixed income	39.4	28.4	10.0
Short-term fixed income	5.8	0.8	0.0
Total	100.0%	100.0%	100.0%

life estate The right of someone to utilize real property for his or her lifetime. For example, a person might give his or her spouse a life estate to a home that would otherwise legally pass to a child at the death of the spouse.

life expectancy A statistical measure of the number of years a person is expected to live. Life expectancy is utilized in many business decisions, including establishing premiums for life insurance and retirement annuities.

life insurance A contract between a life insurance company and the policyholder that pays a stated amount of money to beneficiaries on the death of the insured. —See also CASH-VALUE LIFE INSURANCE; TERM INSURANCE.

life of contract In futures or options trading, the period of time in which trading can occur before the expiration or settlement. In general, a longer life makes an option more valuable.

life settlement The purchase of a relatively healthy person's life insurance policy by a third party for a percentage of the policy's face value. The amount paid depends on the size of the policy and the length of time the policyholder is expected to live. The party that purchases the policy begins paying the premiums at the time of purchase and collects the death benefits when the insured dies. A life settlement differs from a viatical settlement, in which the insured person is terminally ill or has a life-threatening illness.

lifestyle business A small commercial enterprise operated more for the owner's enjoyment and satisfaction than for the profit it earns. For example, a person who enjoys working with stained glass might open a small shop in which she offers classes along with selling materials and her completed work.

life tenant A person entitled to the use of or the income from an asset during his or her lifetime. As an example, a person may stipulate in a will that all of his or her assets are to go to a charity, but that the surviving spouse, designated as life tenant, is to have the use of the income from the deceased's estate for his or her lifetime, following which the remainder of the assets in the estate are to pass to the charity.

lifetime customer value —See CUSTOMER LIFETIME VALUE.

lifetime security The expectation that employment with a company will last until the employee's voluntary retirement.

LIFO —See LAST-IN, FIRST-OUT.

lighten up To reduce, but not eliminate, a particular security position when the investor feels that the security constitutes too much of the portfolio's total value, or when the investor is feeling less bullish on the security. In either case, a residual position in the security is maintained.

light industry An industry that generally requires modest capital investment and uses skilled employees to produce small, high-value products. Electronics companies often fall into the category of light industry. —Compare HEAVY INDUSTRY.

like-kind exchange The sale of real or personal business property when proceeds are invested in property of a similar nature. Under IRS Code Section 1031, like-kind exchanges result in a deferral of capital gains taxes. —Also called *tax-deferred exchange*. —See also SECTION 1031.

like-kind property Investment assets that are similar in nature and can be exchanged without an immediate tax consequence. The definition of like-kind property is fairly broad for real property but more narrowly defined for personal property of a business.

limited company (Ltd.) A firm registered in such a manner as to give its owners limited liability. Limited companies are most often associated with British registration, much as incorporated firms are primarily associated with U.S. registration.

limited distribution Sale of a product within a particular geographic region or through specific stores or companies. For example, a manufacturer might initially limit the distribution of a new battery to a single retail chain.

limited equity cooperative A cooperative housing complex designed for low-income families who become owners and share in management decisions, but are limited in profits that can be earned on resale. The limits on resale profits help maintain a low price for subsequent owners.

limited liability The liability of a firm's owners for no more capital than they have invested in the business. Essentially, the legal separation of ownership and liability means that a stockholder can lose no more than he or she has paid for the shares of ownership, regardless of the firm's financial obligations. Limited liability is one of the major advantages of organizing a business as a corporation. —Compare UNLIMITED LIABILITY.

limited liability company (LLC) A company formed as a combination partnership/corporation in which profits of the business pass through and are taxable to the owners, who are shielded from personal liability.

limited occupancy agreement An arrangement between a seller of real estate and a prospective buyer that permits the prospective buyer to gain temporary use of the property prior to closing the sale.

limited partner Part owner of a limited partnership whose liability is limited to funds the partner has invested in the business.

limited partnership A partnership in which some of the partners have a limited liability to the firm's creditors. —Compare GENERAL PARTNERSHIP. —See also PUBLIC LIMITED PARTNERSHIP; ROLL-UP.

limited-voting stock A class of stock that provides its holders with smaller than proportionate voting rights in comparison with another class of stock issued by the same firm. Limited-voting shares allow another class of stock effectively to control the election of a firm's directors, even though the limited-voting shareholders may have contributed a majority of the firm's equity capital. —Compare SUPERVOTING STOCK.

limited warranty A product guarantee that includes restrictions. For example, a computer manufacturer may offer a warranty on parts for three years, but restrict the warranty on labor to 90 days.

limit move The maximum price change in a commodity futures contract permitted during a single trading session.

limit order An order to execute a transaction only at a specified price (the limit) or better. A limit order to buy would be at the limit or lower, and a limit order to sell would be at the limit or higher. Investors use limit orders when they have decided on the price at which they are willing to trade. —Compare MARKET ORDER. —See also STOP ORDER 1.

limit price The price specified by an investor for a limit order. With a limit order to buy, the price represents the highest price the investor will pay. The price of a limit order to sell represents the lowest price the investor will accept.

line 1. A class of products produced or sold by a company. For example, an appliance company offers a line of refrigerators. **2.** A production or assembly line: *He works on the line where final assembly takes place.* **3.** A relationship in an organization in which one person has responsibility for another.

line and staff An organizational authority structure in which line managers make decisions and take actions that are supported by staff managers.

linear programming A mathematical technique to determine an optimum solution to a problem with many variables that are subject to constraints. Linear programming

line of credit

I am considering opening a line of credit for my business. What kinds of expenses are involved? For example, will I incur a charge even when I have no need for borrowed funds?

In addition to the interest expense charged on any drawn portion of the line of credit, most borrowers will incur costs related to legal and documentation fees, commitment fees paid to the lender at the time of closing, and fees paid throughout the life of the facility on the average unused portion of the line, often referred to as an unused fee. However, the unused fee is a fraction of the stated interest expense on the line.

Lines of credit that are viewed as being highly dependent on the value of the assets securing the facility will often have fees related to the monitoring of the collateral. Some states have certain tax costs associated with loans as well (for example, Florida has documentary stamp fees). If the facility is too large for one lender to facilitate, a syndicate of lenders may be formed to provide the capital. In this instance the borrower would incur arrangement and syndication fees.

■ Brooke Barber, Vice President, Middle Market Banking, Atlanta, GA

---

is utilized in manufacturing decisions to minimize costs and on Wall Street to maximize portfolio returns.

line extension A new product from a company that already markets a similar product. For example, General Mills, manufacturer of Cheerios, extended the brand with seven new varieties, including Honey Nut Cheerios, Apple Cinnamon Cheerios, Berry Burst Cheerios, and so forth. —Also called *flanker brand.*

line manager An employee who manages the day-to-day activities of a group of workers. For example, the senior flight attendant is the line manager of an airplane's cabin crew.

line-of-business reporting —See SEGMENT REPORTING.

line of credit A credit arrangement in which a financial institution agrees to lend money to a customer up to a specified limit. A line of credit, generally arranged before the funds are actually required, provides flexibility for the customer in that it ensures the ability to meet short-term cash needs as they arise. —Compare CLOSED-END CREDIT. —Also called *bank line; credit line; open-end credit; revolver; revolving credit agreement.*

liquid 1. Of, relating to, or being an asset that may be bought or sold in a short period of time with relatively small price changes engendered by the transaction. A U.S. Treasury bill is an example of a very liquid asset. —Compare ILLIQUID 1. **2.** Of, relating to, or being an investment position in which most of the assets are in money or near money. This kind of position generally earns a relatively low return, but allows the company or investor to pay debts and take advantage of other investment opportunities.

liquidate 1. To repay a debt. **2.** To sell a firm's assets and pay off its debts.

liquidate a position To sell all of a particular type of asset. For example, a portfolio manager might decide to liquidate a position in a stock by selling all the shares of that stock held in the portfolio.

liquidated damages The amount agreed upon that will be paid by one party to the other in the event a contract is violated. For example, a contractor may be required to pay liquidated damages in the event a project is not completed by a stipulated date.

liquidated debt Debt that is certain as to amount.

liquidating dividend A pro rata distribution of cash or property to stockholders as part of the dissolution of a business. For example, a firm may be liquidated because the officers believe its stock price does not adequately reflect the value of its assets. All debts and other obligations usually must be satisfied before issuance of a final liquidating dividend. —See also FINAL DIVIDEND 1.

liquidating partner The member responsible for selling and distributing assets and settling debts in a partnership that is in the process of liquidation.

liquidating value The estimated value of a firm in the event that its assets are sold and its debts paid. This value is often stated on a per-share basis so as to indicate some kind of minimum value for a given share of the stock. Liquidating value above the stock's market price indicates the firm is worth more dead than alive.

liquidation 1. The conversion of assets into cash. Just as a company may liquidate an entire subsidiary by selling it to another firm, so too may an investor liquidate by selling a particular type of security. 2. The paying of a debt. 3. The selling of assets and the paying of liabilities in anticipation of going out of business.

liquidity A large position in cash or in assets that are easily convertible to cash. High liquidity produces flexibility for a firm or an investor in a low-risk position, but it also tends to decrease profitability.

liquidity diversification —See LADDERING.

liquidity preference The preference of individuals and organizations to hold wealth in liquid form (cash or savings accounts). Liquidity will be surrendered only when accompanied by higher returns for holding nonliquid assets. Economist John Maynard Keynes cited the combination of liquidity preference and low interest rates to partially explain the lack of investment spending during the extended depression of the 1930s.

liquidity premium The extra return demanded by investors as compensation for holding assets that may be difficult to convert into cash. For example, bonds that seldom trade should offer a higher yield to maturity compared to actively traded bonds of similar maturity and credit risk.

liquidity ratio 1. A measure of a company's ability to meet its short-term obligations achieved through a comparison of financial variables. —See also CURRENT RATIO; QUICK RATIO; WORKING CAPITAL. 2. The value of the trading activity in a stock that is required to change the stock's price by 1%. A high ratio indicates the stock has considerable liquidity. A stock's liquidity ratio is of primary importance to institutions and traders that deal in large volume and that wish to avoid securities with a lack of liquidity.

liquidity risk The risk of having difficulty in liquidating an investment position without taking a significant discount from current market value. Liquidity risk can be a significant problem with collectibles, precious stones, and lightly traded securities. —Also called *marketability risk.*

liquidity trap An economic condition in which interest rate reductions by monetary authorities are ineffective in stimulating economic activity. In this circumstance, individuals, financial institutions, and other businesses become so risk averse they choose to increase liquidity rather than spend and invest.

lis pendens A pending lawsuit, often with regard to real property. A lis pendens for real estate may indicate a question about the property's title.

list **1.** To admit a security for trading on an organized exchange. In order to be listed, the security and the issuer must meet certain minimal standards established by the exchange. These standards may relate to assets, earnings, market value, and stock voting rights. —Compare DELIST. **2.** To place real estate with a broker to sell.

list broker A business that sells listings of sales prospects.

listed property **1.** Certain kinds of business assets, including cars, cell phones, computers, and entertainment equipment, that are subject to special rules of depreciation. Listed-property business use must exceed 50% to qualify for expensing or accelerated depreciation. **2.** Real estate that the owner has listed for sale with a real estate broker.

listed security A security traded on any of the national or regional securities exchanges. Listed securities are generally more liquid than securities that trade only in the over-the-counter market. —Compare UNLISTED SECURITY. —Also called *exchange-traded security.*

listing **1.** Property for sale by a broker. **2.** An agreement between a property owner and a broker to sell a property.

listing requirements Requisites of a firm and the firm's security before the security can be listed for trading on an exchange. Each exchange has its own listing requirements, covering things such as the minimum shares outstanding, the number of shareholders, and the earnings history.

list price The price suggested by the manufacturer and included in catalogs and price schedules. List price is often subject to discounts.

litigant A participant, either plaintiff or defendant, involved in a lawsuit.

litigation The process of pursuing a lawsuit.

live postage The use of postage stamps as opposed to a postage meter or other imprint. Some marketing professionals believe an advertisement with live postage may gain more attention from the recipient.

living benefits Accelerated payments to a life insurance policyholder who is terminally ill. Qualifications for receiving living benefits vary among insurance companies.

living trust A trust created for the trustor and administered by another party during the trustor's lifetime. The living trust may be formed because the trustor is either incapable of managing or unwilling to manage his or her assets. The trust can be revocable or irrevocable, depending on the trustor's wishes. —Also called *inter vivos trust.*

living will A written document in which a person indicates the type of medical treatment that is desired. For example, a living will might specify that no life-sustaining measures be used to prolong a terminal condition.

LLC —See LIMITED LIABILITY COMPANY.

Lloyd's of London A specialist insurance association in which members, including individuals, companies, and partnerships, accept insurance business worldwide through syndicates for their own profit and loss.

load The sales fee the buyer pays in order to acquire an asset. This fee varies according to the type of asset and the way it is sold. Many mutual funds impose a sales charge. As a result of the load, only a portion of the investor's funds go into the investment itself. —Also called *front-end load; sales charge; sales load.*

load fund A mutual fund with shares sold at a price that includes a sales charge—typically 4% to 6% of the net amount invested. Thus, load funds are sold at a price exceeding net asset value, but they are redeemed at net asset value. —See also LOAD; LOW-LOAD FUND; NO-LOAD FUND.

load spread option The allocation of sales charges on mutual fund shares purchased on a contractual plan over a period of years. Sales charges may amount to as much as 20% of any single year's payments during the first four years, provided the total charges for the four years do not exceed 64% of any single year's payments. Also, the total sales charge cannot exceed 9% of contributions of the total value of the contract.

loan A temporary transfer of money or some other asset by a lender to a borrower with a promise of repayment or return to the lender on a specific date. Most loans include a requirement of payment for use of the money or borrowed asset.

loan amortization —See AMORTIZATION.

loan closing —See CLOSING 1.

loan commitment A statement by a lender of the terms under which it will make available a sum of money at some point in the future. For example, a bank enters into a loan commitment with a customer to extend a mortgage loan at a specified rate. —Also called *standby loan commitment.*

loan origination fee A charge by a lender to a borrower for the privilege of obtaining a loan. Origination fees are generally in the form of points that are paid up front in cash. Each point represents 1% of the amount borrowed. —Also called *mortgage discount; points.* —See also OVERAGE 3.

loan portfolio Loans that have been made or bought and are being held for repayment. Loan portfolios are the major asset of banks, thrifts, and other lending institutions. The value of a loan portfolio depends not only on the interest rates earned on the loans, but also on their quality, that is, the likelihood that interest and principal will be paid.

loan-to-value ratio The dollar amount of a loan as a percent of the purchase price or appraised value of the asset being purchased and used as collateral. A high ratio entails greater risk to the lender.

loan value 1. The amount that can be borrowed on a cash-value life insurance policy. **2.** The maximum amount that may be borrowed using a specific asset as collateral. The Federal Reserve specifies the loan value for securities purchased on margin.

lobbyist A person who is compensated for attempting to influence the opinions and decisions of government policymakers and legislators.

LOC —See LETTER OF CREDIT.

local The local branch of a labor union.

local area network (LAN) A group of computers, printers, and associated devices that are interconnected with a common link, generally with a single server. —Compare WIDE AREA NETWORK.

lockbox 1. A service offered by a commercial bank that collects and immediately gives credit for customer payments made to a business client. The business directs its customers to send payments to a post office box that is checked on a regular basis by the bank providing the service. The lockbox service is a cash-management system that allows a business to more quickly gain access to payments received from its customers. **2.** A small box containing an entry key to a home being offered for sale. The box is placed on the front door and is accessible by real estate agents who have a key or combination to the lockbox.

lockdown A prohibition against a firm's employees making changes in the asset composition of their retirement plan. Corporate officials may lock down a retirement plan during a period of administrative changes in the plan. —Also called *blackout period; quiet period.*

locked in **1.** Describing the situation of having a large paper, or unrealized, profit in a security position, with the result being that sale of the security would engender substantial taxation. **2.** Describing the position of a commodities trader when the price of a contract has moved the daily limit and contracts in the commodity cannot be bought or sold.

locked-in interest rate A binding commitment from a lender for a loan at a specified interest rate. The rate guarantee lasts for a fixed period of time, generally 30 to 60 days from the date of the loan application.

locked market A somewhat unusual occurrence in which the bid price and ask price for a security are equal.

lock in To guarantee, as a return or cost. For example, an investor who purchases a noncallable 10% coupon Treasury bond at par locks in a return of 10% annually until the bond matures. The Treasury also locks in a 10% cost for the funds raised through the sale of this bond issue.

lock-in amendment An amendment to a corporate charter that makes it more difficult to void previously approved amendments. For example, a lock-in amendment may require a 60% approval vote to change an existing antitakeover amendment.

lock-in period The time during which a lender guarantees an interest rate to a borrower.

lockout Action by management to prevent employees from entering the workplace and performing their jobs until agreement is reached on a labor dispute. For example, in 2004 the National Hockey League locked out its players for the entire season after labor negotiations ended in a deadlock.

lockup agreement A contractual offer of valuable assets or stock made by a takeover target to the suitor deemed most acceptable to management. A lockup agreement tends to discourage unwanted suitors, but it may penalize the target firm's stockholders because it eliminates counteroffers. —Also called *crown jewel lockup agreement; no-shop provision.*

CASE STUDY Shortly after turning down an acquisition offer for the company, the board of Revlon was faced with a hostile tender offer from the same firm. Pantry Pride offered $47.50 per share, contingent on the Revlon board inactivating a poison pill that would substantially increase the firm's debt in the event an unwanted suitor acquired 20% or more of Revlon's outstanding stock. Pantry Pride filed a lawsuit to invalidate the poison pill and quickly increased its offering price to $56.25 per share. To thwart the Pantry Pride offer, the Revlon board issued substantial amounts of new debt and negotiated a buyout agreement for $57.25 per share with its own management in conjunction with another firm. To kill a Pantry Pride acquisition, Revlon agreed to a lockup agreement that would allow the favored buyer (Forstmann Little & Co.) to purchase two subsidiaries at a bargain price in the event another acquirer (Pantry Pride) acquired 40% of Revlon's outstanding stock.

> The lockup agreement meant that a successful Pantry Pride offer would result in the firm acquiring a much depleted company. Pantry Pride raised its own offer to $58 per share and filed a lawsuit claiming the lockup agreement violated Revlon's fiduciary duty to its shareholders. The court concurred, ruling that after agreeing to sell the firm, Revlon's board had an obligation to its shareholders to obtain the highest possible price.

lockup period The time during which employees and other early investors are prohibited from selling stock in a newly listed company. Investment banks that bring the securities to market establish lockup periods to protect investors in a new issue from large insider selling that can have a major price impact because of a relatively small number of shares available for trading. Lockup periods are usually 180 days from the date of the initial public offering.

logical incrementalism A management philosophy of achieving broad organizational goals by making strategic decisions in small steps. The small steps attempt to resolve conflicting views of participants and reduce risk by capitalizing on knowledge that is gained during the process. Logical incrementalism benefits from flexibility, but is likely to be time-consuming and inefficient.

logistics The planning and managing of the flow of goods, services, and people to a destination. For example, military logistics require moving troops, equipment, and supplies to a combat area.

logo A unique name or graphic design that is identified with an organization or product. For example, the unique Kellogg's script is a logo that easily identifies the firm's products.

London Interbank Offered Rate (LIBOR) The basic short-term rate of interest in the Eurodollar market, and the rate to which many Eurodollar loans and deposits are tied. The LIBOR is similar in concept to that of the prime rate in the United States, except that it is less subject to individual bank management. —Also called *interbank rate.*

London Stock Exchange (LSE) The United Kingdom's largest equity exchange that provides a market for stocks, bonds, and depositary receipts of U.K. and foreign companies. The London Stock Exchange became a publicly traded corporation in 2000.

long —See LONG POSITION 1.

long bond A debt security with a relatively long period remaining until maturity. —Compare SHORT BOND. —Also called *long coupon.*

long coupon **1.** A bond coupon payment representing more than six months of interest. The first coupon of a bond is often for a larger than normal amount because it represents more than six months of interest. **2.** —See LONG BOND.

longevity insurance A financial product that is a combination of a deferred annuity and an immediate annuity. Like a deferred annuity, longevity insurance pays a lifetime income beginning at a specified age. Like an immediate annuity, payments to be received are determined at the time of the investment. For example, an individual might purchase longevity insurance that pays $5,000 per month beginning at age 80. Longevity insurance offers no death benefit and is designed for individuals who expect to live a long life but are concerned they will run out of money.

longevity pay Employee pay based on years of service with the employer. For example, a major state university offers staff employees an annual supplement equal to $50 times the employee's years of service.

longitudinal data Identical data observed over multiple time periods. Monthly data for the consumer price index during the last 20 years is an example of longitudinal data.

long position 1. The net ownership position of a particular security. For example, if an investor owns 500 shares of Wal-Mart common stock, that person is said to be long 500 shares of Wal-Mart. Likewise, the more unusual situation of owning 1,000 shares of a particular stock at a time when 300 shares of the same stock have been sold short produces a long position of 700 shares. Being long indicates an expectation of rising share prices. —Compare SHORT POSITION 1. —Also called *long.* **2.** Net ownership of assets in a brokerage account.

long-range planning Establishing a plan to realize a goal or group of goals over a number of years based on current knowledge about the future. —Compare STRATEGIC PLANNING.

long run In economics, sufficient time for all inputs to be variable, and for firms to be able to enter or exit an industry. Economist John Maynard Keynes is quoted as having said, "In the long run we are all dead." This is one theory on which all economists seem to agree.

long-short fund An investment company that attempts to profit both from long positions in financial assets it considers undervalued and short positions in financial assets it feels are overvalued. For example, a fund may have long positions in stocks of energy companies and short positions in the stocks of financial institutions. Wise investment decisions by a long-short fund portfolio manager will result in the fund's shareholders making money in both up and down markets. Market-neutral funds are a type of long-short fund, but with relatively equal values of long and short positions. —See also MARKET-NEUTRAL FUND.

long-term 1. Of or relating to a gain or loss in the value of a security that has been held over a specific length of time. —Compare SHORT-TERM 1. —See also HOLDING PERIOD. **2.** Of or relating to a liability for which a long period of time (usually one year) remains until payment of the face amount comes due. A long-term bond is a long-term liability. **3.** Of or relating to a contract that is effective for a number of years, although the exact number varies by industry. In sports, for example, a 5-year contract may be considered long-term; for an electric utility, a contract for delivery of coal may last 20 years or more.

long-term capital gain/loss —See LONG-TERM 1.

long-term care Medical and/or social services for people with disabilities or chronic-care needs.

long-term equity anticipation securities (LEAPS) Options that carry expiration dates of up to two years.

long-term lease A lease of ten years or longer. Long-term leases are common in commercial real estate, but unusual in residential real estate.

lookback call (put) option A specialized option that gives its owner the right to purchase (sell) the underlying asset at the lowest (highest) price at which it traded between the effective date and the expiration date of the option. The added advantage of being able to look back makes this option command a relatively high premium.

loophole A flaw or ambiguity in a law or contract that allows someone to legally get around the intent. For example, politicians and political parties are often accused of

low-load fund

Should a low-load or no-load fund outperform a fund with a higher sales charge? If so, why doesn't everyone choose a fund with a low sales charge?

While it is wise to minimize fees and trading costs, it is best to start your search for the right investment without any blinders on. Develop a list of suitable choices and then compare performance net of fees and charges. All mutual funds charge some sort of recurring fee. Mutual funds are investment companies, and the fees they charge provide the revenue to run the company. Some mutual funds—such as no-load and level-load funds— internalize the fees they charge, while others—such as front-end load funds—externalize some of the fees by imposing a sales charge on the investor in addition to the internal management fees. If two mutual funds were exactly alike (two different share classes of the same fund strategy for example), and their performance and internal fees were exactly the same, then the one with the lower load would outperform the other. However, unless you are comparing two almost identical funds, I would not let the load be the sole deciding factor—the cheapest option is not necessarily the best value. With over 8,200 U.S.-based mutual funds to choose from, it is best to first identify quality managers that employ a sound investment process and then look for the least expensive way to participate.

■ Noah L. Myers, CFP®, Principal and Chief Investment Officer, MiddleCove Capital, Centerbrook, CT

taking advantage of loopholes in campaign finance laws. Similarly, businesses and individuals are constantly searching for tax loopholes.

loss The deficiency of the amount received as opposed to the amount invested in a transaction. —Compare GAIN. —See also CASUALTY LOSS; NET LOSS.

loss exposure The amount of potential monetary losses. For example, a person who lives in a $200,000 home and has no homeowner's insurance has a loss exposure of $200,000. The exposure can be reduced or eliminated by purchasing insurance (transferring the exposure) or selling the home. Many casualty insurance companies have reduced their loss exposure in Florida by not renewing homeowner's policies in the state.

loss leader An advertised product sold at below cost in an attempt to attract customers who will buy other, more profitable items. The hope is that losses from the loss leader will be more than offset by profits earned on sales of other items. Milk, sugar, and bread are often used as loss leaders by supermarkets.

loss of income insurance 1. —See BUSINESS INTERRUPTION INSURANCE. 2. —See DISABILITY INCOME INSURANCE.

loss ratio 1. In insurance, the ratio of claims paid to premiums received. A loss ratio of 1.25 results from paying $500,000 in claims while receiving only $400,000 in premiums. 2. In lending, the proportion of nonperforming loans in a loan portfolio.

lot The number of bonds or shares of stock in a single trade. —See also ODD LOT; ROUND LOT.

lot and block system A method of identifying a land parcel using the lot and block numbers of a subdivision plan.

lot line The surveyed boundary of a parcel of real estate.

lowball Of, relating to, or being an unrealistically low bid. —Compare PRICEY.

low-doc loan —See NO-DOC LOAN.

lower of cost or market A method for determining an asset's value such that either the original cost or the current replacement cost, whichever is lowest, is used for financial

lump-sum distribution

What are the tax implications of taking my retirement as a lump-sum distribution?

The tax implications of lump-sum distributions are extremely complex. First, let's clarify that the lump-sum distribution is from pension plans, profit-sharing plans, and stock-bonus plans and not from an IRA. The general rule is that you treat the entire amount as ordinary income in the year you receive the distribution. This (usually) large sum of money could push you into a higher tax bracket and reduce your deductions, due to the IRS's phase-out rules for personal exemptions and itemized deductions. Furthermore, you are subject to a 10% penalty tax on the distribution if you receive it when you are less than 59½ years old (or 55 years old in certain instances).

Taxpayers born before 1936 can compute their tax as if the lump-sum distribution were made evenly over ten years. One must use the 1986 single-payer tax rates in this instance. In addition, taxpayers born before 1936 can also elect to treat the pre-1974 portion of the lump-sum distribution as a capital gain, subject to a 20% tax rate.

The best advice regarding a lump-sum distribution is to roll it over into an IRA if at all possible. This will allow you to continue to defer income taxes until you make withdrawals from your IRA.

■ Peter M. Bergevin, PhD, Professor of Accounting, School of Business, University of Redlands, Redlands, CA

---

reporting purposes. For example, an inventory item originally purchased for $50 that has a current market value of $30 would appear on the firm's balance sheet at $30. The use of lower of cost or market is considered a conservative method of valuing assets.

low-grade 1. Of or relating to debt that has a credit rating of B or below. Low-grade debt offers an above-average yield, but entails substantial risk because promised payments may not be made in a timely manner. **2.** Of or relating to a product of inferior quality. For example, a diamond with flaws may be considered low-grade. Likewise, coal with a high sulfur content is considered low-grade.

low-load fund An open-end investment company with a sales charge ranging from 1% to 3% of the net amount invested by a shareholder, as opposed to charges of 4% to 6% typical of regular load funds and no charges on no-load funds.

low-price leader —See PRICE LEADER 2.

low tech Describing a product that utilizes a low level of technology, often developed many decades ago. A manual can opener purchased today that works in the same manner as one that was manufactured 30 years ago is an example of a low-tech product.

LSE —See LONDON STOCK EXCHANGE.

Ltd. —See LIMITED COMPANY.

lump-sum distribution With retirement plans, the disbursement of an individual's benefits in a single payment. A lump-sum distribution has important income-tax implications; therefore, the individual must investigate this option thoroughly before choosing a single payment.

lump-sum tax A fixed amount of tax paid by everyone regardless of income earned or assets owned. A lump-sum tax is efficient to administer and enjoys a high level of compliance, but is likely to be regarded as inequitable. A poll tax is an example of a lump-sum tax.

luxury tax An excise tax on nonessential goods. A luxury tax may be levied in order to reduce the consumption of a particular item (for example, big vehicles with poor fuel mileage) or to generate revenue (as with a tax on perfume).

■ M

M1 The most restrictive measure of the domestic money supply, which incorporates only money that is ordinarily used for spending on goods and services. M1 includes currency, checking account balances (including NOW accounts and credit union share draft accounts), and traveler's checks. Financial observers closely watch this money measure that is a key indicator of past and future Federal Reserve actions.

M2 A measure of the domestic money supply that includes M1 plus savings and time deposits, overnight repurchase agreements, and personal balances in money market accounts. Basically, M2 includes money that can be used for spending (M1) plus items that can be quickly converted to M1.

M3 A very broad measure of the domestic money supply that includes M2 items plus any large time deposits and money market fund balances held by institutions.

macaroni defense A defensive tactic against a hostile takeover in which the potential target company issues a large number of bonds that must be redeemed at a substantial premium to par in the event the company is taken over. The required redemption substantially expands the cost of a hostile takeover, just as macaroni expands when placed in boiling water.

machine readable Capable of being read or identified by a computer. Floppy disks and UPC bar codes on retail products are machine readable.

macro A sequence of computer commands or keystrokes that can be activated by a single keystroke or word. For example, a macro in a word processing program might input your name, address, phone number, and email address with a single keystroke.

macroeconomics The study of the economy as a whole. Macroeconomics examines topics such as business cycles, inflation, unemployment, balance of trade, and government fiscal policy of taxation and spending. —Compare MICROECONOMICS.

MACRS —See MODIFIED ACCELERATED COST RECOVERY SYSTEM.

Madison Avenue Of or referring to the advertising industry. The term derives from a street in New York City best known as the headquarters for major advertising firms.

mail fraud Illegal use of the U.S. Postal Service in a willful effort to defraud or obtain money or property under false pretenses. Investment scams promising vast riches are a common type of mail fraud.

mailing list 1. A group of people or email addresses on a distribution listing for periodic emails on a particular subject. 2. A listing of individuals, households, or postal addresses to receive direct-mail solicitations.

mail order An order for a good to be delivered via the U.S. Postal Service or another delivery company.

mail-order Of or referring to a business that utilizes an electronic or paper catalog to advertise merchandise and attract orders that are delivered to consumers via the U.S. Postal Service or another delivery company.

maintenance An activity to care for or repair assets such that they retain their value and continue to perform their intended purpose.

maintenance and replacement call A special provision of some bond indentures (especially those of utilities) that permits the borrower to pay off the issue (usually at par) before maturity if the collateral is replaced or disposed of.

maintenance bond A guarantee against defects for a specified period of time following completion of a contract.

maintenance call A call to an investor for additional funds when the market value of securities in the investor's margin account has fallen to the point that the investor's equity (that is, the value of the securities minus the amount owed) does not meet an established minimum. If the investor does not supply the required money or securities, the firm will sell a certain number of securities sufficient to bring the account into conformity. A maintenance call is a type of margin call.

maintenance fee 1. The fee charged by a financial institution to keep an investor's account. For example, some brokerage firms levy a maintenance fee on accounts that have been inactive during a year. Nearly all firms offering sweep accounts charge an annual maintenance fee. **2.** A periodic assessment by a homeowners' or condominium owners' association with funds utilized for common expenses including upkeep, repair, and insurance.

maintenance margin requirement The minimum equity in an account as a percentage of the value of the account. For example, if the maintenance requirement is 25%, the account equity (the market value of the securities minus the amount owed) must equal at least one-quarter the value of the securities in the account. The maintenance margin requirement becomes important when securities purchased on margin fall in price. —Also called *margin requirement; minimum maintenance.* —See also HOUSE MAINTENANCE REQUIREMENT; INITIAL MARGIN REQUIREMENT.

maintenance markup The minimum acceptable markup for a product after allowing for price reductions. For example, a product that costs a retailer $3.50 and has a maintenance markup of $.40 would not be marked down to less than $3.90.

maintenance of membership A labor contract stipulation that employees who are members of a union must continue their membership for the duration of the contract. The maintenance agreement does not require nonmembers to join.

majority The age at which an individual attains legal status as an adult.

majority-owned subsidiary A firm in which more than 50% of outstanding voting stock is owned by the parent company.

majority stockholder A single stockholder or a group of stockholders working in concert who control more than 50% of a corporation's voting stock. —Compare WORKING CONTROL.

majority voting A type of voting right in which stockholders are granted one vote for each director's position for each share held. Thus, the holder of 100 shares would have the right to cast 100 votes for each position for which an election is held. Under this system, any stockholder or group holding 51% of the shares voting is able to control every position up for election. —Compare CUMULATIVE VOTING. —Also called *statutory voting.*

major medical insurance Broad coverage that pays for a portion of expenses incurred due to sickness or injury, generally subject to an annual deductible and a lifetime maximum. Major medical insurance generally excludes cosmetic surgery, convalescent care, occupational injuries, physical examinations, and vision and dental care.

make a market To quote a bid price at which a security will be purchased and an ask price at which the security will be sold. An individual makes a market by quoting the prices at which he or she will buy and sell.

maker **1.** A person who signs a check or issues a promissory note. **2.** The manufacturer of a product.

make-whole call provision A stipulation in a bond indenture that permits the borrower to redeem a bond prior to maturity by making a lump-sum payment equal to the present value of future interest payments that will not be paid because of the early call. The provision makes the bondholder whole by providing compensation for interest payments that are missed because of an early redemption.

make-work Labor entailing token duties that contribute little to the employer.

mala fides —See BAD FAITH.

Malcolm Baldrige National Quality Award An annual award given by the President of the United States to organizations that apply and are judged to be outstanding in seven areas related to quality management and results. The award, named after a former secretary of commerce, was established in 1987 to enhance competitiveness through quality improvements. —Also called *Baldrige Award.*

malfeasance Performing an illegal act. For example, the treasurer of a civic organization diverts some of the organization's money to his personal bank account. —Compare MISFEASANCE; NONFEASANCE.

malicious mischief Deliberate vandalism of property. Spray painting graffiti on a building or intentionally causing a computer to malfunction are examples of malicious mischief.

malingerer An employee who avoids work by feigning illness.

mall A collection of retail establishments, generally under one roof. Large malls are organized with retail shops surrounding a common pedestrian area, with the shops, in turn, surrounded by a large parking area. *Strip malls* are characterized by a row of adjacent stores and restaurants that border a common parking lot. —Also called *shopping center.* —See also OUTLET MALL.

malpractice Failure of a professional person to abide by established standards of practice. Malpractice can occur intentionally, through negligence, or because of ignorance.

malpractice insurance Liability insurance coverage for doctors, lawyers, dentists, teachers, and other professionals against lawsuits claiming negligence in the performance of professional services.

manage To administer the affairs of an organization.

managed account An investment account that is managed by a broker or other professional. Managed accounts are designed for investors lacking the time, interest, or expertise to make their own decisions.

managed care A system to control the access and use of health care in a way that provides adequate services to a controlled group in a cost-efficient manner. Managed-care systems employ or contract with providers to deliver member services.

managed currency A currency whose value in relation to other currencies is intentionally influenced by government authorities. Many emerging market currencies are managed in order to stabilize their value and control their appreciation. —See also DIRTY FLOAT.

CASE STUDY Governments often choose to manage their currencies in an effort to gain a cost advantage in international trade. An artificially cheap currency stimulates exports and dampens imports, resulting in a stronger economy, domestic job growth, and an increase in international reserves. On the negative side, price inflation, asset bubbles, and higher interest rates may accompany a rapidly growing economy. Critics of China's economic policy claimed for years that the People's Bank of China maintained a policy of actively managing the yuan so that it was substantially undervalued relative to other major currencies, especially the dollar. The cheap yuan allowed the government to stimulate exports and domestic job growth. This resulted in huge trade surpluses with the United States that reached $177 billion in 2006. The mammoth U.S. trade deficit was accompanied by the loss of jobs and industrial capacity to China. Under pressure from U.S. businesses and government officials, the assistant governor of the Chinese central bank indicated in mid-2007 that the yuan would gradually become more flexible (decline in value) as the exchange rate was "managed in a rational and balanced manner."

managed earnings Corporate earnings that have been manipulated in order to produce a desired result. Earnings can be managed utilizing a variety of both acceptable and questionable accounting methods. For example, a company might time gains and losses from asset sales to produce steadily rising earnings.

managed economy —See COMMAND ECONOMY.

managed float —See DIRTY FLOAT.

management 1. The core decision-making personnel within an organization. **2.** Directing and coordinating resources in an attempt to attain a defined set of goals.

management accountant An accountant who records and analyzes financial information of the company for which he or she works. Management accountants analyze and interpret financial information that managers require for decision making. —Compare PUBLIC ACCOUNTANT. —Also called *private accountant.* —See also COST ACCOUNTING.

management audit A detailed audit that concentrates on analysis and evaluation of management procedures and the overall performance of an organization. A management audit is undertaken to discover weaknesses and to institute improvements within the organization. —Also called *operational audit; performance audit.*

management buyout —See GOING PRIVATE.

management by exception An organizational system in which managers intervene only when employees fail to meet performance standards or when plans or budgets go awry. Managers compare results with plans and take action when serious differences occur.

management by objectives A system in which managers and employees work together in order to reach a consensus on an organization's objectives. Employee performance is then periodically reviewed in relation to progress in meeting the identified objectives.

management company —See INVESTMENT COMPANY.

management consultant A qualified individual who offers independent management expertise to an organization. Management consultants are often hired to evaluate and offer suggestions for change in organizational structure or technology.

management by exception

What type of organization is best served by a policy of management by exception? It seems as if most managers would have difficulty implementing this type of policy.

All organizations can use management by exception. When routine work results in acceptable performance, no management attention is required. Managers who have properly trained their subordinates should have no problems delegating authority and allowing people to manage their own work. Managers are then able to devote their expertise and attention to nonroutine problems. Some managers have trouble allowing their subordinates to make decisions because of control issues, but this psychological barrier will hinder their careers.

■ Phyllis G. Holland, PhD, Professor and Head, Department of Management,
Langdale College of Business, Valdosta State University, Valdosta, GA

management discussion and analysis A section of a company's annual report that offers management's overview of the year's results along with a vague preview of the upcoming year, including likely developments and major projects.

management fee 1. The money paid to the managers of an investment company. The fee is generally based on a percentage of the net asset value of the fund, with the percentage becoming smaller as the fund's assets grow larger. Fees vary considerably among firms, but average about one-half of 1% of assets. A fund's management fee must be listed in its prospectus and can be found in a number of publications. —Also called *advisory fee.* **2.** The fee charged to manage commercial or residential real estate, generally stated as a percentage of rental income.

management information system (MIS) A formal structure, generally computerized, for collecting and analyzing information relevant to an organization's operations. Information systems are designed to provide managers with information that can be utilized to make better and more timely decisions.

management science Application of quantitative techniques such as linear programming and statistics to managerial decision making.

management style The particular practice used to direct an organization. For example, the leader of an organization may practice an authoritarian management style in which all directives come from the top. Other organizations may operate in a participatory manner that emphasizes group decision making.

manager An employee who is charged with making decisions, leading people, and delegating authority in order to accomplish the goals of the organization. A manager is generally responsible for recognizing and recommending rewards for achievement.

managerial accounting The branch of accounting that provides an organization's management with historical and estimated financial data with which to make current and future planning decisions.

managerial grid A two-dimensional graph or grid that measures the relative importance a leader attaches to the task (measured along the horizontal axis) and the people (measured along the vertical axis). A leader who attaches great importance to the task and little importance to the people involved is considered authoritarian. A leader who attaches great importance to both the task and the people is considered a good team leader.

managing underwriter —See LEAD UNDERWRITER.

mandate **1.** An official order to do something. For example, a corporate executive may issue a mandate that committee members be on time. **2.** An instruction from a court or a court official. **3.** Authorization to do something. For example, a candidate who promised to reduce property taxes during the election campaign assumes a mandate to do so if elected.

mandatorily redeemable shares —See REDEEMABLE SHARES.

mandatory convertible security A debt security that automatically converts to another security, generally shares of common stock, on a specified date. A mandatory convertible differs from most convertible securities in that it does not permit the owner to choose whether or not to convert.

mandatory retirement Forced resignation from employment at a specific age. In the 1970s, nearly 40% of male employees in the United States were subject to mandatory retirement at age 65. Mandatory retirement ended for most employees in 1978 and 1986 with passage of the federal Age Discrimination in Employment Act. —Also called *compulsory retirement.*

mandatory tender bond A bond with a long maturity but a shorter-term (generally six months to five years) mandatory tender date. Unlike an ordinary put bond, a mandatory tender bond is put back to the bondholder, who does not take action to roll the bond into the next tender period. The interest rate is adjusted on the mandatory tender date.

man hour One hour of work, a measure that is frequently used to evaluate productivity. For example, an automobile manufacturer measures its competitiveness and productivity by the number of man hours required to build one vehicle.

manifest A one-page form used by transport companies to list the cargo in a shipment. For example, the Environmental Protection Agency requires waste haulers to have a manifest that includes the type and quantity of waste, the generator of the waste, the transporter, and the storage or disposal facility to which the waste is being shipped.

manipulate **1.** To cause a security to sell at an artificial price. Although investment bankers are permitted to manipulate temporarily the stock they underwrite, most other forms of manipulation are illegal. **2.** To falsify something: *Someone at the company manipulated the financial data in order to inflate profits.* **3.** To influence to one's advantage: *The employee manipulated his supervisor in order to gain a promotion.*

manual[1] A small booklet, generally with information about how to do something.

manual[2] Of or relating to something requiring human effort.

manufactured housing Single-family homes constructed entirely in a factory under a federal building code administered by the U.S. Department of Housing and Urban Development. Manufactured homes are built in a factory, transported to a site, and installed.

manufacturer's representative A sales representative of a manufacturer who attempts to interest wholesale and retail buyers and purchasing agents in the products of the company he or she represents.

manufacturer's suggested retail price (MSRP) The price at which a manufacturer suggests its product be sold to retail buyers. The MSRP may or may not be a realistic appraisal of what consumers are likely to pay. —Also called *sticker price; suggested retail price.*

---

margin account

I plan to open a brokerage account in the near future. Is there a reason to choose a cash account rather than a margin account?

I think that the decision between a cash account and a margin account depends on the client's investment objectives, risk tolerance, and financial resources. By opening a margin account, you can borrow money from your broker to purchase securities, which creates leverage in your account. If the securities that you purchase go up in value, you can make more money than in a cash account. However, if the securities that you purchase on margin go down, you can lose more money than your original investment. If you use margin, you have to be very diligent in monitoring the price movement of your securities and be ready to act, or the outcome could be unpleasant.

■ Richard S. Campbell, CIMA®, Senior Vice President, Wealth Management,
Portfolio Management Director, Smith Barney, Valdosta, GA

---

manufacturing Using labor and capital to convert raw materials into finished or semifinished goods.

manufacturing cost The expense of making a product, including direct labor, direct materials, other direct expenses, and a portion of the overhead.

maple leaf A gold coin minted in Canada.

maquiladora A foreign-owned manufacturing plant in Mexico, generally near the border. Maquiladoras typically import materials and equipment duty-free and use low-paid employees to manufacture and export finished products or semifinished products.

margin **1.** The amount of funds that must be deposited when purchasing securities. —See also INITIAL MARGIN REQUIREMENT. **2.** The equity in an investor's account. —See also MAINTENANCE MARGIN REQUIREMENT. **3.** The difference between the payment received for a good or service and the cost of producing it. A product that is sold for $4.00 and costs $2.75 to produce has a margin of $1.25. **4.** Points added to an index in determining the rate of interest on an adjustable-rate mortgage loan.

margin account A brokerage account that permits an investor to purchase securities on credit and to borrow on securities already in the account. Buying securities on credit and borrowing on securities are subject to standards established by the Federal Reserve and/or by the firm carrying the account. Interest is charged on any borrowed funds and only for the period of time that the loan is outstanding. —Compare CASH ACCOUNT. —Also called *general account.* —See also INITIAL MARGIN REQUIREMENT; MAINTENANCE MARGIN REQUIREMENT.

margin agreement The written document that describes the functioning of a margin account and permits a customer's broker to pledge securities in the account as collateral for loans. A customer must sign a margin agreement before undertaking trades on credit in an account.

marginal analysis Making decisions by comparing the extra benefit with the extra cost of small changes. For example, perhaps a retailer is considering opening her store an hour earlier each morning. Marginal analysis would compare the additional revenues generated by the earlier opening with the extra costs, including labor, electricity, and so forth. The analysis would have to account for the fact that some of the additional sales during the first hour might come from customers who would have

marginal tax rate

How can I determine my marginal tax rate?

Your marginal tax rate is a function of income level, filing status, and statutory tax rates. IRS Form 1040 contains tables based on statutory income tax rates (10%, 15%, 25%, 28%, 33%, and 35% for 2007) and filing status (e.g., single, married filing jointly, and so forth). You find your marginal tax rate by matching your taxable income with the appropriate table.

You should note that your overall marginal income tax rate is usually higher than your federal marginal tax rate because you may be subject to state and municipal income taxes. In addition, income tax credits could reduce your marginal tax rate.

■ Peter M. Bergevin, PhD, Professor of Accounting, School of Business, University of Redlands, Redlands, CA

made purchases later in the day. Marginal analysis is the proper method of making most business decisions. —Also called *incremental analysis.*

marginal cost The additional cost needed to produce or purchase one more unit of a good or service. For example, if a firm can produce 150 units of a product at a total cost of $5,000, and 151 units for $5,100, the marginal cost of the 151st unit is $100. Industries with sharply declining marginal costs tend to be made up of firms that engage in price wars to gain market share. For example, the airlines often discount fares to fill empty seats with customers from competing airlines. —Also called *incremental cost.*

marginal cost of capital The cost to a company of raising additional funds. The marginal cost of capital depends on the current cost of individual sources of capital (common stock, retained earnings, preferred stock, and debt) and the proportions in which the sources will be used. This cost is stated as a percentage and is compared to the return that is expected to be earned on a proposed investment.

marginal player A company that has little impact or influence on the industry in which it operates. For example, a small chain of drug stores is likely to be considered a marginal player in an industry that is increasingly dominated by three or four large companies.

marginal producer A company that can barely eke out a profit at the current price that it receives for its product. Marginal producers are often too small to benefit from economies that result from larger-scale operations.

marginal propensity to consume The proportion of additional disposable income devoted to consumption spending rather than savings. For example, a person who spends $95 of a $100 monthly increase in disposable income has a marginal propensity to consume of 0.95.

marginal propensity to save The proportion of additional disposable income devoted to savings rather than consumption spending. A high marginal propensity to save frees a country's resources for investment use, but too high a propensity to save may result in a recession from lack of consumer spending.

marginal revenue The extra revenue generated by selling one additional unit of a good or service. For example, if a firm can sell 10 units of a product at a price of $25 per unit, total revenue is $250. If, in order to sell 11 units, it must reduce the price to $24, total revenue rises to 11 × $24, or $264. Thus, the marginal revenue of the 11th unit is $264 − $250, or $14.

marginal tax rate The percentage of extra income received that must be paid in taxes. A person's marginal tax rate should be considered in making investment choices. For example, a decision whether or not to purchase municipal bonds is primarily a function of the investor's marginal tax rate. —Also called *tax bracket.* —See also AVERAGE TAX RATE; PROGRESSIVE TAX.

marginal utility The enjoyment or usefulness resulting from using or consuming one additional unit of something. Most products offer declining marginal utility. For example, on a hot day the first cold soft drink is likely to have a much higher marginal utility than the second soft drink. The same may not be true for beer.

margin call A demand for additional funds or securities in a margin account either because the value of equity in the account has fallen below a required minimum (also termed a maintenance call) or because additional securities have been purchased or sold short.

margin of profit —See GROSS PROFIT MARGIN.

margin of safety **1.** The difference between the market value of a firm's assets and the face value of debt using the assets as collateral. A large margin of safety enhances the credit quality of the debt. **2.** The amount by which a firm's revenues exceed breakeven. A large margin of safety means a firm could encounter a substantial reduction in sales and still remain viable. **3.** The amount by which a stock sells below its intrinsic value.

margin requirement **1.** —See INITIAL MARGIN REQUIREMENT. **2.** —See MAINTENANCE MARGIN REQUIREMENT. **3.** —See OPTION MARGIN.

margin stock A stock with qualifications such that it is considered to have loan value in a margin account. This kind of stock usually includes all listed stocks and select over-the-counter stocks meeting Federal Reserve criteria. Stocks not on the margin list must be paid for in full. —Also called *OTC margin stock.*

margin trading The buying and selling of securities in an account in which money is owed to the brokerage firm.

marine insurance Coverage for commercial transportation vehicles and the cargo they transport over land, sea, and air. Marine insurance is often divided into ocean marine insurance, which covers ocean and inland waterway transportation exposures, and inland marine insurance, which provides coverage of property in transit over land.

marital deduction The deduction for tax purposes of property transferred between spouses. For estate and gift purposes, all property transferred between spouses is free of federal taxation.

marital-deduction trust A trust designed to pass assets to a spouse. The trust is used instead of leaving the assets to the spouse directly. The beneficiary receives income from the trust until his or her death, at which time the trust's assets are distributed or the trust is included in the estate of the deceased. —See also QTIP TRUST.

marital property Assets acquired by each spouse during a marriage. Property owned prior to marriage and kept separate during the marriage is generally considered separate, or nonmarital, property. Separate property that is commingled becomes marital property.

markdown **1.** A reduction from the original selling price. For example, retail clothing stores frequently attempt to decrease inventory by offering markdowns on seasonal merchandise. **2.** A decrease in a security price made by a dealer because of changing market conditions. For example, a bond trader may take a markdown in long-term bonds held in inventory when market interest rates rise. —Compare MARKUP 2. **3.**

The difference between the price paid by a dealer to a retail customer and the price at which the dealer can sell the same security to a market maker. —Compare MARKUP 4.

market¹ 1. A place where sellers and buyers meet in order to transact business. **2.** A group of individuals or organizations that are considered potential consumers of a product or service. **3.** A retail establishment where food items are sold. **4.** —See SECURITIES EXCHANGE.

**market² ** To sell a product or service.

marketability The ease with which an asset may be bought and sold. An asset that would be difficult to sell has poor marketability.

marketability risk —See LIQUIDITY RISK.

marketability study An analysis made to determine the likely success of selling a particular product or service. A marketability study is likely to include potential demand, existing competitive products or services, and a recommendation on strategy.

marketable security A security that may be resold by one investor to another. Most securities are marketable; they develop secondary markets for trading. —Also called *negotiable security.*

market analysis 1. An evaluation of the market for a company's goods and services. For example, a company might be interested in the characteristics of consumers who are buying the firm's products, or a comparison of its products with those offered by competitors. **2.** Research that offers assistance in forecasting price trends for stocks and bonds. Market analysis may concentrate on fundamental factors including earnings, inflation, and costs, or it may be directed at technical considerations such as trading volume and price charts.

market area —See TRADE AREA.

market averages —See AVERAGES.

market basket A defined group of products or services used to provide statistical analysis. For example, the consumer price index measures inflation for the market basket of goods and services purchased by households.

market breadth —See BREADTH OF MARKET.

market capitalization The total value of all of a firm's outstanding shares, calculated by multiplying the market price per share times the total number of shares outstanding. For example, at a current price of $50 for each of its 20 million shares of outstanding stock, a firm has a market capitalization of $50 × 20 million, or $1 billion. —Also called *market value.*

market comparison appraisal —See COMPARATIVE MARKET ANALYSIS.

market demand The total demand for a good or service by all consumers.

market economy An economic system based on open and competitive markets in which participants act in their own self-interest and government acts as a referee. Proponents believe a market economy results in the most efficient allocation of resources and the greatest public good.

market efficiency —See EFFICIENT MARKET.

market index —See AVERAGES.

market-indexed CD A certificate of deposit that provides a return based on a specified index, such as the S&P 500, or a commodity, such as gold or silver. These CDs are issued by commercial banks but are generally marketed by brokerage companies.

Terms vary by issuer, but investors are generally guaranteed the return of their principal at maturity.

> **CASE** Some banks and thrift institutions offer certificates of deposit with
> **STUDY** returns linked to a variety of market indexes. For example, a bank
> might offer a CD with principal guaranteed (savers get back at least the
> amount they deposited) and a return based on a gain in the S&P 500 Stock
> Index. In early 2007, EverBank Financial Corporation, a thrift holding company headquartered in Jacksonville, Florida, was offering what it called a
> "MarketSafe Gold Bullion CD" with a yield linked to the upside price performance of the spot price of gold bullion. The CD was available in a 5-year term
> with principal guaranteed by FDIC insurance. The CD offered a yield based
> on 100% of the average price performance of gold bullion, applying ten semiannual pricing dates over the term of the CD. The required minimum investment was $1,500, and the thrift levied no account fees. At the same time, EverBank was offering a 3½–year CD linked to the price performance of the
> Tokyo Stock Exchange REIT Index.

marketing The process of planning and carrying out a program to attract and convince consumers. Marketing includes identifying potential markets, determining an acceptable price, establishing distribution channels, and establishing effective promotions.

marketing information system A procedure to collect, organize, and analyze data that is used to formulate marketing strategies.

marketing intermediary An independent business that assists in the distribution of goods and services produced by other business. For example, a book distributor assists publishers in getting their books into retail outlets.

marketing manager The person responsible for planning and executing an organization's marketing functions, including planning, pricing, and distribution.

marketing mix The combination of marketing variables, including pricing, distribution, packaging, promotion, and personal selling, that a firm uses to sell a good or service.

marketing plan The detailed strategy for pricing, promoting, distributing; and selling a good or service.

marketing research The collection, analysis, and use of data relative to moving a product to consumers.

market leadership The stocks that tend to dominate trading volume during a given period. Some people believe the quality of market leadership indicates future trends for market movement. —Also called *leadership*.

market letter A newsletter containing information on topics such as market trends, security recommendations, economic forecasts, and virtually anything else having an impact on security prices and investor profits. Market letters are provided by most full-service brokerage companies, often for a fee, and by individual investment advisers registered with the SEC.

market line —See CAPITAL MARKET LINE.

market maker 1. One (as a person or firm) that, on a continuous basis, buys and sells a security for one's own account. Market makers usually try to profit from a rapid

marketing plan

I own a small business and don't know squat about marketing. Where can I locate a person or firm that might help me develop a marketing plan? Would this be expensive?

I recommend looking for marketing services through reputable online networking websites, such as LinkedIn. This professional network provides profiles of marketing professionals in a wide variety of disciplines along with personal recommendations for the providers (plus it's free to join and use). Also, don't underestimate the importance of contacting other businesses in your area to see if they have successfully engaged similar services.

Prices for marketing consulting services vary widely depending on the scope of the work being done. Be sure you obtain a detailed proposal and budget before contracting with anyone. The proposal should clearly state what services are being offered, the exact deliverables that will be provided, and how the effectiveness of the marketing plan is going to be measured to ensure a good return on your investment.

▪ E. Mace Lewis, Vice President, Business Development, QD Healthcare Group, Greenwich, CT

---

turnover in security positions rather than from holding those positions in anticipation of gradual price movements. Dealers in the over-the-counter market are market makers. —See also MAKE A MARKET. **2.** A dealer in options on the floor of an options exchange who makes a market in one or more options. The Chicago Board Options Exchange uses market makers.

market metrics Statistics, such as brand awareness, customer satisfaction, market size, and market share, that can be used to help determine the effectiveness of an organization's marketing program.

market multiple —See PRICE-EARNINGS RATIO.

market-neutral fund An investment company that holds approximately equal aggregate values of long positions in stocks expected to outperform the overall market and short positions in stocks expected to underperform the overall market. The goal is to offer higher-than-average returns while using short positions to hedge risk. A market-neutral fund is a specialized type of long-short fund with an approximately equal balance between the two positions. —See also LONG-SHORT FUND.

market-neutral investing An investment strategy that attempts to assemble an investment portfolio with a return that is unaffected by returns in the overall market. For example, an investor might buy shares of a petroleum company the investor considers undervalued and sell short an equal value of shares of a different petroleum company the investor considers overvalued. The investor expects to profit regardless of whether the overall market rises or declines.

market order A customer order for immediate execution at the best price available when the order reaches the marketplace. This, the most common type of order, has the advantage of nearly always being filled, because no price is specified. —Compare LIMIT ORDER. —Also called *at-the-market.* —See also STOP ORDER 1.

market penetration 1. The proportion of the overall market held by a particular product or company. **2.** A strategy to increase market share of a product or service in an existing market. For example, a firm might decide to devote additional funds to advertising in a particular market.

market price 1. The price at which a security trades in the secondary market. **2.** The price at which a good or service normally sells.

market profile The major demographic characteristics and spending patterns of consumers in a particular market.

market rent The amount of rent a real estate unit would command if it were available for occupancy. —See also FAIR MARKET RENT.

market risk **1.** The risk that, because general market pressures will cause the value of an investment to fluctuate, it may be necessary to liquidate a position during a down period in the cycle. Market risk is highest for securities with above-average price volatility and lowest for stable securities such as Treasury bills. **2.** —See SYSTEMATIC RISK.

market segment A unique consumer group that can be identified and targeted. For example, individuals with annual incomes above $100,000 comprise a market segment of potential luxury-car buyers.

market segmentation Separating a market into distinct groups of potential consumers who share common characteristics and interests and who are likely to be attracted to particular products or services.

market sentiment The intuitive feeling of the investment community regarding the expected movement of the stock market. For example, if market sentiment is bullish, then most investors expect an upward move in the stock market.

market share The proportion of industry sales of a good or service that is controlled by a company or by a particular brand sold by the company. Market share is generally measured in terms of the dollar spending of buyers. —Also called *brand share.*

market technician —See TECHNICIAN.

market timing The purchase and sale of securities based on short-term price patterns as well as on asset values. —Also called *timing.*

market to book A ratio comparing the market price of a firm's common stock with the stock's book value per share. Essentially, the market-to-book ratio relates what investors believe a firm is worth to what the firm's accountants say it is worth according to accepted accounting principles. —Also called *price/book ratio; price-to-book-value ratio.*

market value **1.** The price at which an asset currently can be sold. **2.** —See MARKET CAPITALIZATION.

market value clause A property insurance provision that obligates an insurance company to reimburse an insured loss for the current market value of the damaged or destroyed property.

mark to market The adjustment of an account to reflect gains and losses at the end of a trading period. This adjustment is especially relevant in accounts that trade commodity futures, because it is used daily to determine whether the appropriate margin is being maintained. —Compare TAX STRADDLE.

markup **1.** The difference between a product's selling price and its cost, often expressed as a percentage of cost. For example, toothpaste purchased for $2.00 and selling at retail for $2.50 represents a markup of 25%. —See also KEYSTONE MARKUP; MAINTENANCE MARKUP. **2.** An upward revaluation of a security by a dealer because of a rise in the security's market price. A dealer may decide that a markup on a security issue held in inventory is appropriate because of a rising stock market. —Compare MARKDOWN 2. **3.** —See SPREAD 4. **4.** The difference between the price charged by a dealer to a retail customer and the prevailing price at which the same security is being offered by market makers. —Compare MARKDOWN 3.

marriage penalty The increased tax liability assessed a married couple filing jointly compared to the combined tax they would pay if unmarried and filing separate returns. The penalty is greatest when a husband and wife each earn a high income.

married put —See PROTECTIVE PUT.

married taxpayer A taxpayer whose legal marital status is "married" on the last day of the year and is therefore permitted to file a joint return or a return of married filing separately for that tax year. —Compare SINGLE TAXPAYER.

marry a stock To hold a stock for a long period regardless of other investment opportunities or indications that the security should be sold. Most investment advisers consider it unwise to marry a stock, because an investor's needs and the desirability of a particular stock will change over time.

Maslow's hierarchy of needs Psychologist Abraham Maslow's (1908–70) theory of the factors that motivate and sustain human behavior. Maslow theorized that individuals have various layers of needs, beginning with the physiological needs for air, water, and food, and ending with self-actualization and transcendence that result in self-fulfillment. Each layer of needs must be successively satisfied before moving to the next higher level.

Massachusetts Trust A business entity similar to a corporation or limited partnership where investors contribute money or investment assets to a trust and give management authority to a trustee. Individual investors are liable only for the assets held by the trust.

mass communications Communications directed at a very large audience through the use of media including television, radio, newspapers, and the Internet.

mass media Communication channels, including television and newspapers, that reach a large audience.

mass production The automated production of large quantities of identical products on a continuous basis. Mass production is used to produce a homogeneous product at low cost.

master labor agreement An industry-wide employment contract that addresses major issues such as wages and benefits. For example, the Teamsters Union signs a master labor agreement with trucking companies. Master labor agreements often allow additional accords at the local level.

master lease **1.** A lease that allows an existing lessee to lease additional assets under similar terms and conditions as the current lease without being required to negotiate a new contract. **2.** A controlling lease for a property to which any subleases must conform. For example, a sublease cannot be for a longer term than the master lease.

master limited partnership (MLP) —See PUBLIC LIMITED PARTNERSHIP.

master of business administration (MBA) A professional graduate degree designed to prepare the individuals who pursue it for management positions in business. MBA programs typically include coverage of basic business subjects such as marketing, finance, accounting, management, quantitative methods, and economics, plus several electives. —See also EXECUTIVE MBA.

master plan **1.** In real estate, a comprehensive strategy for development and use of a town or large tract of land. **2.** An IRS-approved financial arrangement made available by providers (banks, mutual funds, professional organizations, and insurance companies) for adoption by employers offering a qualified-retirement plan.

master lease

Am I required to obtain permission from the lessor in order to sublease an office or apartment?

The vast majority of leases for residential and commercial properties do not allow the primary tenant to sublease the property unless written permission from the landlord is obtained. Absent any language in the lease that grants permission to do so, the tenant cannot legally sublease. Subleasing is a temporary transfer of occupancy rights to a property granted by the primary tenant, or lessee, to a subtenant, or sublessee. The primary tenant remains fully and legally obligated to the landlord, or lessor, for rent payment and upkeep of property, while the subtenant is obligated only to the primary tenant. Although most leases preclude subleasing, it occurs frequently in residential properties. For example, a college student signs a one-year lease ending July 31, and she subleases to a friend for June and July. Typically the landlord is not aware of this arrangement. If the landlord had to take legal action for late rent, for example, it would be against the primary tenant.

Subleasing may be allowed (with landlord approval) in commercial leases, especially long-term leases to large national or regional companies. When the original lease term has expired, the subtenant must either move out or negotiate a new lease with the landlord. Subleasing is not to be confused with a lease assignment, which is a permanent transfer of all of the legal rights and obligations from the original tenant, or assignor, to a new tenant, or assignee. Most commercial leases allow assignments with the landlord's written permission, which would be granted after the landlord approves the assignee tenant. After the assignment, typically only the new assignee tenant is obligated to the landlord.

▪ Scott Alderman, Broker and President, First Commercial Real Estate, Valdosta, GA

master policy 1. An insurance policy that provides coverage for multiple parcels of real estate. **2.** A single contract issued to an organization by an insurance company that provides group coverage to eligible employees or members.

master-servant rule In law, the principle that an employer is responsible for the acts of its employees during the time they are performing their duties as employees.

matching —See PORTFOLIO DEDICATION.

matching principle 1. In accounting, the notion that expenses should be recorded in the same period in which the expenses were used to earn revenues. **2.** The idea that a business should match the maturity of its liabilities with the maturity of its assets. For example, long-term assets should not be financed with short-term liabilities.

material[1] Of sufficient importance or relevance as to have possible significant influence on an outcome. For example, the possibility that a firm might lose its right to operate a number of television stations because competitors have filed with the Federal Communications Commission for those licenses would be a material fact in preparing the firm's financial statements. —Compare IMMATERIAL.

material[2] Something used in making something else. For example, sheet metal is material used in manufacturing vehicles.

material participation An IRS classification for working in a business on a regular, continuous, and substantial basis. Without material participation, a taxpayer is considered an investor, and losses are considered passive and generally not deductible except against passive income.

matrix A rectangular array of elements in rows and columns such that each element has a unique location that represents two or more sets of factors.

mechanic's lien

Does a mechanic's lien placed on property apply to a new owner if the property is sold? If so, how can I determine if a mechanic's lien is on property I am planning to purchase?

Yes, a mechanic's lien on the title to the property is attached to the land itself, not to the person who created the debt. Reviewing the title to the property will tell you if there is a lien. People trying to enforce mechanic's liens *want* the public to find their notice, so it's usually not a difficult discovery to make on a title. You may do this or have a title search commissioned prior to closing to confirm that there are no outstanding liens on the property.

▪ Joan A. Koffman, Esq., Real Estate Attorney, Koffman & Dreyer, Newton, MA

matrix organization Bringing two or more specialist groups from different departments together to work on an assignment or project.

mature industry An industry in which future growth is so limited that firms in it must grow by taking sales from competitors or by diversifying. The stocks of firms in mature industries often have high dividend yields and sell at low price-earnings ratios. The automotive, petroleum, and tobacco industries are examples of mature industries.

maturing liability A debt that is due to be paid within a short period of time.

maturity 1. The date on which payment of a financial obligation is due. In the case of a bond, the maturity date is the one on which the issuer must retire the bond by paying the face value of the bond to its owners. —See also TENOR. **2.** The date on which an endowment insurance policy is paid up and requires no additional payments.

maturity basis In calculating yield, the premise that a debt will be held to maturity.

maturity value The amount to be paid to the holder of a financial obligation at the obligation's maturity. In the case of a bond, the maturity value is the principal amount of the bond to be paid by the issuer to the owner at maturity.

MBA —See MASTER OF BUSINESS ADMINISTRATION.

mean —See ARITHMETIC MEAN; GEOMETRIC MEAN.

mean term —See DURATION.

mechanic's lien A claim placed on specific real estate in order to secure payment for work performed by a contractor or laborer, or materials provided by a supplier. The lien may result in a forced sale of the property in order to satisfy the claim.

mechanization Using machinery to perform tasks or to assist humans in performing tasks. Mechanization increases capital expenses and reduces labor costs.

media Communications networks, including newspapers, radio, magazines, the Internet, and television, that disseminate information to the public.

media buyer The person with the responsibility for buying and placing advertising space in print and Web media, and time on radio and television. A media buyer may work for the organization doing the advertising, but more likely works for an advertising agency as a buyer for its clients.

median The midpoint of a series of values. For example, a tour group with 90 members and a median age of 60 includes 45 people under 60 years of age and 45 people over 60 years of age.

media rate A special rate offered by the U.S. Postal Service for books, film, printed music, sound recordings, and computer-readable media. Some restrictions apply. —See also LIBRARY RATE.

mediation A process for settling a dispute between two parties. The two sides employ a third party, who attempts to find common ground that will resolve the dispute. Mediation is a less lengthy and less expensive alternative than arbitration. Each side must agree to mediation, and either side may walk away from the process at any time. —Compare ARBITRATION. —See also AMERICAN ARBITRATION ASSOCIATION.

Medicaid A joint state-federal program for state residents who are unable to afford medical care. Medicaid is administered by each state, which sets its own guidelines regarding eligibility and services. Requirements for eligibility typically include age, income, financial resources, physical condition (blind, disabled), and whether a person is a U.S. citizen or lawfully admitted immigrant.

medical expense deduction Unreimbursed expenses for medical care (including dental) of a taxpayer, spouse, and dependents permitted by the IRS as reduction in taxable income. Allowable expenses include payments for diagnosis, treatment, cure, or prevention. The cost of health club dues, funerals, and over-the-counter medications are not permitted. Medical expenses are deductible only to the extent that they exceed 7.5% of adjusted gross income.

Medicare A government-administered health care program for people 65 years of age and over, some disabled people under age 65, and people with kidney failure. Medicare includes Part A (generally without charge), which provides coverage for inpatient hospital care, skilled nursing facilities, hospice care, and some home health care. Medicare Part B requires a monthly premium and provides coverage for doctors' services, outpatient hospital care, and certain medical services not included in Part A.

Medicare tax The tax withheld from employee wages to pay for Medicare benefits. The Medicare tax, at 1.45% of wages, is the smaller part of the FICA (Federal Insurance Contributions Act) tax that also includes Social Security. Medicare taxes are not levied against investment income, royalty income, or any other source of income other than wages.

Medigap (Supplemental Insurance) Policies Health insurance sold by private insurers that offers coverage for gaps (missing coverage) in Original Medicare Plan coverage. Insurance companies are only permitted to offer standardized policies that follow federal and state laws. A husband and wife must each have their own individual Medigap policies for this coverage.

medium of exchange Something that is generally acceptable as payment for goods and services. Currency is a medium of exchange in developed countries.

medium-term bond —See INTERMEDIATE BOND.

medium-term note A corporate debt security offered intermittently or continuously by an agent of the issuer. Despite being called notes, these debt securities generally offer a wide range of maturities.

member bank A banking institution that is a member of the Federal Reserve System. —Compare NONMEMBER BANK.

member firm A securities firm with officers or partners who are members of an organized securities exchange. National brokerage firms are generally members of a number of organized exchanges.

menial Of or relating to work that is uninteresting, requires little skill, and is generally considered demeaning. Garbage collection is an example of menial work.

Merc —See CHICAGO MERCANTILE EXCHANGE.

mercantile **1.** Of or relating to commerce. **2.** Of or relating to the system of mercantilism.

mercantile agency An organization that secures and sells credit information about commercial businesses.

mercantile law —See COMMERCIAL LAW.

mercantilism An early European economic system that encouraged the establishment of colonies to supply the home countries with raw materials that would be turned into finished goods and sold to the colonies. The goals were to build industries at home and accumulate gold from a favorable balance of trade.

merchandise Goods sold to consumers at the retail level.

merchandise allowance Cash or free merchandise offered by a manufacturer or wholesaler to customers who purchase a stipulated amount of goods. For example, a book publisher offers a merchandise allowance of $10 in free merchandise to bookstores that order $150 in books.

merchandise broker An agent who earns commissions by acting as a middleman between sellers and buyers of merchandise. The broker does not own or take possession of the merchandise involved in the transactions that are arranged.

merchandising Planning and executing the promotion of goods and services in an attempt to obtain the greatest value for the seller. Merchandising in a grocery store might include holding promotional events, installing point-of-purchase displays, and issuing cents-off coupons.

merchant **1.** A person who earns an income by buying and selling goods, generally at retail. **2.** A business that agrees to accept debit and credit cards.

merchantable Suitable for being offered for sale. For example, a merchantable log must be of a minimum size to be acceptable to a mill.

merchant bank **1.** An investment bank that commits its own funds by taking a creditor position or equity interest in another firm. For example, a merchant bank may provide temporary financing for a leveraged buyout. **2.** A bank that has entered into an agreement to accept merchant deposits originating from bankcard transactions.

merchant's privilege The legal right of a merchant, or someone acting on behalf of the merchant, to detain for a reasonable time individuals suspected of unlawfully taking the merchant's property. The merchant may confiscate merchandise in plain view, but generally is not permitted to search the detainee. Rules applicable to detention, search, and other aspects of merchant's privilege vary by state. —See also CIVIL RECOVERY.

merge To combine two or more organizations.

Mergent, Inc. A major publisher of financial information in print and online. Formerly the publications department of Moody's Investors Service, its publications include the popular Mergent manuals, *Mergent Bond Record* and *Mergent's Handbook of Common Stocks.*

merger A combination of two or more companies in which the assets and liabilities of the selling firm(s) are absorbed by the buying firm. Although the buying firm may be a considerably different organization after the merger, it retains its original identity. —Compare CONSOLIDATION. —See also DOWNSTREAM MERGER; SYNERGY.

merit good A good or service that public policymakers feel will be under-consumed and should be subsidized. In general, merit goods have positive externalities. For example, a library and public health services are generally considered merit goods. —Compare DEMERIT GOOD.

merit raise An increase in pay based on job performance. For example, an employer may award employees a cost-of-living raise of 3% plus a merit raise of from 0% to 4%. Merit raises are designed to reward and retain employees who exhibit superior job performance.

merit rating Appraisal of an employee's job performance. Merit ratings are often used in determining promotions and raises.

metered mail Packages and letters for which postage has been applied by postage machines. Postage machines can be used for all types of mail other than periodicals. Permits are required for metered bulk mailings.

metes and bounds A legal description of real property using angles and distances from well-known points. "Mete" refers to a limit or limiting mark, while "bounds" refers to boundaries.

me-too product A product that is very similar to products manufactured by other companies and already on the market. For example, a toy manufacturer observes the immense popularity of a competitor's product and decides to produce its own version that is virtually identical.

metric system A system of weights (kilograms) and measures (meters and liters) based on decimals rather than fractions. The French designed the system in the late 18th century.

metropolitan statistical area A designation of the U.S. Office of Management and Budget (OMB) for a county or group of counties with at least one large population center of at least 50,000 inhabitants, plus adjacent territory with a high level of integration with the core. The OMB defines metropolitan areas for purposes of gathering, analyzing, and publishing data. —Formerly called *standard metropolitan statistical area.* —See also MICROPOLITAN STATISTICAL AREA.

mezzanine financing High-yield debt, often issued in connection with a leveraged buyout. Mezzanine real estate loans generally offer relatively high interest rates and the likelihood of eventual ownership of the properties if borrowers are unable to make required loan payments.

microcap 1. Of or relating to the common stock of a company with a small capitalization, usually between $50 million and $250 million. Microcap stocks tend to experience volatile price movements and are subject to investment fraud schemes. In addition, information about small companies that issue these stocks may be difficult to obtain. Many microcap stocks trade over the counter and are quoted on the OTC Bulletin Board or the Pink Sheets. **2.** Of or relating to a mutual fund that holds mostly microcap stocks in its portfolio. Microcap funds tend to exhibit large changes in net asset value.

microeconomics The study of decision making by small economic units, including individuals, households, businesses, and industries. Microeconomics examines issues such as pricing, supply, demand, costs, and revenues. —Compare MACROECONOMICS.

microfinance The granting of financial services and products such as very small loans to assist the exceptionally poor in establishing or expanding their businesses. Microfinance is used in developing countries where budding entrepreneurs do not have access to other sources of financial assistance.

microlender A company or organization that makes small loans to businesses that are generally unable to obtain financing from a regular source. Microlender loans often range from $5,000 to $25,000 at interest rates higher than those charged by commercial banks.

micropolitan statistical area A designation of the U.S. Office of Management and Budget (OMB) for a county or group of counties with at least one large urban cluster of at least 10,000 but less than 50,000 inhabitants. The OMB defines micropolitan areas for purposes of gathering, analyzing, and publishing data. —See also METROPOLITAN STATISTICAL AREA.

mid-cap 1. Of or relating to the common stock of a company with a middle level of market capitalization, usually within the range of $2 billion to $10 billion, although the cutoff points are fuzzy on both ends. **2.** Of or relating to a mutual fund that holds mostly mid-cap stocks.

middle management The tier of managers that answers to and carries out directives from upper management. Middle managers, such as a department manager, are closely identified with managing an organization's day-to-day activities.

mid-month convention The accounting practice where, for purposes of depreciation, real property is placed in service or disposed of at the midpoint of the calendar month. Thus, real property receives one half-month of depreciation in the month in which it is acquired or disposed of.

midterm bargaining Negotiations between a union and employer during the life of a labor contract. Midterm bargaining may involve new issues or a reopener clause, but generally excludes matters covered by the existing agreement.

MIG —See MOODY'S INVESTMENT GRADE.

migrant worker A person engaged in paid labor in a country in which he or she is not a national. Migrant workers often hold jobs that are seasonal or temporary.

military-industrial complex The armed forces and industries with which they have a political and economic relationship. A growing military supports a growing defense industry, and so both lobby for bigger military budgets. The relationship is made even stronger when defense companies hire retired military officers and politicians.

milk 1. To exploit something. For example, a business might take advantage of, or milk, a relationship with a former executive who was elected to public office. **2.** To drain an asset or company of cash. —See also CASH COW.

mill One thousandth of a dollar. Property tax rates are applied in mills per $1,000 of assessed valuation.

millage rate The tax rate expressed in tenths of a cent that is applied to the assessed value of real property. For example, real estate with an assessed valuation of $100,000 in a tax district that levies a 7.5 millage rate results in the owner paying a tax of $750.

mineral lease An agreement between a property owner and another party who is allowed to explore for and extract minerals that are found on the property for a stated time. The property owner receives payments based on the value of the minerals that are extracted.

minimum wage

I am an owner of several fast-food restaurants. I am currently paying my employees a competitive wage, but our business suffers from high employee turnover. Do you think paying employees a little extra, say twenty-five cents per hour, would have much of an impact on the turnover?

No. Minimum-wage jobs are entry-level jobs that employees expect to leave. You would be better advised to look more carefully at turnover patterns and try to alter them rather than reducing overall turnover with very small wage differentials. Probably the best you can do is lengthen the tenure of employees who are productive. Consider "longevity rewards," such as raises or periodic bonuses for those who stay for a certain amount of time. Also consider why employees are leaving. Could your scheduling be more accommodating to your good employees? By paying significantly more than minimum wage, you might be able to increase productivity and reduce turnover, but the cost could outweigh the benefits.

■ Phyllis G. Holland, PhD, Professor and Head, Department of Management,
Langdale College of Business, Valdosta State University, Valdosta, GA

mineral rights Ownership of minerals under a defined surface along with the legal right of access so the minerals can be extracted. Mineral rights can be separated and transferred from land ownership. —Also called *subsurface rights*.

minicoupon bond A bond with a coupon lower than the market rate of interest at the time of issue, resulting in sale of the bond at a discount from face value at issuance. A zero-coupon bond is a special type of minicoupon bond. —Compare ORIGINAL-ISSUE DISCOUNT BOND. —See also DEEP-DISCOUNT BOND.

minimum contact Of or referring to a state or federal requirement that a person or other entity have an association with a legal jurisdiction in order to be the subject of legal action within that jurisdiction. In most instances, a person's presence in a state is considered adequate for minimum contact.

minimum investment The least amount of money required to invest or open an account in a mutual fund. Different funds impose different minimum investments, and a fund may impose different minimum investments for different types of accounts. For example, many mutual funds require lower minimum investments for individual retirement accounts compared to regular accounts.

minimum maintenance —See MAINTENANCE MARGIN REQUIREMENT.

minimum payment The least amount a borrower can pay on a revolving charge account in order to escape a financial penalty. The minimum payment is generally calculated as a percentage of the outstanding balance subject to an absolute minimum such as $10.

minimum pension liability The liability that represents the amount by which an organization's accumulated pension benefits exceed the fair market value of its pension plan assets. The calculation is considered the minimum liability because it calculates benefits using current rather than projected future salaries that are likely to be higher.

minimum tax —See ALTERNATIVE MINIMUM TAX.

minimum tick The smallest possible price movement of a security or contract . —Also called *trading variation*.

minimum wage The rate of pay established by statute or contract as the lowest that an employer may pay employees for performing particular jobs. States sometimes establish a minimum wage that is higher than the federal minimum wage.

mini-tender offer An offer to purchase less than 5% of a company's stock. Investors are at greater danger in a mini-tender offer because it is not subject to many of the SEC disclosure and procedural protections that apply to traditional tender offers.

minor A person who has not yet attained legal age and is not considered legally competent.

minority business A commercial enterprise owned and operated at some specified minimum level by individuals considered as minority as defined by a particular organization or government department. In some instances a single minority owner among a group of owners may suffice for qualification as a minority business. Other organizations may require that minority investors hold at least 51% of ownership to qualify.

minority discount The reduction in value for less than 50% ownership of a business. Minority discount is particularly applicable to a closely held business in which there are a limited number of owners. —Compare CONTROL PREMIUM.

minority interest 1. In accounting, the ownership by the parent company of less than 100% of an affiliated firm. 2. A proportional ownership of a firm that is insufficient to constitute control. Generally, minority interest is viewed as ownership of less than 50% of the voting shares.

minority squeeze-out The elimination of minority shareholders by controlling shareholders.

minus tick —See DOWNTICK.

minutes A written record of the proceedings of a meeting.

MIS —See MANAGEMENT INFORMATION SYSTEM.

miscellaneous itemized deductions Certain expenses, including unreimbursed employee expenses and tax preparation fees, that are permitted as part of itemized deductions used to reduce taxable income. Only miscellaneous itemized deductions (with a few exceptions) that exceed 2% of adjusted gross income can be claimed. Miscellaneous deductions are aggregated with deductions for charitable contributions, medical expenses, mortgage interest, and casualty losses to determine total itemized deductions that are compared with the standard deduction.

misdemeanor A relatively minor crime with maximum punishment of a fine and county or city jail time of up to a year. Misdemeanors include public drunkenness, petty theft, and a variety of traffic violations.

misery index A measure of economic suffering that is calculated by adding the inflation rate and the unemployment rate. For example, an inflation rate of 4% and an unemployment rate of 5% result in a misery index of 9%. A higher index indicates a greater level of economic misery. The index peaked at nearly 21% in 1980.

misfeasance Improper performance of a lawful act. For example, a state highway employee might install a sign in such a way that it is difficult for drivers to see. —Compare MALFEASANCE; NONFEASANCE.

mismanagement Managing ineffectively, incompetently, carelessly, or wrongly. Mismanagement ranges from making poor decisions to breaking rules for personal gain.

misrepresentation Intentionally or unintentionally stating something that is untrue. Misrepresentation can create a liability if it is relied on by someone who suffers a loss as a result. The failure of a seller to identify known structural flaws in a home is a case of misrepresentation.

mission statement A clear and concise declaration of an organization's purpose. For example, Google's stated mission is to "organize the world's information and make it universally accessible and useful." A short mission statement is often followed by the organization's set of values that direct implementation of the mission.

mistake of law A failure to correctly interpret the legal consequences of an action. Mistake of law is not generally permitted as a valid defense of an illegal action.

MIT —See MUNICIPAL INVESTMENT TRUST.

mitigating circumstances Factors that, while not justification for an action such as a crime, should be considered as reasons for reducing the extent of blame. For example, a clerk took money from his employer in order to help pay the medical expenses for his invalid mother.

mitigation of damages 1. In law, a successful plaintiff's obligation to make an effort to minimize further damages. For example, a homeowner whose home suffered damage from a tree limb dropped by a tree service is obligated to take reasonable actions to reduce further damage from water and wind. 2. A defense utilized to reduce a damages award in a liability case. Defendants involved in securities litigation often bring up mitigation of damages as part of their defense. In these cases it is argued that the plaintiffs could, but didn't, take action to reduce the amount of damages.

mix The blend of merchandise offered by a wholesaler or retailer. —See also MARKETING MIX.

mixed economy An economic system in which the private and public sectors work together to solve economic problems. The United States, with privately owned manufacturing and service companies plus government rules and organizations that produce their own goods (highways, electricity, etc.) and services, offers an example of a mixed economy.

MLP —See MASTER LIMITED PARTNERSHIP.

MLS —See MULTIPLE LISTING SERVICE.

mobile home certificate A security issued by Ginnie Mae that is secured by mortgages on mobile homes. Mobile home certificates pass through interest payments and principal repayments to investors.

mode In statistics, the most frequently occurring value in a collection of data.

model 1. An abstraction of reality, generally referring in investments to a mathematical formula designed to determine security values. Economists also use models to project trends in economic variables such as interest rates, economic activity, and inflation rates. 2. A dwelling constructed by a developer that allows potential buyers to inspect the homes, apartments, or condominiums that will be offered for sale. 3. A particular type of vehicle produced by a manufacturer. For example, Escalade is a model offered by the Cadillac Division of General Motors Corporation.

modern portfolio theory —See PORTFOLIO THEORY.

Modified Accelerated Cost Recovery System (MACRS) A depreciation system in which assets are classified according to a prescribed life or recovery period that bears only a rough relationship to their expected economic lives. MACRS represents a 1986 change to the Accelerated Cost Recovery System that was instituted in 1981. The depreciation rates in MACRS are derived from the double-declining-balance method of depreciation. —See also CLASS LIFE.

modified accrual A system of accounting in which revenues are recognized when they become measurable and available to finance expenditures of the fiscal period. Modified accrual is used in government accounting.

modified adjusted gross income Adjusted gross income (the amount on the last line of the first page of IRS Form 1040) without a variety of items including passive losses or income, student loan interest, and qualified tuition expenses. Modified adjusted gross income is used to determine the tax-free status of interest from savings bonds used for education expenses and the deductibility of IRA contributions.

mom and pop store A small retail establishment, often owned and operated by members and relatives of a single family.

momentum The tendency of something to continue movement in a single direction: *The economy may be exhibiting upward momentum with increases in employment and output.*

momentum investor An investor who chooses to acquire the stocks of companies whose stock prices and earnings have been increasing at a faster pace than the overall market.

Monday effect The tendency of stocks to produce lower-than-average returns on Mondays compared to other days of the week. One study indicated most of the poor performance during Mondays occurs during the first hour of trading.

monetarism An economic theory, the proponents of which argue that economic variations, such as changes in prices and output, are primarily the result of changes in the money supply. (Thus, the Federal Reserve Board is the most important economic policymaker in the country.) Proponents of monetarism believe that changes in the money supply precede changes in other economic variables, including stock prices, and that a rational policy calls for moderate, steady increases in the money supply.

monetarist A proponent, usually an economist, of monetarism. Milton Friedman is probably America's best-known monetarist.

monetary gain The gain in purchasing power that is derived from holding monetary assets and/or monetary liabilities during a period of changing prices. An increase in prices tends to devalue monetary assets and monetary liabilities. Thus, if a firm's monetary liabilities exceeded its monetary assets, inflation would tend to produce monetary gains.

monetary items Assets on a firm's balance sheet that are fixed in dollar amount. Cash, short-term loans, and long-term bonds are monetary items.

monetary neutrality The theory developed by classical economists that changes in the money supply have no impact on output or real interest rates. Rather, changes influence the level of price inflation.

monetary policy The Federal Reserve's actions that are designed to influence the availability and cost of money. Specific policy includes changing the discount rate, altering bank reserve requirements, and conducting open market operations. In general, a policy to restrict monetary growth results in tightened credit conditions and, at least temporarily, higher rates of interest. This situation can be expected to have a negative impact on the security markets in the short run, although the long-run effects may be positive because of reduced inflationary pressures. —Compare ACCOMMODA-TIVE MONETARY POLICY.

monetary reserve Foreign currency and precious metals held by a central government and used to settle international transactions and enter into foreign exchange dealings.

monetary standard The backing, if any, of a country's currency. A gold standard means a country issues gold coins and paper notes that can be exchanged for gold. The United States was once on the silver and gold standard.

monetize To convert assets into money.

monetize the debt To convert government debt from interest-bearing securities into money. Although both the securities and the money are considered government debt, the latter can be used to purchase goods and services. Thus, monetizing the debt is considered an inflationary process and, although it may depress interest rates temporarily, it is likely to result in higher interest rates in the long run.

money A generally accepted medium for the exchange of goods and services, for measuring value, or for making payments. Many economists consider the amount of money and growth in the amount of money in an economy very influential in determining interest rates, inflation, and the level of economic activity. There is some disagreement among economists as to what types of things actually should be classified as money; for example, should balances in money market funds be included? —See also MONEY SUPPLY.

money center bank —See MONEY MARKET CENTER BANK.

money illusion The tendency of people to view their income and assets in nominal terms rather than real terms. People suffering a money illusion will consider themselves better off after receiving a 4% raise, even when prices have increased by 4% or more.

money manager —See PORTFOLIO MANAGER.

money market The market for trading short-term, low-risk securities such as commercial paper, U.S. Treasury bills, bankers' acceptances, and negotiable certificates of deposit. The market is comprised of dealers in these securities who are linked by electronic communications.

money market center bank A big commercial bank located in a large metropolitan center. Money market center banks play a leading role in trading financial instruments, determining market interest rates, and providing leadership to commercial banks located outside the money centers. —Also called *money center bank.*

money market deposit account A savings account at a commercial bank or thrift institution that pays a return competitive with money market funds. The number of transactions that may take place each month is limited. Institutions offering the accounts may require a minimum balance in order to receive money market yields.

money market fund A mutual fund that sells shares of ownership and uses the proceeds to purchase short-term, high-quality debt securities such as Treasury bills, negotiable certificates of deposit, and commercial paper. Income earned by shareholders is received in the form of additional shares of stock in the fund (usually priced at $1 each). Although no fees are generally charged to purchase or redeem shares in a money market fund, an annual management charge is levied by the fund's advisers. This investment pays a return that varies with short-term interest rates. Both taxable and tax-exempt varieties of money market funds are offered. —See also AVERAGE MATURITY.

money order A financial instrument that orders a specified sum of money paid to a named party. Money orders are widely available through convenience stores and the U.S. Postal Service.

money purchase plan A defined-contribution pension plan in which the employer contributes a specified amount of cash rather than shares of stock or a percentage of profits.

money supply The amount of money in the economy. Since the money supply is considered by many to be a critical element in determining economic activity, the financial markets attach great importance to Federal Reserve reports of changes in the supply. For example, consistently large increases in the money supply bring fears of future inflation. There are a variety of measures of the supply of money, depending on how strictly it is defined. —Also called *money stock.* —See also M1; M2; M3; MONETARISM.

monopoly¹ A business that is the sole supplier of a particular good or service. Regulated monopolies, such as electric utilities, are generally restricted as to the returns they are permitted to earn. Other monopolies, such as firms with unique products or services derived from patents, copyrights, or geographic location, may be able to earn very high returns. —Compare OLIGOPOLY.

monopoly² Of, relating to, or being a market in which there is a single seller of a particular good or service. For example, electric utilities nearly always operate in monopoly markets. —Compare MONOPSONY.

monopsony Of, relating to, or being a market in which there is a single buyer of a particular good or service. Businesses selling in a market characterized by monopsony are likely to suffer below-average profitability because of the lack of alternative outlets for their products. —Compare MONOPOLY².

Monte Carlo A statistical technique used in investigating a problem in which random numbers are used to perform a series of simulations that produce distributions used to provide guidance on the most likely values.

monthly investment plan An arrangement in which an investor contributes a fixed number of dollars into an investment, most likely a mutual fund, each month. —See also DOLLAR-COST AVERAGING.

Montreal Stock Exchange —See BOURSE DE MONTREAL, INC.

Moody's Investment Grade (MIG) A rating system used by Moody's Investors Service for municipal notes. The rating system classifies notes into four grades: MIG 1, best quality; MIG 2, high quality; MIG 3, favorable quality; and MIG 4, adequate quality.

Moody's Investors Service A leading firm engaged in credit rating, risk analysis, and research of fixed-income securities and their issuers. Moody's ratings help investors judge the credit risks of investing in fixed-income securities. The financial publications department of Moody's was spun off in 1998 to form a new company. —See also MERGENT, INC.

moonlight To work an extra job in order to earn additional income.

moot point An unsettled question about which the answer is without real significance.

morale The state of mind, including confidence and attitude, of an individual or group. Morale affects the quantity and quality of work performed and the ability to achieve assigned tasks.

moral hazard The increased likelihood of a negative outcome because of the personal characteristics or history of a situation. For example, individuals who purchase insurance are likely to exhibit more risky behavior because they know another party will cover financial losses.

moral obligation debt Government or municipal debt that carries an implied pledge of support, but that is not explicitly guaranteed by the full faith and credit of the guarantor organization. Moral obligation debt is generally issued in order to circumvent legal restrictions on borrowing. The securities are rated lower and carry higher yields than general obligation bonds of the same issuer.

moral suasion Using persuasion to encourage certain behavior. For example, to encourage more responsible lending, the chairman of the Federal Reserve mentions during a speech that the Fed is concerned about the quality of loans being made by commercial banks.

moratorium 1. Authority to delay an obligation. For example, a borrower may be legally permitted temporary suspension of payments on a loan. **2.** Suspension of some activity. For example, a zoning authority issues a moratorium on new residential building until environmental and infrastructure concerns are addressed.

Morningstar, Inc. A Chicago-based financial information service best known for its mutual fund publication and mutual fund rating system. The firm's star-based rating system is widely utilized by individual investors in selecting mutual funds.

mortality table A chart indicating probability of death and life expectancy in relation to certain variables such as age, sex, occupation, or socioeconomic class. —Also called *actuarial table.*

mortgage A pledge of specific property as security for a loan. —See also ADJUSTABLE-RATE MORTGAGE; CLOSED-END MORTGAGE; FIRST MORTGAGE; NO-DOC LOAN; REHABILITATION MORTGAGE; REVERSE MORTGAGE; SECOND MORTGAGE.

mortgage-backed revenue bond A municipal bond, the proceeds of which are used to provide funds to financial institutions for making mortgage loans at relatively low interest rates. Interest and principal on the bond are backed by borrower payments on the mortgages. As with other revenue bonds, the quality varies significantly among different issues of these securities.

mortgage banker An organization that makes real estate loans that are then resold to another party. The mortgage banker's income derives from the fees it charges to originate and service the mortgages. Sale of the mortgages gives the mortgage banker more funds to use in making additional loans. —See also WAREHOUSE LENDING.

mortgage bond A long-term debt security that is secured by a lien on specific assets, usually on fixed assets such as real estate. —See also CLOSED-END MORTGAGE; OPEN-END MORTGAGE.

mortgage broker A third party that acts as an intermediary in bringing together borrowers and lenders interested in transacting mortgage loans. Mortgage brokers typically work with multiple lenders, who pay a fee for loans generated by the broker.

mortgage constant The ratio of annual debt service (payment of principal and interest) to the outstanding principal amount of a mortgage. The mortgage constant is the lender's capitalization rate on a mortgage loan.

mortgage discount —See LOAN ORIGINATION FEE.

mortgagee An individual or business that makes loans secured by liens on real property. —Compare MORTGAGOR.

mortgage insurance Insurance coverage to protect the mortgage lender in the event the borrower defaults. Borrowers pay mortgage insurance premiums even though the insurance protects the lenders. —See also PRIVATE MORTGAGE INSURANCE.

mortgage lien A legal claim against real property used as collateral for a loan.

mortgage life insurance Decreasing term life insurance with coverage that pays the outstanding principal on a mortgage. Mortgage life insurance is generally purchased on the life of the family breadwinner so the mortgage will be paid off in the event the breadwinner dies.

mortgage participation certificate A pass-through security that represents ownership in a pool of conventional mortgages put together by Freddie Mac. Freddie Mac guarantees principal and interest on the certificates, and the income is subject to federal, state, and local taxation. —See also PASS-THROUGH SECURITY.

mortgage pool A combination of similar mortgages used as collateral for loans or for participation certificates sold to investors. —Also called *pool*.

mortgage purchase bond A housing revenue bond, the proceeds of which have been used to purchase mortgages from lending institutions. Interest and principal payments are derived from payments on the mortgages underlying the bond issue.

mortgage REIT A real estate investment trust that combines investors' funds with other borrowed money to make loans on real estate. The return earned by the investors depends on the spread between the interest rates charged on the loans made and the interest rates paid on the loans taken out. Earnings on a mortgage REIT are subject to wide fluctuations if the REIT makes short-term loans and takes out long-term loans. —Compare EQUITY REIT.

mortgage servicing Administering a loan, including recordkeeping, payment collection, releasing liens, making certain insurance and taxes are paid, and initiating foreclosure proceedings for loans that are in default. Mortgage servicing is done by lenders and by businesses that receive fee income.

mortgagor An individual or organization that pledges real property as security for a loan. —Compare MORTGAGEE.

most-active list The list of the most active securities in a specific market or in multiple markets during a defined period.

most-favored nation A nation whose imports are treated on the same basis as the nation that receives the most favorable treatment. A reduction in duties on products from one country is extended to any other country that has been recognized with most-favored-nation status.

motion study Analysis of the time and energy spent doing a particular job in an effort to determine how the work can be accomplished more efficiently.

motivation Stirrings within an individual that direct behavior toward an identified goal.

motivational research Studies that attempt to explain the underlying motives of consumer decisions. For example, a financial institution might employ a marketing firm to determine how young professionals decide where to open checking and savings accounts.

motor truck cargo insurance Liability insurance coverage purchased by common and contract truckers for the property of others that they are transporting. Common and contract truckers are liable for the cargo they transport.

mover and shaker A well-known and important person who wields substantial influence in a particular area. For example, Bill Gates is a global mover and shaker in charity work.

moving average A series of successive averages of a defined number of variables. As each new variable is included in calculating the average, the last variable of the series is deleted. For example, suppose a stock's price at the end of each of the last six months is $40, $44, $50, $48, $50, and $52. The four-month moving average in the fifth month is: ($44 + $50 + $48 + $50)/4, or $48. At the end of the sixth month, the four-month moving average is ($50 + $48 + $50 + $52)/4, or $50. Analysts sometimes use moving averages to discover trends in stock prices.

moving expense deduction The deduction permitted for unreimbursed moving expenses involved in relocating to a new job that meets both the distance and time tests established by the IRS. The new job must be at least 50 miles farther from the taxpayer's former home than the old job location. In addition, the taxpayer must work full-time at the new job for at least 39 weeks of the first 12 months following the move.

MSRP —See MANUFACTURER'S SUGGESTED RETAIL PRICE.

multicollinearity In statistics, a situation in which two or more variables that serve as predictors of another variable are correlated to one another. Multicollinearity makes it difficult to determine the relative importance of each predictor on the dependent variable. For example, a researcher wishes to determine the effect of oil prices and weather on the demand for gasoline. Because oil prices are affected by weather, it is more difficult to determine the relative importance of each in its effect on the demand for gasoline.

multiemployer bargaining Negotiations between a labor union and multiple small- and medium-size employers who have banded together for purposes of bargaining with the union. A representative of the employer group generally meets with the union representative to negotiate wages, benefits, and other issues between the employers and unionized employees.

multifamily housing A building comprising two or more dwelling units in the same structure.

multilateral trade Commerce among more than two entities. The North American Free Trade Agreement (NAFTA) is an example of a multilateral trade agreement. —Compare BILATERAL TRADE.

multilevel marketing Selling a good or service through a network of distributors. Essentially, sales take place through word of mouth and at parties rather than in stores. Distributors who successfully recruit additional distributors receive commissions on their own sales and also on the sales of the downline distributors they recruit. Multilevel marketing sometimes turns out to be disguised pyramid operations in which the main order of business is collecting fees from new distributors who wish to join the program.

multimedia An interactive system using a combination of video, audio, static imagery, graphics, and written material.

multinational Of, relating to, or being a company with subsidiaries or other operations in a number of countries. The diversity of operations of such companies subjects them to unique risks (for example, exchange rate changes or government nationalization), but at the same time offers them unique profit opportunities closed to domestic companies.

multiple **1.** In stock-index futures, the number multiplied by the futures price to determine the value of the contract. For example, the 500 multiple of the Standard & Poor's Midcap Index is multiplied by the futures price to determine the value of one contract. Thus, a futures price of $230 would yield a contract value of $115,000 (500 × $230). **2.** —See PRICE-EARNINGS RATIO.

multiple listing Real estate listings of individual brokers that are pooled under an arrangement that allows all brokers who are members of the pool to show and sell the properties. Commissions are shared between the listing broker and selling broker.

Multiple Listing Service (MLS) A group of private databases that provide member real estate agents and prospective buyers with a comprehensive listing of properties that are available for sale and with information about the properties.

multiple management The apportionment of a large portfolio's assets among several managers. This process permits the managers more flexibility, allows for closer monitoring of investments, and creates a competitive atmosphere among the managers. The major disadvantages are higher cost and the potential for a lack of coordination in meeting the fund's overall investment goals.

multiple regression A statistical technique to predict the value of a dependent variable that is influenced by two or more independent variables. For example, a company wishing to predict the success of potential employees might use grades earned in college, the score on a test given by the firm, interviews, and letters of recommendation. The firm would make predictions on the basis of the success or failure of past hires and how they had been rated on the four independent variables.

multiple unit pricing Establishing a single price for the purchase of two or more units of the same product. For example, a store advertises three candy bars for $1.00. Multiple unit pricing is designed to convince consumers they will gain an economic benefit by purchasing more than one unit of a product. This pricing strategy is most effective for low-priced merchandise.

multiplier **1.** The effect of a change in investment spending by business or government on a country's income. For example, a $1 billion increase in investment spending might cause national income to increase by $3 billion. The size of the multiplier depends on the proportion of income that people spend on consumption. **2.** —See GROSS RENT MULTIPLIER. **3.** —See AMERICAN CURRENCY QUOTATION.

multistate tax commission A joint state agency established in 1967 to improve the fairness, efficiency, and effectiveness of state tax systems as they apply to interstate and international commerce. The commission encourages tax uniformity and discourages double taxation. —See also NEXUS.

multitask To carry out two or more activities at the same time. For example, a business executive may respond to emails, write memos, read staff reports, and conduct phone interviews with job applicants during a trip to inspect a new corporate facility.

muni —See MUNICIPAL BOND.

municipal —See MUNICIPAL BOND.

municipal bond The debt issue of a city, county, state, or other political entity. Interest paid by most municipal bonds is exempt from federal income taxes and often from state and local taxes as well. The tax exemption stems from the use to which the funds from a bond issue have been devoted. Municipal bonds with tax-exempt interest appeal mainly to investors with significant amounts of other taxable income. —Also called *muni; municipal; tax-exempt bond.* —See also BOND BUYER INDEX; EX-LEGAL; GENERAL OBLIGATION BOND; REVENUE BOND; TAXABLE MUNICIPAL BOND.

municipal bond fund A mutual fund that invests in tax-exempt securities and passes through tax-free current income to its shareholders. Some municipal bond funds purchase long-term securities that provide a relatively high current yield, but vary substantially in price with changes in interest rates. Other funds choose short-term securities that have lower yields but fluctuate little in value. Municipal bond funds differ from municipal bond unit trusts in that the funds manage the bond portfolios and charge an annual management fee. —See also DOUBLE-EXEMPT FUND; TAX-EXEMPT MONEY MARKET FUND.

municipal bond insurance A guarantee from a third party that principal and interest will be paid to a bondholder. Municipal bond insurance is written by private corporations for a fee paid by issuers hoping to obtain higher credit ratings and lower interest costs. Investors purchasing insured bonds or insured trusts obtain increased safety at the expense of lower yields.

municipal convertible A unique municipal bond that is issued at a large discount from face value because it pays no interest until a specified date, at which time interest payments begin and continue until maturity. For example, a bond issued in 1998 and due in 2025 might begin paying interest in 2008. Essentially, a municipal convertible is a combination of a zero-coupon bond and an ordinary interest-paying bond. Municipal convertibles are traded under a variety of acronyms, including BIGS, CCAB, FIGS, GAINS, PACS, STAIRS, and TEDIS, depending on the underwriter of the particular issue.

municipal investment trust A unit investment trust that holds a portfolio of municipal bonds. Interest and principal received by the trust are passed to the trust's owners. Payments are generally free of federal income taxes and may be free of some or all state income taxes.

municipal note A temporary debt incurred by states, local governments, and special jurisdictions. Municipal notes are usually issued with a maturity length of 12 months, although maturities can range from 3 months to 3 years.

muniments of title Documents such as deeds or titles proving ownership of property.

Murphy's Law The well-worn maxim that "If something can go wrong, it will." The saying is attributed to engineer Edward Murphy, who was stationed at Edwards Air Force Base.

mutual association 1. A nonprofit organization of individuals or entities with a common interest. **2.** —See SAVINGS AND LOAN ASSOCIATION.

mutual company A company owned by its customers rather than by a separate group of stockholders. Many mutual thrifts and insurance companies converted to stock companies, which allowed them to raise funds in the capital markets. —Compare STOCK COMPANY.

mutual fund An investment company that continually offers new shares, and stands ready to redeem existing shares from the owners. Because the shares are purchased directly from and are sold directly to the mutual fund, there is no secondary market in these companies' stock. Individual mutual funds vary substantially in terms of the types of investments, their sales charges (many have none), and their management fees. —Compare CLOSED-END INVESTMENT COMPANY. —Also called *fund; open-end investment company.* —See also CLONE FUND; FAMILY OF FUNDS; LIFECYCLE FUND; LOAD FUND; REGULATED INVESTMENT COMPANY.

mutual insurance company An insurance company that is owned by its policyholders rather than by stockholders. Surplus earnings of mutual insurance companies are returned to policyholders. A number of mutual insurance companies decided to reorganize as stock companies in order to be able to raise additional capital by issuing shares of stock. —Compare STOCK INSURANCE COMPANY.

mutuality of contract An agreement in which each party has an obligation to do or agree to permit to be done something in consideration of the act or promise of the other. In other words, neither party is bound unless both are bound.

mutual savings bank A deposit-gathering thrift institution that chiefly makes mortgage loans. Mutual savings banks, typically located in the northeastern states, are state chartered and organized much like savings and loan associations. —Also called *savings bank.*

mystery shopper An independent shopper who is paid by a company, or the agent of a company, to evaluate one or more of the company's establishments. For example, a restaurant chain may employ mystery shoppers to evaluate the service and food at its restaurants. Mystery shoppers are ordinarily paid a nominal fee in addition to reimbursement of any expenses they incur. —Also called *secret shopper.*

■ N

NAFTA —See NORTH AMERICAN FREE TRADE AGREEMENT.

NAHB —See NATIONAL ASSOCIATION OF HOME BUILDERS.

naked option An opening transaction in an option when the underlying asset is not owned. For example, an investor writing a call option on 100 shares of IBM without owning the stock is writing a naked option. If the option holder calls the stock, the writer must purchase shares in the market for delivery and is therefore caught naked. —Compare COVERED CALL OPTION. —Also called *uncovered option.*

naked position A security position, either long or short, that is not hedged. For example, an investor short 500 shares of IBM with no other position in IBM stock (such as ownership of calls) has a naked position in that security. A naked position is considered aggressive, because it subjects the investor to large potential gains or losses.

naked writer The writer or seller of an option who does not also own the underlying security.

NAM —See NATIONAL ASSOCIATION OF MANUFACTURERS.

named nonowner coverage Automobile insurance protection for individuals who do not own a vehicle. Coverage generally includes liability, collision, and comprehensive, and may also incorporate medical payments and uninsured motorist coverage. Named nonowner coverage may be of interest to individuals who do not own a vehicle but frequently rent vehicles or drive vehicles owned by their employers.

NAR —See NATIONAL ASSOCIATION OF REALTORS.

narrow-based Of or relating to an index or other measuring device composed of a limited number of similar components. For example, the Dow Jones Transportation

Average is narrow based because it is composed only of the stocks of transportation companies. —Compare BROAD-BASED.

narrow basis A market condition in which only a small difference exists between a spot price and futures prices for the same type of contract. —Compare WIDE BASIS.

narrowcasting Distributing customized media content to a specialized audience. Specialized channels on satellite radio are examples of narrowcasting.

narrow market —See THIN MARKET.

NASD —See NATIONAL ASSOCIATION OF SECURITIES DEALERS.

Nasdaq The world's largest electronic stock market, with trades executed through a computer and telecommunications network connecting market makers, electronic communications networks, and order-entry firms. Nasdaq trading commenced in 1971, when the National Association of Securities Dealers owned the system. —Formerly called *National Association of Securities Dealers Automated Quotation System.*

Nasdaq Composite Index An index that indicates price movements of securities in the over-the-counter market. It includes all domestic common stocks in the Nasdaq System (approximately 5,000 stocks) and is weighted according to the market value of each listed issue. The index was initiated in 1971 with a base of 100. Specialized industry indexes are also published.

national account A key customer that is often serviced by a special salesperson or group. For example, a book publisher may employ several people who deal only with national booksellers such as Books-A-Million and Barnes & Noble.

National Association of Home Builders (NAHB) A trade association that promotes the interests of the building industry by pursuing policies that make housing a national priority. The association publishes educational material and actively lobbies local, state, and national politicians.

National Association of Manufacturers (NAM) A Washington, DC–based trade association that represents the interests of U.S. industry in national and international affairs. The NAM lobbies for industry-friendly legislation, including anticounterfeiting laws, restrictions on litigation, and tax benefits for business.

National Association of Realtors (NAR) A trade association of real estate agents and brokers whose stated mission is to help its members become more profitable and successful. The NAR actively lobbies for and against legislation that affects home ownership in general and realtors in particular. It publishes educational materials and requires that its members abide by a code of ethics and standards of practice.

National Association of Securities Dealers (NASD) An association of over-the-counter brokers and dealers that establishes legal and ethical standards of conduct for its members. NASD was established in 1939 to regulate the OTC market in much the same manner as organized exchanges monitor actions of their members. —See also RULES OF FAIR PRACTICE.

National Association of Securities Dealers Automated Quotation System —See NASDAQ.

national bank **1.** A privately owned bank chartered by the U.S. Comptroller of the Currency with membership in the Federal Reserve System and the Federal Deposit Insurance Corporation. **2.** —See CENTRAL BANK.

national brand A product that is marketed and distributed nationally. Examples of national brands include Crest toothpaste, Tommy Hilfiger clothing, and Whirlpool appliances. —Compare STORE BRAND.

National Bureau of Standards —See NATIONAL INSTITUTE OF STANDARDS AND TECHNOLOGY.

national debt The accumulated debt owed to creditors by the federal government. The national debt increases during periods when the U.S. government spends more than it takes in from tax revenues. It declines during periods when tax revenues exceed federal spending.

national income The sum of all of a country's income for a particular period. National income comprises income earned by both labor and capital, and includes wages, interest, profits, pensions, and rent.

National Institute of Standards and Technology A unit of the U.S. Department of Commerce that promotes U.S. innovation and competitiveness by promoting technology and developing measurement methods and standards. The name was changed in 1988 from National Bureau of Standards.

nationalization A government takeover of private property or operations. The government may or may not compensate the property owners. Multinational companies with operations in developing countries have frequently seen their assets nationalized.

CASE STUDY In January 2007 Venezuelan President Hugo Chavez announced that he intended to accelerate the country's socialist revolution by nationalizing some private firms, including telephone and utility companies. Chavez also indicated the country would become more heavily involved in foreign-operated domestic oil projects. The announcement produced a 19% decline in Venezuela's stock market and a major weakening of its currency. U.S.-based AES became a major target of the nationalization. AES is one of the world's largest global power companies, with operations in 26 countries on five continents. In Venezuela the firm owned 82% of a Caracas electric utility that it had purchased in 2000 for $1.6 billion. The Venezuelan utility generated approximately $100 million in annual dividends for the company. Although some analysts thought the 18% public ownership of the utility might provide some protection from nationalization, this was not the case. In February 2007, AES announced that it would be selling its 82% stake in the utility to Venezuela's state-owned oil company for $739 million. As a result, AES expected to record a pretax impairment charge of from $550 to $650 million during the first quarter of 2007.

National Labor Relations Act The 1935 legislation that protects the rights of most workers in the private sector by allowing them to join unions and engage in collective bargaining. The act prohibits employers from committing unfair labor practices to prevent workers from organizing unions or negotiating labor contracts. —Also called *Wagner Act.* —See also UNFAIR LABOR PRACTICE.

National Labor Relations Board (NLRB) An independent federal agency created in 1935 to administer the National Labor Relations Act. The NLRB has a five-member board that decides cases based on records of administrative hearings and a general counsel that investigates and prosecutes unfair labor practice cases. The agency is charged with determining whether employees wish to be represented by a union and with preventing unlawful acts by either employers or unions.

national market system (NMS) A centralized system for reporting transactions and quotations from all qualified market makers. A national market system has been encouraged by the SEC as a trading system that would increase competition among exchanges and market makers, thus providing investors with more liquidity and better prices. Essentially, a national market system is envisioned as a single large market in which market makers are linked by telecommunications with information being freely available. Customer orders would be automatically filled at the best available prices.

National Mediation Board An independent agency that attempts to resolve labor-management disputes in the railroad and airline industries. The board provides mediation services for major disputes and, in rare instances when mediation has failed and transportation services are subject to disruption, may inform the President of the United States. The President, at his discretion, may create a presidential emergency board to delay a work stoppage or lockout for up to 60 days.

National Stock Exchange A regional securities exchange dating to 1885, when a group of businessmen met in Cincinnati, Ohio, to auction the shares of several local companies. Operating as the Cincinnati Stock Exchange, it replaced its trading floor with a geographically dispersed electronic trading system in 1976. The exchange moved its headquarters to Chicago in 1995 and assumed its new name in 2003.

natural business year A 12-month year that ends during a time when a firm's business is at a natural low point. For example a toy manufacturer has a natural year that ends in February or March, when the busy holiday season is over.

natural monopoly An industry in which a business will have such enormous economies of scale that a single firm can effectively and efficiently supply the market at lower cost than two or more firms. A natural monopoly will dominate these industries if government does not impose restrictions. Electric utilities are generally considered natural monopolies.

natural resources Raw materials of personal and commercial value available from the earth.

NAV —See NET ASSET VALUE PER SHARE.

NDA —See NONDISCLOSURE AGREEMENT.

near money Assets that can be converted quickly and easily into cash with virtually no loss in value. Examples of near money are savings account balances and Treasury bills.

negative amortization An increasing loan balance that results from payments that are less than the interest being charged on the loan. The amount by which interest exceeds each payment will be added to the balance of the loan, thus increasing interest charged in subsequent periods.

negative carry The net cost of an investment position when the investment's cost of carry exceeds its current income. For example, buying a bond with a current yield of 6% and financing the purchase with money borrowed at 7% will result in a negative carry. —Compare POSITIVE CARRY. —See also CARRYING CHARGE 1; CARRY TRADE.

negative correlation An inverse relationship between two variables such that as one variable increases, the other variable declines. For example, the sales volume of large vehicles is negatively correlated with the price of gasoline. —Compare POSITIVE CORRELATION.

negative covenant A clause in a loan agreement that prohibits the borrower from an activity. For example, a negative covenant may restrict the payment of dividends or the issuance of new debt. —Compare POSITIVE COVENANT.

negative amortization

Negative amortization seems very risky. Why would a lender make a loan with negative amortization?

Like all loans, the risk a lender is willing to take is not only a factor of its loan policies, but often times may be influenced by market conditions and the need to grow a loan portfolio. That noted, as a matter of practice most lenders would not structure a loan with negative amortization. An example of when a lender would consider providing a loan with negative amortization is when the assets securing the facility are determined to have significant equity value.

▪ Brooke Barber, Vice President, Middle Market Banking, Atlanta, GA

negative income tax Government payments to an individual or household whose reported taxable income is below a specified amount. The negative income tax is a system of income redistribution in which individuals and households are guaranteed a minimum level of income (or tax payments).

negative net worth An excess of liabilities over assets. If the assets are fairly valued, a firm with negative net worth could sell all its assets and then be unable to pay all its outstanding loans. Thus, nothing would remain for the owners. —Also called *deficit net worth.*

negative pledge clause A restriction in a borrowing agreement that limits a borrower's ability to issue new debt having a priority claim on the firm's assets. A negative pledge clause, a part of some debenture agreements, protects the creditors against a dilution of security.

negative yield curve An unusual relationship between bond yields and maturity lengths that results when interest rates on long-term bonds are lower than interest rates on short-term bonds. Negative refers to the downward slope of the curve that is drawn to depict this relationship. —Compare POSITIVE YIELD CURVE. —Also called *inverted yield curve.*

negligence An unintentional failure to exercise due care, or accidentally taking action a reasonable person would not. For example, leaving sharp pieces of glass in your yard is negligent and may be used as the basis for a lawsuit in the event someone is hurt. —See also CONTRIBUTORY NEGLIGENCE.

negotiable 1. Of, relating to, or being a price that is not firmly established. **2.** Of or relating to an instrument that is easily transferable from one owner to another owner. With proper endorsement, most securities are negotiable. **3.** Of, relating to, or being an issue of importance to two or more parties where different options are subject to being changed.

negotiable bill of lading —See ORDER BILL OF LADING.

negotiable certificate of deposit A large denomination ($100,000 and larger) certificate of deposit that is issued in bearer form and that can be traded in the secondary market. Negotiable CDs appeal mainly to companies and institutional investors interested in low-risk investments with a high degree of liquidity. —See also MONEY MARKET.

negotiable order of withdrawal —See NOW ACCOUNT.

negotiable security —See MARKETABLE SECURITY.

negotiated offering A method by which a securities issuer selects an investment banking firm to assist in or guarantee the sale of securities on the basis of discussions and factors, including the best price.

negotiated share repurchase —See GREENMAIL.

negotiation Discussion of a disagreement with the intention of reaching a compromise. For example, a baseball player may enter salary negotiations for a new five-year contract.

Nellie Mae —See SALLIE MAE.

neoclassical economics A school of economics that preceded John Maynard Keynes and the Great Depression. Neoclassical economists believed individuals and business people are rational and make their own best decisions with regard to maximizing utility and profits, respectively.

nepotism Awarding jobs, promotions, raises, and other advantages to relatives and friends, with little consideration of qualifications and performance.

nest egg Funds placed in reserve to provide for an emergency, retirement, or some other purpose.

net 1. The difference between net proceeds from the sale of an asset and the total outlay for the purchase. **2.** The amount that remains after all relevant deductions have been taken. For example, the balance sheet item "net plant and equipment" is the dollar amount of plant and equipment after deducting accumulated depreciation. **3.** The difference between a series of additions and a series of subtractions. For example, a car rental agency has a net of 15 vehicles available for rent after considering returns and previous rentals for the day. **4.** —See NET INCOME.

net assets —See OWNERS' EQUITY.

net asset value —See BOOK VALUE 1.

net asset value per share (NAV) A valuation of an investment company's shares calculated by subtracting any liabilities from the market value of the firm's assets and dividing the difference by the number of shares outstanding. In general, net asset value per share is the price an investor would receive when selling a fund's shares back to the fund. Net asset value per share is similar in concept to book value per share for other types of firms.

net change The points or dollars by which the closing price of a security or a security average has changed from the closing price on the last previous day it traded. For example, a net change of −.50 for a stock indicates a 50¢-per-share decline from the last previous closing price to the present closing price. —Also called *change; price change.*

net contribution —See CONTRIBUTION MARGIN.

net current assets —See WORKING CAPITAL.

net domestic product The economy's output of goods and services less depreciation of the capital stock. Net domestic product is considered by some economists to be a more accurate measure of an economy's health than is the more often used gross domestic product.

net estate The value of an estate's assets less deductions for outstanding debts and funeral and administrative expenses. The federal estate tax is based on the net estate.

net income Income after all expenses and taxes have been deducted. Net income, the most frequently viewed figure in a firm's financial statements, is used in calculating

net estate

What are some methods of reducing a person's net estate so as to limit federal estate taxes?

Depending on its value, an individual's estate may be subject to a federal tax before any distributions are made to the heirs. In 2008 an individual could pass $2,000,000 to anyone estate-tax-free. This figure, sometimes referred to as the "applicable exclusion amount" or "unified credit amount," is scheduled to increase to $3,500,000 in 2009. Once an individual's assets exceed the "applicable exclusion amount," the balance is subject to the estate tax.

An individual can reduce the amount subject to the estate tax through deductions, debts, and estate administration expenses. Deductions can be particularly useful in reducing the amount of estate tax owed. Two deductions—the estate tax charitable deduction and the estate tax marital deduction—are unlimited in scope. This means that an individual can give an unlimited amount of assets to a qualified charity or to a surviving spouse with no estate tax consequences. Thus, in 2008 an individual with a hypothetical $10,000,000 estate could give $2,000,000 to his children and the balance to his wife or a charity and pay no estate taxes at all. Assume that our individual was not charitably inclined and had no interest in benefiting any charities at his death. If he passed all of his assets in excess of the "applicable exclusion amount" to his wife, she would inherit $8,000,000 estate-tax- free. When she died, however, she would only be able to pass $2,000,000 to the children estate-tax-free, leaving $6,000,000 subject to the estate tax. Sophisticated estate planning generally involves giving assets away before death in order to reduce the estate taxes payable at death.

Following are four of the methods most commonly used to reduce the amount of someone's net estate:

1. **Annual gifting.** An individual can give up to $12,000 annually to anyone he or she wishes. If used over time, this technique can reduce a person's net estate by thousands of dollars.
2. **Irrevocable Life Insurance Trust.** This trust usually benefits an individual's spouse and children after the individual dies. The trust enables the individual to transfer life insurance policies out of his or her name for estate tax purposes.
3. **Qualified Personal Residence Trust (QPRT).** This trust is used to transfer the ownership of one or more of an individual's residences to a named beneficiary. After a stated number of years, the individual must pay rent to the beneficiary in order to continue to live in the home; however, the value of the home is not included in his or her estate at death.
4. **Limited Liability Company/Family Limited Partnership (LLC/FLP).** These entities are often used to take advantage of discounting when giving assets away. Instead of receiving some or all of an asset outright, a donee receives an interest in an LLC or FLP. Because such interests are not marketable, they lack controlling interest, and they often represent a minority interest, their value is discounted, or adjusted downward to compensate. Discounts of between 25% and 40% for LLC and FLP interests are not uncommon.

▪ Paul G. Holland, Jr., JD, LLM, Director, Wealth Planning, MiddleCove Capital, Centerbrook, CT

various profitability and stock performance measures, including price-earnings ratio, return on equity, earnings per share, and many others. —Compare GROSS PROFIT. —Also called *aftertax profit; bottom line; net; net profit; profit.*

net income per share —See EARNINGS PER SHARE.

net investment income 1. The amount by which gross investment income (dividends, interest, rents, and royalties) plus capital gains net income exceeds allowable deductions. **2.** For investment companies, income from dividends, interest, and net realized short-term gains, adjusted for management fees and administrative expenses.

Net investment income of investment companies is paid to shareholders as a dividend. —See also NET REALIZED CAPITAL GAINS PER SHARE.

net leasable area The floor space of a building that is available for lease. Net leasable area excludes foyers, hallways, and areas devoted to elevators, air conditioning, and other utilities.

net lease A lease in which the tenant (lessee) is required to pay all maintenance, taxes, and insurance. The tenant is responsible for normal ownership expenses, leaving the lessor free of daily management responsibilities. —Compare GROSS LEASE. —Also called *absolute net; triple net lease.*

net listing A real estate listing in which the agent's commission equals the difference between the selling price and the net sale price stipulated by the owner.

net loss The operating result when expenses exceed revenues for a given period.

net margin —See NET PROFIT MARGIN.

net operating income (NOI) 1. In real estate, all revenues from a property, including rents and income from parking fees, vending machines, etc., less operating expenses for operations and maintenance. **2.** —See OPERATING INCOME.

net operating loss The amount by which deductions exceed income during a year. For a loss to qualify as a net operating loss for tax purposes, the loss must generally be the result of deductions from a trade or business, work as an employee, casualty or theft, moving expenses, or rental property. Net capital losses and personal exemptions are not permitted. In addition, partnerships and S corporations generally cannot use net operating losses. Businesses with a net operating loss can request tax refunds from prior years and carry over any excess losses to future years.

net plant and equipment —See PLANT AND EQUIPMENT.

net present value The discounted value of an investment's cash inflows minus the discounted value of its cash outflows. To be adequately profitable, an investment should have a net present value greater than zero. Net present value is a tool for evaluating an investment proposal.

net proceeds The revenues from the sale of an asset that have been reduced by commissions or other expenses directly related to the sale.

net profit —See NET INCOME.

net profit margin Aftertax net income divided by net sales, a measure of management's ability to carry a dollar of sales down to the bottom line for the stockholders. In other words, net profit margin refers to that which is left for the owners from a dollar of sales after all expenses and taxes have been paid. —Compare GROSS PROFIT MARGIN; RETURN ON SALES. —Also called *net margin.*

net quick assets Current assets readily convertible into cash, minus current liabilities. A large amount of net quick assets often characterizes a conservative firm with a very liquid financial position.

net rate The quoted price by a supplier that can be marked up by a wholesaler or retailer. For example, a tourist attraction may quote a net rate to a tour operator of $15 per person admitted.

net realized capital gains per share For an investment company, the excess of realized long-term capital gains over realized long-term capital losses per share outstanding. —See also NET INVESTMENT INCOME.

net realized value The amount that will be recognized from the sale of an asset less any expenses incurred from the sale. For example, a business owns a vehicle that could be sold for $22,000 after spending $1,500 on minor repairs, painting, and a sales commission. The vehicle's net realized value is $22,000 less $1,500, or $20,500.

net sales Total dollar volume of sales for a period after cash discounts, returns, and freight expenses have been deducted. —Compare GROSS SALES.

net tangible assets per share An assets measure calculated by dividing the difference of tangible assets minus liabilities and the par value of preferred stock by the number of common shares outstanding. Net tangible assets per share is frequently used by investors and raiders seeking undervalued stock.

net transaction A transaction in which no additional fees are paid. For example, securities that are part of a new issue are priced to include all fees.

network effect The increasing value of a good or service as new users are added. For example, a class reunion Internet site becomes a more valuable resource to each user as a greater number of people register and participate.

networking 1. Meeting and interacting with individuals who have similar interests in an effort to build relationships that will produce current and future benefits. 2. Connecting two or more computers in order to share resources, including applications, databases, and hardware.

net working capital —See WORKING CAPITAL.

net worth A measure calculated by subtracting total liabilities from total assets. For an individual, total assets are recorded at current market value. For a company, net worth uses assets as recorded on the balance sheet at historical cost minus any depreciation. —See also EFFECTIVE NET WORTH; OWNERS' EQUITY.

net yield The return earned on an investment after accounting for all expenses, including fees and taxes.

neutral 1. An investment opinion that is neither bullish nor bearish. A neutral opinion for an individual stock generally indicates the stock should not be purchased or sold. 2. Of or relating to an investment position that is likely to produce the best results if the market does not exhibit a major upward or downward movement.

New Deal The social and economic agenda of President Franklin Roosevelt during the Great Depression of the 1930s. Roosevelt's programs included increased government spending, social insurance, and an increased power for the federal government.

new issue A security that is being offered to the public for the first time. New stock issues are often quite risky; the securities may change significantly in price shortly after the initial sale has been completed. Many new issues appear near the end of an extended bull market. —See also INITIAL PUBLIC OFFERING; OFFERING PRICE.

new issue market —See PRIMARY MARKET.

new listing A security that has recently been added to an organized exchange's trading list. The security may have been moved from the over-the-counter market or from a different exchange, or it may be the stock of a firm that recently went public.

new money In corporate or U.S. Treasury debt refunding, the amount by which the par value of new securities exceeds the par value of the securities being refunded. The new money is the additional funds borrowed from the refunding operation.

New York Board of Trade (NYBOT) A leading exchange for trading futures and options contracts in cocoa, coffee, cotton, orange juice concentrate, and sugar. The NYBOT resulted from the 2004 merger of the New York Cotton Exchange and the Coffee, Sugar, and Cocoa Exchange.

New York Mercantile Exchange (NYMEX) A commodity futures and options exchange with two divisions: the NYMEX Division, trading contracts for crude oil, heating oil, gasoline, natural gas, propane, platinum, and palladium, and the COMEX Division, trading contracts for gold, silver, copper, and the Eurotop 100 Index. The current exchange is the result of a 1994 merger of the New York Mercantile Exchange and the Commodity Exchange (COMEX).

New York Stock Exchange (NYSE) The trademarked name of the largest and oldest organized securities exchange in the United States. The NYSE, founded in 1792, currently trades a substantial portion of the nation's listed stocks, including those of most large publicly traded firms. The NYSE merged in 2006 with Archipelago Holdings to form NYSE Group, Inc. One year later NYSE Group merged with Euronext to form NYSE Euronext. The New York Stock Exchange is now operated by NYSE Group, a subsidiary of NYSE Euronext. —See also NYSE ARCA; SECURITIES EXCHANGE.

> **CASE STUDY** On March 7, 2006, the New York Stock Exchange was transformed from a member-owned nonprofit exchange into a publicly traded corporation. The world's best-known exchange that commenced business in 1792 issued shares of ownership to the public in an eagerly awaited IPO. In an effort to remain competitive with other exchanges that had embraced cheaper electronic trading, the NYSE (renamed NYSE Group, Inc.) merged with Archipelago, an electronic trading network, and needed capital and a currency (the newly issued stock) to pay for its modernization. As part of the transformation, seat holders (former owners) received $300,000 in cash, $70,571 in dividends, and 80,177 shares of stock. The stock closed the first day of trading at $80 per share, a major increase from the IPO price. In June of the same year, the exchange beat out a German rival and agreed to acquire Paris-based Euronext, with exchanges in Paris, Amsterdam, Brussels, and Lisbon.

New York Stock Exchange Composite Index A composite index made up of all the stocks listed on the New York Stock Exchange and weighted according to the market value (stock price multiplied by shares outstanding) of each security. The base was set at 50 when the index was established in 1966. The exchange also calculates and publishes specialized indexes.

nexus A level of commercial activity within a legal jurisdiction that is sufficient to require a business to meet the jurisdiction's tax regulations, including the collection and remittance of a sales tax. —See also MULTISTATE TAX COMMISSION.

niche A specialty in which a person or business operates. For example, an individual bookseller might be able to earn a living by dealing only in a specialty, or "niche," area of books that consumers are unable to find elsewhere. Niche markets provide opportunities for small businesses, as they do not have to compete against large corporations, which find the markets too small to enter.

Nikkei Stock Average A price-weighted average of the stock of 225 large companies listed in the First Section of the Tokyo Stock Exchange. The Nikkei Stock Average is the most widely quoted average of Japanese equities.

NINA loan Acronym (no income, no assets) for a loan that does not require the borrower to disclose income or assets on the loan application. —See also NO-DOC LOAN.

niche

I'm interested in starting my own business. Can you suggest some market or product niches that I should investigate?

Niches occur in a market when there are unmet needs. You may be able to supply a product or service that is currently unavailable in a geographic area. You may find smaller groups within an established market that have unique needs that you can address. Because of the commitment (both financial and personal) required in a successful small business, it is important that you are ready to immerse yourself in filling these unmet needs. Therefore, your interests and passions are at least as important as the availability of a niche.

▪ Phyllis G. Holland, PhD, Professor and Head, Department of Management,
Langdale College of Business, Valdosta State University, Valdosta, GA

ninety-day letter A formal notice from the IRS indicating a tax deficiency and requiring a taxpayer response within 90 days. A taxpayer receiving a ninety-day letter may dispute the tax deficiency by petitioning the tax court. —Also called *notice of deficiency.*

NLRB —See NATIONAL LABOR RELATIONS BOARD.

NMS —See NATIONAL MARKET SYSTEM.

no-asset case In Chapter 7 bankruptcies, a case in which no assets are available to satisfy the claims of unsecured creditors.

no cash-out refinancing A mortgage refinancing in which a primary mortgage and secondary mortgages, along with associated expenses, are rolled into a single new mortgage without any cash being paid out to the borrower. —Compare CASH-OUT REFINANCING.

no-doc loan A loan for which the borrower is not required by the lender to provide full supporting documentation for qualifying. For example, a borrower states his income, but may not be required to provide pay stubs or tax returns. No-doc loans carry relatively high interest rates and appeal both to high-risk borrowers and to individuals who don't wish to reveal financial information. For example, a borrower may have unreported income they wish to keep off the record. Low-doc loans are a variation of no-doc loans that require more documentation. —Also called *low-doc loan.* —See also NINA LOAN.

no fault A system of automobile insurance in which all insured persons injured in a vehicular accident are compensated for their injuries without regard to who was at fault. No-fault insurance requires drivers to carry insurance for their own protection at the same time that it limits their right to sue other drivers for injuries. No-fault insurance was designed to reduce the costs of litigation.

NOI —See NET OPERATING INCOME.

noise Random fluctuations that make it difficult to forecast a variable such as the stock market.

no-load DRIP —See SUPER DRIP.

no-load fund An open-end investment company, shares of which are sold without a sales charge. No-load funds sell directly to customers at net asset value with no intermediate salesperson charging a fee. —See also LOW-LOAD FUND.

no-load stock A stock that can be purchased directly from the issuing company whether one is already a stockholder or not. Investors can acquire no-load stocks without paying a brokerage commission or opening an ordinary brokerage account.

nolo contendere The plea of a defendant who does not accept or deny the validity of charges, which are not contested. The plea results in a guilty verdict that cannot be used against the defendant in future legal proceedings.

nominal account In accounting, an account such as an income statement that doesn't relate to an individual customer.

nominal damages A small award made to a plaintiff who has not sustained a substantial injury or loss when the judge or jury wishes to indicate the defendant was at fault.

nominal dollars The actual dollar amount, without adjustment for inflation. For example, the selling price of the average home is $250,000, an increase of $12,500 from the previous year. The price and increase are stated in nominal dollars, and it is not clear if home prices kept up with inflation.

nominal interest rate The stated rate of interest, exclusive of any compounding, that is paid on an investment. For example, annual interest of $80 on a $1,000 investment is a nominal rate of 8%, whether the interest is paid in $20 quarterly installments, in $40 semiannual installments, or in an $80 annual payment. Use of nominal rates can be misleading when comparing returns from different investments. —See also EFFECTIVE RATE OF INTEREST.

nominal quote The approximate price of a security, although no firm bid or ask price is implied. —Compare FIRM QUOTE. —Also called *subject quote.*

nominal return The rate of return on an investment without adjustment for inflation. While nominal return is useful in comparing the returns from different investments, it can be a very misleading indication of true investor earnings on an investment. —Compare REAL RETURN.

nominal scale A list of events or categories without quantitative values or relationships. For example, a retail establishment may maintain a record of customers and whether they are male or female, and adult or minor.

nominal wage The wage of an individual or group without accounting for changes in consumer prices. For example, the statement that employees received a 50¢ raise to $11.50 per hour is in nominal terms, and does not indicate if the raise resulted in an increase in purchasing power.

nominal yield For a fixed-income security, the dollar amount of annual interest or dividends divided by the par value of the security. For example, a $1,000 par value bond that pays interest of $60 annually offers a nominal yield of $60/$1,000, or 6%.

nominee 1. A person or an organization in whose name a security is registered, even though another party holds true ownership. **2.** Someone who has been nominated for an official position. **3.** A person who acts for someone else.

nonacquiescence Announcement that a court decision will not be followed. For example, the IRS may issue a nonacquiescence when it disagrees with an adverse ruling by the U.S. Tax Court.

nonassessable capital stock Capital stock for which owners cannot be assessed additional funds to cover any liabilities of the firm. Thus, an owner of nonassessable capital stock can lose no more than his or her original investment. Nonassessable stock is the dominant kind issued in the United States.

nonassumption clause A provision of a mortgage that prohibits a transfer of the mortgage to another party without consent of the lender. A nonassumption clause can operate to the disadvantage of the borrower, who may wish to sell the property to someone who would benefit from the terms of the mortgage.

noncallable A provision of some bond and preferred stock issues that prohibits the issuer from redeeming the security before a certain date, or, in some cases, until maturity. A noncallable provision operates to the advantage of the investor. —Compare NONREFUNDABLE 1.

noncompete agreement **1.** A clause in an employment agreement in which an employee consents not to compete against the employer following termination of service. The agreement generally includes a specific length of time and the place or area in which competition is prohibited. For example, a salesperson signs an agreement not to contact the firm's customers for three years after leaving employment with the firm. **2.** A contractual arrangement in which a business agrees not to compete with another business. For example, a broadcasting group signs a contract with a cable operator giving the cable operator reduced access to the firm's programming in return for an agreement the cable operator will not buy sports programming from another source.

> **CASE STUDY** An employee of a Minnesota company resigned in 2000 to work for a California firm that made electronic devices similar to those manufactured by his former employer. Following the employee's arrival in California, the new employer filed an injunction to preclude the Minnesota firm from making use of a noncompete agreement that had previously been agreed to by the employee. The Minnesota firm then filed a lawsuit in its home state to enforce the agreement. A Los Angeles County superior court ruled in favor of the California firm and against the noncompete agreement. However, the California Supreme Court subsequently overturned this decision by ruling that the noncompete agreement could be enforced. The decision by the state's high court was somewhat of a surprise, because California law had generally made most noncompete agreements illegal. In practice, the legality and enforcement of these agreements varies widely among the states.

noncompetitive bid A method of purchasing U.S. Treasury bills at the weekly public auction without having to submit a price. With a noncompetitive bid, the investor agrees to purchase a given amount of securities (a minimum of $10,000 and a maximum of $500,000) at the average price set at the auction. Noncompetitive bids permit small investors to participate in the auction.

nonconforming loan A mortgage loan that is not eligible for sale to Fannie Mae or Freddie Mac. A loan may be nonconforming because it exceeds the established limit. A nonconforming loan may penalize a borrower with higher fees or a higher interest rate.

nonconforming use In real estate, the use of property that does not comply with provisions of a zoning ordinance, but is permitted to continue because the use was lawful prior to implementation of current restrictions. —Also called *preexisting use.*

noncontestability clause **1.** A provision in a life insurance policy that prohibits the insurance company from disputing a claim after a specified period. **2.** A provision in a will that is intended to keep beneficiaries from contesting the will's provisions.

noncontributory pension plan A pension plan in which the participating employees are not required to support the plan with contributions. —Compare CONTRIBUTORY PENSION PLAN.

noncumulative Of or relating to a relatively unusual kind of preferred stock on which missed dividends do not have to be made up. —Compare CUMULATIVE.

noncurrent asset An asset that is not expected to be turned into cash within one year during the normal course of business. Noncurrent assets include buildings, land, equipment, and other assets held for relatively long periods. Noncurrent assets are generally more profitable than current assets, but they also entail more risk because they are more difficult to turn into cash and are likely to fluctuate in value more than current assets.

noncurrent liability A liability not due to be paid within one year during the normal course of business. A long-term debt issue is a noncurrent liability.

nondischargeable debts Debts that remain valid following a filing for bankruptcy. Nondischargeable debts generally include federal, state, and local taxes, student loans, debts not listed in the bankruptcy filing, alimony, child support, and court-imposed fines and fees.

nondisclosure agreement (NDA) A contract in which each party promises confidentiality with respect to information that can be disclosed. A nondisclosure agreement may be used to keep secret a trade secret or a salary.

nondiscretionary trust A trust in which the trustee has limited decision-making authority with regard to the investments that can be held by the trust and the manner in which distributions can be made from the trust. —Compare DISCRETIONARY TRUST. —Also called *fixed trust*.

nondisturbance clause A provision in a mortgage that existing leases will be permitted to continue in the event the owner defaults on the loan so long as the tenants fulfill their obligations under the lease. A nondisturbance clause is an important consideration for a tenant who might otherwise remain in lease limbo in the event of a default by the property owner.

nondiversifiable risk —See SYSTEMATIC RISK.

nondiversified management company An investment company that does not agree to be subject to the investment limitations required of a diversified management company. Many venture capital funds, not wishing to be subject to diversification requirements, are classed as nondiversified management companies. —Compare DIVERSIFIED MANAGEMENT COMPANY.

nonequity option An option for which the underlying asset is anything other than stock. Nonequity options include commodity options, currency options, debt options, and stock index options. —Compare EQUITY OPTION.

nonessential function bond —See PRIVATE ACTIVITY BOND.

nonexclusive listing A real estate listing that is open for any broker to sell without sharing the commission with anyone else. —Compare EXCLUSIVE LISTING. —Also called *open listing*.

nonexempt employee A person employed in a position that is subject to minimum wage and the overtime pay provisions of the Federal Labor Standards Act. —Compare EXEMPT EMPLOYEE.

nonexempt property Personal property that may be lost in a Chapter 7 bankruptcy or to a lender who wins a court judgment. —Compare EXEMPT PROPERTY.

nonfamily household A person living alone or sharing a home exclusively with unrelated people, for example, roommates or unmarried partners.

nonfeasance Failure to satisfactorily perform a duty or legally required act. For example, a business may not meet the terms of a contract. —Compare MALFEASANCE; MISFEASANCE.

nonforfeitable The portion of a pension plan that belongs to the employee regardless of future employment. For example, employee retirement benefits at a particular company may be nonforfeitable after 25 years of creditable service or attaining the age of 55.

nonforfeiture provision The right of a life insurance policyholder to: (1) surrender a policy for the cash surrender value; (2) use the cash value to purchase a lesser amount of the same type of insurance; or (3) to exchange the cash value for term insurance of the same face amount as the original policy.

nonintegrated pension plan A defined-benefit retirement plan with benefits that are independent of Social Security retirement benefits. Retirees receiving benefits from a nonintegrated pension plan do not suffer a reduction in their retirement check when Social Security retirement benefits kick in. —Compare INTEGRATED PENSION PLAN.

nonmarketable security A security that may not be sold by one investor to another. This type of security is generally redeemable by the issuer, although within certain limitations. U.S. Treasury savings bonds and most certificates of deposit are nonmarketable securities. —Also called *nonnegotiable security.*

nonmember bank A state-chartered banking institution that is not a member of the Federal Reserve System. —Compare MEMBER BANK.

nonmember firm A firm that is not a member of an organized securities exchange. Nonmember firms must work through member firms to have their orders executed on the exchange.

nonnegotiable security —See NONMARKETABLE SECURITY.

nonoperating income Income derived from a source other than a firm's regular activities. For example, a firm may record as nonoperating income the profit gained from the sale of an asset other than inventory.

nonoperating unit A firm or a firm's subsidiary that operates no assets on its own, but distributes income received from other firms that operate assets leased from the nonoperating company. For example, a railroad may lease its line and equipment to other railroads and merely distribute net income received from the lease payments to the nonoperating railroad's stockholders. —Compare OPERATING UNIT.

nonparametric statistics Statistical procedures used when the researcher has no information about the parameters of the variable. For example, ranking data from highest to lowest by assigning numbers on the basis of sample size is a nonparametric technique. Compared to parametric statistics, nonparametric techniques require fewer assumptions, but tend to be less powerful.

nonparticipating 1. Of, relating to, or being a class of preferred stock that does not have the right to participate with common stock in earnings growth through increases in dividends. Nearly all preferred stock issues are nonparticipating. —Compare PARTICIPATING 1. **2.** Of or relating to a type of life insurance policy in which policyholders do not share in the investment successes or failures of the insurer. —Compare PARTICIPATING 2.

nonperforming asset An asset that produces no income. For example, a loan on which the borrower is not making payments is often described as a nonperforming asset by the lender. Firms often continue to include these assets, which are of questionable value, on their financial statements because they do not wish to show the losses entailed in writing them off. —Compare UNDERPERFORMING ASSET. —Also called *nonperforming loan.*

nonprice competition Competition among firms that choose to differentiate their products by nonprice means, for example, by quality, style, delivery methods, locations, or special services. Firms that desire to differentiate virtually identical products often practice nonprice competition. Companies producing cigarettes, over-the-counter medications, and food products spend large sums on nonprice competition.

nonprobate assets An asset, such as one held in joint tenancy, that does not have to pass through probate in order to be transferred. Nonprobate assets include pension plans, life insurance policies, and jointly held property with survivorship rights. —Compare PROBATE ASSETS.

nonproductive Of or referring to a person or asset that produces little or no useful output.

nonprofit organization An entity that is operated for some public purpose, rather than to pursue and accumulate profits. Certain types of profits are permitted, but they must be used for the benefit of the organization. Congress has established specific standards under which nonprofit organizations may seek tax-exempt status. —Compare FOR-PROFIT.

CASE STUDY A 2006 report by the Congressional Budget Office estimated that in 2002 nonprofit hospitals benefited from $2.5 billion in tax savings that resulted from their corporate tax exemption, plus an additional $1.8 billion in reduced interest expenses from issuing tax-exempt debt securities. The reduced borrowing cost results from the lower interest rate that is acceptable to investors who are not required to pay personal income taxes on interest income derived from tax-exempt securities. The result was that nonprofit hospitals enjoyed a significantly lower cost of capital compared to their for-profit competitors. One study indicated that in 2006 for-profit hospitals had a cost of capital of 12.9%, while nonprofit hospitals had a cost of capital of only 10.8%. The financial advantage accorded these nonprofit organizations results from the expectation they will provide community benefits, including charity care, health screening, health education programs, and emergency room services. More than half of community hospitals providing short-term care are nonprofit, while the remaining institutions were approximately evenly split between for-profit and government-owned hospitals.

nonpublic information Information about a company that is unknown to the public. Insiders, including corporate officers and directors, are prohibited from buying or selling their firm's securities on the basis of nonpublic information.

nonqualifying annuity An annuity not approved by the Internal Revenue Service for tax-deferred pension contributions. A nonqualifying annuity permits the investor to defer taxes on income earned by the annuity, but not to reduce taxable income for contributions made to the annuity.—Compare QUALIFYING ANNUITY. —See also RABBI TRUST.

nonqualifying stock option An option to purchase stock that does not meet certain requirements established by the Internal Revenue Service for favorable tax treatment. Acting on a nonqualifying stock option results in taxable ordinary income on any gain made during the year the option is exercised. —Compare INCENTIVE STOCK OPTION.

nonrated bonds —See NOT RATED.

nonrecognition transaction The sale or exchange of an asset at a gain or loss that is not recognized for tax purposes. A shareholder of a company that is acquired by another company in a stock-only purchase is not required to recognize the transaction for tax purposes unless and until the new shares are sold.

nonrecourse loan A loan in which the lender cannot claim more than the collateral as repayment in the event that payments on the loan are stopped. Thus, a group of investors may purchase an asset with a down payment and the proceeds from a non-recourse loan. In the event that the investment turns sour, the investors are not apt to lose more than the down payment and payments already made on the loan. The lender will absorb the unpaid balance on the loan. —Compare RECOURSE LOAN. —Also called *without recourse.*

nonrecurring charge An expense that is not expected to be encountered again in the foreseeable future.

nonrefundable 1. Describing a provision of some bond issues that prohibits the issuers from retiring the bonds before a specified date, on which funds for the retirement will be raised externally (that is, from outside the issuing firm). Essentially, this provision restricts a borrower from taking advantage of lower interest rates by replacing a bond issue that carries a high coupon rate of interest with a new bond issue that carries a reduced coupon rate of interest. Most bonds are nonrefundable for five to ten years from the date of issue. —Compare NONCALLABLE. **2.** Of or pertaining to a fee or deposit that will not be returned even if the service remains unused or the product is returned. Many inexpensive airline tickets are nonrefundable, even if they are not used.

nonresident alien A person who is not a U.S. citizen, is not a lawful permanent resident (the green card test), or is unable to pass the substantial presence test developed by the Internal Revenue Service. The substantial presence test requires a presence of less than 183 days during the most recent three years to be classified as a nonresident alien. —Compare RESIDENT ALIEN.

nonstock corporation A member-owned corporation that does not issue shares of stock. Nonstock corporations are without any profit motive and are formed to provide a service to their members.

nonstore retailing Offering products for sale outside of a retail store setting. Examples of nonstore retailing avenues include vending machines, mail order, home or office parties, and online computer shopping.

nontaxable income Income items specifically exempted from taxation. On federal returns, the interest from most municipal bonds, life insurance proceeds, gifts, and inheritances is generally nontaxable income.

nonvoting stock Stock in which the holder has no vote in the election of directors, the appointment of auditors, or other matters that may be brought up at the annual meeting. Corporations sometimes create a special class of nonvoting stock to restrict corporate control only to certain groups. Most preferred stock is nonvoting. —Compare VOTING STOCK.

no par Of or relating to a stock with no specific value assigned to it at the time of issue. Whether a stock has a par value or not is no longer of any consequence to investors.

normal distribution In statistics, a bell-shaped distribution of outcomes of a symmetrical nature that is concentrated near the mean. A normal distribution is used to predict the value of a variable.

normal good A product for which demand is directly related to income. Most durable goods are considered normal goods, in that sales increase during periods of increased economic activity and decline during recessions.

normalized earnings Past or forecasted earnings that have been adjusted for cyclical variations. Calculating a moving average of earnings per share over a number of successive periods is often used to normalize earnings.

normal operating cycle —See OPERATING CYCLE.

normal profit In economics, the return an entrepreneur expects from a particular investment in order to commit funds and remain in the business. Normal profit is a function of the risk of the investment plus the return that can be earned on a risk-free investment. Returns higher than a normal profit will attract additional entrepreneurs and increase competition, while returns below a normal profit will cause firms to leave the industry and invest their funds elsewhere.

normal retirement age The youngest age at which a person can retire and draw a pension without a reduction in benefits. The normal retirement age for many plans is 65 years of age. The normal retirement age for Social Security benefits is scheduled to gradually increase to age 67 in 2027.

normal trading unit —See ROUND LOT.

normal wear and tear Physical deterioration of assets as a result of age and normal use.

normative economics Economic analysis that applies personal judgments. Opposing an increase in the minimum wage by claiming it will hurt the poor is an example of normative economics.

North American Free Trade Agreement (NAFTA) A 1994 agreement by the governments of Canada, Mexico, and the United States to stimulate trade and investment by lowering or eliminating trade barriers among the three countries. Provisions of the agreement also addressed worker and environmental concerns. —See also FAST TRACK 2.

North American Industry Classification System A product-oriented classification system utilized to facilitate the collection, tabulation, and analysis of data that is grouped according to similarities in the processes used to produce goods and services. The system was developed in order to provide comparability of economic statistics.

no-shop provision —See LOCKUP AGREEMENT.

no-strike clause A written agreement by a union not to engage in an organized work stoppage, generally in return for a concession by the employer. A no-strike pledge is often accompanied by an agreement for binding arbitration.

notarization A notary public's guarantee that a signature is authentic.

notary public A public official who administers oaths and who certifies signatures and copies of documents.

notarization

My business is required to notarize a large number of documents each year. How do I go about getting one of my employees approved as a notary public? What expenses are involved?

The answer will depend upon the physical location of your business, as the specific application process, eligibility, and costs for becoming a notary vary according to each state. The first step to becoming a notary is to contact your state government to check on eligibility requirements and to request an application. Authority to commission notaries usually falls to the Office of the Secretary of State, although there are exceptions.

General guidelines applicable to most states require the individual be at least 18 years of age, a legal resident of the state in which he or she intends to become a notary and be able to read and write English. A notary applicant does not have to be a United States citizen. Most states will not allow an individual who has been convicted of a felony or of any crime involving fraud or dishonesty to apply for notary status.

States may require a written test, formal notary education, the posting of a bond and of course filing fees. There are states that do not require a test (Minnesota); some that require a test without requiring notary education (Connecticut); and others that may require both notary education and a test (California, Pennsylvania). Information with regard to specific requirements of each state can be obtained from the websites of the National Notary Association (NNA) or the American Society of Notaries (ASN).

With regard to expenses, once again much of it will be state-specific. For example, the state may require the individual to take an educational course prior to application. The state will charge an application or filing fee. Some states, such as Nebraska and Illinois, require the applicant to purchase a bond, while others, such as Connecticut, do not. The notary bond protects the public (not the notary) from losses due to improper notarization. Bonds can be purchased from an insurance company that issues bonds or a bonding company (check your yellow pages). The cost of the bond varies but generally ranges from $50 to $250 per year depending on state requirements.

In addition to educational, filing, and bonding expenses, some states require that the notary purchase a record book (or journal of notarial acts) and a stamp or a seal, while other states, such as Louisiana, consider the notary signature as the notarial seal. Even if these items are not required by a state, purchase of a notary stamp, seal, and record book is still recommended because their use is considered a "best practice" for notaries. With regard to expenses, it is important to note that even if the employer pays for these notary accoutrements, in most states the certificate, stamp (seal), and record book belong to the notary. This means that if the notary leaves his or her place of employment, these items do not stay at the business, but rather go with the notary.

▪ Helen M. Kemp, Division Counsel and Assistant Director,
Retirement and Benefit Services, Office of the State Comptroller, State of Connecticut

note 1. A written promise to pay a specific sum of money on a certain date. —Also called *promissory note.* **2.** —See FOOTNOTE.

note payable A debt owed to a lender and evidenced by a written promise of payment. Notes payable, an entry on the liabilities side of many corporate balance sheets, indicates that a certain dollar amount of loans will be repaid to the lender at a future time.

note receivable A debt due from borrowers and evidenced by a written promise of payment. Notes receivable, an entry on the asset side of many corporate balance sheets, indicates the dollar amount of loans due to be repaid by borrowers.

not for profit —See EXEMPT ORGANIZATION.

notice of default A formal notice sent by a lender to a borrower who is in default of the terms of a loan. The filing of a notice of default is the initial step in the process of foreclosure.

notice of deficiency —See NINETY-DAY LETTER.

notice to quit **1.** A landlord's notice to a renter to vacate the premises. **2.** A tenant's notice to a landlord that the tenant plans to vacate the premises.

not rated Of or relating to an issue of fixed-income securities that has not been rated by an agency such as Moody's or Standard & Poor's. The fact that an issue is not rated does not necessarily mean the securities are risky. —Also called *nonrated bonds.*

novation The substitution of one debt with another debt.

NOW account An interest-bearing account on which checks may be written. Authorized on a national scale in 1981, these accounts pay a relatively small return. Therefore, the balances in NOW accounts should be kept at the minimum necessary to provide needed funds without incurring service charges. —Also called *negotiable order of withdrawal.*

NSF check A check not honored by the bank on which it was written because of insufficient funds in the drawer's account. An NSF check is an overdraft.

nuisance In law, use of land that interferes with someone else's right to use and enjoy neighboring lands. —See also ATTRACTIVE NUISANCE.

null and void Describing a provision or contract that is legally unenforceable. For example, a contract to steal money is null and void, because the act of stealing is illegal. Also, if a contract indicates a date by which time something must be done, and it is not, the contract is null and void.

null hypothesis In statistics, the statement that any difference between groups or variables is due to chance. Statistical analysis is then used to determine if the null hypothesis can be disproved. For example, a marketing research department posits that sales are the same regardless of whether a particular product is placed on the top shelf or bottom shelf of a display. A sample of sales data is then used to determine if the probability of incorrectly stating that the shelf chosen for the display is important.

numbered account An account identified by something other than the owner's name.

nuncupative will A will delivered orally by the testator to witnesses.

NYBOT —See NEW YORK BOARD OF TRADE.

NYMEX —See NEW YORK MERCANTILE EXCHANGE.

NYSE —See NEW YORK STOCK EXCHANGE.

NYSE Arca An all-electronic stock market in which buyers and sellers meet directly (without intermediaries) to trade equity securities and option products. NYSE Arca was formerly known as the Archipelago Exchange, or ArcaEx, prior to its merger with the New York Stock Exchange. NYSE Arca is operated by NYSE Group, a subsidiary of NYSE Euronext.

NYSE Euronext A for-profit publicly traded company formed in 2007 by the merger of NYSE Group, Inc., and Euronext N.V. NYSE Euronext serves as the parent of NYSE Group, which operates the New York Stock Exchange (floor-based trading) and NYSE Arca (electronic trading), and of Euronext, a pan-European exchange.

nuncupative will

Is a nuncupative will easier to challenge? If so, why would someone choose a nuncupative will?

Precisely because of the possibility of mistake, fraud, and perjury, the circumstances in which a nuncupative will is permitted have been narrowly limited in all jurisdictions. Generally, a nuncupative will can only be made by members of the armed forces during war or armed combat and by mariners at sea, and the will ceases to be valid following the expiration of a period of time after the testator has emerged from those circumstances. In some jurisdictions, a nuncupative will can be made during the testator's last illness. The privilege of making a nuncupative will is limited to a narrow group of persons who are deemed unable to make a written will; no one, even persons in this group, should choose a nuncupative will.

■ Stephen F. Lappert, Partner, Trusts and Estates Department, Carter Ledyard & Milburn LLP, New York, NY

O

obligation bond A debt obligation for the purchase of real estate that is for an amount greater than the money that is loaned. The excess obligation creates a personal liability of the borrower for charges such as insurance premiums, property taxes, and unpaid interest.

obligator The person who is bound by an obligation. A borrower is an obligator.

obligee The person to whom an obligation is owed. A creditor (lender) is an obligee.

obsolescence The diminished value of an asset because of reduced productivity compared to alternative assets. Obsolescence is particularly evident in computers, as new models with more memory and faster processors result in obsolescence of older models that remain functional.

OCC —See OPTIONS CLEARING CORPORATION.

occupancy level The proportion of available units in an apartment building, office building, or neighborhood that are occupied. —Compare VACANCY RATE.

occupation The category of employment that serves as a person's principal source of earned income.

occupational analysis Identification of the tasks, skills, and abilities involved in a particular occupation for use in creating job descriptions and establishing remuneration levels.

occupational hazard A typical workplace condition that increases the likelihood of an accident or sickness. Occupational hazards are an important consideration by property and casualty insurance companies in establishing premiums and including limitations on policies.

Occupational Safety and Health Administration (OSHA) The federal agency established in 1971 to establish and enforce standards for a safe and healthy workplace environment. OSHA administers and enforces the Occupational Safety and Health Act passed in 1970.

occupational tax A state or local government fee levied on a business or profession. Most occupational licenses and permits must be renewed annually.

odd coupon —See IRREGULAR COUPON.

odd lot A unit of trading in securities that is made up of fewer than 100 shares of stock or $25,000 face amount of bonds. —Compare ROUND LOT. —See also LOT.

odd-lotter An investor who buys and sells securities in less than the standard unit of trading. Odd-lotters are generally small investors lacking the financial resources to engage in larger trades.

odd pricing Establishing a price that is immediately below an even dollar amount. For example, a shirt is priced at $17.99 rather than $18.00. Odd pricing is used to give the impression of greater value.

OECD —See ORGANIZATION FOR ECONOMIC COOPERATION AND DEVELOPMENT.

OEM —See ORIGINAL EQUIPMENT MANUFACTURER.

off-balance-sheet financing An accounting technique in which a debt for which a company is obligated does not appear on the company's balance sheet as a liability. Keeping debt off the balance sheet allows a company to appear more creditworthy, but misrepresents the firm's financial structure to creditors, shareholders, and the public. The sudden collapse of energy-trading giant Enron Corporation has been attributed in large part to the firm's off-balance-sheet financing through multiple partnerships.

offer 1. A proposition to enter into an agreement. **2.** —See ASK.

offering —See PUBLIC OFFERING.

offering circular An abbreviated prospectus that describes a new securities issue.

offering date The date on which a new securities issue is to be sold.

offering price The price at which an investment is offered to buyers. This price, including any sales fee, is fixed by the underwriting syndicate. —Also called *fixed price*.

offering scale —See SCALE 2.

office building A structure devoted primarily to business involving administrative and clerical work.

Office of Management and Budget (OMB) The federal executive-branch agency charged with assisting the President in preparing and administering the federal budget. The OMB establishes funding priorities, evaluates programs, and ensures reports and proposed legislation are consistent with administration policies.

Office of the Comptroller of the Currency —See COMPTROLLER OF THE CURRENCY 1.

office park A property developed specifically for office buildings, support facilities such as restaurants and convenience stores, and, occasionally, light industry. Office parks are generally located near major highways and interstates to facilitate travel by employees.

official rate In foreign exchange trading, the lawful rate at which an exchange rate is set.

official reserves Gold, SDRs, and foreign currencies held by a country's central bank.

official statement A disclosure of financial and operating information relevant to a municipal bond issue. This statement is similar to the registration statement required of private issuers of securities.

off-peak Of or relating to a period of less than maximum use. For example, retailers typically reduce staffing during off-peak hours. An electric utility may price electricity lower during off-peak periods, when excess capacity is available. The lower rate influences some consumers to change their usage patterns at the same time it allows the utility to utilize its most efficient production facilities. —See also VARIABLE PRICING.

> **CASE STUDY** Giant retailer Wal-Mart announced in early 2007 that the company planned to use labor optimization software to schedule employees according to the number of customers in its stores. At the time of the announcement, the firm was scheduling most of its workers in line with sales, rather than customer traffic. The new software would require the firm's workers to be more flexible (e.g., accept less predictable hours) regarding work during periods of peak and off-peak customer traffic. Employees might be sent home early during off-peak periods when customer traffic was low, or be "on call" to come to work during customer surges. The software could also identify employees who had worked enough hours to approach full-time status. Many of the firm's hourly employees were concerned about the new scheduling plan, which was likely to produce more days of work but fewer hours per day. In addition, some full-time employees who earned a higher wage and received benefits worried that they would be replaced with part-time workers. The scheduling software was likely to benefit customers and stockholders, but not the firm's employees.

off-price store A retail store that sells merchandise at reduced prices compared to other stores. Off-price stores are often located in strip malls and include the chains T. J. Maxx, Steinmart, and Ross.

offset 1. The liquidation of a futures or option position by purchasing (for a short position) or selling (for a long position) an equal number of identical contracts so that no further obligation exists. **2.** Counterbalancing one action or value with another. For example, funds from a customer's savings account can be used to offset interest on a loan.

offshore 1. Of or relating to a financial organization whose headquarters lies outside the United States. Although offshore institutions must abide by U.S. regulations for operations carried on within the United States, other activities generally escape domestic regulation. **2.** Oil and gas operations in the sea.

offshore manufacturing Foreign manufacturing by a domestic company, generally for export to the country in which the domestic firm is located. For example, a U.S. clothing manufacturer establishes a factory in Asia with output exported mainly to the United States.

off-site cost The expense of a remote activity in support of an organization's main pursuit. For example, a financial institution has off-site costs while maintaining records in a remote location. Off-site costs for disposal of drilling wastes can be a major expense for oil and gas companies.

off the balance sheet Describing those assets controlled and liabilities owed by an organization that are not listed on the organization's balance sheet. Lease transactions are sometimes structured so that a major asset is acquired by means of an operating lease rather than a capital lease. —See also OFF-BALANCE-SHEET FINANCING.

off the books Describing a business transaction for which no official record is maintained. Transactions and payments generally take place off the books in order to hide them from government officials, especially the IRS.

OID —See ORIGINAL-ISSUE DISCOUNT.

oil patch A geographical area with substantial deposits of crude oil, natural gas, or oil sands. In the United States, most deposits are in the states of Alaska, Louisiana, Oklahoma, and Texas. Huge reserves of oil sands are in Canada's province of Alberta.

Okun's Law The negative relationship between changes in a nation's unemployment rate and its ratio of actual to potential output. Economist Arthur Okun's research beginning in the 1950s indicated an approximate 1% increase in the unemployment rate was accompanied by a 3% decline in the ratio of actual output to potential output. Subsequent investigations indicated technological changes have caused the ratio to narrow.

oligopoly A market in which a limited number of sellers follow the lead of a single major firm. For example, the domestic tobacco market can be characterized as an oligopoly, with Philip Morris division of Altria being the dominant company in an industry with few participants. —Compare MONOPOLY[1]; OLIGOPSONY. —See also DIFFERENTIATED OLIGOPOLY; DUOPOLY; HOMOGENEOUS OLIGOPOLY.

oligopsony A market in which a limited number of buyers follow the leadership of a single large firm. For example, in a town or region, a large bank may set rates on certificates of deposit that are then adopted by smaller banks and savings and loan associations on their own certificates of deposit. —Compare OLIGOPOLY.

OMB —See OFFICE OF MANAGEMENT AND BUDGET.

ombudsman A person appointed by an organization to receive, investigate, and report on questions and complaints. For example, a city may appoint an ombudsman to listen to and investigate citizen complaints about pubic officials or agencies.

omitted dividend —See PASSED DIVIDEND.

on account 1. A payment that reduces the balance of an outstanding debt. 2. The purchase of a good or service.

on demand When requested. For example, a loan may be payable on demand of the lender.

OneChicago, LLC An electronic exchange formed in 2001 for trading futures contracts on narrow-based indexes and individual common stocks. OneChicago is a joint venture of the Chicago Mercantile Exchange, the Chicago Board Options Exchange, and the Chicago Board of Trade.

one-decision stock A stock that can be bought and held indefinitely such that no second decision to sell is required. The essence of this investment philosophy is that, although temporary aberrations in the stock's price may occur, the stock should outperform the market over an extended period.

one-hundred-percent location The best location for a retail store relative to other sites that are available. The location is generally at a busy intersection with easy access.

one hundred percent statement —See COMMON-SIZE STATEMENT.

one-sided market The market for a security in which only a single side, either the bid or the ask, is quoted. —Compare TWO-SIDED MARKET. —Also called *one-way market.*

one-time rate In advertising, the cost of placing an advertisement that will run once.

one-way market —See ONE-SIDED MARKET.

on order Of or relating to goods that have been ordered but have not yet been delivered to the buyer.

on speculation Preparing something without assurance of acceptance or payment. For example, a writer may author an article on speculation for a magazine.

on-the-job training Learning the tasks and responsibilities of a particular type of employment while engaged in the job as a livelihood.

on the sidelines Of or relating to investors who, having assessed the market, have decided to avoid committing their funds. These investors keep their money in short-term investments, such as money market funds, and wait for a more opportune time to invest. —Also called *sideline*.

open account An arrangement in which a seller allows a customer to buy on credit without a formal borrowing agreement. With no formal guarantee of payment, open accounts can be risky for a seller.

open dating Use of an understandable calendar date (as opposed to a code) on a product's packaging. Open dating allows a retailer to easily determine how long to display a product and helps consumers determine how long they have to use the product. —Compare CLOSED DATING.

open-door policy 1. A national policy of equal trading and development rights for all foreign nations. **2.** A managerial philosophy that employees should be free to ask questions of and share concerns with supervisors at all levels. An open-door policy contrasts with a more formal policy of requiring employees to always go through the chain of command.

open economy An economy that doesn't restrict trade, development, and capital flows with other countries. —Compare CLOSED ECONOMY.

open-end credit —See LINE OF CREDIT.

open-end investment company —See MUTUAL FUND.

open-end lease A lease in which the lessee guarantees the lessor will realize a minimum value for the asset at the end of the lease. With most open-end leases, the lessee has the first opportunity to purchase the asset at the end of the lease.

open-end mortgage A mortgage that permits the issuer to sell additional bonds under the same lien. If the amount of additional bonds is restricted, the mortgage is referred to as a limited open-end mortgage. —Compare CLOSED-END MORTGAGE.

open-enrollment period A defined period (generally one month) during which eligible employees may sign up for insurance coverage or alter their existing coverage. Enrolling during this period does not generally require proof of insurability.

open house A public invitation to inspect an available property during specific hours.

open housing A policy of prohibiting discrimination in the leasing and selling of homes and apartments.

opening 1. The beginning of a trading session. **2.** The initial price at which a security trades for the day. —Also called *opening price*.

opening balance The balance in an account at the beginning of a period.

opening price —See OPENING 2.

opening transaction 1. The initial transaction during a trading day for a particular security. The price at which an opening transaction takes place is important to investors who have placed market orders before the market opens or who have placed at-the-opening orders. —Compare CLOSING TRANSACTION 1. **2.** An option order that establishes a new investment position or that increases the size of an existing investment position. —Compare CLOSING TRANSACTION 2.

open interest The number of contracts for particular futures or an option which, at a given time, are outstanding. A large open interest indicates more activity and liquidity for the contract.

open listing —See NONEXCLUSIVE LISTING.

Open Market Committee —See FEDERAL OPEN MARKET COMMITTEE.

open-market operations The purchase and sale of government securities from a primary dealer in the open market by the Federal Reserve in order to influence the money supply, credit conditions, and interest rates. For example, large purchases of securities will release funds into bank reserves that, in turn, will be used for lending. This action increases the supply of money, and, at least temporarily, pushes down interest rates. —See also FEDERAL OPEN MARKET COMMITTEE.

open-market purchase The buying of stocks and bonds in the securities markets. For example, in order to satisfy the sinking fund requirement of a bond indenture, the issuer may call securities from investors or make open-market purchases. Likewise, a firm wishing to reduce the number of its shares outstanding may make a tender offer to the firm's stockholders or purchase shares in the open market.

open mortgage A real estate loan that permits early repayment of a portion or all of the remaining principal without penalty.

open order —See GOOD-TILL-CANCELED ORDER.

open outcry A public auction in which trading is conducted by calling out bids and offers. Open outcry has been increasingly replaced by more efficient electronic trading systems. Some traders contend that open outcry offers better liquidity with the chance to obtain a better price. —Compare AUCTION MARKET; DEALER MARKET.

open shop An establishment that does not require union membership to gain or retain employment. —Compare CLOSED SHOP.

open space Undeveloped land set aside to provide natural or recreational value to a developed area.

open stock Retail merchandise that can be purchased individually or in small groups rather than only as a complete set. —Compare CLOSED STOCK.

open-to-buy The difference between the amount that has been budgeted for spending on merchandise and the amount that has actually been spent.

open transaction A transaction that has not been finalized by the end of an accounting period. For example, a business makes a sale but has yet to collect payment.

operating company A business that engages in transactions with outsiders.

operating cycle The average length of time between when a company purchases items for inventory and when it receives payment for sale of the items. The operating cycle is equal to the average age of inventories plus the average collection period. A long operating cycle tends to reduce profitability by increasing borrowing requirements and interest expense. —Also called *normal operating cycle.* —See also CASH CONVERSION CYCLE.

operating expense An expense incurred in transacting normal business operations, but outside any manufacturing function. Operating expenses include administrative and selling expenses, but exclude interest, taxes, and cost of goods sold.

operating expense ratio The proportion of gross income that is absorbed in operating expenses. This ratio is widely used in commercial real estate to measure the efficiency with which a property is being managed. —Also called *expense ratio.*

operating income The excess of revenues over expenses derived from normal business operations. Operating income, representing income from ordinary business activities, excludes expenses, such as interest and taxes. Unusual nonrecurring items, such as gains from selling a subsidiary or losses from closing a plant, are not included in the calculation of operating income. —Compare OPERATING LOSS. —Also called *earnings before interest and taxes; net operating income; operating profit.* —See also OPERATING REVENUE.

operating lease A short-term lease (such as that of a cable television connection box on a monthly basis) in which rental payments are made by the lessee and full ownership rights are kept by the lessor. An operating lease contrasts with a capital lease, in which ownership of the asset effectively passes from the lessor to the lessee.

operating leverage The extent to which fixed operating costs magnify changes in sales or revenues into even greater proportionate changes in operating income. For example, a company that substitutes robots or other machinery for laborers also substitutes fixed costs for variable costs and increases its operating leverage. High operating leverage tends to produce volatile earnings. —Compare FINANCIAL LEVERAGE.

operating loss The excess of operating expenses over revenue. As with operating income, operating losses exclude revenues and expenses from operations that are not considered a regular part of the business. —Compare OPERATING INCOME. —Also called *deficit.*

operating profit —See OPERATING INCOME.

operating rate The portion of capacity at which a business operates. For example, an operating rate of 80% indicates that the business is producing 80% of their maximum possible output with existing resources. A low operating rate is generally accompanied by losses or small profits, although the opportunity for profit growth is still great. Conversely, a high operating rate is generally accompanied by high profits, but limited opportunity for further profit improvement.

operating ratio A financial ratio that measures the portion of revenue going to operating expenses.

operating revenue Revenue from any regular source. Revenue from sales is adjusted for discounts and returns when calculating operating revenue. —Compare OTHER REVENUE.

operating statement —See INCOME STATEMENT.

operating strategy An organization's tactical plan for achieving its strategic goals. For example, a company begins developing an operating strategy for achieving its strategic goal of widespread distribution of its products in Europe. The operating strategy might include hiring a marketing manager with international experience, identifying European distributors with which the firm might establish a relationship, and redesigning its products to increase international acceptability.

operating unit A type of operating company that engages in transactions with outsiders and that is owned by another business. For example, in 1995 the stockholders of Capital Cities/ABC approved a $19 billion merger with the Walt Disney Company, whereupon Capital Cities/ABC became an operating unit of Disney. A decade earlier, Capital Cities had acquired ABC. —Compare NONOPERATING UNIT.

opinion leader

How do I go about getting a well-known person to promote my product? Do you have any idea how much it would cost?

Finding an opinion leader is a lot like job hunting. Use your networking skills to uncover opportunities and relationships that you did not know were out there. If six degrees of separation connect everybody in the world, how many connect you and a potential spokesperson? The cost to hire someone to promote your product varies from nothing to millions of dollars.

■ Tom Mesereau, Principal, Mesereau Public Relations, Parker, CO

operational audit —See MANAGEMENT AUDIT.

operational control The authority vested in management to lead the activities of an organization.

operations department —See BACK OFFICE.

operations research Utilizing analytical methods to obtain the optimal solution to an operational problem of an organization. The process involves modeling the system and comparing the outcomes of various decisions. For example, operations research can be used for determining the most efficient routes for a regional trucking firm.

opinion 1. A certified public accountant's written attestation as to the fairness of presentation of financial statements. Anything other than an opinion that the statements have been presented fairly is a matter of serious concern to investors. —Also called *accountant's opinion; auditor opinion.* —See also ADVERSE OPINION; CLEAN OPINION; DISCLAIMER OF OPINION; QUALIFIED OPINION; SUBJECT TO OPINION. **2.** A judge's written explanation of a court decision.

opinion leader A respected and influential person whose views are sought by others. An opinion leader can have a major impact on policy or the commercial success of a product.

opinion of title Written opinion, generally by an attorney, about the validity of a property title. The opinion details research that was undertaken along with any encumbrances that were uncovered.

opinion shopping The search for an accounting firm that will provide the desired opinion for a financial statement. Firms sometimes go opinion shopping when their current auditors consider their accounting practices questionable or unacceptable. Investors should spend extra time investigating firms that have recently changed auditors.

opportunity cost The best alternative that is forgone because a particular course of action is pursued. An example is the interest income that is given up when large balances are kept in a checking account. Likewise, purchasing a home means that less money is available for another investment.

optimum capacity The level of output that results in the lowest average cost. Output at less than optimum capacity results in unused fixed resources, while output at more than optimum capacity causes inefficiencies that increase per-unit costs.

option 1. A contract that permits the owner, depending on the type of option held, to purchase or sell an asset at a fixed price until a specific date. An option to purchase an asset is a call and an option to sell an asset is a put. Depending on how an option is

optimum capacity

Can you provide some guidance on how to determine the optimum capacity for a small manufacturing plant that I own? What kinds of information should I collect in order to determine optimum capacity?

Consider optimum-capacity calculations like stairs with steps, not a steady line going up like an escalator. Most manufacturing lines have optimum levels of production. When I was making Umbroller strollers, the steps for final production were 200 per shift, 600 per shift, 900 per shift, and finally 1800 per shift. Anything in between those numbers of products per shift did not cover our people and machinery costs. At each level on the way up we had to reconfigure the line—more machines, more people, more space. This is what you have to figure out. Component parts tend to be similar, but with single-worker products you can often have a worker run one machine for four hours and another for four hours, or some fractional amounts. The information is more complex to gather when a group is assembling than with single-operator work.

■ Deaver Brown, Publisher, Simplysoftwarecd.com, Lincoln, MA

used, the risks can be quite high. —See also ASIAN OPTION; CONVENTIONAL OPTION; EURO-PEAN OPTION; EXERCISE PRICE; EXOTIC OPTION; EXPIRATION DATE 1; KNOCK-OUT OPTION; LAPSED OPTION; LONG-TERM EQUITY ANTICIPATION SECURITIES; RESTRICTED OPTION; STOCK OPTION 1. **2.** An addition to a basic model. For example, four-wheel drive is an option on many trucks and SUVs. **3.** —See INCENTIVE STOCK OPTION.

optional call The call of a bond by an issuer who wishes to terminate a loan, generally because interest rates have declined since the time of issuance. Optional calls are frequently made at prices slightly higher than par value. Some bond issues are not subject to call; most issues provide a period of years after issuance during which optional calls are prohibited. —See also CALL PROTECTION.

optional cash purchase The buying of shares of stock through a dividend reinvestment plan that are in addition to shares purchased with the dividend. Most dividend reinvestment plans place an upper dollar limit on each shareholder's optional cash purchases.

optional dividend A dividend in which the shareholder may choose among two or more forms of payment. For example, a firm's directors may offer the shareholders a choice between cash or an equal dollar amount of stock.

option holder The owner of an option to purchase (call) or sell (put) an asset such as shares of common stock or a futures contract. The option holder pays the premium and has the alternative of using the option or allowing it to expire. An option holder's loss is limited to the amount of the premium required to purchase it.

option margin The margin requirement to open and maintain an option position. Federal Reserve Regulation T sets minimum option margins, although individual brokerage firms may establish more strict requirements.

option premium —See PREMIUM 2.

Options Clearing Corporation (OCC) An organization established in 1972 to process and guarantee the transactions in options that take place on the organized exchanges. The OCC substitutes its own credit for that of the parties undertaking the options transactions.

option tender bond —See PUT BOND.

option to purchase A contract that gives the option holder the right to purchase property at a specified price until a particular date.

option writer The seller of a call option or a put option in an opening transaction. The option writer receives a premium and incurs an obligation to sell (if a call is sold) or to purchase (if a put is sold) the underlying asset at a stipulated price until a predetermined date. —See also WRITING.

oral contract A verbal agreement that is legally binding but may be unenforceable because of a lack of proof. Oral contracts for real estate are generally unenforceable. —See also PAROL CONTRACT.

oral evidence Spoken testimony that is presented in a trial. —Compare DOCUMENTARY EVIDENCE.

order 1. A customer's instructions to buy or sell securities. **2.** A directive or command from a court or governing authority. **3.** A request to purchase or sell a good or service. For example, a customer at an automobile dealership decides to place an order to buy a new Nissan 350Z. **4.** A sorting or ranking of variables.

order bill of lading A negotiable bill of lading made to the order of the shipper, who can legally sell it to anyone. An order bill of lading allows the shipper to collect for the shipment before it reaches its destination. —Also called *negotiable bill of lading*.

order imbalance An excess of buy or sell orders for securities such that it is impossible to match one type of order with its opposite. Order imbalances usually occur after unexpected news causes a rush to buy or sell a security. —Also called *imbalance of orders*.

orderly market A market in which prices are continually provided by buyers and sellers, and price changes between transactions are relatively small.

order point The inventory level at which an order is automatically placed for additional stock. The order point depends on the expected level of sales, the time required to obtain new stock, and the amount of safety stock that is desired.

ordinal scale A scale of measurement in which data are listed in rank order but without fixed differences among the entries. An example of an ordinal scale would be a best-to-worst ranking of players in the National Basketball Association.

ordinance A law enacted by authority of a county, city, or town. For example, a city enacts an ordinance to prohibit overnight parking on the street. —See also STATUTE.

ordinary annuity An annuity that makes payments at the end of each period. —Compare ANNUITY DUE.

ordinary course of business The customary practices and transactions of a particular business and a particular firm.

ordinary income Income that does not qualify for special tax treatment. Wages, dividends, and interest are ordinary income for individuals.

ordinary income property Property whose sale would result in ordinary income or short-term capital gains. The deduction for tax purposes of a charitable gift of ordinary income property is limited to the donor's cost basis. Ordinary income property includes inventory and short-term capital assets.

ordinary interest Interest calculated on the basis of a 360-day year as opposed to a 365-day year. —Compare EXACT INTEREST.

organic growth

I have read that in evaluating the success of a business, it is better to use organic growth than overall growth. Is this correct and if so, why?

Organic growth is based on the operating expertise of management rather than on the financial manipulations of the merger market. For this reason, organic growth is a better measure of the effectiveness of management and of how managers use organizational resources to create value for shareholders. Growth based on the operating expertise of management cannot be imitated by an individual investor and thus provides something of unique value to the shareholder.

▪ Phyllis G. Holland, PhD, Professor and Head, Department of Management,
Langdale College of Business, Valdosta State University, Valdosta, GA

ordinary loss A loss from the sale or exchange of property that is not considered a capital asset. An ordinary loss is fully deductible against ordinary income.

ordinary shares The European equivalent for shares of common stock. Ordinary shares are held in trust as backing for American Depositary Receipts.

organic growth Revenue growth of a business, excluding any from recently acquired operations. For example, the organic growth of Procter & Gamble in 2006 would exclude any contribution from Gillette, which was acquired by Procter & Gamble during the prior year.

CASE STUDY Managers, financial analysts, and investors consider organic growth an important benchmark when evaluating a firm's operations. Organic growth is generally considered a better measure of a firm's success than is overall sales and earnings, which can be inflated by acquisitions and other nonrecurring events. In early 2007 Procter & Gamble Co. reported second-quarter sales and earnings that were slightly higher than analysts' forecasts. This news should have had a positive effect on the firm's stock price. However, a significant portion of the increases resulted from a weak dollar (P&G has substantial foreign operation), so that organic sales, which excluded acquisitions, divestitures, and the effects of foreign-currency fluctuations, increased only 5%. The disappointing report of organic sales overshadowed the more positive overall sales and earnings report, resulting in a weak stock price at the opening of trading following announcement of the quarterly financial results.

organizational behavior The field of study that examines how individuals and groups behave and perform in organizations.

organizational chart A diagram that outlines an organization's administrative structure.

organizational cost The expenses, including franchise and legal fees, involved in setting up a business. Organizational expenses must be amortized over a period of at least 60 months.

---

organizational cost

What are some actions I can take to reduce the organizational costs of starting a new business?

You want good quality work on the front end of your business from your attorney and your accountant in particular. It is appropriate to shop around for these services, but be careful to be sure that experience is comparable before you conclude that you have found a cheaper provider. You may be able to barter for some services if you have some expertise to trade. You should be aware that experienced advisers may cost more in the short term, but can save you money in the long term by helping you avoid costly mistakes.

■ Phyllis G. Holland, PhD, Professor and Head, Department of Management,
Langdale College of Business, Valdosta State University, Valdosta, GA

---

organizational structure The division of authority and duties within an organization.

Organization for Economic Cooperation and Development (OECD) An international organization of 30 industrialized, market-driven countries that coordinates policy to maximize the economic growth of its members. OECD is known for its publications and statistics related to economic and social issues.

organized labor A group of workers with a common interest who belong to a union.

organized securities exchange —See SECURITIES EXCHANGE.

orientation A program of activities designed to acquaint a new employee with an organization.

original capital Funds contributed to a business by the owners of the business at the time of its incorporation.

original cost —See HISTORICAL COST.

original entry In accounting, a transaction entered in a journal, generally accompanied by a description.

original equipment manufacturer (OEM) A business that manufactures parts or components that are used in products assembled or produced by another company. For example, Delphi is an OEM that supplies navigation and audio systems, instrument panels, steering systems, and a variety of other products to the automotive industry.

original-issue discount (OID) The amount by which a bond is sold below its par value at the time of issue. With the exception of usually tax-free securities (that is, municipals), investors must report a certain portion of the discount as income for tax purposes each year.

original-issue discount bond A bond issued at a discount from par value. The discount occurs when the coupon on the bond is less than the market rate of interest for a bond of similar risk and maturity. —Compare MINICOUPON BOND. —Also called *deep-discount bond.* —See also ZERO-COUPON BOND.

original maturity The period between a security's maturity date and issue date. A bond issued 15 years ago that has an additional 10 years to maturity had an original maturity of 25 years. —See also CURRENT MATURITY.

origination fee A charge by a lender to a borrower for expenses involved in making a loan. An origination fee is designed to cover expenses such as preparation of documents, credit checks, and property appraisal. It is generally calculated as a percentage of the amount borrowed and often serves as a major profit center for lenders.

originator **1.** A financial institution that makes loans that are then resold. **2.** A financial institution that initiates a wire transfer.

OSHA —See OCCUPATIONAL SAFETY AND HEALTH ADMINISTRATION.

OTC —See OVER-THE-COUNTER MARKET.

OTCBB —See OTC BULLETIN BOARD.

OTC Bulletin Board (OTCBB) A real-time quotation service for over-the-counter equity securities not listed or traded on a national securities exchange or on Nasdaq. Securities delisted from the OTC Bulletin Board generally start trading through the Pink Sheets. —Also called *Bulletin Board.*

OTC margin stock —See MARGIN STOCK.

other assets Assets of relatively small value. For financial reporting purposes, firms frequently combine small assets into a single category rather than listing each item separately.

other income **1.** An entry on an income statement that includes income from other than a firm's principal line of business. Dividends, investment interest, and foreign exchange gains are each classified as other income. **2.** For individuals, less common types of income, including gambling winnings, fees from jury duty, prizes, canceled debts, and executor fees.

other liabilities Small and relatively insignificant liabilities. For financial reporting purposes, firms often combine small liabilities into this single category rather than listing each liability separately.

other revenue Revenue from sources other than regular ones. For example, a steel manufacturer would classify interest on customers' overdue accounts as other revenue. —Compare OPERATING REVENUE.

outbid To offer a price that is higher than the existing offers from competitors. For example, an oil company may outbid competitors and win drilling rights to a section of the Gulf of Mexico.

outcry market Buying and selling assets in a face-to-face setting in which bids to buy and offers to sell are shouted to participants. Outcry markets have historically been linked to commodities, but the efficiency of electronic trading is increasingly gaining favor in these markets.

outlaw strike —See WILDCAT STRIKE.

outlet mall A collection of manufacturers' stores, generally under one roof. Outlet malls have become popular shopping destinations for individuals looking for everyday discounts on name-brand merchandise.

outlet store A manufacturer's retail store that usually specializes in irregular and overstocked items at prices lower than can generally be found at other retail stores. —Also called *factory outlet.*

out-of-pocket expenses Personal or job-related expenditures paid by an individual. Unreimbursed job-related expenditures and out-of-pocket expenses involved in charity work are permitted as deductions in calculating taxable income.

out-of-the-money —Used to describe a call option with a strike price above the price of the underlying asset, or a put option with a strike price below the price of the underlying asset. For example, a put option to sell 100 shares of Cisco Systems stock at

$50 per share is out-of-the-money if the stock currently trades at $70. Even though an out-of-the-money option has no intrinsic value, it may have market value. —Compare AT-THE-MONEY; IN-THE-MONEY.

outplacement Assisting employees or former employees in locating jobs with other employers. Outplacement assistance can range from help with drafting a resume to extensive job retraining in trades or professions in demand.

output The volume or dollar amount of production during a specific period.

outside audit —See EXTERNAL AUDIT.

outside director A member of a firm's board of directors who is not employed in another capacity by that firm. An example is the president of one firm who serves as a director of another firm. Some people believe that having some outside directors is necessary to give a board balance and to protect stockholders' interests. —Compare INSIDE DIRECTOR.

> **CASE STUDY** Outside directors make good money for part-time work. In fact, nonemployee directors of many companies are paid more than most working individuals (indeed, most working families) earn during a full year's employment. In its 2007 annual proxy statement, Wyndham Worldwide (formerly part of Cendant Corporation) stated that each nonemployee director would earn an annual retainer of $150,000. Directors earned an additional $5,000 to $20,000 for each committee assignment. Some directors were members of two committees. Nonemployee directors were paid half in cash and half in deferred stock units. In addition to the retainer and committee membership compensation, outside directors each received a $75,000 equity grant that could be exchanged for shares of common stock following retirement or termination of service from the board for any reason. Directors were also provided with company-paid life insurance.

outside the box Describing a way of doing something in other than the usual way, or by means that reject the limits of the status quo. For example, thinking outside the box refers to gaining a new perspective on an issue, as when a creative person takes a failed product and markets it in an innovative manner.

outsourcing Paying another firm to provide goods or services that could be produced internally. For example, an appliance manufacturer may outsource the production of some of its models to other manufacturers that can perform the work more cheaply. Many companies choose to outsource cleaning services. —See also HOMESOURCING.

outstanding capital stock The number of shares of capital stock that have been issued and that are in public hands. Outstanding stock excludes shares issued but subsequently repurchased by the issuer as treasury stock. Outstanding stock is used in the calculation of book value per share and earnings per share. —Also called *shares outstanding; stock outstanding.*

outstanding debt Debt that has not yet been paid. For example, outstanding receivables are debts owed to a firm by its customers. Outstanding payables are debts owed by a firm to its suppliers.

overage **1.** For retail leases, payments in excess of base rent that are derived from a percentage of sales. For example, a retail store in a mall might pay the lessor $10,000 per month plus 2% of sales. **2.** Actual money or goods in excess of the amounts listed on the organization's books. **3.** The difference between the lowest price for a loan product and any higher price paid by a borrower. For example, an overage may be in the form of points.

overboarding An individual serving as a director on the boards of multiple organizations such that it is difficult to devote adequate time to some or all of the positions. Some critics of The Home Depot management pointed to one of the firm's directors, who served on up to ten other boards.

overbooked **1.** In transportation and lodging, an excess of reservations compared to available seats or rooms. Hotels and airlines regularly overbook in order to compensate for customers with reservations who fail to show up. —Also called *oversold.* **2.** —See OVERSUBSCRIBED 1.

overbought Of, relating to, or being the market for a class of assets that has risen very rapidly in the recent past and is likely to suffer short-term price declines in the near future. Determining whether a market is overbought is difficult and is subject to individual interpretation.

overbuilding Building construction that is greater than the market can absorb. Overbuilding can result in falling real estate prices, financial difficulty for contractors, and defaults on real estate loans.

overcharge To cause a customer to pay more than the bona fide price. For example, a clerk charges the regular price rather than the posted sale price of a shirt. Overcharges generally result from computers not being properly updated.

overdepreciation **1.** Depreciation that is more than sufficient to allow for the eventual replacement of the asset being depreciated. —Compare UNDERDEPRECIATION 1. **2.** Depreciation that causes an asset to be carried on a firm's books at a lesser value than it would be worth if it were sold. Overdepreciation produces understated earnings and assets on financial statements. —Compare UNDERDEPRECIATION 2.

overdraft A draft for more than the balance in the account on which the draft is drawn. A bank may honor an overdraft, depending on the importance of the customer and on prior arrangements (if any) to cover overdrafts. —See also NSF CHECK.

overdraft checking account A checking account coupled with a line of credit such that the account holder can write checks for more than the balance in the account without the checks bouncing. Overdrafts are generally subject to a fee, but will save the account holder a merchant's returned-check fee.

overhanging supply A relatively large block of an asset that may, or will, be sold under certain circumstances. For example, a large stockholder may announce a secondary offering of a security. Overhanging supply tends to be bearish for an asset, because both potential buyers and sellers believe price increases of the asset are unlikely.

overhead —See INDIRECT COST.

overheating Of or referring to an economy with strong consumer and business demand for goods and service such that there is concern that costs and prices will start increasing at unacceptable levels. Economies tend to start overheating during the last stages of an extended economic expansion.

overimprovement Development that is too valuable for the parcel of land on which the development occurs. For example, building an upscale shopping mall in a blighted district where land is cheap.

overinsured Having insurance coverage that exceeds a likely loss from damage, injury, or death. For example, a person pays premiums on several overlapping health insurance policies or multiple disability income policies. —Compare UNDERINSURED.

overlapping debt Debt of a municipality that is shared with another political entity. For example, a city may share responsibility with the county in which the city is located for bonds issued by the county to finance a facility such as a public auditorium. —Compare UNDERLYING DEBT 1.

overnight repo A repurchase agreement in which securities are sold provided that they will be repurchased on the following day. Financial institutions use overnight repos as a means of raising short-term money for financing inventories.

overpayment Payment that exceeds the amount due. For example, a taxpayer experiences an overpayment of taxes when withholding credits and prepayments exceed the tax liability for the year. Homeowners sometimes make overpayments in order to reduce the balance on a mortgage more rapidly.

overproduction Production of a good in excess of what is required to meet demand. Overproduction causes a surplus, which is likely to result in reduced prices for consumers.

override 1. A fee paid to managers that is in addition to their regular pay. For example, a sales manager may receive a portion of the commissions paid to other salespeople. —Also called *commission override.* **2.** In taxation, an assessment that is in addition to any automatic increase. **3.** A mechanism for altering an automatic process. For example, equipment may have an override that allows an employee to interrupt its normal operation.

overriding royalty interest A third-party interest in royalty income derived from oil and gas rights.

overrun 1. Production greater than ordered or needed. An overrun may result from an error or because of concern that some units may be of unacceptable quality. **2.** Expenses that exceed the budget. A major cost overrun on a fixed-price government contract may result in the manufacturer losing money on the deal.

oversell 1. To promise more than can be delivered. For example, a salesperson in an appliance store may oversell the performance of a plasma television in an effort to earn a large sales commission. **2.** To continue promoting a good or service after the initial sale has been consummated. Overselling may turn off an impatient buyer.

oversold 1. Of, relating to, or being a market that has declined rapidly and steeply in the recent past and is likely to exhibit short-term price increases in the near future. Determining whether a market is oversold is difficult and is subject to individual interpretation. **2.** —See OVERBOOKED 1.

overstored Describing a town or other geographical area with retail outlets in excess of what is needed to meet consumer demand. —Compare UNDERSTORED.

oversubscribed 1. Or, relating to, or being a new security issue for which there are more requests to purchase securities than there are securities available for sale. For example, brokers may take a sufficient number of preliminary orders for a new issue of stock for which there are insufficient shares available to satisfy the demand. —Also called *overbooked.* **2.** Of, relating to, or being a buyback or takeover attempt in which more securities are offered than the purchaser has agreed to buy. In such a case, the purchaser may decide to buy the additional securities or may buy the agreed-upon number on a pro rata basis.

oversubscription privilege The opportunity to purchase, on a pro rata basis, any remaining shares not already subscribed to in a new stock offering. In a typical new offering using stock rights, new shares are priced below the market price in order to ensure a successful sale. Generally, however, some stockholders will neither use nor sell their rights to buy the new shares, thus leaving some stock unsold, even at the bargain price. The issuer therefore allows the stockholders to oversubscribe in anticipation of extra available shares. —Compare SUBSCRIPTION PRICE.

over-the-counter market (OTC) A widespread aggregation of dealers who make markets in many different securities. Unlike an organized exchange on which trading takes place at one physical location, OTC trading occurs through telephone or computer negotiations between buyers and sellers. Although stocks traded over the counter are often more speculative than listed stocks, virtually all government and municipal bonds and most corporate bonds are traded in the OTC market. —See also OTC BULLETIN BOARD; THIRD MARKET.

over-the-counter medication Nonprescription drugs such as Tylenol, Claritin, and generic formulations that can be purchased at many retail outlets, including discount stores. Over-the-counter medication is less expensive than prescription medication, but generally is not covered by insurance.

over-the-counter retailing Selling merchandise through stores as opposed to selling through mail order or online.

over-the-counter stock A stock not listed on an exchange and trading only in the over-the-counter market.

overtime Hours worked in excess of what is considered standard or normal, generally at a higher rate of pay. Federal and state laws require most employers to pay nonexempt employees an overtime rate of pay of 150% of regular wages.

overtrade 1. To purchase a client's securities at an above-the-market price in return for the client's purchase of part of a new issue. **2.** —See CHURN 1.

overvalued Of, relating to, or being an asset that is selling at a price higher than it logically should. It is difficult, if not impossible, to determine if an asset such as a stock is overvalued. —Compare UNDERVALUED.

overwriting In options trading, the writing of more options than one expects to have exercised. Investors overwrite call options because they consider the underlying stock overvalued. Investors overwrite put options because they consider the underlying stock undervalued.

owner The individual or entity that holds title to an asset.

owner of record —See HOLDER OF RECORD.

owner-operator A person who both owns (or leases) and also operates a business or equipment. Owner-operators are a major factor in the trucking industry, in which independent truckers own or lease the trucks that they drive.

owners and contractors protective liability insurance Liability coverage for negligent acts of contractors and subcontractors hired by the insured. This specialized coverage is written for a specific project and protects the owner, who is responsible for actions of contractors on the project.

owners' equity The owners' interest in the assets of a business. Owners' equity includes the amount invested by the owners plus the profits (or minus the losses) in the enterprise. Owners' equity and liabilities are used to finance a firm's assets. —Also called *net assets; shareholders' equity; stockholders' equity.*

ownership The lawful right to the exclusive possession, use, and transfer of something.

overtime

Are companies required to pay a premium to employees who work overtime or during holidays?

Not necessarily. Under the federal Fair Labor Standards Act (FLSA), only covered, nonexempt workers are entitled to overtime pay at a rate of not less than one and one-half times their regular rates of pay after 40 hours of work in a workweek. Employees who earn certain levels of income and who are engaged in certain duties (such as bona fide executive, administrative, professional, and outside sales employees) are generally exempt from overtime pay. Most states follow the FLSA regulations, with only California, Nevada, Wyoming, and Alaska requiring that overtime for nonexempt employees is due after 8 hours per day (as opposed to after 40 hours per week).

Generally, hours worked on holidays and weekends are treated like hours worked on any other day of the week. There is currently no law that mandates an employer pay an employee a special premium for work performed on these days other than the overtime premium required for work performed in excess of 40 hours in a workweek (or 8 hours in a workday for a few states). A question of overtime often arises when an employee receives a paid day off for a holiday during the week but then must work on Saturday. The answer is that the employee is not entitled to overtime pay for work done on that Saturday unless the work brings the employee in excess of 40 work hours for that week. Whether overtime pay is due for holiday work is based on the number of hours worked for that week and not on the pay received.

Premium pay is a generic term referring to additional pay (not necessarily overtime) given to employees for night, holiday, or Sunday work. Extra or incentive pay for night, holiday, or weekend work must be agreed upon by the employer since it is not federally regulated. However, if more than 40 hours are worked within the workweek, the employer must follow overtime regulations.

The FLSA has no requirement for double-time pay. The only state with double-time regulations is California, which requires all employers to pay double time for an employee who works in excess of 12 hours in a single day or in excess of 8 hours on the 7th consecutive day in a workweek. While employers may not be required by law to pay double time, if an employer has a collective bargaining agreement or other policy stating that employees will be paid double time for certain work, then the employer is obligated to pay employees as required by the agreement. For example, a union contract may require an employer to pay an employee double time for all work done on a holiday or Sunday regardless of the total number of hours worked in a week.

Individual states may differ on overtime exemptions. When the state laws differ from the FLSA, an employer must comply with the standard most protective to employees. Employers should check with their state's Department of Labor with regard to overtime standards. A list of all states and their labor office contact information can be found at: http://www.dol.gov/esa/contacts/state_of.htm.

■ Helen M. Kemp, Division Counsel and Assistant Director,
Retirement and Benefit Services, Office of the State Comptroller, State of Connecticut

 P

PAC 1. —See PLANNED AMORTIZATION CLASS. **2.** —See POLITICAL ACTION COMMITTEE.

package 1. Several products sold as a single unit, usually at a price less than the combined prices of the individual components. For example, a communications company might offer a package of local and long distance telephone service, broadband Internet access, and cable or satellite television. **2.** A combination of television and/

or radio ads offered as a group to a potential advertiser. **3.** A sealed and wrapped container.

packaged goods Consumable goods, including cigarettes, cleaning products, and food items, that are packaged by manufacturers and sold at retail outlets. Packaged goods are consumed and replaced at frequent intervals.

package mortgage A mortgage that includes durable personal property such as appliances along with the real property. Package mortgages are frequently used in new developments, where appliances are included with the homes.

packing list A document prepared by a shipper and included with a shipment that indicates the number and items being shipped, along with any information needed by the transportation company.

Pac Man defense A defensive antitakeover tactic in which the target firm attempts to take over the acquiring firm. The target hopes that the acquiring firm will call off the takeover attempt and look for easier pickings.

paid-in capital Funds and property contributed to a firm by its stockholders. Paid-in capital is generated when a firm issues stock in the primary market, not when the stock is traded in the secondary market. —See also ADDITIONAL PAID-IN CAPITAL; CONTRIBUTED CAPITAL.

paid-in surplus —See ADDITIONAL PAID-IN CAPITAL.

paid-up policy A whole life insurance policy that requires no additional premium payments for the insurance to remain in force. For example, a person may purchase a 30-pay policy at age 20, which means that paying the required premiums will result in the policy being fully paid up when the policyholder reaches age 50.

painting the tape **1.** Illegal trading of a security by manipulators among themselves in order to create the illusion of heavy trading activity, perhaps the kind generated by insiders. The increased trades are then reported on the consolidated tape, a situation that often lures unwary investors into the action. Once the market price of the security escalates, the manipulators will sell out, hoping to make a profit. **2.** Breaking down larger orders into more numerous smaller orders to have more trades appear on the tape and thereby attract investor interest.

paired shares Shares of two firms under common management that are sold as a single unit. A single certificate may be issued to represent ownership in both firms. —Also called *stapled stock.*

pairs trade An investment strategy that matches a short position with a comparable long position in the stock of a company in the same industry. For example, an investor might buy 500 shares of BP and sell short a comparable principal amount of the stock of ExxonMobil. The offsetting positions allow an investor to attempt to profit by selecting the best value in an industry without worrying about changes in the valuation of the sector or the overall market.

P&I —See PRINCIPAL AND INTEREST.

P&L —See PROFIT AND LOSS STATEMENT.

panic buying A flurry of security purchases accompanied by high volume and sharp price increases. During a period of panic buying, buyers do not have time to evaluate fundamental or technical factors, because their primary goal is to acquire securities before the prices rise even more.

panic selling A flurry of selling in a particular security or in securities as a whole. Panic selling is accompanied by particularly heavy volume and sharp price declines as owners scramble to sell before prices drop even more. Panic selling is generally set off by an unexpected event viewed by traders as particularly negative.

paper A short-term unsecured note. This is generally used interchangeably with the term *commercial paper.*

paper company A corporation formed in order to accomplish a specific financial task rather than to produce a good or service. Such a firm usually has few assets other than those of a financial nature.

paper gain —See UNREALIZED GAIN.

paper loss —See UNREALIZED LOSS.

paper money Official paper currency issued by a government or central bank that is acceptable as payment for debts and a medium of exchange.

paper profit —See UNREALIZED GAIN.

par 1. —See PAR VALUE 1. **2.** —See PAR VALUE 2.

paradigm shift A major change in the way of thinking about something or doing something. For example, development of the Internet has resulted in a paradigm shift in the way people gather information.

paradox of thrift In economics, the theory that while it is beneficial for an individual to save a considerable amount of his or her income, the same action by a large proportion of the population will result in recession caused by insufficient aggregate demand. The paradox is that what is good for the individual is not necessarily good for the whole.

paralegal A nonattorney with legal skills who assists and works under the supervision of an attorney. Paralegals can interview clients, conduct legal research, and draft legal documents, but they cannot give legal advice or represent someone in court. —Also called *legal assistant.*

parallel loan A lending arrangement in which two firms in different countries borrow one another's currency. For example, a firm in country A makes a loan in its own currency to a firm in country B at the same time the firm in country B makes a loan in its currency to the firm in country A. The two transactions are designed to offset potential losses from fluctuations in currency exchange rates, but they do subject each participant to credit risk. —Also called *back-to-back loan.*

parameter A value or range of values that defines a system or situation. For example, a contract to build aircraft includes parameters regarding cost, quality, and completion dates.

parasitic marketing —See AMBUSH MARKETING.

par bond A bond that sells at a price equal to its par value, usually $1,000.

parcel A tract of land with a single legal description.

Parcel Post A class of mail offered by the U.S. Postal Service that is used for merchandise, books, circulars, catalogs, and other printed matter. Parcel Post packages can weigh up to 70 pounds and measure up to 130 inches in combined length and distance around the thickest part. Bulk rates are available for firms that send large quantities of packages via Parcel Post.

parent company A company that controls or owns another company or other companies. For example, Union Pacific Corporation is the parent company of operating subsidiary Union Pacific Railroad. —Compare SUBSIDIARY. —See also HOLDING COMPANY.

Pareto's Law A principle of economist Vilfredo Pareto that, in generalized form, holds that 80% of output originates from 20% of input. The 80/20 ratio can be applied to revenues, advertising effectiveness, or management headaches. For example, 20% of advertising produces 80% of results. Likewise, 80% of management headaches are caused by 20% of the employees. —Also called *80/20 rule.*

parity The equivalency of variables. For example, parity exists when an option premium plus the strike price is equal to the market price of the underlying stock. If Amazon.com stock is selling at $17 per share, an option to buy the stock at $15 would be selling at parity if its premium is $2. —See also CONVERSION PARITY.

parking 1. Placing idle funds in a safe, short-term investment while awaiting the availability of other investment opportunities. For example, investors often end up parking proceeds from a security sale in a money market account while searching for other securities to purchase. **2.** Transferring an asset to another party so that true ownership of the asset will be hidden. For example, an investor involved in the take-over of a company may park securities of the company with other investors so that the management of the target company will not know the extent of the investor's stock ownership. Parking for this purpose is generally illegal.

CASE STUDY In June 2005 the Securities and Exchange Commission filed a civil action against Take-Two Interactive Software, Inc., a New York–based publisher and distributor of video and computer games. The action included several former and current executives of the company. The SEC claimed the executives had fraudulently inflated the firm's reported revenue during fiscal years 2000 and 2001 by parking hundreds of thousands of video games with distributors who had no obligation to pay for the product. The SEC claimed the firm fraudulently recorded the shipments as sales and subsequently accepted return of the games, sometimes disguised as purchases of new inventory, in later reporting periods. In this instance, the parking took the form of fraudulently moving product to other firms (and recording the move as sales) when Take-Two executives knew the product would be returned. The SEC claimed the fraudulent accounting practices allowed the firm to improperly recognize $60 million in revenue during 2000 and 2001, and to report aftertax fiscal-year earnings that were inflated by $20 million. In a settlement with the SEC, Take-Two and the executives consented to various penalties, including a corporate payment of $7.5 million.

Parkinson's Law The principle of scholar Northcote that work expands to fill the time available for its completion. For example, if employees are given extra time to complete a task, they will find a way to use the time. The principle has been expanded to other themes, such as: the amount of family junk will expand to fill the attic.

parliamentary procedure Formal rules for the orderly conduct of meetings.

parol contract An oral agreement, or a written agreement without official authentication by seal. A parol contract generally requires valid consideration to be legally binding.

partial equilibrium An analysis of equilibrium in a particular market or sector that ignores the effects in other industries. For example, an economist may want to study the impact of a tax on light bulbs while assuming all things equal in other markets. Partial equilibrium analysis is more useful when the market is narrowly defined.

partial execution

If I place an order to purchase 1,000 shares of a particular stock and the order is filled on three separate executions (say, for example, 200 shares, 500 shares, and 300 shares), will I be required to pay three commissions?

If you place a limit order for a security and get multiple executions in the same trading day, you will incur only one commission. If the same order is executed over multiple trading days, you will incur a commission on the executions each day. A way to avoid this problem is to ask your consultant to execute the trade on a cents-per-share basis to take the guesswork out of your cost.

■ Richard S. Campbell, CIMA®, Senior Vice President, Wealth Management,
Portfolio Management Director, Smith Barney, Valdosta, GA

partial execution Execution of less than the full amount of an order. For example, an investor may place an order to buy 500 shares of GenCorp at $15 or less and get a partial execution if the broker is able to buy only 300 shares at that price. —Also called *partial fill.*

partial fill —See PARTIAL EXECUTION.

partial interest An ownership interest that represents less than the whole. For example, a person may hold the mineral rights to a property, but not own the land.

partial liquidation A distribution or one of a series of distributions by a corporation in cancellation or redemption of all or a part of the firm's stock. For example, a company distributes unused insurance proceeds received when a fire has destroyed a portion of the business, resulting in a cessation of a part of its activities and a contraction in the business.

partial redemption Redemption by an issuer of less than an entire issue of its securities. For example, a corporation may redeem a portion of an outstanding bond issue.

partial release Relinquishment by a lender to its claim on a portion of real property. For example, the developer of a subdivision may gain a partial release as lots in the subdivision are sold and funds received are applied to the mortgage.

partial spinoff Distribution to stockholders, or sale to the public, of shares that represent a minority interest in a firm's subsidiary. A firm may undertake a partial spinoff when it considers the subsidiary is not properly valued by the public as part of the parent firm, or when it wishes to raise funds without giving up total control of the subsidiary.

partial taking Using condemnation to acquire a portion of a property. The U.S. Supreme Court has ruled that compensation must include any loss in value of the remaining property as well as the value of the condemned property.

partial tender offer An offer to purchase less than all the shares of a company by specifying a maximum number of shares that will be accepted.

participating 1. Of, relating to, or being an unusual class of preferred stock that participates with common stock in dividend increases according to a specified formula. For example, a participating preferred issue might require that any increases in dividends on common stock above $2 per share be shared equally with preferred. —Compare NONPARTICIPATING 1. **2.** Of or relating to a type of life insurance in which the insured shares in the insurer's investment success or lack of success. Owners of participating policies receive dividends from the insurer. —Compare NONPARTICIPAT-ING 2. —Also called *with-profits.* —See also VANISHING PREMIUM.

participation certificate A certificate indicating ownership in a pool of assets, generally mortgages.

participation loan **1.** A loan in which one or more lenders share, or participate, with the originating bank in advancing funds to a borrower. A participation loan is useful when the amount of the loan is too large for any single lender. **2.** A loan in which the lender receives consideration in addition to interest. For example, the lender may gain an ownership position in the asset being financed.

participative budgeting Employee input into an organization's budgeting process. Participative budgeting is designed to gain useful information and to motivate employees to help meet the budget.

participative management Involvement of employees and other stakeholders who will be influenced by management decisions in helping to make those decisions. Participative management can increase employee commitment to an organization's goals at the same time it offers fresh insights into how the organization can become more effective.

partition **1.** In law, a court-ordered separation of an estate into proportional interests of the tenants. **2.** A division of commonly owned real property among co-owners.

partner A member of a partnership. —See also LIMITED PARTNER.

partnership A business owned by two or more people who agree on the method of distribution of profits and/or losses and on the extent to which each will be liable for the debts of one another. A partnership permits pass-through of income and losses directly to the owners. In this way, they are taxed at each partner's personal tax rate. —Compare CORPORATION; PROPRIETORSHIP. —See also GENERAL PARTNERSHIP; LIMITED PART-NERSHIP; SILENT PARTNER.

partnership account A financial account in which two or more individuals are equally liable. A partnership account differs from a joint account in that the partnership account may include a written agreement defining the interest of each partner.

partnership life insurance Life insurance on a partner paid for by the other partners. Upon the death of the partner, the insurance company pays an amount equivalent to the value of the deceased partner's ownership stake so that the stake can be purchased from the deceased's heirs.

part-time Of or referring to an employee who works less than the standard number of hours per week. Part-time employees typically do not qualify for insurance or retirement benefits.

party in interest —See REAL PARTY IN INTEREST.

par value **1.** The stated value of a security as it appears on its certificate. A bond's par value is the dollar amount on which interest is calculated and the amount paid to holders at maturity. Par value of preferred stock is used in a similar way in calculating the annual dividend. —Also called *face value; par.* **2.** The minimum contribution made by investors to purchase a share of common stock at the time of issue. Par value is of no real consequence to investors; in fact, many new common stock issues have no stated par value. —Also called *par.* —See also NO PAR. **3.** In foreign exchange, the rate at which a currency is pegged, or fixed.

pass-along audience

Are publishers able to accurately gauge the pass-along audiences of their magazines? If so, how important is the result in pricing advertisements in their publications?

Readership numbers (the total number of estimated readers of a publication, including pass-along audiences) are often more important than general-circulation numbers. In the medical field, for example, the impact factor of a journal is measured by looking at the frequency with which a specific journal is referenced over a set time period. If journal publishers can prove extended readership, using impact factor as one measurement of reach, advertising pricing can be adjusted accordingly.

■ E. Mace Lewis, Vice President, Business Development, QD Healthcare Group, Greenwich, CT

pass-along audience Individuals other than subscribers who are exposed to a publication. For example, pass-along audiences include a family that shares a neighbor's magazine or patrons of a public library. Paid circulation of a periodical or newspaper tends to understate readership because of the pass-along audience.

passbook account A once-popular savings account in which deposits and withdrawals are entered in a small booklet provided by the financial institution. Passbook accounts are very flexible, with no withdrawal penalties, but they typically pay a very low rate of interest.

passed dividend A regular dividend that is omitted by a firm's board of directors. Passed dividends on most issues of preferred stock, but not on common stock, eventually must be made up. —Also called *omitted dividend; unpaid dividend.* —See also DIVIDENDS IN ARREARS.

passenger mile One passenger transported one mile. Commercial and public transportation systems use passenger miles as a measure of traffic. For example, an airplane carrying 80 passengers on a 500-mile flight produces 40,000 passenger miles. Another measure of traffic, revenue passenger miles, includes only paying passengers and is more relevant for commercial transportation companies.

passive activity 1. An activity involving a trade or business in which the taxpayer does not materially participate. 2. Any engagement in real estate rental activity.

passive income (loss) A special category of income (loss) derived from passive activities, including real estate, limited partnerships, and other forms of tax-advantaged investments. Investors are limited in their deduction of passive losses against active sources of income, such as wages, salaries, and pension income.

passive investment management A method of managing an investment portfolio that seeks to select properly diversified securities that will remain relatively unchanged over long periods of time. Passive investment management involves minimal trading, based on the belief that it is impossible to beat the averages on a risk-adjusted basis consistently. —Compare ACTIVE INVESTMENT MANAGEMENT.

passive investor An individual who invests capital but not does participate in management. For example, a person might join a group of other investors to purchase several rental units that will be managed by a real estate professional.

passive portfolio A portfolio of securities that is altered only when another variable, such as market index, is altered.

pass-through entity A legal entity that collects and distributes income and losses to its owners, who wish to protect themselves from personal liability for obligations of the entity. Estates, trusts, partnerships, and S corporations are examples of pass-through entities.

pass-through security A security that passes through payments from debtors to investors. Packages of loans are assembled and sold to investors by private lenders. Although pass-through securities have stated maturities, the actual lives of the securities are likely to be shorter, especially during periods of falling interest rates, when borrowers pay off mortgages early. The security derives its name from the fact that interest and principal payments made by borrowers are passed through monthly after deduction of a service fee. —Also called *pass through.* —See also GINNIE MAE PASS THROUGH; PRODUCTION RATE 2.

past service benefit Retirement plan credit accorded an employee for service prior to the effective date of the plan or prior to the date of participation of the employee. Past service benefits may value past service less than future service (a year of past service does not improve benefits as much as a year of future service), and acquiring past service credit may require a payment by the employee.

patent 1. The original document issued granting public land to an individual. **2.** A government grant giving the owner the exclusive but temporary right to make, use, or sell the item cited in the patent.

> **CASE** Patents offer an incentive to inventors, whose patents give them a **STUDY** limited-time monopoly during which they have exclusive use of their creations. In spring 2007, the U.S. Supreme Court rendered an important decision that made it easier to challenge the rights of patent holders. The case involved an adjustable accelerator in vehicles with electronic engine controls. In general, an invention can be eligible for patent only if it is useful, novel, and not obvious to a person of ordinary skill in the field. A Canadian company operating as a subcontractor for General Motors challenged the patent of a rival company on the basis that the combination of elements involved in the adjustable accelerator was obvious. The district court agreed with the plaintiff, but the U.S. Circuit Court of Appeals, to which patent case appeals are sent, overturned the decision. The court of appeals had historically made obviousness difficult and expensive to prove. This interpretation by the main judicial body overseeing patent law made patents relatively easy to protect. Critics claimed the strict interpretation of obviousness stifled innovation and competition. The Supreme Court ruling negated the circuit court's interpretation of obviousness as applied to patent eligibility. The decision was expected to have important ramifications for technology companies, especially those involved in software design.

Patent and Trademark Office The Department of Commerce agency that processes patent and trademark applications. Successful applications give inventors the exclusive right to their discoveries for a limited time.

patent infringement —See INFRINGEMENT.

patent monopoly A monopoly created by government grant of a patent. For example, the Bell System monopoly on telephone service was based on patents granted in the

1870s. By the 1930s, Bell had thousands of patents that gave it a virtual monopoly on long-distance voice transmission.

patent pending Words attached to manufactured items that indicate that someone has applied for a patent on an invention that is contained in the item. Once a patent has been granted, "patent pending" will be replaced by "covered by U.S. Patent Number xxxxxx."

patent warfare The situation of a company filing multiple patents that are only slightly different from one another in order to protect a profitable product beyond the expiration of the original patent. Patent warfare is particularly common among software companies and pharmaceutical companies.

paternalism A relationship of a company to its employees (or a government authority to its citizens) in which the company, or managers of the company, assume responsibility and make decisions for the employees. For example, management may severely limit the options of employees in the firm's retirement plan.

Patriot Bond A specially inscribed Series EE savings bond issued by the U.S. Treasury beginning December 11, 2001, three months following the September 11 terrorist attacks, to call attention to the country's war effort.

patronage dividend Profits distributed by a cooperative to its members.

pattern —See CHART FORMATION.

pattern bargaining Collective bargaining by a union that seeks to obtain identical terms from a previously signed agreement with a similar company. For example, the United Auto Workers typically bargain with a single auto company and subsequently use pattern bargaining with other unionized automakers.

pauper An extremely poor person who is likely to be living on public charity.

pay 1. To compensate someone for goods received or service performed. **2.** To satisfy part or all of an obligation.

payable That which is owed to another party as a debt.

pay as you go 1. In taxation, withholding taxes from pay. **2.** Paying for goods and services as they are used. An example is long-distance telephone service for which the caller pays for the time used rather than paying a flat monthly fee that includes a specific number of minutes or unlimited calling.

payback period 1. The length of time needed for an investment's net cash receipts to cover completely the initial outlay expended in acquiring the investment. **2.** The number of years the higher interest income from a convertible bond (compared with the dividend income from an equivalent investment in the underlying common stock) must persist to make up for the amount above conversion value paid for the convertible. —Also called *premium recovery period.*

payday loan A small short-term loan that the borrower promises to repay from the next period's paycheck. These loans are used by wage earners who run short of cash before payday. Payday loans typically entail a very high annualized interest rate (often in the triple digits) and a two-week maturity. For example, a $100 loan for two weeks might entail a fee of $15.

paydown In a corporate or U.S. Treasury refunding, the amount by which the face value of the bonds being refunded exceeds the par value of the new bonds being sold. Paydown represents the amount by which the debt is reduced.

payee The individual or organization to whom a payment is to be made.

payer The individual or organization responsible for making a payment.

paying agent A financial institution that makes the payments to the holders of an issuer's securities. For example, an indenture will name a paying agent responsible for making interest and principal payments on a bond issue.

payload Useful cargo that can be carried by a vehicle.

payment Transfer of money, goods, or services to satisfy part or all of an obligation.

payment date 1. The date on which a bill is due. 2. The date on which a dividend will be paid to stockholders or on which interest will be paid to bondholders by the issuers' paying agents.

payment in due course Payment of funds to the holder of a bill of exchange or promissory note on the due date. The payment is made in good faith on the assumption that title to the bill or note is not defective. —See also HOLDER IN DUE COURSE.

payment in kind (PIK) 1. Payment in goods or services that are similar to goods or services that have been provided. Payment in kind contrasts with payment in money. 2. A relatively unusual type of security that allows the issuer to pay the investor with additional shares (in the case of PIK preferred) or with bonds (in the case of PIK bonds) rather than with cash. PIK securities nearly always originate as a result of a leveraged buyout.

payola Undercover payments for the promotion of something. For example, disk jockeys are secretly compensated to play particular songs.

CASE STUDY In April 2007, four major broadcasting companies—CBS Radio, Citadel Broadcasting, Clear Channel Communications, and Entercom Communications—pleaded guilty to Federal Communications Commission charges of payola and agreed to pay the U.S. Treasury $12.5 million. The FCC had claimed the firms' stations had accepted cash and other incentives in return for playing certain music. Receiving payment for airing program material is illegal unless disclosed by the station, which must identify who made the payment. The radio companies also agreed to implement compliance plans and to broadcast the equivalent of 8,400 half-hour segments of music from independent artists. The FCC charges followed a 2005 settlement by Sony BMG Music Entertainment to pay $10 million after an investigation by New York Attorney General Eliot Spitzer. Spitzer claimed the company paid for contest giveaways, covered some of the stations' operational expenses, and provided vacation packages in return for receiving additional airplay. After a series of payola scandals in the late 1950s, federal legislation in 1960 made it illegal to offer money or other inducements to give records airplay without proper disclosures.

pay on death A designation placed on an asset such that, at the death of the owner, the asset passes to a designated beneficiary or beneficiaries who survive the owner. Pay-on-death assets generally avoid probate when the beneficiary survives the owner.

payout 1. In gambling, the money paid on a winning bet. 2. —See DIVIDEND.

payout ratio The ratio from which the percentage of net income a firm pays to its stockholders in dividends is calculated. Companies paying most of their earnings in dividends have little left for investment in new assets that will provide for future earnings growth. —Also called *dividend payout ratio.* —See also DIVIDEND COVERAGE; RETAINED EARNINGS.

pay period The interval at which a worker is paid by an employer. For example, many salaried employees have a monthly pay period.

payroll Wages paid by an employer to employees.

payroll card A stored-value card offered by some companies to their employees as an alternative to payroll checks or direct deposit. Payroll cards are similar to debit cards and can be used to make purchases or withdraw cash at ATMs.

payroll deduction Money withheld from an employee's gross income. Payroll deductions include federal and state withholding for taxes, insurance premiums, and retirement savings plans.

payroll savings plan 1. An agreement between an employer and an employee, who designates that a specific amount of earned income be diverted each period to a designated savings arrangement. 2. A popular arrangement in which an employee designates a periodic deduction from earned income for investment in U.S. savings bonds.

payroll taxes Taxes such as Social Security and Medicare that are paid by employer payroll deductions from wages and salaries.

PDA —See PERSONAL DIGITAL ASSISTANT.

peak The high point reached by a variable: *The demand for gasoline reaches a peak during the summer months.*

pecking order The ranking order of authority in an organization.

pecuniary Of or relating to money.

peer-to-peer (P2P) marketing A promotional program in which customers are encouraged to attract additional customers by promoting a product or service to friends and acquaintances. P2P marketing is practiced by some credit card companies, which offer incentives to cardholders who encourage acquaintances to submit applications.

peg 1. To fix the price of a new security issue during the issuance period through buying and selling it in the open market in order to ensure that the price in the secondary market will not fall below the offering price. —Also called *stabilize.* —See also STABILIZATION PERIOD. 2. To fix the rate at which foreign currencies exchange with one another. 3. To fix the price of a commodity. For example, a government may adopt an agricultural policy of pegging the price of certain commodities such as sugar or wheat.

PEG ratio —See PRICE-EARNINGS/GROWTH RATIO.

penalty plan A mutual fund accumulation plan in which sales fees for the entire obligation are deducted from shares purchased in the first few years that the plan is in effect. In the event that the investors redeem the shares after a short time, only a small portion of the purchase price will be refunded. Sales charges and penalty plans are regulated by the Investment Company Amendments Act of 1970.

pendente lite Latin for "while litigation is pending." For example, a defendant may be required to deposit funds with the court pendente lite to ensure recovery if the case is decided in the plaintiff's favor.

penetration pricing Setting the price of a new product below that charged by the competition in order to gain access to a market. For example, a household products company may charge a low introductory price for a new detergent in order to get consumers to try the new brand in place of their regular detergent. —See also PREDATORY PRICING.

pennying —See FRONT RUNNING.

penny stock A low-priced, speculative stock. Although the maximum price at which a security may sell and still be classified as a penny stock is subject to individual interpretation, $1 is probably the most commonly recognized limit. Many penny stocks are traded in the over-the-counter market and on smaller exchanges.

Pension Benefit Guaranty Corporation A government agency that insures certain corporate pension funds. The corporation, established under the Employee Retirement Income Security Act, is funded by charging companies a premium based on the number of covered employees.

> **CASE STUDY** In January 2007 the Pension Benefit Guaranty Corporation announced that it had become the trustee of the Delta Air Lines Inc. Pilots Retirement Plan. At the time, Delta Air Lines was in bankruptcy. As trustee, the PBGC assumed responsibility for paying pension benefits to over 13,000 active and retired pilots. The responsibility did not include a separate retirement plan for Delta's other employees, which the company continued to sponsor. At the time of the announcement, the pilots' pension plan was underfunded by approximately $3 billion, with $1.7 billion in assets and benefit liabilities of over $4.7 billion. Because the maximum annual guaranteed pension at age 65 for participants in plans that terminated in 2006 was $47,659 (significantly less than some of the pilots had been promised under the Delta plan), the PBGC calculated that it would be responsible for $920 million of the shortfall. This represented the sixth-largest claim in the agency's 32-year history.

pension cost The annual cost incurred by a firm in providing its employees with a pension plan.

pension fund A financial entity that controls assets and disburses income to people after they have retired. Pension funds, which invest in a variety of securities, control such enormous sums that their investment decisions can have significant impact on individual security prices.

pension parachute A pension agreement stating that, in the event of an unfriendly takeover, a firm can use any surplus pension assets to increase pension benefits. A pension parachute is used to make the firm less attractive to takeover, for it prevents the acquiring company from using the excess pension assets to help finance the acquisition.

pension plan An arrangement for paying death, disability, or retirement benefits to employees. Payments into the plan are ordinarily a tax-deductible expense for the firm, but any contribution by employees may or may not be deductible on personal tax returns. Likewise, retirement benefits paid to employees will be wholly or partially taxable. —Compare VESTED BENEFITS. —Also called *retirement plan.* —See also DEFINED-BENEFIT PENSION PLAN; DEFINED-CONTRIBUTION PENSION PLAN.

Pension Protection Act of 2006 Legislation resulting in extensive pension reform, including additional incentives for individuals who save for their own retirement and stiff funding requirements for businesses that offer employer-funded pension plans. The act allows plan providers to offer investment advice and makes it easier for employers to sign up employees in 403(k) and 401(c) retirement plans. The act also affects charitable contributions, funding for long-term care, and college savings plans.

pension reversion Termination of a pension plan by an employer that wishes to capture the amount by which the plan is overfunded. Pension reversions are generally accomplished by using funds in the plan to purchase a fixed annuity from an insurance company. Excess funds beyond the cost of the annuity revert to the company.

pension rollover Reinvestment of a lump-sum pension payout into an individual retirement account. The rollover permits a pension beneficiary to defer taxation until funds are paid out of the individual retirement account. A pension rollover is an alternative to paying taxes on a lump-sum payout, either in one year or by averaging over a number of years.

people-intensive —See LABOR-INTENSIVE.

P/E ratio —See PRICE-EARNINGS RATIO.

percentage depletion Depletion calculated as a percentage of gross income derived from a natural resource. Percentage depletion is independent of the cost of the resource.

percentage lease A leasing arrangement in which the tenant pays fixed monthly rent plus a percentage of revenues generated from the leased property. Percentage leases are common for retail space leased in shopping malls.

percentage-of-completion method A method of recognizing revenues and costs from a long-term project in relation to the percentage completed during the course of the project. Thus, the percentage-of-completion method allows a business profits (or losses) on a project before its completion. —Compare COMPLETED-CONTRACT METHOD.

percentage-of-sales method 1. A widely used method of establishing an advertising budget based on a percentage of past, current, or future sales or profits. For example, a product producing 15% of sales would receive 15% of the advertising budget. **2.** Projecting financial statements on the basis that many of the variables will remain at a fixed percentage of sales. For example, if sales are expected to increase 10% during the next year, the firm will have an additional 10% in inventories, receivables, and accounts payable.

percentile A value on a scale of 0 to 100 that represents the percent of the distribution that is equal to and below the value. For example, a variable at the 80th percentile is equal to or higher than 80% of the components of the distribution.

per diem The fixed daily payment for a service or the maximum daily reimbursement for expenses that are incurred. For example, an insurance company pays health care providers a per diem fee of $120 for each insured patient. Employers generally establish a maximum per diem reimbursement for travel expenses incurred by employees.

perfect competition A market structure in which a large number of small producers and consumers cannot influence prices for identical goods and services, information is freely and readily available, resources have great mobility, and no barriers exist to entry and exit. Perfect competition is a theoretical model that produces maximum efficiency in the use of resources. —Also called *pure competition.* —See also WORKABLE COMPETITION.

perfect hedge A hedge that exactly offsets any gains or losses from an existing investment position. An example of a perfect hedge is the short sale of an owned security in order to lock in an existing profit. Very few hedges are perfect, and most operate merely to offset a portion of losses or gains. —See also RISK HEDGE.

performance **1.** The degree to which a feat is being or has been accomplished. For example, the level of success of a salesperson in achieving a monthly goal of writing orders for new customers. **2.** The return provided by an investment. **3.** In law, satisfying an obligation.

performance appraisal A formal evaluation of an individual's work and achievements during a specified period. Performance appraisals are utilized for determining merit raises and promotions.

performance audit —See MANAGEMENT AUDIT.

performance bond A financial guarantee that a service will be provided or a contract will be satisfactorily completed. For example, a contractor posts a performance bond to guarantee a project will be completed on time.

performance fee A fee paid to an investment manager based on the performance of a client's portfolio, determined by a specified standard. For example, an investment manager might be paid a regular fixed fee plus an incentive fee based on the change in value of the client's portfolio. —Also called *incentive fee.*

performance fund —See AGGRESSIVE GROWTH FUND.

performance stock A stock that investors believe has an excellent chance for significant price appreciation. Performance stock tends to be issued by growth-oriented firms that retain most or all income for reinvestment. The stock usually sells at an above-average price-earnings ratio and experiences large price swings.

peril In property insurance, the potential cause of a loss. For example, wind is a peril cited in homeowners' policies. —Also called *hazard.*

peril point The limit beyond which tariff reduction will cause serious harm to a domestic industry.

period certain annuity —See ANNUITY CERTAIN.

periodic inventory method The calculation of inventories by counting physical inventory at the end of each accounting period rather than updating inventory continuously. Inventory on the balance sheet is determined by the physical count and the method used for valuing inventory. This method is used mostly by small businesses. —Compare PERPETUAL INVENTORY METHOD.

periodic payment plan A plan in which an investor agrees to make monthly or quarterly payments to a mutual fund as a method of accumulating shares over a period of years. The periodic payment plan's stipulation of fixed periodic contributions results in dollar-cost averaging for the investor. —See also PLAN COMPLETION INSURANCE.

periodic purchase deferred contract A deferred annuity purchased with a series of premium payments. For example, an individual might obtain a lifetime monthly income by making annual premium payments to an insurance company prior to retirement. —Compare SINGLE-PREMIUM DEFERRED ANNUITY.

perishable Of or referring to something that is subject to decay or spoilage. There are both perishable (wheat) and nonperishable (gold) commodities.

perjury Knowingly giving false testimony under oath about a material matter. Perjury prosecutions are relatively rare because of the difficulty of proving someone intentionally gave false testimony about a material fact.

perk —See PERQUISITE.

permanent financing The long-term financing that supports a long-term asset.

permanent income hypothesis The economic theory that individuals and families base consumption expenditures on their normal, or permanent, income rather than current income. According to this theory, variations in income, for example, a Christmas bonus, have little impact on consumer spending.

permanent insurance —See CASH-VALUE LIFE INSURANCE.

permit A document granting government authorization to do something. For example, a contractor applies for a building permit to add a bedroom to a home.

permit bond A guarantee that a permit holder will comply with all the rules and regulations governing the permit that has been granted. For example, a bond guarantees a roofer will meet standards mandated by a building permit.

permutations Possible orderings or arrangements of the components comprising a population. For example, a marketing department might examine all the promotional permutations for getting a product to the final consumer.

perpetual bond —See CONSOL.

perpetual inventory method A system of accounting for the value and quantity of inventory by using computers to continuously monitor sales and returns. An occasional physical count is required to confirm the values provided by a perpetual inventory system, which is likely to miss losses from theft. —Compare PERIODIC INVENTORY METHOD.

perpetual warrant A warrant that has no expiration date. Although many warrants have relatively long maturities, few are perpetual.

perpetuity A stream of payments that is expected to last indefinitely.

perquisite A special privilege or fringe benefit as a result of a person's position or employment. For example, a promotion allows an executive to move to a corner office, or a Wall Street investment banker who works late is provided a limousine for transportation home. —Also called *perk.*

per se Latin for "by itself": *Joint price setting by several businesses is considered per se illegal and is grounds for legal action.*

personal digital assistant (PDA) A popular handheld electronic device that performs a variety of business and personal functions including computing, telephone operations, and networking.

personal exemption —See EXEMPTION 1.

personal holding company A corporation with at least 60% of adjusted ordinary gross income being personal holding company income (passive income including dividends, interest, royalties, annuities, rents, and personal service income), and over 50% of the value of the corporation's outstanding stock owned by five or fewer executives. Undistributed corporate earnings are taxed in addition to the regular income tax.

personal identification number —See PIN.

personal income The pretax income of individuals and unincorporated businesses. Personal income is an inferior measure of the economy compared with disposable income; however, personal income is easier to compute and is made available on a monthly basis, while disposable income is calculated on a quarterly basis.

personal injury Wrongful harm, including bodily injury, to someone as a result of negligent or intentional conduct, including false arrest, slander, wrongful eviction, and invasion of privacy.

personal selling

I have taken a new position in sales. Can you provide some pointers on how to be successful at personal selling?

Recognize your personality and play to your strengths. If you have always made friends easily and quickly, your skills lend themselves to "outside" sales that result in immediate transactions. If you tend to have a small but loyal group of friends (like me), you are probably cut out for "inside" sales and long-term clients.

▪ Tom Mesereau, Principal, Mesereau Public Relations, Parker, CO

personal liability An obligation to the full extent of an individual's personal assets. The extent of personal liability is an important consideration in selecting insurance coverage.

personal property All property, tangible and intangible, other than real property. Personal property includes furniture, vehicles, copyrights, and securities. —Also called *personalty*.

personal property floater —See FLOATER 1.

personal savings rate —See SAVINGS RATE.

personal selling The presentation of a persuasive message by a seller to a potential customer or group of customers, generally in a face-to-face meeting. Personal selling can also take place through personal correspondence, telephone conversations, or emails.

personal service corporation A regular corporation whose principal activity is performing personal services (consulting, health care, law, accounting), primarily by the employee-owners. Personal service corporations are taxed at a flat rate of 35% rather than a series of graduated rates as applied to most corporations.

personalty —See PERSONAL PROPERTY.

personnel 1. —See HUMAN RESOURCES 1. **2.** The department of an organization that deals with issues relating to employees and participants.

per stirpes Distribution of an estate in which the descendants of deceased ancestors of the departed receive proportional shares of the estate as if their deceased ancestors had lived. In short, children take the share to which their deceased ancestor was entitled. The size of the proportional shares depends on the kinship.

PERT —See PROGRAM EVALUATION AND REVIEW TECHNIQUE.

Peter principle The observation that managers rise to their level of incompetence. For example, a successful manager is continually promoted to jobs with new responsibilities until reaching a position where incompetence rules out further promotion. Because of the difficulty of demoting someone, this is where the manager remains.

petition 1. A written request to a court that it take a specific action. **2.** A formal request accompanied by signatures of individuals who support the request.

petitioner The person or other entity that requests a court hearing or appeals a lower court ruling. For example, a petitioner might ask a state tax court for a redetermination of a tax deficiency based on a claim that certain income was not taxable by the state.

petition in bankruptcy —See BANKRUPTCY PETITION.

petrodollars The funds that are controlled by oil-exporting countries and have been used to pay for oil imports. Petrodollars are a huge pool of funds available for investment and the purchase of goods and services. Although stated in terms of dollars, the term generally refers to all currencies.

petty cash fund —See IMPREST FUND.

phantom freight Freight charged to the buyer that is different from the actual cost of delivery. For example, a seller adds a freight charge using a basing point of Chicago, regardless of where the shipment actually originates. Thus, a buyer in San Francisco is charged phantom freight if the shipment originated in Reno, Nevada. —See also BASING POINT.

phantom income Income that is subject to taxation but does not provide any cash. Owners of pass-through entities such as partnerships and S corporations are often affected by phantom income. Taxes must be paid on income that is passed through even though it is not accompanied by cash.

phantom stock plan An incentive plan for a firm's executives in which the executives are offered bonuses based on increases in the market price of the firm's stock. A phantom stock plan is supposed to induce the executives to act in the best interests of the shareholders.

> **CASE STUDY** Phantom stock plans are used to reward key employees with the benefits of ownership without actually making them shareholders. A typical plan credits selected employees with a certain number of stock units that each represent a share of the firm's stock. The value of each unit is the same as the value of the firm's stock on the date of the grant. Companies with publicly traded stock simply use the stock's market price. Closely held firms may value their stock by a formula or by formal valuation. In general, phantom stock grant awards have no tax consequences on the grant date to the issuing company or the employee. These plans are particularly attractive to closely held companies with owners who do not wish to give up ownership. However, large publicly traded firms also use these plans. Duke Energy Corporation reported that it awarded phantom stock grants equivalent to 1,181,370 shares in the year ended December 31, 2006, when nearly 3 million units were outstanding. For the years 2005 and 2004, the firm had awarded stock grants of 1,139,880 and 1,283,220, respectively. The firm's awards generally vested over periods ranging from immediate to five years.

phased retirement An employment arrangement in which an employee nearing full retirement works part-time for less than full wages, often while receiving pension income. For example, a university professor teaches half-time for 49% of full salary while drawing full retirement benefits.

Philadelphia Board of Trade The futures subsidiary of the Philadelphia Stock Exchange.

Philadelphia Stock Exchange (PHLX) The oldest organized securities exchange in the United States (founded in 1790), the PHLX serves as a marketplace for stocks, equity options, index options, and currency options. The exchange offers trading in both standardized and customized currency and equity options. The PHLX was the first floor-based stock exchange to change its structure from a seat-based mutual company to a share-based for-profit company.

picketing

Do legal restrictions apply to picketing? For example, can picketing occur on the property of the company being picketed?

Legal restrictions do apply to picketing and are dependent on the type and purpose of the picketing as well as state and federal laws governing the situation. The makeup of the picketers (employee, nonemployee), the purpose of the picket (labor dispute, social issue, personal gripe), and the location of the company (a remote area, a busy street, a shopping mall) are all factors in determining what restrictions may apply and whether picketing can occur on company property. For example, consumer picketing does not enjoy the same level of protection as picketing as part of a labor dispute, while even in that same labor dispute nonemployees do not usually enjoy the same protections with regard to picketing as do actual employees.

With regard to non-labor-related picketing, state or municipal law may implement reasonable "time, manner, and place" restrictions on picketing. States and municipalities may restrict the size of the group picketing, the manner of the picket, the location, the time of the picket, or even restrict a picket within a reasonable distance of "any captive audience," such as patrons waiting in line for events or eating in a seating area. And most states have a ban on targeted residential picketing.

Restrictions with regard to labor-related disputes are more difficult to quantify. Courts and the National Labor Relations Board (NLRB) have recognized the legitimacy of unions' claims for access to private property. The general rule is that picketing is not allowed on company property absent consent or a provision in a collective bargaining agreement, although exceptions have been carved into this rule. If the company's location is remote or fenced in, or there are no public easements surrounding the company, or a union has no other reasonable means of reaching the employer, picketing could be allowed on company property. It is also important to distinguish between picketing and other forms of labor protest. For example, while employees might not be able to enter onto company property to picket, they can distribute literature and solicit on company property during nonwork time and in nonwork areas to organize and conduct other protected activity.

The generic answer is that, except in very limited circumstances, picketing cannot take place on private property without the consent of the owner. However, the fact that property may be privately owned (such as a shopping mall or a sidewalk located entirely on private property) does not automatically make consent of the owner required in all circumstances. A body of law has developed to govern picketing on private property, especially on property that is open to the public. Due to the complexity of the law surrounding pickets, particularly in the area of labor disputes, it is best for a company faced with picketing to consult with its counsel on this issue.

■ Helen M. Kemp, Division Counsel and Assistant Director,
Retirement and Benefit Services, Office of the State Comptroller, State of Connecticut

---

Phillips Curve The relationship between inflation (as measured by wage rates) and the rate of unemployment. According to the relationship illustrated by the concave curve, there is a trade-off between fighting inflation and reducing unemployment.

PHLX —See PHILADELPHIA STOCK EXCHANGE.

physical commodity —See COMMODITY 1.

physical inventory The inventory on hand according to an actual count.

physical life The potential service life of an asset before it physically becomes unable to produce a good or service. An asset is often physically able to continue operating, but at a cost or rate that renders it economically obsolete. The economic life, as op-

piecework

Does the legal minimum wage apply to employees who do piecework?

Yes. The term *piecework* simply describes a type of employment for which an employee is paid a fixed *piece rate* for each unit produced or action performed. A man installing a granite counter in a private home, a dock worker stacking boxes, an auto mechanic doing an oil change, a worker picking apples at an orchard, and a person who sits at home and copies addresses onto envelopes could all be doing piecework depending on how they are paid. The last example (doing work at home) is the most commonly recognized form of piecework and is sometimes referred to as "industrial homework."

All individually covered homework and piecework is subject to the Fair Labor Standards Act (FLSA) minimum wage, overtime, and record-keeping requirements, although there are exceptions for some types of agricultural work. The piece rate must be the one actually paid during non-overtime hours and must be enough to yield at least the minimum wage per hour. The payment to the employee is converted into the "regular rate" for the pay period, and if it is less than the minimum hourly wage, the employer must pay the difference to comply with the state or federal minimum wage, whichever is higher.

The regular rate of pay for an employee paid on a piecework basis is obtained by dividing the total weekly earnings by the total number of hours worked in that week. For example, an employee paid on a piecework basis produces 30 widgets in 45 hours of work. The employee is paid $12 per widget and earns $360. The regular rate of pay for that week is $360 divided by 45, or $8 an hour, which exceeds federal minimum wage (but may not exceed some states' minimum wage) requirements, so the employer does not have to make up the difference. However, the employee is also entitled to overtime pay for each hour over 40. In the above example, in addition to the straight-time pay, the employee is also entitled to $4 (half the $8 regular rate) for each hour over 40 for a total of $20. This amount is combined with the regular rate of pay for a total of $380 due to the employee for the 30 widgets. It is possible for the regular rate to meet or exceed the minimum wage during one pay period and to fall short the next.

The FLSA also requires that certain records be kept of the work done by the employee. The records, at a minimum, must show the number of pieces completed and hours worked on a daily and weekly basis. Individual states may have stricter requirements.

■ Helen M. Kemp, Division Counsel and Assistant Director,
Retirement and Benefit Services, Office of the State Comptroller, State of Connecticut

posed to the physical life, is most important in valuing the asset. —See also ECONOMIC LIFE.

picketing Walking or marching near an organization's premises in protest of something such as wages, employment conditions, or a controversial policy.

pickup A gain in yield that is achieved from swapping bonds. For example, a pickup of 30 basis points comes about when bonds with a 5.70% basis are traded for bonds with a 6.00% basis.

piece rate Employee pay based on the units of production the employee completes. For example, an agricultural worker receives 50¢ for each bushel of oranges that is picked.

piecework Employment in which the employee is paid according to the amount of product produced.

pie chart A circle inside of which variables are represented by wedge-shaped sections based on their proportional importance of the whole. A pie chart might be used to illustrate sales in each of a firm's divisions based on its percentage of total sales.

piercing the veil Holding personally liable the owners, officers, and directors of a corporation or other limited liability company. For example, creditors may be able to pierce the corporate veil when a controlling shareholder uses the corporate structure as a deception to commit fraud.

pier-to-house Describing transportation of containers from the transportation firm's storage location to the consignee.

piggyback 1. Consecutive radio or television commercials of two or more products from the same company. **2.** Placing a truck trailer on a railroad flatcar. **3.** The situation of a broker trading in his or her personal account after trading in the same security for a customer. The broker may believe the customer has access to privileged information that will cause the transaction to be profitable. **4.** —See FOLLOW-ON OFFERING.

piggyback loan —See SECOND MORTGAGE.

piggyback registration The registration of a new issue and already outstanding stock of the same issuer for a single public offering. Thus, a single registration suffices for the primary and secondary offering.

Pigou effect The economic theory of English economist Arthur Pigou that falling prices stimulate consumption, thereby boosting an economy's income and employment. Pigou contended that consumption is based on real net wealth, not current income.

PIK —See PAYMENT IN KIND.

pilot plant An initial production facility, generally on a reduced scale, that is designed to test the feasibility of a new production process or product. Success at a pilot plant can be expected to lead to construction of one or more full-scale facilities.

PIN The personal identification number used by individuals when using an automated teller machine or a debit card.

Pink Sheets The registered name for a privately owned company that operates a centralized quotation service that collects and distributes market maker quotations for securities traded in the over-the-counter market. Pink Sheet quotations include companies that range from businesses in bankruptcy to international firms that do not wish to meet the regulatory requirements of an exchange listing. The service is named for the colored slips of paper on which bid and ask price quotations were once distributed. In 1999 Pink Sheets introduced its Electronic Quotation Service, which provides real-time quotes for OTC equities and bonds. —See also OTC BULLETIN BOARD; YELLOW SHEETS.

pin money Nominal funds available for small purchases.

pip The smallest incremental pricing unit for commodity and currency trading.

pipeline 1. The process through which items pass before their use or distribution to the public. For example, an auto manufacturer may have several new models in the pipeline. **2.** A conduit through which liquids are transported.

pipeline theory —See CONDUIT THEORY.

piracy The unauthorized and illegal duplication of products protected by patents or copyrights. Copying of copyrighted software and unauthorized downloading of movies are examples of piracy.

pit A location on a commodities exchange trading floor where the futures of a particular commodity are traded. —Also called *ring.*

placed in service Describing the date on which an asset becomes available for use: *Hybrid vehicles placed in service prior to 2006 were eligible for a clean-fuel tax deduction of up to $2,000.* For business purposes, the date an asset is placed in service is also the date on which depreciation begins.

placement test An examination designed to determine a person's interests and aptitudes. Placement tests are used by educational institutions to determine the courses a student should take, and by businesses to evaluate a job candidate's likelihood of success.

place of business An establishment where business is conducted. The business may be an office, a retail store, a manufacturing plant, or any other type of commercial or industrial establishment.

place utility The usefulness of a good or service as a function of the location at which it is made available. For example, snowmobiles have greater place utility in Minnesota than in Mississippi. —See also POSSESSION UTILITY.

plaintiff The person or other entity that initiates a lawsuit.

plain-vanilla Of or relating to the uncomplicated version of a particular type of product or asset. For example, a plain-vanilla bond is not convertible and cannot be called. A plain-vanilla washing machine may offer only a single wash cycle. —See also BELLS AND WHISTLES.

plan A design or series of steps for achieving an objective. For example, a software company devises a plan for increasing its market share in Europe.

plan B An alternative plan in the event the main plan proves unsuccessful or impossible to implement.

plan company A company that receives customer payments and purchases mutual fund shares when the customers wish to purchase shares in a fund on a periodic payment plan. Thus, the plan company acts as middleman in collecting the payments and crediting customer accounts.

plan completion insurance A life insurance policy for people who purchase mutual fund shares as part of a periodic payment plan. In the event of the participant's death before completion of the contract, plan completion insurance pays an amount sufficient to complete the remaining payments.

planned amortization class (PAC) A type of collateralized mortgage obligation with a predetermined principal paydown schedule that provides investors with greater cash-flow certainty and a more specific average life. The greater payment certainty comes at the expense of a lower yield to investors.

planned economy —See COMMAND ECONOMY.

planned unit development (PUD) A development project or subdivision with individually owned units plus common property that is owned and maintained by an association of property owners. Planned unit developments have a comprehensive development plan, and buildings are often on smaller lots in order to free more common space.

planning commission A group of appointed or elected citizens who conduct hearings and advise government officials on land-use planning matters, including zoning and development plans.

plan sponsor The entity, generally an employer, that establishes and maintains a benefits plan for employees or members.

plant and equipment The fixed assets that are used to produce the goods and services that a firm sells to its customers. On a corporate balance sheet, plant and equipment are valued at original cost. Plant and equipment become net plant and equipment when adjusted for accumulated depreciation. —Also called *net plant and equipment.*

plastic money Slang for credit card: *He paid for the airline ticket with plastic money.* —Also called *plastic.*

plat A diagram of a piece of land that includes lots, streets, alleys, buildings, and easements.

play —See DIRECT PLAY.

pleading A legal document filed with a court that sets forth a claim, response, or request. A pleading sets forth the cause of a legal action or the defense to a legal action.

pledged asset An asset used as security for a loan. For example, an airline pledges an airliner as collateral for a debt.

plot A measured area of land: *A person bought two burial plots at the local cemetery.*

plow back To reinvest earnings in additional income-producing assets. Firms that plow back earnings rather than pay the earnings in dividends tend to experience more rapid increases in earnings per share.

plowback ratio —See RETENTION RATE.

plug The favorable mention of a company, product, or service in a nonadvertising setting. For example, the host of a television show offers a plug for a new movie starring one of the show's guests.

plus tick —See UPTICK.

PN —See PROJECT NOTE.

pocket money Funds available for incidental expenses: *When the group went to lunch, Jim never seemed to have any pocket money to pay for his meal.* —Also called *spending money.*

point A unit of change in the value of a security or a security index or average. For common and preferred stocks, a point represents a change of $1. For bonds, a point represents a 1% change in face value. For example, a one-point decline in a $1,000 principal amount bond translates to a $10 decline in price. For stock averages and indexes, a point represents a unit of movement and is best interpreted as a percent of the beginning value. For example, a 120-point decline in the Dow Jones Industrial Average that started the day at 12,000 represents a 1% fall in the average.

point-of-purchase display Signs, window displays, counter pieces, literature racks, or other attention-grabbing devices located near a product in order to attract consumer interest and promote sales of the product.

point-of-sale system A comprehensive computerized checkout system that includes a bar-code scanner, receipt printer, cash drawer, credit and debit card scanner, monitor, and inventory management software. A point-of-sale system tracks sales and identifies inventory levels in real time.

points —See LOAN ORIGINATION FEE.

poison pill An antitakeover tactic in which warrants are issued to a firm's stockholders, giving them the right to purchase shares of the acquiring firm's stock (flip-over pill) or their own firm's stock (flip-in pill) at a bargain price in the event that a suitor hostile to management acquires a stipulated percentage of the firm's stock. The poison pill is intended to make the takeover so expensive that any attempt to take control will be abandoned. —Also called *shareholder rights plan.* —See also FLIP-IN PILL; FLIP-OVER PILL; MACARONI DEFENSE; SUICIDE PILL.

> **CASE STUDY** Following a major drop in the price of its common stock, online brokerage firm E*Trade in July 2001 adopted a flip-in poison pill that would help thwart hostile takeover bids for the company. Under what was called a "shareholder rights plan" by the firm, stockholders were issued rights to purchase from E*Trade 0.001 shares of a new series of participating preferred stock at an initial purchase price of $50. The rights plan would be triggered if an individual or group acquired beneficial ownership of 10% or more of the firm's common stock. Issuance of the new preferred stock would make a hostile bid considerably more expensive and, as a result, less likely. Critics of shareholder rights plans claim poison pills help protect ineffective managements while penalizing shareholders who are unable to benefit from higher share values that often result from takeover attempts.

poison-put bond A bond that allows an investor to cash in a security before maturity if the issuer becomes the target of a takeover bid hostile to its management. Poison-put bonds make it expensive for the bidder to buy the target firm, because the bidder will have to raise cash to pay off the owners of the bonds. The bonds can benefit the bondholders, who can cash in the securities if the takeover spawns a new, more highly leveraged high-risk corporate entity. —See also POISON PILL.

policy 1. A written contract issued by an insurance company to a policyholder that serves as evidence of insurance coverage. 2. An established plan or standard course of action that is to be followed.

policyholder A person or organization that pays a premium in return for a contractual right to insurance coverage.

policy loan A loan to a life insurance policyholder by an insurance company that uses the cash value of the policy as security. The debt does not have to be repaid, but if the policyholder should die, the amount of the loan, plus any accrued interest, will be deducted from the amount paid to beneficiaries.

political action committee (PAC) A political group associated with special-interest groups such as unions and corporations (but not political parties) that raises money in order to promote its members' views.

Ponzi scheme —See PYRAMID[1].

pool 1. A temporary affiliation of two or more people formed for the purpose of attempting to manipulate a security's price and/or volume. The pool is necessary in order to acquire the capital needed to manipulate a stock having a large market value. Pools were especially popular in the 1920s and early 1930s, but now have been regulated out of existence. —See also BLIND POOL; TRADING POOL. 2. —See MORTGAGE POOL. 3. A group of insurers and reinsurers who join together to share risks and premiums.

pooling of interests An accounting method for combining, unchanged, the assets, liabilities, and owners' equity of two firms after a merger or combination. Before being discontinued in 2001, pooling was a preferred method of accounting for mergers because it generally produced the highest earnings calculations for the surviving company. —Compare PURCHASE METHOD.

portability 1. The right of an employee to transfer a pension or some other specified benefit to a new job. **2.** The ability of an investor to transfer a proprietary brokerage product, such as a mutual fund, to an account at a different brokerage firm.

portal-to-portal pay Employee compensation based on the amount of time spent by an employee on an employer's property. Portal-to-portal means an employee's compensation begins at the time he or she steps onto the employer's property, not when work actually begins.

portfolio 1. A group of assets. For individuals, a portfolio might include stocks, bonds, rental real estate, bank accounts, and collectibles. For businesses, a portfolio is all of the assets included on the firm's balance sheet. For example, a real estate trust holds a portfolio of office rental properties. —Also called *investment portfolio.*—See also DIVERSIFICATION. **2.** A collection of creative work that can be made available to an employer or potential employer.

> **CASE STUDY** Businesses are constantly assembling and adjusting their portfolios of assets in an attempt to increase the returns they earn and reduce the risks they face. For example, a grocery chain opens new locations while closing or selling underperforming stores. On a smaller scale, retailers adjust the products they offer. A large, diverse company such as General Electric expands in some businesses (lending) at the same time it exits other businesses (insurance). In 2006 beverage giant Coca-Cola acquired Fuze Beverage, LLC in an effort to enhance its product portfolio, which was heavily weighted with carbonated beverages. Financial analysts and Coke's own bottlers had complained the company lacked competitive offerings of noncarbonated beverages that were being demanded by consumers. Fuze had commenced operations in 2001 and had grown rapidly with offerings of tea and energy drinks. Expanding its portfolio to include this new company allowed Coca-Cola to be a stronger competitor in a product area that promised higher sales growth than its existing products.

portfolio beta The relative volatility of returns earned from holding a specific portfolio of securities. A high portfolio beta indicates securities that tend to be more volatile in their price movements than the market taken as a whole. Portfolio beta is calculated by summing the products of each security's beta times the proportional weight of the security in the portfolio. For example, if a portfolio consists of two securities, one valued at $15,000 and having a beta of 0.9 and the other valued at $10,000 and having a beta of 1.5, the portfolio beta is $(0.9)(\$15,000/\$25,000) + (1.5)(\$10,000/\$25,000)$, or 1.14.

portfolio dedication The synchronization of returns on an investment portfolio with known future liabilities. Portfolio dedication applies primarily to investment decisions by institutions such as pension funds and insurance companies. These institutions can estimate future liabilities fairly accurately, and then try to minimize the outlay to satisfy the liabilities. —Also called *dedication; matching.*

portfolio dressing The addition and deletion of securities by an institutional investor before the end of a financial reporting period in order to make the portfolio appear acceptable to investors. Typically, portfolio dressing involves the sale of big losers and the addition of big gainers to convey the impression that the portfolio manager is competent. —Also called *dressing up a portfolio.*

portfolio effect A reduction in the variation of returns on a combination of assets compared with the average of the variations of the individual assets. This effect measures the extent to which variations in returns on a portion of assets held are partially canceled by variations in returns on other assets held in the same portfolio.

portfolio income Investment income, including interest, dividends, royalties, and capital gains.

portfolio insurance The futures or option contracts that serve to offset, in whole or in part, changes in the value of a portfolio. For example, a portfolio manager might sell short stock-index futures to hedge an expected decline in the market value of a portfolio.

portfolio manager A person who is paid a fee to supervise the investment decisions of others. The term is usually used in reference to the managers of large institutions such as bank trust departments, pension funds, insurance companies, and mutual funds. —Also called *money manager.*

portfolio reinsurance The transfer of a portfolio of insurance policies for an entire line of business by the primary insurance carrier to a reinsurance company. Portfolio reinsurance generally means the primary insurer wishes to exit that particular line of insurance.

portfolio theory The theory that holds that assets should be chosen on the basis of how they interact with one another rather than how they perform in isolation. According to this theory, an optimal combination would secure for the investor the highest possible return for a given level of risk, or the least possible risk for a given level of return. —Also called *modern portfolio theory.*

port of entry A designated location where government-appointed officials inspect cargoes, collect duties, and enforce regulations. A port of entry may be established by a country or by a state.

position 1. The ownership status of a person's or an institution's investments. For example, a person may own 500 shares of Google, 350 shares of Boeing, and a $10,000 principal amount of 7% bonds due in 2020. —See also LONG POSITION; SHORT POSITION. 2. The financial condition of a firm, especially with regard to debt. 3. The status of a business or product relative to its competitors. For example, Toyota enjoyed growing sales, a nonunion labor force, and a reputation for quality that gave the company a commanding position in the automotive industry. 4. The net balance in a foreign currency.

positional good A good or service whose quality is judged in relative rather than absolute terms. For example, the desirability of a home is judged on the basis of homes that are owned by neighbors or peers. Likewise, a vehicle may be a positional good desired for its social status rather than its functionality. Positional goods and services generally experience limited availability, which affects their desirability.

position building The continual and gradual accumulation of a firm's shares for a long position, or the borrowing and sale of the shares for a short position.

position day The day on which an investor with a short position in a commodity (that is, the investor who must make delivery) declares an intention to make delivery, if the day is other than the first day permitted.

positioning Determining the manner in which a good or service will be marketed to consumers. For example, company executives discuss whether sales will be hurt by positioning a new food product as a premium item available only at high-end grocery stores. Positioning helps influence how consumers perceive a good or service.

position limit In futures and options trading, the maximum number of contracts that an individual or a group of individuals working together may hold. The position limit is determined by the Commodity Futures Trading Commission for futures, or by the exchange on which the particular contract is traded. —Compare TRADING LIMIT.

positive carry The current net income from an investment position when the current income from the investment exceeds its cost of carry. For example, a Treasury bond with a current yield of 5.2% has a positive carry if its purchase can be financed at 4.9%. —Compare NEGATIVE CARRY. —See also CARRYING CHARGE 1; CARRY TRADE.

positive correlation The relationship between two variables that vary together in the same direction; as one grows larger, the other also grows larger. For example, gasoline prices and sales of fuel-efficient vehicles have a positive correlation. —Compare NEGATIVE CORRELATION.

positive covenant A clause in a loan agreement that requires a specified action by the borrower. For example, a positive covenant may mandate that the borrower maintain a specific level of working capital or issue periodic reports to creditors. —Compare NEGATIVE COVENANT.

positive yield curve The normal relationship between bond yields and maturity lengths that results from higher interest rates on long-term bonds than on short-term bonds. Positive refers to the slope of the curve drawn to depict this relationship. —Compare NEGATIVE YIELD CURVE. —See also FLAT YIELD CURVE.

possession utility The increased value of a product created by the legal right of ownership. For example, a marketing program that increases the desire of consumers to own a particular product also increases the possession utility of that product.

post[1] In accounting, to transfer information from the journal to the ledger.

post[2] The location where transactions in particular securities occur on an organized securities exchange.

postdated check A check with a written date in the future that cannot be deposited or cashed until or after the posted date.

potential dilution The decrease in the proportional equity position of a share of stock that will occur eventually if additional authorized shares are actually issued. This term generally refers to outstanding options and convertible securities likely to be exchanged for shares of common stock at a future time.

pot trust A trust that allows the trustee discretion in distributing assets among beneficiaries. A pot trust is used when the trustor is concerned there may be substantial differences in needs among the trust's beneficiaries, especially children. For example, a parent of three children establishes a pot trust to guard against the possibility one of the children may require greater financial assistance than the other two. Establishing separate trusts for each of the children would provide less flexibility.

pour-over will A will that stipulates the maker's estate will pass (pour) into a trust. For example, a person establishes a trust for the benefit of children. A pour-over will results in the remainder of the estate passing to the trust at the maker's death. A pour-over will can be used to revoke a prior will and to make certain that any missing assets are properly disposed of.

poverty The economic state of an individual or family deemed too poor to afford a minimal standard of living. The formal definition of poverty is a function of annual income compared to family size and age composition.

poverty line The minimum amount of income required for a person or family to meet basic needs. The level of a poverty line is subjective and subject to disagreement. For example, an institution's definition of the poverty line for individuals living in the United States may assume a higher standard for necessities compared to someone living in a developing country.

power center A retail complex comprised of few stores other than several large anchors such as category killers (The Home Depot or Circuit City), warehouse clubs (Sam's or Costco), and discount stores (Target).

power of appointment 1. —See GENERAL POWER OF APPOINTMENT. 2. —See SPECIAL POWER OF APPOINTMENT.

power of attorney A legal document in which a person gives another the power to act for him or her. The authority may be general or it may be restricted to activities such as the handling of security transactions.

power of attorney for health care A legal document that authorizes a person to make medical decisions for the document maker when the document maker is unable to do so. —Also called *health care power of attorney.*

power of sale A section in a mortgage, trust agreement, or will allowing for the sale or transfer of assets under specified conditions. For example, a lender is permitted to sell real property securing a loan in the event the borrower defaults.

Powershares QQQ Trust A market-capitalization-weighted index of the largest and most active nonfinancial domestic and international issues listed on the Nasdaq Stock Market. The index was launched in 1985 to represent Nasdaq's largest companies across major industry groups. —See also QQQQ.

precious metals Relatively rare metals with high economic value as currency and jewelry, including gold, silver, platinum, and palladium.

preclosing The period prior to the closing of a contract when conditions of the contract are confirmed and documents are finalized. For example, the preclosing of a merger between two competing companies might include due diligence regarding antitrust matters.

precomputed interest The interest on a loan that is calculated by multiplying the face value of the loan times the interest rate and either adding the result to the original principal or subtracting the result from funds distributed to the borrower.

precomputed loan An account in which debt is expressed as principal plus interest charges calculated for the full term of the loan.

predate —See ANTEDATE.

predatory lending Abusive lending, often to borrowers who are unlikely to be able to meet the required payments and will, as a result, lose assets used as collateral. Predatory lending typically includes high fees and added charges for questionable products such as credit insurance.

predatory pricing Temporarily charging very low prices, often below cost, in an attempt to drive competitors out of a market. Predatory pricing is generally practiced by large businesses that can afford to lose money on a particular product or group of products at the same time its competitors cannot. While predatory pricing is illegal, it is generally difficult to prove that it is not merely a result of aggressive competition.

preemptible rate The discounted media rate offered to an advertiser on the basis of availability. The advertisement can be preempted by another advertiser that is willing to pay a higher price. Buying advertising at a preemptible rate is similar to buying an airline ticket on standby status.

preemption 1. The priority of federal law over state law when the two conflict. 2. The right of government to seize something. For example, police can confiscate a vehicle used to transport illegal drugs.

preemptive right A stockholder's right to keep a constant percentage of a firm's outstanding stock by being given the first chance to purchase shares in a new stock issue in proportion to the percentage of outstanding shares already held. Not all firms provide the preemptive right, which is more important to stockholders owning a significant part of a company. —Compare PRIVILEGED SUBSCRIPTION. —Also called *subscription privilege.*

preexisting use —See NONCONFORMING USE.

preference item —See TAX PREFERENCE ITEM.

preference stock —See PRIOR PREFERRED.

preferential hiring A hiring practice that favors an identified group for employment. For example, an employer may agree to hire only union members as long as the union is able to provide sufficient candidates to fill demand.

preferred call period —See DEFERMENT PERIOD.

preferred creditor A creditor having priority to payment over one or more other classes of creditors. For example, a borrower must pay holders of first mortgage bonds before payments are made to holders of second mortgage bonds on the same collateral. First mortgage bondholders are the preferred creditors.

preferred dividend coverage The measure of a firm's ability to meet its dividend obligations on preferred stock. The greater the coverage, the less the chance that management will pass a dividend. Several methods are utilized to calculate preferred dividend coverage. The most common is to divide net income by the annual preferred dividend commitment. A more conservative measure is to divide earnings before taxes and fixed charges by fixed charges plus the pretax preferred dividend. The latter is calculated as the preferred dividend divided by one minus the firm's tax rate.

preferred risk A class of insurance for policyholders or potential policyholders who are judged to be less likely than average to suffer an insured loss. For example, a middle-aged woman with an excellent driving record would be considered a preferred risk for automobile insurance. Customers judged to be preferred risks often receive a discount on insurance premiums.

preferred stock A security that shows ownership in a corporation and that gives the holder a claim prior to the claim of common stockholders on earnings and also generally on assets in the event of liquidation. Most preferred stock issues pay a fixed dividend set at the time of issuance, stated in a dollar amount or as a percentage of par value. Because no maturity date is stipulated, these securities are priced on dividend yield and trade much like long-term corporate bonds. As a general rule, preferred stock has limited appeal for individual investors. —See also AUCTION-RATE SECURITY; CALLABLE PREFERRED STOCK; CUMULATIVE; FLOATING-RATE PREFERRED STOCK; PARTICIPATING 1; PREFERRED DIVIDEND COVERAGE; PRIOR PREFERRED; REMARKETED PREFERRED STOCK; SECOND PREFERRED.

pre-IPO An offering of a company's shares prior to the firm's initial public offering. Investing in a pre-IPO tends to be very risky, in part because the planned IPO may never take place. In addition, shares from a pre-IPO are unregistered and are likely to be very difficult to sell until the public offering is completed.

prejudicial error —See REVERSIBLE ERROR.

prelease To promote lease commitments prior to availability of the premises to be leased. For example, builders often prelease the space in a building as a condition for obtaining permanent mortgage financing.

preliminary prospectus —See RED HERRING.

premature exercise Exercise of an option by the owner before the expiration date. Although most options are exercised near expiration, an owner occasionally finds it advantageous to exercise prematurely. For example, the owner of a call may exercise early in order to be the stockholder of record for an upcoming dividend payment. Such an action will often foul up the option writer's plan, in which instance the writer must sell (with a call) or purchase (with a put) the stock earlier than expected.

premises A property and its improvements as designated in a deed, title, mortgage, or an insurance policy.

premium 1. The payment made by an insured to an insurance company that has accepted a transfer of a risk. The amount of the premium is a function of the likelihood and size of a potential loss. —See also DIRECT PREMIUM 2. **2.** The price at which an option trades. The amount of the premium is affected by various factors, including the time to expiration, interest rates, strike price, and the price and price volatility of the underlying asset. —Also called *option premium.* **3.** The amount by which a bond sells above its face value. —Also called *bond premium.* **4.** The excess by which a warrant trades above its theoretical value. **5.** The amount by which a convertible bond sells above the price at which the same bond without the convertible feature would sell. **6.** A free or reduced-price item offered as an incentive to undertake some action. For example, a savings institution offers frequent-flyer points to customers who invest $10,000 in a one-year certificate of deposit. —See also DIRECT PREMIUM 1.

premium bond A bond that sells at a price above its par value. An investor must be careful about purchasing a bond that is selling at a premium because of the possibility of a call by the bond's issuer for sinking fund requirements or for refunding. Except for convertible bonds, the size of a bond's premium usually can be expected to decline as the bond approaches maturity, at which time it will be redeemed at par.

premium income Fees in the form of premiums received by an investor who sells short a call option or put option. For example, an investor holding shares of BP can earn premium income by writing covered call options that allow the buyer of the calls the right to purchase the option writer's BP shares at a fixed price until a stated date.

premium pay A wage rate higher than normal for working overtime, holidays, days off, or under especially hazardous conditions.

premium rate 1. The cost of insurance coverage for a specified time. For example, term life insurance may have a premium rate of $1.50 for each $1,000 of coverage. **2.** The unusually high charges entailed in calling certain telephone numbers. For ex-

premium bond

My broker says I shouldn't purchase bonds that sell above par. Is this good advice?

Not necessarily. All else equal, a bond may be priced at a premium because it has a high coupon rate or is deemed to have a relatively safe credit rating—characteristics which many may find desirable. Both discount bonds and premium bonds can be the right choice depending on numerous conditions, including your views on the upcoming movement in interest rates. For example, premium bonds tend to have a lower duration, which can result in lower volatility and prove safer during a sudden rise in interest rates. There are many factors to evaluate when considering investing in bonds, and the decision should not be made exclusively on whether the bond is above or below par.

■ Noah L. Myers, CFP®, Principal and Chief Investment Officer, MiddleCove Capital, Centerbrook, CT

ample, a typical scam informs a person they must call a particular telephone number in order to claim a valuable prize. The call results in the caller paying a premium rate for each minute of time on the telephone.

premium recovery period —See PAYBACK PERIOD 2.

prenuptial agreement A written agreement by a couple who plan to marry in which financial matters, including rights following divorce or the death of one spouse, are detailed. —See also COHABITATION AGREEMENT.

prepackaged bankruptcy A Chapter 11 bankruptcy settlement in which the reorganization and main provisions have been agreed to by creditors and owners in advance of the filing.

prepaid expense An expenditure for an item that will provide future benefits. For example, a firm may pay an insurance premium only once a year, resulting in an expense that provides benefits throughout a 12-month period. The unexpired part of the premium is carried on the firm's balance sheet as a current asset.

prepaid income Compensation received in advance of a promised service or delivery of a good. Prepaid income is generally taxable in the year in which it is received, unless a taxpayer uses the accrual method of accounting, in which case the income is reported as the service is performed.

prepaid interest The interest on a loan that has been paid but is not due until a following period. The Internal Revenue Service does not permit taxpayers to claim prepaid interest as an itemized deduction on tax returns.

prepayment A payment made prior to the date it is due. For example, borrowers sometimes make an extra principal payment, or prepayment, in order to reduce the outstanding balance on their loan.

prepayment clause A provision in a loan agreement that allows the borrower to repay a loan ahead of schedule, although a penalty may apply.

prepayment penalty The charge assessed a borrower for early repayment of a loan. A prepayment penalty makes it less likely a borrower will refinance a loan following a drop in market rates of interest.

prepayment risk The risk to a lender that part or all of the principal of a loan will be paid prior to the scheduled maturity. Prepayments generally occur when market rates of interest decline following the loan origination. Prepayment generally results in reduced cash flow to the lender, who must reinvest proceeds from the prepayment at a reduced interest rate. —Also called *call risk.*

prerefunded bond A bond secured by an escrow fund of U.S. government obligations that is sufficient to pay off the entire issue of refunded bonds at maturity. The rating of the refunded bond generally assumes the rating of the government obligations (highest rating) at the time the fund is established. —See also ARBITRAGE BOND.

prerefunding The placing of funds with a trustee in order to retire a bond issue as a liability before the call date. —Also called *advance refunding.* —See also ARBITRAGE BOND.

presale The marketing and sale of properties prior to or during construction. Builders and developers often offer discounted prices on presales.

prescriptive right Public rights that are acquired to private lands through use. For example, the public gains prescriptive right by having used a popular trail that leads through private property from a road to a beach. The right of access through use is essentially an easement.

present fairly The standard for an independent auditor's presentation of financial statements according to generally accepted accounting principles. The auditor's report offers an opinion as to whether the financial statements present fairly the firm's financial position, results of operations, and cash flow.

present value (PV) The current value of future cash payments when the payments are discounted by a rate that is a function of the market interest rate. For example, the present value of $1,000 to be received in two years is $812 when the $1,000 is discounted at an annual rate of 11%. Conversely, $812 invested at an annual return of 11% would produce a sum of $1,000 in two years. —Compare FUTURE VALUE. —See also NET PRESENT VALUE.

president A leading decision maker of a company. The president, who reports to the board of directors, is sometimes the company's chief executive officer.

presidential election cycle The tendency of the stock market to move in four-year cycles, with rising markets occurring during the period before presidential elections. The presidential election cycle is based on observation of past market movements and on the theory that holds that incumbent presidents manipulate the economy before elections in such a way that bull markets ensue. —Also called *election cycle.*

presold 1. Of, relating to, or being a new security issue that is sold out before all the specifics of the issue have been announced. In the case of a bond issue, this term usually means that sufficient orders for the issue have been placed before announcement of the coupon rate(s). **2.** Describing dwellings that a developer has sold prior to construction. For example, half of a proposed condominium's units may be presold prior to the beginning of construction.

presorted mail Mail prepared so as to bypass certain postal operations in order to qualify for a discounted postal rate. Pieces must be grouped according to ZIP code or carrier route or carrier walk sequence. Presorted first-class mailing requires at least 500 addressed pieces of mail. —See also ZONED RATE.

press clipping service —See CLIPPING SERVICE.

press kit An assortment of promotional materials that is distributed to the media in an effort to generate publicity about a person, product, or organization.

prestige pricing Establishing a high price for a product or service in an effort to create an image of high quality. Prestige pricing appeals to consumers who believe price and quality are related.

pretax income Reported income before the deduction of income taxes. Pretax income is sometimes considered a better measure of a firm's performance than aftertax income because taxes in one period may be influenced by activities in earlier periods. —Also called *earnings before taxes; pretax.*

pretax loss A loss reported before tax benefits are considered.

pretax writedown An accounting reduction in the value of an asset, measured before any effect by income taxes.

pretax yield The rate of return on an investment before taxes have been considered. As with other measures of yield, pretax yield is usually stated on an annual basis.

pretermitted heir A person such as a child or spouse who would normally be included in a will but was accidentally omitted. For example, a child is born or adopted after a will is executed. Some states allow a pretermitted spouse to claim the portion of an estate that would pass to a spouse when no will existed.

preventative maintenance Regular inspection, cleaning, overhauling, and replacement in an effort to prevent future problems that result in downtime and more expensive repairs. For example, an automobile owner replaces a timing belt at 60,000 miles in order to reduce the likelihood of a future engine failure.

price The cost of a good or service.

price/book ratio —See MARKET TO BOOK.

price break 1. A reduction in per-unit price if an order exceeds a specified quantity. **2.** A temporary reduction in the price of a product. For example, a retailer may advertise a weekend price break for a car stereo.

price change —See NET CHANGE.

price discrimination Charging different prices to different consumers for the same good or service. Price discrimination requires that the seller be able to effectively segment markets, or else buyers at a low price will be able to profit by selling to other buyers being charged a higher price. Price discrimination is regularly practiced by airlines that sell seats on the same plane at many different prices. —See also DUMPING 2.

price-earnings/growth ratio (PEG ratio) A valuation tool that compares a stock's price-earnings ratio with the firm's expected growth in earnings per share. Most advocates of this tool believe choosing a stock with a PEG ratio of less than one will tend to produce above-average returns.

price-earnings ratio (P/E ratio) A common stock analysis statistic in which the current price of a stock is divided by the current (or sometimes the projected) earnings per share of the issuing firm. As a rule, a relatively high price-earnings ratio is an indication that investors believe the firm's earnings are likely to grow. Price-earnings ratios vary significantly among companies, among industries, and over time. One of the important influences on this ratio is long-term interest rates. In general, relatively high rates result in low price-earnings ratios; low interest rates result in high price-earnings ratios. —Also called *earnings multiple; market multiple; multiple; P/E ratio.* —See also FORWARD P/E; TRAILING P/E.

price-earnings relative The price-earnings ratio of a stock in relation to the price-earnings ratio of the overall stock market, generally as measured by the S&P 500. This ratio is used as a tool to help determine if a stock's P/E ratio is reasonable.

price elasticity —See ELASTICITY.

price fixing Two or more sellers (buyers) colluding to charge (pay) the same price in a particular market for a good or service. The law prohibits nearly all attempts to fix prices.

> **CASE STUDY** Five large music companies and three large music retailers agreed in October 2006 to settle a lawsuit over alleged price fixing during the late 1990s. The companies did not admit wrongdoing, but agreed to refrain from using minimum-advertised pricing, the practice of establishing minimum retail prices that served as the basis for the lawsuit. The defendants claimed minimum-advertised pricing was actually procompetitive because it helped protect independent music retailers from cutthroat competition by big discounters such as Wal-Mart. As a result, they claimed, the practice increased the number of retailers. The agreement required the defendants to pay $67 million and to distribute $75 million in compact disks to public and nonprofit groups. A government official indicated that halting the retail pricing plan could cause prices to drop by as much as $5 per CD.

price gouging Taking advantage of a lack of competition and selling at an especially high price. For example, auto dealers are known to engage in price gouging when a much-sought-after model is in short supply.

price index 1. —See CONSUMER PRICE INDEX. **2.** —See PRODUCER PRICE INDEX.

price inelasticity —See INELASTICITY.

price leader 1. A business whose pricing decisions heavily influence the pricing decisions of its competitors. Price leadership is most common in an industry dominated by a large firm. —See also OLIGOPOLY. **2.** A business that offers the best price in a given market. For example, Wal-Mart is a grocery price leader in many of the markets in which it operates. —Also called *low-price leader.*

price lining Pricing a product at different levels in order to appeal to different segments of the market. For example, an appliance manufacturer creates a dishwasher that it sells in different versions (basic, midline, and premium) at different prices to appeal to different segments of buyers. Price lining is targeted at consumers for whom price is important in choosing the model of a product they should purchase. —Also called *product line pricing.*

price range —See RANGE 2.

price-sales ratio (P/S ratio) A financial ratio that compares a firm's stock price with its sales per share (or its market value with total revenue). It is used by some analysts to find companies that may be temporarily undervalued in the stock market. A low P/S ratio is thought to characterize a firm with the potential for a significant turnaround, because sales are already being made and improvement need only take place in the margin the firm is able to earn on each dollar of sales.

price skimming Establishing a high price for a product or service before competitors have had sufficient time to introduce competing products or services. For example, the manufacturer of a new type of cell phone initially charges a very high price, which it expects to lower after competitors make it to market with similar models. Price skimming is a way for a manufacturer to take advantage of its temporary monopoly.

price stabilization Intervention in the market in an effort to reduce price volatility. —See also PEG.

price support A government policy of guaranteeing a minimum price for a product, generally by purchasing the product from the producer.

price system A means of organizing economic activity by using price to allocate goods and services.

price target The projected price of a security.

price-to-book-value ratio —See MARKET TO BOOK.

price war Intense competition in which competing businesses repeatedly lower prices in an attempt to gain customers. Price wars most often occur in industries, such as airlines, that have high fixed costs.

pricey Of, relating to, or being an unrealistically high offer to sell. An offer to sell a house for $350,000 when similar homes have been selling for $300,000 is pricey. —Compare LOWBALL.

pricing The determination of the price at which something will be sold. For example an investment banking firm will establish the price at which a new issue of bonds will sell. If the price is set too high or the yield is set too low, the issue will not sell out. If the price is set too low or the yield is set too high, the issuer will pay more than necessary in interest to sell the bonds.

prima facie Describing something that is seemingly so obvious that nothing in addition is required to prove its truth. For example, a shopper running out of a store entrance carrying goods that have not been paid for is prima facie evidence of theft.

primary beneficiary The first person or other entity named to receive the proceeds from an estate, a trust, a retirement plan, or a life insurance policy. —See also SECONDARY BENEFICIARY.

primary boycott An effort by an organized group to discourage members of the group and other consumers from buying products from a specific company. —Compare SECONDARY BOYCOTT.

primary commodity A commodity in its natural state. For example, silver ore as opposed to processed silver used in jewelry.

primary contractor —See GENERAL CONTRACTOR.

primary data Original data that is gathered and evaluated. For example, a research group may conduct a telephone survey in order to gather primary data to help determine likely voters for a particular candidate for office. —Compare SECONDARY DATA.

primary dealer A government securities firm to which the New York Federal Reserve Bank sells directly and from which it buys directly in an attempt to control the money supply. —Compare REPORTING DEALERS. —See also OPEN-MARKET OPERATIONS.

primary demand 1. Consumer demand for final goods and services. —Compare DERIVED DEMAND. 2. In marketing, consumer demand for a general product category as compared to a particular brand.

primary distribution A sale of a new issue of securities in which the funds go to the issuer. —Compare SECONDARY DISTRIBUTION. —Also called *primary offering*.

primary lease The main lease between an owner and tenant under which subleases exist.

primary market The market in which new, as opposed to existing, securities are sold. Investors who purchase shares in a new security issue are purchasing them in the primary market. —Compare SECONDARY MARKET. —Also called *new issue market.*

primary offering —See PRIMARY DISTRIBUTION.

primary shares Shares in a stock offering in which proceeds go to the issuing company. Primary shares have not been previously traded and are not included in shares outstanding prior to the offering. —Compare SECONDARY SHARES.

primary trend The main direction in which a variable is moving. An upward primary trend in stocks is considered a bull market, while a downward primary trend is a bear market. —See also SECONDARY TREND.

prime 1. Of or relating to a debt security rated AAA or Aaa. **2.** —See PRIME RATE.

prime paper The highest grades of commercial paper as determined by the rating agencies. Prime paper includes those having Moody's ratings of P-3 and above.

prime rate A short-term interest rate quoted by a commercial bank as an indication of the rate being charged on loans to its best commercial customers. Even though banks frequently charge more and sometimes less than the quoted prime rate, it is a benchmark against which other rates are measured and often keyed. —Also called *prime.*

prime tenant —See ANCHOR TENANT.

principal 1. The face amount of a bond. Once a bond has been issued, it may sell at more or less than its principal amount, depending on changes in interest rates and the riskiness of the security. At maturity, however, the bond will be redeemed for its principal amount. —Also called *principal amount.* **2.** Funds put up by an investor. **3.** The person who owns or takes delivery of an asset in a business transaction. For example, the owner of a home (the principal) contracts with a broker to list the home for sale.

principal amount —See PRINCIPAL 1.

principal and interest (P&I) A payment, generally monthly, on an amortized loan that includes interest charges and a portion of principal.

principal, interest, taxes, and insurance The components of a monthly mortgage payment when insurance and taxes are paid into an escrow account. The monthly payment includes only principal and interest when insurance and taxes are paid separately by the borrower.

principal market The main market in which a security trades. The principal market for the common stock of most large corporations in the United States is the New York Stock Exchange, even though most of this stock also trades on one or more other exchanges and in the over-the-counter market. —See also CONSOLIDATED TAPE.

principal place of business 1. The location of a firm's head office. **2.** The location where the majority of activities relative to a business take place. For example, whether or not a home office is considered a principal place of business is a factor in determining whether a taxpayer can claim a home office deduction.

principal residence The dwelling in which a person spends most of his or her time. The courts and the IRS consider a number of factors, including voter registration, and address on driver's license and tax returns when there is a question about a person's principal residence.

principal risk The possibility an investment will be worth less when it is sold than when it was purchased. Principal risk is high for tangible assets and for common stocks compared to most fixed-income investments such as bonds, preferred stock, and certificates of deposit.

principal stockholder A stockholder who owns a large number of voting shares in a firm. For SEC purposes, a person who owns 10% or more of a firm's voting stock is considered a principal stockholder.

principal sum The amount payable on an insurance policy. For example, the beneficiary of a life insurance policy receives a principal sum of $50,000 upon the death of the insured.

principal trade A securities transaction in which the executing brokers are trading from inventory and are thus acting as dealers.

priority A relative position or claim to something. In bankruptcy, for example, the claim of a secured bondholder has priority over the claim of an unsecured bondholder.

Priority Mail A premium service offered by the U.S. Postal Service that offers delivery of documents and packages (70 lb. maximum) in two to three days.

prior-lien bond A bond with a priority claim over other bonds, both secured and unsecured, of the same issuer.

prior period adjustment Correction of a material mistake in reported income in an earlier financial statement. Although prior period adjustments affect retained earnings, they are not used to alter income in the current period. —Also called *retroactive adjustment.*

prior preferred A class of preferred stock that has preference over one or more other classes of preferred stock of the same issuer. Preference may be with respect to payment of dividends and/or claims on assets. —Compare SECOND PREFERRED. —Also called *preference stock.*

prior service cost The expense to an employee to purchase service credits used in determining the employee's retirement benefits. For example, a teacher pays $10,000 to purchase three years of service performed in a different state. Purchase of the credits will result in an increase in the teacher's annual retirement income.

private accountant —See MANAGEMENT ACCOUNTANT.

private activity bond A type of municipal bond issued when funds are to be used for a nonessential purpose. Private activity bonds pay taxable interest unless specifically exempted by the federal government. Private activities for which tax-exempt bonds may be issued include airports, electric and gas distribution systems, government mass transportation systems, solid waste disposal facilities, and student loans. Except for nonprofit college and hospital bonds, interest from tax-exempt private activity bonds is subject to the alternative minimum tax. —Compare ESSENTIAL FUNCTION BOND. —Also called *nonessential function bond; private purpose municipal bond.* —See also MUNICIPAL BOND.

private brand A product purchased by a retailer for resale with the retailer's own brand name. Most grocery chains buy canned vegetables and other products for sale with their own brand name.

private corporation —See PRIVATELY HELD COMPANY.

private equity firm An investment company that pools investor funds that are utilized, generally in combination with large amounts of borrowed capital, for the acquisition of underperforming businesses. Private equity firms often choose to replace management, revamp operations, and recapitalize the balance sheet in an effort to improve profitability and increase the value of the acquired business before offering it for sale.

Private Export Funding Corporation A private entity created in 1970 to assist in financing U.S. exports. The organization is owned by commercial banks, industrial companies, and financial services companies engaged in financing, producing, or exporting U.S. goods and services.

private foundation A tax-exempt organization founded with private money to support charitable activities. Nonoperating private foundations make grants to charitable organizations, while operating private foundations distribute funds directly for charitable activities. —Compare PUBLIC CHARITY.

private law 1. A private bill passed by the House of Representatives and Senate that affects only a private individual or individuals. —Compare PUBLIC LAW. **2.** A law that defines legal rights and relationships between two or more parties, such as a contract between a landlord and tenant.

private letter ruling An Internal Revenue Service response to a taxpayer's question about an interpretation of the tax implications of a particular transaction. A private letter ruling applies only to the particular circumstances of the taxpayer who requested the ruling.

private-limited partnership A partnership with a maximum of 35 accredited partners that is able to avoid registration with the Securities and Exchange Commission.

privately held company A firm whose shares are held within a relatively small circle of owners and are not traded publicly. —Also called *private corporation*.

private mortgage insurance Coverage for borrower defaults provided to mortgage lenders by private insurance companies. —See also MORTGAGE INSURANCE.

> **CASE STUDY** Lenders often require private mortgage insurance (PMI) when a borrower puts less than 20% down on a home mortgage. The insurance protects the lender in the event the borrower defaults on the loan. The Homeowners Protection Act of 1998 established certain rules for automatic termination and borrower cancellation of private mortgage insurance on home mortgages. For home mortgages signed on or after July 29, 1999, PMI must generally be terminated automatically when the loan reaches 22% equity, based on the original property value. For example, a $150,000 home is purchased with $15,000 (10%) down. Private mortgage insurance should be automatically canceled when the outstanding balance on the mortgage is reduced to $117,000 (78% of the original property value). The automatic cancellation does not apply if payments by the borrower are not current, or if the loan is considered "high risk." It also does not apply to FHA or VA loans or to loans with lender-paid PMI. Some states have enacted laws relative to private mortgage insurance, even for mortgages signed prior to July 29, 1999.

private placement The sale of an issue of debt or equity securities to a single buyer or to a limited number of buyers without a public offering. A private placement is generally conducted by an investment banker who acts as an agent in bringing together the seller and the buyer(s).

private purpose municipal bond —See PRIVATE ACTIVITY BOND.

privatization The conversion of a public enterprise to a private enterprise. For example, a government-owned railroad or airline may undergo privatization if ownership shares of the enterprise are sold to individual and institutional investors.

privileged subscription The issuance of new stock in which existing stockholders are given preference in purchasing new shares up to the proportion of shares they already own. Thus, an owner of 5% of all the issuing firm's outstanding stock would be permitted to buy up to 5% of the new issue at a special price below the current market price. —Compare PREEMPTIVE RIGHT. —See also RIGHTS OFFERING.

privity 1. The contractual relationship or mutual interest between two parties, such as a landlord and tenant. 2. Private knowledge held jointly with another party. —See also VERTICAL PRIVITY 2.

probability A quantitative measure of the likelihood of something occurring: *Tenants of the mall gave the new restaurant a 20% probability of remaining in business for a year.*

probability distribution The distribution of possible outcomes to an event, along with the probability of each potential outcome. This statistical tool is used to measure the risk associated with events such as shooting craps, playing cards, or investing in securities.

probate The proof that a will is valid and that its terms are being carried out. Probate is accomplished by an executor/executrix, who is paid a fee based on the size of the estate that passes through the will. Certain trusts and jointly owned property pass to beneficiaries without being subject to probate and the attendant fee. —See also NONPROBATE ASSETS.

probate assets Assets in an estate that are subject to probate and will pass according to the terms of the will of the deceased or, absent a will, state statute. —Compare NONPROBATE ASSETS. —Also called *probate estate.*

probate bond —See FIDUCIARY BOND.

probate estate —See PROBATE ASSETS.

probationary employee 1. A recently hired employee who must demonstrate an ability to perform a job, and who can be dismissed without cause. 2. An employee who is being disciplined by an employer.

proceeds 1. The amount received from the sale of an asset. The term usually refers to the amount received before deduction of commissions or other costs related to the transaction. —See also NET PROCEEDS. 2. Funds given by a lender to a borrower.

process manufacturing A manufacturing method in which value is added through a product's transformation. For example, petroleum is refined and transformed into gasoline. —Compare DISCRETE MANUFACTURING.

procurement The combined activities of acquiring services or goods, including ordering, arranging payment, obtaining transportation, inspection, storage, and disposal.

procuring cause The effort of the person who brings about a desired outcome. For example, the work of a salesperson that results in a sale such that the salesperson is entitled to a commission.

produce 1. To manufacture something. For example, the Chevrolet Division of General Motors Corporation produces Corvettes in Bowling Green, Kentucky. 2. To cause something to occur or exist. For example, a tariff on Canadian timber produces high lumber prices in the United States. 3. To grow or bring forth: *Farmers in the plains produce huge amounts of wheat.*

producer cooperative A group of producers who band together to process or market their products. SunKist, SunMaid, Blue Diamond, and Ocean Spray are each examples of producer cooperatives.

producer goods Intermediate goods such as raw materials and equipment that are used in the production of consumer goods.

producer price index A comprehensive index of price changes at the wholesale level. Because wholesale price changes eventually find their way into consumer prices, the producer price index is closely watched as an early indicator of future retail price changes. —Formerly called *wholesale price index.* —Compare CONSUMER PRICE INDEX. —Also called *price index.* —See also GDP DEFLATOR.

product advertising The promotion of a particular good or service that is designed to increase demand. Newspaper, magazine, and television ads for a particular brand of beer are examples of product advertising.

product development process The progression of stages over which an organization develops an idea through to launching a good or service. Stages might include creating, developing, testing, and launching.

product differentiation —See DIFFERENTIATION.

production 1. Using labor and materials to create and build a product. **2.** Extracting natural resources from the ground. **3.** Customer orders generated by a salesperson: *Each person in the office had a production goal for the month.*

production control Using planning and scheduling to coordinate workers and materials in an efficient production process. Production control in a vehicle-manufacturing plant would involve monitoring inventory, ordering parts and materials, and scheduling assembly.

production possibilities frontier In economics, the graph depicting all possible combinations of two or more goods, assuming the efficient use of resources. The frontier is generally drawn as a concave curve and illustrates the tradeoff of one good for additional production of another good. The goal is to increase productivity and shift the curve outward.

production rate 1. The number of units of output that are produced during a given period. **2.** In finance, the coupon rate of interest on a Ginnie Mae pass-through security.

productive Describing the degree to which a person, machine, factory, land, or some other thing is able to produce goods and services.

productivity The efficiency with which output is produced by a given set of inputs. Productivity is generally measured by the ratio of output to input. An increase in the ratio indicates an increase in productivity. Conversely, a decrease in the output/input ratio indicates a decline in productivity.

product liability The legal responsibility of a manufacturer or distributor of a product to make restitution for injuries or damage resulting from use of the product.

product liability insurance Insurance coverage for liability of a manufacturer or distributor of goods because of damages that result from use of the goods.

product life cycle —See LIFE CYCLE.

product line A group of related products offered for sale by a company. For example, a publisher has a product line of state and regional maps that it distributes to truck stops.

product line pricing —See PRICE LINING.

product manager —See BRAND MANAGER.

product mix The composition of goods and services produced and/or sold by a firm. A limited product mix tends to increase the firm's risk at the same time it increases the potential for large profits. Thus, a firm specializing in a niche market in electronics is likely to experience either great success or large losses, depending on how demand and competition develop for its specialized output. —Also called *sales mix*.

profession An occupational group of people who have learned specialized skills that allow them to serve the public need. Teaching, engineering, medicine, law enforcement, and architecture each are considered professions.

professional corporation A legal entity that is formed to provide professional services such as law or medicine to the public. Shareholders of a professional corporation must normally be licensed in order to offer the services for which the corporation was formed. For example, shareholders of a legal professional corporation must be licensed attorneys.

professional liability insurance —See ERRORS AND OMISSIONS INSURANCE.

profit 1. In investments, the selling price less the purchase price when the result is positive. **2.** —See NET INCOME.

profitability ratio A comparison of two or more financial variables that provide a relative measure of a firm's income-earning performance. Profitability ratios are of interest to creditors, managers, and especially owners. —Compare RETURN ON COMMON STOCK EQUITY; RETURN ON EQUITY; RETURN ON INVESTMENT; RETURN ON SALES. —See also COMMON-SIZE STATEMENT; GROSS PROFIT MARGIN; NET PROFIT MARGIN.

profit and loss statement (P&L) —See INCOME STATEMENT.

profit center A segment of a business for which costs, revenues, and profits are separately calculated, with the manager of the segment being responsible for and judged on the performance of that segment. For example, a large corporation with diversified interests in paper manufacturing, trucking, and fast food may regard each of these three businesses as a profit center.

profiteer A person or entity that takes advantage of a situation in order to make what most people would consider an excessive profit. For example, if during a natural disaster the only operating gasoline station in town raised its prices 50%, it would be considered a profiteer.

profit margin 1. The relationship of gross profits to net sales in a business. Net sales are determined by subtracting returns and allowances from gross sales, whereupon the cost of goods sold is then subtracted from net sales to obtain gross profit. Gross profit is divided by net sales to obtain the profit margin—an excellent indicator of a firm's operating efficiency, its pricing policies, and its ability to remain competitive. —See also GROSS PROFIT MARGIN. **2.** The net profit margin of a business, which is calculated by deducting operating expenses and cost of goods sold and dividing the result by net sales. This term is less often used to indicate net profit margin.

profit motive The desire of an investor and business executive to earn an income on invested funds.

profit-sharing plan A savings plan offered by many firms to their employees in which a part of the firm's profits is funneled into a tax-deferred employee retirement account. These plans give employees additional incentive to be productive. —Also called *employee profit sharing*.

---

pro forma earnings

Are pro forma earnings sometimes a better measure of a firm's success than earnings reported according to generally accepted principles?

It depends on who computes the pro forma earnings and financial statements. An independent analyst should certainly adjust GAAP-based financial statements in order to produce greater information and more useful insights. One should not rely on pro forma financials disclosed by the reporting entity. Numerous studies confirm the bias of firm-based pro formas. In short, companies tend to include or emphasize favorable financial information and exclude or downplay harmful disclosures in their pro forma financial statements.

■ Peter M. Bergevin, PhD, Professor of Accounting, School of Business, University of Redlands, Redlands, CA

---

profit squeeze A reduction in earnings, perhaps caused by a poor business climate, increased competition, or rising costs. For example, higher fuel prices are likely to cause a profit squeeze among airline companies.

profit taking The general widespread selling of securities or of a particular security after a significant price rise as investors realize, or take, their profits. Although profit taking depresses prices, it does so temporarily. The term usually implies that the market is trending upward. —Also called *taking profits.*

pro forma earnings Income not necessarily calculated in accordance with generally accepted accounting principles. For example, a company might report pro forma earnings that exclude depreciation expense and nonrecurring expenses such as restructuring costs. In general, pro forma earnings are reported in an effort to put a more positive spin on a company's operations.

pro forma financial statement A financial statement constructed from projected amounts. A firm might construct a pro forma income statement based on projected revenues and costs for the following year. Likewise, a firm may wish to develop a set of pro forma statements to determine the effect of a projected stock buyback.

program budgeting Establishing a budget by grouping expenditures and revenues into functional activities, or programs. Rather than having a budget item for capital equipment that might be spread over many different programs (as is done in line-item budgeting), a program budget would include only proposed capital expenditures for a specific program.

Program Evaluation and Review Technique (PERT) A management technique for projecting activities and events that will lead to the completion of a project. A PERT diagram includes different paths, along with the estimated time required to achieve a successful completion.

programmer A person who writes, tests, and maintains source code that computers must follow in order to perform their functions. Programmers generally work under specifications provided by software engineers or systems analysts.

program trading An arbitrage operation in which traders take a long or short position in a portfolio of stock and the opposite position in one or more futures contracts in the same portfolio. Program trading is undertaken in order to take advantage of a difference in market values between two essentially identical portfolios of securities. Both sides of the trade are closed out on or near the day the futures contract expires, when the values of the positions should be equal. Because of the size of the trades and the complexity of the technique, program trading is practiced almost exclusively by large institutions. —Compare BASIS TRADING.

progressive tax A tax with a rate that increases as the amount to be taxed increases. For example, a taxing authority might levy a tax of 10% on the first $10,000 of income and increase the rate by 5% per each $10,000 increment up to a maximum of 50% on all income over $80,000. A progressive tax often uses high rates on relatively large incomes and tends to encourage tax shelters. The federal income tax, many state income taxes, and the unified gift-estate tax are progressive taxes. —Compare REGRESSIVE TAX.

progress payments Funds distributed to a contractor, subcontractor, or supplier as a project moves through stages toward completion. Progress payments are a pay-as-you-go system in which workers and suppliers are paid intermittently throughout the course of the project.

projected benefit obligation The present value, as of the calculation date, of all promised future benefits. The obligation is based on estimated future benefit and salary levels and on the assumption the plan will not be terminated. The net liability of a plan equals the amount by which the projected benefit obligation exceeds plan assets.

project management Planning and coordinating a project from its inception to its completion. The project manager oversees the scheduling of resources and attempts to make certain the project meets its budget guidelines.

project note (PN) A short-term debt security issued by a municipality to finance a federally sponsored real estate project, with repayment guaranteed by a pledge from the U. S. Department of Housing and Urban Development. These securities are considered very high grade.

promissory note —See NOTE 1.

promotion **1.** An advancement in job rank, generally at higher pay. **2.** An activity designed to increase the demand for a good or service. For example, an advertising firm designs a promotion for a new hybrid vehicle being introduced by an automobile manufacturer.

promotional allowance Funds given by a manufacturer to a middleman or retailer for promoting its product. For example, a household products company gives a grocery chain a promotional allowance for placing their new detergent in a special display at the end of the aisle. —Also called *push money.*

promotional partnership An agreement between businesses to promote a product. For example, a fast-food chain may partner with an entertainment company to promote a new movie.

promotion mix The combination of personal selling, public relations, advertising, sales promotion, sponsorships, direct mail, and trade shows that are utilized in promoting a good or service. The appropriate mix is the combination that produces the best results for a given budget.

proof of claim In law, written proof from a creditor that a debt is owed. For example, a proof of claim, along with supporting evidence, is filed by a creditor in bankruptcy court to demonstrate a claim for the amount owed the creditor by the bankrupt party.

proof of loss Documentation given an insurer by a policyholder to substantiate an insured loss. Such documentation might include a bill of sale for, or a recent photo of, property that has been lost. In the case of a death, a death certificate is required for payment of death benefits.

property 1. Something valuable, tangible or intangible, that is owned. **2.** A trait or attribute of something. For example, a desirable property of bonds is the semiannual interest payment.

property dividend A stockholder dividend paid in a form other than cash, scrip, or the firm's own stock. For example, a firm may distribute samples of its own product or shares in another company it owns to its stockholders. In general, a property dividend is taxable at its fair market value.

property insurance Insurance coverage that protects property against physical damage or loss from fire, theft, and other means. Business owners may want expanded coverage for data, paper, and records kept at the place of business. —See also HOME-OWNER'S INSURANCE.

property line The legal boundary of a tract of land as established by survey.

property management Leasing, subleasing, and renting the real estate of others in return for compensation.

property report A written description of a property that is prepared by a developer and must be provided to potential purchasers.

property rights The legal rights to ownership of an asset and any profits associated with its use.

property tax —See AD VALOREM TAX.

proportional tax —See FLAT TAX.

proportionate redemption A partial stock buyback in which a stockholder maintains the same ownership percentage after selling a portion of his or her shares back to the issuer.

proprietary Of or relating to private ownership with exclusive rights of use protected by copyright, patent, or trademark. For example, a proprietary good such as the antidepressant drug Prozac is protected by patent such that it can be manufactured and sold only by Eli Lilly & Co.

proprietary interest Partial or complete ownership of something. For example, an inventor has a proprietary interest in an invention that has been licensed under a royalty arrangement to a manufacturer.

proprietary lease An agreement with the corporate owner of a cooperative building that gives a shareholder the exclusive right to occupy one of the building's units.

proprietor The owner of a business.

proprietorship A firm with a single owner, chiefly one who acts as the manager of the business. Business income, expenses, taxes, liability for debts, and contractual obligations are inseparable from the owner's personal finances. —Compare CORPORATION; PARTNERSHIP. —Also called *sole proprietorship.* —See also UNLIMITED LIABILITY.

pro rata —Used to refer to something on a proportional basis. For example, in a rights offering, rights are distributed to stockholders on the basis of the number of shares already held by each stockholder. Thus, the pro rata distribution enables the stockholders to purchase new shares in proportion to the old shares they already own.

pro rata cancellation Insurer cancellation of coverage prior to policy expiration, with reimbursement to the policyholder equal to the daily earned premium times the number of days of coverage remaining.

pro rata distribution clause The provision in a property insurance policy that provides proportional coverage of two or more buildings on the basis of the proportional value of each building to the total value of buildings included in the policy. Pro rata distribution becomes applicable when a policyholder is underinsured.

prorate To allocate something such as cost among two or more parties. For example, when a home is sold, the electric bill during the month of sale may be prorated between the buyer and seller, depending on the number of days each occupied the home during the month.

prospect¹ 1. To look for customers. For example, a registered representative may join a civic organization to prospect for new customers. **2.** To explore for something valuable, such as oil or gold.

prospect² A potential customer. For example, families with young children are good prospects for a toy retailer.

prospect list A list of prospective customers. For example, a broker might acquire a list of physicians, dentists, or owners of private aircraft, assuming that at least some of these people have money to invest and would consider becoming customers.

prospectus A formal written document relating to a new securities offering that delineates the proposed business plan or the data relevant to an existing business plan—information needed by investors to make an educated decision on whether to purchase the security. The prospectus includes financial data, a prospective on the firm's business history, a list of its officers, a description of its operations, and mention of any pending litigation. A prospectus is an abridged version of the firm's registration statement filed with the SEC. —See also OFFERING CIRCULAR; RED HERRING.

prosperity In economics, a period of relative abundance with strong business profits and little unemployment.

protected strategy An investment strategy with a goal of limiting risk. For example, purchasing a stock and a put on the stock establishes a limit on the amount of money that may be lost, since the put protects against losses derived from a declining value of the stock. Although protected strategies limit losses, they also generally penalize potential profits.

protectionism The establishment of barriers to the importation of goods and services from foreign countries in order to protect domestic producers. Protectionism generates higher consumer prices. It is also likely to penalize domestic exporters, because foreign countries are apt to retaliate with trade barriers of their own.

protective covenant —See COVENANT 2.

protective put A put option owned in conjunction with the corresponding stock. A protective put guarantees the holder will receive, at minimum, proceeds that equal the exercise price of the put. For example, an investor could hold 100 shares of Coca-Cola while also holding a put on Coca-Cola stock. The protective put shelters the investor in case the stock's price declines in the market. —Also called *married put.*

prototype The trial version of a product that serves as a model for potential development. For example, a vehicle manufacturer introduces a prototype sports car at the annual auto show. The prototype may eventually move forward into production, depending on how it is received by the public.

proved reserves The quantity of minerals expected to be recoverable under current economic and operating conditions. The amount of proved reserves is important in valuing the stock of a company with significant holdings in natural resources.

provisional rating A bond rating conditional upon the successful completion of a specific project or the fulfillment of a stipulated condition. —Also called *conditional rating*.

proxy The written authority to act or speak for another party. Proxies are sent to stockholders by corporate management in order to solicit authority to vote the stockholders' shares at the annual meetings.

proxy fight A contest between two or more opposing forces to solicit stockholders' proxies and, in effect, to gain control of the firm through the election of directors. It is usually quite difficult to wrest control from the existing management through a proxy fight, but suitors sometimes use the tactic in takeover attempts.

proxy statement The material accompanying solicitation of a proxy from stockholders. The proxy statement lists the items to be voted on, including nominees for directorships, the auditing firm recommended by directors, the salaries of top officers and directors, and resolutions submitted by management and stockholders. Proxy statements are required by the SEC.

prudent man rule A federal and state regulation requiring trustees and portfolio managers to make financial decisions in the manner of a prudent man, that is, with intelligence and discretion. The prudent man rule requires care in the selection of investments, but does not limit investment alternatives. —See also INVESTMENT-GRADE; LEGAL LIST.

P/S ratio —See PRICE-SALES RATIO.

psychic income Nonmonetary satisfaction gained from employment. For example, someone working in a low-paid job helping the poor may enjoy a substantial amount of psychic income.

psychographics Consumer characteristics with regard to attitudes, habits, lifestyle, opinions, and values. Marketing people are interested in consumers' attitudes and personality traits that affect purchasing decisions.

P2P marketing —See PEER-TO-PEER MARKETING.

public accountant An accounting professional who renders a wide range of accounting services on a fee basis, including audits, taxes, and consulting for clients that may include businesses, governmental organizations, and individuals. —Compare MANAGEMENT ACCOUNTANT. —See also CERTIFIED PUBLIC ACCOUNTANT.

public adjuster An independent insurance adjuster who investigates insurance claims for the insured.

public charity A nonprofit organization, including a hospital, religious organization, or educational institution, that receives the majority of its financial support from a broad segment of the general public. Public charities are exempt from federal income taxes. —Compare PRIVATE FOUNDATION.

public corporation **1.** A corporation with shares of stock that are publicly traded on an exchange or in the over-the-counter market. **2.** A corporation established for a specific public purpose by government, but with a large degree of financial and operational independence from the government authority that created it; for example, a municipal hospital.

public debt The accumulated borrowing of the U.S. government. Borrowing is required when federal spending exceeds tax revenues.

public distribution The sale of a new securities issue to individual investors. The sales fee for the distribution, usually absorbed by the issuer, is included in the offering price.

public domain 1. The status of material or products that are available to anyone because they are not subject to copyright or patent protection. Some material cannot be copyrighted, while much material now in the public domain was once subject to copyright that has expired. **2.** Government-owned lands.

public good A good for which it is difficult to exclude anyone from benefiting and for which additional consumers can be added without diminishing the enjoyment of anyone else. National defense and police protection are public goods most efficiently supplied by government. —Also called *collective good.*

public housing Government-owned and -operated dwellings made available to low-income individuals and families for modest rents.

public law A bill or resolution passed by a governmental authority that has been enacted into law. Public laws deal with relationships between individuals and the state, and include criminal law and constitutional law. —Compare PRIVATE LAW 1.

public limited partnership A limited partnership that provides an investor with a direct interest in a group of assets (generally, oil and gas properties). Public limited partnership units trade publicly, like stock, and thus provide the investor significantly more liquidity than ordinary limited partnerships. —Also called *master limited partnership; publicly traded partnership.* —See also ROLL-UP.

publicly held 1. Of, relating to, or being securities that are freely transferable among investors. For example, stock owned by institutional investors is publicly held, but unregistered stock held by a firm's founder is not publicly held. **2.** Of, relating to, or being a publicly traded company.

publicly traded company A company whose shares of common stock are held by the public and are available for purchase by investors. The shares of publicly traded firms are bought and sold on the organized exchanges or in the over-the-counter market. Such companies are regulated by the SEC.

publicly traded fund —See CLOSED-END INVESTMENT COMPANY.

publicly traded partnership —See PUBLIC LIMITED PARTNERSHIP.

public offering The sale of an issue of securities to the public, an activity that usually occurs with the assistance of an investment banker who purchases the securities from the issuer and then resells them to the public. —Also called *distribution; offering; public sale.*

public offering price The price at which securities are offered for sale to the public. The price usually includes any sales commission.

public record Information acquired and maintained by state, local, and federal authorities that is made available for public inspection. Public records include real estate transactions, lawsuit filings, and building permits.

public relations Providing information and promotional material in an effort to influence attitudes and opinions relative to a person, company, or other entity.

public relations

I have decided that I need assistance in promoting my business. What factors are most important in selecting a public relations firm?

It's important to find a PR firm that knows your industry. Just like mechanics that specialize in domestics *and* imports, PR firms that try to be all things to all people will not be focused enough to represent your company in the in-depth manner you need. Either that or the learning curve will drain your budget and test your patience.

■ Tom Mesereau, Principal, Mesereau Public Relations, Parker, CO

public sale 1. —See PUBLIC OFFERING. **2.** Government-owned surplus property offered for sale to the general public. **3.** An auction of goods that is open to the public.

Public Securities Association A trade group of banks, brokers, and dealers engaged in underwriting and trading federal, state, and local government securities.

public utility A private business that provides an essential public service while operating in an industry that has large economies of scale. Public utilities are offered a fair return on their capital in return for tight regulation by government. Electric utility companies are examples of public utilities, although governments have permitted many of these businesses to form unregulated subsidiaries.

public works Projects such as highways and sewage disposal facilities that are paid for and constructed by governments for public use.

PUD —See PLANNED UNIT DEVELOPMENT.

puffery Exaggeration and overstatement in support of something. Puffery is frequently used in advertising when products are described as best, most useful, best values, and so forth.

pull strategy A marketing program designed to generate consumer demand for a product. A successful program will cause consumers to pull the product through the distribution chain. Pull strategies include manufacturers issuing free or cents-off coupons, placing advertisements on radio or television, or offering free samples at selected locations. —Compare PUSH STRATEGY.

pulsing Advertising in concentrated bursts rather than continuously. Pulsing can overcome the problems of deteriorating ad quality and listener fatigue that may occur with continuous advertising.

pump and dump Market manipulation in which a thinly traded stock is accumulated, promoted, and subsequently sold at an artificially high price to unsuspecting investors. Internet chat rooms where investors gather investment information from unknown parties facilitate this illegal practice.

pump priming Government fiscal policy aimed at stimulating economic growth by increasing deficit-financed expenditures. The additional government expenditures are expected to prime the pump for greater business and consumer spending.

punch list An inventory of things to do or that need to be corrected. For example, a building contractor may have a punch list of problems that need to be taken care of prior to a particular date.

pulsing

Is pulsing of advertising more effective with particular types of goods and services? If so, can you provide some examples?

Pulsed advertising can be very effective after you have had a product on the market for a while and want to either reinforce the message of your product or communicate new information about your product or service. Be sure to have a good mix of advertising vehicles (print, online, television, etc.) to ensure maximum impact.

▪ E. Mace Lewis, Vice President, Business Development, QD Healthcare Group, Greenwich, CT

punitive damages Court-awarded monetary damages that exceed the actual losses of the plaintiff. Punitive damages are designed to punish the defendant and serve as a deterrent for others who might commit the same act.

pur autre vie In law, describing one's interest in property for another person's lifetime. For example, a son may have the right to a vacation home for the lifetime of his father.

purchase Something that is acquired in exchange for payment. A purchase contrasts with a gift or something acquired through an inheritance.

purchase method A method of accounting for a merger or combination in which one firm is considered to have purchased the assets of the other firm. If the price paid for the acquired firm exceeds the market value of the acquired firm's assets, the difference is recorded as goodwill on the acquiring firm's balance sheet. The goodwill must be written off over a period of years. —Compare POOLING OF INTERESTS.

purchase money mortgage A mortgage or trust deed given by the purchaser to the seller as partial payment on the purchase price. A purchase money mortgage is an example of seller financing.

purchase order A buyer's written order to a supplier indicating all of the terms of a proposed transaction. A purchase order obligates the buyer if accepted by the supplier.

purchasing power 1. Consumer ability to purchase goods and services. Increased purchasing power represents proportionately larger increases in income than increases in the cost of goods and services. 2. The ability to purchase goods and services with a fixed amount of money. Within this narrower application, purchasing power is inversely related to the consumer price index. Increased purchasing power is a signal that future increases in economic activity are likely.

purchasing power parity A theory that currency exchange rates are in equilibrium when purchasing power in the countries is equalized. For example, if a basket of goods costing 100 euros in Germany costs $140 in Valdosta, Georgia, the currencies should exchange at a rate of 1.40 dollars to the euro. Purchasing power parity can be thwarted by transportation costs, trade barriers, and a lack of competitive markets. —Also called *law of one price.*

purchasing power risk The risk that unexpected changes in consumer prices will penalize an investor's real return from holding an investment. Because investments from gold to bonds and stock are priced to include expected inflation rates, it is the unexpected changes that produce this risk. Fixed income securities, such as bonds and preferred stock, subject investors to the greatest amount of purchasing power risk because their payments are established at the time of issue and remain unchanged regardless of the inflation rate.

pure competition —See PERFECT COMPETITION.

pure play An investment that is concentrated in a particular industry or operation. An investor who believes that snowmobiles are the wave of the future will search for a pure play in snowmobiles. In other words, the investor seeks out a company that does nothing other than manufacture and sell snowmobiles. Likewise, Whirlpool Corporation is more of a pure play in household appliances than is General Electric, the latter generating much of its revenues from other operations, including healthcare, commercial finance, and broadcasting.

pure risk A risk for which there is a possibility of loss, but no possibility of gain. The possibility of a vehicle being involved in an accident is an example of a pure risk. Most pure risks are insurable. —Compare SPECULATIVE RISK.

purpose statement A document that states the use to which proceeds of a loan that is backed by securities are to be put. The borrower agrees not to use the funds to purchase securities in violation of Federal Reserve credit regulations.

push money 1. Extra compensation paid by a manufacturer or employer to a salesperson for selling a particular product. For example, an appliance manufacturer offers a bonus for selling a washer or dryer from a line that has been discontinued. —Also called *spiff.* 2. —See PROMOTIONAL ALLOWANCE.

push strategy Promoting a product to members of the sales force and retailers rather than to eventual consumers. An example would be advertising appliances in a trade magazine read by appliance retailers. —Compare PULL STRATEGY.

put¹ 1. An option that conveys to its holder the right, but not the obligation, to sell a specific asset at a predetermined price until a certain date. In most cases, puts have 100 shares of stock as the underlying asset. For example, an investor may purchase a put option on GenCorp common stock that confers the right to sell 100 shares at $15 per share until September 21. Puts are sold for a fee by other investors, who incur an obligation to purchase the asset if the option holder decides to sell. Investors purchase puts in order to take advantage of or hedge the possibility of a decline in the price of the asset. —Compare CALL¹ 1. —Also called *put option.* —See also TRANSFERABLE PUT RIGHT. 2. Sale of an issue of bonds before maturity by forcing the issuer to buy at par. Few bond issues permit the holder this option. 3. In leasing, the required purchase of the leased asset by the lessee at the conclusion of a lease using an agreed-upon formula.

put² To force the seller of a put option to purchase shares of stock at the stipulated price. Puts are exercised by the owner only when the market price of the underlying stock is less than the strike price. —Also called *put to seller.*

put bond A relatively unusual bond that allows the holder to force the issuer to repurchase the security at specified dates before maturity. The repurchase price, usually at par value, is set at the time of issue. A put bond allows the investor to redeem a long-term bond before maturity, but the yield generally equals the one on short-term rather than long-term securities. —Also called *option tender bond.* —See also MANDATORY TENDER BOND; POISON-PUT BOND; YIELD TO PUT.

put option —See PUT¹ 1.

puttable common stock The shares of common stock that are sold with rights to put the shares back to the issuer at a specified price. —Compare CALLABLE COMMON STOCK.

put to seller —See PUT².

PV —See PRESENT VALUE.

P value In statistics, the probability that a difference between two groups occurred because of chance. For example, two groups of people with the same medical problem are treated with different medications. A lower P value for any difference in outcomes indicates a lower probability that the difference was a result of chance. Results with a low P value are considered statistically significant.

pyramid¹ A classic investment fraud in which the operator pays promised high returns to current investors from the contributions made by new investors. Thus, funds are never invested in any productive assets, but are simply paid out as a return to existing owners. The operator must continue to attract more and more investors in order to pay a return to those who have already committed their funds. —Also called *financial pyramid; Ponzi scheme.*

pyramid² To use profits derived from a profitable security position in combination with borrowed money in order to acquire an even larger investment position. Pyramiding, which is very risky, allows an investor the possibility of greater profits by using a given amount of funds to control the maximum amount of securities.

Q

QQQQ The ticker symbol and Wall Street name for the Powershares QQQ Trust, a popular exchange-traded fund based on the Nasdaq 100 Index. This fund serves as a proxy for large-cap Nasdaq stocks, including Microsoft, Oracle, Cisco, and Intel. —Also called *cubes.*

QTIP Trust A marital-deduction trust in which the surviving spouse receives income from the trust's assets for life, but the trust's principal is left to someone else, usually children. A QTIP trust controls the eventual beneficiaries, while at the same time taking advantage of the marital deduction and providing an income for the surviving spouse. —Also called *Qualified Terminable Interest Property Trust.*

qualified charity A charitable organization that meets Internal Revenue Service standards for accepting donations that are tax deductible to the donor. The organization must be engaged in one or more of eight designated activities, and it cannot attempt to influence legislation or use earnings to benefit a private shareholder. —Also called *charity.*

qualified endorsement Endorsement of a negotiable instrument when the endorser adds a restriction in an attempt to escape liability in the event the instrument is not honored. For example, the endorser of a check may add "without recourse."

qualified lead A potential customer who meets standards established by the seller. For example, a vacation timeshare pays a marketing company for the names and addresses of families who meet an established income and age requirement.

qualified opinion The opinion of a certified public accountant that a firm's financial statements deviate in some respect from a clean opinion according to generally accepted accounting principles. For example, the auditor was unable to audit and verify an area of the financial reports. —Compare CLEAN OPINION.

qualified charity

How do I determine if an organization is considered a qualified charity? I want to make certain a contribution will be tax deductible.

In order to encourage charitable giving, the U.S. tax code provides incentives to taxpayers who make contributions to qualified charities. An income tax deduction is available for contributions to qualified charities, and an estate tax deduction is available for transfers made to qualified charities at death.

Generally, a qualified charity includes a corporation, trust, fund, or foundation created under the laws of the United States or any state or possession of the United States that is operated for one or more of the following purposes: religious, charitable, educational, scientific, literary, the prevention of cruelty to children or animals, or the promotion of amateur sports competition. In addition, contributions to war veterans' organizations, domestic fraternal societies, certain nonprofit cemetery companies, and the United States or any state or possession, or any political subdivision of a state, are also deductible.

As a donor, you may ask the organization whether it is a qualified charity or you may check with the IRS to determine if an organization is a qualified charity. The IRS lists qualified charities in Publication 78. This list is found at www.irs.gov/app/pub78. You may also call the IRS directly at 1-877-829-5500.

▪ Paul G. Holland, Jr., JD, LLM, Director, Wealth Planning, MiddleCove Capital, Centerbrook, CT

qualified organization Organizations approved by the Internal Revenue Service to accept tax-deductible contributions. Organizations other than churches and governments must generally apply to the IRS to become a qualified organization.

qualified plan An employer-sponsored tax-deferred employee benefit plan that meets the standards of the Internal Revenue Code of 1954 and that qualifies for favorable tax treatment. Contributions by an employer and an employee accumulate without being taxed until payouts are made at the employee's retirement or termination.

qualified replacement property Securities of a domestic corporation that serve as a replacement and allow for deferral of taxes on the gains of stock sold to an employee stock ownership plan.

qualified residence A dwelling on which mortgage interest qualifies for deductibility under Internal Revenue Service rules. The IRS permits deductions for interest paid on loans to finance a taxpayer's principal residence and one other qualified residence.

qualified residence interest Deductible interest paid on mortgage debt to acquire, construct, or improve a qualified residence. Interest on home equity loans is considered qualified residence interest.

Qualified Terminable Interest Property Trust —See QTIP TRUST.

qualified transfer An amount paid on behalf of an individual as tuition to an educational organization or to any person who provides medical care to such an individual. A qualified transfer is not treated as a transfer of property by gift for purposes of calculating a gift tax.

qualify 1. To meet requirements for obtaining credit. For example, a potential homebuyer must comply with lender-established standards with regard to income and credit history in order to qualify for a mortgage loan. **2.** To meet the standards established for obtaining a job. For example, a firm may stipulate that job applicants possess an earned college degree in accounting plus two years' experience to qualify for a job opening. **3.** To include a stipulation in a contract. For example, a contract to purchase a home is qualified with a restriction that the structure must be moved from the property within six months of purchase.

qualifying annuity An annuity approved by the Internal Revenue Service in which the contributions may be deducted from taxable income. The effect of contributing to a qualifying annuity is deferred taxes on the contributions from the time the contributions are made to the time any withdrawals are made. Qualifying annuities are used for individual retirement accounts, Keogh plans, and profit-sharing plans. —Compare NONQUALIFYING ANNUITY.

qualifying child A person who satisfies four criteria established by the IRS for relationship, residence, age, and support. Being able to claim a qualifying child may enable a taxpayer to claim several tax benefits, such as head of household filing status, exemption for a dependent, the child tax credit, the child and dependent care credit, and the earned income credit.

qualifying dividends Dividends that meet Internal Revenue Service regulations for exclusion or partial exclusion from federal income taxes, or that benefit from a reduced tax rate. For example, corporations are permitted to exclude a portion of all of the qualifying dividends received from stock owned in domestic corporations. The Jobs and Growth Tax Relief Reconciliation Act of 2003 offered a reduced tax rate on qualifying dividends paid by an American company or a qualified foreign company. A minimum holding period is required in order to benefit from the reduced tax rate.

qualifying relative A person who satisfies five criteria established by the IRS for citizenship, support, tax filing status, income, and relationship. A qualifying relative can be claimed as a dependent for federal income tax purposes.

qualifying stock option —See INCENTIVE STOCK OPTION.

qualitative analysis Subjective study of something using nonmathematical methods. For example, a firm considering a merger evaluates the other firm's management quality, labor relations, and customer satisfaction. —Compare QUANTITATIVE ANALYSIS.

quality assurance A formal arrangement of actions to reasonably ensure the quality of a good or service will meet a firm's standards. —Also called *quality control.* —See also SIX SIGMA.

quality circle A relatively small group of employees who meet regularly to discuss issues relating to their employment. Quality circles are designed to improve employee morale, job efficiency, management procedures, and the quality of a firm's products.

quality control —See QUALITY ASSURANCE.

quality of earnings —See EARNINGS QUALITY.

quant A person who has strong skills in mathematics, engineering, or computer science, and who applies those skills to the securities business. For example, a pension fund may employ a quant to put together an optimal portfolio of bonds to meet the fund's future liabilities.

quantitative analysis Mathematical study of something. For example, an economist makes an economic forecast to management after analyzing many quantitative factors, including currency exchange rates, inflation, interest rates, and changes in the money supply. —Compare QUALITATIVE ANALYSIS.

quantity discount A reduction in price per unit for orders that meet minimum quantity standards established by the seller. A quantity discount may apply to a single order or to a series of orders placed within a certain period. —Also called *volume discount.*

quantity theory of money The economic theory that price inflation is directly related to changes in the quantity of money in circulation. According to the theory, an increase in the money supply will place upward pressure on the prices of goods and services, but will have a limited impact on employment and output. Assumptions underlying the quantity theory of money have changed over the years, and current adherents generally believe the Federal Reserve should refrain from policies that result in sudden increases or decreases in the money supply. Rather, the Fed should gradually increase the supply of money to accommodate real economic growth.

quarter 1. One quarter of a point. For bond quotes, a quarter represents one quarter of 1% of par, or $2.50. For stocks, a quarter represents a quarter of a dollar, or 25¢. **2.** A three-month period that represents 25% of a fiscal year.

Quarterly Income Preferred Securities (QUIPS) Preferred stock that represents interest in a limited partnership formed for the sole purpose of lending proceeds of the equity issue to the parent company. Dividends to holders of QUIPS are paid from tax-deductible interest paid by the parent corporation.

quarterly return 1. The rate of return, expressed as a percentage, earned on an investment during a three-month period. **2.** A tax return submitted at three-month intervals. For example, IRS form 941 is a quarterly return to be filed by employers, who are required to disclose number of employees, wages paid, taxes withheld, Social Security and Medicare taxes, sick pay, and other information for the quarter.

quasi contract An obligation created by the court in an effort to make things fair and avoid an injustice. For example, if a lawn services mows your lawn rather than the yard of your neighbor who contracted for the service, you will be responsible for the cost under a quasi contract if you watched the company doing the work, knowing it was being done on the wrong property. You will not be responsible for the cost if you were away from home and unaware the service was being performed.

quasi-public corporation A privately operated firm having legislatively mandated public responsibilities. A quasi-public corporation may have publicly traded shares of stock. Fannie Mae is a quasi-public corporation established to make a secondary market in mortgages. The firm is privately owned but publicly traded, and its shares of common stock are listed on the New York Stock Exchange.

queue A series of things arranged according to their order of arrival. For example, a queue of customers waiting to be served or a series of jobs waiting to be printed.

queuing theory A mathematical analysis of waiting lines. For example, a traffic engineer uses queuing theory to set the timing for stoplights along a major thoroughfare. A hospital manager uses queuing theory to establish staffing levels.

quick asset A current asset that is easily convertible into cash with no loss of value. Quick assets are often calculated as current assets minus inventories. —See also NET QUICK ASSETS.

quick ratio A relatively severe test of a company's liquidity and its ability to meet short-term obligations. The quick ratio is calculated by dividing all current assets with the exception of inventory by current liabilities. Inventory is excluded on the basis that it is the least liquid current asset. A relatively high quick ratio indicates conservative management and the ability to satisfy short-term obligations. —Compare CASH RATIO. —Also called *acid-test ratio.* —See also CURRENT RATIO; NET QUICK ASSETS.

quid pro quo An equal exchange that a person or firm makes with another person or firm. In the securities industry, institutional investors provide orders to brokerage firms as a quid pro quo for in-depth research.

quiet enjoyment The right of a property owner or tenant to enjoy the property without outside interference. Leases frequently include a covenant giving the tenant the right of quiet enjoyment. The lessor is prohibited from interfering with the tenant's use of the property as long as the tenant pays the rent and abides by the terms of the lease.

quiet period 1. The period during which a security issue is in registration and the issuer is not permitted to promote the issue. The quiet period begins during the filing period and ends 25 days after the security begins trading. 2. —See LOCKDOWN.

quiet title suit Legal action to validate the title to property. Quiet title actions generally occur when a question exists about ownership of a particular piece of real estate. A court decision favoring the plaintiff of the suit will allow a filing for a valid title.

QUIPS —See QUARTERLY INCOME PREFERRED SECURITIES.

quitclaim deed A deed that transfers an ownership interest in real property but makes no guarantee regarding title to the property. For example, a divorced spouse uses a quitclaim deed to transfer ownership of a home to the former partner. A quitclaim deed makes no guarantees regarding the possibility of other ownership interests in the asset.

quorum The minimum number of members who must be present in order to conduct business.

quota A maximum or minimum limit on quantity. For example, the appliance department of a retail store has a monthly sales quota, or minimum number of units that are expected to be sold. Applied to imports, a quota designates the maximum quantity of a product that may be brought into a country during a specified period. —See also TARIFF 1; TRIGGER PRICE.

quota sample A sample chosen by the interviewer or researcher based on requirements for specified groups or subgroups. For example, an interviewer must select an equal number of males and females, but can choose which individuals to include in each category. Without random selection, a quota sample is likely to introduce bias.

quotation A statement or listing of the price for something. For example, a salesperson offers a potential buyer a quotation of $23,500 for a vehicle. A quotation of $15.01–$15.03 for stock means a potential buyer is willing to pay $15.01 per share (the bid), and a seller is asking $15.03 per share (the ask). —Also called *quote.*

R

r² —See COEFFICIENT OF DETERMINATION.

rabbi trust A nonqualified deferred compensation arrangement in which an employer contributes funds to the irrevocable trust for the benefit of an employee. Assets held in a rabbi trust are subject to claims by creditors of the employer in the event the employer declares bankruptcy.

racket An illegal activity designed to achieve wealth for the perpetrators. For example, the owner of a used-car lot turns back the odometers on the vehicles offered for sale.

racketeering Carrying on an illegal activity, or racket, to make money. Racketeering is generally applied to structured groups such as child pornography rings or union members involved in labor racketeering.

rack jobber A wholesaler that provides racks filled with merchandise in space that is leased from retailers. For example, a rack jobber might provide displays with music CDs in a series of convenience stores. The rack jobber and convenience stores split revenues from sales of the CDs in some agreed-upon manner.

Radio Frequency Identification (RFID) A technology in which an electronic tag stores and transmits information that identifies an object or group of objects to which the tag is attached. RFID is used as a substitute for bar-code technology, which provides much less information and must be scanned. For example, RFID can store and relay information about the location and date of a product's manufacture. RFID tags can be active (include their own power source—these are more expensive) or inactive.

rag content A measure of paper quality that represents the percentage of cloth fibers relative to pulp fiber. A high rag content tends to make paper thick and stiff.

raider A person or firm that attempts a takeover of a company. —Compare TARGET COMPANY; WHITE KNIGHT. —Also called *corporate raider.* —See also GREENMAIL; JUNK FINANCING; SHARK REPELLENT.

raiding 1. An attempt to purchase a sufficient number of shares of a company's stock through a tender offer so that control of the target's operations can be taken away from its current management. —Also called *venture arbitrage.* 2. An attempt by a labor union to enroll workers who are members of a different union.

rain insurance Insurance coverage that reimburses a promoter for losses if an event is canceled or postponed because of rain. Coverage can be adjusted for specific amounts of rain and generally includes losses from reduced ticket sales.

rainmaker An employee who brings a substantial amount of profitable business to a firm. For example, an attorney switches firms and many of his clients follow.

rally A fairly sharp, short-term general rise in security or commodity prices after a period of little movement or of declining prices.

ramp up To increase. For example, an auto manufacturer plans to ramp up production for one of its best-selling vehicles.

RAN —See REVENUE ANTICIPATION NOTE.

R&D costs —See RESEARCH AND DEVELOPMENT COSTS.

random digit dialing Dialing telephone numbers according to computer-generated random sets of seven-digit numbers. Random digit dialing has the advantage of including unlisted numbers and is used for telephone survey samples.

random number generator An object or routine that can produce a random sequence of integers. Random number generators are used in gambling (bingo and slot machines) and statistical sampling.

random sample A sample collected in a random manner such that all choices within a population have an equal chance of selection. —See also STRATIFIED RANDOM SAMPLING.

random variable A variable that can assume multiple values based on a unique probability distribution.

random-walk hypothesis The hypothesis that states that past stock prices are of no value in forecasting future prices, because past, current, and future prices merely reflect market responses to information that comes into the market at random. In short, price movements are no more predictable than the pattern of the walk of a drunk.

range 1. The difference between the largest and smallest variables in a sample or population. Range is used in statistics as a measure of dispersion. 2. The high and low prices reached by a security within a given period. A large range in relation to a security price tends to indicate greater price volatility and risk for an investor. —Also called *price range.*

rank and file Regular members of an organization such as a labor union. Rank and file excludes officers and leaders.

ratable 1. Proportional. 2. Describing something that can be evaluated or rated, generally with respect to taxation. A ratable estate is taxable according to its value.

rate 1. A price or charge relative to some basis such as units or time. For example, a plumber's rate for labor is $25 per hour. 2. —See INTEREST RATE.

rate base The valuation of a utility's assets for the purpose of determining the rates the utility is permitted to charge its customers. Exactly what a utility should be permitted to include in its rate base is often a point of contention between the utility and its customers.

rate card A list of prices, generally printed on a small piece of paper and used for presenting detailed price information to potential customers. For example, a salesperson from the television station checks his rate card before quoting the price of a 30-second advertisement on the 6 p.m. news.

rate covenant A provision for a municipal revenue bond issue that sets requirements for charging revenue on the facility that is being financed by the bond issue. For example, a rate covenant might require that the rates from customers of a city sewage plant be sufficient to ensure adequate maintenance and repair for the facility. A rate covenant is included in a bond agreement to protect the bondholders' interests.

rated policy An insurance policy issued to someone considered a greater than average risk. For example, a life insurance company set a higher premium on the rated policy it sold to a professional racecar driver.

rate of return 1. —See CURRENT YIELD. 2. —See TOTAL RETURN. 3. —See RETURN ON INVESTMENT.

rate relief An action taken to allow a regulated company, such as a utility, to charge higher rates (that is, the prices it charges its customers) so that it can generate greater revenues. Public utilities frequently seek rate relief by filing a request for rate increases with public regulatory bodies.

ratified sales contract A legally binding and enforceable agreement that has been agreed to by both the buyer and seller. Used primarily in real estate, the contract specifies the price, proposed closing and occupancy dates, type of mortgage financing sought by the buyer, and any contingencies.

ratify To approve or confirm something. For example, members of the union ratify a new labor agreement.

rating 1. The grading of a security with respect to a characteristic or a set of characteristics, such as safety and growth. Rating is most often applied to debt securities, which are graded according to the issuer's ability to pay interest and principal when due. —See also BOND RATING; DOWNGRADING; MOODY'S INVESTMENT GRADE; NOT RATED; STOCK RATING; UPGRADING 1. 2. A measure of audience size for a radio or television

ratio analysis

How accurate are the results of ratio analysis? Is seems as if a lot of items that businesses include on their financial statements are not what they seem. For example, companies include assets as marketable securities that, in truth, are not marketable at all.

Ratio analysis is only as good as the inputs that produce the ratios' outputs. To the extent that the measurements are flawed, inconsistent over time, or incomparable among firms, ratio results will provide little, if any, information. The analyst must standardize ratio inputs, so far as the financial data permit, in order to use ratios in financial analysis.

Generally accepted accounting principles and ethical disclosure practices are also important factors in using ratios. As your comment implies, reporting securities without an actual market in the financial statements overstates assets and would create a favorable bias in many ratios, such as the current ratio. The Financial Accounting Standards Board clarified its definition of fair (market) value in 2007. That financial statement closed many loopholes regarding market-based disclosures. That FASB ruling, as with all others, will only be effective if management conforms to the spirit of the standard and tries to report economic reality.

■ Peter M. Bergevin, PhD, Professor of Accounting, School of Business, University of Redlands, Redlands, CA

program. **3.** The rank assigned to something. For example, *Consumer Reports* publishes frequency-of-repair ratings for appliances.

rating agencies Companies that grade securities so as to indicate the quality of the securities for investors. The two major rating services are Moody's Investor Services and Standard & Poor's Corporation. —See also CREDIT RATING AGENCY REFORM ACT OF 2006.

rating trigger A provision in a loan agreement that initiates a specific action in the event of a change in a firm's credit rating. For example, a downgrade in a firm's credit rating may set off accelerated debt repayment in a backup credit line.

ratio The relation between two quantities when compared with one another mathematically. For example, the most frequently used ratio among investors is the price-earnings ratio. Financial analysts, investors, and managers use ratios to evaluate many factors, such as the attractiveness of a stock or the operating efficiency of a company. —Also called *financial ratio.* —See also ACTIVITY RATIO; DEBT MANAGEMENT RATIO; LIQUIDITY RATIO; PROFITABILITY RATIO.

ratio analysis A study of the relationships between financial variables. Ratios of one firm are often compared with the same ratios of similar firms or of all firms in a single industry. This comparison indicates if a particular firm's financial statistics are suspect. Likewise, a particular ratio for a firm may be evaluated over a period of time to determine if any special trend exists. —Compare TREND ANALYSIS. —See also HORIZONTAL ANALYSIS; VERTICAL ANALYSIS.

rationing A systematic method for limiting access to a good or service when demand exceeds supply. For example, a store imposes a limit on the number of sale items each customer may purchase.

ratio scale A measurement system in which numbers are assigned based on the magnitudes of the objects being measured. Measurements of length, weight, and time are ratio scales. For example, a six-foot person is 20% taller than a 5-foot person. Similarly, a baseball game lasting three hours is 50% longer than a game lasting two hours.

raw land Unimproved land in its natural state. Raw land does not have man-made improvements such as streets and sewers.

raw material The goods used in the manufacture of a product. For example, a furniture manufacturer is likely to have raw materials such as hardware, lumber, and metal tubing on hand. Raw material is carried as an inventory item in the current assets section of a firm's balance sheet.

reach The extent of the audience exposed to an advertising message. For example, an advertisement in the local newspaper will reach 50,000 subscribers.

reaction A decline in security prices following a period of rising security prices.

read the tape To observe security price and volume information as it appears on the consolidated tape. Some traders read the tape in an attempt to spot irregular trades or price movements that signal buying or selling opportunities.

reaffirmation agreement Agreement by a debtor who has declared bankruptcy to continue paying on a debt, generally in order to hold possession of an asset that would be subject to repossession. For example, a person who has declared Chapter 7 bankruptcy signs a reaffirmation agreement on a vehicle loan in order to maintain possession of the vehicle.

re-aging A lender's increasing the term of a loan agreement when the borrower has missed one or more payments. Re-aging changes the account from "delinquent" to "current" at the same time it leaves unchanged the principal amount owed. Re-aging of a significant number of customer loans can make the firm's loan portfolio appear of higher quality than it actually is.

real asset A physical asset such as gold or timber. Real assets tend to be most desirable during periods of high inflation. —Compare FINANCIAL ASSET.

real estate Land, its buildings, and improvements thereto. —Also called *real property.*

real estate broker A person or business entity that earns commission or fee income by representing sellers and buyers in real estate transactions. Real estate brokers act as intermediaries and are licensed by the state in which they conduct business.

real estate closing —See CLOSING 1.

real estate commission The state agency that licenses and regulates real estate agents, and that administers real estate laws.

real estate investment trust (REIT) A company that purchases and manages real estate and/or real estate loans. Some REITs specialize in purchasing long-term mortgages, while others actually buy real estate. Income earned by a trust is generally passed through and taxed to the stockholders rather than to the REIT. —See also EQUITY REIT; MORTGAGE REIT.

real estate limited partnership A limited partnership in which one or more general partners acquire, manage, and sell real estate for the benefit of limited partners who enjoy limited liability from partnership debts and legal claims. Income and losses of the partnership are passed through to the partners.

real estate mortgage investment conduit (REMIC) A type of pass-through mortgage-backed security established in the Tax Reform Act of 1986. REMICs can vary in both maturity and risk, and are backed by mortgage or participation loans.

real estate owned Real property owned by a lender as a result of foreclosure.

Real Estate Settlement Procedures Act A 1974 federal statute requiring specified disclosures to real estate borrowers and outlawing kickbacks that increase the expense of real estate settlements. Lenders are required to spell out costs associated with settlements, outline lender servicing and escrows account practices, and describe business relationships between settlement service providers.

real income Income, as of a person, group, or country, that has been adjusted for changes in the prices of goods and services. Real income measures purchasing power in the current year after an adjustment for changes in prices since a selected base year. If money income increases more than consumer prices, real income increases. If money income increases less than consumer prices, real income declines. Declines in real income are unfavorable for those suffering the declines and for firms selling goods and services to them.

real interest rate The nominal current interest rate minus the rate of inflation. For example, an investor holding a 10% certificate of deposit during a period of 6% annual inflation would be earning a real interest rate of 4%. The real interest rate is a more valid measure of the desirability of an investment than the nominal rate is.

realization principle An accounting standard that recognizes revenue only when it is earned. Generally, realization occurs when goods are sold or a service is rendered.

realized gain The amount by which the net proceeds from the sale of an asset exceed its cost of acquisition. When gains are realized, they become income for tax purposes. —Compare UNREALIZED GAIN.

realized loss The amount by which an investment's acquisition cost exceeds the net proceeds from its sale. A realized loss, as opposed to a paper loss, may be used to reduce taxable income. —Compare UNREALIZED LOSS.

real market The quotes from a dealer who is willing to buy and sell a security in relatively large volume. Dealers uninterested in trading a security may provide quotes, but do not expect anyone to act on them.

real party in interest The person or entity that will benefit from a successful court action. For example, an insurance company reimburses an insured business for fraud committed by an employee. The insurance company then sues the employee for recovery in the name of its insured client. In this instance, the insurance company will benefit from any recovery and is the real party in interest. —Also called *party in interest.*

real property —See REAL ESTATE.

real return The inflation-adjusted rate of return on an investment. If an investor earns a return of 12% during a year when inflation is 4%, the real return is 8%. —Compare NOMINAL RETURN.

real rights The rights attached to tangible assets, in particular, real property.

real-time Of or relating to the actual time during which something occurs; that is, current as opposed to delayed. For example, real-time stock price quotations are generally available to investors with Internet brokerage accounts.

realtist A member of the National Association of Real Estate Brokers, an organization of predominantly black real estate brokers that was formed in 1947.

Realtor A real estate broker or agent who is a member of the National Association of Realtors. The term is registered by the National Association of Realtors, and its members are required to abide by the organization's code of ethics.

real wages Wages adjusted for changes in purchasing power. For example, a wage increase of 4% during a period of 5% inflation results in a decline in real wages.

real yield security A debt security on which the coupon rate is periodically reset to a level that reflects changes in the consumer price index plus a real yield spread. A real yield security transfers the risk of unexpected inflation from the creditor to the borrower. Series I savings bonds are an example of a real yield security.

reappraisal lease A lease agreement that includes an adjustable lease payment in accordance with scheduled independent reappraisals of the property's value.

reasonable care Care a prudent person would exercise in similar circumstances. Reasonable care is a subjective standard used in legal proceedings to determine negligence.

reasonable time The amount of time necessary to do what is required. This is vague terminology used in interpreting contracts that do not include specific times.

reassessment **1.** A reevaluation of property for the purpose of establishing a new tax base. Periodic reassessments are standard practice in most districts, which update valuations according to recent sale prices. **2.** Reconsideration of a rule or strategy. For example, a company's directors decide on reassessment of a merger proposal after accounting irregularities are discovered in the other firm's financial statements.

rebalance an account To buy and sell securities so as to maintain a predetermined ratio of selected categories in an investment account. Following an extended bull market in equities, for example, an investor who wishes to own a portfolio of 60% equities and 40% bonds would need to rebalance the account by selling stock and buying bonds.

rebate A refund of a portion or all of a purchase.

rebranding Marketing the same product under a different identity. For example, the owner of a restaurant decides to change the name from "Jake's Place" to "The Inn on the Lake" in order to signify a more upscale eating establishment.

> **CASE STUDY** In one of the most expensive and, to many, confusing rebrandings in history, AT&T announced in early 2007 that Cingular Wireless would become AT&T. The name change came about after AT&T acquired BellSouth Corporation at the end of 2006. The two companies jointly owned Cingular Wireless, which in 2004 had acquired AT&T Wireless after it was spun off from parent AT&T. But this had been a different AT&T that divested the wireless operation. The earlier AT&T was purchased in 2005 by SBC, one of its former operating companies that immediately assumed the better-known name of its former parent. Confusing? Think of former AT&T Wireless subscribers who became Cingular Wireless subscribers before becoming AT&T subscribers. Some AT&T subscribers had never made the first change and were continuing to use AT&T Wireless phones when Cingular announced the change to AT&T. The Cingular brand name had been born only six years before the latest rebranding. After spending billions of dollars promoting the Cingular name, AT&T officials refused to provide an estimate on the cost of the latest rebranding.

recall **1.** An order or request that dismissed employees return to work. **2.** A company's announcement that merchandise it manufactured or sold should be returned for repair or replacement. For example, in 2000 Bridgestone/Firestone announced that, for safety reasons, it was undertaking a voluntary recall of nearly 6.5 million of certain types and sizes of tires it had manufactured. **3.** Removal of an elected official by public petition.

recapitalization A change a company makes in the long-term financing mix it uses. For example, a firm may borrow long-term funds (that is, it may sell bonds) in order to acquire the money needed to repurchase a block of its outstanding stock. Because recapitalization will often affect the level and the volatility of earnings per share, it is of interest to stockholders. Recapitalization often occurs when a firm attempts to reorganize while in bankruptcy proceedings. —See also DIVIDEND RECAPITALIZATION.

> **CASE** Hospital operator Health Management Associates announced in **STUDY** early 2007 that it would undertake a corporate recapitalization by issuing $2.4 billion in new debt in order to raise funds that would be used to pay its common stockholders a one-time dividend of $10 per share. The dividend would represent a nearly 50% return on the stock, which was selling for approximately $21 per share. The recapitalization was designed to fend off private equity firms that often utilize debt to finance the acquisition of a target company's shares. Companies that already have substantial amounts of debt are much less likely to be subject to an unwelcome takeover attempt. The recapitalization by Health Management Associates was able to take advantage of favorable interest rates, but it resulted in a substantial drop in the firm's credit rating. Recapitalizations often work to the advantage of shareholders and the disadvantage of creditors.

recapture clause The section of a lease agreement that permits the lessor to terminate a lease prior to the end of the scheduled term. For example, the landlord of a commercial complex terminates the lease of a tenant that fails to meet sales projections that are part of the lease agreement.

recapture of depreciation 1. The extent to which the price received from selling a depreciated asset represents recovery of depreciation taken in prior years. For example, an asset purchased for $10,000, depreciated to a book value of $6,000, and sold for $9,000 would result in a recapture of $3,000. —Also called *depreciation recapture.* **2.** Loss of government benefits because a company failed to maintain promised investment or employment levels. For example, many communities grant extensive tax abatements and other economic benefits to entice businesses to locate nearby. In turn, the businesses promise a minimum amount of investment and employment. **3.** Repayment of benefits gained from government subsidized low-interest financing when a home is sold for a gain within a specified period from the date of purchase.

recapture rate The portion of the capitalization rate required to compensate for the decline in value of a wasting asset over the expected holding period. The recapture rate is added to the discount rate to determine the appropriate capitalization rate for an asset.

recasting debt Modifying a firm's debt. A company may decide to recast its debt in order to gain flexibility with regard to stock repurchases and dividend payments.

receipt Written acknowledgement of a transaction in which something of value was received.

receivables —See ACCOUNTS RECEIVABLE.

receivables aging —See AGING.

receivables turnover —See ACCOUNTS RECEIVABLE TURNOVER.

recapture clause

Do most lease agreements include a recapture clause that allows a lessor to terminate a lease? Can the clause be subject to interpretation such that a lessor can take advantage of the clause to get rid of a tenant?

Recapture clauses are usually contained in long-term commercial leases to large corporate tenants. The primary purpose of the recapture is to give the landlord the option to terminate the lease if the tenant asks the landlord to approve an assignment or sublease. The tenant would make such a request either to get out of its lease obligation or because market rents are higher than the rent currently paid by the tenant and the tenant can make money by sub-leasing this property and finding cheaper space elsewhere. If the landlord determines that an assignment or sublease of the property to another tenant is more profitable than the existing lease with the current tenant, the landlord would invoke the recapture clause, terminate the lease, and deal with the proposed new tenant.

Even though the existing tenant might be forced to forgo the opportunity to make a "profit" from subleasing, it is likely that such a tenant is satisfied simply to be able to walk away from its lease obligation, since that was the tenant's primary motivation in the first place. The specific language of a recapture clause can vary based on how strong a negotiating position is held by the parties. If the tenant is stronger than the landlord (Wal-Mart compared to an individual, for example), the tenant would never agree to an open-ended recapture clause whereby the landlord could arbitrarily terminate the lease if a better deal came along. If the landlord is stronger, the tenant might be forced to agree to a recapture clause, but should be certain that the lease specifies the circumstances that may trigger the recapture right.

▪ Scott Alderman, Broker and President, First Commercial Real Estate, Valdosta, GA

receiver A person assigned by a court to handle the affairs and assets of a business in bankruptcy proceedings. The receiver is charged with overseeing the firm for the benefit of its creditors and stockholders.

receiver's certificate The short-term debt that is issued by the receiver of a firm in bankruptcy proceedings. Receivers' certificates are of high quality because they have first claim on the bankrupt firm's assets.

receivership The state of an organization whose operations and assets have been placed in the legal custody of a receiver for the protection of creditors and other affected parties. An organization in receivership may be liquidated, or it may eventually emerge to continue operations, although likely in a different form. —See also BANKRUPTCY.

receive versus payment (RVP) A settlement procedure in which a customer instructs that the delivery of a security will be made immediately upon receipt of proceeds from the sale of the security. —Compare DELIVERY VERSUS PAYMENT.

receiving clerk An employee who inspects the quantity and quality of goods received from suppliers.

receiving report A document with a detailed listing of shipments received by a company.

recession An extended decline in general business activity. The National Bureau of Economic Research formally defines a recession as three consecutive quarters of falling real gross domestic product. A recession affects different companies in different ways. For example, companies selling consumer durables are affected to a greater extent than companies such as grocery stores that sell necessities.

reciprocal buying An arrangement in which two or more organizations purchase one another's goods and services. For example, a multibusiness firm enters into a buying and selling arrangement with businesses that are its customers and suppliers.

reciprocal immunity The tax immunity that interest payments on federal securities have against state and local authorities, and that interest payments on state and local securities have against federal authorities. Although not specifically stated as such in the U.S. Constitution, reciprocal immunity has been recognized by the U.S. Supreme Court.

reciprocity A mutual agreement of equal treatment. For example: countries enter into a treaty that lowers tariffs; a group of states agree to accept one another's teaching certificates.

reckoning 1. Counting or problem solving. **2.** Amount due.

recognized gain The taxable portion of a gain from a tax-free exchange. Cash received as a component of a like-kind exchange is generally recognized as taxable.

recompense Compensation for service, loss, or goods. For example, the city provided recompense for citizens who were injured during the mishap.

reconciliation The process of balancing two or more things: *Consumers should take time for a monthly reconciliation of their bank statement and check register.*

reconsign To alter the destination or consignee of freight during shipment. For example, Union Pacific reconsigns a railroad car to Denver from its original destination of Salt Lake City.

reconveyance Removing a lien and returning title to property to the equitable owner when the obligations of a debt have been met.

record date The date on which a firm's books are closed during the process of identifying the owners of a certain class of securities for purposes of transmitting dividends, interest, proxies, financial reports, and other documentation to them. For example, only the common stockholders who are listed on the record date will receive the dividends that are to be mailed on the payment date. —Also called *date of record.* —See also EX-DIVIDEND; INTEREST DATES.

recording Noting the terms of a legal document in a book of public record. For example, details of a mortgage on real property are recorded with the county clerk.

records management Systematic life-cycle management of records that includes identification, collection, classification, storage, retrieval, and, eventually, disposition.

recoup To regain what has been lost. For example, an investor sells an asset at a price sufficient to offset a previous loss.

recourse The right of a lender to demand payment from a guarantor of a loan in the event the primary borrower defaults. For example, Lender A sells a loan with recourse to lender B. Lender B can seek payment from Lender A in the event the borrower defaults.

recourse loan A loan in which the lender can claim more than the collateral as repayment in the event that payments on the loan are stopped. Thus, a recourse loan places the borrower's personal assets at risk. —Compare NONRECOURSE LOAN.

recovery 1. The rising price of an asset. For example, following an extended decline in the price of precious metals, investor expectations of future inflation may generate recoveries in gold and silver prices. **2.** Increased economic activity during a business cycle, resulting in growth in the gross domestic product. **3.** Collection of all or a portion of a debt previously considered uncollectible. **4.** Valuable materials remaining after processing. For example, waste processing may result in the recovery of materials that can be reused. **5.** Compensation obtained from a judicial proceeding. **6.** Proceeds from the sale of an asset that represent depreciation that has already been taken.

recovery fund An account funded by licensed real estate brokers for the compensation of individuals who have suffered wrongdoing in dealings with real estate brokers and agents.

recovery of basis A distribution that represents a return of cost and that is nontaxable.

recovery period The stipulated period during which a company fully depreciates an asset. Recovery periods for various kinds of assets are established by the government and often bear only a loose relationship to the profitable life of an asset.

recruiter A person responsible for identifying and evaluating candidates for available positions.

recruiting Soliciting appropriate persons for employment or membership in an organization.

recycling Reclaiming and altering the physical form of resources that have been, or would normally be, discarded as waste. Recycling is differentiated from reuse, which does not alter the physical form of the discarded resource. Sanitizing and refilling soft drink or beer bottles for resale is an example of reuse, not recycling.

red Of or relating to a firm or the operations of a firm that are deemed unprofitable. The term derives from the color of ink used to show losses on financial statements. —Compare BLACK.

redeem To convert into cash. For example, a mutual fund shareholder can choose to have shares redeemed by selling them to the fund. A company may decide to redeem a portion of its outstanding bonds by calling them prior to the maturity date.

redeemable shares Ownership shares that the issuing business may repurchase. Some redeemable shares are mandatorily redeemable and must be repurchased by the issuer on a particular date or on the occurrence of a specified event, such as the death of an owner.

redemption **1.** The retirement of a security by repurchase. Although generally used in reference to the repurchase of a bond before maturity, the term also applies to stock and mutual fund shares. —See also PARTIAL REDEMPTION. **2.** The acceptance of a vendor coupon by a retailer, distributor, or manufacturer for full or partial payment of a good. **3.** Payment to a governmental authority of delinquent taxes and associated costs incurred during a tax lien process.

redemption date The date on which a debt security is scheduled to be redeemed by the issuer. The redemption date is the scheduled maturity date or, if applicable, a call date.

redemption fee **1.** The fee charged to repurchase an asset. For example, hedge funds often levy a stiff redemption fee when an investor decides to cash in his or her shares prior to a certain date. **2.** —See DEFERRED SALES CHARGE.

redemption premium —See CALL PREMIUM.

redline

Is it illegal to redline? If so, are there any exceptions when it is legal?

Yes. Redlining—named for lenders who actually drew a red line around a neighborhood on a map, refusing mortgages to buyers in areas considered "risky"—is against the law. Banking practices received congressional scrutiny in the Fair Housing Act of 1968, which prohibited discrimination, and the Home Mortgage Disclosure Act of 1975, which required the release of data on bank lending. Unfortunately, despite these attempts to stop discriminatory practices, many believe that some lenders still deny mortgage loans based on the neighborhoods in which the applicants live.

There are no exceptions by which redlining is statutorily legal, but some may argue that the current federal regulations are themselves a form of redlining. And others may argue that financial institutions have a right to stop lending mortgage money in, for example, a declining economic area or market environment. If a bank can show that a specific mortgage loan or that lending in a specific area will significantly and adversely affect its business opportunities or bottom line in the future, is that redlining or prudent financial investing?

■ Joan A. Koffman, Esq., Real Estate Attorney, Koffman & Dreyer, Newton, MA

redemption price 1. The price at which an open-end investment company will buy back its shares from the owners. In most cases, the redemption price is the net asset value per share. **2.** —See CALL PRICE.

redevelopment The rehabilitating or clearing and improving of already developed urban property. For example, a redevelopment project may rehabilitate an abandoned warehouse and convert it into retail shops and loft apartments.

red herring A prospectus that is given to potential investors in a new security issue before the selling price has been set, and before the issuer's registration statement has been approved for accuracy and completeness by the SEC. This document, which provides details of the issue and facts concerning the issuer, is so named because of a statement on it, printed in red, that the issue has not yet been approved by the SEC. —Also called *preliminary prospectus.*

rediscount To discount a negotiable instrument a second time. A central bank adds liquidity to the banking system by rediscounting (buying at a discount) high-quality debt instruments.

rediscount rate —See DISCOUNT RATE 1.

redline A refusal to lend to individuals or businesses or to insure properties that are located within a particular geographical area, generally a deteriorating urban neighborhood. Redlining discriminates on the basis of location.

red tape Time-consuming procedures insisted on by bureaucracies, often related to some level of government.

reduction certificate A document provided by a lender indicating the remaining balance on a loan.

reduction in force —See RIF.

reengineering Rethinking the structural design of a business process in an effort to improve efficiency, reduce cost, or enhance quality. For example, an auto manufacturer reengineers its design process in order to expedite the introduction of new fuel-efficient vehicles.

CASE STUDY Taco Bell, under new CEO John Martin, engaged in a major reengineering effort in the early 1980s. Martin initiated changes to increase the quality of the firm's offerings and reduce the time spent on food preparation and paperwork. One initiative, called the "K-Minus Program," created a system in which food was prepared in central commissaries and shipped to kitchenless (hence, the term *K-minus*) restaurants. The commissaries cooked the meat, ground the beans, and chopped the cheese and vegetables (other than tomatoes) that were shipped prepacked to the restaurants. The reengineering allowed the firm to improve the quality of its products, reduce employee accidents (no chopping), save on preparation time, and reduce store space devoted to kitchen activities. One report indicated the K-Minus Program saved Taco Bell $7 million per year. The firm was able to grow its sales from $500 million in 1982 to $3 billion ten years later.

re-exports Goods imported into a country that are subsequently exported, either to the country of origin or a different country.

referee 1. A court-appointed officer who takes testimony, gathers evidence, and reports back to the court. **2.** A person who is appointed to settle a dispute.

referral A person or business steered to a business by an existing customer. For example, a person who needs repair work on a vehicle is referred to a particular mechanic by a satisfied customer of the mechanic.

refi Slang for refinance, especially with regard to mortgages.

refinance 1. To extend the maturity of a loan. **2.** —See REFUND 1.

reformation Alteration of a contract to more accurately represent the intentions of the parties at the time the contract was signed. For example, an insurance contract that was issued without a type of coverage that was agreed to both by the agent and the client may undergo reformation.

refund 1. To retire securities with the funds that have been raised through the sale of a new security issue. Refunding usually occurs after a period of falling interest rates, when firms issue new debt in order to retire existing debt having high coupon rates of interest. —Also called *refinance.* —See also CALL PROVISION; NONREFUNDABLE 1; PREREFUNDED BOND. **2.** To return money to a customer who returns a good or is dissatisfied with a purchase. **3.** To return to a taxpayer excess taxes that have been paid.

refundable credit An IRS tax credit payable to a taxpayer even though it may exceed the taxpayer's tax liability. The earned income tax credit for low-income working individuals and families is an example of a refundable credit.

refund annuity An annuity that provides fixed payments as long as the annuitant lives, and that guarantees repayment of the amount paid in. If the annuitant dies before receiving the amount paid in for the annuity, the balance is paid to the beneficiary.

refunding bond A bond that is issued for the purpose of retiring an outstanding bond. Issuers refund bond issues to reduce financing costs, eliminate covenants, and alter maturities —See also PREREFUNDING.

regional bank A bank with deposit gathering and lending concentrated in a particular geographic area of the country. For example, a regional bank may serve four southeastern states.

regional exchange A securities exchange that specializes in the stocks and bonds of companies with a regional, rather than a national, interest. The regional exchanges provide the only organized trading in many of these securities. They also list and trade many of the securities traded in one or more of the national exchanges.

regional shopping center A large retail shopping complex of 300,000 to 900,000 square feet, including one or two full-line department stores. Regional shopping centers typically draw customers from a radius of 40 to 50 miles.

registered bond —See REGISTERED SECURITY.

registered company A corporation that has filed an SEC registration form and that is subject to SEC reporting requirements.

registered competitive market maker **1.** A dealer registered with the National Association of Securities Dealers to make a market in one or more securities. A registered competitive market maker must offer firm bid and ask prices. **2.** A floor trader on the New York Stock Exchange.

registered exchange A securities exchange that has filed, and has had accepted, a registration statement with the SEC. All the larger securities exchanges in the United States are registered with the SEC, as required by the Securities Exchange Act of 1934.

registered investment adviser A professional investment adviser who manages the investments of others and is registered with the SEC as part of the Investment Advisers Act of 1940. Registered investment advisors have a fiduciary duty to act in the best interest of their clients and disclose any conflicts of interest. They are required to register annually with the SEC.

registered investment company An investment company that is registered with the SEC and meets the requirements of the Investment Company Act of 1940 with respect to income distribution, fee structure, and diversification of assets.

registered mail A special first-class mailing service of the U.S. Postal Service with numbered receipt and designated valuation. Registered mail receives special handling and is designed for sending valuables.

registered options trader A member of an organized options exchange who is a market maker in certain options assigned by the exchange. A registered options trader holds a position similar to a specialist on a stock exchange.

registered representative An employee or a partner in a brokerage firm who is registered to handle customer accounts. —Also called *account executive; broker; stockbroker.*

registered secondary distribution The sale of a block of previously issued securities following registration with the SEC. Securities sold in a registered secondary offering are likely to come from an institutional investor who acquired the securities in a private placement.

registered security **1.** A security, the certificate of which has the owner's name imprinted on its face. A record of current owners is kept by the issuer for purposes of transmitting checks, proxies, reports, and so forth. Nearly all securities are registered. —Compare BEARER FORM. **2.** A security that has been registered with the Securities and Exchange Commission. —See also REGISTRATION.

registered trader —See FLOOR TRADER.

registrar **1.** A firm that updates stock records using information sent by the transfer agent. Essentially, the registrar makes certain that the issued certificates correspond with those that have been canceled. **2.** A business that is authorized to enter and maintain a record of Internet domain names. **3.** A person or entity in charge of rec-

---

regressive tax

Why is the payroll tax that funds Social Security and Medicare considered a regressive tax?

Social Security tax is paid on income up to a certain level. For instance, in 2008 an individual paid the statutory tax rate of 6.2% on all income up to $102,000, for a maximum tax of $6,324. Taxes paid on income up to a fixed level are not regressive—everyone pays the same percentage rate, based on income. However, for someone who earned above $102,000 in 2008, the actual average tax rate paid was less than 6.2%. For example, a person who earned $204,000 would have paid the maximum tax of $6,324, or only 3.1% of income. This makes the tax regressive—the more you earn, the lower your tax rate is as a percent of your income.

Medicare taxes are not regressive; everyone pays the same percentage of their earnings, and there is no cap on income. Medicare taxes would be considered a proportional tax.

▧ Michael W. Butler, PhD, Professor of Economics, Angelo State University, San Angelo, Texas

---

ords. For example, a college registrar maintains records of all students during their enrollment.

registration The preparation of a security issue for public sale. For registration, the issuer hires an underwriting firm to prepare a registration statement that is submitted to the SEC or to a state authority. As part of this process, an investment banker brings in a public accounting firm to audit the issuer's financial condition. —See also COOLING-OFF PERIOD 1; GUN JUMPING 2; PIGGYBACK REGISTRATION.

registration statement A document filed with the SEC containing detailed information about a firm that plans to sell securities to the public. Required data include financial statements, the reason for the issue, and details on the firm's business. Certain issues (such as those under $500,000, intrastate sales only, private placements, and bank securities) are exempt from this requirement. —See also DEFICIENCY LETTER; OFFICIAL STATEMENT; PROSPECTUS.

registry of deeds Official real estate title documents maintained by a government office such as a county recorder. The registry is open to public access.

regression analysis The measurement of change in one variable that is the result of changes in other variables. Regression analysis is used frequently in an attempt to identify the variables that affect a certain stock's price.

regression coefficient A mathematical measure of the relationship between a dependent variable and an independent variable. For example, a financial theorist might attempt to determine the effect of increased dividends on a stock's price by calculating the regression coefficient between the price of the stock and its dividends per share. In this instance, the stock price is the dependent variable and the dividend payment is the independent variable.

regressive tax A tax that has a rate that declines as the amount to be taxed increases. In terms of income, federal and state taxation of cigarettes is regressive because low-income smokers pay a higher rate of taxation in terms of their income than high-income smokers do. A system of regressive taxation tends to free more funds for investment because high-income individuals tend to save a greater portion of their income. However, a regressive tax is often considered socially and politically unacceptable. —Compare PROGRESSIVE TAX.

regular-way contract A security transaction in which delivery of the certificate by the selling broker and delivery of cash by the buying broker are to occur three business days after the trade date. A regular-way contract is the usual method for handling stock and corporate and municipal bond transactions. Government securities and options settle one business day following the trade date. —Compare CASH CONTRACT.

regulated futures contract A futures contract traded on a national securities exchange registered with the SEC and subject to deposits and withdrawals in a system of mark to market.

regulated investment company An investment company that meets certain standards and, as a result, does not have to pay federal income taxes on distributions of dividends, interest, and realized capital gains. Essentially, this income is passed through to the stockholders, who, in turn, are taxed. To qualify as a regulated investment company, a firm must derive at least 90% of its income from dividends, interest, and capital gains. It also must distribute at least 90% of the dividends and interest received. It must have a minimum diversification of its assets.

Regulation A An SEC regulation that permits companies raising less than $5 million in a 12-month period to file with the SEC a printed copy of an offering circular in place of a regular registration statement.

Regulation A issue A type of new security issue that requires a much shorter prospectus and carries with it reduced officer and director liability for misleading and/or false statements.

Regulation D An SEC regulation that permits some smaller companies to offer and sell securities without registering the transaction. The regulation applies to companies that seek to raise less than $1 million in a 12-month period and to companies that raise up to $5 million, as long as the securities are sold to accredited investors or to 35 or fewer individuals.

Regulation FD An SEC regulation that mandates a company must release material information to all investors simultaneously. Material information released inadvertently must be made publicly available within 24 hours. Some critics contend Regulation FD causes increased volatility in stock prices.

Regulation T A Federal Reserve regulation that specifies the maximum initial credit extension that may be given to investors in securities. The initial margin requirement has varied from 40% to 100% since the regulation was established under provisions of the Securities Exchange Act of 1934. Listed stocks, convertible bonds, and many over-the-counter stocks are covered by Regulation T. —See also FREERIDING; FROZEN ACCOUNT 2.

Regulation U A Federal Reserve regulation that controls bank loans made to customers for the purpose of purchasing and carrying listed stocks.

Regulation Z A Federal Reserve regulation that implements the Truth in Lending Act, requiring lender disclosure of credit terms in a meaningful way. For example, all creditors are required to use the same credit terminology and expression of rates. The regulation has been amended many times since its implementation in 1968. —See also CONSUMER CREDIT PROTECTION ACT OF 1968.

regulatory agency A governmental authority charged with overseeing and supervising a particular area of economic activity. For example, the Food and Drug Administration is the regulatory agency that oversees the introduction of new pharmaceutical products.

regulatory climate The term applied to the latitude with which a regulated firm or industry is permitted to pursue an adequate return on its stockholders' investments. This term is often used in reference to utilities, which are required to obtain approval for rate changes. A favorable regulatory climate generally causes investors to value a company more highly, because they expect its earnings to be greater. Regulatory climate is also likely to have a strong influence on where a company locates its operations.

rehabilitation mortgage A loan with proceeds devoted to repairing and improving a property. For example, the FHA Section 203(k) program provides insurance for loans used for rehabilitation and repair of single-family properties.

rehabilitation tax credit The federal tax credit for expenses incurred in the renovation, restoration, and reconstruction of certain buildings. The credit is calculated as a percentage of costs for rehabilitation of buildings placed in service prior to 1936 and buildings certified as historic structures.

rehypothecate To repledge stock as collateral for a loan. In practice, this term means to pledge securities (by a brokerage firm) for a bank loan when the securities have already been pledged to the firm by one of its customers. The brokerage firm essentially passes along the collateral in order to obtain a loan to finance the customer's account.

reimbursement Payment to compensate someone for an expense that has been incurred. For example, a job applicant receives reimbursement for travel expenses.

reindustrialization Modernization and redevelopment of industrial facilities, generally with the help of government grants and tax incentives.

reinforcement advertising Promotions designed to retain a customer base by reassuring purchasers they made the correct choice. For example, a dealer or manufacturer sends former customers information about awards and other news concerning a product that has been purchased.

reinstatement **1.** Restoration of insurance coverage that has lapsed because of nonpayment of premiums. **2.** Having a delinquent loan brought up to date when the borrower pays all past due payments and fees. **3.** The return of a suspended or terminated employee to a former job.

reinsurance A transfer of the risk assumed by one insurance company to one or more other insurance companies. In short, reinsurance is insurance for insurers. For example, an insurance company that writes substantial amounts of homeowners' policies in Florida has an interest in transferring a large portion of the risk of loss to other insurance companies that write homeowners' policies in other areas of the country.

reinvestment plan —See DIVIDEND REINVESTMENT PLAN.

reinvestment privilege The prerogative of a mutual fund shareholder to have dividends used to purchase additional shares in the fund. Most mutual funds give their shareholders reinvestment privileges, and most do not charge fees for the purchase of the new shares.

reinvestment rate The annual yield at which cash flows from an investment can be reinvested. The reinvestment rate is of particular interest to people holding short-term investments, such as certificates of deposit or Treasury bills, or long-term investments that produce large annual cash flows, such as high-coupon bonds.

reinvestment risk The possibility that the cash flows produced by an investment will have to be reinvested at a reduced rate of return. For example, the owner of a certificate of deposit faces the risk that lower interest rates will be in effect when the certificate matures and the funds are to be reinvested.

REIT —See REAL ESTATE INVESTMENT TRUST.

related party transaction A business deal between two parties when one of the parties has influence over the other. For example, a public corporation does substantial business with a firm owned by one of its directors. Related party transactions offer the possibility of a conflict of interest.

relationship selling Establishing a long-term customer relationship in an effort to generate repeat business. Relationship selling may be directed at especially important customers and may include a liberal return policy and access to high-level executives.

release 1. To make an asset available. For example, a lender releases real estate from a mortgage lien after the loan has been fully repaid. **2.** To free a person from an obligation. For example, a tenant is released from a lease.

release clause Stipulation in a loan agreement that allows the borrower to repay a specific amount of the debt and gain release of a portion of the property used as security for the loan. For example, a borrower gains a release of one of five rental properties used as security for a blanket loan.

reliability The degree to which a person, measure, or object is dependable. For example, vehicles manufactured by certain companies are considered to have above-average reliability.

reload In corporate compensation, to replace exercised stock options with new options on the same stock. For example, a corporate executive who exercises options for 50,000 shares of stock is granted options for an additional 50,000 shares.

relocate To move to a new location. For example, airplane manufacturer Boeing Corporation decided to relocate its corporate headquarters from Seattle to Chicago.

relocation clause Stipulation in a lease that permits a landlord to move a tenant to another location in the same building.

relocation service A business that assists a firm's employees in moving to another city. The service typically includes taking charge of selling the employee's current home, arranging the move of personal goods, and purchasing a home in the new location.

remainder Interest in an estate that is postponed until the termination of a prior estate. For example, a couple transfers assets to a trust with the stipulation that they receive trust income during their lifetime. At their deaths, the remainder is transferred to a person or organization named by the grantors.

remainderman A person or organization that is to receive the remaining interest in a property or estate after prior interests have been satisfied.

remargin To deposit additional cash or securities in a margin account when equity in the account is judged to be insufficient to meet the maintenance margin requirement.

remarketed preferred stock A type of preferred stock in which the dividend rate is determined periodically by a remarketing agent. The agent resets the dividend rate so that the preferred stock can be tendered at par or resold at the original offering price. —Compare AUCTION-RATE SECURITY.

renegotiate

I have been having difficulty making my mortgage payments. How can I best convince my lender to renegotiate the loan?

You should immediately contact your lender by phone and document all communications in writing. Ignoring the problem will *not* solve it. Write to the lender about your credit history, your years of mortgage payments, your care and maintenance of your home—all of this will show the lender that you are a continuing good credit risk, despite falling on hard times now. Telling the truth about your financial situation is also important. It's hard to admit when your luck has turned, but doing so honestly and completely is the way to convince a lender to help you now, rather than to foreclose on your house. And, don't give up. There are many home-owners with similar plights; it will take persistence to succeed at renegotiating your current loan.

▪ Joan A. Koffman, Esq., Real Estate Attorney, Koffman & Dreyer, Newton, MA

remediation Action to correct damage to the environment. For example, ABC Chemical Company was required to spend millions of dollars on remediation of toxic waste before offering a property for sale.

remedy Legal relief for a wrong, or enforcement of a right. For example, the injured party of a breached contract is offered remedy in the form of monetary damages.

REMIC —See REAL ESTATE MORTGAGE INVESTMENT CONDUIT.

remit To send payment for goods or services.

remittance Funds sent from one party to another. For example, a retailer's Internet site generally includes remittance information for goods that are ordered.

remonetization Reinstating a commodity or some other item as money. Some individuals concerned about inflation and excess money creation by central banks advocate the remonetization of gold and silver.

remuneration Compensation for services. Payment to a consultant is a type of remuneration.

renegotiate To change the conditions and terms of a contract. For example, a borrower may ask to renegotiate the terms of a mortgage when market rates of interest drop below the rate specified in the mortgage. Professional athletes frequently demand to renegotiate their contracts after a particularly productive year.

renewable natural resource A natural resource that reproduces itself. For example, forests are a major renewable resource in the southeastern United States. Precious metals and oil are nonrenewable natural resources.

renewal Extension of an agreement. Renewal of an insurance policy extends coverage for an additional period. Renewal of a loan results in an extension of the period when principal must be repaid.

renewal option The right, but not the obligation, of a party to extend an agreement. For example, a retailer in a shopping center has the right to renew the current lease, although with a possible change in the required lease payment.

rent 1. Regular payment for the use of property. 2. —See ECONOMIC RENT.

rent control Government restrictions on the price a landlord may charge for the use of real property. Rent control is effective only when the maximum allowable price is below the price that would be established in a free market.

rent roll A document for a rental facility that lists the tenants and the terms for each of their respective leases.

rent-up period The time immediately following completion of construction when the owner/landlord is actively seeking tenants. An owner may offer special deals in an effort to reduce the rent-up period.

reopener clause Provision in a labor contract allowing one or either party to reopen negotiations for the entire agreement or specific portions of the agreement. The purpose of a reopener clause is to allow one party to force the other party to renegotiate portions of the agreement covered by the reopener clause. —See also MIDTERM BARGAINING.

reorder point The inventory level at which a reorder is placed automatically. The reorder point is a function of the minimum acceptable amount of inventory, the daily consumption of inventory, and the amount of time required between when an order is placed and inventory is received.

reorganization 1. The restatement of assets to current market value, along with a restructuring of liabilities and equity to reflect the reduction in asset values and negotiations with creditors. Reorganization is used as an attempt to keep a financially troubled or bankrupt firm viable. —See also CHAPTER 11. **2.** Altering the organizational structure of an entity: *The new CEO began a reorganization of the firm by removing a layer of management and consolidating seven divisions into three.* —Also called *corporate reorganization.*

reorganization plan A plan filed with a bankruptcy court judge by a company in Chapter 11 proceedings in which the disbursement of assets is stipulated. The plan must be approved by the firm's creditors and by the court. A reorganization plan results in new securities being given to creditors in trade for old securities.

rep —See SALES REPRESENTATIVE.

repatriate To bring home assets that are currently held in a foreign country. Domestic corporations are frequently taxed on the profits that they repatriate, a factor influencing the firms to leave overseas the profits earned there.

repetitive manufacturing The continuous flow of discrete units, generally at high speed, until completion. The manufacture of compact disks with music or software are examples of goods produced in repetitive manufacturing.

replacement cost The current cost of replacing an asset with an equivalent asset.

replacement cost accounting An accounting system that values assets and liabilities according to their replacement cost rather than their historical cost. Replacement cost accounting incorporates the effects of changing prices and the resultant changing values of the items that are listed in a firm's financial statements.

replacement cost insurance Insurance coverage that replaces or repairs damaged property without an allowance for depreciation. Damaged property is replaced on the same premises with other property of similar quality and materials as long as the cost is not more than coverage limits spelled out in the policy.

replacement period The period during which certain assets can be replaced without recognition of a gain for tax purposes. In most cases, property that is damaged, destroyed, stolen, requisitioned, or condemned and replaced with other property or money (insurance or condemnation settlement) does not result in a taxable gain if the replacement occurs within two years.

replacement reserve Funds set aside in escrow to provide for anticipated maintenance expenses and replacement of short-lived assets. For example, a condominium home-owners' association establishes a replacement reserve to pay for heating and cooling equipment, painting, a new roof, and so forth. —Also called *reserve fund.*

replevin Legal action to recover possession of personal property. For example, a secured creditor institutes replevin to gain possession of assets used as collateral for a loan in default.

repo **1.** Short for repossessed or repossession. **2.** —See REPURCHASE AGREEMENT.

repo rate The rate of interest (annualized) on a repurchase agreement.

reporting currency The currency in which financial statements are prepared and presented.

reporting dealers Any of various independent dealers in government securities who report their trading activity and security positions to the Federal Reserve. Because the Federal Reserve uses purchases and sales to influence the money supply, information from reporting dealers plays an important part in monetary policy. —Compare PRIMARY DEALER. —See also OPEN-MARKET OPERATIONS.

reposition To change consumer perception of a product so as to place it in a different market segment. For example, a household products company may introduce a premium toothpaste and, at the same time, reduce the price and discontinue most advertising for an existing brand that it wishes to reposition as a popular entry in this category.

> **CASE STUDY** Marlboro, the world's best-selling cigarette and what many consider its most valuable brand, was the subject of what is almost certainly the most successful product repositioning in history. Having initially marketed it as a cigarette for women ("Mild as May," with ads featuring sophisticated females) following its 1924 introduction, manufacturer Philip Morris decided to reposition Marlboro with a more masculine image following cancer health warnings in the 1950s. In the middle of the decade, Marlboro ads began featuring tattooed men who were portrayed as rugged and independent. The firm's advertising touting "man-sized taste" and a flip-top box initially utilized different types of Marlboro men, but eventually settled on the cowboy as its featured character. The cowboy's rugged lifestyle in Marlboro country, backed by music from "The Magnificent Seven," attracted an increasing number of male smokers, to make Marlboro number one.

repossession Reclaiming an asset, generally as a result of a borrower defaulting on a loan.

repricing Exchanging newly issued incentive stock options priced at the current market price for previously granted options that are out-of-the-money. Critics claim repricing rewards managers of companies with stock prices that have declined.

reproduction cost The current cost of constructing an exact duplicate of something using the same materials and workmanship.

repudiation Rejection of an agreement. For example, a company issues a public statement of repudiation of its promise to provide health insurance for all retirees.

repurchase agreement (RP) The sale of an asset with a simultaneous agreement to repurchase the asset at a specified price on a given date. Essentially, this process involves taking out a loan and using the asset as collateral. —Compare REVERSE REPURCHASE AGREEMENT. —Also called *repo.* —See also OVERNIGHT REPO.

required rate of return 1. The minimum rate of return that an investment must provide, or must be expected to provide, in order to justify its acquisition. For example, an investor who can earn an annual return of 5% on certificates of deposit may set a required rate of return of 9% on a more risky stock investment before considering a shift of funds into the stock. An investment's required rate of return is a function of the returns available on other investments and the risk level inherent in a particular investment. **2.** The minimum rate of return required by an investor, a stipulation that limits the types of investments the investor can undertake. For example, a person with a required rate of return of 14% would generally have to invest in relatively risky securities.

required reserves The reserves against deposits that commercial banks and thrifts are required to hold in either cash or deposits at the Federal Reserve. —Compare EXCESS RESERVES. —See also RESERVE REQUIREMENT.

requisition A formal request for a service or product.

reschedule 1. To negotiate different terms for a loan, generally with smaller payments and a longer maturity. **2.** To establish a new place or time for something: *Bad weather required the company to reschedule its deliveries.*

rescind To cancel an agreement. For example, a developer rescinds a contract to purchase a piece of property that was found to contain substantial amounts of toxic waste.

rescission The cancellation of an agreement and reversion to the original position. For example, a company cancelled a previous exercise of an incentive stock option because of a substantial drop in the price of the stock acquired through the exercise. The rescission results in the employee surrendering stock in exchange for money that was paid for the stock.

rescue financing Providing funds in the form of equity or debt to a financially troubled business facing insolvency or attempting to emerge from bankruptcy.

research and development costs (R&D costs) The costs that are incurred during the development and introduction of new products to the market, or during the improvement of existing products. Although R&D costs tend to penalize current profits, they should eventually benefit the firm when new products developed as a result of the research become profitable themselves. Many analysts regard a high proportion of sales revenue devoted to R&D as a positive sign relative to a firm's profit potential and future stock price.

research department The group of individuals in a brokerage firm or institutional investment house that analyzes companies, economic matters, and securities. The research departments in institutional investment houses assist in selecting investments and devising investment strategies. Brokerage firm research departments assist the registered representatives in making customer purchase suggestions.

reseller A person or company that is authorized to sell someone else's products. A communications company that does not own its own transmission facilities but resells time purchased from other carriers is an example.

reservation 1. Property set aside for a specific purpose: *The state government allocated funds for a 10,000-acre wildlife reservation surrounding the lake.* 2. A booking with an established time and place for an event or activity.

reserve deficiency A shortage in funds set aside as a reserve for a specific purpose. For example, during a recession a firm may find the reserve fund covering allowance for bad debts deficient when the actual amount of bad debts exceeds expectations. A reserve deficiency will penalize the firm's profits if the firm has to set aside additional funds to offset the deficiency.

reserve for bad debts —See ALLOWANCE FOR DOUBTFUL ACCOUNTS.

reserve for contingencies A part of retained earnings that are set aside for potential future losses. For example, a firm may establish a reserve account to cover the possibility of losing a lawsuit to which it is a party.

reserve fund 1. Monies held under an indenture agreement by the trustee of a bond issue. For example, the trustee for a revenue bond issue maintains a reserve fund to offer lender protection against the possibility of a shortfall of revenues. 2. —See REPLACEMENT RESERVE.

reserve price The lowest price a seller is willing to accept for an item being auctioned. Only the seller is aware of the reserve price. —Also called *upset price.*

reserve requirement The required percentage of customer deposits that banks and thrifts must hold in cash or in deposits at the Federal Reserve. This requirement is set by the Federal Reserve. Changes in the required percentage are used by the Fed to influence credit conditions. An increased percentage requirement means fewer funds available for lending and a resultant rise in interest rates. —See also MONETARY POLICY.

reserves 1. The funds that are earmarked by a firm from its retained earnings for future use, such as for the payment of likely-to-be-incurred bad debts. The existence of such a reserve informs readers of the firm's financial statements that at least a part of the retained earnings will not be available to the stockholders. —See also ALLOWANCE FOR DOUBTFUL ACCOUNTS; RESERVE FOR CONTINGENCIES. 2. In banking, currency held in vaults plus deposits at Federal Reserve banks. —Also called *legal reserves.* 3. Gold and foreign currency held by a central bank.

reserve stock control Determining the inventory level by adding deliveries and subtracting distributions from the previous inventory level. For example, if beginning inventory is 500 units, and 250 units are added and 200 units are distributed or sold, the current inventory should be 550 units. Reserve stock control allows a firm to maintain a running total of inventory without counting the physical stock.

reset note A debt security with terms that can be reset on one or more dates during the life of the note. At the time the terms are changed, the holder usually has the right to redeem the security.

resident alien A noncitizen who has been granted permanent residency and enjoys most of the rights of citizenship. —Compare NONRESIDENT ALIEN.

resident buyer A person who resides in or near a major merchandising hub and who provides information on products and pricing to potential customers. A resident buyer may serve as an agent for multiple companies or be an employee of a single firm.

residential broker A real estate professional who specializes in the listing and sale of individual homes and condominiums.

residential mortgage A loan to purchase residential real estate that serves as security for the loan. Interest paid on a home mortgage secured by a main home or second home is generally deductible for tax purposes.

residential service contract An insurance contract purchased by a home buyer to cover the cost of specified repairs or replacements during a defined period.

resident manager A full-time, live-in resident of an apartment complex who has the responsibility for managing and coordinating maintenance, housekeeping, and administrative duties.

residual security A security with the potential for diluting earnings per share. A convertible bond is a residual security because conversion of the bond by an investor will result in more shares of common stock outstanding and a reduction in earnings per share.

residual value 1. The price at which a fixed asset is expected to be sold at the end of its useful life. Residual value is used in calculating some types of depreciation. —Also called *salvage value; scrap value.* **2.** The anticipated value of a vehicle at the expiration of a lease. A high residual value should result in a lower monthly lease.

residuary beneficiary —See RESIDUARY LEGATEE.

residuary estate The portion of an estate that remains after all debts, taxes, and fees are paid and specific gifts are distributed. Specific gifts that cannot be distributed (for example, the beneficiary has already died) become part of the residuary estate.

residuary legatee The person designated by a will to receive property not specially designated for others. For example, an unmarried man leaves his home to his sister and everything else to his disabled brother, who is the residuary legatee. —Also called *residuary beneficiary.*

res ipsa loquitor A legal claim that the facts are obvious and no further evidence need be offered to demonstrate negligence on the part of a defendant.

resistance level A price at which a security or the market itself will encounter considerable selling pressure. —Compare SUPPORT LEVEL.

res judicata Final judgment in a legal dispute. According to the doctrine of res judicata, the losing party in a legal judgment cannot litigate the same issue in a different court.

resolution 1. A formal statement of an opinion or decision. For example, directors of a corporation approve a resolution to support an aggressive affirmative action program. **2.** Solution to a problem: *As yet, there is no resolution of the state's budget crisis.*

resource allocation The manner in which scarce resources are distributed. From a business standpoint, this relates to how management distributes capital among its various operations. From a consumer's viewpoint, resource allocation relates to how goods and services are distributed among consumers. Efficient resource allocation results in a more productive economy. —Also called *allocation of resources.*

respondeat superior Legal doctrine that an employer is responsible for employee actions undertaken during the course of their employment. Under respondeat superior, a hospital can be sued for negligent acts of a doctor working for the hospital.

respondent 1. The party in a lawsuit that responds to a legal action initiated by another party. —Also called *defendant.* **2.** A person or other entity that has replied to a query.

response A reply to a question or stimulus: *Consumer response to the firm's new advertising campaign was poor.*

response bias The influence on the answer a respondent gives of what he or she believes the questioner wants to hear. In some cases a question may be poorly worded, so as to favor a particular response. For example: "With the recent increases in the cost of living, are you satisfied with the candidate's proposal to raise taxes?"

restatement The altered presentation of a portion or all of an earlier financial statement. For example, a firm may issue a restatement of its previously published balance sheet and income statement because it has discovered some heretofore unknown information that should have been included on the initial statements.

restitution Court-ordered payment to a successful plaintiff by the defendant of a legal action.

restraining order A court-ordered directive that forbids certain actions. A restraining order may be temporary or permanent. For example, a company seeks a restraining order to prevent another business from using a similar logo.

restraint of trade Activities such as fixing prices or colluding to regulate supplies that impede free competition. A contract that restrains commerce among states is an illegal restraint of trade.

restraint on alienation Provision in a deed or will that restricts the ability to transfer ownership of real property. For example, a will might include a restraint on alienation that prohibits property left to a beneficiary from ever being sold or transferred to a specified son or any of the son's descendants.

restricted account A brokerage margin account in which the customer cannot purchase any additional stock on margin without putting up more equity. An account is restricted when its debit balance is greater than the loan value of the securities within the account. —Also called *blocked account.*

restricted option An option in which an uncovered opening transaction cannot be made. An option becomes restricted when it closes at a price under $50 (1/2 point) and is out-of-the-money by more than 5 points. Restricted options are not prohibited for covered transactions or spreads.

restricted retained earnings The retained earnings that are unavailable for the payment of dividends to common stockholders. For example, dividend arrearages on cumulative preferred stock must be paid before any dividend payments can be made to common stockholders. Therefore, the arrearages will result in restricted retained earnings. —Also called *restricted surplus.*

restricted security A security that has not been registered with the SEC and therefore may not be sold publicly. These securities frequently enter portfolios of institutional investors through private placements and are sometimes registered at a later date. —Also called *letter bond; letter security; letter stock; unregistered security.*

restricted stock grant An offer, sometimes extended to corporate managers, that allows the purchase of stock, generally at a bargain price if specified conditions are met. Restrictions may include a minimum length of employment or a specified rate of earnings growth. Voting rights and dividends revert to the recipient at the time of the grant.

restricted surplus —See RESTRICTED RETAINED EARNINGS.

restrictive covenant —See COVENANT 2.

restructuring A significant rearrangement of a firm's assets and/or liabilities. A firm's restructuring may include discontinuing a line of business, closing several plants, and making extensive employee cutbacks. A restructuring generally entails a one-time charge against earnings. —Compare DEBT RESTRUCTURING.

restructuring charge The expense of reorganizing a company's operations. A restructuring charge is an infrequent expense that generally results from asset writedowns or facility closings. It is not considered an extraordinary item and must be considered when calculating a firm's income from continuing operations.

resumé —See CURRICULUM VITAE.

retail Of or describing a business that sells services and products to the final consumer. Wal-Mart, Sears, Target, and Gap are each examples of retail businesses. —Compare WHOLESALE.

retail credit Credit extended to individuals for household, family, and other personal expenditures. Retail credit includes both open-end and closed-end credit.

retail display allowance A discount offered by manufacturers or distributors to retailers who display products in a favored location. For example, a soft-drink bottler offers a retailer a special price for placing a large retail display near the store entrance.

retail inventory method A method for valuing inventory in which retail sales for a period are deducted from the retail value of beginning goods plus the retail value of purchases for the period. The result is converted to cost based on the ratio of cost to the retail price. The accuracy of this method of inventory valuation is dependent on the mix of goods sold being the same as the mix of goods available for sale.

retail outlet A store that purchases goods from manufacturers or wholesalers and sells directly to consumers, generally in small quantities.

retainage Funds withheld by a client from a contractor until construction is complete.

retained earnings The accumulated net income that has been retained for reinvestment in the business rather than being paid out in dividends to stockholders. Net income that is retained in the business can be used to acquire additional income-earning assets, which result in increased income in future years. Retained earnings is a part of the owners' equity section of a firm's balance sheet. —Also called *earned surplus; surplus; undistributed profits.* —See also ACCUMULATED EARNINGS TAX; APPROPRIATED RETAINED EARNINGS; RESTRICTED RETAINED EARNINGS; STATEMENT OF RETAINED EARNINGS.

retained earnings statement —See STATEMENT OF RETAINED EARNINGS.

retainer A fee paid in advance for future services. For example, a business too small to afford a full-time attorney assures that it will have legal representation by paying a retainer to a law firm.

retaliatory eviction Terminating a lease and evicting a tenant who makes a complaint or files a legal action against the landlord.

retention rate The proportion of net income that is not paid in dividends. For example, a firm earning $80 million after taxes and paying dividends of $20 million has a retention rate of $60 million/$80 million, or 75%. A high retention rate makes it more likely a firm's income and dividends will grow in future years. —Also called *earnings retention ratio; plowback ratio.*

retirement 1. The disposal of a fixed asset at the end of its useful life. Retirement may result in a gain or loss, depending on any compensation received for the asset and whether the asset is carried at a positive book value. **2.** The voiding of a firm's own stock that has been reacquired and is being held as Treasury stock. **3.** Permanently leaving employment.

retirement age The age at which an employee can retire and receive retirement benefits. Early retirement is nearly always accompanied by a reduction in benefits compared to those that would be received when retirement is deferred until the full retirement age is reached. Social Security pays reduced benefits when a person is covered and chooses to draw benefits prior to reaching his or her full retirement age.

retirement fund Assets of an individual, family, or organization that are earmarked for retirement benefits.

retirement plan —See PENSION PLAN.

retroactive Applicable to a previous time. For example, an employer grants an especially productive employee a raise retroactive to the beginning of the calendar year.

retroactive adjustment 1. A change applied to a previous incident or amount. For example, a public service commission orders a retroactive adjustment to utility rates. **2.** —See PRIOR PERIOD ADJUSTMENT.

retrocession Reinsurance of reinsurance. For example, a reinsurer purchases business from an insurance company that it subsequently reinsures, in whole or part, with another reinsurance company.

return 1. —See YIELD 1. **2.** Merchandise brought back to the seller for a refund, credit, or an exchange for different merchandise. **3.** The tax form on which individuals and businesses submit information about income and expenses to tax authorities.

return of capital —See CAPITAL DIVIDEND.

return on assets (ROA) —See RETURN ON INVESTMENT.

return on common stock equity A measure of the return that a firm's management is able to earn on common stockholders' investment. Return on common stock equity is calculated by dividing the net income minus preferred dividends by the owners' equity minus the par value of any preferred stock outstanding. For firms with no preferred stock, return on common stock equity is identical to return on equity. —Compare PROFITABILITY RATIO.

return on equity (ROE) A measure of the net income that a firm is able to earn as a percent of stockholders' investment. Many analysts consider ROE the single most important financial ratio applying to stockholders, and the best measure of performance by a firm's management. Return on equity is calculated by dividing net income after taxes by owners' equity. —Compare PROFITABILITY RATIO. —See also RETURN ON COMMON STOCK EQUITY.

return on investment (ROI) A measure of the net income a firm's management is able to earn with the firm's total assets. Return on investment is calculated by dividing net profits after taxes by total assets. —Compare PROFITABILITY RATIO. —Also called *rate of return; return on assets.*

return on sales The portion of each dollar of sales that a firm is able to turn into income. Because of severe competition, regulation, or other factors, some firms or industries have low returns on sales. This is generally the case for grocery chains, for example. In some instances, a low return on sales can be offset by increased sales. Return on sales varies significantly from industry to industry. —Compare NET PROFIT MARGIN; PROFITABILITY RATIO.

Reuters A London-based business information company that provides news and financial data to individuals, professionals, and media organizations around the world.

revaluation An increase in the value of one currency in relation to other currencies. Revaluation is generally undertaken by a government because of pressure from trading partners that are running large trade deficits and want their businesses to become more price competitive. —Compare DEVALUATION.

revenue The inflow of assets that results from sales of goods and services and earnings from dividends, interest, and rent. Revenue is often received in the form of cash, but also may be in the form of receivables to be turned into cash at a later date.

revenue anticipation note (RAN) A short-term municipal obligation with repayment to be made from a revenue source other than taxes.

revenue bond A municipal debt on which the payment of interest and principal depends on revenues from the particular asset that the bond issue is used to finance. Examples of such projects are toll roads and bridges, housing developments, and airport expansions. Revenue bonds are generally considered of lower quality than general obligation bonds, but there is a great amount of variance in risk, depending on the particular assets financed. —Compare AUTHORITY BOND.

revenue enhancement An increase in revenues, especially by way of increased taxes. Revenue enhancement includes reducing taxpayer deductions and eliminating tax credits.

revenue neutral A change in the tax code such that the amount of tax revenues that will be collected by government remains unchanged. For example, a decrease in marginal tax rates is accompanied by an elimination of certain deductions.

revenue procedure A statement from the IRS or state tax authority intended to provide guidance to taxpayers with regard to the administration of laws and regulations. For example, the IRS issues a revenue procedure for helping to determine whether individuals employed by colleges and universities are exempt from Social Security taxes.

revenue ruling The written guidance that is provided taxpayers by the Internal Revenue Service. Although revenue rulings apply to individual situations, they are often of general interest because of the manner in which the IRS interprets a particular tax problem. —Also called *letter ruling; ruling.*

reversal **1.** An appeals court ruling that overturns a previous court decision. **2.** Negative news, prospects, or financial results for a business, as, for example, when a major customer decides to take its business to a competitor. **3.** An accounting entry that offsets another entry.

reversal effect The theory that stock prices overreact to relevant news, so that extreme investment performance tends to reverse itself. Some studies indicate that short-term overreaction may lead to long-term reversals as investors recognize and correct past pricing errors.

reversal pattern In technical analysis, a chart formation that indicates a market top or a market bottom. A reversal pattern, which usually occurs after a major movement in the price of a stock or in the entire market, is an indication that investors should adjust their positions to take advantage of the coming change in market direction.

reverse —See REVERSE REPURCHASE AGREEMENT.

reverse acquisition An acquisition in which the company taken over becomes the surviving entity. A reverse acquisition is sometimes used to acquire and convert a private company into a public company without being required to go through a lengthy registration process.

reverse annuity mortgage —See REVERSE MORTGAGE.

reverse channel The path taken when products move from the user back to the seller or manufacturer, as, for example, when empty printer cartridges or returnable bottles are returned by consumers to retailers.

reverse discrimination Hiring and promotion policies practiced against a majority group. Affirmative action favoring a minority group results in reverse discrimination.

reverse leverage The situation in which the cost of borrowed funds is higher than the return earned on assets that were acquired with the borrowed money.

reverse leveraged buyout An equity investment in a company that is troubled by excessive debt. The equity infusion produced by the buyout is intended to reduce debt to a more manageable level.

reverse mortgage A mortgage in which a homeowner's equity is depleted by a lump sum distribution or a series of payments from the mortgage holder to the homeowner. Selection by the homeowner of a series of payments means the amount borrowed increases as the annuity payments continue. A reverse annuity mortgage is used primarily by elderly homeowners who wish to convert the equity in their homes into cash, either as a single amount or a series of payments. —Also called *reverse annuity mortgage.*

CASE STUDY Reverse mortgages have gained popularity as retirees decide to meet a portion of their living expenses by liquidating the wealth that has accumulated in their homes. These loans are only available to individuals 62 years of age or older who live in their homes. The amount of money that can be obtained from a reverse mortgage depends on the appraised value of the home, the age of the homeowner, and the current interest rate. The older the borrower, the lower the interest rate, and the more valuable the home, the greater the amount of funds that can be borrowed. Funds may be drawn as a lump sum, as a series of fixed monthly payments for a lifetime or a predetermined period, or as a line of credit that may be drawn on as needed. The home can never be taken from the homeowner, and no repayment is ever required as long as the homeowner stays current on taxes and insurance while continuing to live in the home. Funds received from a reverse mortgage are not considered income and, as a result, are not taxable. On the downside, the fees and costs involved in a reverse mortgage can be considerable. Expenses include an origination fee to cover the lender's operating expenses (several thousand dollars), a mortgage insurance premium to cover the possibility the loan servicer may go out of business (2% of the maximum claim amount), an appraisal fee ($300 to $400), closing costs ($800 to $1,000), and a monthly service fee set-aside of $30 to $35.

reverse preference In international trade, a tariff benefit offered by a developing country for goods imported from a developed country in return for tariff reductions granted by the developed country.

reverse repurchase agreement The purchase of an asset with a simultaneous agreement to resell the asset on a given date at a specified price. The result is simply a loan at a prescribed rate for a predetermined period while holding the asset as collateral. —Compare REPURCHASE AGREEMENT. —Also called *reverse.*

reverse stock split A proportionate reduction in the shares of stock held by shareholders. For example, a one-for-four split would result in stockholders owning one share for every four shares owned prior to the split. A reverse stock split has no effect on a firm's financial and operational performance and is often designed only to boost the market price of the stock so it won't be delisted from trading on an exchange that imposes a minimum share-price requirement. —Compare SPLIT. —Also called *split down.*

reverse swap The exchange of one bond for another such that an earlier investment position is reestablished to the position that existed before an earlier swap. For example, an investor might swap intermediate-term bonds for long-term bonds to take advantage of a steeply sloped yield curve. As the yield curve flattens, the investor might engage in a reverse swap by exchanging the long-term bonds for intermediate-term bonds.

reversible error A mistake in a trial court that is sufficiently important to justify reversing the judgment of a lower court. For example, the court fails to give proper instructions to a jury. —Also called *prejudicial error.*

reversing entry An accounting journal entry that exactly offsets a previous entry. For example, a business issues bonds on October 1 with the first semiannual interest payment due on April 1 of the following year. Interest expense is debited and interest payable is credited at the end of the first year. A reversing entry the following year credits interest expense and debits interest payable.

reversing trade In futures trading, a trade that brings an investor's position in a particular contract back to zero. The purchase of a stock index contract that has previously been sold short is an example of a reversing trade.

reversion The return of property to the prior owner or grantor. For example, leased property goes back to the lessor at the termination of the lease. Under a reversion clause, unspent funds from a federal grant must be returned to the government.

reversionary factor The number that is divided into a future amount in order to calculate the future amount's present value. For example, the reversionary factor to calculate the present value of $1,000 to be received in five years at an annual discount rate of 6% is $1/(1.06)^5$.

reversionary interest The ownership interest of a person in property held in life estate by someone else. For example, a person gives a home to his mother for her lifetime. At the mother's death, the home will revert to the grantor, who has a reversionary interest in the property.

reversionary trust A trust whose property will, on specified circumstances, revert to the grantor.

reversionary value The anticipated value of an asset on a specified date in the future. Reversionary value is an important consideration in determining the appropriate lease payment for a vehicle. A large reversionary value will reduce the lease payment.

revocable transfer A transfer of property that can be revoked. A will is an example of a revocable transfer, because the document can be changed prior to death.

reversionary trust

When might a reversionary trust be used?

A reversionary interest is often found in the "qualified personal residence trust" and the "grantor retained annuity trust," which are popular estate-planning vehicles. In these trusts, the grantor retains the use of the trust property (the grantor retains the use of the residence in the qualified residence trust and retains a fixed annuity amount in the grantor retained annuity trust) for a specified period of years. If the grantor dies during this period, the terms of the trust direct that all or a portion of the trust property will be paid ("revert") to the grantor's estate, either at the grantor's death or at the expiration of the specified term. A reversion might also be included in an inter-vivos trust for the benefit of the grantor (sometimes called a "living trust") if the trust indenture does not direct the disposition of the grantor's property at the grantor's death and the grantor desires that the property pass under his or her will.

▪ Stephen F. Lappert, Partner, Trusts and Estates Department, Carter Ledyard & Milburn LLP, New York, NY

revocable trust A trust that may be terminated by the grantor or that is set up to terminate automatically at a specific date. Revocable trusts are often used to turn daily decisions regarding certain assets over to someone else. They are also used to reduce probate fees, to reduce delays in distributing assets, and to keep assets from becoming a matter of public record. A revocable trust—an important estate-planning tool—may serve to reduce federal estate taxes, but generally will have no effect on income taxes. —Compare IRREVOCABLE TRUST.

revocation Cancellation of something. For example, an unhappy parent visits her attorney to ask about a revocation of her will, which named her only child as sole heir.

revolver —See LINE OF CREDIT.

revolving credit agreement 1. A consumer loan that requires a minimum payment that is less than the outstanding balance. Balances carried forward incur an interest charge. 2. —See LINE OF CREDIT.

revolving fund An account that recycles funds. For example, a public authority operates a fund that makes mortgage loans to small business owners. Principal and interest payments from borrowers are credited to the fund and used to make additional loans.

rezone A change in the designated use of a parcel of land. For example, the planning commission recommends that property be rezoned from residential to commercial in order to permit the construction of an office building.

RFID —See RADIO FREQUENCY IDENTIFICATION.

rich 1. Of, relating to, or being an asset judged by some investors to be overvalued. For example, a new issue of stock may carry an offering price that many analysts consider rich. 2. Describing a person with substantial wealth.

rider An appendage that adds special provisions to an insurance contract. For example, home health care may be offered as a rider for a nursing home policy.

RIF (reduction in force) The separation or downgrading of employees as a result of reorganization, lack of work, or a shortage of funds. A RIF is generally expressed as a percentage of an organization's work force.

right A certificate that permits the owner to purchase a certain number of shares, or, frequently, a fractional share of new stock from the issuer at a specific price. Rights are issued to existing stockholders in proportion to the number of shares the stockholders already own. Rights then may be combined with cash to purchase the new shares, or they may be sold to other investors. —Also called *stock right; subscription right.* —See also EX-RIGHTS; PREEMPTIVE RIGHT.

right of accumulation The right that is granted to buyers by some mutual funds permitting the buyers to count existing holdings of the fund along with new purchases when determining the size of the sales fee on the new shares. This right applies to funds that charge fees on a sliding scale, whereby the more shares that are purchased, the lower the fee that is charged on a percentage basis. Thus the fee charged on succeeding purchases is determined by all purchases, past and present, not just by new purchases.

right of first refusal An arrangement that allows a party to purchase an asset by matching the offer of any other potential buyer. For example, a lease agreement may give the lessee the right of first refusal to purchase the leased asset in the event the lessor decides to sell at the termination of the lease.

right of redemption The reasonable opportunity given to owners of property lost through a tax sale to reacquire the property. Redemption must normally occur within a specified period and entails a penalty plus the price paid for the property.

right of rescission The right of a borrower to cancel certain credit contracts without penalty within three business days from the date of a loan application. Any down payment or fees must be returned to the borrower. The right of rescission is part of the Truth in Lending Act.

right of survivorship —See JOINT TENANCY WITH RIGHT OF SURVIVORSHIP.

right of way 1. The right to cross through land belonging to someone else. 2. The authority of a vessel, vehicle, or person to proceed in preference to others.

rights off —See EX-RIGHTS.

rights offering The distribution to existing owners of rights to purchase shares of stock as part of a new stock offering. A company uses a rights offering when it sells new shares to existing shareholders rather than selling new shares to the entire investment community. The rights are used as a means to distribute new shares to existing holders on the basis of the shares each holder already owns. —See also OVERSUBSCRIPTION PRIVILEGE; PREEMPTIVE RIGHT.

rights on Of or relating to stock that trades so that new buyers, rather than sellers, will receive rights that have been declared but not yet distributed. —Compare EX-RIGHTS. —Also called *cum rights.*

right to work Prohibition of requiring union membership as a condition for continuing employment. Companies often prefer to locate in right-to-work states because their employees cannot be required to join a union, thus making unions less powerful.

ring —See PIT.

ring fencing The legal walling off of certain assets or liabilities within a corporation. For example, a firm may form a new subsidiary to protect, or ring-fence, specific assets from creditors.

riparian rights The right of a landowner to use water on or bordering his or her property. Riparian rights are common in the eastern United States, but not in the western United States, where water is often in short supply.

rising-coupon security —See STEPPED COUPON BOND.

risk The uncertainty of an outcome. When applied to investments, risk is the uncertainty of the return that will be earned. For example, a company incurs a risk when entering a new market because of the uncertainty as to how their product will be received by consumers. Risk for businesses results from a variety of factors that range from not being able to accurately forecast interest rates to unexpected inflation (or deflation). —See also BUSINESS RISK; EVENT RISK; FINANCIAL RISK; FOREIGN EXCHANGE RISK; INTEREST RATE RISK; LIQUIDITY RISK; PURCHASING POWER RISK.

risk adjusted Of or relating to a variable, such as the return on an investment, that has been altered in order to account for the differences in risk among variables of the same type. For example, financial managers adjust expected returns on various investment projects for risk in order to make them comparable.

risk arbitrage The simultaneous purchase and sale of assets that are potentially, but not necessarily, equivalent. For example, Firm A may make an offer to acquire Firm B by exchanging one share of its own stock for two shares of Firm B's stock. If the stock of Firm A is trading at $50 and the stock of Firm B is trading at $23, the risk arbitrager would buy shares in Firm B and sell short one-half this number of shares in Firm A. If the buyout offer is approved, the two stocks will exchange on a one-for-two basis, and the arbitrage position will be profitable. The risk is that the buyout will be unsuccessful, and the exchange of stock will not take place. Risk arbitrage is also used in situations involving reorganizations and tender offers. —Also called *equity arbitrage.*

risk aversion The tendency of investors to avoid risky investments. Thus, if two investments offer the same expected yield but have different risk characteristics, investors will choose the one with the lowest variability in returns. If investors are risk averse, higher-risk investments must offer higher expected yields. Otherwise, they will not be competitive with the less risky investments.

risk capital —See VENTURE CAPITAL.

risk-free return The annualized rate of return on a riskless investment. This is the rate against which other returns are measured. —See also EXCESS RETURN.

risk hedge The taking of an offsetting position in related assets so as to profit from relative price movements. For example, an investor might purchase futures contracts on gold and sell short futures contracts on silver in the belief that gold will become relatively more valuable compared with silver over the life of the contracts.

riskless investment An investment with a certain rate of return and no chance of default. Although various investments (for example, savings accounts and certificates of deposit at insured institutions) meet these requirements, a Treasury bill is the most common example of a riskless investment.

risk management Identifying potential risks and making decisions so as to reduce the possibility and/or impact of the risks. For example, an investor attempts to reduce risk by choosing conservative investments or assembling a diversified portfolio. Businesses sometimes use futures contracts to avoid risk in the foreign exchange market. Household products companies try to avoid major mistakes by introducing new products in test markets.

risk premium The extra yield over the risk-free rate owing to various types of risk inherent in a particular investment. For example, any borrower other than the U.S. government usually must pay investors a risk premium in the form of a higher interest rate on loans to account for the fact that the risk of default is less on U.S. government securities than on credit instruments of other borrowers. Businesses expect to earn a substantial risk premium when they invest in developing or unstable companies.

risk profile The degree to which various risks are important to a particular individual.

risk retention The assumption of certain risks as opposed to paying another party to assume the risks. For example, a corporation may decide to pay the health expenses of its employees rather than purchase a health insurance plan. Similarly, an individual with an older vehicle may decide to retain the risk of damage to the vehicle and forgo collision and comprehensive insurance.

risk-return tradeoff The direct relationship between the risk of an investment and its expected return. Businesses and investors will generally avoid a risky investment opportunity unless the expected return is high enough to justify the risk. Stocks are generally considered riskier investments than bonds, but can still be a desirable investment choice because stocks offer higher expected returns. Low-risk investments such as money market funds, certificates of deposit, and U.S. Treasury securities typically offer low returns compared to more risky investments.

ROA —See RETURN ON ASSETS.

road show A series of presentations to investors describing an upcoming issue of securities. A road show is designed to drum up interest in the issue among potential investors.

Robert's Rules of Order Formal procedures used by many organizations for conducting their meetings. The rules of order were developed by Civil War army officer Henry Robert.

Robinson-Patman Act Federal legislation enacted in 1936 to protect small independent retailers and suppliers from predatory practices by multistore chains. The act required that sellers sell to everyone at the same price.

robot 1. An automated self-contained electronic or mechanical device that performs mechanized, repetitive tasks. —See also STEEL-COLLAR WORKER. **2.** Automated software with artificial intelligence that searches and indexes websites. —Also called *crawler; spider.*

robotics The science of designing, manufacturing, and using robots.

rod A unit of length equivalent to 16.5 feet.

ROE —See RETURN ON EQUITY.

ROI —See RETURN ON INVESTMENT.

role playing Simulating a situation by assuming the role of one of the participants. For example, a college placement service utilizes role playing in helping students prepare for interviews.

roll —See ROLL OVER.

rolling stock Any of various readily movable pieces of transportation equipment such as automobiles, locomotives, railroad cars, and trucks. Rolling stock generally makes good collateral for loans because the equipment is standardized and easily transportable among firms or locations. —See also EQUIPMENT TRUST CERTIFICATE.

Roth IRA

I am getting ready to open an IRA. How do I choose between a Roth IRA and a regular IRA?
It depends largely on federal and state income tax considerations. While the Roth IRA has tax-free earnings, you pay taxes on the money that you put in the Roth IRA. The regular IRA has tax-free contributions, but withdrawals after retirement are taxed. If you think you will be in a higher marginal tax bracket after you retire, you would be better off receiving tax-free distributions when you retire. If you think you will be in a lower marginal tax bracket when you retire, but are in a high bracket now, you would be better off with a regular IRA.

■ Michael W. Butler, PhD, Professor of Economics, Angelo State University, San Angelo, Texas

---

rollout Introduction of a new product or service: *The public appeared less than overwhelmed by Microsoft's rollout of its new Vista operating system.*

rollover **1.** The reinvestment of money received from a maturing security in another similar security. Rollover usually applies to short-term investments such as certificates of deposit, commercial paper, and Treasury bills. —See also IRA ROLLOVER; PENSION ROLLOVER. **2.** The obtaining of funds from a new loan for use in paying off the balance of a maturing loan. —See also REFUND 1; REFUNDING BOND.

roll over To reinvest funds from a maturing security into a similar security. —Also called *roll.*

rollover loan An unusual loan with a long amortization period and a fixed interest rate that is periodically reset on the basis of some stipulated standard.

roll-up A public limited partnership in which a number of existing limited partnerships are pooled into a single partnership.

rotating shift A work schedule with hours that change at prescribed intervals. For example, a person may work four days from 8:00 a.m. to 4:00 p.m., four days from 4:00 p.m. to midnight, and four days from midnight to 8:00 a.m. The cycle is then repeated.

Roth 401(k) An employer-sponsored savings plan in which employees have income withheld from their paycheck for contribution to a retirement account. Unlike a regular 401(k), a Roth 401(k) requires that taxes be paid upfront on income contributed to the account. Tax benefits are transferred to the distribution period, when withdrawals of contributions and investment income are tax-free, assuming qualifications regarding age and plan length are satisfied. Any matching employer contributions are maintained in a separate account and subject to taxation upon withdrawal.

Roth IRA A special type of individual retirement account in which contributions are made with aftertax dollars, but distributions are tax-free as long as certain requirements, including holding period and age, are met. All earnings within the account are free of taxation.

round lot The standard unit of trading in a particular type of security. For stocks, a round lot is 100 shares or a multiple thereof, although a few inactive issues trade in units of 10 shares. For corporate, municipal, and government bonds, a round lot is usually considered to be $100,000 of principal amount of securities per trade. Customers involved in securities transactions in lots other than round lots are often penalized somewhat because the trades require more broker and dealer effort. —Compare ODD LOT. —Also called *even lot; normal trading unit.* —See also LOT.

round trip The purchase and sale of the same security. —Also called *round turn*.

routing **1.** The path to be taken: *The distribution manager decided on the most efficient routing for the delivery van.* **2.** The forwarding of data packets across multiple networks to the appropriate address.

royalty The compensation that is paid to the owner of an asset based on income earned by the asset's user. For example, an oil company pays royalties to the owners of mineral rights, and a book publisher compensates its authors with royalty payments.

royalty interest The proportional ownership interest of the owner of oil and gas rights in income produced by the asset. —See also OVERRIDING ROYALTY INTEREST.

royalty trust An ownership interest in certain assets, generally crude oil or gas production and real estate. Unlike the usual corporate organization, a trust arrangement permits income and tax benefits to flow through to the individual owners. Thus, some investors argue that a trust produces more value for the owners.

RP —See REPURCHASE AGREEMENT.

rubber check —See BOUNCE 3.

rule of 72 The mathematical rule used in approximating the number of years it will take a given investment to double in value. The number of years to double an investment is calculated by dividing 72 by the annual rate of return. Thus, an investment expected to earn 10% annually will double the investor's funds in 72/10, or 7.2 years. Dividing 72 by the number of years in which the investor wishes to double his or her funds will yield the necessary rate of return.

rule of 78s A mathematical formula for calculating the amount of interest to be rebated to a borrower who repays or refinances an amortized loan prior to the scheduled maturity. The calculation assumes the initial payments of an installment loan go mostly toward interest, so that consumers receive a meager refund when they prepay a loan. Most installment-loan agreements now use simple interest, so the rule of 78s is not applicable. —Also called *sum-of-the-years method*.

Rules of Fair Practice The rules of conduct that have been established for members of the National Association of Securities Dealers and that require, among other things, fair prices, reasonable charges, firm quotations, and ethical practices. Failure to follow these rules may result in fines or expulsion from NASD.

ruling **1.** A decision by a court. **2.** —See REVENUE RULING.

run A demand for their funds by a large number of frightened depositors of a financial institution. Financial institutions normally keep on hand only a small proportion of deposits, so a run can result in the failure that depositors fear. Federal deposit insurance was introduced to give depositors confidence their funds are safe.

running ahead The illegal purchase or sale of a security by a broker for his or her personal account before execution of customer orders in the same security. If a brokerage firm issues a negative report on a company, a broker acting on the report for his or her own account before telling clients about the report would be running ahead. —See also FRONT RUNNING.

running yield —See CURRENT YIELD.

run of paper Instruction to a newspaper by an advertiser that an advertisement can be placed in any position in the paper. Choosing run of paper generally results in a reduced charge to an advertiser. —Compare FULL POSITION.

run of schedule A radio or television advertisement that can run at the broadcaster's convenience.

runup A sharp, short-term increase in the market value of an asset or asset class.

run with the land A real estate covenant that binds all current and future owners of a property. For example, a covenant may prohibit commercial use of a property.

rural Of or pertaining to a geographical area that is undeveloped or lightly developed and sparsely populated. Rural areas are characterized by farms, forests, and prairies. —Compare URBAN.

rurban Of or pertaining to the outer limits of an urban area where residential and commercial areas coexist with agriculture. Rurban areas are eventually consumed by development.

Russell Indexes Any of three market-value-weighted indexes of U.S. stocks: Russell 1000, Russell 2000, and Russell 3000. Russell 1000 includes the 1,000 largest capitalization U.S. stocks. Russell 2000 consists of the next 2,000 largest capitalization U.S. stocks and is often used as a measure of small stock performance. Russell 3000 is composed of all the stocks included in the two other indexes.

rust belt The Northeast and Upper-Midwest, where many of America's manufacturing facilities became technologically and economically obsolete.

RVP —See RECEIVE VERSUS PAYMENT.

▪ S

sabotage To intentionally destroy property or obstruct normal operations: *Workers unhappy with their new contract decided to sabotage the firm's delivery vehicles by pouring sand into the gas tanks.*

sack To fire or terminate an employee: *The directors unanimously voted to sack the CEO after the firm's owners suffered several years of earnings disappointments.*

safe harbor 1. A regulation that protects individuals or corporations from the legal consequences of certain actions they undertake. For example, firms filing forecasts with the SEC have a safe harbor from individuals or businesses that use the forecasts and are subsequently damaged (that is, they lose money), as long as the forecasts were prepared in good faith. Taxpayers are offered safe harbor for favorable tax treatment of certain transactions by following guidelines issued by the Internal Revenue Service. 2. A tactic in which the target of an unfriendly takeover makes itself less attractive by taking a specific action. For example, a takeover target pays a large cash dividend to shareholders. —See also SCORCHED EARTH.

> **CASE STUDY** Federal legislation passed in 1996 allowed safe harbor 401(k) plans that eliminated the need for companies to undertake nondiscrimination testing. The program was particularly attractive to small businesses because it permitted owners and key employees to make maximum salary deferral contributions. Prior to this legislation that became effective in 1999, many small companies and professional firms elected not to participate in 401(k) retirement programs. Safe harbor plans require that an employer either match employee contributions (100% of each participant's first 3% of salary and 50% of the next 2% of salary) or provide a nonelective contribu-

tion equal to 3% of salary for all eligible employees. Matching contributions must be vested immediately, and distributions cannot occur until age 59½ or termination of employment, whichever occurs first. All employees at least 21 years old and with one year of service (1,000 hours) must be allowed to participate in a safe harbor 401(k) plan.

safekeeping The keeping of assets, including securities, by a financial institution. Brokerage firms provide safekeeping for securities left in customer accounts.

safety margin The amount in excess of the minimum requirement. For example, a borrower maintains a balance of $6,000 in his or her account, a safety margin of $1,000 above the lender's compensating balance requirement of $5,000. An engineer builds in a safety margin by utilizing components that are stronger than called for by the manufacturer.

safety stock The minimum amount of inventory of a particular item that is maintained to insure against being unable to satisfy customer demand. For example, a produce company maintains a safety stock equal to 10% of monthly sales, in case of unexpected demand. Reducing safety stock results in lower inventory costs, but makes it more likely a firm will lose sales.

salariat Salaried workers.

salary Regular compensation paid by an employer to an employee. Salary does not include benefits such as health and life insurance premiums paid by an employer.

salary continuation plan An arrangement in which an employer agrees to continue payment of an employee's salary for a specified time at the employee's death, retirement, or disability. The employer may self-insure the plan or purchase a life insurance policy on the employee with the employer as beneficiary. Proceeds from the policy would go to pay future salary benefits.

salary reduction plan A retirement plan that permits an employee to set aside a portion of salary in a tax-deferred investment account selected by the employer. Contributions and the income they earn are sheltered from taxes until the funds are withdrawn. —Also called *401(k) plan.* —See also ROTH 401(K).

sale 1. Price reductions by a retailer. **2.** A transaction in which a good or service is transferred to a buyer in return for cash received by the seller.

sale and leaseback The sale of a fixed asset that is then leased by the former owner from the new owner. A sale and leaseback permits a firm to withdraw its equity in an asset without giving up use of the asset. —Also called *leaseback.*

CASE STUDY In March 2007 Air India announced that it planned to enter into a sale-and-leaseback agreement for six 20-year-old Airbus A-310 aircraft already in its fleet. Proceeds from the sale would be used to supplement working capital and help make loan payments required on the acquisition of 68 new Boeing aircraft. At the time of the announcement, the airline had received one bid of $78 million, with a leasing arrangement requiring a monthly rental fee of $247,000 per aircraft. The lease was for a term of five years. The sale-and-leaseback arrangement would allow the firm to raise needed capital at the same time it maintained use of the six aircraft.

sale and leaseback

Can you provide an example of how a sale and leaseback can benefit a business?

A sale-leaseback transaction offers a company numerous benefits, including the ability of the seller to realize 100% of the current market value of the asset and use the proceeds to reinvest into its core operating business while maintaining use of the asset. Sale-leaseback transactions also diversify the funding sources of capital for a company outside the typical debt and equity markets and provide long-term capital with no financial covenants. The transaction provides the seller with the ability to deleverage its balance sheet and can offer tax benefits given that the rent/lease payments are tax-deductible.

■ Brooke Barber, Vice President, Middle Market Banking, Atlanta, GA

sale-in, lease-out (SILO) A financial arrangement in which a tax-exempt entity sells an asset to a private investor or investment group and then leases the asset back. For example, a city sells an office building to a private investment group that leases the building back to the city. The transaction offers the investment group tax advantages, such as depreciation expense, that are not available to the city. Legislation in 2004 restricted use of these arrangements.

sales The revenue from the sale of goods and services. Sales exclude other types of revenue such as dividends, interest, and rent.

sales charge —See LOAD.

sales contract An agreement between a seller and a buyer with conditions and terms of the sale, including the product or service being offered, an agreed-upon price, relevant warranty information, and the date on which the sale is to be finalized.

sales engineer A salesperson who possesses substantial technical knowledge, generally including an engineering degree and previous work experience. Sales engineers are typically hired to sell complex products purchased by large companies, and they interface with customers by demonstrating how the products can be used to improve efficiency, increase reliability, and so forth.

sales incentive Additional compensation paid to a salesperson who exceeds a predetermined quota established by the employer. A sales incentive may be a nonmonetary item (trip, vehicle use, etc.), a fixed amount of money, or a percentage of the dollar amount of sales above the quota.

sales journal A book of credit sales listed in chronological order.

sales load —See LOAD.

sales mix —See PRODUCT MIX.

sales office A manufacturer's office that supports the activities of the firm's sales agents. A national corporation may establish regional sales offices to provide its agents with recordkeeping, product technical specifications, and customer credit information.

salesperson An individual who represents and sells products and/or services for a manufacturer, wholesaler, or retailer.

---

salesperson

What characteristics make for a successful salesperson?

A successful salesperson consistently brings value to the customer. That value is provided if the salesperson:

- understands the dynamics of the customer's marketplace,
- knows the specific needs of his or her customers and how to meet them,
- consistently brings new ideas and suggestions to the customer,
- flawlessly executes on services sold (or provides quality products on a consistent basis),
- follows up consistently, and
- maintains ethical business practices.

> ▪ E. Mace Lewis, Vice President, Business Development, QD Healthcare Group, Greenwich, CT

---

sales portfolio A listing of items that are available for sale including pricing and technical specifications.

sales price The payment made by a buyer to a seller for the purchase of a good or service.

sales promotion A program designed to increase sales of a designated service or product. For example, an automobile manufacturer initiates a sales promotion for its SUVs by offering dealer incentives and consumer rebates. Sales promotions may also include increased advertising, reduced prices, zero-percent financing, and sweepstakes.

sales representative A commissioned salesperson employed to sell goods and services to individuals, businesses, and other organizations. —Also called *rep*.

sales returns and allowances An entry on the income statement to account for the value of goods that are returned by customers. Sales returns and allowances is subtracted from gross sales in the calculation of net sales.

sales revenue The dollar amount of sales for cash and on credit during a period.

sales tax A government levy on retail sales that is collected by retailers at the point of sale. A sales tax may be structured to exempt certain classes of products (groceries, drugs) or services.

sales-type lease A lease by a manufacturer or dealer that meets the criteria for a capital lease. For example, an automobile dealer offers a 60-month lease on full-size trucks.

Sallie Mae The common name for SLM Corporation, parent firm of several subsidiaries engaged in education lending, debt collection, and college savings programs. Sallie Mae provides a secondary market in student loans, the majority of which are government guaranteed. This organization was the first government-sponsored enterprise to be transformed into a private company. As such, the firm lost the implied government backing of its debt that is enjoyed by Fannie Mae and Freddie Mac. SLM Corporation is also the parent company of Nellie Mae, a major provider of higher education loans for students and parents. —Formerly called *Student Loan Marketing Association*.

salvage value —See RESIDUAL VALUE 1.

sample **1.** A subset chosen from a population. For example, a marketing researcher interviews a sample of visitors to the shopping mall in an effort to determine the types of mall advertising that have been most effective. A sample should be representative of the population from which it is drawn. **2.** A product given without charge to a potential customer by a manufacturer, distributor, or retailer.

sampling **1.** Selecting and examining a subset of a population in order to reach certain conclusions about the characteristics of the population: *The manufacturer found that extensive sampling of its products allowed it to pinpoint quality problems and improve its manufacturing process.* **2.** Offering small or inexpensive samples of a product in an effort to encourage subsequent purchases. Manufacturers frequently use sampling during the introduction of a new product.

S&L —See SAVINGS AND LOAN ASSOCIATION.

S&P —See STANDARD & POOR'S.

S&P 500 —See STANDARD & POOR'S 500 STOCK INDEX.

sandwich lease A lease in which the lessee becomes the lessor by subletting the property to someone else. For example, Frank signs a three-year lease with a payment of $3,000 per month. Frank then subleases the property to Joe for $3,500 per month.

Santa Claus rally A rise in security prices that occurs during the last week of the calendar year and during the first few days of the new year. —Also called *year-end rally.*

Sarbanes-Oxley Act The congressional legislation that regulates certain corporate financial activities and improves the accuracy of financial statements. Among other things, the act prohibits personal company loans to directors and officers, requires certification of financial statements by a firm's chief executive officer and chief financial officer, protects employee whistleblowers, increases criminal penalties for securities law violations, requires disclosure of off-balance-sheet financing, and calls for improvement in the accuracy of pro forma financial statements. The act was passed in 2002 in response to widely publicized corporate accounting scandals.

satisfaction piece An official instrument that acknowledges an obligation has been satisfied. For example, a lender acknowledges that a debt has been satisfied.

saturated Describing a market in which nearly all potential customers have been reached and use of a product or service is currently near a maximum. For example, a town is saturated with supermarkets.

savings account An account in a depository institution in which funds are deposited at interest but withdrawals cannot by made by check.

savings and loan association (S&L) A deposit-gathering financial institution that is primarily engaged in making loans on real estate. Depositors own some S&Ls, while others are organized as profit-making institutions with stock that is publicly traded. —Also called *federal savings and loan association; mutual association.* —See also THRIFT.

savings bank —See MUTUAL SAVINGS BANK.

savings bond A nonmarketable security issued by the U.S. Treasury in relatively small denominations for individual investors. Two categories of bonds are currently available for purchase. Interest on these bonds is exempt from state and local, but not federal, taxation. —Also called *United States savings bond.* —See also SERIES EE SAVINGS BOND; SERIES HH SAVINGS BOND; SERIES I SAVINGS BOND; TREASURY DIRECT.

savings rate The percentage of disposable income that remains after consumption expenditures. The savings rate of individuals and families in the United States has historically been among the lowest of any industrialized country, and in the early 2000s was actually negative. —Also called *personal savings rate.*

Say's Law The principle of Jean Baptiste Say (1767–1832) and fellow classical economists that posits that supply creates its own demand. The basis of Say's Law is that there can be no general glut of goods, because additional supply will create additional demand: Who would work to create more goods and services unless they intended to spend their income on other goods and services? The principle holds up better in a barter economy than in a modern economy.

SBA —See SMALL BUSINESS ADMINISTRATION.

SBIC —See SMALL BUSINESS INVESTMENT COMPANY.

scab A derogatory term for someone who accepts employment or continues to work while other employees are on strike. —See also STRIKEBREAKER.

scalage 1. An allowance given a buyer for the likelihood that a product will shrink or leak prior to delivery. **2.** A proportional reduction in size.

scale 1. The wage rate for a particular job classification. **2.** The schedule of yields (or prices) at which an underwriter offers a serial bond issue to the public. The schedule reflects yields at the various maturities being offered. —Also called *offering scale.* —See also INVERTED SCALE. **3.** Proportional representation of an object's dimensions in a drawing or plan of the object.

scale order A specialized brokerage order that requests multiple executions at varying prices for the same security; for example, when an investor who wishes to liquidate a security position in a rising market spaces orders to sell specified numbers of shares at ten-cent price intervals.

scalper 1. A market maker who assigns excessive markups or markdowns on security transactions. Such activity is in violation of National Association of Securities Dealers rules. **2.** An investment adviser who takes a position in a security before publicly recommending the security for purchase. The scalper then sells the security at a profit after the recommendation has caused investors to buy the security and push its price higher. This type of activity must be disclosed to buyers. **3.** An in-and-out trader who attempts to profit on relatively small price changes. **4.** An individual who purchases something thought to be in short supply and then attempts to resell it at far above the purchase price: *A scalper standing outside the stadium was offering to sell two World Series tickets.*

scarcity An insufficient supply of something relative to the demand. Scarcity results in higher prices to buyers and, generally, higher profits to sellers.

scatter diagram A chart that displays two sets of data, one represented on the horizontal axis and the other on the vertical axis. Each observation is represented by a dot on the chart. Scatter diagrams are used to study possible relationships between two variables.

scenic easement An easement whose sole purpose is scenic preservation. A scenic easement results in restrictions so as to preserve the affected property in an undeveloped or natural state.

schedule 1. A tax form. **2.** A listing of times and locations for activities at an event.

Schedule B The federal income tax form for listing gross dividends and/or gross taxable interest income payments that total more than $400 during the tax year.

Schedule C The federal income tax form for listing the profit or loss from a business.

Schedule D The federal income tax form for listing gains and losses from capital assets that have been sold (or bought, in the case of a short sale) during the tax year.

scorched earth An antitakeover strategy in which the target firm disposes of those assets or divisions considered particularly desirable by the raider. Thus, by making itself less attractive, the target discourages the takeover attempt. Such a strategy is almost certain to penalize the shareholders of the target firm. —Compare CROWN JEWEL 2.

SCORE —See SERVICE CORPS OF RETIRED EXECUTIVES.

S corporation A corporation that qualifies for and chooses special tax status under the Internal Revenue Code. Corporate gains and losses are passed through to shareholders, who escape double taxation (corporate tax plus a tax on dividends) and are offered the protection of limited liability.

scrap value —See RESIDUAL VALUE 1.

screen To examine a quantity of things with the goal of selecting a limited number that meet certain predetermined requirements. For example, an investor might screen all electric utilities for stock that offers a dividend yield of 8% or more and a price-earnings ratio of 8 or less. Similarly, an employer screens applicants for job openings.

scrip 1. A certificate of value issued for a specific purpose and without government authority. For example, a company issues employees at a remote mining operation scrip that can be used for purchases in the company store. **2.** A certificate that can be exchanged for a fractional share of stock. Scrip is distributed as the result of a spinoff, a stock dividend, or a stock split in which the stockholder would be entitled to a fractional share of stock. For example, the owner of a single share would receive scrip for one-half a share in the event the issuer declared a three-for-two stock split.

scrip dividend An unusual type of dividend involving the distribution of promissory notes that call for some type of payment at a future date. Scrip dividends generally signal that a firm is short of cash. —Compare LIABILITY DIVIDEND.

SDR —See SPECIAL DRAWING RIGHTS.

seal 1. An embossed impression affixed to a document that guarantees the document's authenticity. **2.** The device used to emboss or imprint a document and guarantee its authenticity.

sealed bid 1. A purchase offer that is delivered to the seller or the seller's agent in a sealed envelope so that it remains secret from other bidders. **2.** An offer to sell or to perform work that is delivered in a sealed envelope to a potential customer. Government agencies are often required to solicit sealed bids for major procurements.

seasonal adjustment Recalculation of a set of data to remove the effect of recurring seasonal influences. For example, the seasonal variation in the prices of fruits and vegetables can have a substantial impact on the consumer price index unless the index calculation includes a seasonal adjustment. In practice, the Bureau of Labor Statistics publishes the CPI both with a seasonal adjustment and without a seasonal adjustment.

seasonal unemployment Unemployment that results from the seasonal nature of certain types of employment. For example, the seasonal nature of agriculture and tourism creates substantial unemployment during certain periods of each year.

sealed bid

What is the best way to go about determining the price to submit in a sealed bid? I have passed on several opportunities to bid on business because I wasn't quite sure how to determine the amount to bid.

Sealed bids are tricky. Three points are critical to understand before bidding: First, will they absolutely agree to buy at some defined cost or less? Second, what is that cost? And finally, what do you expect your competitors to bid at? The last question is the hardest; but if you have been in the business for a while, you will have a pretty good idea of that number. Knowing your own costs is straightforward. If you have lots of opportunities compared to resources to execute, you can try to get the highest reasonable price possible. If you have fewer opportunities, you have to cut your bid more to "get the business." Better to bid a bit high and safely than not to bid at all.

▪ Deaver Brown, Publisher, Simplysoftwarecd.com, Lincoln, MA

seasonal variation A regularly recurring change in the value of a variable. For example, electric utilities generally experience significant seasonal sales variations in electricity. Likewise, toy manufacturers have sales increases before Christmas.

seasoned 1. Of, relating to, or being a security issue that has traded in the secondary market long enough to establish a track record for price variability and trading volume. 2. Of, relating to, or being an outstanding loan with a record of timely payments.

seat Membership on an organized securities exchange. Because the number of seats on an exchange is generally fixed, membership may be acquired only by purchasing a seat from an existing owner at a negotiated or an offered price.

SEC —See SECURITIES AND EXCHANGE COMMISSION.

SECA —See SELF-EMPLOYMENT CONTRIBUTIONS ACT.

secondary beneficiary The recipient of a bequest only if predeceased by the primary beneficiary. For example, Joe names his wife as primary beneficiary and his only child as secondary beneficiary of his estate. Joe's child is the secondary beneficiary and will inherit the estate only if Joe's wife is already deceased at Joe's death. —See also PRIMARY BENEFICIARY.

secondary boycott An organized boycott of a business or other entity in an effort to keep the entity from conducting business with another business or entity. —Compare PRIMARY BOYCOTT.

secondary data Data already gathered for one use that is then utilized for another purpose. For example, a person researches income distribution using data collected by the Department of Commerce. —Compare PRIMARY DATA.

secondary distribution The sale of a block of existing, not newly issued, securities with the proceeds going to the present holders rather than to the issuing firm. An especially large secondary distribution may put pressure on the security's price until the additional shares or bonds have been assimilated in the market. —Compare PRIMARY DISTRIBUTION. —Also called *secondary offering.* —See also REGISTERED SECONDARY DISTRIBUTION; SPOT SECONDARY DISTRIBUTION.

secondary market The market in which existing securities are traded among investors through an intermediary. Exchanges such as the New York Stock Exchange and Nasdaq facilitate the trading of securities in the secondary market. —Compare FOURTH MARKET; PRIMARY MARKET; THIRD MARKET. —Also called *aftermarket.*

secondary offering —See SECONDARY DISTRIBUTION.

secondary shares Shares in a stock offering in which proceeds go to other investors rather than the issuing company. Secondary shares have been previously traded and will not result in an increase in shares outstanding. —Compare PRIMARY SHARES.

secondary stock The stock of a smaller firm listed on the New York Stock Exchange, or nearly any stock traded on the American Stock Exchange, the regional exchanges, or in the over-the-counter market. These generally volatile stocks often exhibit price movements different from those of the large blue chips. —Also called *second-tier stock.*

secondary strike —See SYMPATHY STRIKE.

secondary trend A movement of a variable that is opposite that of the primary trend. For example, even during a bull market, when the primary trend of stock prices is upward, downward secondary trends frequently occur. —See also PRIMARY TREND.

second home A dwelling occupied part-time by someone who owns a primary residence. Interest paid on loans secured by a primary home and second home are generally deductible for taxpayers who choose to itemize deductions.

second mortgage A real estate mortgage with a subordinate claim to another mortgage on the same property. The second mortgage is more risky to the lender than the first mortgage; thus, it carries a higher rate of interest. —Also called *piggyback loan.* —See also SOFT SECOND LOAN.

second preferred A class of preferred stock that has a subordinate claim to dividends and assets relative to another class of preferred stock of the same issuer. —Compare PRIOR PREFERRED.

second stage capital Funds provided for a relatively new but growing business that has insufficient cash flow to provide adequate working capital. —Compare FIRST STAGE CAPITAL.

second-tier stock —See SECONDARY STOCK.

secret shopper —See MYSTERY SHOPPER.

section An area of land equal to one square mile, or 640 acres.

Section 8 Housing Private rental units that qualify for federal subsidies on behalf of low-income tenants who pay a limited portion of their income for rent. A Section 8 Home Ownership Program permits certain voucher recipients to use the vouchers to purchase single family homes, condominiums, and manufactured housing.

section 501(c)(3) organization An entity, often described as a charitable organization, that is organized and operated exclusively for purposes set forth in section 501(c)(3) of the IRS Code. These organizations may not participate in campaign activities for or against political candidates, may not attempt to influence legislation, and none of their earnings can accrue to a private shareholder or individual. Meeting these standards allows the organizations to obtain federal tax-exempt status and to receive tax-deductible contributions.

Section 1031 A part of the IRS Code that permits owners of investment property to defer the capital gains tax on the exchange of property of a like kind. The deferral of capital gains applies to a like-kind exchange of rental real estate, but not to like-kind exchanges of stocks, bonds, and partnership interests. —See also LIKE-KIND EXCHANGE.

Section 1231 property Depreciable assets, including vehicles, buildings, and machinery, used in a trade or business and held for over one year. Net gains on the sale of Section 1231 property are subject to capital gains treatment, except for depreciation recapture, which is taxable as ordinary income. Ordinary loss deductions are permitted in years in which a business incurs net Section 1231 losses.

sector 1. A group of securities (such as airline stocks) that share certain common characteristics. Stocks that are particularly interest sensitive are considered a sector. 2. An industry or field of economic activity: *The housing sector can be expected to encounter substantial difficulty if long-term interest rates experience a major increase.*

sector fund An investment company that concentrates its holdings among securities or other assets sharing a common interest. For example, a sector fund may limit its holdings to foreign securities from a particular country or geographic region (for example, Korea Fund or Pacific Fund). Likewise, it may specialize in the securities of energy-related firms or in companies that produce precious metals. Sector funds permit investors to concentrate on a specific investment segment and yet diversify their investments among various issuers. Sector funds entail more risk but offer greater potential returns than funds that diversify their portfolios. —Also called *special-purpose fund; specialty fund.*

sector rotation An investment strategy involving the movement of investments from one industry sector to another in an attempt to beat the market. For example, an investor might rotate investments among consumer durables, technology, and energy securities as economic fundamentals and valuations in each of these sectors change. —Also called *group rotation.*

secular trend The relatively consistent movement of a variable over a long period. A stock in a secular uptrend is an indicator that the security has experienced an extended period of rising prices.

secular trust A nonqualified deferred compensation arrangement for key employees and executives with contributions and trust income considered as taxable income to the beneficiary. Assets in a secular trust are not subject to claim by creditors of the employer in the event of the employer's bankruptcy.

secured creditor A creditor having a claim that is protected by specific assets. For example, the owner of a mortgage bond can force the sale of, or can take possession of, a particular asset if the borrower fails to meet the terms of the lending agreement. —Compare UNSECURED CREDITOR.

secured debt —See SECURED LIABILITY.

secured lease obligation bond (SLOB) A debt obligation serviced by lease payments on a single asset. The debt may be secured only by the lease or by a combination of the lease and a lien on the asset being leased. SLOBs are used primarily by electric utilities to finance power stations.

secured liability A debt that is guaranteed with a pledge of assets. Secured bonds are often secured with real estate or equipment. —Also called *secured debt.*

secured transaction A loan for which the lender receives a security interest in an asset pledged as collateral. The transaction is secured by the lender being able to take control of the pledged asset in the event the borrower defaults.

Securities Act Amendments of 1975 The legislation that gives the SEC authority to develop a national market in securities, thereby making the system more competitive and more efficient. The amendments have had limited success in producing a fully integrated market system.

Securities Act of 1933 A landmark securities law intended to improve the flow of information to potential investors in new security issues and to prohibit certain selling practices relating to those issues. Issuing firms are required to register their securities with the federal government, and investment bankers must provide investors with a prospectus. Secondary issues, private offerings, and certain small issues are usually exempt from requirements of the act.

securities analyst —See FINANCIAL ANALYST.

Securities and Exchange Commission (SEC) The U.S. government agency, established in 1934, charged with protecting investors and maintaining the integrity of the securities markets. The SEC requires public companies to disclose meaningful financial information to the public, and it oversees participants in the securities business, including stock exchanges, broker-dealers, investment advisers, mutual funds, and public utility holding companies. The commission is composed of five presidentially appointed commissioners, four divisions, and 18 offices.

securities exchange A facility or network for the organized trading of securities. The major national exchanges are the American Stock Exchange, Chicago Board Options Exchange, Nasdaq, and New York Stock Exchange. —Also called *exchange¹; market¹; organized securities exchange; stock exchange.*

Securities Exchange Act of 1934 Landmark legislation that established the SEC and that gives it authority over proxy solicitation and registration of organized exchanges. In addition, the act sets disclosure requirements for securities in the secondary market, regulates insider trading, and gives the Federal Reserve authority over credit purchases of securities. When established, the act reflected an effort to extend and overcome shortcomings of the Securities Act of 1933. These two pieces of legislation are the basis of securities regulation in the twentieth and twenty-first centuries. —See also FOREIGN CORRUPT PRACTICES ACT; WILLIAMS ACT.

Securities Investor Protection Act of 1970 An act that established the Securities Investor Protection Corporation. The legislation responded to the generally unstable condition of the brokerage industry in the late 1960s.

Securities Investor Protection Corporation (SIPC) A government-sponsored organization created in 1970 to insure investor accounts at brokerage firms in the event of the brokerage firms' insolvency and liquidation. The maximum insurance of $500,000, including a maximum of $100,000 in cash assets per account, only covers customer losses due to insolvencies, not losses caused by security price fluctuations. SIPC coverage is similar in concept to Federal Deposit Insurance Corporation coverage of customer accounts at commercial banks.

Securities Law Enforcement Remedies Act Federal legislation enacted in 1990 that provides the SEC with additional enforcement powers, especially over corporate officers and directors who demonstrate "substantial unfitness."

securities loan **1.** A loan made to an investor for the purpose of buying securities. The loan is secured by the securities. **2.** The lending of securities by one broker-dealer to another broker-dealer. Securities loans generally occur when broker-dealers need to borrow securities for delivery on customers' short sales.

securities markets The physical locations and dealer networks on which securities trade. Technological innovations have been moving the securities markets from trading floors to electronic interfaces.

securitized Of, related to, or being debt securities that are secured with assets. For example, mortgage purchase bonds are secured by mortgages that have been purchased with the bond issue's proceeds.

security 1. An instrument that, for a stock, shows ownership in a firm; for a bond, indicates a creditor relationship with a firm or with a federal, state, or local government; or signifies other rights to ownership. 2. Collateral used to guarantee repayment of a debt.

security deposit A required payment by a lessee to a lessor, generally at the beginning of a lease. The deposit helps guarantee that the lease will not be violated and the leased property (vehicle, apartment, house) will be in acceptable condition at the end of the lease.

security depository A centralized location in which security certificates are placed and stored for later transfer. (Transfers usually take place by book entry rather than by physical movement.) —Also called *depository.* —See also DEPOSITORY TRUST COMPANY.

security interest The legal right of a lender to take a borrower's property in order to secure payment of an obligation. For example, a bank assumes a security interest in a vehicle purchased by a customer using funds borrowed from the bank.

security rating 1. —See BOND RATING. 2. —See STOCK RATING.

security valuation model An analytic tool for valuing securities in which a series of mathematical relationships is used to determine the price at which a security should sell. Accuracy using a model depends not only on the validity of the relationships, but also on the precision of the estimates of other variables required by the model.

seed money Funds provided to finance the initial stages of a new venture. Seed money may be utilized to conduct research, develop the prototype for a product, or determine if an idea is workable or economically viable.

segment An identifiable part of a business organization. For example, a large corporation might have a number of segments, including industrial, aerospace, and leisure products. —Also called *business segment.*

segmentation Grouping customers according to homogeneous attributes. For example, an automobile manufacturer with a full line of vehicles uses segmentation by income level in planning the marketing of its products. Small, entry-level vehicles are marketed to individuals and families with modest incomes, while wealthy individuals are market targets for the firm's luxury vehicles. Segmentation allows a business to focus its marketing where it will be most productive.

segment reporting A type of financial reporting in which a firm discloses information by identifiable industry segments. For example, Procter & Gamble reports revenues, income, assets, depreciation, and capital expenditures for each of three segments: beauty and health, household products, and Gillette. Segment reporting is required by the SEC as part of its attempt to provide stockholders and the public with better financial data. —Also called *line-of-business reporting.* —See also INDUSTRY SEGMENT.

segregation of duties Separating certain areas of responsibility and duties in an effort to reduce fraud and unintentional mistakes. For example, an employee who accepts cash payments should not also have responsibility for making bank deposits and reconciling bank statements.

seigniorage The difference between the face value and the manufacturing cost of coins and currency. A central bank enjoys substantial positive seigniorage from printing and issuing currency, but can suffer negative seigniorage from minting coins.

> **CASE STUDY** U.S. Mint officials announced in late 2006 they were planning to implement rules prohibiting the melting down of pennies and nickels. The statement followed several years of rapidly rising commodity prices that resulted in negative seigniorage for both coins. Pennies, comprised of 2.5% copper and 97.5% zinc, had a metal content value of 1.12¢ and an overall cost, including production expenses, of 1.73¢ each at the time of the announcement. Nickels, with 75% copper and 25% zinc content, had a metal value of 6.99¢ and an overall cost of 8.34¢ each. The mint was also planning to require that shipments of the two coins to foreign countries be capped at $100 worth of coins. The news resulted in some people calling for abolishing the penny and altering the content of the nickel, much as the government did in the 1960s when dimes and quarters had a high silver content.

seisin In law, possession of an asset. For example, the owner of an apartment building has seisin.

selective distribution Selling a product or service through a limited number of outlets. Selective distribution reduces competition, allows a manufacturer to establish higher quality standards for service, and can reduce distribution expenses.

self-amortizing loan A debt requiring the borrower to make a series of equal periodic payments that gradually pay down the balance of the loan. Each payment is comprised of both interest and principal. Conventional mortgage loans and vehicle loans are self-amortizing.

self-directed IRA An individual retirement account that permits its owner wide latitude as to types of assets and control over the investments within the account. A self-directed IRA generally refers to IRAs established at brokerage firms in which customers may buy and sell securities. Brokerage firms may charge an annual fee in addition to commissions on any trades in an account.

self-employed Of or describing an individual who operates a trade, business, or profession, either by himself or herself, or as a partner. Self-employed individuals are required to pay Social Security and Medicare taxes in addition to income taxes.

Self-Employment Contributions Act (SECA) Federal legislation passed in 1954 that requires owners of small businesses such as S corporations and partnerships to pay the full premiums for Social Security and Medicare. SECA taxes are calculated as a percentage of net income from self-employment, and half the SECA payment is deductible in calculating federal income taxes.

self-employment income Gross earnings from a trade or business, minus allowable business deductions and depreciation.

self-employment retirement plan —See KEOGH PLAN.

self-employment tax Social Security and Medicare tax required of self-employed persons. Unlike employees of a business, who share this tax with their employer, self-employed persons must pay the full amount of the tax. Two deductions result from the Social Security tax: half the tax can be used to reduce net earnings; also, half the tax can be used as a deduction on IRS Form 1040. —See also SELF-EMPLOYMENT CONTRIBUTIONS ACT.

self-insure To assume the risk of a loss by setting aside money in a reserve fund rather than paying premiums to transfer the risk to an insurance company. For example, the owner of an older vehicle may decide to self-insure against potential damage to the vehicle that would normally be covered by collision or comprehensive insurance.

self-proving will A will that is accepted by the probate court as valid without requiring evidence, including the testimony of witnesses to the will. Requirements for a self-proving will are subject to state law. For example, some states require that witnesses sign an affidavit in the presence of a notary public.

self-regulatory organization (SRO) A member-operated organization that establishes and enforces minimum standards and rules of conduct. The National Association of Securities Dealers is an example of a self-regulatory organization.

self-tender An offer by a firm to repurchase some of its own securities from stockholders, generally on a pro rata basis from those shares offered for sale. A self-tender may be preferable to purchasing the securities in the open market, because a self-tender is quicker and will not disrupt public trading in the securities. A self-tender is similar to a buyback, except that buybacks often refer to repurchases from special groups or a few large holders. —Also called *stock repurchase plan.*

sell To dispose of an asset. —Compare BUY².

seller financing An agreement in which the current owner of an asset provides all or part of the financing for its sale. Seller financing is generally used as an inducement to a buyer who finds borrowing through normal channels to be expensive or impossible. Seller financing can prove advantageous to a seller who has relatively poor investment alternatives for money received from the sale.

seller's market A market in which the demand for an asset swamps supply to the point that prices rise above the level that would have been expected under more usual circumstances. As an example, new vehicle models that catch the public fancy typically result in a seller's market, in which dealers can charge eager buyers more than the suggested retail price. —Compare BUYER'S MARKET.

selling agent or broker A person who sells something for someone else, generally in return for a commission based on a percentage of the sale price.

selling climax A period of very high volume and sharp downward movement in the stock market. A selling climax generally signals the end of a prolonged bear market. —Compare BUYING CLIMAX. —Also called *climax.*

selling concession —See CONCESSION 1.

selling, general, and administrative expenses (SG&A) Corporate overhead costs for a period, including expenses such as advertising, salaries, and rent. SG&A is found on a corporate income statement as a deduction from revenues in calculating operating income. —See also OPERATING EXPENSE.

selling group A group of investment bankers that assists a syndicate or an underwriter in the sale of a new security issue but is not responsible for any unsold securities.

selling panic A period of rapidly falling asset prices as investors and speculators attempt to liquidate investment positions without regard to price. Selling panics occur when individuals and institutions believe they must sell a particular type of asset at once, before prices fall further. —Compare BUYING PANIC.

selling short —See SHORT SALE 1.

sell-off A general decline in security prices. This term generally refers to a short- or intermediate-term decline rather than to an extended period of falling prices.

sell short against the box —See SHORT AGAINST THE BOX.

sell signal An indication provided by a technical tool, such as a chart of a stock's price, that the stock should be sold. For example, the fall of a stock below its upward trendline is often interpreted as a sell signal. —Compare BUY SIGNAL.

semiannual Twice per year. For example, bond interest is typically paid on a semiannual basis. —Also called *biannual.*

semimonthly Twice per month: *Many companies pay their employees semimonthly.*

semivariable cost An expense that has both a fixed component and a variable component such that the expense is directly related to sales, but not in the same proportion. For example, operation of a vehicle entails semivariable costs, with fuel as a variable expense and depreciation as a fixed expense. A firm's delivery van can be driven twice as much and help generate twice as much in sales revenue without operation of the vehicle costing the firm twice as much.

senior debt A class of debt that has priority with respect to interest and principal over other classes of debt and over all classes of equity by the same issuer. In the event of financial difficulties or liquidation of the borrower's assets, holders of senior debt will have a priority claim. Most loans from financial institutions and certain high-grade debt securities such as mortgage bonds are senior debt. Because senior debt has a relatively secure claim, it is less risky from the point of view of the lender and it pays a lower rate of interest compared with debt of the same issuer having a subordinate claim. —Compare JUNIOR DEBT.

seniority 1. The basis of an employment system in which a worker's status derives from his or her length of service. Some organizations use seniority to determine salary, layoffs, office location, job preference, promotions, and so forth. **2.** The condition or status of a security that has priority over other securities by the same issuer with respect to the payment of income (that is, interest or dividends) and repayment of principal. As an example, for the same issuer, bonds have seniority over preferred stock, and preferred stock has priority over common stock. —See also JUNIOR SECURITY.

sensitivity analysis A statistical technique in which inputs are changed one at a time or in combination while the effect upon a particular variable such as output, sales, or profits is observed. For example, price, packaging, and size are changed to determine the effect upon sales.

sensitivity training Instructional and self-help sessions in which individuals meet in small groups or one-on-one with a counselor to discuss how they feel about particular issues.

sentiment index A numerical guide to investor feeling toward the securities markets that is constructed to determine whether certain segments of the investment community are bullish or bearish. The index is used by technical analysts to determine whether stock should be bought or sold. Sentiment is evaluated by looking at a variety of measures, including the incidence of short sales by specialists, mutual fund cash positions, and the amount of margin debt. —Compare ADVISERS' SENTIMENT.

SEP —See SIMPLIFIED EMPLOYEE PENSION PLAN.

separate property The property that is entirely owned by one spouse, even in a community-property state. Separate property generally includes property received as an inheritance or as a gift, or property owned by one spouse before marriage.

separate return A tax return filed separately by each spouse, in which income and deductions attributable to that spouse are listed. Spouses may choose to file separate returns or to file a joint return combining incomes and deductions. —Compare JOINT RETURN.

Separate Trading of Registered Interest and Principal of Securities (STRIPS) Treasury securities that have had their coupons and principal repayments separated into what effectively become zero-coupon Treasury bonds. The components, issued in book-entry form, carry the full backing of the U.S. Treasury. Like other zero-coupon bonds, these securities are subject to wide price fluctuations. They also subject the owner to an annual federal income tax liability even though no direct interest is paid.

separation of service The conclusion of employment because of retirement, resignation, or termination by a worker with his or her employer.

sequential access Recovering and reading data or records in the order in which they are stored. Locating a song or some other data on a cassette tape is an example of sequential access, because the user must read through all the preceding data to reach the desired point on the tape.

serial bonds Bonds issued under a single indenture simultaneously with groups of the bonds scheduled to mature periodically. For example, a municipality may issue $40 million of bonds with $2 million scheduled to mature each year for 20 years. Many bond issues are a combination of serial bonds and term bonds.

serial correlation The relationship that one event has to a series of past events. In technical analysis, serial correlation is used to test whether various chart formations are useful in projecting a security's future price movements. —Also called *autocorrelation*.

Series EE savings bond A U.S. Treasury obligation that pays a fixed interest rate and is sold to investors in denominations as low as $50 at a 50% discount from face value. Series EE bonds issued between May 1997 and April 2005 earn a variable rate of interest at 90% of the average yield on five-year Treasury securities for the previous six months. Series EE bonds issued after April 2005 earn a fixed rate of interest. Bonds may be redeemed after one year, but a three-month interest penalty is assessed for redemptions during the first five years. Federal income taxes on interest earned may be paid each year or may be deferred until the savings bond is redeemed. Interest earned on savings bonds is exempt from state and local taxation. —See also PATRIOT BOND.

Series HH savings bond A U.S. Treasury obligation issued in multiples of $500 that pays interest every six months. The security has a maturity of ten years, but may be redeemed after being held six months. The U.S. Treasury discontinued issuing Series HH bonds in 2004.

Series I savings bond A nonnegotiable U.S. Treasury obligation that pays semiannual interest based on a combination of a fixed rate established by the Treasury and the semiannual inflation rate as measured by changes in the consumer price index. Series I bonds are issued at face value in amounts that range from $50 to $10,000. The bonds have a maturity of 30 years, but may be redeemed beginning one year after issuance. —See also TREASURY INFLATION-PROTECTED SECURITIES.

CASE STUDY Series I savings bonds are an easily accessible investment that provides the unusual combination of inflation protection with absolute safety of principal. The bonds are available at financial institutions or online in denominations as low as $25, and there are no purchase or redemption charges. They can be redeemed one year after purchase, although a three-month interest penalty is assessed when redemptions occur within five years of the purchase date. Redemptions after five years incur no penalty. I bonds earn a return that is a combination of a fixed rate plus the inflation rate. The fixed rate is announced each May and November and applies to all bonds issued during the six months beginning with the announcement date. This portion of earnings remains the same for the life of the bond. The inflation rate is announced each May and November, and is combined with the fixed rate to determine the earnings rate for each six-month period. Thus, the earnings rate for a Series I savings bond changes each six months. Earnings from Series I bonds can be postponed until redemption for federal tax purposes and are exempt from all state and local taxes. Overall, the Series I savings bond is a high-quality investment that offers a modest return protected against inflation.

Series 7 An examination required of potential registered representatives and designed to test the candidates' basic understanding of the securities industry. The multiple-choice test, developed by the New York Stock Exchange, is administered by the National Association of Securities Dealers. —Also called *General Securities Registered Representative Examination.*

service 1. Delivery of work by a person or group for the benefit of someone else. **2.** Assistance offered by a business to its customers. For example, an appliance dealer is known to offer excellent service to its customers.

service business A company that earns income by performing work or offering expertise to individuals and businesses. Vehicle repair, home health care, and financial planning are examples of service businesses.

service charge A fee, either a fixed amount or a percentage of a bill, charged to customers for a service. For example, a restaurant may levy a 15% service charge on the food and drink bill of parties with six or more customers. A utility may include a monthly service charge to cover meter reading and billing. A credit card company is likely to levy service charges for late payments or for exceeding the credit limit on an account.

Service Corps of Retired Executives (SCORE) A volunteer organization of active and retired businesspeople who offer assistance to individuals starting or operating small businesses. SCORE offers low-cost educational seminars and free one-on-one counseling sessions, either in person or via email. The organization has nearly 400 chapter offices and is headquartered in Washington, D.C.

service department The section of a manufacturing or retail business that provides assistance to the firm's customers. The service department of a manufacturer takes care of exchanging or repairing faulty products, responds to questions, and may follow up sales with a customer satisfaction survey. The service department of a retailer offers credit applications, accepts payments, places merchandise on layaway, and takes care of returns.

service economy The portion of an economy devoted to service activities such as financial services, education, sales, research, and entertainment. Technological improvements have allowed developed countries to transfer resources from agriculture and manufacturing to providing services.

service sector The part of the economy that includes individuals and businesses that produce services rather than goods. The service sector includes education, finance, communications, health care, utilities, wholesale and retail trade, and transportation. In the mid-1980s employment in the United States was evenly divided between service jobs and production jobs. The split has since changed, such that the service sector provides a significant majority of jobs in the United States.

servicing Taking care of the administrative tasks related to an outstanding loan, including sending notices, collecting payments, and handling defaults.

set aside¹ 1. Land withdrawn from agricultural production. **2.** Jobs or contracts that are reserved for bidding by minorities and minority-owned businesses.

set aside² To negate or overrule a previous court order.

setback Minimum horizontal distance between a structure and the property line or some other established boundary.

setoff 1. The amount by which a defendant claims an award should be reduced because of an offsetting claim by the defendant against the plaintiff. For example: A plaintiff has been awarded $100,000. The defendant does not dispute the award, but claims the plaintiff owes the defendant $25,000 from another transaction. Thus, the defendant claims to owe the plaintiff only $75,000. **2.** The amount by which a tax refund can be used to offset a government obligation. For example, Alabama legislation in 2004 permitted state courts to intercept state income tax refunds as setoffs to delinquent fine accounts in criminal and traffic cases.

settle 1. In law, to resolve a dispute between a plaintiff and a defendant. **2.** To pay an obligation. **3.** To finalize a securities transaction by transferring cash to the seller and the security to the buyer.

settlement 1. The transfer of the security (for the seller) or cash (for the buyer) in order to complete a security transaction. —See also DELAYED SETTLEMENT; EARLY SETTLEMENT. **2.** Distribution of estate assets to beneficiaries. **3.** Agreement between parties to a lawsuit. **4.** —See CLOSING 1.

settlement date 1. The date on which either cash (for a buyer) or a security (for a seller) must be in the hands of the broker in order to satisfy the conditions of a security transaction. —Compare TRADE DATE. —See also DELAYED SETTLEMENT. **2.** The date on which a real estate transaction is complete and ownership is handed over to the buyer.

settlement month The month in which delivery is to take place in a futures contract. Most futures positions are reversed (that is, long positions are sold and short positions are covered) before their respective settlement months.

settlement period The period between the trade date and the settlement date. The settlement period on most securities is three business days. The settlement period for options is one business day.

settlement price In futures trading, an official price established at the end of each trading day by using the range of closing prices for a particular contract. This price, similar to the closing price for stock, is used to determine margin requirements and the following day's price limits.

settlement sheet —See CLOSING STATEMENT.

settlor —See GRANTOR 2.

setup cost The expense of establishing a new procedure. For example, a vehicle manufacturer incurs substantial setup costs when switching a production line to a new model. Establishing a business on the Internet can entail substantial setup costs.

Seven-S framework A model for managing an organization based on the explicit factors of strategy, structure, and systems, and the human factors of shared values, skills, staff, and style. The framework was developed in the late-1970s by Tom Peters and Robert Waterman as consultants for McKinsey and Company.

severalty —See TENANCY IN SEVERALTY.

severance damages Payment for the loss of value to the remaining portion of a tract of land, the other portion of which has been condemned and taken for public use. The state condemns land for highway construction. Payment to the landowner would include the value of the land taken plus severance damages for repairs to the remaining property incurred by the landowner following construction of the highway.

severance pay Payment by an employer to an employee upon termination of employment. The amount of severance pay is often a function of an employee's annual income and length of service.

sexual harassment Verbal or physical conduct of a sexual nature when submission or rejection affects an individual's employment or work performance, or when such conduct creates an intimidating, hostile, or offensive work environment. The U.S. Equal Employment Opportunity Commission expects employers to communicate to employees that sexual harassment will not be tolerated.

SG&A —See SELLING, GENERAL, AND ADMINISTRATIVE EXPENSES.

SGL —See SPECULATIVE GRADE LIQUIDITY RATING.

shadow price The monetary value assigned to a good or service when the market price is unavailable or incomplete. For example, the shadow price of electricity takes into account environmental costs such as air and water pollution as well as direct production costs.

shakedown **1.** Extortion. Hoodlums telling a shop owner they will leave him alone for $100 per week is an example of a shakedown. **2.** A test operation to determine if something works as expected. For example, the manager invites friends and neighbors to a complimentary meal during a shakedown of a new restaurant.

shakeout A reduction in the number of firms that operate in a particular industry. An example of a shakeout is the decline in the number of commercial banks in the United States. Shakeouts often occur when an industry has experienced a period of rapid growth in demand followed by overexpansion by manufacturers. Large, diversified companies able to survive a weak business climate tend to benefit from shakeouts.

shakeup A sudden and major change in an organization: *After several quarters of losses, the firm's directors decided to undertake a shakeup and replace all of top management.*

sham Counterfeit. For example, deals arranged solely to skirt income taxes are generally considered by the courts to be sham transactions.

sham trust An abusive trust that lacks economic substance and serves no legitimate purpose. Income and expenses are assigned to the true owner, not the trust.

share 1. A single unit of a class of ownership in a corporation, represented by a stock certificate. 2. A single unit of ownership in a mutual fund. 3. A portion of something. For example, a business has 20% of the market for a particular product.; thus the firm's market share is 20%.

shared-appreciation mortgage An unusual real estate loan introduced in the early 1980s in which the lender offers a below-market interest rate in return for sharing a portion of any profits when the real estate is sold. Shared-appreciation mortgages are most popular when rates on mortgage loans are high.

shared-equity mortgage A home loan in which the lender provides a portion of the down payment in return for partial ownership of the home. Proceeds from a sale of the home are shared proportionally to ownership between the borrower and lender.

shareholder —See STOCKHOLDER.

shareholder derivative suit A special type of class action lawsuit filed by one shareholder or by a limited number of shareholders on behalf of all the other shareholders in a firm. An example is a suit filed against a mutual fund's management in which the litigants claim excessive management and distribution fees.

shareholder of record —See HOLDER OF RECORD.

shareholder rights plan —See POISON PILL.

shareholders' equity —See OWNERS' EQUITY.

share repurchase plan A corporation's plan for buying back a predetermined number of its own shares in the open market. Institution of a share repurchase plan derives from management's view that the company has limited outside investment opportunities and that its shares are undervalued. Repurchase of the shares will decrease the amount of outstanding capital stock, increase earnings per share, and, it is hoped, result in an increase in the price of the stock.

shares authorized —See AUTHORIZED CAPITAL STOCK.

shares outstanding —See OUTSTANDING CAPITAL STOCK.

shark An investor or firm that is hostile to the target firm's management and that is interested in taking over the firm.

shark repellent A strategy used by corporations to ward off unwanted takeovers. Examples of this antitakeover measure include making a major acquisition, issuing new shares of stock or securities convertible into stock, and staggering the election of directors. Shark repellents often benefit corporate officers more than the stockholders. —Also called *takeover defense.* —See also POISON PILL.

shelf offering A new security issue that is part of a larger issue that has been registered with the Securities and Exchange Commission. Companies are permitted to sell securities that are part of a shelf offering for up to two years without reregistering the issue with the SEC.

shelf registration A simplified method of registering securities that permits corporations to file a relatively uncomplicated registration form with the SEC and, during the next two years, issue the securities. Shelf registration is supposed to provide more flexibility for corporations when they are raising funds in the capital markets.

shelf talker A sign or card attached to a shelf in a retail store that calls shoppers' attention to the nearby shelved product. For example, a card with "new" in bright red letters might be used to identify a new product.

shelf talker

Has any research been done to indicate the effectiveness of shelf talkers? If effective, this seems an inexpensive method for spurring sales.

Research shows shelf talkers are the most powerful influence on increasing a product's sales once it is on the shelf. The power of shelf talkers is so great that major retailers generally restrict them to major brands such as Kraft, Procter & Gamble, Coca-Cola, and Johnson & Johnson, and to themselves. Smaller companies can work through this challenge by providing in-shelf, clip-strip, power-wings/end-panel, and floor displays. Target prohibits all of these to maintain its cool, uncluttered image. Wal-Mart permits displays but carefully restricts shelf talkers. Grocery, drug, and dollar chains provide the best opportunities for smaller companies to put in displays and shelf talkers.

■ Deaver Brown, Publisher, Simplysoftwarecd.com, Lincoln, MA

shell corporation A corporation that has no active business operations and few or no assets. Shell corporations are often formed to acquire the assets of an existing corporation. They are sometimes formed to avoid taxes or liability. —See also BLANK-CHECK COMPANY.

shelter¹ —See TAX SHELTER.

shelter² To protect one's income from taxation. Some taxpayers shelter their income by investing in such activities as oil drilling ventures.

Sherman Antitrust Act An 1890 federal antitrust law intended to control or prohibit monopolies by forbidding certain practices that restrain competition. In the early 1900s, the U.S. Supreme Court ruled that the act applied only to unreasonable restraints of trade, and thus could be used only against blatant cases of monopoly.

shift A work period: *New employees were assigned to the late shift, beginning at 10:00 p.m.*

shift differential Additional pay offered by employers to convince employees to choose shift work. For example, a company offers an additional 50¢ per hour to employees who work evenings.

shift work A work period other than the normal period of 8:00 a.m. to 5:00 p.m. For example, applicants for employment at a telecommunications company that must provide 24-hour service to its customers are offered shift work.

shipper A person or company whose name appears on a bill of lading as tendering a shipment. —Also called *consignor*.

shop¹ **1.** A dealership in securities. **2.** A small retail store such as a barber shop or butcher shop. **3.** A small workplace for building, repairing, or manufacturing. **4.** —See UNION SHOP.

shop² **1.** To offer something for sale: *The real estate firm learned its neighbor had decided to shop his business.* **2.** To examine goods or services at different establishments: *The owner of the delivery service needed to shop for a new van.*

shopping center —See MALL.

shopping product A consumer product on which someone will spend considerable time and effort gathering relevant information about price, quality, resale value, etc., before making a decision to buy. Diamonds, cars, and high-end bicycles are examples of shopping products.

shop steward A union member who is elected by other union employees to handle their complaints and represent their interests.

short 1. —See SHORT POSITION 1. **2.** —See SHORT POSITION 2. **3.** —See SHORT SALE 1.

short against the box To sell an owned security short, usually in order to carry a profit on the security into the next tax year. Delivery may be made by using the owned shares or by purchasing new shares in the market. The Taxpayer Relief Act of 1997 largely eliminated shorting against the box as a means to defer a gain into a future year. —Also called *sell short against the box.*

short bond A debt security with a short period remaining until maturity. —Compare LONG BOND. —Also called *short coupon.*

short coupon 1. —See SHORT BOND. **2.** The first interest payment on a newly issued bond that includes less than the usual six months' worth of interest. For example, a bond issued on February 1 with interest payment dates of June 1 and December 1 would make an initial interest payment equal to four months' interest.

short cover To purchase a security that has previously been sold short in order to close out the position. Although short covering may occur at any time, the term is often used in reference to the actions of investors with short positions who repurchase stock in strongly rising markets in order to cut their losses or protect their profits. This procedure produces even more strength in the market. —Also called *cover.* —See also SHORT SQUEEZE.

shortfall An amount that is less than anticipated. For example, a shortfall in the payment of receivables may cause a firm to secure a loan from the bank.

short form An abbreviated document. For example, the federal government and various state governments offer numerous short forms for qualified businesses and individuals to use in reporting income. Many legal documents are also available in short form.

short hedge An investment transaction that is intended to provide protection against a decline in the value of an asset. For example, an investor who holds shares of Nextel and expects the stock to decline may enter into a short hedge by purchasing a put option on Nextel stock. If Nextel does subsequently decline, the value of the put option should increase and offset the decline in the stock.

short interest The number of shares of a particular stock that have been sold but have not yet been repurchased. Many analysts consider a large short position in a given stock bullish, because it represents future demand for the security as purchases are made to replace borrowed certificates.

short position 1. A net investment position in a security in which the security has been borrowed and sold but not yet replaced. Essentially, it is a short sale that has not been covered. —Compare LONG POSITION 1. —Also called *short.* **2.** An investment position in which the investor either has written an option or has sold a commodity contract, with the obligation remaining outstanding. —Also called *short.*

short rate The higher cost paid by an advertiser who fails to utilize the contracted space or time that qualifies for a reduced advertising rate.

short run A period of time during which businesses can increase production with existing capacity, but not increase capacity. For example, an automobile manufacturer can increase production in its current facilities, but does not have adequate time to add new facilities.

short sale **1.** The sale of a security that must be borrowed to make delivery. Short sales usually, but not always, entail the sale of securities that are not owned by the seller, who anticipates profiting from a decline in the price of the securities. —Also called *selling short; short.* —See also GHOST STOCK; SHORT AGAINST THE BOX; SHORT COVER. **2.** The sale of real property when the outstanding mortgage exceeds proceeds from the sale. For example, a family buys a $250,000 home that is financed with a loan of equal amount (no money down). A year later the home is sold for $225,000 when the outstanding balance on the mortgage is $248,000. —See also DEBT-DISCHARGE INCOME.

short squeeze The pressure on short sellers to cover their positions if prices increase sharply or there is difficulty in borrowing the security the sellers are short. The rush to cover produces additional upward pressure on the price of the stock, which then causes an even greater squeeze. —Also called *squeezing the shorts.*

short-term **1.** Of or relating to a gain or loss on the value of an asset that has been held less than a specified period. For individual tax purposes, an asset held for a year or less is classified as short-term. —Compare LONG-TERM 1. —See also HOLDING PERIOD. **2.** Of or relating to a debt security in which a short time remains until the face value is paid to the investor. Exactly what constitutes short-term is subjective, although five years and under may be considered the norm. **3.** Of or relating to business assets that are expected to be converted to cash within one year, and to business liabilities that are due within one year.

short-term capital gain/loss —See SHORT-TERM 1.

short-term debt Debt of a business or other entity that is due to be paid within one year. Short-term debt is a component of current liabilities on a firm's balance sheet.

short-term discount notes The promissory notes issued by municipalities at a discount from face value. Essentially, short-term discount notes are a form of tax-exempt commercial paper.

short-term municipal bond fund —See TAX-EXEMPT MONEY MARKET FUND.

short weight Describing a product, package, or shipment with a weight less than stated. The Customs Department of the Government of Hong Kong in 2007 fined seafood stall owners from $680 to $3,000 for supplying crabs of short weight.

shrinkage The loss of inventory encountered in the regular course of business. For example, a firm engaged in transporting grain can expect to lose part of its product to weather, careless handling, and various other factors. A retailer may lose inventory to theft by customers and employees. —Also called *leakage.*

shrinking asset —See WASTING ASSET.

shrinkwrap A thin plastic that manufacturers use to wrap their products. Heat is used to shrink the plastic for a tight fit. Shrinkwrap is used to combine two or more products in a single unit and to seal a product so that it cannot be opened prior to purchase.

shutdown **1.** The closing of an organization or an end to its doing business: *A major budget disagreement in late 1995 between President Clinton and a Republican Congress resulted in a government shutdown.* **2.** A halt in production: *Lack of inventory resulted in a shutdown of the company's production line.*

shyster A disreputable person, generally in the practice of politics or law.

shrinkage

I am concerned about increased shrinkage at my retail business. Can you suggest some easy-to-implement methods to address this problem?

Unfortunately, you must view both employees and customers as sources of shrinkage and remove as much temptation as possible from both groups. Customers should know that store employees are aware of their presence, and employees should be able to see all parts of the store. This may require some rearrangement of your space to provide sight lines from the cash register or mirrors when direct observation is not possible. Keep small, valuable items under lock and key. Establish a reputation for prosecuting shoplifters.

There are ways you can reduce employee theft as well. Try to be sure that there are at least two employees present at all times. Know how many keys you have and who has them. Be sure that everyone enters and exits the store through one door (preferably at the front). Examine all parcels leaving the store, including packages being carried out by employees— including managers—and garbage. Reward honesty in employees, share shrinkage data and reward reduction in losses, and provide a generous staff discount.

■ Phyllis G. Holland, PhD, Professor and Head, Department of Management, Langdale College of Business, Valdosta State University, Valdosta, GA

SIC —See STANDARD INDUSTRIAL CLASSIFICATION SYSTEM.

sick pay Payments by an employer to an employee who is unable to work because of illness. Most states do not require employers to offer a sick-leave benefit, although many employers do so voluntarily. Sick pay is considered taxable income to the employee.

sideline —See ON THE SIDELINES.

sideways market —See FLAT MARKET.

sight draft A draft that is payable on demand. —Compare TIME DRAFT.

signal To provide information. For example, an unexpected dividend increase may signal investors that a firm's directors are more optimistic about future profits than previously thought.

signature guarantee A written guarantee by a financial institution (nearly always a commercial bank or stock exchange member firm) that a particular signature is valid. A signature guarantee is often required on a certificate or other official document to be mailed.

signing bonus Money offered to a new employee, or an employee whose contract is expiring, as an incentive to join, or remain, with the organization. Many signing bonuses are paid in a lump sum on hire, while others are split, with part paid upfront and the remainder paid after a specified period. Signing bonuses are attractive to employers that do not wish to commit to a high salary.

silent partner A member of a partnership who does not take active part in management and who is not publicly recognized as a partner.

Silicon Valley The region in California south of San Francisco where there is a heavy concentration of companies involved in computers, software design, the Internet, and other high-technology endeavors. The name derives from silicon, a common material used in the manufacture of computer chips.

SILO —See SALE-IN, LEASE OUT.

silver parachute An agreement for employee severance benefits in the event control of the firm changes hands. A silver parachute is less lucrative and is extended to more employees than is a golden parachute.

silver standard A monetary system in which the basic currency unit is defined in terms of a specific quantity of silver and money convertible into silver. As with the gold standard, the silver standard takes monetary policy out of the hands of government officials, who are often prone to pursue inflationary policies.

simple interest The interest that is paid on an initial investment only. Simple interest is calculated by multiplying the investment principal times the annual rate of interest times the number of years involved. —Compare COMPOUND INTEREST.

SIMPLE IRA A savings incentive match plan for employees of small businesses with 100 or fewer employees. The plan is similar to, but more flexible than, a regular IRA. Employees enter into a qualified salary reduction agreement to contribute a percentage of their annual compensation to a tax-deferred retirement account. The employer may either match employee contributions or contribute a fixed percentage of all employees' pay. All earnings grow tax-deferred. SIMPLE is an acronym for Savings Incentive Match PLan for Employees of small employers.

simple linear regression An expression of the value of one variable (the dependent variable) as a function of another variable (the independent variable). For example, the wholesale price of gasoline might be expressed as $1.00 + 0.05(oil price per barrel).

simple trust A trust in which the trustee is required to distribute all income currently. A simple trust is not permitted to make charitable gifts or receive a charitable gift deduction. —Compare COMPLEX TRUST.

simplified employee pension plan (SEP) A special type of joint Keogh plan–individual retirement account that is created for employees by employers and that permits contributions from each party. The SEP was developed to give small businesses a retirement plan that was easier to establish and administer than an ordinary pension plan.

simulation A mathematical exercise in which a model of a system is established, then the model's variables are altered to determine the effects on other variables. For example, a financial analyst might construct a model for predicting a stock's market price and then manipulate various determinants of the price, including earnings, interest rates, and the inflation rate, to determine how each of the changes affects the market price.

simultaneous survey —See COINCIDENTAL SURVEY.

single-entry bookkeeping A simplified accounting system that records transactions with a single entry rather than as a debit and credit. Single-entry bookkeeping does not track assets and liabilities, and makes it more difficult to detect errors. For example, an entry for purchasing supplies does not identify whether the purchase was made with cash or on credit.

single-family housing A residential dwelling designed for one family. Single-family housing includes detached homes, patio homes, townhouses, condominiums, and cooperatives.

single interest insurance Coverage for only one of several parties that have an insurable interest in a property. For example, a bank purchases single interest insurance to cover possible damage to a vehicle on which it has an outstanding loan. The policy provides coverage for the bank's interest, but not the borrower's interest in the vehicle.

single-life annuity A stream of regular retirement benefits during the lifetime of the recipient. No payments are made to a beneficiary at the death of the recipient. —Compare JOINT AND SURVIVOR ANNUITY.

single-premium deferred annuity A deferred annuity purchase having one lump-sum premium payment. Single-premium deferred annuities offer the tax benefit of increasing in value tax-free until distribution takes place. Thus, an investor could pay a large single premium, have the investment build up free of taxes for a period of years, and then receive partially taxable annuity payments at retirement. A single-premium deferred annuity is more flexible than an individual retirement account, but unlike contributions by some individuals to an IRA, a premium to purchase a deferred annuity is not deductible for tax purposes. —Compare PERIODIC PURCHASE DEFERRED CONTRACT.

single-premium life insurance An insurance policy that requires a single upfront premium for paid-up coverage for the lifetime of the insured. This type life insurance is heavily weighted toward being an investment plan that provides tax-deferred accumulations.

single state municipal bond fund —See DOUBLE-EXEMPT FUND.

single stock future A contract in which opposite parties agree to buy and sell a stock at a set price on a certain date. Unlike a stock option, in which the owner of the option has a right to either buy (call) or sell (put), both parties in a single stock future contract have an obligation. —See also ONECHICAGO, LLC.

single taxpayer A person who, on the last day of the year, is unmarried or legally separated under a divorce or separate maintenance decree issued by the state, and who does not qualify for another filing status. The filing status on the last day of the year generally determines the filing status for the entire year. —Compare MARRIED TAXPAYER.

sinking fund The assets that are set aside for the redemption of stock, the retirement of debt, or the replacement of fixed assets.

sinking fund call An issuer's call of a portion of an outstanding bond issue to satisfy the issue's sinking fund requirement. A sinking fund call is generally at par value, with the bonds to be called determined by lot. Most bond issues provide investors with a period of protection between the date on which the issue is originally sold and the date on which the first sinking fund call takes place. —See also EXTRAORDINARY CALL; OPTIONAL CALL.

sinking fund provision A stipulation in many bond indentures that the borrower retire a certain proportion of the debt annually. The retirement may be effected by calling the bonds from the investors (if interest rates have declined) or by purchasing the bonds in the open market (if interest rates have increased). —Compare DOUBLING OPTION. —Also called *bond sinking fund.* —See also FUNNEL SINKING FUND.

sin stock Stock of a company that derives all or a significant portion of its revenues from socially questionable activities such as gambling, selling alcoholic beverages, or manufacturing and distributing tobacco products. Some organizations and investment companies avoid investing in sin stocks. For example, the foundation of a university may decide to avoid owning the stocks of any companies engaged in the manufacture and/or distribution of alcoholic beverages or tobacco products.

sin tax A government levy on goods or services considered by many citizens to be socially objectionable. Cigarettes and liquor are two favorite targets for the levying of a sin tax. Taxes on gambling and legalized prostitution would also be considered sin taxes. A government that wants additional revenues can try to make a case that additional sin taxes will reduce consumption of an objectionable good or service. Proponents claim people can always quit using the good or service if they want to avoid the tax.

SIPC —See SECURITIES INVESTOR PROTECTION CORPORATION.

sit-down strike An act of organized disobedience in which employees refuse to work and also refuse to leave their place of employment.

site **1.** A piece of property. **2.** Land on which some development is being undertaken.

site assessment The process by which the Environmental Protection Agency determines whether a tract of land has uncontrolled or abandoned hazardous waste and qualifies for cleanup using money from the Superfund trust fund.

SIV —See STRUCTURED INVESTMENT VEHICLE.

Six Sigma A process management system that uses statistical analysis to evaluate and enhance operational efficiency in order to improve product or service quality. Six Sigma was developed at Motorola in the mid-1980s and received widespread publicity in the late 1990s when it was utilized by Jack Welch at General Electric. —See also FIVE WHYS.

> **CASE STUDY** Six Sigma is a statistical methodology for implementing a strategy of quality improvement and waste reduction. The process was pioneered in the 1980s by Motorola to improve customer satisfaction through a reduction in manufacturing defects. The first stage of the process is to identify the factors that are the primary culprits in customer dissatisfaction. Each factor is then examined to determine an acceptable range of outcomes and identify opportunities for improvement. The Six Sigma methodology gained widespread exposure when Jack Welch embraced it at General Electric. Welch's assistants subsequently left GE and carried the methodology to their new firms. The Home Depot adopted Six Sigma in 2001 when Robert Nardelli arrived from GE to head the giant Atlanta-based home improvement company. Nardelli centralized operations and initiated a program of staffing cuts and improved productivity. Although sales and profits improved, the firm's stock price languished, and Nardelli was gone from Home Depot by early 2007. Some critics claim the Six Sigma system is designed for manufacturing and is not easily transferable to service companies.

size **1.** The market for a security in which a relatively large volume is being offered for sale or in which a large volume can be absorbed. Size in a security is more important for institutional investors than it is for individuals, because most individuals usually do not trade in sufficiently high volume to warrant concern about the size of the market. **2.** The number of units bid for and offered in the current quote.

sizzle In advertising, excitement as opposed to substance. For example, an advertising campaign for a new sports car promotes the thrill of driving rather than reliability and comfort.

---

slotting allowance

Slotting allowances seem to be another form of payola. Shouldn't they be illegal?

Major brands and opening price-point product lines rarely if ever have to pay slotting allowances, or slotting fees. In fact, in my more than 30 years of selling opening price-point brands, no retailer has ever asked me for slotting fees. Slotting fees are requested in two instances, both of which make economic sense for the retailer and supplier alike—if they elect to participate. The first is when a brand desires preferred positioning in the store, such as on an end-cap, where sales are over 500% greater than in line (along the aisle), or at the front counter, where sales can be 1,000% greater. The second instance is for marginal or new higher-priced products that are risky for the retailer to carry. In that instance a retailer sometimes will accept a slotting fee in exchange for placement. For these reasons, there are arguments for keeping slotting fees legal.

▪ Deaver Brown, Publisher, Simplysoftwarecd.com, Lincoln, MA

---

skim **1.** To confiscate money before it is counted or reported. In the simplest case, for example, a clerk skims a small amount of cash from a register. In a more elaborate scheme, a firm's controller skims substantial funds by falsifying bank deposit slips received from the organization's bookkeeper. **2.** Charging high prices for a short period while a product is unique and in large demand. The price is ultimately lowered when competing products are introduced. For example, car dealers charge more than the suggested retail price for a new model in great demand. After several years, the same model is offered at a discount when competitors introduce their own new products.

SKU —See STOCKKEEPING UNIT.

slack[1] Extra time to complete a project: *The project manager built slack into the schedule in the event complications were encountered with government approvals.*

slack[2] Of or describing a business environment with weak demand and unused business facilities: *January is a slack season for retail sales.*

slamming Switching a user's service without the person's consent. For example, many individuals discovered in the late 1990s and early 2000s that their long-distance telephone service had been changed without their knowledge or permission. To a lesser extent, consumers' electric service was the subject of slamming.

slander A false and malicious oral statement that harms a person's reputation. Some speech, such as that by public officials during official duties, may be protected from charges of slander. In general, a lawsuit based on slander must be initiated within a year of a slanderous statement. —See also LIBEL.

sleeping beauty A firm with valuable assets not effectively used by its management. Such a firm has high profit potential and value, and is therefore a prime candidate for takeover.

SLM Corporation —See SALLIE MAE.

SLOB —See SECURED LEASE OBLIGATION BOND.

slotting allowance A one-time payment by a manufacturer or vendor to a retailer in order to ensure shelf space in the retailer's store(s) or in its warehouses. Slotting allowances are controversial and play a major role in new product introductions.

slowdown **1.** A reduction in economic growth or an actual decline in economic activity. A slowdown is likely to result in the Federal Reserve lowering short-term interest rates in order to stimulate the economy. **2.** An intentional reduction in productivity

---

small business

My spouse and I are considering the purchase of a local business. What are some of the pitfalls of a husband and wife working together, and how can we prevent problems before they develop?

What has worked for my wife and me for the last 12 years is this:

1. Determine specific responsibilities for each person and stay out of each other's way. For example, I perform all of the accounting functions while Mona handles the database work. We share the account work, but we are aware of what projects each other is working on.

2. When someone lets a detail slip through the cracks, focus on fixing it instead of focusing on the mistake. Mistakes do happen, and if you let them bother you—like most of us did when working in office environments early in our careers—you cannot leave them behind.

3. Do your best to leave your work talk at the office. It is way too easy to fall into the habit of discussing business at all hours.

■ Tom Mesereau, Principal, Mesereau Public Relations, Parker, CO

---

by employees. For example, in 2000, pilots at United Airlines engaged in a slowdown that resulted in nearly 24,000 flight cancellations. The United pilots engaged in the slowdown in order to gain a better labor contract.

slump A decline in something: *Even a rising stock market can be expected to encounter an occasional slump when investors take profits and sell stocks.*

slush fund A pool of money available for distribution with little accountability required. For example, an office manager may have a slush fund for coffee and occasional employee gifts; or a corporation may maintain a secret slush fund used to bribe government officials.

small business An independently owned and operated business that is not dominant in its field. Qualifying as a small business depends on the industry in which the business operates and the organization that selects the standards. For example, a firm that qualifies as a small business in retailing is different from that of a firm in manufacturing. In general, a small business has from 100 to 500 employees.

Small Business Administration (SBA) An independent agency of the federal government that operates an extensive network of field offices dedicated to aiding and counseling small businesses. The SBA offers management assistance and help with financial and federal contract procurement. —See also CERTIFIED LENDERS PROGRAM.

Small Business Investment Company (SBIC) A privately owned and operated financial institution created to provide equity capital and long-term credit to qualified small businesses. The program was created by Congress in 1958 to assist small businesses in obtaining financing that was unavailable through normal channels. SBICs can qualify for government-backed long-term loans.

small business issuer An issuer of securities that has less than $25 million in annual revenues and outstanding publicly held stock worth no more than $25 million. Public offerings by small businesses are subject to special SEC registration rules.

small-cap **1.** Of or relating to the common stock of a relatively small firm having little equity and few shares of common stock outstanding. Small-cap stocks tend to be subject to large price fluctuations; therefore, the potential for short-term gains and losses is great. **2.** Of or relating to mutual funds that invest in the stock of small-cap companies. —See also MICROCAP 2.

small claims court A court with limited jurisdiction that handles civil claims for relatively small amounts of money. Trials are generally informal affairs in which the parties represent themselves and the judge has wide discretion over evidence that is permitted.

small claims division A division of the Federal Tax Court that hears cases involving disputed tax liabilities of $50,000 per year or less. A taxpayer can present his or her case and evidence alone or accompanied by a CPA, attorney, or enrolled agent. A loss by a taxpayer in small claims division cannot be appealed.

small investor A person who occasionally buys and sells securities, generally in relatively small amounts.

smart money The funds controlled by investors who should have special knowledge of the right kinds of investments to make. Essentially, the term refers to funds controlled by insiders or to institutional money. The implication is that if the individual investor can figure out where the smart money is going, he or she can follow suit and make above-average profits. Many researchers believe that smart money is no more likely to earn above-average returns than funds invested by typical investors.

smokestack industry A basic manufacturing industry, such as the automobile, rubber, and steel industries, that has limited growth potential, and earnings and revenues that vary cyclically with general economic activity.

snail mail Mail sent via the U.S. Postal Service, as opposed to email. Snail mail is slow (like a snail) and often takes days for delivery, compared to email messages, which are delivered almost instantaneously.

snowball To increase at an increasing rate: *Negative press reports about the firm's financial condition snowballed following the resignation of the chief executive officer.*

social investing The approach of limiting one's investment alternatives to securities of firms whose products or actions are considered socially acceptable. For example, an investment manager might decide to eliminate from consideration the securities of all firms engaged in the manufacture of tobacco or liquor products. —Also called *ethical investing.* —See also GREEN INVESTING.

socialism A political and economic system based on collective ownership of the means of production and distribution. Socialists claim that their system of government and worker ownership bases production on human needs rather than on the profit motive.

social responsibility Proceeding with an awareness that the actions of a person or organization affect others. For example, a company's management feels a social responsibility to offer affordable health insurance to its employees.

Social Security Act Federal legislation passed in 1935 that created a social insurance program funded through payroll taxes paid by employers and their employees. The legislation was initiated by President Franklin Roosevelt and passed during the Great Depression, when many Americans had lost most or all of their savings because of bank failures and a major stock market crash. The legislation created a pay-as-you-go program in which current employees pay taxes that are used to support current retirees. —See also INTEGRATED PENSION PLAN.

Social Security credits Credits toward retirement, survivor, and disability benefits that are secured by earning a prescribed amount of annual income subject to Social Security taxes. An individual can earn a maximum of 4 credits per year, with a minimum of 40 credits required to qualify for retirement benefits. Disability and survivor benefits may require fewer credits. Credits earned for Social Security also count toward Medicare eligibility at age 65.

Social Security disability income Benefits paid to a qualified disabled person and certain members of the disabled person's family. To qualify for benefits, a person must have worked in jobs covered by Social Security and must have a medical condition that meets Social Security's definition of disability. Benefits usually continue until a person is able to return to work on a regular basis.

Social Security tax The federal tax paid by employers and employees on employee earned income. The tax levied on current employers and employees is used to pay for retirement, survivor, and disability benefits of current recipients. The employer is responsible for withholding the tax from employee paychecks and forwarding the funds to the government. Self-employed individuals are responsible for paying both parts of the tax. —See also FEDERAL INSURANCE CONTRIBUTIONS ACT.

soft currency A national currency that has experienced a substantial depreciation in value relative to other currencies. The depreciation may result from inflation, a weak economy, or currency exchange restrictions. A soft currency may be difficult to convert into other currencies because individuals and governments are concerned its value will depreciate further. —Compare HARD CURRENCY. —Also called *soft money*.

soft dollars Payment for brokerage firm services that is provided by commissions generated from trades. Thus, an investor who does significant trading might be provided with "complimentary" subscriptions to market letters or an at-home quote system. Payment is disguised in the form of large commissions paid to the brokerage firm. —Compare HARD DOLLARS.

soft goods Textiles and clothing. In retailing, dry goods are distinguished from hardware, groceries, and appliances. —Compare HARD GOODS. —Also called *dry goods*.

soft landing A slowing of economic growth that avoids a recession and the accompanying high unemployment. The Federal Reserve may pursue a restrictive monetary policy to achieve a soft landing when the economy has been expanding at an unsustainable rate.

soft loan A loan in which favorable repayment terms have been granted to the borrower. For example, a loan may have a below-market rate of interest or an extended grace period. Soft loans are often offered to developing countries.

soft market A market for a good or service that exhibits little demand in comparison to the availability of products or services: *The significant increase in oil and gasoline prices is likely to result in a soft market for large vehicles.*

soft money 1. —See SOFT CURRENCY. **2.** Contributions given to political parties for purposes other than supporting specific candidates for office. For example, soft money can be used for party-building activities such as recruiting new members. In truth, it is often difficult to know where soft money is being spent. **3.** Research or project funding that is not expected to be recurring. For example, a university receives a grant to hire scientists for a research project.

soft second loan A second mortgage with payments that are forgiven, deferred, or subsidized in some fashion, generally until resale of the mortgaged property.

> **CASE STUDY** A program developed by Massachusetts state government and private partnerships uses soft second loans to increase affordable housing opportunities for low- and moderate-income first-time homebuyers.

> Funds obtained through the program can be used to secure financing from private-sector lenders that charge reduced closing costs and accept a modest down payment. The program works by breaking the total mortgage amount into a first mortgage and a subsidized interest-only second mortgage. Splitting the mortgage allows the borrower to avoid private mortgage insurance. The first mortgage can be for up to 77% of the purchase price, while the second mortgage and down payment make up the remaining 20% and 3%, respectively. The subsidy for the second mortgage is gradually phased out over ten years, after which the borrower begins making payments on the total principal and interest. The borrower is responsible for repaying the subsidy if the home is resold within five years of its purchase. Repayment is limited to the lesser of the subsidy or 20% of the net appreciation if the borrower lives in the home for five years or longer.

soft spot An area of weakness: *The firm's soft spot was its inability to develop a technologically superior product that would command a higher price.*

sole proprietorship —See PROPRIETORSHIP.

solvent 1. Able to meet debts or discharge liabilities. —Compare INSOLVENT. **2.** Describing the situation of having assets in excess of liabilities.

sources and uses of funds statement —See STATEMENT OF CASH FLOWS.

sovereign debt A financial liability of a national government. U.S. Treasury bonds are an example of sovereign debt.

sovereign immunity The principle that a government (sovereign) or governmental entity is immune from private lawsuits unless it gives consent.

sovereign risk The risk of owning the security of an issuer in a country other than the one in which the investor lives. For example, an investor residing in the United States incurs sovereign risk in purchasing a bond issued by the government of Brazil. This risk stems from the fact that a foreign country may nationalize its private businesses, stop paying interest, or repudiate its debt.

sovereign-wealth fund Investment assets held by a sovereign entity in another sovereign's currency. A sovereign-wealth fund results when a country runs current account surpluses and accumulates more reserves than are required for ordinary needs. For example, China announced in May 2007 that it would invest $3 billion of its foreign exchange reserves in the private-equity firm Blackstone. Later the same year, Abu Dhabi invested $7.5 billion for a 5% stake in Citibank. Some individuals have expressed concern that sovereign-wealth funds may invest for political as well as financial motives.

spam Unsolicited and unwanted email.

span of control The number of subordinates a manager is expected to supervise. A wide span of control reduces expenses, but requires more management skill and may reduce effective feedback.

SPDR —See STANDARD & POOR'S DEPOSITARY RECEIPT.

SPE —See SPECIAL PURPOSE ENTITY.

spec house A house constructed on speculation that a buyer will be located. —See also SPECULATIVE BUILDING.

span of control

Is there a rule of thumb that addresses the number of subordinates a manager can effectively control?

While it is theoretically possible to determine an appropriate span of control, there are many factors that determine the number of subordinates a manager can supervise. Some of these factors are the type of work being supervised (when jobs are easy to learn and/or self-directed, the span of control can increase), the characteristics of the manager (how comfortable the manager is with delegation and the manager's abilities), the manager's job (the time available for supervising others), and the characteristics of subordinates (how well-trained they are and how comfortable they are with decision making). Organization culture may also dictate closer supervision or more delegation. An organization that has rules and procedures carefully defined may tolerate a larger span of control than one in the same industry with less reliance on routines. Large spans of control yield organizations with few levels of hierarchy, while small spans of control yield many levels of middle and upper management.

■ Phyllis G. Holland, PhD, Professor and Head, Department of Management,
Langdale College of Business, Valdosta State University, Valdosta, GA

---

special agent **1.** An Internal Revenue Service employee who combines accounting and law enforcement skills to investigate financial crimes. **2.** A person who has been granted limited authority by someone else to undertake a specific task.

special assessment A charge levied against specific parcels of real property with proceeds used to defray all or a portion of the cost of improvements that will benefit the property. For example, a special assessment by a homeowners' association raises funds to pay for new sidewalks.

special assessment bond A municipal bond with debt service limited to revenues from assessments against those who directly benefit from the project the funds have been used to finance. This type of bond is more risky than a general obligation bond of the same issuer if it is not also secured by a full-faith-and-credit pledge.

special call —See EXTRAORDINARY CALL.

special cash account —See CASH ACCOUNT.

special dividend —See EXTRA DIVIDEND.

Special Drawing Rights (SDR) Reserve assets created by the International Monetary Fund in 1969 and allocated to member countries to use as a supplement to gold and convertible currencies in settling international accounts. The value of an SDR is based on a basket of international currencies.

specialist A member of a securities exchange who is a market maker in one or more securities listed on the exchange. The specialist is the person on the exchange floor to whom other members go when they wish to transact or leave an order. Specialists are assigned securities by the exchange and are expected to maintain a fair and orderly market in them. —Also called *assigned dealer.* —See also BOOK¹ 1.

specialist's book —See BOOK¹ 1.

specialist unit A group of people or firms acting together to maintain an orderly market in securities assigned by an exchange. Specialist units may act as agent or as principal in executing trades on the floor of the exchange. —Also called *unit.*

special multiperil policy Commercial insurance coverage that incorporates several forms and endorsements into a single policy. A special multiperil policy typically offers coverage for buildings, contents, liability for bodily injury and property damage, and medical payments to others.

special power of appointment The legal authority granted to a person to distribute the grantor's property to a specified group. For example, a person may grant to her attorney a special power of appointment to distribute her household and personal items, but only to her children. —Compare GENERAL POWER OF APPOINTMENT. —Also called *power of appointment.*

special-purpose acquisition company —See BLANK-CHECK COMPANY.

special purpose entity (SPE) A semi-independent business organization formed to carry out a specific function. For example, a company might form an SPE to purchase some of the firm's assets. The SPE uses the assets as collateral for a loan, with proceeds going to pay the company for the purchased assets. The assets and corresponding debt become balance sheet entries of the SPE, not the corporation. Companies that wish to eliminate troublesome assets and/or debts from their financial statements sometimes abuse the use of special purpose entities.

special-purpose fund —See SECTOR FUND.

special situation A currently undervalued stock that can suddenly increase in value because of imminently favorable circumstances. For example, a firm may be about to bring a new, potentially profitable product to market. If everything turns out favorably, the gains in the firm's stock could be quite large. Another special situation might derive from the impending liquidation of a company. Special situations are usually quite risky, but offer the possibility of big gains in value.

special tax bond A municipal bond with debt service limited to the revenues generated by a special tax. A bond issue to finance a convention center with the interest and principal payments limited to taxes received from a levy on motel and restaurant sales is an example of a special tax bond. Certain special tax bonds are also secured by the full faith and credit of the issuer; they have the additional security of being general obligations.

specialty advertising Promotion by imprinting the name of a product or place of business on pens, key chains, calendars, coffee cups, caps, T-shirts, and other small items that are given to members of a target audience. Specialty advertising allows a company to place its logo, slogan, or name before a customer multiple times.

specialty fund —See SECTOR FUND.

specialty retailer A retail business with a narrow but deep product line likely to appeal to a selective group of buyers. For example, a bicycle shop offers bicycles at a wide range of prices and bicycle-related products difficult to find elsewhere.

special use permit Written government authorization to engage in specified activities that have the potential to result in undesirable impacts under existing laws. For example, an organization may be granted a special use permit for a parade or rally. Individuals are required to obtain a special use permit for commercial operations in the Florida Keys National Marine Sanctuary.

special warranty deed A deed that guarantees a title without claims or defects for the period the property has been owned by the seller. No warranties are offered for earlier periods.

specie Money such as gold and silver coins that have intrinsic value.

specific charge-off method An accounting procedure for deducting credit losses in which debts deemed wholly or partially worthless are charged off against income

special warranty deed

Why would a buyer of property accept a special warranty deed?

A special warranty deed means that the seller is responsible only for problems that he or she caused, and not for anything that occurred before the seller became the owner. This type of deed should not be a buyer's first choice and, if the buyer has bank financing, it may not be accepted by the lender. For example, if the seller had previously deeded the property to another party, had granted an undisclosed option to purchase, or had permitted a lien to be placed on the property, the seller could be in breach of the warranty of title. However, if the title is impaired because *someone else* forged a prior owner's signature, or sold the property in violation of a court order, the seller would not be liable because the seller did not personally cause the problem. If consenting to a special warranty deed is the only way a buyer can acquire the property, and a title insurance company agrees to fully insure the title, the buyer may purchase the property with a certain degree of comfort. Nevertheless, accepting a special warranty deed should be a choice of last resort.

■ Joan A. Koffman, Esq., Real Estate Attorney, Koffman & Dreyer, Newton, MA

reported in the same tax period. This method of accounting for uncollectible debts contrasts with accumulating a reserve for bad debts.

specific identification A method of inventory control in which each inventory item is identified for purposes of cost and sales. Specific identification is generally used on large, relatively valuable items such as vehicles or construction equipment that can have a major impact on a taxpayer's reported income. Individual investors often use specific identification when selling securities.

specific lien The lien of a secured creditor against a specific piece of property. Home mortgages and auto loans for which particular assets are pledged as collateral are examples of specific liens.

specific performance A legal remedy requiring a defendant to perform obligations stipulated in a valid contract or agreement.

specific tariff A customs duty assessed on a per unit basis rather than on market value. For example, a specific tariff on a particular type of grain might be established at 20¢ per pound. —Compare AD VALOREM TARIFF.

speculation The taking of above-average risks to achieve above-average returns, generally over a relatively short period. Speculation involves buying something on the basis of its potential selling price rather than on the basis of its actual value.

speculative Of or relating to an asset or a group of assets with uncertain returns. The greater the degree of uncertainty, the more speculative the asset.

speculative building Construction for which no buyer has been identified. A builder or construction company engaged in speculative building assumes the risk that a completed project will be difficult to sell at an acceptable price, in which case substantial financing charges may be incurred. —See also SPEC HOUSE.

Speculative Grade Liquidity rating (SGL) Assessment of a firm's ability to meet obligations coming due during the next 12 months. The SGL rating system was developed by Moody's Investors Service to provide guidance in regard to a company's liquidity risk and the possibility of default. Rating assignments range from SGL–1 (very good) to SGL–4 (weak).

speculative risk A risk for which it is not possible to determine if the result will be a loss or gain. Playing blackjack for money is an example of a speculative risk. Speculative risks are generally not insurable. —Compare PURE RISK.

speculator A person who is willing to take large risks and sacrifice the safety of principal in return for potentially large gains. Certain decisions regarding securities clearly characterize a speculator. For example, purchasing a very volatile stock in hopes of making half a point in profit is speculation, but buying a U.S. Treasury bond to hold for retirement is an investment. It must be added, however, that there is a large gray area in which speculation and investment are difficult to differentiate.

spending money —See POCKET MONEY.

spendthrift clause A trust or will provision that disallows claims against trust assets resulting from pledges by the beneficiary in anticipation of receipt of the assets. For example, a beneficiary borrows money using assets held by the trust as collateral that will be transferred to the lender.

spider 1. —See STANDARD & POOR'S DEPOSITARY RECEIPT. **2.** —See ROBOT 2.

spiff —See PUSH MONEY 1.

spike A sudden, short-term change in the price of something that just as suddenly returns close to its previous level. For example, a stock that has consistently traded in a $10- to $12-per-share range may suddenly move to a price of $14 and then return to $12. The sudden rise to the $14 price is a spike.

spillover —See EXTERNALITY.

spinning The allocating of shares of a hot initial offering by a securities firm to the personal account of a corporate executive in anticipation of gaining future business from the executive's firm.

spinoff The distribution to stockholders of the stock of a subsidiary held by a parent company. Usually the distribution is not taxable to the stockholders until the new shares have been sold. —Compare SPLITOFF. —See also PARTIAL SPINOFF.

> **CASE STUDY** On December 8, 2006, the directors of Duke Energy approved a spinoff to Duke Energy shareholders of all the shares of wholly owned subsidiary Spectra Energy. Spectra Energy represented all of the assets and liabilities of Duke Energy's natural gas business, including distribution, transmission, storage, and gathering. Shareholders of Duke Energy would receive 0.5 shares of Spectra Energy common stock for each share of Duke Energy common stock held. For example, the owner of 300 shares of Duke Energy would receive 150 shares of Spectra Energy. Following the spinoff, Duke shareholders could sell or retain the Spectra Energy shares they had received. They also had the option of retaining their Spectra Energy stock and disposing of their Duke Energy shares. The spinoff allowed investors to have a direct investment in the specific industry. Separate shares of stock would also allow Spectra Energy management more flexibility in raising capital for expansion and acquisitions. The spinoff was tax-free to Duke Energy shareholders.

spin off To distribute stock of a subsidiary to stockholders of the parent company. For example, directors of Union Pacific Corporation voted to spin off the firm's natural resource operations by distributing to Union Pacific stockholders shares of Union Pacific Resources.

splintered authority Shared control of the same decisions between two or more individuals or organizations. For example, decisions on the manufacture of a new fighter aircraft have to be approved both by the contractor and the air force.

split A proportionate increase in the number of shares of outstanding stock without a corresponding increase in assets or in funds available, as would be the case in a new stock offering or in an acquisition that uses stock as payment. Essentially, a firm splits its stock to reduce the market price and make the shares attractive to a larger pool of investors. A 4-for-1 split would result in an owner of 100 shares receiving 300 additional shares, or an after-split total of 4 shares for every 1 share owned before the split. —Compare REVERSE STOCK SPLIT. —Also called *stock split.*

split commission A sales fee divided between two or more people.

split dollar life insurance Cash value life insurance in which premiums and benefits are shared by two or more parties. For example, a business and one of its key employees purchase a $1 million policy on the employee's life, with premiums split equally between the business and the employee. At the employee's death, benefits are allocated between the two on an agreed-upon basis. Split dollar insurance is especially beneficial to younger employees, who may have difficulty affording the premiums required for a large policy.

split down —See REVERSE STOCK SPLIT.

split-fee option —See COMPOUND OPTION.

split funding The purchase of more than one financial product with the same payment. For example, some financial programs combine life insurance and a mutual fund in the same package, with each customer payment being split between the two.

split gift A gift from one partner in a marriage to someone outside the marriage when one-half of the gift is assumed by law to have been made by each spouse. A split gift permits the annual gift tax exclusion per recipient to effectively be doubled when the gift originates from a married couple.

splitoff An exchange of the stock of a subsidiary for a pro rata surrender of stock in the parent corporation. A splitoff is similar to a spinoff, but in the case of the splitoff, a smaller (or no) decline in the stock of the parent corporation should take place. —Compare SPINOFF.

split offering 1. The sale of a new bond issue that is composed of serial bonds and term bonds. Many municipal issues are sold as split offerings. 2. A security offering that consists of new and previously issued securities of the issuer. For example, a corporation may undertake an issue of common stock that is composed of new shares and shares being held as Treasury stock.

splitoff IPO —See EQUITY CARVE-OUT.

split rating A condition that occurs when a bond is rated differently by the rating agencies. For example, a bond is rated AA by one agency and A by another agency. A split rating may occur because one rating agency places a different emphasis on certain variables or because it views a particular item (such as a recent acquisition by the issuer) differently than the other rating agency.

split ratio The ratio by which the number of a firm's outstanding shares of stock are increased following a stock split. For example, a two-for-one split results in twice as many outstanding shares, with each share selling at half its presplit price. A higher split ratio results in a greater reduction in the price of the stock.

split-run Describing an advertising program in which different advertisements for the same product or service are used to determine their relative effectiveness. For example, a car manufacturer pays for two advertisements of equal size but with different copy to be run in the same magazine.

split shift A employee work schedule that includes two or more segments during each working day. For example, to handle peak customer activity during lunch and dinner, restaurant personnel often work split shifts. Similarly, university professors with night classes may work a split shift that involves teaching during mornings or afternoons and returning to work in the evening.

split up The distribution of all of a firm's assets, generally in the form of stock distributions, such that the firm ceases to exist.

split-up value The aggregate dollar value of a firm's various parts if they were to be sold separately. Many takeovers occur because of a difference between the stock market values and the split-up values of the target companies.

spokesperson 1. An individual whose job it is to speak to the media or public on behalf of a business or other organization. 2. A well-known individual who is paid to represent a product or organization. For example, baseball great Joe DiMaggio was a long-time spokesperson for Mr. Coffee.

sponsor 1. An institutional investor or a brokerage firm that has a position in a security and influences other investors to establish a position in that security. 2. An individual, business, or other organization that pays part or all of the expenses for a radio or television program. 3. An individual, business or other organization that takes responsibility for managing and/or financing an organized activity: *The bank served as a sponsor of the annual festival.* 4. The individual or entity that establishes or helps establish a mutual fund. 5. A general partner who organizes and promotes a limited partnership. 6. —See UNDERWRITER 1.

sponsored American Depositary Receipt An American Depositary Receipt in which the company whose shares are held in custody has direct involvement in issuance of the ADRs. The foreign company registers the receipts with the Securities and Exchange Commission and chooses a single depositary bank. Holders of sponsored ADRs have all the rights of common stockholders, including the right to receive reports, the right to vote, and the right to receive dividends. —Compare UNSPONSORED AMERICAN DEPOSITARY RECEIPT.

spot advertising Advertising in selected geographic markets as opposed to advertising on a national scale. For example, an advertising agency purchases radio promotions in small markets.

spot commodity A commodity that is available for immediate delivery.

spot market —See CASH MARKET.

spot month The nearest month in which a currently traded futures contract is due for delivery.

spot price —See CASH PRICE.

spot rate The price at which currency is trading in the cash market. A transaction at the spot rate requires delivery within two business days.

spot secondary distribution A secondary distribution by security holders not affiliated with the issuer such that the distribution does not require registration with the SEC.

spot zoning Rezoning a parcel of land for a use that is not compatible with the use and zoning of surrounding property. For example, a corner lot in a residential area may be rezoned as commercial to allow construction of a convenience store.

spousal IRA An individual retirement account in the name of a nonworking spouse. A spousal IRA may be funded by the working spouse up to a maximum amount established by law. There is also a limit on total combined annual contributions to the IRAs of the working and nonworking spouses.

spousal remainder trust An irrevocable trust that may be set up for any length of time in order to pass assets to a spouse. Between the time that the trust becomes effective and the time that the assets are passed, income earned by the trust is taxable to a named beneficiary at the beneficiary's tax rate.

spread 1. A position taken in two or more options or futures contracts to profit through a change in the relative price relationships. Purchasing an option to expire in October and selling an option on the same asset expiring three months earlier is one example of a spread. **2.** The difference in price between two futures contracts that are identical except for delivery date. **3.** The difference between a financial institution's lending rate and the cost of funds. **4.** The difference between the bid and ask prices for a particular security. A large spread often indicates inactive trading of the security. —Also called *bid-ask spread; markup.* **5.** —See UNDERWRITING SPREAD. **6.** The difference in yields between two fixed-income securities. —See also BASIS POINT.

spreading The establishment of a long position in an option and a short position in another option of the same class but with a different strike price or expiration date, or both. Spreading is supposed to achieve profit from a difference in relative price movements of two options of the same class.

spreading agreement A clause in a loan contract that provides additional collateral that can be claimed by the lender.

spread-load contractual plan A contractual plan for purchasing shares of a mutual fund in which sales charges are not concentrated in the first payment or in the first few payments made by the investor.

spread order An order to buy and to sell options of the same class but with different strike prices and/or expiration dates in which the customer specifies a spread between the option sold and the option purchased.

spreadsheet A worksheet on which financial data are laid out in rows and columns for comparative purposes. For example, a financial analyst might use a spreadsheet to determine how a firm's sales and profit margins have varied throughout a period of quarters or years. —Also called *worksheet.*

spread to Treasury The difference in yield between a fixed-income security and a Treasury security of similar maturity. Treasury securities are the standard by which all other fixed-income securities are measured.

springing convertible A convertible security that includes warrants to purchase additional shares of the issuer's common stock. Certain prescribed events, such as a hostile tender offer or the accumulation of a large block of stock by a single group, cause the exercise price of the warrants to drop or spring. This unusual security is issued primarily to deter a corporate takeover by making the takeover more expensive.

springing power of attorney A power of attorney that becomes effective upon a specific event, such as an illness or disability of the principal. The document may provide that a specific person, such as the principal's physician, will determine when the principal is unable to handle his or her own affairs.

sprinkling trust A family trust in which the trustee has the power to distribute income to the beneficiaries according to their individual needs rather than according to a specified formula.

squatter's rights —See ADVERSE POSSESSION.

squeeze 1. The use of coercion in an attempt to obtain money from someone. For example, a squeeze is put on a delinquent borrower who is told to make a payment or a report will be made to the credit bureau. **2.** A period of tight money when interest rates are high and loans are difficult to obtain.

squeeze-out The forcing of stockholders to sell their stock. Majority holders of a company's stock may attempt a squeeze-out of minority stockholders in order to take complete control of the firm.

> **CASE STUDY** In October 2001 the only three directors of a North Carolina business announced their intention to acquire all the firm's outstanding stock they did not already own for $8.00 per share in cash. At the time of the proposed buyout, the three directors owned 78% of outstanding shares, which had been trading in the $4.00 to $5.00 range. Although the majority of minority shareholders voted in favor of a merger that would result from the buyout, a dissident shareholder filed a class action lawsuit challenging the proposal. The shareholder claimed a breach of fiduciary duty on the part of the directors as a result of unfair dealing, unlawful coercion, and unfair price. A trial court dismissed the lawsuit in 2002, a decision upheld by an appeals court two years later. The dissident shareholder had been squeezed out of his ownership in the firm.

squeezing the shorts —See SHORT SQUEEZE.

SRO —See SELF-REGULATORY ORGANIZATION.

SSI —See SUPPLEMENTAL SECURITY INCOME.

stabilization The goal of government fiscal and monetary policy designed to temper business cycles. During a recession, for example, the Federal Reserve reduces short-term interest rates and Congress increases government spending. The opposite actions should be undertaken when the economy is growing at an unsustainable pace.

stabilization period The time elapsing between the offering of a security issue for sale and its final distribution, during which the underwriter enters the secondary market in order to stabilize the price of the security. The underwriter attempts to keep the secondary market price of the security from falling below the offering price. —See also PRICE STABILIZATION.

stabilize —See PEG 1.

staff 1. Individuals who have positions with an organization and hold a contract of employment. **2.** Employees assigned to assist a superior with an assigned task.

staff authority Authority to advise or counsel others with line authority. For example, a human resources director may advise department heads on job applicants. In certain circumstances, staff members are given additional authority within the particular functional area in which they operate.

stagflation An economic condition that is characterized by slow growth, rapidly rising consumer prices, and relatively high unemployment.

staggered maturities In an investor's portfolio, bonds with differing maturity dates. For example, an investor may accumulate a $250,000 portfolio of bonds such that $10,000 face value of bonds matures each year for 25 years.

staggered terms Membership terms for a firm's directors that expire in different years. A firm with 12 directors might have four-year terms, with 3 seats up for election each year. Staggered terms make it more difficult for a raider to gain control of a board.

staggering maturities —See LADDERING.

stagnation An extended period of slow economic growth accompanied by relatively high unemployment.

stake An ownership position in a business. For example, Warren Buffett's Berkshire Hathaway has acquired a substantial stake in many businesses.

stakeholder Any party that has an interest in an organization. Stakeholders of a company include stockholders, bondholders, customers, suppliers, employees, and so forth.

stake-out investment An investment that provides an initial stake in a company in anticipation of additional investments in the same firm.

stand-alone company An independent operating firm. For example, a large diversified firm may consider spinning off a subsidiary because, as a stand-alone company, the subsidiary would command a higher price-earnings ratio than the parent.

standard 1. A basis of reference against which other things or activities can be compared: *The firm established a standard for potential employees.* 2. The foundation of a monetary system. For example, gold was once the foundation of some monetary systems.

Standard & Poor's (S&P) A registered service mark for a service that furnishes financial and statistical data for use in computers to the specifications and/or orders of others. Standard & Poor's Corporation is an investment advisory service that publishes financial data. This subsidiary of McGraw-Hill also rates debt securities and distributes a series of widely followed stock indexes. Major publications include *The Outlook, Stock Reports, Industry Survey,* and *Stock Guide.*

Standard & Poor's Depositary Receipt (SPDR) An interest in a trust that holds shares of all stock in the S&P 500. Ownership of an SPDR allows an investor to track the entire market through a single investment. These receipts trade on the American Stock Exchange at about one-tenth the value of the S&P 500. —Also called *spider.*

Standard & Poor's 500 Stock Index (S&P 500) An inclusive index made up of 500 stock prices, including 400 industrials, 40 utilities, 20 transportation, and 40 financial issues. The index is constructed using market weights (stock price multiplied by shares outstanding) to provide a broad indicator of stock price movements.

Standard & Poor's 400 Stock Index (S&P 400) A broad-based index of 400 industrial stock prices weighted on the basis of market value (stock price multiplied by shares outstanding). It includes listed and over-the-counter stock but is heavily influenced by the stock of large corporations. The index is based on a value of 10 during the period 1941–43.

Standard & Poor's 100 Stock Index (S&P 100) A market-capitalization-weighted measure of 100 major, blue chip stocks representing diverse industry groups. It is best known by the ticker symbol OEX.

Standard & Poor's ratings Evaluations of credit quality and equity values by Standard & Poor's Corporation. Equity ratings are published as "stars," with five stars indicating a "strong buy" and one star indicating a "strong sell." Credit ratings indicate S&P's assessment of a borrower's ability to meet a specific financial obligation. —See also CREDIT RATING.

standard cost The estimated cost of manufacturing something. Standard cost is frequently used to calculate the cost of a firm's inventories.

standard deduction The minimum deduction from income allowed a taxpayer for calculating taxable income. Individuals with few itemized deductions elect the standard deduction in place of itemizing deductions. —Formerly called *zero bracket amount.*

standard deviation A statistical measure of the variability of a distribution. An analyst may wish to calculate the standard deviation of historical returns on a stock or a portfolio as a measure of the investment's riskiness. The higher the standard deviation of an investment's returns, the greater the relative riskiness in the amount of return. —See also RISK; VARIANCE 1.

standard industrial classification system (SIC) A classification of businesses and business units by type of economic activity. The system uses single-digit to four-digit classifications, depending on how narrowly the business unit is defined. There are 11 single-digit groupings and more than 1,000 four-digit groupings.

Standard Mail Mail that qualifies for a lower postage rate but requires a minimum of 200 pieces or 50 pounds per mailing. In addition, the sender is required to pay an annual fee in order to qualify for the lower rate. This class applies to mail that formerly qualified as third-class and fourth-class mail.

standard metropolitan statistical area —See METROPOLITAN STATISTICAL AREA.

standard mileage rate The deduction permitted by the IRS for the expense of operating a motor vehicle. A taxpayer can choose to use the standard mileage rate as opposed to maintaining a detailed record of expenses that are actually incurred. The IRS identifies three standard mileage rates depending on whether the vehicle is used for business purposes, charitable causes, or for medical or moving purposes. The standard mileage rate is based on an annual study of the fixed and variable costs of operating a motor vehicle.

standard of living The quality of life enjoyed by an individual, family, or group of people. Economists often view standard of living in terms of real income, or money income adjusted for the cost of living, plus additional adjustments for the effects of pollution, health, leisure time, and so forth.

standard opinion —See CLEAN OPINION.

standard score —See Z SCORE.

standard wage rate Basic remuneration per unit of time or output excluding overtime, bonuses, or benefits.

standby fee 1. The fee paid to an underwriter who agrees to purchase unsold securities as part of a standby underwriting agreement. **2.** —See COMMITMENT FEE.

standby loan commitment —See LOAN COMMITMENT.

standby underwriting Describing an agreement by underwriters to purchase the portion of a new securities issue that remains after the public offering. A standby underwriting agreement eliminates the issuer's risk of not selling the issue out, but it increases the investment bankers' risk.

standing order 1. Instructions to a vendor to supply specified goods or services at regular intervals up to a predetermined date or until receiving notice from the purchaser. 2. Instructions to a financial institution to pay fixed sums at regular intervals to a particular party.

standstill agreement A written agreement between two firms whereby the actions of one firm with respect to the other are limited until a specified date. For example, Firm A may sell Firm B a block of Firm A's stock with the stipulation that Firm B will acquire no additional shares in Firm A for five years.

stapled stock —See PAIRED SHARES.

stare decisis In law, to follow precedent and apply established principles in future cases where the facts are essentially the same.

start-up company A new business.

start-up costs Expenses that will be incurred before a new business is able to open its doors or start production and generate revenues. Start-up costs include fees, paying for a place to conduct business, acquiring equipment, living expenses while getting a business ready for operation, and so forth.

state bank A bank organized under a state, rather than a federal, charter.

stated capital —See LEGAL CAPITAL.

stated value A value assigned to common stock by the firm's management for purposes of financial statements. Stated value, used in place of par value, is calculated on a per-share basis by dividing the stated capital resulting from a new issue of common stock by the number of new shares issued. Stated value is unrelated to the stock's market price and is of little importance to the shareholders.

statement A written presentation, as of financial data. —See also ACCOUNT 2; FINANCIAL STATEMENT.

statement analysis An analysis of an organization's financial and operating condition through the use of financial statements. Statement analysis is used by financial analysts to determine the value of a firm's securities.

statement of affairs A financial statement of an organization's assets according to realizable values and liabilities according to priority of claim. A statement of affairs is prepared for organizations in or contemplating bankruptcy.

statement of cash flows A financial statement listing how a firm has obtained its funds and how it has spent them within a certain period. This statement, developed from the income statement and from changes in balance sheet entries between two dates, provides insights into the manner in which the firm's management raises and invests money. —Also called *application of funds statement; flow of funds statement; funds statement; sources and uses of funds statement.*

statement of financial condition —See BALANCE SHEET.

statement of financial position —See BALANCE SHEET.

statement of retained earnings A financial statement that lists a firm's accumulated retained earnings and net income that has been paid as dividends to stockholders in the current period. —Also called *retained earnings statement.*

state trading company A government-owned or -controlled enterprise that imports and/or exports goods and services. These organizations are typically formed to assist with exports that generate foreign exchange and stimulate domestic employment opportunities. They also centralize buying of imports.

static budget A budget based in a fixed set of assumptions. For example, the manufacturing division establishes a budget at the start of the fiscal period that cannot be altered, no matter what occurs with respect to prices, demand, or the economy. —Compare FLEXIBLE BUDGET.

statistic A number calculated from data representing a population. For example, the annual revenue of Microsoft is a statistic.

statistical inference Estimating the properties of an unknown distribution from a sample of that distribution. For example, an interview of 100 individuals who tried a new brand of frozen pizza indicated 60 would switch from their old brand to the new brand. Using statistical inference, the company decided it was worthwhile to move ahead with marketing the new brand.

statistically significant Of or relating to a result that is unlikely to be a consequence of chance: *Results of a 10-year trial for a new drug allowed researchers to show the decline in toe fungus by individuals taking the drug was statistically significant.*

statistical quality control The use of statistical techniques to analyze quality and identify the causes of quality variation. Statistical process control is utilized to ensure uniform results by calling attention to variations that are outside established parameters.

statistical sampling Selecting one or more representative units of a population in an effort to understand characteristics of the overall population. Statistical sampling is used to draw conclusions about a population without examining all of the items comprising the population: *The firm's auditors used statistical sampling to judge the accuracy of its accounts receivable.*

statistics The branch of mathematics that deals with the collection, organization, and evaluation of data. Statistics is useful to businesses that wish to evaluate the characteristics of various populations. For example, statistics might be used to determine what types of advertising are most effective in attracting the attention of wealthy retirees.

status symbol An asset or activity that influences the perception of a person's social status. For example, individuals often select a home or vehicle more as a status symbol than for its functionality.

statute A written law enacted under federal or state legislative authority. A statute may be perpetual or limited in duration.

statute of frauds State law requiring that certain instruments be in writing and signed. Designed to prevent fraud, a statute of frauds generally applies to leases, contracts to transfer real property, and wills.

statute of limitations The time limit established by law to enforce certain rights or to file lawsuits. For example, a taxpayer has three years from the filing date to collect a tax refund. A Colorado resident has two years to file a medical malpractice suit.

statutory audit A legally required examination of an organization's annual accounts and financial records.

statutory foreclosure A foreclosure without the need for judicial action. Statutory foreclosures are more expedient and less costly for a lender than judicial foreclosures. Many states allow the sale of property by a mortgage holder without supervision of the court. —Compare JUDICIAL FORECLOSURE.

statutory investment —See LEGAL INVESTMENT.

statutory merger A merger in which one of the merged organizations continues as a legal entity.

statutory notice Required notice of an intended action. For example, state law requires an employee be given a minimum period of notice of termination. Along other lines, following an audit, the Utah State Tax Commission sends the taxpayer a statutory notice unless full payment has been received after sending the preliminary notice. The statutory notice serves as a legal and binding assessment of the taxpayer's tax liability.

statutory voting —See MAJORITY VOTING.

stealth tax —See HIDDEN TAX.

steel-collar worker A robot that performs a job of a human.

steer 1. To direct potential home buyers or renters away from or toward particular neighborhoods based on race. **2.** To set a course by providing direction: *The new CEO had steered the company back to profitability.*

step-payment lease —See GRADUATED LEASE.

stepped coupon bond A bond with interest coupons that change to predetermined levels on specific dates. Thus, a stepped coupon bond might pay 4% interest for the first five years after issue and then step up the interest every fifth year until maturity. Issuers often have the right to call the bond at par on the date the interest rate is scheduled to change. —Also called *dual coupon bond; rising-coupon security; step-up coupon security.*

stepped-up basis An increase in the cost basis of an asset for tax purposes. For example, inherited property assumes a stepped-up basis if it increased in value subsequent to the date it was acquired by the deceased person. —Also called *basis.*

stepping in front —See FRONT RUNNING.

step-up A scheduled increase in the exercise or conversion price at which a warrant, an option, or a convertible security may be used to acquire shares of common stock. For example, a warrant may permit its owner to purchase ten shares of stock at $20 per share up to a specified date and at $22.50 per share thereafter until the warrant expires. The step-up works to the disadvantage of the holder, however. It is not a feature of most of these securities.

step-up coupon security —See STEPPED COUPON BOND.

sterile investment An investment vehicle that provides no current income. Examples of a sterile investment include a stock without a dividend, a bond that trades flat, or tangible assets such as gold, art, and baseball cards.

steward 1. A person who manages the resources of others: *She was an excellent steward of the foundation.* **2.** An employee who serves as elected representative of union members.

sticker price —See MANUFACTURER'S SUGGESTED RETAIL PRICE.

stiff To fail to pay or deliver something as scheduled: *The shop owner got stiffed by one of his customers who moved out of town.*

stipend A regular payment, generally for services rendered. For example, an employee required to move to a new location may receive a stipend to cover six months of living expenses.

stipulated fact A particular piece of information that has been agreed to by parties on opposite sides of a dispute.

stipulation 1. An agreement between the parties or attorneys engaged in a legal dispute. 2. A restriction to an agreement. For example, a person agrees to buy a used car, but only if the power steering is repaired.

stochastic Describing a variable or a system's output that is subject to chance or probability. In a stochastic system a change in one variable may have a less than predictable effect on another variable. For example, a company that is considering doubling spending on quality control will be uncertain of the extent to which quality will improve. —Compare DETERMINISTIC.

stock 1. An ownership share or ownership shares in a corporation. —See also BEARER STOCK; COMMON STOCK; PREFERRED STOCK; STOCK CLASS. 2. Merchandise on hand at a manufacturer, distributor, or retailer: *The clothing store had plenty of stock available for the big sale.*

stock appreciation right Executive compensation that permits an employee to receive cash or stock equal to the amount by which the firm's stock price exceeds a specified base price.

stock average —See AVERAGES.

stockbroker —See REGISTERED REPRESENTATIVE.

stock buyback —See BUYBACK.

stock certificate —See CERTIFICATE 1.

stock class 1. A category of capital stock issued by a company and having specific rights or characteristics. Most firms have only a single class of stock outstanding. Thus, every share has exactly the same rights as every other share. But some companies have two or more classes of capital stock, designated as class A, class B, and so forth. For example, one class may have controlling voting rights, but both classes may share equally in dividends. In general, a firm issues different classes of stock when it wishes to sell one class to the public and reserve another class for its founders. —Also called *class; classified stock; dual-class stock.* —See also COMMON STOCK. 2. A category of stock issued by a mutual fund. Funds sometimes issue multiple classes of stock. A fund, for example, may have one class of shares that carries a sales fee and another class of shares that has a contingent deferred sales fee and a 12b–1 fee, but no initial sales fee. Both classes of shares would be based on the same portfolio of securities.

> **CASE STUDY** In May 2007, Rupert Murdoch's News Corp. offered $5 billion—$60 per share—in an uninvited takeover attempt of financial publisher Dow Jones & Company. The offer represented a premium of 65% over the prior day's closing price of $36.33, although it was still substantially under the high price of $76.75 that had been reached in 2000. The large premium offered by News Corp. was necessitated by Dow Jones's equity capitalization, which included two stock classes. The firm's outstanding stock consisted of nearly 62 million shares of common stock plus 20 million shares of supervot-

ing class B stock. Owners of common stock could cast one vote per share, while class B shareholders, mostly members of the Bancroft family, enjoyed ten votes per share. Although family members held slightly less than 25% of all outstanding shares of Dow Jones, they controlled nearly 65% of voting power through their ownership of 82% of the supervoting class B shares. While a premium of 25% or 30% might have easily swayed shareholders of a company with only a single class of common stock, News Corp. was required to offer enough of a premium to convince family members to part with one of the country's last family-owned publishing empires.

stock company A company owned by stockholders, with the ownership evidenced by transferable certificates. —Compare MUTUAL COMPANY.

stock dividend A dividend made up of shares of the paying firm's stock. A stock dividend is often used in place of or in addition to a cash dividend if the firm wishes to conserve cash. Unlike a cash dividend, a stock dividend is usually not taxable to the shareholder when it is received, but rather when it is sold. Stockholders who are supposed to receive a fractional share will often receive a check for the amount equal to the market value of the fractional share. Payment of a stock dividend is indicated in stock transaction tables in newspapers by the symbols *b* and *t*. —See also SCRIP DIVIDEND.

stock exchange —See SECURITIES EXCHANGE.

stockholder An individual or organization that owns common stock or preferred stock in a corporation. —Also called *shareholder.*

stockholder derivative suit A lawsuit filed by one or more of a company's stockholders in the name of the company. A derivative suit is filed when the firm's management will not or cannot sue in the name of the company. For example, a stockholder may enter a derivative suit against the firm's chief executive officer to recover funds from a questionable or an improper act by that officer. —Also called *derivative suit.*

stockholder of record —See HOLDER OF RECORD.

stockholders' equity —See OWNERS' EQUITY.

stock index —See INDEX[1].

stock index future A contract for the future delivery of a sum of money based on the value of a stock index (in most cases, 500 times the index). Unlike other futures contracts, in which a given commodity is specified for delivery, stock index futures call for cash settlements, because it is not possible to deliver an actual index. This future can be used to speculate on the future direction of the stock market (rather than just a few stocks) or to hedge a portfolio of securities against general market movements.

stock index option A contract that gives its owner the right to buy (call option) or sell (put option) a stock index at a fixed value until a specified date. Options are traded on the S&P 500, the S&P 100, the NYSE Composite Index, and the Major Market Index, along with specialized indexes. These options work exactly like regular stock options, except that an index rather than a particular stock is the underlying asset. As with stock index futures, delivery must be in cash, because it is not possible to deliver an index.

stock insurance company An insurance company that is owned by shareholders who have invested in the firm by purchasing shares of its common stock. Stockholders of an insurance company may or may not also be policyholders. Stock insurance companies are able to tap the financial markets for capital, which gives them a financial advantage over mutual insurance companies. —Compare MUTUAL INSURANCE COMPANY.

stockkeeping unit (SKU) Code established by a merchant that identifies a specific unit of inventory. For example, a retailer assigns a SKU of B6698-6 to a brown, size 6 shoe of a particular style.

stock ledger —See STOCK REGISTER.

stock market The group of organizations, institutions, and individuals engaged in the systematic trading of financial securities for themselves and others.

stock option 1. An option to buy or sell a specific number of shares of stock at a fixed price until a specified date. —See also CALL[1] 1; CAPPED-STYLE OPTION; INCENTIVE STOCK OPTION; PUT[1] 1. 2. —See INCENTIVE STOCK OPTION.

stockout cost Revenue lost because a lack of inventory results in a firm being unable to fill all of its customer orders. For example, if an electronics store underestimates demand for a new laptop computer, it will lose customers to a store that has secured adequate stock. —See also SAFETY STOCK.

stock outstanding —See OUTSTANDING CAPITAL STOCK.

stockpile To acquire and store something for future use. For example, an automobile manufacturer stockpiles a part out of concern employees of the supplier will soon go on strike.

stock power A form, separate from a stock certificate, that can be used to transfer stock. A stock power is useful when an investor wishes to deliver an unsigned certificate in one envelope and the stock power form for transfer of the certificate in another envelope. —Compare BOND POWER.

stock purchase plan A program offered by a corporation that allows its employees to purchase shares of the firm's stock, often at a slight discount from market value. Some employers agree to match employee purchases up to a specified amount. Stock purchase plans are designed to promote employee loyalty by offering employees an ownership stake in the company for which they work. —See also DIRECT STOCK PURCHASE PLAN; EMPLOYEE STOCK OWNERSHIP PLAN.

stock rating The grading of a stock, generally with respect to its expected price performance or safety. A number of publications, such as *Value Line,* publish stock ratings regularly. Of the major ratings firms, only Standard & Poor's rates stocks. —Compare BOND RATING. —Also called *security rating.*

stock record An account of the securities being held by a brokerage firm.

stock register A record listing the issues, transfers, and retirements of a firm's stock. —Also called *stock ledger.*

stock repurchase plan 1. —See BUYBACK. 2. —See SELF-TENDER.

stock right —See RIGHT.

stock split —See SPLIT.

stock symbol The letter or sequence of letters used to identify a security. For example, on the consolidated tape, T is used for AT&T Corporation, CVG for Convergys Corporation, and XOM for ExxonMobil. Symbols are also used to identify securities on video display terminals.

stock turnover —See INVENTORY TURNOVER.

stock warrant —See WARRANT.

stop-and-go tactic The tax-reduction or -deferment technique in which income and deductions are moved from one year to another. This technique involves advancing deductions and delaying income. For example, an investor may wait to recognize stock gains by selling early in the next year.

stop order 1. An order to buy or to sell a security when the security's price reaches or passes a specified level. At that time the stop order becomes a market order, and the executing broker, usually the specialist, obtains the best possible price. A stop order to buy must be at a price above the current market price, and a stop order to sell must have a specified price below the current market price. 2. An order from the SEC suspending a registration statement when an omission or a misstatement has been found.

stop payment An instruction to a financial institution to not pay a check that has been issued but not yet presented for payment.

stop transfer An order to stop the transfer of ownership of a particular stock or bond certificate, a situation that generally occurs after an investor has notified a transfer agent that a certificate has been lost or stolen.

store An enterprise engaged in selling goods and services.

store brand A product that is manufactured and packaged for a particular store or retail chain. For example, grocery chains often sell store brands of soft drinks and canned vegetables at a price lower than similar products with well-known brand names. Even with a lower retail price, store brands often offer a higher profit margin to retailers. —Compare NATIONAL BRAND.

storekeepers burglary and robbery insurance A combination of several different burglary and robbery coverages in a single form that is designed for small retail stores. Coverage includes robbery of a guard, robbery inside and outside the premises, safe burglary, property damage as a result of burglary or robbery, burglary of merchandise, and theft from a messenger.

story bond A bond so unusual or having such complicated features that salespeople are frequently called on to explain its intricacies to customers. Story bonds sometimes offer slightly higher yields than ordinary bonds as a way of convincing investors that they are worth holding.

straddle 1. In futures, the purchase of a contract for delivery in one month and sale of a contract for delivery in a different month on the same commodity. 2. In options, the purchase or sale of both a call and a put, generally with the same strike price and expiration date. The buyer of a straddle benefits from large price fluctuations in the underlying asset, while the seller of a straddle, who collects the premiums, benefits from small price changes in the underlying asset.

straight bill of lading A nonnegotiable written receipt provided by a shipper for a consignment that must be delivered directly to the specified party.

straight debt Debt that does not include any features other than payment of interest and repayment of principal. For example, straight debt cannot have a feature that permits bondholders to convert the debt into shares of common stock. —See also CONVERTIBLE SECURITY.

straight life annuity An annuity that makes payments to the recipient only for the duration of his or her lifetime. No minimum number of payments and no minimum sum to be paid are guaranteed. All payments end upon the recipient's death. This annuity is desirable for someone with no dependents who wishes to obtain the largest possible payments.

straight-line depreciation A method of recording depreciation such that the original cost minus the estimated salvage value of an asset is written off in equal amounts during each period of the asset's life. For example, a machine costing $10,000 with an estimated life of five years and no salvage value would be depreciated $2,000 ($10,000/5) annually, using straight-line depreciation. If the machine had an estimated salvage value of $4,000, annual straight-line depreciation would amount to $1,200. —Compare ACCELERATED DEPRECIATION.

straight-line production A method of organizing production in which an unfinished product moves along a straight line from one assembly team to the next. Parts, tools, and equipment are staged along the line to improve efficiency and reduce the time required to manufacture and assemble the product.

straight-through processing The direct exchange of cash and securities. Straight-through processing is a major objective for cross-border transactions, which are generally much more costly to settle compared to domestic transactions.

straight time Regular work hours not subject to overtime or bonus pay.

strategic planning The process of making systematic decisions about proposed future outcomes. The process includes evaluating an organization and the environment in which it operates, establishing long-term goals, and mapping a plan to achieve the goals that have been identified. Strategic planning assumes and incorporates the likelihood of a changing environment that will require adjustments in the identified goals and the process of achieving them. —Compare LONG-RANGE PLANNING.

strategy A plan of action for achieving an objective.

stratified random sampling A sampling procedure in which a population is separated into subgroups (strata) and then samples are selected from each subgroup. Stratified random sampling is used when homogeneous subgroups can be identified within a heterogeneous population. For example, the population of a geographic area is separated into subgroups based on age.

straw man 1. A person who purchases an asset or undertakes some action for another person who wishes to remain anonymous. —Also called *front man.* **2.** A weak or misleading argument that is offered so that it can easily be disproved to make a point or win an argument.

street Short for the U.S. financial markets, especially those in New York City.

street name —Used to describe registration of a customer-owned security in the name of the brokerage firm holding the certificate. A security is held in street name to simplify trading because no delivery of or signature on the certificate is required, or because the certificate is being used as collateral in a margin account.

street price The normal price at which something could be purchased. For example, the list price of the laptop computer is $799, although the street price is about $100 less.

street smarts Practical wisdom that allows a person to be successful: *The business tycoon was a high school dropout, but he possessed street smarts.*

stretch IRA An individual retirement account in which the period of tax-deferred earnings within the IRA stretches beyond the lifetime of the person who set up the IRA. Stretch IRAs can result in huge accumulations and payouts, depending on the assumptions regarding the rate of return that will be earned and the length of time funds are to accumulate.

strike¹ The collective action of workers who refuse to perform their job duties. Strikes are generally associated with labor unions, taking place when members reach an impasse with an employer over wages, benefits, or a major job issue. —See also SYMPATHY STRIKE; WILDCAT STRIKE.

strike² To stamp a coin blank with a design.

strike benefits Pay and other assistance received by striking workers who have lost compensation from their employer. Strike benefits are generally considered taxable income. —Also called *strike pay.*

strikebreaker A worker hired by a company to replace someone on strike. —See also SCAB.

strike notice A document presented by a union to an employer or mediator indicating that employees will go on strike beginning at a specified time and date.

strike pay —See STRIKE BENEFITS.

strike price The exercise price at which the owner of a call option can purchase the underlying stock, or the owner of a put option can sell the underlying stock.

strike vote A vote by employees to determine if they are willing to initiate a collective work stoppage. A positive vote to strike does not necessarily mean a strike will occur.

strip mall —See MALL.

stripping —See COUPON STRIPPING.

STRIPS —See SEPARATE TRADING OF REGISTERED INTEREST AND PRINCIPAL OF SECURITIES.

strong dollar A dollar that is valuable relative to foreign currencies. A strong dollar exchanges for more units of other currencies compared with the units for which it could be exchanged in the past. A strong dollar tends to hurt U.S. firms that rely heavily on foreign sales, because the firms' products will cost more in terms of the foreign currencies. —Compare WEAK DOLLAR. —See also EXCHANGE RATE.

structural unemployment Unemployment that results from a mismatch between the skills needed by employers and the skills possessed by workers. Rapidly changing technology requires employees with new skills at the same time it makes old skills obsolete. Structural unemployment can exist in a strong economy that is near full employment. —Compare CYCLICAL UNEMPLOYMENT.

structure Something that is constructed on or erected from the ground: *The developers announced the new office building would be one of the largest structures in the city.*

structured investment vehicle (SIV) A special type of conduit that utilizes third-party borrowing in addition to short-term debt to finance the purchase of long-term assets. For example, an SIV might acquire a portfolio of mortgaged-backed securities with short-term debt plus proceeds from an issue of commercial paper secured by the acquired assets. An SIV must be marked to market (not always an easy task) and portfolio assets sold to repay investors in the event debt cannot be refinanced.

structured note A medium-term derivative debt security that has one or more special features such as an interest payment based on an equity index, a foreign exchange index, or a benchmark interest rate. Issuers of structured notes often hedge these securities with their own transactions in the derivatives market. Structured notes tend to be complex and are aimed primarily at sophisticated investors.

stubs The shares of equity in a firm that is financed almost completely with debt. Stubs are often created when firms go through a leveraged buyout or pay big cash dividends in order to fend off a takeover.

Student Loan Marketing Association —See SALLIE MAE.

style investing An active portfolio management strategy that uses certain signals to determine whether to switch into identifiable equity segments, in particular, whether to move from growth stock to value stock or the reverse, or from small-cap stock to large-cap stock or the reverse.

subagent In real estate, an agent who works for and owes a fiduciary duty to a client's agent. For example, a subagent may work with potential buyers but have a fiduciary duty to the selling agent. A subagent is subject to the same duties as the agent.

subcontractor An individual or business with specific expertise that is employed by a general contractor to perform a specific part of the work on a project: *The job of providing electrical wiring in the new office building was awarded to a subcontractor from Indianapolis.*

subdivide To partition a tract of land into multiple sections that are offered for sale: *The investor group purchased a field just outside town with the intention of subdividing the property for a new housing development.*

subdivision A parcel of land that has been legally divided into two or more lots or tracts for the purpose of sale or development.

subindex An index based on a particular category of components that make up a larger index. For example, the Nasdaq Composite Index is subdivided into subindexes for categories including banks, computers, industrials, insurance, and telecommunications. Tracking subindexes provides an indication of how particular segments of the market are performing.

subject quote —See NOMINAL QUOTE.

subject to mortgage A condition in a property sale agreement under which the buyer agrees to make monthly mortgage payments on the existing mortgage, although the seller of the property remains liable for the payments in the event the buyer defaults. This differs from an assumable mortgage, in which the buyer assumes full responsibility for an existing mortgage. —See also ASSUMABLE MORTGAGE.

subject to opinion An audit opinion by a certified public accountant that a firm's financial statements are fairly presented subject to the outcome of an uncertain future event. A major lawsuit, the outcome of which could significantly affect the firm, may be unresolved at the time of the audit; such a situation is an example of a factor influencing the opinion.

sublease An agreement in which the right to use leased property is transferred to another party. Subleases are generally for a portion of the leased property or for a shorter term than the master lease.

subliminal Of or describing a stimulus too weak to be perceived. Some advertising strategies make use of subliminal messages. For example, companies pay to have their products appear in movies and television programs so that viewers will be unconsciously influenced to purchase the products.

suboptimize To make the best of one part of the whole without making the best of the whole. For example, a plant manager moves her best employees to the production department and maximizes its efficiency, but the loss of good employees in the shipping department results in so many inefficiencies that the plant's overall output is less than optimal.

subordinated debenture An unsecured bond with a claim to assets that is subordinate to all existing and future debt. Thus, in the event that the issuer encounters financial difficulties and must be liquidated, all other claims must be satisfied before holders of subordinated debentures can receive a settlement. Frequently, this settlement amounts to relatively little. Because of the risk involved, the issuers have to pay relatively high interest rates in order to sell these securities to investors. —See also CONVERTIBLE SECURITY.

subordinate interest A loan secured by another claim and subordinate to a senior interest.

subpoena A written order from a court requiring someone or something to be present at a specific time and place at a deposition or other proceeding.

subprime loan Credit granted to a borrower who does not meet regular lending standards. The borrower may have a poor credit history, income verification problems, or a spotty employment record. Subprime loans carry a higher interest rate and subject the lender to greater risk of nonpayment than regular loans. —See also ALT-A LOAN.

> **CASE STUDY** Loans of questionable quality (many were of unquestionably poor quality) drew big and small lenders seeking above-average returns in the low-interest-rate environment of the years 2002 to 2007, and especially during 2005 and 2006. Nowhere was aggressive lending more evident than in residential real estate, where individuals were often able to obtain mortgages with no money down and no proof of income. The easy availability of credit brought high times to lenders, brokers, and homebuilders until the bubble burst in early 2007, when many financially strapped borrowers stopped making required payments on their loans. Being unable to make payments wasn't such a problem when home prices were rising and borrowers could refinance or sell the mortgaged real estate at a profit. It became a major problem, however, when home prices stopped rising and actually began declining in many markets. One of the major lenders in the subprime mortgage market was New Century Financial, a company formed with venture capital in 1995. The firm became the country's second largest subprime lender, and in February 2005 branded itself as a "New Shade of Blue Chip." Approximately two years later, the firm announced it was restating financial statements and would not be accepting new loan applications. Lenders had cut off credit to the company and were demanding repayment for some of their loans. New Century's common stock began trading on the Pink Sheets after having been delisted from the New York Stock Exchange, and the firm filed for bankruptcy in April 2007. Other subprime lenders were suffering similar fates, and many had already dropped out of what had become a very risky business.

subrogation Satisfying someone else's obligation and then attempting to collect from the party that owes the debt. For example, an insurance company satisfies the claim of one of its clients and then seeks reimbursement from the person or other entity that caused the damage.

subscribe 1. To use rights for ordering securities sold as a new issue. **2.** To declare interest in something.

subscription period The span of time during which a new issue of securities may be bought by investors. A subscription period will typically last a week or two, after which the rights to subscribe will expire at no value.

subscription price The price at which rights holders may acquire shares in a new securities issue. The subscription price is usually set at slightly less than the market price so as to ensure that it will be successfully sold. —Compare OVERSUBSCRIPTION PRIVILEGE. —See also RIGHTS OFFERING.

subscription privilege —See PREEMPTIVE RIGHT.

subscription ratio The number of rights required to purchase a single share of a security in a rights offering.

subscription right —See RIGHT.

subscription warrant —See WARRANT.

subsequent events Material events that occur between the date of a firm's financial statements and the date on which the financial statements are released. For example, a firm may have become involved in litigation subsequent to the date of the financial statements. Some subsequent events result in adjustments being made in the financial statements, while other subsequent events require only that the events be disclosed.

subsidiary A company controlled or owned by another company. For example, the trucking company Overnite Transportation is a wholly owned subsidiary of Union Pacific Corporation. If a subsidiary is wholly owned, all its stock is held by the parent company. —Compare HOLDING COMPANY; PARENT COMPANY.

subsidiary ledger A record of second-level accounts, the balances of which equal the related accounts in the general ledger. Subsidiary ledgers are used to maintain records of separate accounts such as sales and purchases.

subsidy A government payment or other benefit to a producer (consumer) to encourage the production (consumption) of particular products or services. For example, the state of Wisconsin provides an interest-rate subsidy to municipalities that borrower money to finance wastewater treatment plants.

subsistence theory of wages —See IRON LAW OF WAGES.

substitute —See SWAP².

substitute check A front and back paper reproduction of an original check, including all the information that is required for automated processing. Depository institutions are permitted to truncate checks and create an electronic image that is transmitted to another financial institution for processing. A paper reproduction of the electronic image can be delivered to depository institutions that require paper checks.

substituted basis —See CARRYOVER BASIS 2.

substitute goods Goods that serve the same purpose, such that an increase in demand for one will result in a decreased demand for the other. For example, coffee and tea are substitute goods. —Compare COMPLEMENTARY GOODS.

substitution bond swap The sale of one bond combined with the purchase of another, virtually identical bond that offers a slightly higher yield.

substitution effect The extent to which a price change in a good or service will cause consumers to substitute other goods or services. For example, an increase in the price of cable service will cause some consumers to drop cable service for satellite or fiberoptic service.

subsurface rights —See MINERAL RIGHTS.

subtenant A person who rents property from a lessee: *The brokerage firm that leases the entire second floor of the office building subleases unneeded space to a subtenant.*

subtotal The total of a portion of a series of numbers. For example, the firm's total revenue report included subtotals for revenues generated from each country in which it operates.

subvented lease A subsidized lease. For example, an automobile manufacturer may reduce the lease payment and make a lease more attractive by overestimating the residual value of a leased vehicle.

sucker rally A sharp, abbreviated upturn in stock prices that occurs during a major bear market.

suggested retail price —See MANUFACTURER'S SUGGESTED RETAIL PRICE.

suggestion box A container into which employees or customers can anonymously deposit slips of paper on which they have offered advice or an opinion.

suicide clause A provision in a life insurance policy that denies payment of insurance benefits in the event of the policyholder's suicide within a specified period from the time the policy was purchased.

suicide pill A poison pill provision so devastating to the target of a takeover attempt that the target company may have to be liquidated to satisfy its creditors. For example, the company's directors may institute a suicide pill giving stockholders the right to exchange their stock for debt if a raider acquires more than a specified percentage of the company's outstanding shares. The tremendous increase in debt will effectively doom the target company if the takeover attempt is successful.

suit **1.** A legal action initiated by one party against another. **2.** Slang for an executive or officer of an organization.

suitability rule A National Association of Securities Dealers guideline that requires a brokerage firm to have reasonable grounds for believing a recommendation fits the investment needs of a client.

suitor A company that offers to purchase another firm.

summary possession action A legal filing to take possession of a rental property. A summary possession action can be taken by an owner, a landlord, a tenant who has been wrongfully put or kept out of a rental unit, or by the next tenant whose rental term has commenced.

summons A plaintiff's document that is issued by the court to inform a defendant he or she has been sued. The defendant must file a reply or appear in court on the appropriate date or suffer a default judgment for the plaintiff.

sum-of-the-years'-digits method (SYD) A system for calculating the annual depreciation expense for a capital asset. The calculation involves identifying the number of years over which the asset will be depreciated and summing all of the numbers while counting back to one. This becomes the denominator in the ratio used to determine annual depreciation. The numerator is the number of years remaining in the life of the asset. For example, suppose an asset has a five-year life. The denominator is 5 + 4 + 3 + 2 + 1, or 15. The first year's depreciation is 5/15, or 0.33 times the asset's cost. Depreciation for the second year is 4/15 times the asset's cost.

sum-of-the-years method —See RULE OF 78s.

sunk cost A past outlay or loss that cannot be altered by current or future actions.

sunset industry A mature industry with declining sales and a bleak outlook. Many people consider newspapers to be part of a sunset industry, as individuals increasingly get their news electronically.

sunset provision A clause in a law that automatically repeals the law on a specific date. For example, legislation passed in 2001 scheduled a phaseout of the federal estate tax over 10 years. The legislation also included a sunset provision that reinstated the tax to its original level in 2011.

sunshine law A legal guarantee of public access to meetings, records, votes, and deliberations of public governmental bodies unless otherwise provided by law. Sunshine laws are designed to open government decision making to public scrutiny.

super DRIP A dividend reinvestment plan that offers direct purchase of a firm's shares. A super DRIP allows an investor to buy initial shares from the firm, often with no transaction charge. —Also called *no-load DRIP.*

superfund A federal trust account established by law in 1980 and used by the Environmental Protection Agency to respond to chemical emergencies and to clean up and control hazardous waste sites. Legislation establishing the superfund authorizes prosecution of those responsible for the release of hazardous waste.

superior good A good that consumers buy more of as they grow wealthier. Designer handbags, upscale jewelry, and luxury cars are examples of superior goods that are purchased in greater numbers as consumer incomes rise. —Compare INFERIOR GOOD.

supermajority provision A part of a corporation's bylaws that requires an unusually high percentage of stockholder votes in order to bring about certain changes. For example, a firm may require that 80% of shares approve a resolution to call a meeting of stockholders for any purpose other than the annual meeting. This provision makes a corporate takeover more difficult. —See also BOARD-OUT CLAUSE.

supermarket A retailer offering a large variety of food items, including canned and boxed goods, meats, dairy products, and fruits and vegetables. Many supermarkets offer related products, such as health and beauty aids, magazines, and small household products.

superstore An especially large retail store that serves as a one-stop shopping destination by offering a wide variety of goods that range from groceries to appliances. A superstore is also likely to offer services such as a banking center, photo center, and automotive service center. For example, many superstores allow consumers to buy groceries, have their photos developed, and eat lunch while the oil is being changed in their vehicle.

supervoting stock A class of stock that provides its holders with larger than proportionate voting rights compared with another class of stock issued by the same company. For example, Dow Jones & Company has two classes of common stock: supervoting class B has ten votes per share, compared to the firm's regular common stock with one vote per share. At the end of 2001, class B shares composed only about 20% of outstanding common stock but enjoyed nearly three-quarters of the total voting power. Supervoting stock permits a limited number of stockholders to retain or gain control of a company without having to own more than 50% of all common stock outstanding. —Compare LIMITED-VOTING STOCK. —Also called *control stock.*

supplemental agreement A modification to an existing agreement. For example, a supplemental agreement may add, delete, or replace some of the wording in an earlier agreement.

Supplemental Security Income (SSI) A federal needs-based assistance program to help aged, blind, and disabled people who have little or no income. The program is administered by the Social Security Administration but funded out of general tax revenues.

supplemental unemployment benefits Employer-financed payments to a terminated employee. The payments are considered taxable wages and are subject to withholding, but not to Social Security or Medicare taxes.

supplemental wages Wages paid by an employer that are not paid at a regular hourly rate or in a predetermined fixed amount. Supplemental wages include bonuses, commissions, sick pay, noncash fringe benefits, and other irregular payments. An employer may choose to report tips and overtime pay as either regular wages or supplemental wages.

supplier A person or business that serves as a source for goods and services. For example, Sysco Corporation is a major supplier to the food service industry.

supply¹ The quantity of a good or service a supplier is willing to bring to market at a given price during a specified time interval. —Compare DEMAND.

supply² To provide something.

supply-chain management Developing, administering, and improving the reliability and efficiency with which a business acquires the factors of production. For example, a firm works with suppliers to schedule deliveries during slack periods when employees are not busy with other tasks.

supply curve A graphical representation of the quantity supplied of a good or service at various prices. The supply curve generally slopes upward, indicating additional units being supplied at higher prices. —Compare DEMAND CURVE.

supply-demand analysis An evaluation of a good or service on the basis of factors affecting its supply and demand. Supply-demand analysis is supposed to determine if an imbalance exists or will exist between supply and demand for a good or service. For example, if the supply of a good is expected to exceed demand, its price can be expected to decline. Supply-demand analysis incorporates information on manufacturing capacity, currency exchange rates, consumer incomes, interest rates, and many other factors that influence availability and purchases.

supply price The price at which a good or service will be offered in the quantity demanded by the market.

supply-side economics The school of economics that concentrates on devising and promoting ways to increase the output of goods and services in the long run. The defining idea of supply-side economics is that marginal tax rates should be reduced to provide incentives to supply additional labor and capital, and thereby promote long-term growth.

support level A price at which a security or the market will receive considerable buying pressure. A support level develops as investors miss purchasing a stock just before a price rise and resolve to buy the stock if it again reaches that level. —Compare RESISTANCE LEVEL.

surcharge A fee added to an existing charge. For example, a freight company adds a fuel surcharge to cover a recent spike in the cost of gasoline and diesel fuel. A surcharge may be either a fixed amount per transaction or an amount calculated as a percentage of the charge.

> **CASE** In early 2007 the Surface Transportation Board ordered railroads to
> **STUDY** alter the method they were using to establish surcharges to recover
> increased fuel costs. The railroads had implemented the surcharges following
> a big run-up in petroleum prices. The federal order followed charges by ship-
> pers that the railroads were using surcharges to boost profits in addition to
> recovering higher fuel charges. The railroads had set the surcharges as a per-
> centage of base shipping rates that didn't necessarily reflect mileage or fuel
> charges. Heavy demand for transportation services allowed the railroads to
> raise base rates, which in turn resulted in the firms generating additional rev-
> enues and profits from the surcharges. The federal order was likely to cause
> the railroads to base the surcharge on mileage rather than on base rates in
> order to more closely track fuel expenses.

surety bond A contract involving three or more parties in which one of the parties
(the surety) agrees to fulfill an obligation or provide monetary compensation to another of the parties (the oblige) in the event the third party (the principal) defaults.
Surety bonds are used to guarantee construction agreements, court appearances, and
lost stock certificates.

surplus 1. Equity in excess of par value. Surplus includes additional paid-in capital
and retained earnings. **2.** —See RETAINED EARNINGS.

surrender 1. To terminate a life insurance policy or annuity prior to maturity or
death of the insured. **2.** To voluntarily cancel a lease.

surrender value —See CASH SURRENDER VALUE.

surtax A tax in addition to the regular tax. For example, many cities and counties
levy a sales tax that is in addition to the state sales tax. For a period of time the federal
government required individuals to pay a 10% surtax on taxable income above a
specified amount. Thus, the marginal rate of 36% became a marginal rate of 39.6%.

survey 1. A map or diagram of a parcel of land, including its boundaries, dimensions,
important reference points, and structures. **2.** A collection of information derived
from responses to questionnaires or interviews. —See also COINCIDENTAL SURVEY.

survey area The geographic area in which an issue is sampled or evaluated. For example, a redevelopment agency examines economic and physical problems in a survey
area in which it may initiate a redevelopment program.

surviving company The company that emerges in control following a business combination. The surviving company is generally one of the firms entering the combination, but may be a new company formed by the combination. For example, BP,
formerly British Petroleum, was the surviving company from the merger of British
Petroleum and Amoco Corporation.

surviving spouse A widower or widow. A surviving spouse has certain privileges and
responsibilities with respect to assets, income, rights, and liabilities that were jointly
or individually held by the deceased spouse.

survivorship 1. The right to ownership of an asset because of outliving the person
with which the survivor had an undivided interest. **2.** A life insurance policy that
insures two lives and does not pay death benefits until the death of both insureds.

suspended trading The temporary suspension of trading in a security. Trading in a
security may be suspended if, for instance, a major announcement by the issuing

company is expected to influence significantly the security's price. The temporary halt in trading is intended to give the financial community enough time to hear the news. —Also called *trading halt.*

suspense account In accounting, a temporary account used for recording expenditures and income items until they can be reviewed, identified, and appropriately allocated.

suspension 1. The temporary halting of an activity such as making payments or producing a product until corrective action is taken. For example, a government agency suspends financial assistance until the recipient makes changes in its accounting procedures. **2.** Discipline of an employee who is placed on temporary status without pay or duties.

swap¹ A contract in which two parties agree to exchange future payment streams. In the most common type of swap arrangement, one party agrees to pay fixed interest payments on designated dates to a counterparty who, in turn, agrees to make return interest payments that float with some reference rate such as the rate on Treasury bills or the prime rate. —See also COUNTERPARTY RISK; CREDIT-DEFAULT SWAP.

swap² To trade one asset for another. For example, an investor who believes interest rates will rise swaps a bond with a 20-year maturity for a bond with a 5-year maturity. —Also called *exchange²; substitute; switch.*

swap order A specialized security order in which a customer specifies that two transactions be made only if a given price differential can be achieved. For example, an investor might specify that 500 shares of one security be purchased and 500 shares of another security be sold only if the former can be executed for $5 per share less than the latter. —Also called *switch order.*

sweat equity Improvements to property produced by labor of the owner of the property. For example, a couple increases the value of their home (and the value of their equity in the home) by working nights and weekends to remodel the bathroom.

sweatshop A workplace in which employees are mistreated with long hours, low wages, an inhospitable environment, unsafe conditions, and so forth.

sweep To automatically move cash balances into an interest-earning money market fund. Certain brokerage firms offer to perform this activity for some or all of their accounts.

sweep account —See ASSET MANAGEMENT ACCOUNT.

sweepstakes A lottery in which winners are selected in a random manner. Sweepstakes are used as a promotional tool by businesses in an attempt to attract new customers or increase revenue from existing customers. For example, a credit card company offers a free vacation as a prize to cardholders, who receive a sweepstakes entry with each use of their card.

sweetener An addition to an agreement that makes it more appealing. An example of a popular sweetener is the addition of warrants (options to buy stock) to a bond in order to make the bond marketable with a lower interest cost.

sweetheart deal A collusive, unethical transaction between two parties. For example, unethical union officials may gain personal benefits by agreeing to a sweetheart deal that grants concessions to the employer.

swing loan —See BRIDGE LOAN.

swing shift —See SHIFT WORK.

switch 1. —See SWAP[2]. **2.** To move funds out of one mutual fund and into another mutual fund. —Also called *convert.* —See also TELEPHONE SWITCHING.

switch order —See SWAP ORDER.

SWOT analysis A strategic planning tool in which an organization, business plan, or project is evaluated by analyzing its *s*trengths, *w*eaknesses, *o*pportunities, and *t*hreats. The analysis is designed to identify the important factors affecting the achievement of an objective.

SWX Swiss Exchange An all-electronic securities exchange formed from the 1995 merger of exchanges in Geneva, Basel, and Zurich. The exchange offers trading in equity securities, investment funds, exchange-traded funds, bonds, Eurobonds, and options.

SYD —See SUM-OF-THE-YEARS'-DIGITS METHOD.

sympathy strike A collective action by workers to not perform their jobs because of a dispute with management by a separate group of workers. For example, in the summer of 2005 ground workers of British Airways staged a sympathy strike at London's Heathrow Airport with laid-off workers of the firm's catering service. —Also called *secondary strike.*

syndicate[1] A consortium of individuals or companies formed to pursue a particular business venture that syndicate members would find difficult to undertake individually. For example, investment banking firms form underwriting syndicates to bid on new security issues that are to be resold to individual and institutional investors. The underwriting syndicate disbands when the security offering has been completed. —Also called *underwriting syndicate.* —See also SELLING GROUP.

syndicate[2] To distribute shares of ownership in a partnership or joint venture. For example, a brokerage firm may syndicate ownership in certain oil and gas properties.

syndicate manager A major underwriting firm that forms a syndicate in order to distribute participations to members. The manager of a securities issue allocates the securities among other firms in the group, but is itself generally responsible for the largest share of the issue.

synergy An increase in the value of assets as a result of their combination. Expected synergy is the justification behind most business mergers. For example, the 2002 combination of Hewlett-Packard and Compaq was designed to reduce expenses and capitalize on combining Hewlett-Packard's reputation for quality with Compaq's impressive distribution system.

synthetic asset The combination of securities and/or assets in such a way that they produce the same financial effect as would the ownership of an entirely different asset. For example, selling a put option and buying a call option on a commodity produce the same financial effect as actually owning the underlying commodity.

synthetic lease A financing method that confers certain aspects of ownership to the lessee, who, for accounting purposes, treats the arrangement as an operating lease. Neither the asset nor the lease is included on the lessee's balance sheet. A synthetic lease is a type of off-balance-sheet financing that results in a company understating its financial obligations.

systematic risk Risk caused by factors that affect the prices of virtually all securities, although in different proportions. Examples include changes in interest rates and consumer prices. Although it is not possible to eliminate systematic risk through diversification, it is possible to reduce it by acquiring securities (for example, those of utilities and many blue chips) that have histories of relatively slowly changing prices. —Compare UNSYSTEMATIC RISK. —Also called *market risk; nondiversifiable risk.* —See also BETA 1.

systematic sampling A method of statistical sampling in which the population is divided into intervals, and a single selection is sampled from each interval. For example, suppose an auditor wishes to sample 50 invoices from a population of 1,000 invoices arranged in chronological order. Dividing the population of 1,000 by 50 yields 20 intervals. Thus, each 20th invoice is chosen, beginning with a random starting point between 1 and 20. If 3 is chosen as the random starting point, invoices selected will be 3, 23, 43, 63, and so forth.

systematic withdrawal plan —See WITHDRAWAL PLAN.

systems programmer 1. An individual who writes programs that enable a computer system to operate properly. **2.** The person in an organization who is responsible for the performance of the organization's computer system. A systems programmer might install and integrate a new software program or recommend to management a new operating system.

 T

TAB —See TAX ANTICIPATION BILL.

tabloid A newspaper approximately half the physical size of a regular ("broadsheet") newspaper. The smaller size is generally easier to hold, especially for commuters, and is popular among publishers in the United Kingdom. The smaller size is often associated with newspapers that concentrate on sensationalism (murders, kidnappings, salacious stories) and have many large photographs.

T-account A diagram represented by a capital T that is used in double-entry bookkeeping to enter debits and credits for business transactions. The account title is listed horizontally across the top. Debits are entered below the title on the left side while credits are listed below the title on the right side.

tactic A limited and often short-term plan of action designed to help carry out a strategy. For example, an aging actor offers to appear in a movie for a nominal salary as a tactic to restart his career.

tactical objective An intermediate goal that is part of a comprehensive strategy of achieving a given result. For example, a company wishes to increase its return on assets (net income divided by total assets) from a current 12% to 15%. A tactical objective in reaching this goal might include reducing energy consumption by 10%.

Taft-Hartley Act Federal antiunion legislation passed by Congress in 1947 over a veto by President Harry Truman. The act prohibited closed shops and required that a majority of employees approve a union shop. The legislation prohibited unions from contributing to political campaigns and allowed companies to refuse to bargain with unions.

tag sale An individual, neighborhood, or estate sale in which each item is tagged or labeled with a price.

take¹ 1. To accept the price offered by a potential buyer. **2.** To seize assets: *After the borrower had missed three payments, the used auto dealer took the vehicle he had sold her.*

take-out loan

Are take-out loans arranged prior to the time when the short-term loan is obtained? If not, it seems like an awfully risky arrangement.

Take-out loans are not always arranged prior to the closing of a short-term real-estate loan. If a take-out loan is not in place, the lender can mitigate the risks by structuring the terms of the short-term loan to ensure that it can be refinanced via a permanent financing source and by requiring varying levels of up-front equity to insulate the lender from potential declines in value. The lender will also ensure that pro forma rental rates and occupancy levels are acceptable and that the project could support debt payments at stabilization should a refinance not be obtained.

Equally important to a lender in mitigating refinance risk is a client's history. Lenders evaluate the past performance of the client in delivering previous projects and successfully repaying the related loan. Some lenders may also look to the personal (or corporate) financial strength of the individual borrower/owner to determine what level of financial support they offer to bridge the gap between the loan and any potential refinance shortfall.

■ Brooke Barber, Vice President, Middle Market Banking, Atlanta, GA

take² 1. Funds received from a transaction or series of transactions. For example, a neighbor brags about her take from yesterday's garage sale. **2.** Taking or attempting to take illegal income or bribes: *The employee selling company secrets was on the take.*

take a bath To lose a large portion of the money invested in a particular product or asset. For example, a company took a bath on its new watermelon-flavored toothpaste that few customers even tried.

take a flier To commit funds to a speculative investment: *A wealthy investor took a flier on a penny stock recommended by his brother-in-law.*

take a position To buy or sell securities in order to establish a net long or a net short position.

take-away acquisition The purchase of a company that has an outstanding offer to be acquired by another firm. For example, General Electric attempted to acquire Honeywell International for $45 billion shortly after Honeywell had received a $40 billion offer from United Technologies. Take-away acquisitions can be risky for the acquiring firm, which often has insufficient time to conduct a thorough analysis of the acquired company.

take delivery 1. To accept a commodity to be delivered as part of a long futures contract. For example, the buyer of a gold futures contract who will need the metal on the delivery date may plan to take delivery rather than close out the contract. **2.** To accept certificates for securities that have been purchased. **3.** To accept a receipt for goods delivered by a shipper.

takedown 1. An investment banker's share of a new security offering. **2.** The price paid by an underwriter for securities to be sold as part of a new issue.

take-home pay The amount of salary or wages remaining after taxes, insurance, retirement contributions, and other deductions have been withheld.

take-or-pay agreement A contractual agreement in which one party agrees to purchase a specific amount of another party's goods or services or to pay the equivalent cost even if the goods or services are not needed. Take-or-pay contracts are frequently employed by electric utilities, which use the agreements as collateral for loans to build plants to generate electricity.

> **CASE STUDY** Take-or-pay agreements linking sellers and buyers through long-term contracts are common in the energy business, where producers are required to make huge initial expenditures, and consumers often need a steady long-term supply of energy. The agreements require a purchaser to pay for a prespecified minimum quantity of coal, gas, or electricity, regardless of whether the purchaser actually takes delivery. In certain instances, a purchaser who must pay but cannot use product in one year may be permitted to take extra product the following year. Likewise, the producer guarantees to deliver a minimum quantity. PetroChina financed a 2,400-mile natural gas pipeline on the basis of signing long-term take-or-pay contracts with 40 customers. A little less than half the sales were to residential customers and another quarter of sales were to industrial customers. These were generally considered low-risk agreements. The remaining gas was contracted mostly to power plants owned by municipal governments or companies owned by municipal governments. There was some concern that municipal governments would be unable to sell enough electricity to make use of all the gas specified in the take-or-pay agreements. It was unclear how the contracts would be enforced in the event of a dispute. In addition, coal was less expensive than gas at the time the pipeline was completed, thereby making it less likely the municipal governments would want all the gas they had agreed to take.

take out 1. The extra funds generated in an account when an investor sells one block of securities and buys another block at a lower total cost. For example, a customer may sell $50,000 face amount of bonds at 85 and then purchase $50,000 face amount of a different bond at 80. **2.** A bid for a seller's remaining position in a security.

take-out loan In real estate, a permanent loan with a long-term maturity that replaces a short-term loan. For example, a builder completes an apartment building and replaces an existing construction loan with a 25-year mortgage.

take-out merger —See CLEANUP MERGER.

takeover The acquisition of controlling interest in a firm. Although the term is often used to refer to acquisition by a party hostile to the target's management, many takeovers are friendly. —See also FRIENDLY TAKEOVER; RAIDER; UNFRIENDLY TAKEOVER.

takeover defense —See SHARK REPELLENT.

takeover stock A stock that, for various reasons, has good potential for being taken over by another firm. Stocks of companies holding large amounts of cash and having little debt often come into play as takeover stocks. —See also IN PLAY; SPLIT-UP VALUE.

takeover target —See TARGET COMPANY.

takeunder Acquisition of controlling interest in a firm when the purchase price is less than the trading price of the target's stock. For example, a small company may encounter difficulty competing with larger competitors such that the smaller firm's management actively seeks a buyer. Takeunders often involve companies that have put themselves up for sale, causing speculators to bid up their stock prices above what acquiring firms are willing to pay.

CASE Well-known clothing marketer OshKosh B'Gosh, Inc. agreed in May **STUDY** 2005 to a $312 million takeunder by Georgia-based Carter's, Inc. The 110-year-old firm had announced in February 2005 the possibility of a sale following a news leak that Goldman, Sachs & Co. had been retained to explore strategic alternatives for the Wisconsin-based firm. The news came approximately a month after an announcement of an increase in the firm's quarterly sales and a decline in its quarterly net loss. The firm's stock price increased by nearly 50%, from $19 on February 1 to $27.38 on February 17. Carter's paid $26 cash for each OshKosh B'Gosh share, a significant discount to the market price immediately preceding the buyout offer. The takeunder resulted in losses for speculators who took late positions in the stock while anticipating higher offers from interested suitors. Carter's indicated that it intended to continue marketing OshKosh B'Gosh as a separate brand and would improve profit margins by reducing offerings, outsourcing manufacturing, and closing underperforming stores.

taking In law, seizing private property without fair compensation to the owner. Taking can also include the imposition of severe restrictions that results in the devaluation of property.

taking inventory Counting or weighing stock that is available for sale. Taking inventory allows a firm to determine if the amount of stock available for sale is within a normal range for its type and size of business. It can also help to pinpoint areas of concern when profit margins are unsatisfactory. For example, a grocer may determine it has been subject to employee theft.

taking profits —See PROFIT TAKING.

tallyman An individual who counts or weighs (maintains a tally) goods that are being shipped or received.

TAN —See TAX ANTICIPATION NOTE.

tandem Of or relating to entering into two trades at the same time. For example, an investor who sells a July futures contract and buys a September futures contract is engaging in a tandem trade.

tangible asset An asset, such as a building or piece of equipment, that has physical properties. —Compare INTANGIBLE ASSET. —Also called *hard asset*. —See also NET TANGIBLE ASSETS PER SHARE.

tangible personal property Personal assets that can be touched or felt, excluding real estate. Tangible personal property includes vehicles, livestock, and equipment. It does not include stocks, bonds, and savings accounts.

tape 1. —See TICKER TAPE. **2.** —See BROAD TAPE.

tap fee The charge for hooking homes and businesses up to a water and sewer system.

tare weight The weight of a shipping container including necessary packing materials but excluding any goods that are to be transported. For example, the weight of an empty railcar or truck trailer.

target audience A selected group considered to be the most appropriate recipients of an advertisement, message, or program. For example, a target audience might be teenage females, retirees, or members of a particular ethnic group. Businesses tend to choose advertising messages that are likely to appeal to a target audience. For example, manufacturers of recreational vehicles advertise in travel magazines, while beer companies choose to advertise during televised football games.

target company A firm that is the object of a specific action unwanted by its management, such as a takeover attempt or an antitrust suit. —Compare RAIDER. —Also called *takeover target.* —See also IN PLAY; TAKEOVER; TOEHOLD PURCHASE.

targeted jobs tax credit A tax credit offered to businesses undertaking activities that create jobs among targeted classes of the population. For example, a state may allow tax credits for establishing or adding to a corporate headquarters or for constructing or improving an infrastructure project. A 1978 federal program offered a tax credit to employers for a portion of the wages paid to individuals in groups subject to high rates of unemployment.

target fund —See LIFECYCLE FUND.

target market The group of consumers for which a product is manufactured or a service is offered. For example, the publisher of a book about a university's national championship football team would identify male graduates of the school as a target market.

target price **1.** The price that an investor or a security analyst expects a security to achieve. Generally, when a security achieves the target price, it is time to close out a position in it. **2.** The price at which an investor hopes to purchase an asset. For example, a company desiring to take over another firm may set a target price for the firm. **3.** The selling price for which a product or service is developed. For example, an editor at a publishing company proposes a series of children's books with a target price of $7.95.

target-retirement fund —See LIFECYCLE FUND.

tariff **1.** A tax levied on a good imported into a country. In most instances, tariffs are intended to make imported goods more expensive than and thus less competitive with domestic products. —Also called *duty.* —See also AD VALOREM TARIFF; COUNTERVAILING DUTIES; GENERAL AGREEMENT ON TARIFFS AND TRADE; SPECIFIC TARIFF; TRIGGER PRICE. **2.** The rates or charges for a firm's service or product. For example, a parking garage posts a schedule of its tariffs at the entrance. A common carrier has a schedule of tariffs for various types of goods it will transport.

> **CASE STUDY** A tariff imposed by a country can serve both as a source of revenue and as a barrier that protects a targeted group of businesses and their employees, but often at the expense of nearly everyone else. For example, a tariff on imported vehicles helps the domestic automobile industry and its suppliers, but penalizes car buyers, who are forced to pay higher prices and may have fewer choices. In some instances a country and the affected industries may decide a tariff no longer serves the purpose for which it was imposed. Such was the case with tariffs on aluminum imported into the European Union. In May 2007 the EU announced a trade agreement between the Gulf Cooperation Council and the European Union that would reduce by half the tariff on aluminum imported by the EU. The EU agreed to assess the situation in two years, with the possibility of eliminating the remaining tariff. Aluminum making requires large amounts of energy, the expense of which had increased dramatically. As a result, the production of aluminum was moving from the United States and Europe to energy-rich regions such as the

Middle East. The EU wanted to reduce the cost of imported aluminum and other raw materials that could be fabricated in Europe into finished goods.

tariff war A series of increases in tariffs between two or more countries attempting to gain a trade advantage. For example, a U.S. increase in tariffs on imported clothing from China is followed by a Chinese increase in tariffs on beef imported from the United States.

task force A temporary group of individuals organized to undertake a specific mission. For example, a corporate CEO forms a task force to address high costs of the firm's health insurance plan.

task management A formalized process for achieving an identified result. For example, prior to taking off, an airline pilot initiates a series of procedures to assure the integrity of the airplane.

tax A levy by government on income, property, purchases, or assets of individuals and businesses. Money raised through taxes is used to pay for government purchases of goods and services.

tax abatement An elimination or reduction in taxes granted by a taxing authority. For example, tax abatement may be offered to a property owner who guarantees a minimum amount of job creation.

taxable equivalent yield The pretax yield that provides the same return as a specified aftertax yield. Taxable equivalent yield is calculated by dividing tax-free yield by the difference obtained from subtracting the applicable tax rate from 1. For example, for an investor who pays taxes at a rate of 40%, an aftertax yield of 6% has a taxable equivalent yield of $0.06/(1 - 0.4)$, or 10%.

taxable estate The adjusted gross estate less any allowable marital deduction or charitable deductions. The taxable estate is the base on which the estate tax is calculated, although the actual tax due will be affected by any state death taxes and gift taxes that have been assessed.

taxable income The amount of income that is subject to taxation. Taxable income is what remains after accounting for allowable adjustments and deductions.

taxable municipal bond A municipal bond on which interest paid to the bondholder does not qualify as tax-exempt for federal tax purposes because of the use to which the bond proceeds are put by the municipal borrower. Although taxable municipal bonds are subject to federal taxation, most are not subject to taxation by the state in which the municipal issuer is located.

taxable value —See ASSESSED VALUE.

taxable year The 12-month period for which taxable income is calculated. For individuals, the taxable year is nearly always the same as the calendar year. For businesses, the taxable year is nearly always the same as the fiscal year.

Tax and Loan Accounts U.S. Treasury accounts at commercial banks that are funded by taxes received directly from the public and excess funds transferred by the Treasury. The Treasury uses the accounts to maintain general account target balances that are used for operating purposes.

tax anticipation bill (TAB) A short-term U.S. Treasury obligation that is issued at a discount and that may be used at face value upon maturity or a few days before to pay a federal tax obligation. These securities appeal primarily to corporations and relatively large investors with significant tax obligations.

tax anticipation note (TAN) A short-term municipal obligation that is sold to provide funds for government operations until taxes have been received. At that time, the receipts are used to repay the debt. These generally low-risk securities appeal primarily to larger investors.

tax arbitrage An investment or business strategy that takes advantage of tax rate differences among assets, markets, or business units. For example, a family-owned business hires a family member who is subject to an income tax rate lower than the rate paid by the business. A business may practice tax arbitrage by utilizing transfer pricing in order to shift expenses to a high-tax state or country.

> **CASE STUDY** Tax arbitrage using low-cost tax-exempt bonds to finance the purchase of higher-yielding taxable securities is prohibited under the tax code and the Department of the Treasury's regulations. For example, a nonprofit hospital or university is prohibited from issuing tax-exempt bonds and using the proceeds to acquire higher-yielding investments or to replace funds that were used directly or indirectly to acquire higher-yielding investments. A nonprofit institution is permitted to issue tax-exempt bonds for financing investments in operating assets, including buildings and equipment. Nonprofit hospitals and universities often accumulate large investment portfolios, courtesy of donors who gain tax benefits by giving money or other assets to the nonprofit institutions. A nonprofit wanting to spend capital funds can skirt the tax arbitrage prohibition by issuing tax-exempt bonds rather than utilizing its portfolio assets to finance buildings and equipment. The portfolio assets remain intact and continue to earn a return higher than the interest paid on the tax-exempt bonds. Using this broad definition of tax arbitrage (utilizing proceeds from tax-exempt bond issues rather than available portfolio assets), the Congressional Budget Office estimated that in 2002 nonprofit hospitals were earning returns from tax arbitrage on almost $11 billion of tax-exempt debt.

tax assessor The public official who evaluates property for purposes of taxation. —Also called *assessor*.

tax audit —See AUDIT 2.

tax avoidance The reduction of a tax liability by legal means. For example, high-income individuals avoid significant federal income taxes by purchasing and holding municipal bonds. —Compare TAX EVASION.

tax base The resources that are available for taxation. For example, the tax base for many counties that level a property tax is the value of property in the county subject to taxation. An evaluation of the tax base is of particular importance in certain municipal bond issues secured by tax revenues.

tax basis —See BASIS 2.

tax benefit rule The tenet that a state or local tax refund resulting from deducting the tax in an earlier period is taxable only to the extent that the deduction resulted in reduced taxes in the earlier period. The entire amount of the refund may not be taxable if the taxpayer was subject to the alternative minimum tax or enjoyed unused tax credits.

tax bracket —See MARGINAL TAX RATE.

Tax Court The federal court of record for providing a judicial forum in which taxpayers can dispute tax deficiencies determined by the IRS. The Tax Court is comprised of 19 appointed members, senior judges, and special trial judges who travel nationwide to conduct trials in various locations.

tax credit A reduction in the amount of taxes owed. For example, corporations are permitted a credit on U.S. taxes for taxes paid to foreign governments, and individuals could, for a number of years, claim a tax credit for a portion of expenditures for certain energy-saving home improvements. A tax credit is more valuable than a deduction of an equal amount because the credit results in a reduction in tax owed rather than a reduction in taxable income. —See also FOREIGN TAX CREDIT.

tax deduction —See DEDUCTION.

tax deed The deed to the government-claimed property of a delinquent taxpayer that is conveyed to the purchaser at a public sale.

tax deferral The delay of a tax liability until a future date. For example, an IRA may result in a tax deferral on the amount contributed to the IRA and on any income earned on funds in the IRA until withdrawals are made. At the corporate level, accelerated depreciation of assets results in a delay in tax liabilities. Tax deferral, which is legal, means a postponement, not elimination, of a tax liability. —Also called *deferral of taxes.*

tax-deferred annuity —See TAX-SHELTERED ANNUITY.

tax-deferred exchange —See LIKE-KIND EXCHANGE.

tax-deferred income Income that is earned but that is neither received nor taxed until a later date. For example, interest earned on U.S. Treasury bills is received and taxed at maturity. Likewise, U.S. savings bonds provide appreciation of value on which holders may defer paying taxes until the security is cashed in. —Compare TAX-FREE INCOME; TAX-SHELTERED INCOME.

tax-efficient fund A mutual fund that manages its investment portfolio so as to minimize the tax liability of its shareholders. A tax-efficient fund attempts to minimize capital gains distributions by reducing portfolio turnover, and to minimize dividend payments to shareholders by concentrating on investments in companies with low dividend payouts. —Also called *tax-managed mutual fund.*

tax evasion The illegal avoidance of taxes. Intentionally failing to include some cash sales when reporting income to the Internal Revenue Service is an example of tax evasion. —Compare TAX AVOIDANCE.

tax-exempt bond —See MUNICIPAL BOND.

tax-exempt income —See TAX-FREE INCOME.

tax-exempt money market fund An open-end investment company that invests in short-term tax-exempt securities. These funds usually pay relatively low current income but are very liquid. They appeal to higher-income investors who seek a temporary investment. —Also called *short-term municipal bond fund.*

tax-exempt organization —See EXEMPT ORGANIZATION.

tax-exempt property Real property that is not subject to ad valorem taxes. Local communities typically exempt from taxation property owned by religious organizations, educational institutions, nonprofit institutions, and various levels of government. A 2002 report by the city of Boston, Massachusetts, indicated half the city's land area was exempt from taxation.

tax gap

Could moving from an income tax to a national sales tax or value-added tax help close the gap between the amount of taxes people should pay and the amount they actually pay?

Yes, taxes would be much more difficult to avoid and compliance would improve. In effect, the merchant becomes the tax collection agent and collects the tax at the time the tax liability is due. Additionally, the cost of collecting these taxes would be much less than collecting federal income taxes, unless, of course, Congress adds special provisions to these relatively simple taxes.

■ Michael W. Butler, PhD, Professor of Economics, Angelo State University, San Angelo, Texas

tax foreclosure Government taking of real property due to nonpayment of taxes by the property's owner.

tax-free exchange An exchange of assets between taxpayers in which any gain or loss is not recognized in the period during which the exchange takes place. Rather, taxpayers are required to adjust the basis of assets exchanged.

tax-free income Income received but not subject to income taxes. For example, interest from most municipal bonds is free of federal income taxes and often from state and local income taxes as well. —Compare TAX-DEFERRED INCOME; TAX-SHELTERED INCOME. —Also called *tax-exempt income.*

tax gap The difference between the amount of taxes the government should collect and the amount of taxes the government actually collects. The tax gap is a result, mostly, of individuals and businesses understating income and overstating deductions and exemptions. Taxpayers who do not file returns on time also contribute to the tax gap.

tax haven A country or other political entity that offers outside businesses and individuals a climate of minimal or nonexistent taxation. In some cases, the low taxes apply not only to those levied by the tax haven itself, but also to the possibility of reducing or avoiding taxes levied in the investor's home country.

tax incentive A tax benefit offered in order to encourage or discourage targeted activities. For example, the federal government offered tax credits for buying hybrid (electric/gas) vehicles and tax incentives for rehabilitating historic buildings.

tax incidence The relative burden of a tax among different groups. For example, people with large vehicles who drive a lot of miles pay a larger than average share of a gasoline tax. Tax incidence is an important consideration in tax policy because it affects how people act. A higher gasoline tax is likely to result in people choosing to drive less and to do so in more fuel-efficient vehicles. —Also called *incidence of tax.*

tax indexing —See INDEX[2].

tax lien A legal claim placed against property because of nonpayment of taxes by the property owner. A tax lien assumes priority over all other claims on the same property.

tax loophole —See LOOPHOLE.

tax loss carryback —See CARRYBACK.

tax loss carryforward —See CARRYFORWARD 1.

tax-loss selling The sale of securities that have declined in value in order to realize losses that may be used to reduce taxable income. Tax-loss selling occurs near the end of a calendar year so that the loss can be used in that tax year to offset ordinary income or gains on other security transactions. Thus, tax-loss selling occurs mainly among stocks that have declined in price. —Compare TAX SELLING.

tax-managed mutual fund —See TAX-EFFICIENT FUND.

tax map A map maintained by a tax assessor's office that shows the location and boundaries of individual properties within a taxing district.

tax neutrality A government system of collecting revenues such that the flow of the factors of production are unaffected. In other words, the tax does not affect how firms conduct business. Although a portion of resources is transferred to government, there are no secondary effects of taxation.

taxpayer A person, organization, or other entity that is subject to taxation. Taxpayers include individuals, corporations, partnerships, estates, trusts, and a variety of other entities.

taxpayer identification number (TIN) For an individual, his or her Social Security number. For a business or fiduciary, its Employer Identification Number (EIN). Employers are required to have a new employee certify his or her taxpayer identification number on IRS Form W-9.

tax planning The process of systematically making decisions with regard to their impact on taxation. For example, deciding whether to sell securities and realize a capital loss in order to offset an earlier capital gain realized on another sale. Likewise, making a decision on the timing of withdrawals from an Individual Retirement Account also involves tax planning.

tax preference item An item that can legally be omitted in order to reduce taxable income when calculating an individual's tax liability by ordinary means. However, the item must be included when calculating the individual's alternative minimum tax. For example, interest paid by certain municipal bonds that is ordinarily omitted in calculating taxable income must be included when calculating the alternative minimum tax. —Also called *preference item.*

tax rate The proportional amount of taxes paid on a given income or the given dollar value of an asset. If the tax is calculated on the basis of total income, it is the average tax rate. If the tax is calculated only on extra units of income, the rate is the marginal tax rate.

tax rate schedules A list of basic formulas provided by the IRS for calculating a taxpayer's federal income tax liability. Separate schedules are available for the different filing categories: single, married filing jointly or widow(er)s, married filing separately, and head of household. Taxpayers with a taxable income of $100,000 or more must use a tax rate schedule to calculate the annual tax liability. —See also TAX TABLE.

Tax Reform Act of 1986 Tax legislation that significantly reduced marginal income tax rates for individuals and corporations as well as curtailed many deductions and eliminated numerous preference items. The act was designed to be revenue-neutral and, in general, it benefited high-income and low-income individuals, and corporations that do not spend large amounts of money on long-lived equipment. Although an original goal had been to simplify the tax system, no simplification was evident in the final legislation.

tax sale

What are some of the pitfalls of investing in tax liens?

There is a considerable amount of due diligence that needs to be exercised in making a good investment in a tax sale. Can you afford the expenses you will incur in your due diligence? Considerations of things like searching for additional liens against the property, doing title searches, surveying the property, inspecting the house, and researching the real estate market where the house is located are a few of the important considerations. There is a lot of risk involved. Can you afford the risk? Most small investors are probably not capable of making successful investments in tax liens.

■ Michael W. Butler, PhD, Professor of Economics, Angelo State University, San Angelo, Texas

tax refund Payment by the government to a taxpayer who has paid more taxes than were due. A tax refund can result from a variety of reasons, including a taxpayer's incorrectly calculating his or her tax liability. Taxpayers sometimes overestimate their tax liability and pay too much in estimated taxes.

tax return An official form supplied by the IRS or other tax authority on which individuals and companies enter all information relevant to calculating their tax liability.

tax roll A record of a taxing authority's taxable land parcels including descriptions, owners, and assessed valuations.

tax sale The public auction by government of property on which taxes are unpaid. A tax sale does not automatically convey title to the purchaser, because the delinquent taxpayer has a specified period in which to pay the taxes owed, plus interest and court costs, in order to recover ownership. Essentially, the purchaser buys the lien and becomes a creditor to the delinquent taxpayer.

tax selling The sale of securities to establish gains or losses for income-tax purposes. Significant tax selling often occurs in December, especially following a bear market, as investors seek to realize losses to offset previous realized gains or other income. An investor may engage in tax selling to establish gains when he or she expects to be paying a higher marginal tax rate the following year. —Compare TAX-LOSS SELLING.

tax shelter An investment that produces relatively large current deductions that can be used to offset other taxable income. Popular tax shelters include real estate projects and gas and oil drilling ventures. —Also called *shelter*. —See also ABUSIVE TAX SHELTER.

tax-sheltered annuity (TSA) A retirement plan that permits an employee of a tax-exempt charitable, educational, or religious institution to contribute a certain portion of wages or salary into a tax-sheltered fund. Contributions serve to reduce taxable income in the year they are contributed. Taxes on income earned in the plan are deferred. Both past contributions and income are fully taxable when withdrawals are made. —Also called *403(b) plan; tax-deferred annuity.*

tax-sheltered income Income that is received and that would ordinarily be taxable but, because of certain noncash deductions such as depreciation, is protected from taxation. For example, rent that has been earned from a rental property is generally sheltered by depreciation on the property being rented. —Compare TAX-DEFERRED IN-COME; TAX-FREE INCOME.

tax shield —See DEDUCTION.

tax status The category in which a taxpayer chooses to file a local, state, or federal tax return. Tax status alternatives for a federal return are single, married filing jointly or widow(er), married filing separately, and head of household.

tax straddle A combination of two similar futures contracts (one bought and one sold) that tend to move in opposite directions, so that a loss on one is offset by a gain in the other. The contract showing the loss is sold in the current year (shortly before year's end), while the contract showing the gain is sold in the next year. The net effect is to push taxes back one year. This practice ended with legislation that requires all gains and losses in futures contracts to be realized for tax purposes at the end of each year. —Compare MARK TO MARKET.

tax swap The sale of a security that has declined in price since the purchase date and the simultaneous purchase of a similar, but not substantially identical, security. The purpose of the swap is to achieve a loss for tax purposes while continuing to maintain market position. —See also WASH SALE.

tax table An IRS-provided table listing the tax liability for annual taxable income of up to $100,000 for various categories of taxpayers. Taxpayers with taxable income of $100,000 and more are required to use the tax rate schedules to determine their tax liability.

tax treaty An agreement between two or more taxing authorities with regard to sources of income and the rates at which these sources will be taxed. Tax treaties are designed to prevent double taxation of income earned in one country by a resident of another country.

tax umbrella A corporation's tax loss carryforwards that may be used to shelter profits in future years.

tax wedge The tax-related difference between the cost to employ a worker and the worker's take-home pay. Social Security taxes and income tax withholding reduce workers' paychecks below the workers' cost to the employer.

tax year The 12-month period for which tax is calculated. For most individual taxpayers, the tax year is synonymous with the calendar year.

T bill —See TREASURY BILL.

team building A planned program to enable a group of individuals to work toward a common goal. Team-building exercises include defining the team goal and identifying the factors that might inhibit progress in achieving the goal.

teaser ad 1. A short television clip designed to interest viewers in an upcoming program. 2. An advertisement that offers a premium to attract consumers to a good or service.

teaser rate An especially low interest rate offered for a short-term period by a lender. Teaser rates are widely offered by credit card companies to attract consumers to open accounts and transfer outstanding loan balances. Teaser rates are also a feature of many adjustable-rate mortgages. —Also called *introductory rate.*

technical analysis The study of relationships among security market variables, such as price levels, trading volume, and price movements, so as to gain insights into the supply and demand for securities. Rather than concentrating on earnings, the economic outlook, and other business-related factors that influence a security's value, technical analysis attempts to determine the market forces at work on a certain security or on the securities market as a whole. —Compare FUNDAMENTAL ANALYSIS.

technical correction A temporary downturn in the price of a stock or in the market itself following a period of extensive price increases. A technical correction takes place in a generally increasing market when there is no particular reason that the increases should be interrupted other than the fact that investors have temporarily slowed securities purchases. —Compare TECHNICAL RALLY.

technical default Default under an indenture agreement for other than nonpayment of interest or principal. For example, a borrower may fail to maintain a stipulated level of net working capital.

technical indicator A variable used when technically analyzing the market to determine when to invest and which stocks to select. Technical indicators include price trends, volume, and odd-lot sales.

technically strong —Used to describe a security or the whole market when most technical indicators point toward a price rise. For example, a stock may be technically strong because it has twice attempted and failed to break through a particular price level.

technically weak —Used to describe a security or the whole market when technical indicators point toward a price decline. For example, small investors may step up odd-lot purchases of securities, the number of stocks hitting new highs may be small, and market volume on days the averages are rising may be light. Together these things indicate a technically weak stock market.

technical obsolescence A decrease in value of a product or service caused by advances in technology. For example, older aircraft have become technically obsolete in part because they are not fuel efficient. This was not as important when oil was selling for $25 per barrel as when oil sells for $100 per barrel. Likewise, dry cleaning became a less valuable service because of the development of new fabrics. —Compare FUNCTIONAL OBSOLESCENCE.

technical rally A temporary rise in a security price or in the general market during a downward trend. Technical rallies are considered interruptions to a general trend. —Compare TECHNICAL CORRECTION.

technician A person who uses technical analysis to determine the selection and timing of security purchases and sales. —Also called *market technician.*

technological unemployment The reduction in the need for labor because of changes in technology. For example, the introduction of UPC scanners at retail checkout counters permits fewer employees to perform the same amount of work compared to when prices had to be input into a register. Likewise, utilization of robots in manufacturing plants has reduced the number of employees required to produce most products.

telecommunications The transmission and reception of voice, data, and video through electronic means.

telecommuting Utilizing telecommunications to perform a job from home or some other location that is remote from a regular workplace. Telecommuting allows an employee to save the cost and time of commuting to work, and at the same time to address family concerns such as caring for young children or an ill family member.

telecottage A relatively small, community-based telecommunications center that offers residents access to education and work. Telecottages were initially established as community development efforts in rural areas of Europe.

telemarketing Use of the telephone to market and sell goods and services. The Federal Trade Commission maintains a Do Not Call Registry for individuals who do not wish to receive unsolicited calls at home.

telephone switching The movement of an investor's funds from one mutual fund to another mutual fund on the basis of an order given via telephone.

template 1. A reusable form or pattern utilized to create objects with an identical shape. For example, a template is used to spray-paint symbols on a parking lot. **2.** An electronic document with established margins, text, and graphics that can be used to create standardized documents and records: *The business requires employees to file expense statements on a template available on the firm's website.*

tenancy The right to use and occupy real property: *Their lease gave the family a two-year tenancy in the home.*

tenancy at sufferance Tenancy by someone who no longer legally enjoys the right of tenancy. For example, a college student remains in an apartment after termination of the lease.

tenancy at will Tenancy that is subject to termination at any time by either the tenant or landlord. For example, a family continues to reside in a rented home after expiration of the lease while the owner attempts to sell the property.

tenancy by the entirety A type of asset ownership limited to married couples in which each spouse holds an equal share of the asset, but neither may sell or give away an interest without the other's permission. If one spouse dies, the deceased's share automatically passes to the surviving spouse. —Compare TENANCY IN COMMON.

tenancy for years Tenancy for a stated period of time or until a specific occurrence. For example, itinerant farm workers have the right to occupy the property until the crops have been harvested.

tenancy in common A type of asset ownership for two or more persons in which, upon the death of one owner, his or her share passes to heirs if a will is left or to the estate if no will is left, rather than to the co-owners. Transactions involving the property require written permission of all owners. —Compare JOINT TENANCY WITH RIGHT OF SURVIVORSHIP; TENANCY BY THE ENTIRETY.

tenancy in severalty Ownership by one person or entity (for example, a corporation). —Also called *severalty.*

tenant 1. A person or entity who makes payments for the use of property owned by someone else. **2.** One who permanently or temporarily possesses land under some kind of title. **3.** The occupant of real property.

tenant fixtures Fixtures added to leased property by a tenant, who is legally permitted to remove the fixtures at the termination of the lease. For example, the tenant of an office suite adds new lighting fixtures that can be moved to a new property at the end of the current lease.

tenant improvements Alterations to a leased space to meet the requirements of a tenant. For example, soundproofing, reconfigured interior space, and upgraded electrical wiring may be required. Tenant improvements may be paid for by the tenant, the landlord, or shared according to some agreed upon formula.

10b5-1 plan An investment plan that permits officers, directors, and other insiders of publicly traded companies to arrange future stock transactions that can be completed even though nonpublic information later becomes available. The plan allows for greater trading flexibility for corporate insiders who would otherwise face restrictions resulting from material nonpublic information.

ten-day window The span of time between the point when an individual or a company buys 5% or more of a firm's stock and the point at which the purchase must be publicly reported.

tender¹ 1. An unconditional offer to perform part of a contract. For example, notice of intention to deliver a commodity according to terms of a futures contract. **2.** A barge or small boat used to transport supplies or people. **3.** —See LEGAL TENDER.

tender² To offer shares of stock to the issuing firm as part of the company's buyback.

tender of delivery A buyer's duty to accept and pay for goods, assuming the seller has given proper notification necessary for the buyer to take delivery.

tender offer An offer made directly to stockholders to purchase or trade for their securities. A tender offer often contains restrictions, such as the minimum number of shares to be tendered for the offer to be effective or the maximum number of tendered shares that will be accepted. A tender offer may be made by a firm to its own shareholders to reduce the number of outstanding shares, or by an outsider wishing to obtain control of the firm. —Compare HOSTILE TENDER OFFER. —See also CREEPING TENDER OFFER; EXCLUSIONARY TENDER OFFER; MINI-TENDER OFFER; PARTIAL TENDER OFFER; SELF-TENDER; TWO-TIER TENDER OFFER; WILLIAMS ACT.

tenement 1. Property that is leased from someone else. **2.** A building suitable for human habitation. **3.** An apartment building housing large numbers of low-income families.

1040 The standard IRS form used by individuals to file annual income taxes. Alternate versions of 1040 are available, including 1040A (taxable income under $50,000 with no business ownership or itemized deductions), 1040EZ (taxpayers with no dependents, income under $50,000, and interest income of $400 and less), and 1040NR (U.S. nonresident aliens). —Also called *Form 1040.*

10–K An annual report of a firm's operations filed with the SEC. Compared with the typical annual report sent to stockholders, a 10–K is much less physically attractive; however, it contains many more detailed operating and financial statistics, including information on legal proceedings and management compensation. A firm's stockholders may obtain a free copy of the 10–K by writing to the corporate treasurer. —Also called *Form 10–K.*

1099–DIV An annual statement to investors and to the Internal Revenue Service by payers of dividends that lists the amount of taxable dividend payments for the year. Also included, if appropriate, is any backup withholding required by law.

1099–INT An annual statement to savers and the Internal Revenue Service that shows the amount of taxable interest payments received from an institution during the year. Interest included on 1099–INT forms includes interest paid on savings accounts, money market funds, interest-bearing checking accounts, and taxable bonds. Municipal bond interest is not included on a 1099–INT form.

tenor The term of a contract, generally with respect to a repayment of money. For example, a short-term loan may have a tenor of six months.

10–Q A quarterly unaudited financial report filed by firms that have securities listed with the SEC. The 10–Q is a less detailed, more frequently filed version of the 10–K. —Also called *Form 10–Q*.

tenure 1. The length of time in a person's current employment. **2.** The right to use and occupy property either under ownership or lease. For example, oil companies can bid on tenure rights to explore and produce oil on government property.

tenure in land —See LAND TENURE.

ten-year tax option A formula used to calculate a tax on the ordinary income portion of a lump-sum distribution of a qualified retirement plan. The tax is paid in one sum for the year the distribution is received. Taxpayers are permitted to select this option one time.

term 1. The period during which a loan will remain outstanding. For example, a bond may have a term of ten years, after which the borrower will pay the principal. **2.** The length of time that a person is to serve in an official capacity. For example, a firm's directors may be elected for terms of three years each.

term bonds Any of various bonds that mature on the same date. Corporate bond issues are often of the term variety because all the bonds of a given issue are scheduled to mature simultaneously. Municipalities often issue a combination of serial and term bonds, with periodic retirements of serial bonds and then redemption of a block of term bonds during the final year. —See also SERIAL BONDS.

term certificate A certificate of deposit with a maturity of one year or more.

terminable marital trust A trust in which the surviving spouse has use of the trust's income, but not its assets. These assets will pass to others (most likely children) at the death of the spouse.

terminal value The dollar value of an asset at a specific future time. For example, a $1,000 certificate of deposit that earns an annual return of 9% has a terminal value of $1,539 in five years.

termination benefits Benefits due an employee who terminates employment. For example, an employer may continue health, dental, and employer-paid life insurance for three months past the last date of active employment. —See also COBRA.

termination fee The one-time charge for terminating or transferring an individual retirement account. If a financial institution charges a termination fee, the fee must be spelled out in the original agreement that is signed when the account is opened. Some institutions, particularly banks and savings and loans, may not charge termination fees.

term insurance A type of life insurance in which the insurance company pays a specified sum if the insured dies during the coverage period. Term insurance includes no savings, cash values, borrowing power, or benefits at retirement. On the basis of cost, it is the least expensive insurance available, although policy prices can vary significantly among firms. Renewable term insurance offers coverage that can be renewed by the policyholder regardless of health. —Compare CASH-VALUE LIFE INSURANCE.

term loan A loan with a stated maturity of three to ten years that often requires only that the borrower make interest payments until the maturity date, when the entire principal is due. —Compare AMORTIZED LOAN.

terms 1. The conditions of a contract. **2.** The payment provisions in a sales contract. For example, a distributor of merchandise might stipulate payment terms of a 2% discount for payment within 10 days, with full payment required by 30 days.

test market

What factors do businesses consider when selecting test markets?

A fairly comprehensive needs assessment must be done in order to select a test market. Some factors to consider when evaluating a market include:

- assessing the number of customers available,
- determining the presence and relative success of any competitors in the area,
- understanding the demographics of the customer base, and
- gauging how easy or hard it will be for your salespeople to reach your targeted customers.

■ E. Mace Lewis, Vice President, Business Development, QD Healthcare Group, Greenwich, CT

terms of trade The relative price of a country's exports compared to the cost of its imports. A country's terms of trade improve when its export prices rise relative to its import prices.

term structure of interest rates —See YIELD CURVE.

term to maturity The number of years within which the issuer of debt promises to meet the requirements of an indenture agreement. —See also YIELD CURVE.

testament —See WILL.

testamentary trust A trust created by a person's will, and thereby not effective until the death of the testator. Testamentary trusts are used chiefly by wealthy individuals who are concerned about their beneficiaries' ability to administer large amounts of assets.

testate Of, relating to, or being a person who has made a valid will. —Compare IN-TESTATE.

testator A person who has made and signed a valid will.

testimonial —See ENDORSE 2.

testimonium A clause in a legal instrument that includes the date and other information associated with the signing of the document.

test market The population group or geographic region selected for promoting the sale of a new product or service. For example, a major grocery chain chooses central Indiana as a test market for upscale convenience stores.

test marketing Evaluating the commercial viability of a new product or service by offering it for sale in a limited geographical area. For example, a company is satisfied with the sales of a new flavored coffee during test marketing and decides to offer the product in a wider distribution area.

test statistic A value calculated from a sample of data that summarizes the sample and addresses the hypothesis posed by the investigator.

theoretical value The calculated price at which a security should sell. Depending on investor expectations and market imperfections, a security may sell at a price above or below its theoretical value.

Theory of Constraints A management philosophy of continuous improvement achieved by identifying and managing the most important constraint that affects quality and productivity. Successfully dealing with one constraint is followed by identifying and handling the next most important problem. For example, a business may determine that delivery delays are the result of excessive absenteeism. Initiating a bonus pay system may successfully deal with this constraint. The Theory of Constraints is credited to Israeli-born scientist and business consultant Eliyahu Goldratt.

Theory X The pessimistic management theory that employees are generally lazy, dislike work, resist change, and care little about organizational goals. If Theory X is accurate, managers need to adopt an authoritarian style in order to maximize the productivity of employees.

Theory Y The optimistic management theory that employees are generally creative and view work as fulfilling. Managers should offer a creative and participative atmosphere that will stimulate employees to be productive in achieving the organization's goals.

Theory Z The Japanese management style popularized in the 1980s that assumes employees have an interest in good working relationships with management and other employees. Management generally has high confidence in employees, who are encouraged to participate in the management decision making. Employees are viewed as long-term assets who will stay with the same firm throughout their careers.

the Street —See WALL STREET.

thin capitalization A financial structure heavily weighted toward debt, generally undertaken in order to gain the tax advantage of deducting interest expenses. The Netherlands proposed a "thin capitalization rule" that disallowed a tax deduction for interest expenses on excess debt. Excess debt was defined as the extent to which total debt exceeded three times total equity.

thinking outside the box —See OUTSIDE THE BOX.

thin market A market for a security in which there are relatively few offers and bids. A thin market causes reduced liquidity and makes it more difficult to buy or sell the security without affecting its price. —Compare DEEP MARKET; TIGHT MARKET 2. —Also called *narrow market.*

third market The over-the-counter dealer market in stock that is listed on organized exchanges such as the New York Stock Exchange. The third market developed in the 1960s when institutional investors became dissatisfied with the liquidity and brokerage commissions for large security trades on the exchanges. —Compare FOURTH MARKET; SECONDARY MARKET.

third party An individual or other entity who is not a direct party to a contract or agreement, but who somehow has an interest in or is affected by it. For example, an insured driver is at fault in a traffic accident that damages the car of another person, who becomes the third party. The insured driver and his or her insurance company are the direct parties to the contract.

third-party check A check that has been endorsed once and is being cashed or deposited by a second endorser. For example, a check on First Valdosta Bank is made out to Bill, who endorses the check and gives it to Karin, who then endorses the check for deposit to her account. Many businesses do not accept payment by third-party checks.

third-party sale Sale of a product to an intermediary who in turn sells or gives away the product to the final consumer. For example, newspapers are purchased in bulk by a hotel for free distribution to guests, the third parties.

Thomson Financial A major provider of information, analytical tools, and consulting services to the financial community. The firm, a division of Thomson Corporation, is best known to investors for its First Call segment, which publishes consensus earnings estimates. —See also FIRST CALL.

three-martini lunch A leisurely, generally expensive lunch during which executives discuss business and indulge in alcoholic beverages. Use of the term generally implies the participants took too much time, spent too much money, and drank too many alcoholic beverages.

thrift A financial institution that derives its funds primarily from consumer savings accounts. The term originally referred to those institutions offering mainly passbook savings accounts, but the industry evolved through financial deregulation to the point where these accounts often provide only a small source of funds for many thrifts. The term often refers to savings and loan associations, but can also mean credit unions and mutual savings banks.

thrift shop A retail establishment operated by a charity that sells donated secondhand merchandise, including clothing, books, and small appliances. Volunteers staff many thrift shops. —Compare CONSIGNMENT SHOP.

thrifty Describing someone who spends money only after careful evaluation.

through rate The cost of shipping goods from the point of origin to final destination. The through rate is particularly relevant when two or more shippers are involved in taking care of a single shipment.

tick A movement in the price or price quotation of a security or contract. —See also DOWNTICK; MINIMUM TICK; UPTICK.

ticker An automated quotation system on which security transactions are reported after they occur on an exchange floor. Even though the newer systems are electronic and no longer actually tick, the name of the old mechanical device has stuck.

ticker symbol The abbreviation by which a security appears on stock quotation machines. For example, T represents AT&T, GY represents GenCorp, C represents Citicorp, and CVG represents Convergys.

ticker tape The narrow continuous rolls of paper on which stock transactions were printed before the electronic age made the old system obsolete. The term now refers to the flow of prices appearing on the electronic tickers of brokerage firms. —Also called *tape*. —See also BROAD TAPE.

tick mark The symbol used by accountants on audit work papers to indicate a procedure has been completed.

tied loan In international trade, a government agency loan that requires the foreign borrower to purchase products from or spend money in the lender's country.

tie-in agreement —See TYING CONTRACT.

tie-in promotion A joint promotion of two or more products or services. For example, in 2006 boxes of Post Great Grains cereal included a free trial package of Starbucks coffee as a value-added item for consumers. The tie-in promotion was intended to increase sales of both the cereal and the coffee.

tiered market A securities market in which investors favor certain groups or types of stock, with the result that the favored securities sell at higher price-earnings ratios than do other securities with similar characteristics. Favored groups tend to rotate as investors' interests and perceptions change.

tight market 1. A market in which the supply of a good or service is limited compared to demand. For example, a community in eastern Wyoming's coal country experiences a tight market in rental housing during the energy boom. Tight markets result in rising prices. **2.** A market for securities in which competition is intense and spreads are narrow. In a tight market, dealers must make up in volume what they lose on a narrowing of the spread. —Compare DEEP MARKET; THIN MARKET.

tight money A condition of the money supply in which credit is restricted and interest rates, consequently, are relatively high. Tight money generally has a negative effect on asset values. —Compare EASY MONEY.

tight ship An organization with strict rules and firm controls. For example, a company brings in a new CEO who promises to run a tight ship.

till A tray or box where money is kept, as, for example, a cash register.

time-and-a-half A rate of pay that is 150% of normal, generally for working overtime or during holidays. —See also DOUBLE TIME.

time-and-motion study Measuring and evaluating the time required to complete a specific task. The study is undertaken in an effort to detect inefficiencies and make improvements that will increase productivity.

time card A card used to record the time that an employee arrives at and departs from work. Most time cards are time stamped when they are inserted into a recording or stamping device. The time card is inserted upon arrival and again at departure, thus providing the employer with a record of the number of hours at work.

time deposit An interest-bearing savings deposit or certificate of deposit at a financial institution. Although the deposits formerly included only deposits with specific maturities (such as certificates of deposit), they now are considered to include virtually all savings-type deposits. —Compare DEMAND DEPOSIT.

time draft A draft that is payable a certain number of days after it has been presented. —Compare SIGHT DRAFT.

time horizon The interval during which an investment program is to be completed. An investor's time horizon is very important in determining the types of investments that should be selected. For example, investments that would be appropriate for an individual's retirement in 30 years are seldom suitable for reaching a short-term goal. —Also called *horizon.*

time management The employment of techniques to improve productivity by using time more effectively. For example, a manager might maintain a time log for recording his or her activities in order to determine how much time is wasted.

time series A set of variables with values related to the respective times the variables are measured. Thus, a weekly record of sales throughout a period of years is a time series. Time series are often used to project future values by observing how the value of a variable has changed in the past.

times fixed charges —See FIXED-CHARGE COVERAGE.

time share Joint ownership of real property that gives each owner a specified time interval for occupancy. Initial offerings in these arrangements entailed buying a specific week each year. Current offers are generally more flexible, allowing owners to choose their week from within groups of weeks or to buy points that can be traded for weeks. Time-share owners are also generally offered an opportunity to join a network that allows them to trade for time at other facilities. Time-share ownership often entails a substantial annual fee to pay for maintenance, taxes, insurance, and management.

times interest earned —See INTEREST COVERAGE.

time spread —See CALENDAR SPREAD.

timetable **1.** The period during which a goal or series of goals is to be achieved: *The construction firm's timetable indicated the new building would be ready for occupancy by the end of January.* **2.** A schedule of events along with the times at which the events are to occur. For example, a train line's timetable provides a chronological listing of departure times and destinations.

time utility The increase in consumer satisfaction gained by making a good or service available at the appropriate time. For example, offering fresh donuts and hot coffee early in the morning, or selling imprinted T-shirts immediately following a championship game is an effort to effect time utility.

time value The portion of an option premium in excess of the option's intrinsic value. For example, a call option that allows the holder to buy 100 shares of a $25 stock for $20 (the strike price) has an intrinsic value of $500. The time value is $150 if the option trades for $650.

time value of money The concept that holds that a specific sum of money is more valuable the sooner it is received. Time value of money is dependent not only on the time interval being considered, but also the rate of discount used in calculating current or future values.

time-weighted return A rate-of-return measure of portfolio performance that gives equal weight to each period included in the study, regardless of any differences in amounts invested in each period.

timing —See MARKET TIMING.

timing difference The time difference between the point at which a transaction affects items for financial reporting purposes and the point at which it affects the same items for tax purposes. For example, purchase of a fixed asset depreciated by an accelerated method for tax purposes, but by straight-line for reporting purposes, creates a timing difference for depreciation expense.

TIN —See TAXPAYER IDENTIFICATION NUMBER.

tin parachute An employee-protection plan that guarantees severance pay, outplacement assistance, and health and life insurance benefits to all employees who lose their jobs because of a corporate takeover. A generous tin parachute serves to make a takeover more expensive and less likely.

tip **1.** Information unavailable to the general public that, if accurate, could produce extraordinary profits for an investor who acts on it in a security transaction. **2.** —See GRATUITY.

tippee A person who is given inside information.

TIPS —See TREASURY INFLATION-PROTECTED SECURITIES.

tipster A person who provides inside information.

title **1.** A legal document that is evidence of an ownership interest in property. —See also AFTER-ACQUIRED TITLE. **2.** The right of ownership of property.

title defect A legal claim on property by someone other than the owner(s). For example, a person might claim to hold a lien on the property. A title defect affects an owner's ability to sell property. —Compare CLEAR TITLE.

title insurance An insurance contract that protects a home buyer against financial losses caused by a defect in the title to the property. The cost of title insurance is a function of the value of the property.

title insurance company A business that examines the validity of the title to real property and, if satisfied, guarantees there are no encumbrances or defects.

title report A written statement of the condition of a title to real property with regard to claims, easements, or other defects.

title search An exhaustive search of public records relating to the chain of ownership of a piece of property. —Also called *examination of title.* —See also ABSTRACT OF TITLE.

title-theory state A state in which the buyer of property receives title from the seller and then gives that title to the mortgage holder. The lender returns the title to the buyer when the mortgage is paid. The buyer enjoys use of the property during the term of the mortgage, even though the lender holds the title. —Compare LIEN-THEORY STATE.

toehold purchase The acquisition of a minority position in a target company before establishing a much larger stake. Toehold purchases are often used by investors who wish to influence management decisions or acquire controlling interest at a future date. A toehold purchase of less than 5% of the outstanding common stock allows a party to buy stock in a company without filing a notice with the SEC and with the target company.

> **CASE STUDY** Private equity firms and hedge funds sometimes make a toehold purchase in a target company as a way to lower the overall cost of an acquisition. For example, a private equity firm might purchase up to 5% of a target's stock at market prices before making an offer to acquire the remaining shares at a substantial premium. The acquiring firm might also obtain a minority position in order to pressure the board to make certain changes. Either action may well cause other investors to become interested in the firm and enter into a bidding contest for its shares. In November 2005, Carl Icahn announced he had acquired 9.3% of the stock of Canadian-based Fairmont Hotels and Resorts, the owner or operator of over 80 properties including several of Canada's most historic properties. At the time of the announcement, Icahn said that he wanted the firm's management to take steps to increase the firm's undervalued share price. He also stated that the firm's shareholders would benefit if a larger hotel operator acquired the company. The following month Icahn launched a $1.19 billion cash offer of $40 per share to obtain a controlling interest in the company. The firm's directors urged shareholders to reject the offer and later agreed to a $45-per-share cash buyout by a Saudi prince and a Los Angeles–based real estate investment fund. Although Icahn failed in his takeover bid, his toehold purchase put the firm in play and produced a substantial profit for the activist investor.

tokenism Minimal and insincere hiring of minorities to create the appearance of inclusiveness and compliance with affirmative action.

Tokyo Stock Exchange (TSE) The largest securities exchange in Japan. The Tokyo Stock Exchange, established in 1878, trades equities electronically in four sections: the first section for stocks of the largest Japanese companies; the second section for stocks of smaller companies with lower trading volumes; the third section for foreign securities; and the fourth section for growth and emerging stocks. The Tokyo Stock Exchange also trades bonds, options, and futures.

toll 1. A fee. For example, drivers may be required to pay a toll to use a road or cross a bridge. Callers may be charged a toll to place a telephone call outside their calling area. 2. Loss or suffering from an activity, event, or condition: *The pension fund's poor financial condition took a toll on employees.*

tombstone An advertisement for a securities issue. The ad lists the security, some of the security's specifics, and a bracketed list of the members of the syndicate selling the issue in the order of the members' importance. The term derives from the fact that the notice appears as a matter of record after the sale has been completed.

top The highest level to which a stock, a market index, or some other asset will rise. A top may be short-term or long-term, depending on the type of price movement being evaluated. —Compare BOTTOM.

top a bid To make a bid higher than the prevailing bid.

top-down Of or relating to making investment decisions by first focusing on economic forecasts and then evaluating prospects for individual industries and companies. —Compare BOTTOM-UP 2.

topper fee The penalty fee paid to a potential acquirer by a target company that accepts a higher subsequent offer from another firm. This special type of breakup fee is included in the acquisition agreement between the target company and the original acquiring firm that has been spurned.

Toronto Stock Exchange (TSE) The main Canadian exchange for trading large-cap equity securities. The TSE moved from traditional floor trading to electronic trading in 1997, and in April 2000 demutualized to become a for-profit corporation. The Toronto Stock Exchange accounts for approximately 95% of all equity trading in Canada. Small-cap Canadian stocks are traded in Vancouver on the Canadian Venture Exchange.

Torrens System A system for the registration of real property such that a buyer can rely on the name showing on the land title. The Torrens System allows a purchaser to buy property without a title search and without concern about the manner in which the seller became an owner. This system of land registration is popular in Australia, parts of Canada, and in some states of the United States.

tort A civil (as opposed to criminal) wrong resulting in injury caused intentionally or by carelessness. Litigation involving a tort may result from such things as an automobile accident, assault, medical malpractice, product liability, trademark infringement, and slander.

total asset turnover A financial ratio that indicates the effectiveness with which a firm's management uses its assets to generate sales. A relatively high ratio tends to reflect intensive use of assets. Total asset turnover is calculated by dividing the firm's annual sales by its total assets. Sales are listed on the firm's income statement and assets are listed on its balance sheet. —Also called *asset turnover.*

total capitalization —See CAPITALIZATION.

total cost The total amount of money expended to establish an investment position. Total cost includes commissions, accrued interest, and taxes in addition to the principal amount of securities traded.

total disability The physical or mental inability to perform the essential duties of the person's regular occupation or a similar occupation for which the person is generally qualified. The definition of total disability can vary and is very important in attempting to qualify for disability benefits from an insurance company. Social Security tends to use a strict definition of disability.

total loss Damage so extensive that the cost of repair exceeds the value of the property. For example, a casualty insurance company might declare a damaged vehicle a total loss and purchase the vehicle from the insured rather than pay to have it repaired.

total quality management (TQM) A set of management practices directed toward continuous improvement that results in a high quality of products and services. The underlying foundation of TQM is that everyone needs to participate in order to achieve long-term quality goals. —See also BUSINESS PROCESS REENGINEERING.

total return The sum of dividend, interest, or other regular income plus any gain in value. Total return is generally considered a better measure of an investment's return than regular income alone. —Also called *rate of return.*

total volume The aggregate amount of trading in a security on a particular security exchange, or in a specific type of security such as stocks, bonds, options, or futures contracts.

Totten trust A trust in which the assets are deposited for a beneficiary, but the grantor has complete control of the trust, including the right to reclaim the assets. The assets pass to the beneficiary upon the death of the grantor but are taxed as part of the grantor's estate.

tout 1. To foster interest in something. For example, a broker might tout a security to a client in the hope that the client will purchase the security. **2.** To offer gambling advice for a fee.

townhouse One of a row of adjoining houses, generally with two or more floors. Most townhouses are designed with the kitchen and a living area on the main floor and two or more bedrooms on upper floors.

TQM —See TOTAL QUALITY MANAGEMENT.

trace To follow or track something. For example, a firm's auditor might trace a transaction, or a freight company may be asked by a customer to trace a missing shipment.

tracking error The difference in the return earned by a portfolio and the return earned by the benchmark against which the portfolio is constructed. For example, if a bond portfolio earns a return of 5.15% during a period when the portfolio's benchmark (say, for example, the Lehman Brothers Index) produces a return of 5.06%, the tracking error is .09%, or 9 basis points.

tracking stock A common stock that provides holders with a financial interest in a particular segment of a company's business. Essentially, a tracking stock is a proxy for the value of the subsidiary if it were independent and publicly traded. Tracking stocks are generally issued by corporations that feel their firms are not being fully valued by investors.

tract A parcel of land, generally held for development or some other specific purpose.

tract house One of many similar homes, generally constructed by a single developer, on a tract of land. Tract homes are built in a limited variety of sizes, floor plans, and colors that are repeated over and over.

trade¹ 1. The purchase or sale of an asset. —See also TRANSACTION. **2.** The occupation or business in which a person is employed: *The woman next door is employed in the diamond trade.*

trade² To buy or sell an asset, frequently with only short intervals of ownership: *Our friend read a book on how to get rich by trading residential properties.* —See also FLIP-PING.

trade acceptance A bill of exchange drawn by the seller on the buyer that guarantees payment on a specific date. The trade acceptance can be sold at a discount in the secondary market.

trade advertising Advertising directed at wholesalers and distributors that resell goods to the public. For example, an appliance manufacturer advertises its products in a magazine sent to retailers.

trade agreement A treaty between two or more countries that agree to certain terms of commerce that may include tariffs, quotas, and environmental or employment issues. —See also NORTH AMERICAN FREE TRADE AGREEMENT.

trade allowance 1. A price reduction offered to retailers or distributors in an effort to stimulate sales of a product. —Also called *trade discount.* **2.** An allowance for cargo losses that result from the nature of the product carried. For example, a small proportion of petroleum products may leak or remain in a pipeline.

trade area The geographic region in which a good or service is available and from which a company generates most of its sales. For example, a local retail store may have a trade area with a 50-mile radius. —Also called *market area.*

trade balance —See BALANCE OF TRADE.

trade barrier A government restriction that limits international trade of goods and services. For example, in March 2002, President Bush established a trade barrier by imposing quotas on the importation of certain types of steel into the United States.

trade credit The sale of goods or services when the seller provides short-term credit. Trade credit results in accounts receivable for the seller and accounts payable for the buyer. Trade credit is offered as an incentive to customers. —See also TERMS 2.

trade date The date on which an order to buy or sell a security is executed. Most security orders require payment or delivery within three business days of the trade date. —Compare SETTLEMENT DATE 1. —Also called *transaction date.*

trade deficit The amount of goods and services that a country imports that is in excess of the amount of goods and services it exports. Large trade deficits may result in unemployment and a reduction in economic growth in the country with the deficit. —Compare TRADE SURPLUS.

trade discount —See TRADE ALLOWANCE 1.

trade diversion In international trade, a change in the sources of origin for a country's imports caused by adjustments in trade practices. For example, government quotas imposed on car imports from Asia shift demand to importing additional vehicles manufactured in Europe.

trade fixture Personal property attached to real property by a tenant in order to pursue a trade or business. Trade fixtures remain the property of the tenant, who has the right of removal before or at the termination of the lease.

trade magazine A periodical publication directed toward a particular industry or profession rather than the general consumer. For example, *Fleet Owner* is a trade magazine targeted at executives and managers of commercial trucking fleets.

trademark A distinctive proprietary emblem, insignia, or name that identifies a particular product or service. A trademark is an intangible asset that may be protected from use by others. —See also GENERIC MARK.

trade mission A group of individuals sent by a government and/or business interests to a foreign country in an effort to stimulate exports to that country.

trade name The name under which a company conducts business.

trade promotion An activity designed to influence the pricing, sales, and profitability of a good or service. For example, a manufacturer may reduce a product's list price in return for a retailer agreeing to purchase a larger quantity.

trader A person who buys and sells things with the goal of profiting from short-term price swings. For example, a stock trader buys and sells securities.

trade rate A reduced price for a good or service offered to a specific group. For example, a hotel chain may offer a trade rate to travel writers.

trade secret Information regarding an idea, process, data, or anything else an organization considers confidential. Trade secrets are designed to give an organization a head start against competitors in offering goods and services.

trade show An organized gathering of members of a particular industry during which they display or demonstrate their products and services for potential customers. Trade shows are often open only to members of the media and people associated with the particular industry.

trade surplus The amount of goods and services that a country exports that is in excess of the amount of goods and services it imports. A trade surplus increases economic activity in a country but also may result in higher prices and interest rates if the economy is already operating at near capacity. —Compare TRADE DEFICIT.

trade union —See LABOR UNION.

trade war An escalating competition between two or more countries that take actions, including imposing duties and quotas, to restrict imports from the other participants. For example, in 2002 the United States escalated a dispute over Canadian softwood lumber by imposing a 27% duty on imports of this product from its northern neighbor. —See also TARIFF WAR.

trading authorization A written document that gives another party the power to enter orders for an investor's account. The other party may be an employee of the broker-dealer handling the account, a spouse, or someone else designated by the client in the trading authorization.

trading bloc A group of countries that have associated to promote and manage trade activities. Trading blocs are formed to encourage trade of goods and services among members.

trading desk A desk where securities are traded. Trading desks are found in most large financial institutions, including banks, insurance companies, and brokerage firms where bonds, stocks, and futures are bought and sold. —Also called *desk*.

trading dividends The purchase and sale of equity securities with the goal of maximizing dividend income. Corporate investors may engage in trading dividends to take advantage of the tax benefit of dividend income for corporations.

trading halt —See SUSPENDED TRADING.

trading limit The number of commodity contracts that a person may trade during a single day. The limit is established by the Commodity Futures Trading Commission or by the exchange on which the particular contract is traded. —Compare POSITION LIMIT.

trading on the equity The use of borrowed money to increase the return on an investor's capital. Suppose an investor is able to borrow 50% of the funds required for a $10,000 investment that returns 16% annually. If interest on the loan is 6%, the investor can earn $1,600 ($10,000 at 16%) minus interest of $300 ($5,000 at 6%), or $1,300 on an investment of $5,000 ($10,000 minus $5,000 borrowed), for a return of 26% ($1,300/$5,000).

trading pool A pool in which the stock is manipulated by purchases and sales in the open market. For example, pool operators affect a stock's price and volume by making purchases in the open market, thereby attracting the interest of other investors.

trading range The high and low prices between which a stock, bond, futures contract, option, or an average of these financial products has been traded or is expected to trade.

trading unit —See UNIT OF TRADING.

trading variation —See MINIMUM TICK.

traffic **1.** The number of people who visit or walk near a retail store: *The coffee shop is located near the entrance to the mall, where there is a considerable amount of traffic.* **2.** Visitors to a website: *Placing a banner ad on the search engine site generated a lot of traffic for the advertiser.* **3.** Transmissions over a communications network.

trailer fee —See TRAILING COMMISSION.

trailing commission A commission paid annually to a sales agent for as long as a client's money remains in an account. —Also called *trailer fee.*

trailing earnings The earnings per share for a firm's most recently completed fiscal year.

trailing P/E The price-earnings ratio of a firm's common stock calculated as the current stock price divided by the previous year's earnings per share. —Compare FORWARD P/E.

trait theory The theory that leadership effectiveness can be explained by particular characteristics or personality traits that lead people naturally into leadership roles. Commitment, courage, integrity, and imagination tend to be characteristics of leaders.

tranche A class of bonds. Collateralized mortgage obligations are structured with several tranches of bonds that have various maturities.

transaction An agreement among parties to transfer all or part ownership of something. —See also TRADE[1] 1.

transaction costs The expense incurred in buying or selling something. Transaction costs for buying and selling securities include commissions, markups, markdowns, fees, and any direct taxes. Real estate purchases or sales typically result in substantial transaction costs. All or a portion of transaction costs may be embedded in the price and difficult to determine.

transaction date —See TRADE DATE.

transaction exposure The risk of loss caused by changes in currency exchange rates when a company's payables and receivables are denominated in a foreign currency. Derivatives are used to hedge against changes in currency exchange rates and reduce transaction exposure.

transaction processing In computers, the continuous processing and updating of files. For example, a large retail chain is likely to utilize transaction processing in inventory control when stores report real-time sales data to a central computer. —Compare BATCH PROCESSING.

transfer 1. To record a change in asset ownership. **2.** To deliver an asset to the buyer. For example, a security is transferred to the buyer's broker by the seller's broker.

transferable put right An option granted by a corporation to its shareholders that permits the shareholders to sell stock back to the corporation at a stipulated price. Shareholders who do not wish to exercise the options are permitted to sell the put rights to other investors. Issuing transferable put rights is an alternative to a tender offer or open market purchases as a form of share repurchase.

transfer agent A company, generally a bank or trust company, appointed by a firm to transfer that firm's securities. The transfer agent is also likely to maintain the current record of security owners for transmitting dividends, reports, security distributions, and so forth.

transfer development rights A zoning privilege for the development of one parcel of land that can be transferred to a different parcel of land. In most instances this involves shifting the potential development of agricultural land to areas nearer to municipal services. Transfer development rights allow a landowner to separate and sell development rights.

transfer notice —See DELIVERY NOTICE 1.

transfer on death A legal agreement that, upon the death of its maker, passes ownership of certain assets to beneficiaries while bypassing probate. A transfer-on-death agreement generally results in assets passing with minimal delay and may result in reduced probate fees. Assets passed through this agreement remain subject to estate taxation.

transfer payment A payment by an individual or organization for which no good or service is received. Medicaid payments by government to low-income individuals are examples of transfer payments.

transfer price The price at which an item is transferred internally between two units of the same company. For example, an oil company engaged in drilling, refining, and marketing must determine the price of the product as it passes through the chain from oil field to service station in order to determine the profitability of each stage.

transfer tax 1. A tax on the transfer of property that is sold. **2.** A tax on the transfer of assets by gift or by death.

transformational leadership Motivating people by using energy, enthusiasm, and passion to sell a vision.

transient worker —See ITINERANT WORKER.

transit advertising Promotions placed in public locations. Transit advertising includes billboards, displays on buildings or public transportation vehicles, and signs in terminals or on the inside of buses or subways.

transition economy The economic system of a country that is in the process of shifting from being centrally planned to becoming a market structure.

transit zone An area adjacent to a port in which goods are stored for the benefit of a neighboring country without port facilities. Goods that enter and exit the transit zone are not subject to duties or quotas of the host country. A transit zone is a limited version of a free trade zone.

translation The expression of amounts denominated in one currency in terms of another currency by using the rate at which the two currencies are exchanged. For example, a firm with foreign operations might express sales made in euros in terms of U.S. dollars. —Also called *foreign currency translation.*

translation gain The gain that results when a firm translates amounts stated in one currency into terms of another currency. For example, a U.S. company that translates euros into U.S. dollars following a period of a weakening dollar will report a translation gain because the euros exchange for a greater number of dollars.

translation loss The loss that results when a firm translates amounts stated in one currency into terms of another currency. The loss is incurred when the firm translates from a currency that has declined in value relative to the currency into which the amounts are being converted.

transmittal letter A cover letter, generally brief, that accompanies another item such as a document. The transmittal letter includes the purpose and a description of the item being sent.

transnational 1. Of or describing a business with operations in more than one country. **2.** Describing a shipment that moves between two or more countries.

transparency The full, accurate, and timely disclosure of information. Transparency makes it more likely that assets will be accurately valued.

transparent market A market in which current quotation and trade information is readily available to all interested participants.

transshipment 1. The transfer of goods from one conveyance to another for further transport. For example, fish may be transferred from a small fishing vessel to a larger cargo ship. **2.** Shipping goods to an intermediate destination where they are reshipped to the ultimate buyer. For example, a munitions manufacturer ships weapons to a country for reshipment to another country, where weapon sales are prohibited by the manufacturer's government.

travel and entertainment expenses Expenses incurred by a business for employee travel and entertainment that are ordinary and necessary in carrying on a trade or business. Certain IRS regulations apply in order to be able to deduct travel and entertainment expenses for tax purposes. For example, only 50% of food, beverage, and entertainment expenses are generally permitted as deductions. Reimbursed travel and entertainment expenses incurred by an employee are not included in wages and cannot be deducted. Unreimbursed expenses by an employee are generally permitted as an itemized deduction, subject to the 2% adjusted gross income limit.

treasurer A corporate financial officer who often has the responsibility for preparing financial reports, releasing financial information, and filing tax returns. The treasurer may or may not be the firm's main financial decision maker.

Treasuries All bonds backed by the U.S. government that are issued through the Department of the Treasury. The safety of Treasuries is the benchmark against which all other debt securities are measured. Interest received from U.S. Treasury securities is not subject to taxation by state and local governments, although it is taxable by the

Treasury Inflation-Protected Securities (TIPS)

I am concerned about inflation and have heard that TIPS provide a good hedge against rising consumer prices. Can you explain how these securities work? How do I buy them?

TIPS are marketable securities whose principal is adjusted by changes in the consumer price index. With inflation (a rise in the index), your principal increases. With deflation (a drop in the index), your principal decreases but never drops below the amount of your original investment. TIPS pay interest every six months at the fixed rate; however, the amount of interest may vary up or down depending on your principal adjustment.

You can purchase TIPS directly from the U.S. Treasury and also through banks and broker-dealers. To set up an account directly with the Treasury, go to http://www.treasurydirect.gov.

■ Richard S. Campbell, CIMA®, Senior Vice President, Wealth Management,
Portfolio Management Director, Smith Barney, Valdosta, GA

---

federal government. —See also SEPARATE TRADING OF REGISTERED INTEREST AND PRINCIPAL OF SECURITIES.

Treasury bill A short-term debt security of the U.S. government that is sold in minimum amounts of $10,000 and multiples of $5,000 above the minimum. Bills with 13-week and 26-week maturities are auctioned each Monday, and 52-week bills are sold every 4 weeks. These obligations, which are very easy to resell, may be purchased through brokers, commercial banks, or directly from the Federal Reserve. —Also called *T bill.* —See also BANK-DISCOUNT BASIS; CERTIFICATE OF INDEBTEDNESS.

Treasury bill auction The weekly Monday auction for 13-week and 26-week Treasury bills and the monthly auction for 52-week Treasury bills. The Federal Reserve conducts the auctions on a competitive-bid basis. A portion of the issues is set aside for investors who do not wish to enter a specific bid, but who will purchase the securities at the average price paid by competitive bidders.

Treasury bond Longer-term, interest-bearing debt of the U.S. Treasury. Treasury bonds are quoted and traded in thirty-seconds of a point.

Treasury Department —See DEPARTMENT OF THE TREASURY, U.S.

Treasury Direct A U.S. Treasury book-entry security system that allows investors to purchase and maintain U.S. Treasury securities, including bills, notes, bonds, TIPS, and U.S. savings bonds. The system is generally designed for investors who plan to hold securities until maturity, although securities held in an account can be sold at current market prices through brokers or many financial institutions. Treasury securities that have already been issued can only be purchased through brokers or dealers in the secondary market.

Treasury Inflation-Protected Securities (TIPS) Negotiable bonds issued and guaranteed by the U.S. Treasury with returns that are indexed to compensate bondholders for inflation. Indexing is accomplished by adjusting the principal amount of TIPS upward to adjust for changes in the consumer price index. These securities were first issued in 1997. —See also SERIES I SAVINGS BOND.

Treasury note Intermediate-term (1–10 years), interest-bearing debt of the U.S. Treasury that may be purchased through a bank or brokerage firm or directly from the Federal Reserve. An active secondary market makes it easy to resell a Treasury note.

treasury stock The shares of a firm's stock that have been issued and then repurchased. Treasury stock is not considered in paying dividends, voting, or calculating earnings per share. It may be retired or reissued. —See also RETIREMENT 2.

tree diagram A drawing showing all of the possible outcomes from an event, based on subsequent events and decisions that follow those events. A tree diagram begins with one event, which branches into two or more subsequent events, which each branch into multiple events, and so forth. Each event is accompanied by its respective probability.

trend The relatively constant movement of a variable throughout a period of time. The period may be short or long, depending on whether the trend itself is short-term or long-term. For example, a rising market is taken to mean that prices of most stocks are in an upward trend.

trend analysis The analysis of past changes in a variable's value to determine if a trend exists and, if so, what the trend indicates. A firm's marketing department is likely to be interested in sales trends for each of the firm's products. —Compare RATIO ANALYSIS.

trendline In statistics, a line on a chart indicating the direction of a variable over time. In technical analysis of securities, a straight line or two parallel straight lines indicate the direction in which a security has been moving and, many technicians believe, the direction in which it will continue to move. When a variable breaks through a trendline, the beginning of a new trend is indicated.

trial and error A process of experimenting with different possibilities in an effort to determine which option works best or produces the desired outcome. For example, a company might try several options for packaging a new product in order to determine which option produces the most sales. Those options that do not produce satisfactory results—the errors—are rejected.

trial balance A list of general ledger account balances that indicates whether debits and credits are equal.

trial court The court in which a lawsuit is filed and a first hearing is held.

trial offer An offer by a manufacturer, distributor, or service company to a potential customer to try a product or service without charge. Trial offers often require the recipient to cancel within a specific time in order to keep from receiving additional merchandise or services at the regular price. For example, a publisher might offer three free issues of a magazine, after which the recipient must either cancel or be billed for a subscription.

trial size Product packaging of a smaller-than-normal size that is offered at a nominal price in an effort to attract new customers.

trickle down In economics, the theory that increased wealth and income for businesses and wealthy individuals will filter, or trickle down, to those on a lower rung of the economic ladder. The theory holds that granting tax breaks to businesses will result in increased profitability, expansion, and the hiring of additional employees such that increased wealth and profits at the top trickle down as increased incomes for individuals.

trigger point The event or condition that initiates a predetermined action. For example, the New York Stock Exchange halts trading in stocks when the Dow Jones Industrial Average declines by a specified number of points (the trigger point) in a trading session.

trigger price The specific price of an imported item below which a quota or tariff will be put into effect. A trigger price is imposed to keep foreign competitors from under-cutting prices charged by domestic companies in the domestic firm's home market.

triple A —See AAA.

triple A tenant A financially strong tenant that is much sought after by landlords.

triple net lease —See NET LEASE.

triple tax exempt Of, relating to, or being a municipal bond, trust, or fund paying interest that is free of federal, state, and local income taxation for individuals residing in certain localities. This situation results from the fact that most, but not all, states and localities exempt municipal bond interest from taxation if the bonds are issued within that particular state. Triple tax exemption is of particular interest to investors residing in high-tax states and localities, such as New York City.

triple witching hour The hour before the market closing when options and futures on stock indexes expire on the same day, thereby setting off frenzied trading in futures, options, and underlying securities. Traders and arbitrageurs unwind investment positions and produce large price movements in securities. The triple witching hour occurs on the third Fridays of March, June, September, and December. —See also EXPIRATION FRIDAY.

troubled debt restructuring —See DEBT RESTRUCTURING.

troubleshooter Someone who identifies and solves problems. For example, a firm experiencing substantial inventory shortages hires a security consultant to serve as a troubleshooter. Some business executives who can turn a troubled company around are considered troubleshooters.

troy weight A system of measuring mass, especially for precious metals, including gold and silver. One ounce typically used in the United States is equal to 0.91 troy ounces.

truckload The quantity of freight required to fill a trailer or to qualify for truckload rates.

true lease A lease that meets IRS requirements for the lessor to claim ownership and the lessee to claim the entire lease payment as an expense for tax purposes. To qualify, any purchase option must be at fair market value at the end of the lease. —Also called *fair market value lease.*

truncation 1. In mathematics and computing, reducing the number of digits to the right of the decimal point by dropping those that are least significant. **2.** —See CHECK TRUNCATION.

trust A legal arrangement whereby control over property is transferred to a person or organization (the trustee) for the benefit of someone else (the beneficiary). Trusts are created for a variety of reasons, including tax savings and improved asset management. —See also CHARITABLE LEAD TRUST; CHARITABLE REMAINDER TRUST; CLIFFORD TRUST; DISCRETIONARY TRUST; MARITAL-DEDUCTION TRUST; QTIP TRUST; SHAM TRUST.

trust account An account in a financial institution such as a bank, credit union, or trust company that is established under a trust agreement and administered by a trustee for the benefit of another person. For example, an attorney administers a trust account for safekeeping of a client's funds. —See also IMPOUND ACCOUNT.

trust certificate —See COLLATERAL TRUST BOND.

trust company A legal entity, generally affiliated with a commercial bank, that serves as an intermediary or agent on behalf of individuals or businesses as a guardian, trustee, or conservator of trust funds and estates.

trust deed 1. —See DEED OF TRUST. 2. —See INDENTURE.

trustee An appointed person or institution that manages assets for the benefit of someone else. Trustees are most often trust corporations or trust departments of commercial banks that manage the assets for a fee based on a percentage of the size of the trust (usually under 1%). A trust may be very restrictive or it may allow the trustee wide discretion, depending on the grantor's wishes.

trustee in bankruptcy A court-appointed agent charged with the administration, liquidation, and distribution of the assets of a bankrupt company or individual. The trustee acts on behalf of interested parties, primarily creditors.

trustee's sale The public sale by a trustee of property in foreclosure. The appointed trustee distributes proceeds of the sale to creditors holding unpaid debts.

trust fund Property held in trust and administered for the benefit of someone.

Trust Indenture Act of 1939 The legislation that established rights for security holders under indenture agreements. The act sets standards for trustees, requires financial reports by the issuers to the trustees, and mandates disclosure of owners' rights under the indenture agreements.

trust instrument The written document creating a trust and its instructions.

trustor The person or organization that creates a trust.

Truth in Lending Act —See CONSUMER PROTECTION ACT OF 1968.

TSA —See TAX-SHELTERED ANNUITY.

TSE 1. —See TOKYO STOCK EXCHANGE. 2. —See TORONTO STOCK EXCHANGE.

t-test A statistical method to determine whether differences in means or proportions between two groups of data are significant, or to determine whether a mean or proportion differs significantly from a specified value. For example, a t-test might be used to determine whether the mean number of sick days for a company's employees during a year was significantly different from 4.2, the mean number of sick days in the industry the same year.

tuition tax credit —See HOPE SCHOLARSHIP TAX CREDIT.

tulip bubble The famous speculative period in 17th-century Holland when crazed bidding from merchants, speculators, and individuals sent tulip bulb prices to great heights only to be followed by a sudden fall. Stories surfaced that the Dutch were bidding up to a year's salary for especially desirable bulbs.

turkey An investment that has performed poorly. There were many turkeys during the dot-com bust of 2001.

turnaround 1. The process of moving from a period of losses or low profitability into a more profitable stage. A turnaround may be triggered by a number of factors, including a better use of assets or the development of new products and services. 2. A security that is in the process of reversing a declining price trend. 3. The purchase and sale of a security on the same day.

turnaround time The time required to complete an assignment or job. For example, an airline attempts to minimize the turnaround time required to get a plane back in service after a completed flight. A short turnaround time results in more trips and greater revenue.

turnkey Describing a system or project ready for immediate use—the end user need only open the door or turn it on. For example, a business may be offered as a turnkey operation, in which case a buyer can immediately begin operations. Likewise, a turnkey software program can be installed and used immediately.

turnover 1. The trading volume of the market or of a particular security. 2. The number of times that an asset is replaced during a given period. For example, an inventory turnover of five indicates that the firm's inventory has been turned into sales and has been replaced five times. 3. Replacement of employees: *A fast-food restaurant paying minimum wage suffers high turnover.*

turnover rate 1. The trading volume in a particular stock during a period (generally one year) as a percentage of the total number of shares of that stock outstanding. The turnover rate adjusts for the differences in outstanding shares and provides a measure of the relative activity in a stock. 2. For an investment company, the volume of shares traded as a percentage of the number of shares in the company's portfolio. A high turnover rate may indicate excessive trading and commissions. 3. The number of employees replaced as a proportion of the average number of employees.

turn the corner To reverse a series of negative events: *The CEO reported that last quarter's improvement in sales was a sign the firm had turned the corner after several years of declining revenues.*

12b–1 fee A type of mutual fund expense in which the fund's operators use a portion of the firm's assets to pay for costs of distributing the fund. The fee is included in the fee table of a fund's prospectus. National Association of Securities Dealers' rules establish an annual limit on the size of the fee. The name is derived from the SEC rule that describes the fee. —Also called *distribution fee.*

twenty-day period —See COOLING-OFF PERIOD 1.

twisting An attempt to convince an individual to sell one product and purchase another product, primarily so the salesperson can earn additional commissions. In the brokerage business, twisting is usually called *churning.* Twisting, the more general term, also applies to the sale of other products, such as insurance policies.

two-sided market The market for a security in which a bid price and an ask price are both quoted. —Compare ONE-SIDED MARKET. —Also called *two-way market.*

two-step mortgage A special type of adjustable-rate mortgage that offers a reduced rate of interest for a specified number of years (generally five to seven) after which the interest rate adjusts to a fixed market rate for the remainder of the term. Unlike most adjustable-rate mortgages, the interest rate on a two-step mortgage is adjusted only one time. —Also called *hybrid mortgage.*

two-tailed test In statistics, testing a hypothesis when it is acceptable to reject a hypothesis because the sample statistic is either too large or too small. For example, a petroleum company wants to determine if a new additive to gasoline has an effect on mileage. The null hypothesis is the additive does not affect mileage. The hypothesis is rejected if the additive either increases or decreases mileage.

two-tier tender offer An offer to purchase a sufficient number of stockholders' shares so as to gain effective control of a firm at a certain price per share, followed by a lower offer at a later date for the remaining shares. For example, an investor may offer $50 per share for up to 51% of a firm's outstanding stock and then, having gained control, offer $40 for each of the remaining shares. —Compare ANY-AND-ALL BID. —See also APPRAISAL RIGHT; BACK-END VALUE; BLENDED PRICE; FAIR PRICE AMENDMENT.

12b-1 fee

Is there any reason to choose a mutual fund that levies a 12b-1 fee? For example, can I expect a fund with a 12b-1 fee to outperform a similar fund that does not charge the fee?

Approximately 70% of mutual funds (measured by share class) levy a 12b-1 fee, so the results of any thorough search or screen are sure to include solid investment candidates both with and without 12b-1 fees. Keep in mind that the presence of a 12b-1 fee does not necessarily indicate a more expensive fund. A fund that charges a 1% management fee plus a .25% 12b-1 is still less expensive than a fund without a 12b-1 that charges 1.5% in other fees. Originally enacted in 1980, the 12b-1 fee was intended to help a then-struggling mutual-fund industry defray marketing and distribution expenses. However, the proliferation of share classes has increasingly blurred the lines between 12b-1 fees and sales loads. Some funds still offer just one share class, but many offer five or more. As of this writing, there are approximately 8,200 U.S.-based mutual funds, and the many with multiple share classes produce over 22,000 total variations. It is within these share classes that the issue of 12b-1 fees gets opaque. Exploring a few of the most common share classes (A, B, C) can illuminate the issue. In general, A-share funds (including load-waived A shares and even some no-load funds) have 12b-1 fees equal to 25 basis points (1/4 of 1%) of the fund's assets on a yearly basis. B and C shares do not carry a front-end sales load (often 4% to 5.75%) like traditional A shares, but the 12b-1 on B and C shares can be as high as 1%. At that level, the 12b-1 can start to rival the other internal costs of managing the fund. I wouldn't be overly concerned with a 25-basis-point 12b-1, as it wouldn't take much for a skilled asset manager to overcome that hurdle and still add value on a net basis. I would be more hesitant to saddle that same manager with a 100-basis-point additional fee—especially if it was permanent (most B shares eventually exchange for lower-cost A shares in six to ten years, but C shares can impose the fee indefinitely). Ultimately, having many choices can improve your end result, but you should explore each option fully and choose the one that is most closely aligned with your interests and objectives.

▪ Noah L. Myers, CFP®, Principal and Chief Investment Officer, MiddleCove Capital, Centerbrook, CT

two-tier wage plan A compensation plan in which new employees are paid at a reduced rate compared to experienced employees. Two-tier plans are particularly attractive to businesses that experience high labor turnover.

CASE STUDY Two-tier wage plans gained traction in the face of globalization, which forced U.S.-based production facilities to compete with foreign plants enjoying much lower labor costs. Labor unions nearly always strenuously oppose two-tier compensation plans, in part because the arrangements fly in the face of the important union principle "equal pay for equal work." Dual-tier pay systems also tend to damage labor harmony and create worker and public perception of a weak union. U.S. companies exercised a powerful bargaining weapon against labor unions when the firms threatened to move jobs overseas through outsourcing or acquiring offshore production facilities. In January 2005, the United Auto Workers ratified a new six-year contract with heavy equipment manufacturer Caterpillar, Inc. under which new hires would make $10 to $15 per hour (depending on job classification), compared with the firm's then current workers, who had started at an hourly wage of $20 to $22. The contract also called for annual lump-sum payments rather than yearly wage increases. The union indicated that the proposal of a two-tier system was accepted in an effort to preserve jobs. California grocery workers represented by the United Food and Commercial Workers Union had accepted a similar two-tier compensation system the prior year.

two-way analysis of variance A statistical analysis in which two independent variables, or factors, are examined with regard to their impact on a dependent variable and on one another. For example, a researcher might want to examine the effect of age and sex on productivity. The researcher would examine the effect of age on productivity, the effect of sex on productivity, and the effect of different combinations of age and sex on productivity.

two-way market —See TWO-SIDED MARKET.

tycoon An influential and wealthy business person. For example, Bill Gates and Steve Jobs are tycoons of the first order.

tying contract An agreement that requires a customer to purchase one good or service in order to be able to purchase another good or service. For example, an automobile dealer requires customers to purchase an extended warranty as a condition of being able to buy a vehicle in great demand. Tying contracts are generally illegal under the Sherman Antitrust Act. —Also called *tie-in agreement.*

type I error In a statistical test, the mistake of rejecting a true hypothesis. For example, a firm hypothesizes that a new product will enjoy mean weekly sales of at least 1,000 units. Sample results indicate that mean weekly sales are significantly less than 1,000, and so the hypothesis is rejected. However, another firm introduces an identical product, and mean weekly sales turn out to be more than 1,000 units.

type II error In a statistical test, the mistake of accepting a false hypothesis. For example, a company hypothesizes that a new type of radial tire will last for a mean of more than 50,000 miles. Based on sample results, the hypothesis is accepted. However, after the product is put on the market, it turns out that the mean mileage is significantly less than 50,000 miles.

■ U

UCC —See UNIFORM COMMERCIAL CODE.

UGMA —See UNIFORM GIFTS TO MINORS ACT.

ullage The amount by which a container lacks being full. For example, ullage indicates available storage space for petroleum products.

ultra vires In law, activities of a business or other body that are outside the scope of its authority or charter. For example, directors of a corporation finance a merger with shares of stock that have not been authorized by shareholders.

umbrella liability insurance Special coverage for especially large monetary damages a person or other entity is obligated to pay another party. This insurance derives its name from its coverage of awards that exceed regular liability protection included in homeowner's insurance, automobile insurance, and business insurance. For example, a homeowner's policy might include $100,000 of liability coverage while umbrella liability insurance will often have a limit of $1 million or more.

umbrella pricing A market situation in which several large firms dominate an industry and maintain relatively high prices such that smaller firms with higher costs are also able to operate profitably.

unamortized bond discount When a bond is originally sold at a discount from par value, the difference between the par value and the proceeds from selling the bond that have not yet been assessed as an interest expense to the borrower. A firm issuing a bond at below par value must charge off the difference to interest expense throughout the issue's life. Unamortized bond discount is the portion of the discount that has not yet been shown as an expense. —Also called *bond discount.*

unamortized bond premium When a bond is originally sold at a premium to par value, the difference between the par value and the proceeds from selling the bond that have not yet been subtracted from interest expense.

unappropriated retained earnings Accumulated earnings that have not been appropriated for specific purposes (for example, payment on a debt) and are available for distribution to shareholders. —Compare APPROPRIATED RETAINED EARNINGS.

unaudited statement A financial statement prepared by an auditor but not in accordance with generally accepted auditing standards. Unaudited statements are prepared to less rigorous standards than audited statements. —Compare AUDITED STATEMENT.

unauthorized strike —See WILDCAT STRIKE.

unbalanced growth Economic growth characterized by the expansion of some sectors much more rapidly than other sectors. For example, technology may be advancing at a much more rapid pace than energy or manufacturing. Unbalanced growth may result from unequal availability of capital, a poor distribution of entrepreneurial abilities, or government policies.

unbiased estimator In statistics, a sampling statistic (if the sampling process was repeated indefinitely) that is equal to the true value of the population parameter. For example: The sample mean of a properly chosen, random sample is an unbiased estimator of the population mean. The average of all sample means, for random samples of a fixed size, is equal to the mean of the population from which the samples were chosen.

unbundling The separation and separate pricing of products and services by financial institutions. When deregulation resulted in price competition and the introduction of new products, financial institutions found it increasingly necessary to offer and price each product separately.

uncollected funds A deposit or a portion of a deposit that has not yet been collected by a financial institution. Financial institutions typically prohibit customers from writing checks on uncollected funds.

uncollectible account Sales on account that cannot be collected. The customer (debtor) may be insolvent or simply refuse to pay. Sellers that are able to accurately estimate uncollectible accounts provide for an expense in the period during which the sales take place. An allowance for uncollectible accounts is reported on the balance sheet as a deduction from accounts receivable.

unconscionability Legal defense against the enforcement of a contract that is so one-sided that a normal person would find it unconscionable. For example, an elderly person signs a contract for repair of a roof at a cost much higher than would be charged by a reputable contractor. Unconscionability results from an unfair bargaining position that may be related to a variety of factors, including a language barrier or mental frailty.

uncovered option —See NAKED OPTION.

underbanked 1. Of or describing individuals who use few traditional financial services such as credit cards and checking accounts. The underbanked often purchase money orders, utilize check-cashing services, and pay bills in cash. **2.** Describing an investment banking firm that is experiencing difficulty attracting other firms to underwrite a new security offering.

> **CASE STUDY** According to one estimate, nearly 40 million individuals living in the United States do not have a transaction account or credit score. An equal number of people have a bank account, but have such a low credit score that they are excluded from nearly all but the most expensive lending sources. The unbanked and underbanked are often immigrants, widows, ethnic minorities, and individuals who have filed for bankruptcy. They buy money orders at convenience stores, cash checks at check-cashing services, and borrow money through payday lending services. In each case they pay very high fees. Or they go to their nearest Wal-Mart, which offers all these services. In an effort to expand its offering of financial services, Wal-Mart applied in Utah for an industrial-bank charter. Approval of the charter would be accompanied by federal deposit insurance and allow the giant retailer to process its own credit-card transactions. Wal-Mart indicated it intended to open limited-service banks within its stores but did not plan to open bank branches if the charter were granted. The application brought heavy opposition from the commercial banking industry, especially from small banks that would face new competition. In March 2007 the firm announced that it had withdrawn its application for a charter.

undercapitalized Of, relating to, or being a firm that has insufficient long-term equity to support its assets. A rapidly growing company that finds itself financing its operations primarily with short-term loans may be undercapitalized.

underclass The lowest and least privileged class of individuals in a society. An underclass is typically characterized by high dropout rates from school, receipt of public assistance, high rates of unemployment, and households headed by females. Members of the underclass are typically outside the mainstream of a society.

underdepreciation 1. Depreciation that is insufficient to allow for the eventual replacement of the asset being depreciated. Underdepreciation is generally caused by rising prices for replacement assets. —Compare OVERDEPRECIATION 1. **2.** Depreciation that causes an asset to be carried on a firm's books at a greater value than it would have if it were sold. Underdepreciation results in overstated earnings and assets on the firm's financial statements. —Compare OVERDEPRECIATION 2.

underemployed Individuals working at jobs that don't fully utilize their knowledge and skills. The classic example is someone with a PhD driving a cab. Underemployment often results from lack of mobility.

underground economy Commerce that escapes notice by the government. Illegal activities, including selling illegal drugs, are included in the underground economy. Barter of goods that is not reported and escapes taxation is also a major part of the underground economy.

underhanded Of or describing a person or activity that is deceitful: *To head off managers bailing out to competing firms, the underhanded CEO falsely promised that the firm was not contemplating any layoffs.*

underinsured Having insufficient insurance coverage to offset a loss from damage, injury, or death. —Compare OVERINSURED.

underleveraged Of, relating to, or being a firm that has insufficient debt in its capital structure. Because bond interest is deductible for tax purposes and is generally fixed in amount for a long period of time, some use of debt can often result in a larger return on the owners' investment. Whether a company is underleveraged is usually a matter of opinion.

underlying asset **1.** The physical or financial asset to which a security holder or a class of security holders has a claim. An analyst may believe that a stock is underpriced on the basis of the value of the firm's underlying assets and the potential earning power of those assets. **2.** The asset that underlies and gives value to a security. The underlying asset of a stock option is the stock that the option can be used to purchase. Likewise, the underlying asset of a convertible bond is the stock for which the bond can be exchanged. The market value of a security is directly affected by changes in the value of any underlying asset into which it may be exchanged. For example, the market value of an option on a futures contract is directly affected by the value of the futures contract.

underlying debt **1.** Debt of a municipal organization for which a higher municipal organization is at least partially responsible. For example, hospital authority debt may be guaranteed by a county such that the hospital debt is underlying the debt of the county. —Compare OVERLAPPING DEBT. **2.** A first mortgage on real estate when the same property is being used as collateral for other debt. For example, a first mortgage is the underlying debt when a home equity loan on the same property is also outstanding. —Also called *underlying mortgage.*

underlying mortgage —See UNDERLYING DEBT 2.

undermargined Of or relating to a brokerage account in which the dollar value of the margin (market value of the assets minus the amount owed) has fallen below the percentage of value set by the maintenance margin requirement.

underpay To pay less than is deserved: *Most people would consider nursing home employees to be underpaid based on the work they are required to perform.*

underpayment penalty The penalty assessed by tax authorities when a taxpayer's withholding and estimated tax payments (plus any overpayment from the prior year) are substantially less than the tax that is owed. The IRS does not assess an underpayment penalty when a taxpayer has paid at least 90% of the tax owed or when withholding plus estimated taxes paid equal 100% of the prior year's tax liability.

underperforming asset An asset that earns a lower rate of return than it would be capable of earning if it were properly used. A firm with underperforming assets is a prime target for takeover. —Compare NONPERFORMING ASSET.

underpricing The pricing of a new security issue at less than the prevailing price of the same security in the secondary market. Underpricing helps ensure a successful sale.

underreporting Taxpayers' understating of income or overstating of deductions, exemptions, and tax credits. Underreporting is the major cause of the tax gap.

undersecured claim Debt secured with collateral that has a value of less than the amount of the debt. For example, a lender offers 100% financing for the purchase of a new vehicle, which immediately becomes a used vehicle that loses thousands of dollars in value. The lender has an undersecured claim.

understored Describing a town or geographic area in which there is a shortage of retail outlets to meet consumer demand. —Compare OVERSTORED.

undersubscribed Of or relating to a new issue of securities for which demand from investors is less than the number of securities to be issued.

under the counter Of or describing a secret transaction. For example, prescription drugs were illicitly purchased under the counter.

undervalued Of, relating to, or being an investment that is selling at a price lower than it logically should be selling. Whether an investment is undervalued is a subjective judgment. —Compare OVERVALUED.

underwater **1.** Describing a loan in which the amount owed is greater than the value of the asset being used as collateral for the loan. For example, the market value of a home is less than the outstanding balance on the loan that financed the home's purchase. **2.** Of or relating to a stock option for which the option exercise price is higher than the market price of the stock.

underwithheld Money withheld by an employer from an employee's paychecks that is insufficient to cover the employee's income tax liability. Being underwithheld means the employee will be required to pay taxes when his or her annual tax return is filed. —See also UNDERPAYMENT PENALTY.

underwrite **1.** To assume the risk of securities' sale by purchasing the securities from the issuer for resale to the public. Investment bankers often assume this underwriting function in order to guarantee that the issuer will receive all the funds needed from the sale. —See also BEST-EFFORTS BASIS 1; HOT ISSUE; INVESTMENT BANK; PEG 1; STANDBY UNDERWRITING. **2.** In insurance, to accept a risk in return for premium payments by the insured.

underwriter **1.** An investment banker who acts to guarantee the sale of a new securities issue by purchasing the securities for resale to the public. —Also called *sponsor.* —See also AGREEMENT AMONG UNDERWRITERS; INVESTMENT BANK; LEAD UNDERWRITER. **2.** A company that accepts the risks of others. For example, many insurance companies are underwriters for casualty losses sustained by their clients.

Underwriters Laboratories An independent, not-for-profit organization engaged in product testing and certification. Products that are tested and meet the standards established by Underwriter Laboratories are permitted to carry the "UL" label.

underwriting agreement A written contract between a company planning a public securities issue and the managing underwriter of that issue. The agreement specifies the particulars of the issue such as dates, fees, offering price, and the responsibilities of the parties. —Compare AGREEMENT AMONG UNDERWRITERS.

underwriting spread The difference in the price that an investor pays for a new security issue and the price paid the issuer by the lead underwriter. The underwriting spread is a function of a number of variables, including the size of the issue and the riskiness, or price volatility, of the security. —Also called *spread.*

underwriting syndicate —See SYNDICATE[1].

undistributed profits —See RETAINED EARNINGS.

undivided interest Complete or partial ownership of the entirety of an asset such that claims of co-owners cannot be separated. For example, an individual may hold a 25% undivided interest in a vacation home. The owner has the right to three months' use (25% of the year) of the home. Undivided interest of real property donated to a charity qualifies for a tax deduction.

undivided profit The undistributed net income that has not yet been included as part of retained earnings.

undue influence Pressure that causes someone to do something he or she would not have otherwise done. For example, an elderly person making out a will is subject to undue influence from a companion who wishes to be named as a major beneficiary. Evidence of undue influence may invalidate a contract or will.

unearned discount **1.** A discount inappropriately taken by a customer when payment is made after the manufacturer's stated discount period has elapsed. For example, a company buys merchandise from a manufacturer that offers a 2% discount when payment is made within 10 days. The company taking delivery of the merchandise does not pay for 15 days, but claims the discount anyway. **2.** A secret discount offered to one or more customers without being offered to other customers. **3.** For financial institutions, loan interest deducted in advance and not yet applied to income.

unearned income **1.** Individual income, such as dividends, pension payments, and capital gains, that is derived from something other than personal services. —Compare EARNED INCOME. **2.** For a business, income that has been received but not yet earned. For example, a computer manufacturer sells a three-year warranty that customers pay in full when they purchase equipment. Only a portion of the payment is recorded as earned income during the first year, while the remainder is considered unearned income that will be applied in subsequent years.

unearned interest Prepaid interest received but not treated as income by a lender. For example, installment loans often result in unearned interest that must be returned to the borrower if the loan is repaid early.

unearned premium In insurance, the portion of a premium that is applicable to the unexpired part of the insurance term. For example, a casualty insurance company receives an annual premium from a customer purchasing a homeowner's policy. After three months of coverage, three-quarters of the premium remains unearned. —Compare EARNED PREMIUM.

unemployable Describing a person who is unable to engage in activities necessary for paid employment. The inability to work may result from a variety of reasons, including health problems or lack of skills.

unemployment The economic situation of people looking for work and being willing to work at the prevailing wage, but unable to find a job. —See also CYCLICAL UNEMPLOYMENT; FRICTIONAL UNEMPLOYMENT; SEASONAL UNEMPLOYMENT; STRUCTURAL UNEMPLOYMENT.

unemployment compensation Monetary payments from a joint federal-state program to workers who become unemployed through no fault of their own as determined by state law. Payments continue for a limited period or until the unemployed worker locates new employment. The program is designed to provide partial income replacement while unemployed workers search for new employment and to help stabilize the economy during economic downturns. Unemployment compensation is funded by an employer payroll tax that is based on wages paid to covered employees.

unemployment rate The proportion of unemployed persons in the labor force. Unemployed persons include individuals 16 years of age and over without work who were available for work and made an effort to locate employment during the period being measured.

unencumbered Of or relating to an owned asset that does not have a claim against it. Real estate not being used as collateral for a loan and on which all taxes are current is unencumbered. —Compare ENCUMBRANCE 1.

unexpired cost The future benefits that remain from ownership of an asset being used in the production process. Unexpired cost for an asset is equal to historical cost less accumulated depreciation. This measure of cost is primarily used for financial reporting purposes within the firm. —Compare EXPIRED COST.

unfair competition A commercial activity that confuses or deceives the public about a product or service. For example, in January 2007 Cisco Systems filed a lawsuit claiming trademark infringement and unfair competition relative to Apple, Inc. introducing its "iPhone," a trademark that Cisco registered in June 2000.

unfair labor practice Action by an employer or union that violates terms of the National Labor Relations Act or other federal or state legislation. For example, employers are prohibited from discriminating against employees who engage in union activities, and unions are prohibited from refusing to bargain with the employer of the employees it represents. —See also NATIONAL LABOR RELATIONS BOARD.

unfreeze To remove restrictions or controls. For example, the IRS might agree to unfreeze a bank account after the taxpayer settles his disputed tax obligation.

unfriendly takeover The acquisition of a firm despite resistance by the target firm's management and board of directors. —Compare FRIENDLY TAKEOVER. —Also called *hostile takeover.* —See also KILLER BEE; RAIDER.

unfunded 1. Describing a financial obligation for which no money is available. For example, a pension plan is unfunded when benefits are paid only from current contributions. **2.** Of or being a government mandate unaccompanied by the necessary funds to accomplish the mandate. For example, the state requires that all school systems offer prekindergarten, but fails to allocate any funds to compensate the systems for additional classrooms or teachers that are required.

unified credit A credit used against federal taxes due on estates and large gifts. Under current law, the unified credit is sufficient to offset taxes on multimillion dollar estates and large gifts. Thus, the combination of estate value and large gifts must exceed several million during a person's lifetime before any taxes must be paid to the federal government.

uniform capitalization rules The requirement that certain taxpayers capitalize rather than expense direct and indirect costs incurred in the production of personal property. The effect is to move expenses from the period of production to the period of sales. This results in a higher taxable income in years when more products are produced than sold.

Uniform Commercial Code (UCC) A set of laws governing commercial transactions designed to standardize state regulation of business practices, including sales, transportation, financing, leases, storage, and so forth. For example, the Uniform Commercial Code permits a creditor to inform other creditors about a borrower's assets being used as collateral. All states other than Louisiana have adopted the entire UCC.

Uniform Gifts to Minors Act (UGMA) Uniform state laws that facilitate irrevocable gifts to a minor by eliminating the requirement of a guardian or trust. A custodian, who may be the donor, is appointed to manage the gift, but full rights to the principal and income reside with the minor, who gains control upon reaching the applicable age (usually 18 or 21). Earnings are reported to the IRS using the minor's Social Security number.

Uniform Settlement Statement A required document listing all the closing costs in a real estate transaction or refinancing. The statement is prepared by the lender and made available to the borrower, seller, and buyer on or before a mortgage loan settlement.

unilateral contract An agreement in which one party makes a conditional promise. For example, a business may promise to pay an asphalt company $6,000 if the company will pave the firm's parking area. The promise is conditional on the asphalt company accepting and completing the job. —Compare BILATERAL CONTRACT.

unimproved property Land without significant structures or other improvements that would increase its value.

unincorporated association A contractual relationship among individuals who have come together for a specific purpose. Unlike a corporation, an unincorporated association does not have an existence that is independent from its members, and it cannot hold assets in its own name.

uninsured motorist insurance Vehicle insurance coverage that pays for losses from an accident caused by a hit-and-run driver or an uninsured motorist, up to the policy limits. The coverage includes property damage and bodily injury. Payment requires proof that the other party was at fault.

union An association of workers that promotes employee interests, including pay, benefits, and working conditions.

union label An attachment or mark that identifies a product as being produced by union labor. The label is useful for consumers who wish to buy (or not buy) because of the manufacturer's affiliation (nonaffiliation) with a union.

union scale The rate of pay required by a union contract: *Members of the band playing in the casino lounge are paid union scale.* The rate applies whether or not the employee is a union member.

union shop A place of employment where employees subject to a collective bargaining agreement must become members of a union within a specified time of being hired. —Also called *shop¹*. —See also CLOSED SHOP.

unique impairment In life insurance, distinctive factors that set apart an applicant from standard applicants. For example, an applicant may suffer from a health problem, causing the company to decline coverage.

unique selling proposition A marketing strategy of differentiating a product or service by concentrating on unique features that are not offered by competitors. For example, Procter & Gamble introduced Crest in 1955 as the first fluoride toothpaste to be proven effective in preventing cavities and tooth decay. The company promoted an endorsement for Crest by the American Dental Association.

unissued capital stock Corporate capital stock that has been authorized but not yet issued. Management of a firm will often ask its stockholders to authorize many more shares of stock than are actually needed in order to provide flexibility for the issuance of more shares later without stockholders' approval.

unit 1. One portion of a business. For example, GE Commercial Finance is a unit of General Electric. **2.** —See SPECIALIST UNIT. **3.** —See UNIT OF TRADING. **4.** —See UNIT SHARE.

unitary elasticity Of or relating to the demand for a good or service when revenues of the seller are unaffected by a change in price. For example, a price increase of 5% will result in a reduction in demand of 5%; a price reduction of 10% will result in an increase in demand of 10%. —See also ELASTIC; INELASTIC.

unitary tax A state corporate income tax on worldwide income. Although unpopular with corporations, governments institute unitary taxes to foil firms that use creative accounting techniques to transfer their income to states or countries with low income-tax rates. Unitary taxes are typically based on a combination of sales, payroll, and property attributed to a state.

unit convertible A security that is convertible into a package of assets or securities rather than into a specified number of shares of a single common stock.

United Parcel Service (UPS) The Atlanta-based transportation and logistics company that is the world's largest package delivery company.

United States government securities —See GOVERNMENTS.

United States International Trade Commission —See INTERNATIONAL TRADE COMMISSION, U.S.

United States person For federal tax purposes, a citizen or resident of the United States, a partnership or corporation created in the United States or under the law of the United States or any state, a trust or estate other than a foreign trust or estate, or any other person who is not a foreign person. —Compare FOREIGN PERSON.

United States savings bond —See SAVINGS BOND.

unit growth Growth in sales expressed in terms of the actual number of units as opposed to the dollar value of the units that have been sold. Measuring growth in units, rather than in dollars, eliminates the effect of inflation and better illustrates real growth.

unit investment trust An unmanaged portfolio of investments assembled by an investment adviser and sold in units to investors by brokers. Units of a trust usually sell for $1,000 including a sales commission of approximately 4% at the time of the initial offering. Sponsoring brokers usually maintain a secondary market for the units, the value of which depends on the value of the securities held by the trust. —Also called *fixed trust*.

unit labor cost An important measure of productivity calculated by dividing total labor compensation (including benefits) by real output. An increase in unit labor costs will result in a reduction in profitability unless a firm can pass along higher labor costs to its customers. Economists view increases in unit labor costs as an important indicator of potential inflation.

unit of trading The minimum quantity of a security required for regular trading purposes. The unit of trading for most stocks is 100 shares. —Also called *trading unit; unit.*

unit sales Sales measured in terms of physical units rather than dollars. Financial analysts often use unit sales data when evaluating the health of a company.

unit share A combination of securities that is traded as a single package. For example, a share of common stock and a warrant may be traded as a unit. —Also called *unit.*

units-of-production method An accounting technique in which depreciation is assigned to each unit of output. For example, a truck costing $50,000 and expected to be driven 100,000 miles results in depreciation of $50,000/100,000, or 50¢ per mile. This method of assigning depreciation is unreliable unless production units can be estimated accurately.

unit train A train hauling a single commodity to a designated destination. For example, a unit train that hauls coal between a mine and a power plant.

unity-of-command principle The management theory that a subordinate should report to only a single person.

universal life insurance A combination of term life insurance and a tax-deferred savings plan paying a variable return. This combination was developed during the early 1980s when interest rates rose to very high levels and caused the public to view regular whole life policies unfavorably. —See also VARIABLE UNIVERSAL LIFE INSURANCE.

universal product code (UPC) A unique 12-digit number assigned to merchandise. The first 6 digits identify the vendor and the next 5 digits identify the product. The last digit, called a *check digit*, verifies the UPC has been read correctly. A product's UPC is typically placed next to a computer-readable bar code. —See also CHECK DIGIT.

unjust enrichment Benefiting at the expense of someone else without legal justification. For example, charging admission for people to view a commercial movie without notifying or paying the copyright owner. An unjust enrichment claim must show: (1) a benefit to the defendant, (2) a loss to the plaintiff, and (3) a violation of equity and justice.

unlimited liability The liability of the owner of a business for all the obligations of the business. An owner's personal assets can be seized if the business's assets are insufficient to satisfy claims against it. The placement of personal assets at risk is a great disadvantage of proprietorships and general partnerships. The ability to limit the amount of liability to which an owner is subject is a major reason for the formation of corporations and limited partnerships. —Compare LIMITED LIABILITY.

unlisted security A security that trades only in the over-the-counter market. —Compare LISTED SECURITY.

unload 1. To sell an investment, generally at a loss. **2.** To quickly sell a large amount of merchandise, either to raise cash or avoid a loss in value. **3.** To remove cargo from a container or vehicle.

unoccupancy The status of a property that is not being lived in. The limits of insurance applying to unoccupied premises are often reduced if the unoccupancy extends beyond a specified period. For example, an insurance company might agree to one-half the value of a claim for a damaged property that had been unoccupied for over 120 days.

unoccupied —See VACANT.

unpaid dividend 1. A declared dividend that has not yet been paid. **2.** —See PASSED DIVIDEND.

unqualified opinion —See CLEAN OPINION.

unrealized gain The increased market value of an asset that is still being held compared with its cost of acquisition. Unrealized gains are not usually taxable. —Compare REALIZED GAIN. —Also called *book profit; paper gain; paper profit.*

unrealized loss The reduction in value of an asset that is being held compared with its original cost. An unrealized loss usually must be realized by closing out the position before it can be recognized for tax purposes. —Compare REALIZED LOSS. —Also called *book loss; paper loss.* —See also WASH SALE.

unrecorded deed A document that transfers ownership of property without the document being publicly recorded. Unrecorded deeds escape public notice but can prove troublesome to the parties involved.

unrecovered cost 1. Payments into an annuity that have not been distributed at the annuitant's death. **2.** —See BOOK VALUE 1.

unregistered security —See RESTRICTED SECURITY.

unrelated business income For a tax-exempt organization, this is income from a trade or business that is regularly carried on and not substantially related to the tax-exempt status of the organization. Unrelated business income is generally taxable, although dividends, interest, certain rental income, royalties, and gains and losses from disposition of properties are excluded when calculating unrelated business income.

unreported income The difference between income that is reported voluntarily and income that should be reported. Although primarily applied to income taxes, unreported income is applicable to other issues, such as divorce proceedings. —See also TAX GAP.

unsecured creditor A creditor with a claim for which no specific assets are pledged. A debenture holder is an unsecured creditor. —Compare SECURED CREDITOR.

unsecured liability A liability for which no specific collateral is held by a creditor. Essentially, payment on an unsecured liability is assured by the promise of the borrower.

unskilled Describing a person who is lacking training or expertise. Unskilled workers tend to earn low wages in jobs requiring manual labor.

unsought good A category of goods or services that consumers either do not know about, or know about but would rather not think about. For example, a coffin is generally considered an unsought good.

unsponsored American Depositary Receipt An American Depositary Receipt representing shares of a foreign company not directly involved in issuance of the ADR. Unsponsored ADRs are originated by a bank(s) that independently purchases the foreign firm's shares, holds the shares in trust, and sells the ADRs through brokerage firms. The depositary bank, rather than holders of the ADRs, retains the right to vote shares held in trust. —Compare SPONSORED AMERICAN DEPOSITARY RECEIPT.

unstated interest Additional interest that must be declared on an installment contract when the contract calls for inadequate or no interest. Both stated and unstated interest must be included in interest income for tax purposes.

unsystematic risk The risk that is specific to an industry or firm. Examples of unsystematic risk include losses caused by labor problems, nationalization of assets, or weather conditions. This type of risk can be reduced by assembling a portfolio with significant diversification that a single event affects only a limited number of the assets. —Compare SYSTEMATIC RISK. —Also called *diversifiable risk.*

unwind 1. To close out a relatively complicated investment position. For example, an investor who practices arbitrage by taking one position in stocks and the opposite position in option contracts would have to unwind by the date on which the options would expire. **2.** To rectify a transaction in which a mistake has been made. For example, because of a misunderstanding, a brokerage firm may have bought the wrong stock for a customer. The firm must then unwind the erroneous trade by selling the stock just purchased and buying the correct stock.

UPC —See UNIVERSAL PRODUCT CODE.

up/down volume ratio A measure calculated by dividing a stock's aggregate trading volume during days when the price increases by the aggregate trading volume during days when the price declines. This technical tool attempts to provide guidance as to whether a stock is being accumulated or distributed. A high up/down volume ratio is considered a bullish indicator.

up front Of or relating to immediate payment: *The seller demanded that the buyer pay 25% of the price up front.*

upgrading **1.** An increase in the quality rating of a security issue. An upgrading may occur for a variety of reasons, including an improved outlook for a firm's products, increased profitability, or a reduction in the amount of debt the firm has outstanding. An upgrading generally can be expected to have a positive influence on the price of the security. —Compare DOWNGRADING. **2.** Making changes in order to improve something: *Upgrading their inventory software realized efficiencies and savings for the company.* **3.** An increase in the quality of securities held in a portfolio.

upkeep The maintenance and repair tasks necessary to keep assets in good working condition.

upselling Suggesting that a customer purchase a more expensive or extra good or service. For example, a good waiter engages in upselling when calling a diner's attention to appetizers and desserts that might not normally be ordered. Upselling is also practiced extensively by telemarketers. Internal upselling refers to a sales pitch made by or on behalf of the same seller in the initial transaction. External upselling is a pitch by someone different from the seller of the initial transaction.

> **CASE STUDY** The Federal Trade Commission enforces a Telemarketing Sales Rule (TSR) that provides important protections for a consumer presented with upselling. Among other things, the TSR requires disclosure of all information that is relevant to the consumer's decision to accept the offer before the consumer authorizes payment for the purchase. It also requires the consumer's informed consent before billing information is submitted for payment. In April 2006 an executive of the Direct Marketing Association requested an FTC advisory opinion as to whether a particular type of marketing program qualified under TSR as upselling. The solicitation was one that was made in conjunction with an inbound call to a financial institution from a customer requesting account, transaction, balance, or payment information. After responding to the consumer's request, the financial institution offered information about a service (for example, credit monitoring) and asked if the customer was interested in learning more about the product. A positive response resulted in the call being transferred to a marketing company that pitched the service. The Direct Marketing Association contended the solicitation did not constitute upselling because the initial transaction (providing information about the account) did not involve a seller. However, the FTC was of the opinion the solicitation did involve upselling and was not exempt from the Telemarketing Sales Rule.

upset price —See RESERVE PRICE.

upside potential The potential price or gain that may be expected in a security, security average, or other asset, generally stated as the dollar price or the dollar amount of gain that may reasonably be expected in the particular security or security average. For example, an analyst may feel that a stock currently selling at $25 per share has an upside potential of $40. —Compare DOWNSIDE RISK.

upstream Of or relating to earnings or operations at a firm that are near or at the initial stages of producing a good or service. For example, exploration and production are upstream operations for a large integrated oil company. —Compare DOWNSTREAM.

uptick An upward price movement for a security transaction compared with the preceding transaction of the same security. —Compare DOWNTICK. —Also called *plus tick.*

uptime The amount of time equipment or a system is in service and operating. —Compare DOWNTIME.

uptrend A series of price increases in a security or in the general market. Some investors believe a security tends to take on a certain inertia; as a result, these investors search for a stock in an uptrend, thinking that it will probably continue to move in the same direction. —Compare DOWNTREND.

upwardly mobile Pertaining to a person or segment of the population that is likely to quickly advance in economic and social standing. For example, some consider that a law degree from an ivy league school will help a person to become upwardly mobile. —See also VERTICAL MOBILITY.

urban Of or relating to a geographic area that is heavily developed and densely populated. —Compare RURAL. —See also RURBAN.

urban renewal Redevelopment of an established but physically deteriorated urban area in order to improve housing, commerce, and social activities. Government urban renewal projects are undertaken in the hope that improved property values and increased tax revenues will pay for the cost of the renewal.

usable bond A bond that may be used at face value in combination with a warrant to purchase shares of common stock. Essentially, the issuer allows warrant owners to substitute the bond for cash when the warrants are exercised. Ownership of this type of bond is, like ownership of a convertible bond, a speculation on the direction of interest rates and also on the direction of the price of the underlying stock.

U.S. citizen Any person born or naturalized in, and subject to the jurisdiction of, the United States.

useful life The period during which a depreciable asset will be productive. An asset's useful life is likely to be different than its life for depreciation purposes as determined by the Internal Revenue Service. —Compare CLASS LIFE.

user fee A charge for the use of a particular good or service. For example, an entrance fee to a state park or the rental of equipment at a pubic facility. Many government-operated facilities are financed by both tax revenues and user fees.

U.S. savings bond —See SAVINGS BOND.

usufructuary right The right to use and enjoy property owned by another. For example, in 1837 several Chippewa Bands gave land to the United States in return for usufructuary rights to hunt, fish, and gather on the land.

usury law A state law that restricts the interest rate that can be charged on specified types of loans.

utility **1.** In economics, a measure of satisfaction. For example, some middle-aged men gain substantial utility from driving sports cars, even though these vehicles are expensive and impractical. **2.** A business that provides an essential service, generally under government regulation. Electric companies, gas transmission firms, and local telephone companies are utilities. **3.** A software program designed to perform a specific task related to managing a computer's resources. For example, a defragmenter program can detect and restructure fragmented files.

V

vacancy rate The percentage of available rental units that remain unoccupied or un-rented. A high vacancy rate tends to pressure landlords to lower rents or offer incentives in order to fill unoccupied units. —Compare OCCUPANCY LEVEL.

vacant Describing a property without an occupant. —Also called *unoccupied.*

vacant land Land without usable structures, although it may have improvements such as utilities.

vacate **1.** To set aside: *The appeals court vacated an earlier court ruling that the city must remove its Christmas decorations.* **2.** To move out of a property: *The tenant was asked to vacate the apartment after the landlord received numerous complaints of excessive noise.*

vacation pay Compensation due an employee during established vacations.

VA loan A mortgage made by an approved lender and guaranteed by the U.S. Department of Veterans Affairs. VA loans have low down payments and are restricted to qualified members of the military, veterans, reservists, and their unmarried surviving spouses. Loans are made to obtain homes, condominiums, manufactured homes, and to refinance loans.

valuable consideration Some defined benefit, such as money or performance, that is promised as part of an agreement. Contracts must generally include valuable consideration in order to be legally enforceable.

valuation A process for calculating the monetary value of an asset. Valuation is subjective and often results in wide disparities for the perceived values of most assets.

value **1.** The monetary worth of something: *The painting has a value of at least $150,000.* **2.** A number resulting from a calculation or analysis.

value-added tax (VAT) A tax levied on increases in a product's value at each stage of production and distribution. The value-added tax, essentially an invisible sales tax included in the final price, is ultimately paid by consumers. For example, a candy maker paying $10,000 for ingredients used in the manufacture of chocolate bars that are resold for $15,000 would be required to pay a tax on the $5,000 of value added to the product. Proponents argue that substituting the value-added tax for the current federal income tax would stimulate consumer saving. —Compare CONSUMPTION TAX.

value chain The successive stages during which value is created when producing, distributing, and servicing a product. Distinct stages in the value chain may include: (1) receiving and distributing raw materials, (2) converting raw materials into a finished product, (3) identifying customers and distributing the product, and (4) providing customer support. Identifying the value chain allows a firm to refine its operations in an effort to improve quality, add efficiencies, and increase profits.

value date 1. The date on which parties agree to settle a transaction. For example, a futures contract calls for settlement on a specific date. 2. The date on which a financial institution makes funds available to a depositor.

valued policy An insurance contract in which the insurer agrees to pay the limit of the liability in the event of a total loss. For example, the home of an insured owner burns down and would cost $225,000 to rebuild. A valued policy with a $275,000 limit would pay the homeowner the policy limit of $275,000.

value in exchange The value of something in terms of the goods or services for which it can be exchanged. While specie (for example, a gold coin) possesses an intrinsic value, paper money is generally desirable only for its value in exchange.

value-in-use pricing Establishing a price based on a product's value to the customer as opposed to the manufacturer's cost of production. This method of pricing is effective only when consumers have no effective substitutes. For example, a pharmaceutical company may price a specialty cancer drug at a very high level, regardless of the firm's cost of production, based on the drug's value to the limited number of people who have few alternatives. On the other hand, aspirin, which has a very high value for many people, is typically sold at a low price because of competitive pressures.

value investing The selection of securities to be bought and sold on the basis of the value of a firm's assets. For example, an investor may search for the stock of a company in which current assets exceed total liabilities on a per share basis by more than the market price of the stock. Value investing emphasizes asset value more than earnings projections. —See also ASSET VALUE.

Vancouver Stock Exchange —See CANADIAN VENTURE EXCHANGE.

vanishing premium In participating life insurance policies, elimination of the normal annual premium payment when a policyholder chooses to substitute dividends received the previous year. A vanishing premium is possible only when the dividend received equals or exceeds the required premium. Holders of participating policies can choose to use premiums to acquire additional life insurance coverage or to make required premium payments.

variable Something, such as stock prices, earnings, dividend payments, interest rates, and gross domestic product, that has no fixed quantitative value. —See also DEPENDENT VARIABLE; INDEPENDENT VARIABLE.

variable annuity An annuity with payments to the annuitant that vary depending on the investment success of a separate investment account underlying the annuity. Because the invested funds are primarily in common stock, this annuity offers greater potential rewards and greater attendant risks than annuities supported by fixed-income securities. —Compare FIXED ANNUITY. —See also HYBRID ANNUITY.

variable cost The costs of production that vary directly in proportion to the number of units produced. Variable costs often include labor expenses and raw material costs, because labor and raw material usually must be increased to increase output. Firms for which variable costs represent a high proportion of total costs are usually less likely to experience large fluctuations in earnings, because changes in sales and revenues are accompanied by nearly equal changes in costs. —Compare FIXED COST.

variable coupon renewable note (VCR) A renewable note on which interest is reset on a weekly basis according to a predetermined formula. A VCR continues to renew at quarterly intervals unless the owner directs the issuer to repay the principal.

variable interest rate An interest rate on a loan that adjusts at regular intervals based on a specified index. For example, a loan may have a rate that adjusts each six months to 1% above the prime rate. A loan with a variable interest rate tends to entail greater risk for the borrower.

variable life insurance Life insurance that relates benefits to the value of a separate investment account underlying the annuity. This insurance is designed to prevent erosion of benefits by inflation. The size of the benefits will vary.

variable pricing A policy of pricing a good or service at different levels for different customers or sales events at different times. For example, an electric utility serving customers in Georgia may charge a higher price per kilowatt hour during summer months, when air conditioning is in heavy use and the utilities are required to put inefficient generators in service. Many movie theaters offer lower prices during matinees, when demand is typically light. —Also called *flexible pricing*.

variable-rate certificate of deposit A certificate of deposit that pays a rate of interest that changes at predetermined intervals according to a specified formula or a key interest rate. This savings instrument is most appropriate if the investor expects short-term interest rates to rise before the certificates mature.

variable-rate demand obligation A floating-rate debt obligation that has a nominal long-term maturity as well as an option allowing the investor to put (sell) the obligation back to the trustee, generally at par plus accrued interest.

variable-rate mortgage —See ADJUSTABLE-RATE MORTGAGE.

variable-rate note —See FLOATING-RATE NOTE.

variable-rate preferred stock —See FLOATING-RATE PREFERRED STOCK.

variable universal life insurance A blend of universal and variable life insurance that allows flexible premiums (within a range) and gives the policyholder a choice of investments. Cash values accumulate tax deferred, and the death benefit can vary depending on investment results. Variable universal life insurance is best suited for young individuals who have a basic understanding of investing.

variance 1. A statistical measure of the variability of measured datum from the average value of the set of data. A high variance, indicating relatively great variability, also indicates that the average is of minimal use in projecting future values for the data. Standard deviation is the square root of variance. —Compare COVARIANCE. —See also RISK. **2.** In real estate, an exception to current zoning requirements that permits an owner to utilize land in a manner not normally permitted. For example, a property owner might seek a variance to build a self-storage facility in an urban redevelopment zone. **3.** In accounting, the difference between actual and budgeted costs for labor and raw materials used in production.

variety store A retail establishment that offers a wide assortment of inexpensive and frequently purchased merchandise, including health and personal care items, candy, boxed or packaged food, and housewares. A single-price store is an example of a variety store.

VAT —See VALUE-ADDED TAX.

VCR —See VARIABLE COUPON RENEWABLE NOTE.

velocity The number of times money is spent during a specified period. A high velocity of money indicates consumers and businesses are quickly spending the money they receive. Velocity is a component of the quantity theory of money, which economists utilize to explain the effects of changes in the money supply on prices, output, and gross domestic product.

vendee The buyer of goods, services, or real property.

vendor The seller of goods, services, or real property. Giant food service operator Sysco Corporation is a well-known vendor.

vendor's lien A seller's claim to property that has been delivered until the buyer has paid in full.

venture A commercial endeavor in which an entrepreneur risks his or her resources in return for an expected profit.

venture arbitrage —See RAIDING 1.

venture capital A pool of risk capital, typically contributed by large investors, from which allocations are made available to young, small companies that have good growth prospects but are short of funds. Small investors can buy new issues or participate in mutual funds that specialize in the supply of venture capital. —Also called *risk capital*.

venture capital fund An investment company that invests its shareholders' money in new, very risky, but potentially very profitable, business ventures. —See also NONDIVERSIFIED MANAGEMENT COMPANY.

venture investing The acquiring of a stake in a start-up company by a brokerage firm or analyst by obtaining discounted, pre-IPO shares. Critics claim venture investing causes analysts to have a vested interest in seeing a stock appreciate in value and so be more likely to issue favorable recommendations.

venture team 1. In marketing, an independent task force assigned to a project involving new product development. 2. In management, a group of individuals who manage a new business enterprise.

vertical analysis The comparison of an item on a financial statement with a different item on the same statement. For example, an analyst may study a firm's balance sheet to compare the level of current assets with the level of current liabilities in order to measure liquidity. Analysts often study a firm's income statement to compare net income with total sales. —Compare HORIZONTAL ANALYSIS.

vertical conflict Organizational disagreements between individuals or groups at different hierarchical levels. For example, account executives may feel supervisors are not allowing them to offer big enough discounts to retain major customers.

vertical equity The principle that holds that individuals in different income groups should be taxed at different rates. —Compare HORIZONTAL EQUITY.

vertical integration Acquiring suppliers and distributors so as to control more stages of the production process. For example, a meatpacker acquires feedlots, a packaging company, and a distributor such that it controls the animals it processes from near birth until final sale. Major oil companies such as ExxonMobil are vertically integrated. —See also BACKWARD INTEGRATION; FORWARD INTEGRATION.

vertical marketing Promoting a product or service to specific industries. For example, a manufacturer of camping supplies targets promotions toward sporting goods stores. —Compare HORIZONTAL MARKETING.

vertical merger A merger between two firms involved in the same business but on different levels. As an example, a meat processing company may merge with a food distributor. The merger permits the firms to gain greater control of the manufacturing or selling process within that single industry. —Compare HORIZONTAL MERGER.

vertical mobility The ability of qualified individuals and classes of individuals to improve their position with regard to income, responsibilities, and social standing.

vertical privity 1. In real estate, a relationship in which the entire estate, including benefits and burdens, passes from the original party to successors. For example, a buyer must abide by restrictive covenants agreed to by the original owner. 2. The contractual relationship that exists between manufacturer, seller, and buyer.

vertical security exchange The exchange of one security for a different security (that is, stock for debt or debt for stock).

vertical specialization 1. Managerial organization in which tasks move along a chain of command. For example, a manager hands down an assignment to middle management. —Compare HORIZONTAL SPECIALIZATION. 2. In international trade, using imported intermediate parts and creating a good that is later exported.

vertical union —See INDUSTRIAL UNION.

vested benefits Pension benefits that belong to an employee independent of his or her future employment. An employee usually becomes vested after five years of employment with the same firm, although there are numerous exceptions requiring longer employment. —Compare PENSION PLAN.

vesting Gaining legal ownership of retirement funds. Employer contributions to a retirement plan do not become the property of the individual until vesting occurs. For example, an employer may require three years of employment for partial vesting and five years of employment for full vesting.

viatical settlement The purchase of a terminally ill person's life insurance policy for a certain percentage of the policy's face value. The amount paid depends on the size of the policy and the length of time the policyholder is expected to live. The company that purchases the policy begins paying the premiums at the time of purchase and collects the death benefits when the insured dies. —See also LIFE SETTLEMENT.

vicarious liability The liability of one party for the action or inaction of another party, even though the party held liable is not directly responsible for any injury. For example, a company may be held liable for the actions of an employee, or a parent may be held liable for injury caused by a child.

> **CASE STUDY** In 1999 testimony before a U.S. Senate subcommittee, Enterprise Rent-A-Car Vice President Ray Wagner spoke in favor of legislation that would restrict litigation involving vicarious liability of motor vehicle rental companies. Wagner stated he felt it was unfair to subject car rental companies to unlimited liability for the acts of renters. Unlimited liability was a fact of life for rental companies in several states, including Connecticut, Iowa, Maine, New York, Rhode Island, and the District of Columbia. A problem the firms faced was that vehicles might be rented in one state but involved in an accident in another state with liberal liability laws. Several cases were cited during the testimony, including one in which Thrifty rented a car in Toronto to an individual who was involved in an accident while driving the car in New York. The police report indicated the driver of the rental car was driving too fast and following too close. A three-day jury trial resulted in Thrifty being held vicariously liable under New York law and required to pay $1.1 million in damages to the plaintiff. In another case, four British sailors

rented a car from Alamo in Fort Lauderdale, Florida, to drive to Naples, Florida. While driving to Naples, the driver of the car fell asleep and allowed the car to leave the road and crash into a canal. The driver and two passengers were killed, and the fourth passenger was seriously injured. Alamo, as owner of the car, was held vicariously liable, even though no negligence was attributed to the firm. The jury ordered that Alamo pay the plaintiffs $7.7 million, an award that was affirmed on appeal.

vice president (VP) A senior executive who is second in command to the president and may occasionally stand in when the president is absent. Many businesses have multiple vice presidents, often with specialized titles such as vice president for finance or vice president for marketing.

vig —See VIGORISH.

vigorish The fee charged by a bookmaker or gaming operator. For example, the casino dealer takes a fee at the poker table. —Also called *juice; vig.*

viral marketing A marketing technique whose strategy is to gain access to social networks that will voluntarily pass along an advertising message. For example, a soft-drink manufacturer develops an advertising message in the form of a humorous video clip or interactive game that is posted on the Internet. Viewers enjoy the clip or game and pass it along to their friends, who in turn send it to their own friends. Viral marketing can result in an advertising message gaining wide exposure at a modest expense.

CASE STUDY Viral marketing can be a low-cost method for gaining widespread notice for a product or service. A company can get the initial word out and let others do the work of spreading that word among potential consumers. The classic case of the successful use of viral marketing was Hotmail's including a link to its Web address on messages sent by people using the firm's Web-based email service. Each message sent using Hotmail included the promotion: "Get Your Private, Free Email at http://www.hotmail.com." Interested recipients of an email from a Hotmail user could click on the link and quickly sign up for the free service. These new users would then spread the word with their own emails. Another example of viral marketing is the inclusion of "tell-a-friend" links on Web pages. These links make it easy for people to spread the word about a contest or some other promotion to their friends. Advertisers offering a contest will often provide bonus entries for users who utilize the "tell-a-friend" links to submit the email addresses of contacts. An email with information about the promotion or contest is then sent to these addresses.

virtual corporation 1. A business that has few employees and outsources nearly all its work. 2. A consortium of businesses that pursue a common goal. For example, several companies work together to produce a technologically advanced product.

visible supply New security issues, primarily bonds, scheduled for sale during the next month.

VITA —See VOLUNTEER INCOME TAX ASSISTANCE PROGRAM.

vocational rehabilitation A program of services designed to allow people to return to or remain in the labor force. For example, the Department of Veterans Affairs offers vocational rehabilitation services for veterans who have suffered a service-related disability.

void[1] To invalidate. For example, a party may void a contract if the other party fails to disclose all material facts.

void[2] Describing a contract or agreement that has no legal effect.

voidable Of or referring to a contract or agreement that can be judged unenforceable. For example, a contract may be missing an essential element.

volatile Tending to be subject to large and rapid variations. For example, the price of gold is frequently described as being volatile during periods when its price is rapidly rising and falling. Likewise, a person who exhibits rapid changes in behavior or mood is said to have a volatile personality.

volume The amount of trading sustained in a security or in the entire market during a given period. Especially heavy volume may indicate that important news has just been announced or is expected.

volume discount —See QUANTITY DISCOUNT.

voluntary accumulation plan A plan to acquire additional shares in a mutual fund on a more or less regular basis, at the discretion of the shareholder.

voluntary bankruptcy A bankruptcy initiated by the organization entering the bankruptcy rather than by that organization's creditors. Organizations generally enter voluntary bankruptcy to protect themselves from creditors' claims. —Compare INVOLUNTARY BANKRUPTCY. —See also CHAPTER 7; CHAPTER 11.

voluntary compliance A system of taxation that relies on individual taxpayers to report their income, calculate the appropriate taxes, and file a tax return.

voluntary conveyance The voluntary transfer of title to real property, generally from a borrower to a lender in order to satisfy the balance due on a defaulted loan.

voluntary dissolution Termination of an organization's legal existence by a vote of directors and shareholders or members.

Voluntary Employees Beneficiary Association An employer-sponsored employee benefit plan in which the employer gains a current tax deduction for contributions that grow tax-deferred. Plan assets are protected from creditors, and an employer is given wide latitude in structuring the benefits. The plan is generally set up as a trust with a bank acting as trustee.

voluntary lien A claim placed on real property by a lender with the consent of the property owner. For example, a person purchases a home by willingly taking out a mortgage that serves as a lien on the property.

Volunteer Income Tax Assistance Program (VITA) A program wherein certified volunteers sponsored by various organizations offer free tax help to moderate-income people who cannot prepare their own tax returns.

voting rights The type of voting privileges and the amount of control held by the owners of a class of stock. —See also CUMULATIVE VOTING; MAJORITY VOTING; NONVOTING STOCK; PROXY; SUPERMAJORITY PROVISION.

voting stock Stock for which the holder has the right to vote in the election of directors, in the appointment of auditors, or in other matters brought up at the annual meeting. Most common stock is voting stock. —Compare NONVOTING STOCK. —See also SUPERVOTING STOCK.

voting trust certificate A trust-issued certificate that evidences stock ownership but reserves voting rights for the trust. Voting trust certificates are exchanged for stock when voting power must be consolidated. Thus, holders of certificates have all the usual rights of stockholders with the exception of voting rights.

voucher 1. A document or coupon that can be exchanged for goods, services, or money. For example, a tour operator gives each group member a set of vouchers that can be redeemed for meals and accommodations. **2.** A document that substantiates a transaction.

voucher register In accounting, a journal in which accounts payable and their payments are recorded.

VP —See VICE PRESIDENT.

vulture fund A pool of investment money used to purchase distressed financial assets or real estate at bargain prices. Vulture funds are relatively risky but offer large potential profits. The performance of a vulture fund is dependent on the skill of the fund's managers in identifying and purchasing undervalued assets that can be turned into profitable investments.

vulture investor An investor who attempts to profit by buying debt of bankrupt or credit-impaired companies. Vulture investors are generally interested in the debt of problem companies that hold substantial tangible assets.

W

wage Money paid for services rendered.

wage and salary administration The establishment and management of an organization's compensation policy, including the maintenance of employment records and the setting of job classifications, wage brackets, overtime policy, and salary review plans.

Wage and Tax Statement (W-2) The IRS form that employers are required to send each year to the IRS and each employee for whom income, Social Security, or Medicare tax was withheld, or would have been withheld had the employee not claimed more than one allowance or an exemption from withholding. —Also called *Form W-2*.

wage assignment A document in which an employee voluntarily transfers the right to receive wages to a creditor. Wage assignments represent a form of security arrangement in which collateral is a portion of an employee's future wages.

wage bracket 1. The pay range for a specific occupation. **2.** In tables provided by tax authorities, the pay range that determines the appropriate amount of income tax to be withheld from employee wages.

wage ceiling 1. The high end of a wage bracket. For example, a school system may have a wage bracket of $35,000 to $45,000 for new teachers, depending on a person's discipline, education, and experience. In this school system, the wage ceiling for new teachers is $45,000. **2.** The maximum amount of wages used to calculate some variable such as pension or Social Security contributions.

wage controls Government regulation of employee pay. The federal government and numerous state governments have enacted minimum wage rates as a form of wage controls. In some instances governments have chosen to restrict allowable wage increases in an attempt to restrain inflation, particularly during times of war. Critics

claim that wage controls distort economic decision making and result in an inefficient allocation of resources.

wage drift The change in the amount by which actual earnings exceed negotiated
earnings. For example, employers in a region of the country experiencing labor
shortages may offer bonuses or overtime that exceed a nationally negotiated wage
agreement.

Wage Earner Plan —See CHAPTER 13.

wage floor The minimum wage that can be paid. A wage floor may be established by
legislation, union negotiations, or corporate policy.

wage incentive The offer of additional compensation for better performance. For example, an employer offers employees a bonus if monthly output exceeds a specified
level. Wage incentives might also be offered for improvements in quality or reductions in accidents.

wage-price spiral The interrelation between wages and prices such that an increase
in one results in an increase in the other, which results in another round of increases.
For example, workers see rising consumer prices and demand an increase in wages
that causes their employers to raise prices because of their higher labor costs.

wage-push inflation Consumer and producer price increases that result from higher
labor costs. For example, professional football signs a new labor agreement that calls
for a major escalation in player salaries, and as a result, teams increase the price of
game tickets.

wage rate The established pay for a defined period of work. For example, a local
contractor pays $15 per hour. Wage rate is generally stated on a pretax basis and is
exclusive of any benefits such as employer-paid insurance.

wage scale A schedule of wages for employees within a facility, organization, or industry.

wage stabilization The object of a government program designed to restrain increases in wage rates as part of an effort to contain inflation. For example, toward this end,
a government board may be given authority to approve or reject wage agreements
negotiated between employers and employees.

Wagner Act —See NATIONAL LABOR RELATIONS ACT.

waiting period —See COOLING-OFF PERIOD 1.

waiver The voluntary relinquishment of a claim, right, or privilege. For example, an
organization in severe financial difficulty may ask employees to agree to a waiver for
a portion of their next paycheck.

waiver of premium A provision in some life insurance contracts that forgives scheduled premium payments in the event the insured becomes disabled and can no longer
work.

walk-in A new customer who simply walks into the office or store. For example, a
medical practice may accept walk-ins.

walkout A work stoppage caused when employees leave their place of employment
as a sign of protest.

wallflower An out-of-favor security, company, or industry.

Wall Street The main street in New York City's financial district. The term is often
used to denote the entire financial district in New York or the world of U.S. finance
and investments. —Also called *the Street.*

WAN —See WIDE AREA NETWORK.

war chest Liquid assets accumulated by a firm to use in a potential acquisition or in defending itself against a takeover attempt. A substantial war chest adds security and enhances investment opportunities, but is likely to be a drain on short-term profitability.

warehouse club A very large retail outlet that offers members low prices for buying in bulk. Warehouse clubs, including Costco, Sam's Club, and BJ's Wholesale Club, typically require an annual membership fee and offer few frills.

warehouse lending A specialized form of credit offered by commercial banks and other large lenders to companies involved in the mortgage banking business. Essentially, warehouse lending involves offering mortgage bankers a line of credit to provide financing to homebuyers until the loan is closed and can be offered for sale to investors. Loan documentation is held by the warehouse lender as collateral for the line of credit.

warehouse receipt Written acknowledgment by a warehouser of the receipt of goods being held in storage. Warehouse receipts can be used to settle futures contracts by guaranteeing the quality and quantity of goods being stored.

wares Articles of commerce being offered for sale.

warrant A security that permits its owner to purchase a specific number of shares of stock at a predetermined price. For example, a warrant may give an investor the right to purchase five shares of XYZ common stock at a price of $25 per share until October 1, 2013. Warrants usually originate as part of a new bond issue, but they trade separately after issuance. —Also called *equity warrant; stock warrant; subscription warrant.* —See also DEBT WARRANT; PERPETUAL WARRANT; USABLE BOND.

warranty A guarantee. For example, a manufacturer or seller may provide a warranty that a product will be repaired or replaced if it fails to work as advertised. A seller of real property includes a warranty that the title is clear. —See also IMPLIED WARRANTY; LIMITED WARRANTY.

warranty deed A deed to real property in which the seller guarantees the title is clear and that the buyer will be protected against all claims.

warranty of habitability The implied guarantee by a landlord that a rental property is livable, safe, and sanitary. Failure to rid a rental property of insect infestation is a breach of a warranty of habitability. A breach of warranty may allow a tenant to sue for rent reduction.

warranty of merchantability —See IMPLIED WARRANTY.

wash sale The illegal purchase or repurchase of an asset within 30 days of the sale date of a basically identical asset that was sold in order to claim a tax loss. For example, if an investor sold a security at a loss and then immediately repurchased the same security or a basically identical security, the Internal Revenue Service would consider the transaction a wash sale and disallow the loss for tax purposes.

wash trade A transaction designed to make it appear that a purchase and sale has occurred even though no change in ownership was effected. For example, an investor might simultaneously buy and sell shares in one company through two different brokerage firms in order to create the appearance of substantial trading activity that will draw in other investors. Wash trades are illegal.

waste¹ 1. Unused materials considered undesirable that remain from a production process, as, for example, rock and other excess material that result from mining ore. **2.** A reduction in the value of real property because of damage or neglect by a tenant.

waste² To carelessly misuse assets: *The boy wasted the inheritance from his aunt.*

wasting asset An asset that tends to decline in value over time as its expected life is used up. For example, a factory machine or an automobile is a wasting asset. A natural resource such as timberland or a coal mine becomes a wasting asset as trees are harvested or coal is mined. —Also called *shrinking asset.*

watch list A roster of securities that are under scrutiny for a special reason. For example, a watch list may be established for stock that has exhibited an unusual trading volume or for debt securities that have reduced quality ratings.

water and sewer bond A revenue bond issued by a municipality to finance the building or extension of water and sewer systems. Interest and principal payments on the bond are derived from and are limited to revenues received from charges to the users of the systems.

watered stock Stock that is issued with a value considerably in excess of the value of the assets that support it. The term may be derived from the practice of feeding cattle salt to induce them to drink large amounts of water just before they are sold, thereby increasing their weight. Thus, the buyer—whether of stock or of livestock—pays for more than is actually received.

WATS —See WIDE AREA TELEPHONE SERVICE.

waybill A document issued by a freight carrier indicating the shipper, point of origin, route, destination, intended recipient, and carrier charges.

weak dollar A dollar that is of smaller value relative to foreign currencies. A weak dollar exchanges for fewer units of other currencies compared with the units for which it could have been exchanged in the past. A weak dollar tends to help U.S. firms that rely heavily on foreign sales because the firms' products will cost less in terms of the foreign currencies. A weak dollar hurts consumers of foreign goods because these goods cost more in terms of U.S. dollars. —Compare STRONG DOLLAR. —See also EXCHANGE RATE.

weak link theory The principle that holds that the successful completion of a process that requires a series of interrelated events is dependent on the success of the weakest link in the process. This is a play on the strength of a chain being dependent on the strength of its weakest link.

weak market A market in which prices are falling because the quantity supplied exceeds the quantity demanded. For example, the United States experienced a weak housing market in 2007 and 2008, when there were more sellers than buyers.

wealth effect The relationship between personal wealth and consumer spending. According to the wealth effect, consumers have a tendency to spend a larger proportion of personal income as their wealth increases. The wealth effect was used to explain increases in consumer spending in the late 1990s, when stock prices boomed.

wealth tax A tax based on the market value of assets that are owned. An ad valorem tax on real estate and an intangible tax on financial assets are both examples of a wealth tax. Although many developed countries choose to tax wealth, the United States has generally favored taxing income.

wearout factor The tendency of an advertising campaign or technique to be used to the extent that it is no longer effective. For example, a corporate advertiser uses the same advertising segment over and over during a season of baseball broadcasts.

weekend effect The tendency of securities to perform better on Fridays than on Mondays. Some technical analysts contend the weekend effect is primarily the result of the Monday auctions of U.S. Treasury securities.

weight 1. A measure of the heaviness of paper, generally on the basis of pounds per 500 sheets. **2.** In statistics, the importance assigned to a coefficient.

weighting The assigning of a measure of relative importance to each of a group of variables that are combined. For example, if an investor has 70% of his or her invested funds in stock A, which provides a current yield of 3%, and the remaining 30% of the invested funds in stock B, which provides a current yield of 5%, the weighted current yield of both securities is $(0.70)(0.03) + (0.30)(0.05)$, or 3.6%.

welfare state The term used to describe the result of a social policy in which government assumes responsibility for the welfare of its citizens. The degree of responsibility can vary but generally includes retirement income, health insurance or care, and employment assistance. A welfare state is accompanied by high tax rates to provide funding for government services.

well-heeled Wealthy. A person with a substantial amount of assets is said to be "well-heeled."

wellness program Comprehensive services designed to promote and maintain the good health of employees or members. A wellness program might include education, availability of exercise facilities, organized activities, and free health examinations.

wheel of retailing The lifecycle of retailers, moving from an entry position with low prices to gain market share to eventually moving upscale with higher-quality products aimed at more affluent consumers. Japanese automobile manufacturers moved along this cycle after entering the U.S. market with inexpensive vehicles that captured market share and then gradually moving upscale with higher-priced vehicles that offered higher margins to the manufacturers.

when-distributed 1. —Used to refer to a security that trades after the date of issue but before the time at which the certificates are delivered. **2.** Of or relating to a security on which a distribution is scheduled but has not yet occurred.

when-issued —Used to refer to a security that has not yet been issued but that will be issued in the future. Trading in when-issued securities often occurs between the time a new security is announced (for example, the time when a stock is split) and the time the certificates are actually issued.

whipsaw A quick price movement followed by a sharp price change in the opposite direction. An investor expecting a continuation in the direction of a security's price movement is likely to experience whipsaw in a volatile market. This risk is very important to short-term traders, but inconsequential to long-term investors.

whisper number An unofficial estimate of a financial variable (generally, earnings or revenues) that will be reported by a corporation. A whisper number may be different from published estimates by financial analysts or earnings guidance provided by corporate management.

whistleblower An employee or former employee who reports misconduct by one or more members of an organization. For example, an employee reports that members of management are participating in an illegal surveillance program.

CASE STUDY The Tax Relief and Health Care Act of 2006 established an IRS Whistleblower Office that administers a program to uncover tax cheating and oversee appropriate rewards to whistleblowers who substantially contribute to uncovering violations of the tax laws. Violations include deliberately underreporting or omitting income, overstating deductions, maintaining multiple sets of books, hiding assets or income, and claiming personal expenses as business expenses. The new whistleblower law was aimed at uncovering significant violations involving tax fraud or underpayments of over $2 million (including tax, penalties, and interest). Individual tax cheats must have an annual taxable income exceeding $200,000 in order for a whistleblower to qualify for a reward under the law. Rewards vary from 15% to 30% of the amount the IRS collects as a result of information provided by the whistleblower. A tip that is not the original source of information is subject to a smaller reward. The IRS does not pay potential rewards of $100 or less, and payments will not be approved until a case is complete and the IRS has collected the taxes and penalties it is due. A less ambitious IRS whistleblower law paid cumulative rewards of under $30 million in the five years prior to 2006. According to the IRS, only 8% of claims filed under the previous law had resulted in reward payments.

whistleblower laws Federal, state, and local laws that protect a whistleblower from retaliation and other illegal treatment. The federal False Claims Act permits a whistleblower to file a claim in federal court. Other laws allow a whistleblower to file a complaint with a governmental agency.

white-collar Of or referring to salaried employees who perform work requiring some degree of intellectual skill rather than manual labor. —Compare BLUE-COLLAR.

white-collar crime Nonviolent illegal activities for financial or personal gain. Examples of white-collar crime include fraud, blackmail, forgery, identity theft, bribery, embezzlement, and counterfeiting.

white elephant A business, real property, or other asset that is a headache to own and difficult to dispose of. For example, a small business may require considerable time from the owner, who nonetheless loses money or earns very little income.

white goods 1. Major appliances, including washers, dryers, stoves, water heaters, and freezers, that were at one time nearly always finished in white porcelain. 2. Cloth items including napkins, towels, sheets, and curtains.

white knight A person or company that rescues a target firm from a takeover attempt by buying the firm. —Compare RAIDER. —See also HOSTILE TENDER OFFER; SHARK REPELLENT; WHITE SQUIRE.

whitemail A takeover target's sale of a large number of its own shares at a bargain price to a friendly party. Whitemail causes a takeover to become more difficult and expensive because a corporate raider must purchase additional shares from a party friendly to the target company.

white paper A research report on a specific topic, often accompanied by a proposed solution to a problem that occasioned the report. For example, an interdisciplinary group of employees might be assigned to write a white paper on how the firm can reduce energy costs.

white-shoe Referring to or being a well-established firm, generally in the area of finance or law, that does business with wealthy clients.

white squire An investor sympathetic with management who holds a block of stock in a company that is or could be subject to an unfriendly takeover.

white squire defense An antitakeover strategy in which a takeover target places a block of its stock in the hands of an investor deemed sympathetic to management. Having a white squire decreases the possibility of a takeover because the suitor must acquire a significantly greater proportion of the remaining shares in order to complete the takeover. However, the white squire may become disenchanted and put its block of stock up for sale, or it may itself mount a takeover attempt.

whole life insurance —See CASH-VALUE LIFE INSURANCE.

whole loan A mortgage loan sold in the secondary market when the buyer assumes the entire loan along with its rights and responsibilities. A whole loan is differentiated from investments in which the buyer becomes part owner of a pool of mortgages.

wholesale Of or describing a business that sells to other businesses. For example, a produce company distributes fruits and vegetables at wholesale to area restaurants and grocery stores. —Compare RETAIL.

wholesale money Funds borrowed in large amounts from financial institutions rather than from small lenders.

wholesale price index —See PRODUCER PRICE INDEX.

wholly owned subsidiary A company that is totally owned by another company. For example, American Airlines is a wholly owned subsidiary of AMR Corp. A wholly owned subsidiary may have publicly traded preferred stock and debt, but all of its common stock is owned by a parent company and is unavailable for purchase.

wide area network (WAN) A telecommunications network that uses dedicated lines or satellites to connect remote users that operate from a wide geographical area. —Compare LOCAL AREA NETWORK.

Wide Area Telephone Service (WATS) A telecommunications service offered primarily to commercial users at a fixed rate or a special low rate. The service may apply only to incoming calls, only to outgoing calls, or both. For example, a food manufacturing company may use a WATS service that allows customers to make free (to the customers) calls to the firm.

wide basis A market condition in which there is a relatively large difference between a spot price and futures prices for the same type of contract. —Compare NARROW BASIS.

widget A general term for an unspecified device. For example, an economist might discuss the marginal cost of manufacturing a widget.

widow-and-orphan stock A stock characterized by smaller than average price movements, a relatively high dividend, and little likelihood of dividend reduction or serious financial problems. A widow-and-orphan stock is a conservative investment with limited possibility for large gains or losses.

wildcat strike A temporary work stoppage that has not been authorized by a union. In early 2007, over 200 postal workers in Leeds, England, took part in a wildcat strike because of the large amount of junk mail they were being required to carry. —Also called *outlaw strike; unauthorized strike.*

wildcatter A person in the oil business who drills exploratory wells outside lands with existing production. Wildcatters tend to be risk takers who are willing to suffer numerous losses in search of a major oil find.

will A legal document describing the desired distribution of a person's assets at death. —Also called *testament.* —See also SELF-PROVING WILL.

Williams Act A 1968 addition to the Securities Exchange Act of 1934 that requires investors who own or tender more than 5% of a firm's stock to furnish certain information to the SEC. The act also established a minimum period during which a tender offer must be held open. Required information includes the reason for the acquisition, the number of shares owned, and the source of the funds used for the purchase.

Wilshire 5000 Total Market Index A very comprehensive market-capitalization-weighted index composed of over 6,500 stocks. The Wilshire 5000 included 5,000 stocks when it was created in 1974, but has since been expanded. Wilshire Associates calculates numerous other indexes, including the Wilshire 4500, which excludes stocks composing the S&P 500.

windfall An unexpected profit or gain. For example, a business receives a windfall when it holds substantial inventories of a good that experiences a rapid increase in price.

winding up The process of liquidating an organization by selling assets, paying off creditors, and distributing any excess holdings to owners or members.

window 1. A period of time during which an action can be expected to generate a successful result. For example, underwriters may have a window for corporate debt issues sandwiched between two periods of heavy U.S. Treasury offerings. **2.** —See DISCOUNT WINDOW.

window dressing An adjustment made to a portfolio or financial statement to create a more positive appearance than is actually the case. For example, a manager may decide to provide window dressing to a portfolio by selling stock that has declined in value and replacing it with stock that has increased in value. Such activity creates the impression of successful portfolio management. Likewise, a firm might adjust its current assets and liabilities prior to the release of its financial statement

window period The time interval during which a company permits its executives and key employees to trade its stock. —See also BLACKOUT PERIOD 1.

winner's curse The likelihood that the winning bidder in an auction of several bidders will pay too high a price.

wire house A relatively large, multioffice brokerage firm that uses electronic communications to transmit customer orders for execution.

wire transfer —See ELECTRONIC FUNDS TRANSFER.

withdrawal plan An option offered by some open-end investment companies whereby an investor can receive payments at regular intervals. Withdrawal plans are generally used by people who wish to use their accumulated funds for retirement purposes. —Also called *systematic withdrawal plan.*

withholding 1. The holding back of a portion of wages, dividends, interest, pension payments, or various other sources of income for payment of taxes to the U.S. Treasury. —See also BACKUP WITHHOLDING. **2.** The illegal holding back of a portion of securities allocated as part of a new issue to a member of an underwriting syndicate. The underwriter may wish to keep the securities or resell them to a designated party so as to profit from an expected price rise soon after the issue has been offered to the public.

without recourse —See NONRECOURSE LOAN.

without reserve —See ABSOLUTE AUCTION.

with-profits —See PARTICIPATING 2.

workable competition A market structure that results in efficient production without achieving the strict standards of perfect competition. The concept of workable competition is often applied by governmental authorities in guiding regulatory policy for oligopolies in energy and communications.

worker buyout 1. An attempt by an employer to reduce the size of its workforce by offering financial incentives to employees who agree to terminate their employment with the firm. Workers may be required to surrender retirement and health benefits as a condition for receiving the financial incentives. **2.** Acquisition of a business by its employees. Worker buyouts generally occur when a business is in bankruptcy or severe financial difficulty and employees are concerned about losing their jobs.

worker capitalism A system in which employees own part or all of the firm for which they work. Proponents of worker capitalism believe employees will be more productive if they have a stake in the profits resulting from their labor. Employee Stock Ownership Plans were developed on this premise.

workers' compensation insurance Medical and disability insurance coverage that employers are required to provide to employees who may encounter job-related accidents or illnesses. Laws governing workers' compensation vary by state, but coverage is likely to include lost-wage benefits, medical and rehabilitation benefits, and benefits to dependents in the case of an employee death.

workers' compensation laws Legislation to ensure that employees who are injured during their employment or suffer a work-related illness receive monetary compensation. The employer is liable for providing compensation regardless of whether or not the employer is negligent. Federal legislation provides coverage for federal employees and certain workers engaged in interstate transportation, while state statutes establish coverage for other workers.

working capital The amount of current assets that is in excess of current liabilities. Working capital is frequently used to measure a firm's ability to meet current obligations. A high level of working capital indicates significant liquidity. —Also called *net current assets; net working capital.* —See also CURRENT RATIO; QUICK RATIO.

working control The ownership of a sufficient amount of a firm's voting stock (not necessarily more than 50%) to determine corporate policy. —Compare MAJORITY STOCKHOLDER.

working papers 1. In accounting, documents that serve as evidence of work performed by auditors. Working papers include information on how an auditing engagement is designed and executed. **2.** A legal document required of minors to prove they are of legal age for employment. —Also called *employment certificate.*

working poor People who work but qualify as being below the official poverty level.

work in process The partially finished goods that are held in inventory for completion and eventual sale. —Also called *goods in process.*

workload The amount of work a person is expected to complete, generally within a specified period.

work order A written request for an individual or department to perform an identified task.

workout The process of a debtor's meeting a loan commitment by satisfying altered repayment terms. For example, a firm in Chapter 11 bankruptcy proceedings might reach an agreement with its creditors for ways in which the firm's obligations can be worked out.

work permit A government-issued document authorizing the holder to legally work. For example, individuals who are not U.S. citizens or legal foreign residents are likely to need a work permit in order to gain legal employment. —See also WORKING PAPERS 2.

worksheet 1. A piece of paper or an electronic document with preliminary information that is used in completing a report or project. For example, a taxpayer may use a worksheet for calculating her federal income tax. **2.** —See SPREADSHEET.

work simplification Arranging a task so that it can be accomplished as efficiently as possible. For example, a hospital hires a consulting firm to develop a work simplification process for admitting patients.

work station 1. A single-user computer connected to a local-area network. **2.** An area devoted to an employee's accomplishing an assigned task. For example, a sandwich shop has four work stations, with employees adding ingredients at each station according to the type of sandwich requested by a customer.

work stoppage An interruption of work as a result of an employee strike or an employer lockout. For example, in 2005, a work stoppage involving the New York City Metropolitan Transit Authority and the Transit Workers Union idled 35,000 employees.

workweek 1. The standard number of hours an employee is expected to work during a seven-day period. **2.** For purposes of establishing overtime pay, seven consecutive 24-hour periods. For example, an organization may define its workweek to begin at midnight on Sunday and run through 11:59 p.m. on Saturday.

World Bank A financial institution owned and managed by nearly 200 member countries that provides financial and technical assistance to developing countries. Assistance includes low-interest or interest-free loans and grants for education, health, communications, and infrastructure. The World Bank is comprised of the International Bank for Reconstruction and Development, which focuses on middle-income and creditworthy poor countries, and the International Development Association, which provides assistance to the world's poorest countries.

world fund —See GLOBAL FUND.

worth The value of something, either in monetary or nonmonetary terms.

wrap account A special investment account in which all of the account's assets are entrusted to a professional money manager. All expenses relating to the account, including professional advice and commissions, are wrapped into a single annual fee that generally ranges from 1% to 3% of the total market value of assets in the account. Wrap accounts are designed for individual investors who choose to have a professional money manager handle a part or all of their investments. These accounts usually require minimum initial investments of at least $25,000.

wraparound annuity An annuity contract in which the investor has a measure of control regarding the investments that are in the plan, and in which the income generated by those investments is sheltered from taxation until withdrawal. The Internal Revenue Service no longer permits tax deferral through a wraparound annuity.

wraparound mortgage A real estate loan in which an existing mortgage is combined with a new junior mortgage. The borrower makes full payment to the holder of the wraparound mortgage, who in turn makes the required payment to the original mortgage holder. For example, a person purchases a home from a seller who has an outstanding mortgage. Rather than take out a new mortgage to pay the seller, who will in turn pay off the existing mortgage, the buyer makes monthly payments to the seller that cover the required payment on the original mortgage plus whatever additional amount is required to service money advanced from the seller. The buyer is not required to qualify for, or absorb the expense of, a new mortgage.

wrap-up insurance An umbrella insurance policy that covers all parties involved in a particular project or series of projects. For example, an owner or general contractor may purchase wrap-up insurance for the construction of a shopping mall or an apartment building. Wrap-up insurance is relatively expensive, but the costs may be shared among covered parties. Coverage usually includes general liability, workers' compensation, employer's liability, and umbrella liability. Additional coverage, such as errors and omissions insurance, may be added.

wrinkles —See BELLS AND WHISTLES.

writ A written legal order requiring a specific action or inaction. For example, a writ of habeas corpus is a court order for a detaining authority to bring a detainee before the court in order to determine if the detention is legal. A writ of execution might direct a sheriff to give a plaintiff possession of property.

writedown A reduction in the value of an asset carried on a firm's financial statements. For example, the firm's accountants, believing the inventory is overvalued, may decide to take a writedown by reducing inventory valuation. Unlike a writeoff, a writedown does not result in elimination of the asset.

> **CASE STUDY**   The New York Times Company announced in early 2007 that it would take a $814.4 million writedown on the value of two of its newspapers. New England's flagship newspaper, the Boston Globe, had been purchased by the Times in 1993 for $1.1 billion, and the Worcester Telegram & Gazette was bought for just under $300 million seven years later. A continuing deterioration in circulation and advertising revenues was plaguing the newspaper industry, thereby reducing the value of its properties and occasioning the writedown. The result was a quarterly loss of $648 million, or $4.50 per share, although earnings excluding the charge were a positive $88 million, or $.61 per share. The writedown caused a reduction of assets and equity on the firm's balance sheet. A company official commented that while the profitability of the print media remained challenging, the firm's digital properties were very promising.

writeoff A reduction to zero in the value of an asset carried on a firm's financial statement. Companies often hesitate to make writeoffs, because they reduce profits reported to stockholders.

write off To reduce the balance (that is, the book value of an asset or a group of assets) in an account to zero by recognizing the recorded value as an expense. For example, a firm may write off a technologically obsolete asset shown on its balance sheet as

wrongful termination

As a small business owner, what steps should I take to make certain I am not accused of wrongful termination by one of my employees?

The first step is to hire an employment attorney to help you set up business-specific policies and procedures designed to prevent claims of wrongful termination—and then to follow them. The second step occurs prior to the actual hire of an applicant. Obtain the written consent of the applicant to check references, and perform a background check to investigate the applicant's Social Security number, previous reviews by prior employers, motor vehicle records, or other records applicable to the job for which the applicant is being considered. Do a simple Google search. Eliminate applicants who refuse to sign a release for the information and give misleading information on a resume or in an interview.

Once employees are hired, set out clear job duties and expectations—the more objective the better. Let employees know exactly what they are expected to do and in what time and manner. Develop work rules and consequences for violating them, and make sure employees know what these rules and consequences are! Discipline (don't punish) employees in a consistent manner for violation of the rules (don't play favorites). If you have to be flexible and waive a rule, do so only for a legitimate business reason. A company is more apt to become embroiled in employment-related litigation because it is "nice" and makes an exception to a rule than if it sticks to its rules and polices. Adopt a written policy prohibiting sexual harassment that is part of a broader anti-harassment policy that prohibits illegal discrimination generally. Develop a procedure for employees to utilize in case of a complaint of harassment or discrimination. Send supervisors (and employees if possible) to anti-harassment and diversity training.

For all complaints and disciplinary problems, conduct an impartial investigation and *make findings*—even if the complaint turns into a "he said, she said" saga. If an employee does not perform satisfactorily, document, document, document, so in the event of a lawsuit, you'll be able to show that you warned the terminated employee and gave the employee both a chance to explain and a chance to improve. Never retaliate against an employee for filing a complaint; statistically, more companies are successfully sued for retaliation than for the actual termination. When you terminate an employee, have someone from Human Resources or another manager present, do not get into an argument about the merits of the discharge, and use clear and concise language as to why the employee is being terminated. The reason you give the employee verbally should be the same one that appears on the unemployment notice or pink slip. Inconsistency is the hobgoblin of wrongful termination claims. Don't try to figure out if the terminated employee is entitled to unemployment benefits—leave that to the state's unemployment department.

For problem employees, check with labor counsel before terminating. Also consider offering a severance package in exchange for release of all claims (a guideline is two weeks pay for every year of service), and get counsel's help writing the release to be signed in exchange for the payment.

■ Helen M. Kemp, Division Counsel and Assistant Director,
Retirement and Benefit Services, Office of the State Comptroller, State of Connecticut

having monetary value. The asset will then be deleted from the balance sheet, and income during the period will be reduced (or losses will be increased) by an equivalent amount. —Also called *charge off.*

writer The person who creates an option by selling an option contract in an opening transaction. For example, an investor may be the writer of a call or a put. —See also NAKED WRITER.

writeup An accounting increase in the book value of an asset without an accompanying expenditure of funds. For example, if a firm accounts for inventory on the basis of market value, the firm may need a writeup of inventory during a period of price inflation.

writing The sale of an option in an opening transaction. The option writer incurs a potential obligation to buy (if a put is written) or to sell (if a call is written) an asset at a particular price.

written-down value **1.** The accounting value following a writedown of an asset that was considered overvalued. **2.** —See BOOK VALUE 1.

wrongful termination Discharge of an employee for illegal reasons. Wrongful termination includes dismissal that violates collective bargaining laws, is a form of sexual harassment, is in retaliation for the employee having filed a complaint, or is in violation of federal or state antidiscrimination laws.

W-2 —See WAGE AND TAX STATEMENT.

X-inefficiency The ineffectiveness with which resources are utilized to produce outputs. X-inefficiency often results from a lack of competition, which leads to wasteful spending, overcapacity, and political lobbying to maintain legal protection.

x-mark signature The signature by an individual who is unable to write his or her name.

Yankee bond A dollar-denominated bond sold in the United States by a foreign-domiciled issuer. U.S. investors can thereby purchase the securities of foreign issuers without being subject to price swings caused by variations in currency exchange rates. Yankee bond prices are influenced primarily by changes in U.S. interest rates and the financial condition of the issuer.

year bill A 12-month U.S. Treasury bill. Unlike 13- and 26-week Treasury bills, which are auctioned weekly, year bills are auctioned only once a month.

year-end The end of an organization's fiscal year.

year-end dividend —See FINAL DIVIDEND 2.

year-end rally —See SANTA CLAUS RALLY.

year to date (YTD) January 1 until the current date. Financial publications frequently provide information for a security's YTD return, or the return provided by the security since the beginning of the calendar year.

yellow-dog contract An employment contract that prohibits an employee from joining a labor union during the period of employment. Yellow-dog contracts were popular during the early 1900s but are now illegal.

Yellow Sheets A privately owned centralized electronic and print quotation service for corporate, convertible, high-yield, and foreign bonds. Yellow Sheets derives its name from the yellow paper on which taxable debt quotations are distributed. Electronic quotations are in real time, and printed quotations are distributed weekly. —See also PINK SHEETS.

yield **1.** The percentage return on an investment. A given investment can have a variety of yields because of the many methods used to measure yield. For example, a bond's yield may be stated in terms of its returns if held to maturity, if held to the call date, or if held to the put date; or the yield may be calculated simply on the basis of the interest the bond pays compared with its current market price. —Also called *return.* —See also CURRENT YIELD; DIVIDEND YIELD; YIELD TO AVERAGE LIFE; YIELD TO CALL; YIELD TO MATURITY; YIELD TO PUT. **2.** Revenues raised by government with a particular tax: *The 1% sales tax proposed by the county commission will produce an annual yield of at least $1 million.* **3.** In agriculture, the amount of crops produced. For example, a Washington navel orange tree should produce an average yield of 100 fruits per year.

yield advantage The additional current return from holding a convertible security as opposed to owning the stock into which the convertible can be exchanged.

yield basis A method of quoting a bond's price in terms of its yield rather than in terms of its dollar value. Because bonds are bought and sold on the basis of yield, yield is generally a more informative measure of value than a bond's dollar price. Treasury securities are usually auctioned on a yield basis.

yield curve At any particular time, the relation between bond yields and maturity lengths. The yield curve usually has a positive slope, because yields on long-term bonds generally exceed yields on short-term bonds. The shape of a yield curve is influenced by a number of factors, including the relative riskiness between long-term and short-term securities, and investors' expectations as to the level of future interest rates. —Also called *term structure of interest rates.* —See also EXPECTATIONS HYPOTHESIS; FLAT YIELD CURVE; NEGATIVE YIELD CURVE; POSITIVE YIELD CURVE.

CASE STUDY Short-term interest rates tend to be much more volatile than long-term interest rates. Thus, the yield curve is somewhat like a rope, with rapid up-and-down movements on the left end, which displays short-term rates, and gradual changes on the right end, which depicts long-term rates. Somewhat surprisingly, the two ends of the yield curve don't always move in the same direction. The Federal Reserve attempts to work its economic magic by influencing short-term rates. In particular, the Fed sets the discount rate (the rate at which banks can borrow from the Fed) and establishes a target for the federal funds rate (the rate at which banks borrow reserves from one another). A Federal Reserve decision to reduce short-term rates in an attempt to stimulate the economy can cause long-term rates to increase if lenders and investors are concerned a stronger economy will be accompanied by higher inflation. Inflationary expectations have a direct effect on long-term interest rates. On September 18, 2007, the Federal Reserve announced it was reducing the target rate for federal funds from 5.25% to 4.75%. This half-point decline was larger than anticipated and was accompanied by an increase in stock prices and declines in other short-term rates, including CD rates, Treasury bill rates, and the prime rate (the rate offered by banks to high-quality borrowers). On the same day that short-term rates declined, the rate on 10-year U.S. Treasuries experienced a slight increase. One month later, the rate on 10-year Treasury bonds was even higher.

yield curve

I have noticed that short-term CDs are currently yielding more than CDs with longer maturities. Should I take advantage of the higher short-term rates even though I don't expect to need the funds for many years?

It depends. You must consider the reinvestment risk. That is, what will your reinvestment rate be when the short-term CD matures? If the yield curve falls and both long- and short-term rates are lower, you may lose money. You may be better off taking a long-run view of your investment strategy. On the other hand, if you stand to make a substantial return on your short-term CD investment, the potential return may well offset the reinvestment risk. Yield curves are normally upward sloping, so there may be a good chance you can reinvest at a higher rate when the short-term CDs mature.

■ Michael W. Butler, PhD, Professor of Economics, Angelo State University, San Angelo, Texas

yield equivalence Equal aftertax returns on different investments. As an example, for an investor in a 25% marginal tax bracket, a corporate bond with a taxable return of 6% has yield equivalence with a tax-free bond returning 4.5%.

yield spread The difference in yield, at a given time, between two bonds or between different segments of the bond market. For example, the yield spread between AAA-rated bonds and A-rated bonds may be one half of 1% at a particular time. Likewise, the yield spread between long-term taxable and nontaxable bonds may be 2%. Yield spread may be caused by any of various factors, including maturity difference, risk difference, or taxability difference.

yield to average life The average yield on a fixed-income security, assuming an average life for the security. In the case of bonds, average life may be significantly less than the number of years until maturity because of sinking fund requirements. Thus, the investor may be forced to sell the bond back before maturity.

yield to call The annual return on a bond, assuming the security will be redeemed at the call price on the first date permitted. This measure of yield includes interest payments and price depreciation because bonds are quoted in this way only if they sell above the call price.

yield to maturity (YTM) The annual return on a bond held to maturity when interest payments and price appreciation (if priced below par) or depreciation (if priced above par) are considered. Bond quotations are generally on a yield-to-maturity basis, although an investor who sells a bond before maturity may earn a yield different from the yield to maturity as calculated at the time the security was purchased. —See also INTERNAL RATE OF RETURN; MATURITY BASIS.

yield to par call The annual return from owning a bond, assuming a redemption on the first date the bond can be called at face value.

yield to put The annual yield on a bond, assuming the security will be put (sold back to the issuer) on the first permissible date after purchase. Bonds are quoted in this manner only if they sell at a price below the put price. Therefore, the yield includes interest and price appreciation.

yield to worst The lowest possible yield from owning a bond when all potential call dates prior to maturity are considered.

YTD —See YEAR TO DATE.

YTM —See YIELD TO MATURITY.

yuppie A young urban professional who earns a good income and enjoys impressing others with an affluent lifestyle.

▪ Z

Zacks Investment Research A firm that compiles earnings estimates and brokerage firm investment recommendations for thousands of publicly traded firms.

zero —See ZERO-COUPON BOND.

zero-based budgeting A method of allocating financial resources such that each budgeting entity must justify all of the period's planned expenditures. Thus, funds allocated in one period are not influenced by the allocation or use of funds in the prior period. Zero-based budgeting is designed to improve the efficiency of an organization by directing funds to the parts of the organization that are most deserving rather than to those that received the bulk of last period's funds.

zero bracket amount A largely outdated reference to the *standard deduction.*

zero-cost collar The investment position of being short a call option and long a put option for stock already owned. The premium received from selling the call option is used to pay for the purchase of the put. The collar is designed to protect an investor against a decline in the price of the stock without the investor being required to sell the stock and pay a tax on capital gains.

zero-coupon bond A bond that provides no periodic interest payments to its owner. A zero-coupon bond is issued at a fraction of its par value and increases gradually in value as it approaches maturity. Thus, an investor's income from a zero-coupon bond comes solely from appreciation in value. Zero-coupon bonds are subject to very large price fluctuations. The tax consequences of taxable issues often make zero-coupon bonds more suitable for tax-deferred accounts such as IRAs than for regular investments. —Also called *accrual bond; capital appreciation bond; zero.* —See also SEPARATE TRADING OF REGISTERED INTEREST AND PRINCIPAL OF SECURITIES.

zero-coupon certificate of deposit A certificate of deposit that pays no periodic interest and that is sold at a discount from face value (that is, maturity value). A zero-coupon CD is essentially the same as any other CD in which the investor leaves interest to compound.

zero inventory Maintaining a minimum level of inventory as part of a goal to reduce costs and increase profitability. Although an actual level of zero inventory is unlikely, a strategy to reduce inventory should result in lower expenses associated with warehousing, spoilage, and so forth. The term is sometimes used synonymously with just-in-time inventory.

zero population growth A state of stable population in which the birth rate plus immigration is equal to the death rate plus emigration.

zero-sum game A situation in which one person's gain must be matched by another person's loss. If taxes and transaction costs are not considered, many types of investing, such as options and futures, are examples of zero-sum games.

zombie A company that remains in business even though it is technically bankrupt and almost surely headed for the graveyard.

zoned rate A postal rate structure for certain Priority Mail, periodicals, and package services offered by the U.S. Postal Service. Rates are based on weight and distance traveled (or zones crossed).

zoning Regulation of the use of land and structures within a particular geographic area. For example, zoning regulation may allow only single-family detached homes on a particular tract of land. —See also INCLUSIONARY ZONING.

zoning map A map illustrating locations and boundaries of zoning districts throughout a city, county, or other political subdivision.

zoning ordinance An article of land use regulation by a government authority. A zoning ordinance may specify the maximum height of a structure, the minimum size of a lot, the use of a building, and so forth.

Z score In statistics, a Z score represents the number of standard deviations that a particular value of a variable is from the mean. The Z score = [(specific value of a variable) − (mean of the variable)] ÷ (standard deviation of the variable). A Z score indicates how different a specific value is from the mean. —Also called *standard score; Z value.*

Z value —See Z SCORE.

About the Author

David L. Scott is Professor Emeritus of Finance at Valdosta State University, where he taught finance and investing for thirty-two years. Prior to his tenure at Valdosta State, he was a professor at Florida Southern College. Dr. Scott has conducted workshops, written numerous articles, and authored more than two dozen books on business finance, personal finance, and investing. He has been a guest on numerous radio shows and has appeared on CNBC and NBC's *Today*. Dr. Scott was born in Rushville, Indiana, and received degrees from Purdue University and Florida State University before earning a PhD in economics from the University of Arkansas.